THE BARBOUR COLLECTION OF CONNECTICUT TOWN VITAL RECORDS

THE BARBOUR COLLECTION OF CONNECTICUT TOWN VITAL RECORDS

MADISON 1826–1850
MANCHESTER 1823–1853
MARLBOROUGH 1803–1852
MERIDEN 1806–1853
MIDDLEBURY 1807–1850
MONROE 1823–1854
MONTVILLE 1786–1850
NAUGATUCK 1844–1853

Compiled by
Nancy E. Schott

General Editor
Lorraine Cook White

Copyright © 2000
Genealogical Publishing Co., Inc.
Baltimore, Maryland
All Rights Reserved
Library of Congress Catalogue Card Number 94-76197
International Standard Book Number 0-8063-1602-0
Made in the United States of America

INTRODUCTION

As early as 1640 the Connecticut Court of Election ordered all magistrates to keep a record of the marriages they performed. In 1644 the registration of births and marriages became the official responsibility of town clerks and registrars, with deaths added to their duties in 1650. From 1660 until the close of the Revolutionary War these vital records of birth, marriage, and death were generally well kept, but then for a period of about two generations until the mid-nineteenth century, the faithful recording of vital records declined in some towns.

General Lucius Barnes Barbour was the Connecticut Examiner of Public Records from 1911 to 1934 and in that capacity directed a project in which the vital records kept by the towns up to about 1850 were copied and abstracted. Barbour previously had directed the publication of the Bolton and Vernon vital records for the Connecticut Historical Society. For this new project he hired several individuals who were experienced in copying old records and familiar with the old script.

Barbour presented the completed transcriptions of town vital records to the Connecticut State Library where the information was typed onto printed forms. The form sheets were then cut, producing twelve small slips from each sheet. The slips for most towns were then alphabetized and the information was then typed a second time on large sheets of rag paper, which were subsequently bound into separate volumes for each town. The slips for all towns were then interfiled, forming a statewide alphabetized slip index for most surviving town vital records.

The dates of coverage vary from town to town, and of course the records of some towns are more complete than others. There are many cases in which an entry may appear two or three times, apparently because that entry was entered by one or more persons. Altogether the entire Barbour Collection--one of the great genealogical manuscript collections and one of the last to be published--covers 137 towns and comprises 14,333 typed pages.

TABLE OF CONTENTS

MADISON	1
MANCHESTER	49
MARLBOROUGH	87
MERIDEN	119
MIDDLEBURY	177
MONROE	201
MONTVILLE	231
NAUGATUCK	249

ABBREVIATIONS

ae. --------------- age
b. ----------------born, both
bd. ---------------buried
B.G. -------------Burying Ground
d. ----------------died, day, or daughter
decd. ------------deceased
f. ----------------- father
h. ----------------hour
J.P. --------------Justice of Peace
m. ---------------married or month
res. --------------resident
s. ----------------son
st. ---------------stillborn
w. ---------------wife
wid. ------------widow
wk. ------------week
y. ---------------year

THE BARBOUR COLLECTION OF CONNECTICUT TOWN VITAL RECORDS

MADISON VITAL RECORDS
1826-1850

	Vol.	Page
ALLINGTON, Mary L., m. Timothy A. **MEIGS**, b. of Madison, Oct. 24, 1841, by Rev. Samuel N. Shephard	1	52
ATKINS, William, of Berlin, m. Celia A. **TALMAGE**, of Madison, Nov. 10, 1837, by Samuel B. C. West	1	5
BACON, Henry, m. Jane A. **SCRANTON**, b. of Madison, Apr. 22, 1846, by Rev. Samuel N. Shephard	2	109
William Andrew, m. Mary **NORTON**, July 2, 1827, by Rev. Samuel N. Shephard	1	7
BAILEY, Jeremiah B., s. Jeremiah B., b. Nov. 11, 1828	1	81
Sarah Jean, d. George R. & Lois L., b. Mar. 31, 1852	2	40
BALDWIN, William, of Branford, m. Amelia **SHELLEY**, of Madison, Nov. 25, 1847, by Rev. Samuel N. Shephard	2	120
BARNES, Clara B., of Branford, m. Oswell C. **TALLMADGE**, Nov. 4, 1849, by [Rev. George] S. Hare	2	140
BARTLETT, BARTLET, Daniel, m. Mary **EVARTS**, b. of Madison, Oct. 15, 1848, by Rev. Samuel N. Shephard	2	119
David, of Enfield, Mass., m. Marriett **STEVENS**, of Madison, Nov. 6, 1847, by Rev. James P. Terry	2	115
Timothy, of Guilford, m. Hannah **BENTON**, July 27, 1829, by Rev. Samuel N. Shephard	1	6
Timothy, of Guilford, m. Hannah **BENTON**, of Madison, July 27, 1829, by Rev. Samuel N. Shephard	1	8
BASSETT, Charles, m. Mary Ann **CONWAY**, b. of Guilford, July 22, 1849, by Rev. Geo[rge] L. Hare	2	122
Charles Henry, [s. Nathan F. & Adah], b. Feb. 20, 1830	1	81
Ellsworth, m. Cynthia **HOEL**, Nov. 23, 1831, by Rev. Samuel N. Shephard	1	9
Frances, [s. Nathan F. & Adah], b. Mar. 28, 1828; d. Aug. 24, 1829	1	81
Jane Elizabeth, [d. Nathan F. & Adah], b. May 7, 1832	1	81
Maria S., m. Nathan **HOWELL**, b. of Madison, Nov. 24, 1843, by Rev. Samuel N. Shephard	2	104
Olive Clark, [d. Nathan F. & Adah], b. Apr. 11, 1834	1	81
Susan R., of Madison, m. Madison A. **TREAT**, of New Milford, Aug. 11, 1849, by Rev. Geo[rge] L. Hare	2	122
Susan Roxanna, [d. Nathan F. & Adah], b. Oct. 12, 1826	1	81
BEEBE, Samuel D., of Norwich, m. Cynthia S. **GRISWOLD**, of Madison, Apr. 9, 1851, by Rev. Samuel N. Shephard	2	141
BENTON, Abigail, wid., of Madison, m. Albert B. **WILDMAN**, of Guilford, Apr. 29, 1838, by Rev. Samuel N. Shephard	1	75

BARBOUR COLLECTION

	Vol.	Page
BENTON (cont.)		
Abigail G., of Madison, m. Albert B. **WILDMAN**, of Guilford, Apr. 29, 1838, by Rev. Samuel N. Shephard	1	30
Amanda, m. Jonathan **DUDLEY**, Nov. 26, 1828, by Rev. Samuel N. Shephard	1	15
Daniel, m. Abigail **GRAVE**, Nov. 29, 1832, by Rev. Samuel N. Shephard	1	9
George, m. Maria **BISHOP**, b. of Madison, Sept. 6, 1832, by Stephen A. Loper	1	8
Green, of Maidison, m. Charlotte **WRIGHT**, of Killingsworth, Nov. 23, 1831, by Rev. Samuel N. Shephard	1	9
Hannah, m. Timothy **BARTLET[T]**, of Guilford, July 27, 1829, by Rev. Samuel N. Shephard	1	6
Hannah, of Madison, m. Timothy **BARTLET[T]**, of Guilford, July 27, 1829, by Rev. Samuel N. Shephard	1	8
Mary P., m. Daniel **SMITH**, b. of Guilford, Sept. 3, 1837, by Rev. S. N. Shephard	1	73
Phebe Ann., of Madison, m. Ely S. **CAMP**, of Durham, Apr. 21, 1836, by Rev. Stephen Hayes, of North Madison	1	12
Polly, m. Joseph R. **DOUD**, b. of North Madison, Jan. 3, 1834, by Rev. Luke Wood, Killingworth	1	15
Youngs E., of Guilford, m. Mary Ann **ELY**, of Madison, Jan. 16, 1828, by Rev. Aaron Dutton, of Guilford	1	7
BIDWELL, Edwin, m. Maria C. **LEE**, b. of Madison, June 8, 1848, by Rev. Samuel N. Shephard	2	117
BISHOP, Amos, m. Rhoena **WILCOX**, Dec. 27, 1831, by Rev. Samuel N. Shephard	1	9
Curtiss B., of Madison, m. Catharine **COAN**, of Wallingford, [June] 27, [1841], by Rev. Judson A Root	1	231
Eber J., [s. Amos & Rachel], b. Apr. 10, 1822	2	2
Eber J., m. Betsey W. **WILCOX**, Mar. 5, 1846, by Rev. Samuel N. Shephard	2	112
George, m. Nancy M. **EVARTS**, b. of Madison, Feb. 19, 1846, by Rev. Samuel N. Shephard	2	112
James H., m. Nancy B. J. **STONE**, May 16, 1847, by Rev. David Smith	2	114
Joel B., m. Amanda **DUDLEY**, b. of Madison, Feb. 6, 1843, by Rev. Lent S. Hough	2	102
John M., m. Cynthia **HULL**, b. of Madison, Apr. 1, 1844, by Rev. Henry Chase, at 44 Market St., New York. Recorded Aug. 18, 1890	2	115
Jonathan J., [s. Amos & Rachel], b. Nov. 5, 1811; d. Dec. 21, 1834	2	2
Josephine Estelle, d. Eber J. & Betsey W., b. Sept. 5, 1852; d. Apr. 29, 1853	2	40
Laura, m. Benjamin B. **WOODFORD**, Aug. [ ], 1827, by Rev. Samuel N. Shephard	1	68

MADISON VITAL RECORDS 3

	Vol.	Page
BISHOP (cont.)		
Levi, m. Polly M. **COE**, b. of Madison, Feb. 14, 1828, by Rev. Samuel N. Shephard	1	7
Maria, m. George **BENTON**, b. of Madison, Sept. 6, 1832, by Stephen A. Loper	1	8
Mary M., [d. Amos & Rachel], b. Jan. 14, 1809	2	2
Rachel, w. of Amos, d. Feb. 10, 1829, ae 49	2	2
Wealthy A., [d. Amos & Rachel], b. May 13, 1816	2	2
Wealthy A., m. George N. **WILLCOX**, b. of Madison, Apr. 12, 1843, by Rev. L. S. Hough	2	102
BLAKE, Alpheas B., of North Guilford, m. Achsah **SCRANTON**, of Madison, Oct. 16, 1838, by Rev. Samuel N. Shephard	1	77
BLATCHLEY, Alfred, m Caroline **NORTON**, May 25, 1829, by Rev. Samuel N. Shephard	1	8
BOARDMAN, Emulous, of Middletown, m. Amanda **STONE**, of Madison, Mar. 12, 1835, by Rev. Stephen Hays	1	76
BRADLEY, Amanda, of Madison, m. Benjamin **LYNDS**, of Chester, Sept. 24, 1840, by Rev. S. N. Shephard	1	46
Arba Lovel, [s. Benjamin & Fanny], b. July 19, 1832	2	3
Asa, of North Haven, m. Cynthia **MUNGER**, of Madison, May 4, 1830, by Rev. Samuel West	1	7
Ashbel Benjamin, [s. Phinehas & Chloe], b. Oct. 28, 1818	2	39
Candice Lewis, d. [Benjamin & Candace], b. Feb. 5, 1815; d. Apr. 18, 1833	2	3
Catharine, m. Phinehas M. **DUDLEY**, b. of Madison, Sept. 8, 1827, by Rev. Pierpoint Brockett, of Killingworth	1	13
Concurrence, [child of Phinehas & Lois], b. Nov. 5, 1827; d. Sept. 4, 1829	2	39
Cynthia Rebecca, [d. Phinehas & Lois], b. Mar. 24, 1839	2	39
Elizabeth Roxanna, [d. Phinehas & Lois], b. Jan. 15, 1816	2	39
Emily Roxanna, [d. Tallcot & Margarette Azubah], b. June 20, 1839	2	2
Eunice, w. of Tallcot, d. July 5, 1828	2	2
Ezra George, [s. Phinehas & Lois], b. Dec. 7, 1825	2	39
Fanny M., m. William L. **GRIFFING**, b. of Madison, July 16, 1849, by Rev. Samuel N. Shephard	2	123
Fanny Margarett, [d. Benjamin & Fanny], b. May 29, 1830	2	3
George R., d. Oct. 10, 1834, ae 31 y.	2	37
Harriet had s. James Harvey, b. Nov. 8, 1821	2	3
Henrietta Louisa, [d. Benjamin & Candice], b. Apr. 16, 1814	2	3
Henry Clay, [s. Phinehas & Lois], b. Feb. 25, 1832	2	39
Henry Crane, [s. Tallcot & Margarette Azubah], b. Mar. 2, 1832	2	2
James Harvey, s. Harriet, b. Nov. 8, 1821	2	3
John Tibballs, s. Tallcot & Eunice, b. Apr. 28, 1827	2	2
Lanson West, [s. Benjamin & Fanny], b. Oct. 30, 1826	2	3
Louisa C., m. Abram P. **SCRANTON**, Jan. 22, 1851, by Rev. Samuel N. Shephard	2	139

	Vol.	Page
BRADLEY (cont.)		
Louisa Concurrence, [d. Phinehas & Lois], b. Dec. 28, 1829	2	39
Lynde Gilead, [d. Benjamin & Fanny], b. May 9, 1823	2	3
Margaret B., m. Samuel F. **WILLARD**, b. of Madison, Apr. 8, 1851, by Rev. Samuel N. Shephard	2	141
Margaret Bushnell, d. Tallcot & Margarette Azubah, b. Aug. 15, 1830	2	2
Mary Meriam, [d. Phinehas & Lois], b. Feb. 23, 1835	2	39
Minor, of Guilford, m. Mrs. Parma **MUNGER**, of Madison, Nov. 9, 1848, by Rev. Samuel N. Shephard	2	123
Narrissa, m. Frederick **DOUD**, b. of Madison, Aug. 21, 1833, by Rev. William Case, of Chester	1	14
Nathan N., d. Apr. 25, 1841, ae 75 yr.	2	37
Richard Clark, [s. Phinehas & Lois], b. Feb. 24, 1837	2	39
Sarah Amelia, d. W[illia]m F. & Sophia W., b. Feb. 26, 1841	2	2
William F., of New Haven, m. Sophia **WILLARD**, of Madison, July 17, 1839, by Rev. Sam[ue]l N. Shephard	1	77
W[illia]m Frances, [s. Benjamin & Candice], b. Oct. 4, 1810	2	3
William Talcott, [s. Tallcot & Margarette Azubah], b. May 27, 1835	2	2
BRISTOL, Charles, [s. Uri & Naomi], b. Sept. 10, 1832	2	3
Daniel, [s. Uri & Naomi], b. Dec. 7, 1836	2	3
Eliza, of Madison, m. John **DAVIDSON**, of Mereden, June 5, 1836, by Rev. Stephen Hays, of North Madison	1	18
Harvey, of N. Killingworth, m. Alpha **THERYERS**, of Madison, Jan. 1, 1833, by Rev. Samuel N. Shephard	1	76
Maria, m. Austin **KELSEY**, b. of Madison, June 19, 1836, by Rev. Stephen Hays	1	42
Washington, [s. Uri & Naomi], b. Oct. 8, 1829	2	3
William, of Middletown, m. Lucy M. **DOWD**, of Madison, July 1, 1846, by Rev. Samuel N. Shephard	2	112
BROWN, Samuel U., m. Mary Ann **DOWD**, Mar. 17, 1850, by [Rev. Geo[rge] S. Hare]	2	140
BUCKINGHAM, John A., m. Clarrissa **NORTON**, b. of Madison, Jan. 25, 1849, by Rev. Samuel N. Shephard	2	121
BUELL, John C., of Killingworth, m. Julia **STEVENS**, of Madison, Sept. 17, 1834, by Rev. Stephen Hays	1	76
BURT, James, of Springfield, Mass., m. Diantha **STEVENS**, of North Madison, Jan. 1, 1834, by Rev. Stephen Hays, of North Madison	1	8
BUSH, Martha E., of Madison, m. Joel W. S. **PECK**, of New Haven, Oct. 22, 1851, by Rev. Samuel N. Shephard	2	142
BUSHNELL, Ann Augusta, [d. W[illia]m C. & Cynthia A.], b. May 18, 1840	2	3
Cornelius Scranton, [s. Nathan & Chloe], b. July 18, 1828	2	2

MADISON VITAL RECORDS

	Vol.	Page
BUSHNELL (cont.)		
Elizabeth M., of Madison, m. Frederick W. **HALL**, of Guilford, Mar. 14, 1832, by Rev. Samuel N. Shephard	1	33
Mary A., m. John **STORRER**, b. of Madison, Jan. 17, 1843, by Rev. Samuel N. Shephard	2	102
Mary A., of Madison, m. William V. **DOOLITTLE**, of New Haven, July 16, 1845, by Rev. Samuel N. Shephard	2	110
Mary Judson, [d. Nathan & Chloe], b. Sept. 21, 1822	2	2
Nathan Townsend, [s. Nathan & Chloe], b. Jan. 18, 1825	2	2
Samuel W., [s. Nathan & Chloe], b. Mar. 16, 1827; d. Apr. 25, 1827	2	2
W[illia]m C., m. Cynthia A. **GRISWOLD**, b. of Madison, Oct. 11, 1837, by Rev. S. N. Shephard	1	77
CADWELL, William H., of Saybrook, m. Clarrissa R. **COE**, of Madison, Sept. 18, 1848, by Rev. Samuel N. Shephard	2	118
CAHOON, CAHOONE, Abigail, of Killingworth, m. Ezra **DOWD**, of Madison, July 15, 1840, by Rev. S. N. Shephard	1	53
Albert, of Killingworth, m. Susan Amelia **GRIFFING**, of Madison, Feb. 1, 1846, by Rev. George F. Kettell	2	108
CAMP, Albert, of Durham, m. Marittee **WILLARD**, of Madison, Jan. [ ], 1828, by Rev. Samuel N. Shephard	1	10
Ely S., of Durham, m. Phebe Ann **BENTON**, of Madison, Apr. 21, 1836, by Rev. Stephen Hayes, of North Madison	1	12
Janette R., m. George **WILLARD**, b. of Madison, May 30, 1849, by Rev. Samuel N. **SHEPARD**	2	121
CHESTER, Charles A., of East Haddam, m. Martha E. **DUDLEY**, of Madison, Sept. 17, 1848, by Rev. David Smith	2	120
CHITTENDEN, Catharine Amelia, m. Augustus C. **WILCOX**, June 21, 1837, by Rev. Samuel N. Shephard	1	71
Chapman Warner, s. Samuel & Sarah, b. Dec. 17, 1818	1	83
Dency, of Madison, m. William **REDFIELD**, of Killingworth, Nov. 26, 1835, by Rev. Stephen Hays	1	61
Elizabeth Ann, d. Jonathan & Hannah B., b Aug. 12, 1835	1	84
Henry, of Killingworth, m. Emeline **CRAMPTON**, of Madison, Jan. 6, 1830, by Rev. Samuel N. Shephard	1	11
Henry Augustine, s. Samuel & Sarah, b. May 31, 1814	1	83
Hosmer Ely, s. Samuel & Sarah, b. Feb. 10, 1816	1	83
Joel, Capt., d. Apr. 13, 1843, ae 57 y.	1	162
John Newton, s. Samuel & Sarah, b. Dec. 25, 1827	1	83
Jonathan Samuel, s. Jonathan & Hannah B., b. Sept. 29, 1832	1	84
Joseph, d. Apr. 14, 1844	1	162
Luranda Collins, d. Samuel & Amanda, b. May 19, 1809	1	83
Lusanda C., m. Timothy L. **LEE**, b. of Madison, Nov. 24, 1831, by Rev. Samuel N. Shephard (Luranda)	1	46

	Vol.	Page
CHITTENDEN (cont.)		
Mary M., m. Dwight **HUMISTON**, Nov. 6, 1845, by Rev. David Baldwin	2	107
Samuel Conkling, s. Samuel & Amanda, b. Sept. 22, 1811	1	83
William Ferdinand, s. Samuel & Sarah, b. Aug. 1, 1825	1	83
CLANNING, Eliza, of Killingworth, m. Charles **POST**, of Saybrook, July 27, 1835, by Rev. Samuel N. Shephard	1	59
CLARK, Richard P., of Saybrook, m. Philena **HOEL**, of Madison, Apr. 11, 1830, by Rev. Samuel N. Shephard	1	11
Samuel E., of Saybrook, m. Wealthy **CRAMPTON**, of Madison, May 2, 1830, by Rev. Samuel N. Shephard	1	11
Thomas H., of Haddam, m. Mary **FOWLER**, of Madison, Oct. 7, 1835, by Rev. Aaron Dutton, of Guilford	1	12
COAN, Caroline Antoinette, d. Rev. Geo[rge] & Mabel M., b. Nov. 9, 1824	1	83
Catharine, of Wallingford, m. Curtiss B. **BISHOP**, of Madison, [June] 27, [1841], by Rev. Judson A. Root	1	231
George Munger, s. Rev. George & Mabel M., b. Apr. 13, 1823	1	83
Hannah, m. Samuel Butler **HILL**, b. of Madison, Feb. 13, 1838, by Rev. Simeon Scranton	1	35
COE, Abigail Hoyt, [d. Benjamin G. & Caroline], b. Aug. 17, 1824	2	5
Benjamin, [s. Benjamin G. & Caroline], b. Apr. 11, 1822; d. Oct. 18, 1845	2	5
Benjamin G., m. Emeline **PRATT**, Nov. 30, 1846, by Rev. Samuel N. Shephard	2	113
Catharine Amelia, [d. Benjamin G. & Caroline], b. May 1, 1838	2	5
Charles Augustus, [s. Thomas & Sarah M.], b. Aug. 30, 1838; d. Mar. 24, 1840	2	4
Chloe Roxanna, [d. William & Chloe], b. May 2, 1821	2	5
Clarissa, [d. Heman & Polly], b. July 13, 1808	2	4
Clarrissa, m. Horace L. **DUDLEY**, b. of Madison, Sept. 30, 1829, by Rev. Samuel N. Shephard	1	16
Clarrissa R., of Madison, m. William H. **CADWELL**, of Saybrook, Sept. 18, 1848, by Rev. Samuel N. Shephard	2	118
Edwin, [s. Heman & Polly], b. Aug. 17, 1810	2	4
Elias Thomas, [s. William & Chloe], b. Dec. 25, 1832	2	5
Eliza Maria Dee, [d. Simeon & Chloe M.], b. Apr. 12, 1835	2	7
Elizabeth, of Madison, m. Henry L. **REDFIELD**, of Clinton, Oct. 27, 1839, by Rev. W[illia]m Albert Hyde, of Westbrook	1	62
Emeline, [d. Heman & Polly], b. Feb. 8, 1813	2	4
Emeline, m. Daniel **PAINE**, July 22, 1834, by Rev. Samuel N. Shephard	1	59
Emily Amelia, [d. Thomas J. & Rebecca], b. May 13, 1825; d. Feb. 15, 1826	2	5

MADISON VITAL RECORDS 7

	Vol.	Page
COE (cont.)		
Emily Rebecca, [d. Thomas J. & Rebecca], b. Jan. 3, 1837	2	5
Fanny Artemisia, [d. Jonathan & Betsey], b. Nov. 1, 1837; d. Apr. 3, 1839	2	5
Frances Eliza, [s. Jonathan & Betsey], b. Feb. 19, 1826	2	5
Frederick William, [s. William & Chloe], b. Sept. 18, 1814	2	5
George Humphrey, [s. Jonathan & Betsey], b. Feb. 28, 1829	2	5
Henry Martin Dee, [s. Simeon & Chloe M.], b. Mar. 15, 1830	2	7
Hiram Leander Dee, [s. Simeon & Chloe M.], b. Sept. 21, 1833	2	7
Horace Nelson, [s. Thomas J. & Rebecca], b. Mar. 13, 1832	2	5
John Newton Dee, [s. Simeon & Chloe M.], b. July 4, 1828	2	7
John P., m. Elizabeth H. **HOWD**, b. of Madison, Apr. 17, 1848, by Rev. Samuel N. Shephard	2	117
Jonathan Bronson, [s. Jonathan & Betsey], b. Mar. 6, 1835; d. May 25, 1882	2	5
Joseph Alexander, [s. Heman & Polly], b. Feb. 3, 1830	2	4
Julius Selden Dee, [s. Simeon & Chloe M.], b. Feb. 28, 1823	2	7
Lydia A., of Madison, m. Charles **SMITH**, of Derby Conn., Mar. 3, 1844, by Rev. Nathan Tibballs	2	106
Lydia Adeline, [d. Jonathan & Betsey], b. Mar. 13, 1822	2	5
Margaret Gleason, d. Frederick W[illia]m & Elizabeth, b. Sept. 15, 1839	2	5
Mary A., m. John L. **DOWD**, b. of Madison, May 20, 1846, by Rev. Samuel N. Shephard	2	109
Mary Ann, [d. Thomas J. & Rebecca], b. Apr. 18, 1827	2	5
Polly M., m. Levi **BISHOP**, b. of Madison, Feb. 14, 1828, by Rev. Samuel N. Shephard	1	7
Samuel N., m. Sarah R. **WHEDON**, b. of Madison, Sept. 1, 1846, by Rev. Samuel N. Shephard	2	112
Samuel Newell, [s. Thomas J. & Rebecca], b. Apr. 16, 1823	2	5
Sarah A., m. Charles E. **WILLARD**, b. of Madison, May 10, 1847, by Rev. Samuel N. Shephard	2	114
Sarah Augusta, [d. Thomas & Sarah M.], b. Aug. 31, 1840; d. Feb. [ ], 1846	2	4
Sarah E., m. Charles P. **KIRTLAND**, Apr. 2, 1851, by Rev. Geo[rge] S. Hare	2	140
Sarah Emily, [d. Jonathan & Betsey], b. Apr. 2, 1831	2	5
Thomas, [s. Heman & Polly], b. Mar. 14, 1815	2	4
Wellington Sabastian, [s. Heman & Polly], b. July 14, 1817	2	4
William, m. Lydia **SMITH**, b. of Madison, Oct. 14, 1850, by Rev. Samuel N. Shephard	2	139
William Henry, [s. Jonathan & Betsey], b. Apr. 4, 1824	2	5
COLLINS, Lewis W., of Corinth, Vt., m. Sarah O. **FIELD**, of Madison, May 7, 1843, by Rev. Lent S. Hough	2	103

	Vol.	Page
COLLINS (cont.)		
Sarah O., of North Madison, m. Samuel C. **DORR**, of Lyme, Aug. 19, 1849, by Rev. Geo[rge] L. Hare	2	123
CONKLEY, Henrietta E., of Madison, m. Edward **COWLES**, of Avon, Dec. 4, 1831, by Rev. Samuel N. Shephard	1	11
CONKLING, Abigail L., m. Orrin H. **DOUD**, b. of Madison, Sept. 25, 1830, by Rev. Samuel N. Shephard	1	16
Abigail M., m. Erastus **DEE**, b. of Madison, Oct. 3, 1839, by Rev. Lewis Foster, of Clinton	1	80
Abigail Meigs, [d. Richard C. & Almira], b. Jan. 9, 1818	2	4
Ann Eliza, [d. Richard C. & Almira], b. Feb. 22, 1830	2	4
Antoinette B., of Madison, m. John L. **SEWARD**, of Guilford, Jan. 17, 1849, by Rev. Samuel N. Shephard	2	120
Antoinette Betsey, [d. Stephen & Betsey], b. Feb. 24, 1823	1	84
Augustus Y., m. Amoret **ROWE**, b. of Fair Haven, Apr. 11, 1848, by Rev. Samuel N. Shephard	2	116
Ellen Augusta, [d. Richard C. & Almira], b. Mar. 11, 1837* (*1836 in small figures)	2	4
Fanny L., of Madison, m. Levi **WALKER**, of East Haven, Oct. 22, 1846, by Rev. Samuel N. Shephard	2	113
Fanny Lucretia, [d. Richard C. & Almira], b. Jan. 10, 1820	2	4
Frances Jane, [d. Richard C. & Almira], b. Dec. 25, 1824; d. [ ], 1825	2	4
Hamilton Washington, [s. Richard C. & Almira], b. Mar. 7, 1835* (*1834 in small figures)	2	4
Horton L., m. Maria J. **DOWD**, b. of Madison, Apr. 19, 1840, by Rev. S. N. Shephard	1	230
James Usher, [s. Richard C. & Almira], b. Apr. 4, 1823; d. Aug. 8, 1824	2	4
Jehiel M., d. Dec. 25, 1841, ae 44	2	37
Joseph Benjamin, [s. Richard C. & Almira], b. Dec. 21*, 1832 (*12th in small figures)	2	4
Leonanddos Woolworth, [s. Stephen & Betsey], b. Feb. 13, 1828	1	84
Marg[a]ret Lucy, [d. Stephen & Betsey], b. May 23, 1820	1	84
Mary Landon, [d. Stephen & Betsey], b. Apr. 14, 1825	1	84
Richard Christopher, [s. Richard C. & Almira], b. Nov. 19, 1821	2	4
Roxanna Catharine, [d. Richard C. & Almira], b. Mar. 17, 1826* (*1827 in small figures)	2	4
Roxanna L., of Madison, m. Joseph **STANNARD**, of Killingworth, Apr. 22, 1828, by Rev. Samuel N. Shephard	1	63
Samuel Meigs, [s. Richard C. & Almira, b. Dec. 11, 1833	2	4
Sarah, m. Titus **KELSEY**, Oct. 26, 1836, by Rev S. N Shephard	1	42
William F., m. Roxanna **HILL**, b. of Madison, Sept. 14, 1851, by Rev. Samuel N. Shephard	2	141
William Frederick Augustus, [s. Richard C. & Almira], b. Mar. 11, 1816	2	4

MADISON VITAL RECORDS 9

	Vol.	Page
CONWAY, Mary Ann., m. Charles BASSETT, b. of Guilford, July 22, 1849, by Rev. Geo[rge] L. Hare	2	122
COOPER, James J., of Wallingford, m. Hannah C. WALKLEY ,of North Madison, Aug. 26, 1832, by Rev. Jared Andrew, of North Madison	1	10
Sarah, of Madison, m. Edwin DUDLEY, of Killingworth, Mar. 31, 1839, by Rev. Simeon Scranton	1	79
COWLES, Edward, of Avon, m. Henrietta E. CONKLEY, of Madison, Dec. 4, 1831, by Rev. Samuel N. Shephard	1	11
COX, Mary A., of Middletown, m. John A. LUCAS, June 27, 1850, by [Rev. Geo[rge] S. Hare]	2	140
CRAMPTON, Abigail M., m. Orrin S. FOWLER, b. of Madison, Jan. 11 ,1830, by Rev. Samuel N. Shephard	1	24
Daniel B., of Madison, m. Hancy P. DICKINSON, of East Haddam, Mar. 6, 1839, by Rev. Amos L. Favore	1	230
Electa had s. William Washington YOUNG, b. Aug. 12, 1822	1	150
Elizabeth m. John R. WILCOX, b. of Madison, Apr. 13, 1829, by Rev. Samuel N. Shephard	1	68
Emeline, of Madison, m. Henry CHITTENDEN, of Killingworth, Jan. 6, 1830, by Rev. Samuel N. Shephard	1	11
Henrietta H., m. Julius A. HILL, b. of Madison, Sept. 16, 1835, by Rev. Samuel N. Shephard	1	34
Mary L., had d. Mary Roxanna NICHOLAS, b. Jan. 13, 1822	1	118
Rachel, d. David & Rachel, b. Oct. 8, 1777	1	94
Russell, of Madison, m. Mary LEETE, of Guilford, Sept. 9, 1835, by Rev. Aaron Dutton, of Guilford	1	12
Sally Adeline, of Madison, m .Samuel W. MAYNARD, of Durham, Aug. 4, 1841, by Rev. Hudson A. Root	1	51
Samuel R., m. Mary Ann EVARTS, Oct. 29, 1839, b. of Madison, by Rev. Samuel N. Shephard	1	230
Wealthy, of Madison, m. Samuel E. CLARK, of Saybrook, May 2, 1830, by Rev. Samuel N. Shephard	1	11
William B., m. Betsey M. WHEDON, b. of Madison, Oct. 16, 1844, by Rev. Samuel N. Shephard	2	109
CROWELL, Henry G., of Boston, Mass., m. Martha E. TORREY, of Madison, [Sept.] 24, [1850], by Rev Reuben Torrey	2	138
CRUTTENDEN, Barbara Roxanna, d. William & Roxanna, b. Oct. 5, 1829; d. Oct. 3, 1834	1	82
Benjamin, d. Apr. 16, 1844, ae 51 y.	1	162
Catharine Amelia, d. Abraham, Jr. & Urania, b. Feb. 13, 1815	1	82
Edmund, d. Feb. 11, 1830, ae 62 y.	1	162
Elizabeth Jemima, d. Abra[ha]m & Urania, b. June 13, 1823	1	82
Eunice, d. Edmund & Hannah, b. Sept. 11, 1802	1	84

	Vol.	Page
CRUTTENDEN (cont.)		
Gilbert, s. David & Hannah, b. July 20, 1822; d. Nov. 17, 1825	1	82
Harvey Edward, s. Abra[ha]m & Urania, b. Jan. 8, 1821	1	82
Joel Nathan, s. Abra[ha]m & Urania, b. Dec. 16, 1817; d. Apr. 25, 1837	1	82
Jonathan, s. David & Hannah, b. May 18, 1817	1	82
Lydia, d. David & Hannah, b. Sept. 6, 1819	1	82
Rachel, d. Edmund & Hannah, d. Nov. 4, 1822, ae 25 y.	1	162
Roxanna, w. of W[illia]m, b. Sept. 14, 1798; d. May 20, 1835	1	162
William, s. Edmund & Hannah, b. Nov. 30, 1806	1	82
William, m. Roxanna **FIELD**, b. of Madison, Mar. 8, 1828, by Rev. Samuel N. Shephard	1	10
William Edmund, s. William & Roxanna, b. Feb. 13, 1835; d. Nov. 29, 1835	1	84
DAVIDSON, John, of Mereden, m. Eliza **BRISTOL**, of Madison, June 5, 1836, by Rev. Stephen Hays, of North Madison	1	18
DAVIS, Bela, m. Sarah **SCRANTON**, this evening [Dec. 25, 1827], by Rev. David Smith, of Durham	1	13
Cornelia Elizabeth, [d. Bela & Sarah], b. Dec. 9, 1832	2	8
Daniel, of Madison, m. Elizabeth L. **ROSS**, of Saybrook, Sept. 26, 1852, by Rev. W. W. Brown	2	144
Deborah Ann, [d. Levi & Mary Ann], b. Dec. 9. 1827	2	8
George N., of North Killingworth, m. Mary M. **DAVIS**, of North Madison, Jan. 8, 1834, by Rev. Stephen Hays, of North Madison	1	15
George Washington, [s. Bela & Sarah], b. Aug. 3, 1838	2	8
Irwin Smith, [s. Bela & Sarah], b. Nov. 29, 1828	2	8
Judson Edwards, [s. Levi & Mary Ann], b. June 15, 1841	2	8
Mary Mrs., of Madison, m. Harvey **HALE**, of Madison, July 5, 1829, by Rev. Samuel West	1	32
Mary M., of North Madison, m. George N. **DAVIS**, of North Killingworth, Jan. 8, 1834, by Rev. Stephen Hays, of North Madison	1	15
Watson, of Killingworth, m. Olive C. **HALE**, of Madison, Sept. 21, 1831, by Rev. F. W. Sizer, of Durham	1	14
William Henry, [s. Bela & Sarah], b. Aug. 30, 1840	2	8
DAY, Bridget, [d. John & Catharine], b. [ ], in Ireland	1	119
Catharine, [d. John & Catharine], b. [ ], in America	1	119
George Henry, [s. John & Catharine], b. [ ], in America	1	119
John, [s. John & Catharine], b. [ ], in Ireland	1	119
Mary, [d. John & Catharine], b. [ ], in Ireland	1	119
Michael, [s. John & Catharine], b. [ ], in Ireland	1	119
Thomas, [s. John & Catharine], b. [ ], in Ireland	1	119
DEE, Elias K., m. Betsey **ROOT**, Nov. 25, 1829, by Reynold Webb, J.P.	1	14

MADISON VITAL RECORDS

	Vol.	Page
DEE (cont.)		
Erastus, m. Abigail M. **CONKLING**, of Madison, Oct. 3, 1839, by Rev. Lewis Foster, of Clinton	1	80
Hetty Ann, of Madison, m. Jason Seward, Jr., of Guilford, Jan. 20, 1847, by Rev. Samuel N. Shephard	2	113
DeFORREST, Edwin, m. Martha **LEETE**, July 14, 1850, by [Rev. Geo[rge] S. Hare]	2	140
DEMING, Levi, of Newington, m. Caroline **SCRANTON**, of Madison, Sept. 21, 1842, by Rev. Samuel N. Shephard	2	100
DENISON, Hannah, m. Achilles **WILLARD**, b. of Madison, May [ ], 1829, by Rev. Samuel N. Shephard	1	69
DICKINSON, Charlotte A., of Haddam, Conn., m. Horace **GARDINER**, of Springfield, Mass., Nov. 27, 1836, by Rev. Stephen Hays	1	28
Hancy P., of East Haddam, m. Daniel B. **CRAMPTON**, of Madison, Mar. 6, 1839, by Rev. Amos L. Favore	1	230
Margaret M., of Haddam, m. James C. **SCRANTON**, of Madison, Jan. 3, 1836, by Rev. A. F. Beach	1	66
DINGWELL, Levi H., m. Sarah **DOUD**, Oct. 9, 1834, by Rev. Samuel N. Shephard	1	18
DOAN, Joseph C., of Middletown, m. Nancy M. **SCRANTON**, of Madison, Mar. 27, 1836, by Rev. A. F. Beach	1	17
DOLAN, Julia, m. John **McFADDEN**, b. of Ireland, Nov. 10, 1851, by Rev. Samuel N. Shephard	2	142
DOOLITTLE, DOELITTLE, Amanda, of Madison, m. Orland W. **ISBELL**, of Killingworth, Sept. 9, 1829, by Rev. David Metcalf	1	38
Emily M., of Madison, m. Nathan **LANE**, of Killingworth, June 18, 1843, by Rev. L. S. Hough	2	103
Mary Janette, [d. Abram A. & Adelia], b. Oct. 3, 1838	2	8
William V., of New Haven, m. Mary A. **BUSHNELL**, of Madison, July 16, 1845, by Rev. Samuel N. Shephard	2	110
DORR, Samuel C., of Lyme, m. Sarah O. **COLLINS**, of North Madison, Aug. 19, 1849, by Rev. Geo[rge] L. Hare	2	123
DOWD, DOUD, Abigail T., d. Julius & Clarrissa, b. Apr. 22, 1813	1	88
Achillus, m. Susan **WILCOX**, b. of Madison, Sept. 19, 1838, by Rev. S. N. Shephard	1	80
Alfred G., m. Harriet C, **SCRANTON**, b. of Madison, Nov. 28, 1833, by Rev. Samuel N. Shephard	1	16
Alpha Maria, [d. James H. & Alpha], b. June 20, 1847	2	7
Angeline, d. Julius & Clarrissa, b. Nov. 18, 1809	1	88
Angeline, m. Elijah W. **HARRIS**, b. of Madison, June 5, 1828, by Rev. Samuel N. Shephard	1	32
Angenora, [d. Joshua & Mary L.], b. Nov. 13, 1816	1	89
Angenora, of Madison, m. Orrin **HULL**, of Wallingford, [, 1839], by Rev. Samuel N. Shephard	1	37
Augustus M., m. Rebecca E. **FIELD**, b. of Madison, Oct. 22, 1845, by Rev. Samuel N. Shephard	2	111

BARBOUR COLLECTION

	Vol.	Page
DOWD, DOUD (cont.)		
Austin, m. Abigail **SCRANTON**, b. of Madison, Oct. 26, 1835, by Rev. Stephen Hays, of North Madison	1	17
Benjamin, [s. Galen & Mary], b. Sept. 2, 1819; d. Apr. 3, 1821	2	6
Benjamin, [s. Galen & Mary], b. Sept. 28, 1821; d. Nov. 3, 1822	2	6
Caroline, d. Julius & Clarrissa, b. Apr. 27, 1821	1	88
Catharine, d. Julius & Clarrissa, b. Apr. 27, 1821	1	88
Charles Ferdinand, [s. Wyllys W. & Rebecca], b. Apr. 25, 1825	2	7
Charles H., m. Mary R. **SCRANTON**, Oct. 6, 1841, by Rev. Sam[ue]l N. Shephard	1	53
Charles Hamilton, [s. Galen & Mary], b. Oct. 7, 1817	2	6
Chloe R., of Madison, m. Hiram **STEVENS**, of Killingworth, Apr. 24, 1834, by Stephen Hays	1	65
Cyrus Bradley, s. Frederick & Narcissa, b. Feb. 22, 1835	1	89
David, of Madison, m. Mrs. Densey **WILCOX**, of Killingworth, Sept. 18, 1837, by Rev. Stephen Hays	1	79
David D., m. Mary **HARRIS**, b. of Madison, Jan. 15, 1829, by Rev. Samuel N. Shephard	1	15
David S., m. Julia **DOUD**, b. of Madison, Feb. 5, 1836, by Rev. Stephen Hays	1	18
Delia Frances, [d. Galen & Mary], b. Mar. 11, 1826	2	6
Delia Frances, m. Lawrence A. **FIELD**, b. of Madison, Dec. 24, 1845, by Rev. George F. Kettell	2	108
Edgar Charles, [s. Martin L. & Marriet], b. June 28, 1835	2	6
Edmune, [s. Joshua & Mary L.], b. Dec. 28, 1818; d. Dec. 1, 1820	1	89
Edmund Augustus, [s. Joshua & Mary L.], b. June 14, 1823; d. Oct. 29, 1824	1	89
Eliza S., of Madison, m. Asahel **STENT**, of Brandford, Sept. 17, 1843, by Rev. L. S. Hough	2	104
Elizabeth, [d. Galen & Mary], b. July 3, 1813; d. Jan. 10, 1816	2	6
Elizabeth H., m. John P. **COE**, b. of Madison, Apr. 17, 1848, by Rev. Samuel N. Shephard	2	117
Elizabeth Kelsey, [d. Samuel K. & Jerusha], b. Jan. 2, 1828	2	6
Ellen A., of Madison, m. Joseph C. **MOULTHROP**, of North Branford, May 22, 1845, by Rev. Samuel N. Shephard	2	107
Ellen Maria, [d. Samuel K. & Jerusha], b. Aug. 16, 1836	2	6
Ezra, of Madison, m. Abigail **CAHOONE**, of Killingworth, July 15, 1840, by Rev. S. N. Shephard	1	53
Frederick, s. Timothy & Sarah, b. June 20, 1803	1	87
Frederick, m. Narrissa **BRADLEY**, b. of Madison, Aug. 21, 1833, by Rev. William Case, of Chester	1	14
George, m. Louisa **WILCOX**, b. of Madison, Feb. 1, 1831, by Rev. Samuel N. Shephard	1	16

MADISON VITAL RECORDS 13

	Vol.	Page
DOWD, DOUD (cont.)		
George L., m. Matilda L. **DOWD**, b. of Madison, May 4, 1837, by Rev. Stephen Hays	1	78
Giles, [s. Joshua & Mary L.], b. Sept. 13, 1833	1	89
Harriet Ann, [d. Wyllys W. & Rebecca], b. Nov. 3, 1831	2	7
Harriet M., of Madison, m. Edward **WILCOX**, of Berlin, Sept. 28, 1838, by Rev. Samuel N. Shephard	1	30
Henry, [s. Galen & Mary], b. Apr. 17, 1823; d. July 31, 1823	2	6
Henry Manfred, [s. Wyllys W. & Rebecca], b. May 17, 1835	2	7
Herman S. T., s. Julius & Clarrissa, b. Sept. 17, 1823	1	88
Hiram Sanford, [s. Ezra & Abigail], b. Mar. 19, 1841	2	6
Horace H., s. Julius & Clarrissa, b. Apr. 16, 1815	1	88
James Harvey, m. Alpha **HILL**, Oct. 25, 1835, by Rev. David Baldwin	1	17
Jane R., of Madison, m. William L. **HEALD**, of North Haven, Mar. 26, 1845, by Rev. Samuel N. Shephard	2	109
Jane Rebecca, [d. Wyllys W. & Rebecca], b. Mar. 20, 1827	2	7
Jerusha, w. of Sam[ue]l K., b. June 3, 1841	2	6
Joel, [s. Joshua & Mary L.], b. Apr. 8, 1815	1	89
John L., m. Mary A. **COE**, b. of Madison, May 20, 1846, by Rev. Samuel N. Shephard	2	109
John Luther, [s. Wyllys W. & Rebecca], b. May 14, 1821	2	7
Joseph R., m. Polly **BENTON**, b. of North Madison, Jan. 3, 1834, by Rev. Luke Wood, Killingworth	1	15
Joseph T., s. Julius & Clarrissa, b. Apr. 22, 1825	1	88
Judson Hill, s. James H. & Alpha, b. Aug. 28, 1838	1	89
Judson Hill, [s. James H. & Alpha], b. Aug. 28, 1838	2	7
Julia, m. David S. **DOUD**, b. of Madison, Feb. 5, 1836, by Rev. Stephen Hays	1	18
Julia Ann, d. Timothy & Sarah, b. Mar. 8, 1806	1	87
Julius Albert, s. Julius & Clarrissa, b. Aug. 22, 1806	1	87
Julius N., m. Mary Ann **MUNSON**, b. of Madison, May 4, 1837, by Sam[ue]l N. Shephard	1	78
Laura C., d. Julius & Clarrissa, b. Mar. 18, 1808	1	87
Lucy M., of Madison, m. William **BRISTOL**, of Middletown, July 1, 1846, by Rev. Samuel N. Shephard	2	112
Maria J., m. Horton L. **CONKLING**, b. of Madison, Apr. 19, 1840, by Rev. S. N. Shephard	1	230
Mary Ann, m. Samuel U. **BROWN**, Mar. 17, 1850, by [Rev. Geo[rge] S. Hare]	2	140
Mary Elizabeth, [d. Galen & Mary], b. July 28, 1824; d. Nov. 30, 1831	2	6
Mary Woods, [d. Martin L. & Marriet], b. Nov. 2, 1837	2	6
Matilda L., m. George L. **DOWD**, b. of Madison, May 4, 1837, by Rev. Stephen Hays	1	78
Nancy Amelia, [d. Wyllys W. & Rebecca], b. Dec. 22, 1838	2	7
Nathan Hill, [s. James H. & Alpha], b. Mar. 28, 1841	2	7

	Vol.	Page
DOWD, DOUD (cont.)		
Orrin H., m. Abigail L. **CONKLING**, b. of Madison, Sept. 25, 1830, by Rev. Samuel N. Shephard	1	16
Polly, d. Timothy & Sarah, b. Sept. 19, 1795	1	87
Polly, [d. Joshua & Mary L.], b. June 1, 1821	1	89
Polly A., of Madison, m. John **STENT**, of Branford, Nov. 6, 1842, by Rev. L. S. Hough	2	101
Rachel, [d. Joshua & Mary L.], b. May 27, 1825	1	89
Rachel, m. Alvah O. **WILCOX**, b. of Madison, Sept. 26, 1826, by Rev. Erastus Scranton, of Orange	1	68
Richard E., s. Julius & Clarrissa, b. Apr. 16, 1811	1	88
Roxanna, d. Timothy & Sarah, b. Oct. 19, 1793	1	87
Rufus, of North Madison, m. Betsey **THOMAS**, Oct. 29, 1837, by Rev. Sam[ue]l N. Shephard	1	79
Samuel Edward, s. Achillus & Susan A., b. Oct. 24, 1840	2	6
Samuel K., m. Jerusha **WILCOX**, b. of Madison, Aug. [ ], 1827, by Rev. Samuel N. Shephard	1	13
Sarah, d. Timothy & Sarah, b. Feb. 17, 1800	1	87
Sarah, m. Levi H. **DINGWELL**, Oct. 9, 1834, by Rev. Samuel N. Shephard	1	18
Sarah Louisa, d. Abner H. & Cynthia A., b. Jan. 15, 1841	2	6
Selden Demetrius, [s. Joshua & Mary L.], b. May 30, 1831	1	89
Sidney A., s. Julius & Clarrissa, b. Jan. 26, 1817	1	88
Susan R., m. Sereno H. **SCRANTON**, b. of Madison, Sept. 29, 1833, by Rev. Samuel N. Shephard	1	66
Tamson Eliza, [d. Wyllys W. & Rebecca], b. May 21, 1823	2	7
Thomas Ward, [s. Galen & Mary], b. Aug. 21, 1815	2	6
Timothy B., s. Julius & Clarrissa, b. Jan. 23, 1819	1	88
William G., m. Ellen A. **FIELD**, July 26, 1849, by Rev. Samuel N. Shephard	2	124
William Galen, [s. Galen & Mary], b. Feb. 18, 1828	2	6
William Wickham, [s. Joshua & Mary L.], b. Nov. 21, 1828	1	89
Wyllys Wadsworth, [s. Wyllys W. & Rebecca], b. July 25, 1829	2	7
DUDLEY, Abigail, d. Timothy & Theodora, b. Mar. 6, 1816	1	87
Abigail, m. Henry **LEE**, b. of Madison, Nov. 13, 1850, by Rev. Samuel N. Shephard	2	139
Abigail M., m. Franklin **ROSE**, b. of Madison, Sept. 9, 1849, by Rev. E. S. Huntington	2	137
Amanda, m. Joel B. **BISHOP**, b. of Madison, Feb. 6, 1843, by Rev. Lent S. Hough	2	102
Amelia Rosette, [d. Horace L. & Clarissa], b. June 18, 1837; d. Sept. 24, 1838	2	7
Benjamin Timothy, s. Timothy & Theodora, b. Feb. 13, 1821	1	87
Charles Edgar, [s. Horace L. & Clarissa], b. June 22, 1831; d. Sept. 19, 1832	2	7
Charles Edgar, [s. Horace L. & Clarissa], b. Sept. 6, 1833	2	7
Edwin, of Killingworth, m. Sarah **COOPER**, of Madison, Mar. 31, 1839, by Rev. Simeon Scranton	1	79

MADISON VITAL RECORDS 15

	Vol.	Page
DUDLEY (cont.)		
Everett W., m. Jane S. **MUNGER**, b. of Madison, Apr. 23, 1848, by Rev. Reuben Torrey	2	116
Harriet N., of Madison, m. George B. **HILLIARD**, of Killingworth, Nov. 28, 1833, by Rev. Samuel N. Shephard	1	34
Harriet Newell, d. Timothy & Theodora, b. Mar. 20, 1814	1	87
Horace L., m. Clarrissa **COE**, b. of Madison, Sept. 30, 1829, by Rev. Samuel N. Shephard	1	16
Jason, [s. Phinehas M. & Catharine], b. Oct. 15, 1834	2	7
Jonathan, m. Amanda **BENTON**, Nov. 26, 1828, by Rev. Samuel N. Shephard	1	15
Joseph W., m. Sivilla **NETTLETON**, b. of Madison, Oct. 25, 1843, by Rev. Samuel N. Shephard	2	104
Juliana, w. of Ebenezer, d. Sept. 18, 1852, ae 69 y.	1	164
Lancelott, [s. Phinehas M. & Catharine], b. Mar. 11, 1829	2	7
Lancellotte, m. Susan **HULL**, Jan. 26, 1851, by [Rev. Geo[rge] S. Hare]	2	140
Louisa, of Madison, m. Jason **SEAWARD**, 2d, of Guilford, Nov. 6, 1828, by Rev. Aaron Dutton	1	63
Maria, m. Stephen **WILLARD**, b. of Madison, June [ ], 1829, by Rev. Samuel N. Shephard	1	69
Martha E., of Madison, m. Charles A. **CHESTER**, of East Haddam, Sept. 17, 1848, by Rev. David Smith	2	120
Maryette, of Guilford, m. Daniel W. **WATERHOUS[E]**, of Saybrook, Oct. 23, 1833, by Rev. Samuel N. Shephard	1	70
Mary Lee, [d. Horace L. & Clarissa], b. May 25, 1835	2	7
Phinehas M., m. Catharine **BRADLEY**, b. of Madison, Sept. 8, 1827, by Rev. Pierpoint Brockett, of Killingworth	1	13
Polly, m. Frederick A. **NORTON**, July 3, 1842, by Rev. L. S. Hough	2	101
Rebecca, of Madison, m. Jehiel P. **WAY**, of Chester, June 6, 1849, by Rev. Samuel N. Shephard	2	122
Sally M., m. John A. **HILL**, Nov. 23, 1832, by Rev. Samuel N. Shephard	1	33
Samuel, m. Mary C. **SMITH**, Nov. 24, 1839, by Rev. Sam[ue]l N. Shephard	1	53
Sarah Matilda, d. Timothy & Theodora, b. Nov. 21, 1818	1	87
William, m. Clarrissa A. **FOWLER**, b. of Madison, June 8, 1836, by Rev. Samuel N. Shephard	1	78
ELLIOTT, John, D. D., Rev., d. Dec. 17, 1824, ae 56 y. Was pastor in East Guilford, since South Madison	1	170
ELY, John, Rev., d. Nov. 2, 1827, ae 64 y.	1	170
Mary Ann, of Madison, m. Youngs E. **BENTON**, of Guilford, Jan. 16, 1828, by Rev. Aaron Dutton, of Guilford	1	7
EVARTS, Amanda, wid. of Austin, d. Apr. 8, 1844, ae 49	1	170
Amanda, wid. [of Austin], d. Apr. 8, 1844, ae 49	2	38
Austin, s. Roswell & Ruth, b. Feb. 18, 1800	2	38
Austin, m. Amanda **NORTON**, May 15, 1822	2	38
Austin, d. Aug. 5, 1843, ae 43	1	170

BARBOUR COLLECTION

	Vol.	Page
EVARTS (cont.)		
Austin, d. Aug. 5, 1843, ae 43 y.	2	38
Caroline Charlotte, [d. Joel & Delia], b. May 16, 1828	1	92
Clarrissa A., of Guilford, m. John **GRISWOLD**, of Madison, July 28, 1836, by Rev. S. N. Shephard	1	27
Edward Webster, s. Leaming & Clarrissa, b. Oct. 17, 1831	1	92
Eliza Cornelia, [d. Joe & Delia], b. Aug. 19, 1817	1	92
Emily, [d. Joel & Delia], b. Apr. 2, 1820; d. Feb. 15, 1840	1	92
Emily, d. Joel, d. Feb. 15, 1840	1	170
Henry Austin, [s. Austin & Amanda], b. Feb. 28, 1837	2	38
Hysielton (?) Osborne, [s. Joel & Delia], b. June 10, 1831	1	92
Joel, d. July 27, 1839, ae 64 y.	1	170
Joel Ellsworth, [s. Joel & Delia], b. Apr. 10, 1826	1	92
Maria, [d. Joel & Delia], b. Mar. 11, 1816	1	92
Mary, m. Daniel **BARTLETT**, b. of Madison, Oct. 15, 1848, by Rev. Samuel N. Shephard	2	119
Mary Ann, m. Samuel R. **CRAMPTON**, b. of Madison, Oct. 29, 1839, by Rev. Samuel N. Shephard	1	230
Mary E., m. George **HEMMINGWAY**, b. of New Haven, May 5, 1852, by Rev. Samuel N. Shephard	2	143
Mary Lucretia, [d. Austin & Amanda], b. Jan. 12, 1823; d. Sept. 6, 1824	2	38
Nancy M., m. George **BISHOP**, b. of Madison, Feb. 19, 1846, by Rev. Samuel N. Shephard	2	112
Nancy Maria, d. Leaming & Clarrissa, b. Nov. 20, 1827	1	92
Oliver Wolcott, [s. Austin & Amanda], b. Oct. 29, 1832	2	38
Polly Minerva, [d. Joel & Delia], b. Jan. 15, 1824	1	92
Roger Griswold, [s. Austin & Amanda], b. Aug. 27, 1827	2	38
Samuel Justin, [s. Joel & Delia], b. Mar. 15, 1819; d. Apr. 20, 1819	1	92
Samuel Justin, [s. Joel & Delia], b. Nov. 19, 1822; d. Jan. 5, 1823	1	92
William, Jr., of Guilford, m. Sophronia **STEVENS**, of North Madison, May 31, 1832, by Jared Andrews	1	19
William Roswell, [s. Austin & Amanda], b. Mar. 20, 1825	2	38
Worthington Edwards, [s. Joel & Delia], b. Apr. 19, 1834	1	92
FAIRFIELD, Anne, of West Springfield, Mass., m. Caleb **MUNGER**, of North Madison, Jan. 5, 1834, by Rev. Stephen Hays	1	50
FENN, Benjamin S., of Canaan, m. Sally **SCRANTON**, of Madison, May 17, 1835, by Rev. Samuel N. Shephard	1	25
FIELD, Bethia, d. Feb. 10, 1835, ae 72	2	9
C. Elvina, m. A. E. **STONE**, Aug. 31, 1853, by Rev. W. B. Lee, of Fair Haven (C. Elvira)	2	145
Caroline Elvira, d. Joel & Rachel, b. Nov. 4, 1827	2	9
Edmund Franklin, [s. Kirtland & Frances], b. Jan. 1, 1845	2	9
Eliza Abigail, [d. George & Mary J.], b. Feb. 6, 1834	1	95
Ellen A., m. William G. **DOWD**, July 26, 1849, by Rev. Samuel N. Shephard	2	124
Frances Elizabeth, [d. Kirtland & Frances], b. Oct. 18, 1846	2	9

MADISON VITAL RECORDS 17

	Vol.	Page
FIELD (cont.)		
George, m. Mary **LEETE**, b. of Madison, Aug. 29, 1830, by Reynold Webb, J.P.	1	24
George Florenline, [s. George & Mary J.], b. Apr. 14, 1837; d. Oct. 28, 1838	1	95
Georgianna, m. George A. **SHELLEY**, b. of Madison, Apr. 10, 1849, by Rev. Samuel N. Shephard	2	121
Jane Eliza, [d. Frederick & Lucy], b. Jan. 3, 1841	2	9
Jemima, of Madison, m. Jeremiah A. **HALL**, of Wallingford, Nov. 1, 1835, by Rev. Stephen Hays	1	34
Julia Ann., m. Col. Jared **WILLARD**, b. of Madison, Nov. 8, 1835, by Rev. Stephen Hays	1	71
Julius, of Madison, m. Mary Ann **IVES**, of Killingworth, June 2, 1850, by Rev. Reuben Torrey	2	138
Kirtland, m. Frances E. **GRIFFETH**, b. of Madison, Nov. 2, 1841, by Rev. Samuel N. Shephard	1	26
Lawrence A., m. Delia Frances **DOWD**, b. of Madison, Dec. 24, 1845, by Rev. George F. Kettell	2	108
Mabel, m. Heman **STONE**, Jr., b. of Madison, Nov. 6, 1828, by Rev. Zolva Whitmore, of Guilford	1	64
Martha Jane, [d. George & Mary J.], b. Dec. 27, 1838	1	95
Mary, m. John **MEIGS**, Apr. 2, 1801	2	17
Mary A., d. Martin, d. Sept. 18, 1837, ae 25	2	9
Mary Elizabeth, [d. Frederick & Lucy], b. Nov. 20, 1837	2	9
Oswell Warren, [s. George & Mary J.], b. Dec. 4, 1830	1	95
Rebecca E., m. Augustus M. **DOWD**, b. of Madison, Oct. 22, 1845, by Rev. Samuel N. Shephard	2	111
Rodolphus Leete, [s. George & Mary J.], b. July 11, 1832	1	95
Roxanna, m. William **CRUTTENDEN**, b. of Madison, Mar. 8, 1828, by Rev. Samuel N. Shephard	1	10
Samuel, m. Susan **NORTON**, b. of Madison, May 10, 1832, by Rev. Samuel N. Shephard	1	25
Sarah O., of Madison, m. Lewis W. **COLLINS**, of Corinth, Vt., May 7, 1843, by Rev. Lent S. Hough	2	103
Thomas S., m. Julette **WILCOX**, b. of Madison, Nov. 16, 1847, by Rev. Samuel N. Shephard	2	119
FITCH, Delia A., m. Henry **SCRANTON**, Aug. 15, 1848, by Rev. Samuel N. Shephard	2	118
FORBES, Benjamin F., of Branford, m. Malinda F. **SHELLEY**, of Madison, Nov. 25, 1847, by Rev. Samuel N. Shephard	2	119
FOSTER, Alfred, s. Orrin & Rachel, b. May 12, 1816; d. Apr. 26, 1817	1	94
Alpha, m. Abraham **MAINE**, Jan. [ ], 1828, by Rev. Samuel N. Shephard	1	49
Alpha Luranda, d. Orrin & Rachel, b. May 12, 1816	1	94
Caroline, d. Orrin & Rachel, b. Mar. 13, 1804	1	94
Chloe Maria, d. Orrin & Rachel, b. Jan. 24, 1800	1	94
Clarrinda Orret, d. [Frederick & Roxanna], b. Sept. 14, 1823	2	9
Clarrissa Amelia, d. Orrin & Rachel, b. Dec. 18, 1812	1	94
Daniel Alfred, .s. Orrin & Rachel, b. July 24, 1821	1	95
David Stone, s. Orrin & Rachel, b. Apr. 11, 1802	1	94

	Vol.	Page
FOSTER (cont.)		
Eliza Ann, d. Orrin & Rachel, b. Feb. 19, 1808	1	94
Eliza Ann, m. Luman **JOHNSON**, b. of Madison, Sept. 17, 1829, by Rev. Samuel N. Shephard	1	39
Emily A., m. Henry D. **KNOWLES**, b. of Madison, June 13, 1852, by Rev. Samuel N. Shephard	2	144
Harriet, d. Orrin & Rachel, b. July 11, 1818	1	95
Jane Frances, [d. Frederick & Roxanna], b. June 28, 1826	2	9
Leander, s. Orrin & Rachel, b. Mar. 19, 1806	1	94
Lucinda, m. Zenas **NORTON**, b. of Madison, Jan. 2, 1832, by Rev. Samuel N. Shephard	1	55
Lydia A., m. Timothy F. **WILCOX**, b. of Madison, Mar. 27, 1845, by Rev. Samuel N. Shephard	2	109
Lydia Almira, [d. Frederick & Roxanna], b. June 11, 1820	2	9
Marvin, m. Eliza Ann **SHELLEY**, b. of Madison, Sept. 5, 1831, by Rev. Samuel N. Shephard	1	25
Mary Roxanna, [d. Frederick & Roxanna], b. Apr. 4, 1831	2	9
Orpha, m. Joel R. **NORTON**, b. of Madison, Nov. 22, 1827, by Rev. Samuel N. Shephard	1	55
Orrin, b. Mar. 18, 1776	1	94
Prudence, w. of Saul, d. Feb. 25, 1834, ae 80	2	9
Saul, d. July 16, 1842, ae 86	2	9
Sophia Manerva, d .Orrin & Rachel, b. Apr. 12, 1810	1	94
Susan M., m. William H. **JOHNSON**, b. of Madison, June 6, 1841, by Rev. Judson A. Root	1	39
Susan Matilda, d. Orrin & Rachel, b. Mar. 30, 1823	1	95
FOWLER, Catharine, w. of Reuben R., d. Apr. 12, 1841	2	37
Clarrissa A., m. William **DUDLEY**, b. of Madison, June 8, 1836, by Rev. Samuel N. Shephard	1	78
Frederick, of Northford, m. Ellen A. **SCRANTON**, of Madison, Aug. 30, 1849, by Rev. Samuel N. Shephard	2	124
Maria, m. Josiah **MUNGER**, Jr., b. of Madison, Apr. 14, 1828, by Rev. Aaron Dutton, of Guilford	1	49
Mary, of Madison, m. Thomas H. **CLARK**, of Haddam, Oct. 7, 1835, by Rev. Aaron Dutton, of Guilford	1	12
Orrin S., m. Abigail M. **CRAMPTON**, b. of Madison, Jan. 11, 1830, by Rev. Samuel N. Shephard	1	24
Reuben Lewis, s. Reuben & Adah, b. Sept. 7, 1822	1	95
FRANCIS, Daniel, of Killingworth, m. Dolly **RICHMOND**, of Madison, Aug. 5, 1827, by Rev. Samuel West	1	24
James, of Durham, m. Ruth Ann **WILLARD**, of Madison, Oct. 12, 1830, by Rev. Samuel N. Shephard	1	24
GARDINER, Horace, of Springfield, Mass., m. Charlotte A. **DICKINSON**, of Haddam, Conn., Nov. 27, 1836, by Rev. Stephen Hays	1	28
GARDNER, Charlotte A., m .Asa **STEVENS**, 2d, b. of Madison, July 30, 1848, by Rev. Reuben Torrey	2	119
Horace, d. June 25, 1846, ae 29 y.	2	36
Lucina Ann, d. Horace & Charlotte, b. Sept. 14, 1845	2	36

	Vol.	Page
GAYLORD, Charles L., of Middletown, m. Catharine L. MUNGER, of Madison, Apr. 7, 1848, by Rev. Reuben Torrey	2	116
GLADWIN, Josiah B., of Middletown, m. Eliza A. MUNGER, of Madison, May 13, 1838, by Rev. Samuel N. Shephard	1	27
Josiah B., of Guliford, m. Mary S. WILLCOX, of Madison, May 5, 1844, by Rev. L. S. Hough	2	105
GOLDTHWAIT, Ebenezer, of Granby, Mass., m. Elmira PARDEE, of Madison, Apr. 29, 1830, by Rev. Samuel West	1	27
GRAVE, Abigail, m. Daniel BENTON, Nov. 29, 1832, by Rev. Samuel N. Shephard	1	9
Ann Augusta, [d. Hubbard & Betsey], b. June 12, 1830; d. Apr. 14, 1833	2	10
Elias Cleveland, [s. Hubbard & Betsey], b. June 12, 1820; d. Aug. 16, 1822	2	10
Frances M., of Madison, m. William D. MEIGS, of New Haven, Sept. 27, 1849, by Rev. Samuel N. Shephard	2	124
Frances Meriam, d. John & Rebecca, b. Aug. 13, 1824	1	98
Mary, [d. Hubbard & Betsey], b. Apr. 23, 1828	2	10
Mary, m. Gustavus K. REDFIELD, b. of Madison, May 2, 1848, by Rev. Samuel N. Shephard	2	117
Roxann, m. Benjamin KELSEY, b. of Madison, Apr. 8, 1838, by Rev. Samuel N. Shephard	1	43
Susan, m. Samuel GRISWOLD, b. of Madison, Nov. 29, 1832, by Rev. Samuel N. Shephard	1	27
William Cleveland, [s. Hubbard & Betsey], b. Aug. 13, 1826; d. Jan. 22, 1827	2	10
GREEN, Lucy, of Madison, m. Nicholas HEMINGWAY, of Wallingford, Nov. 24, 1836, by Rev. Stephen Hays	1	35
GRIFFETH, GRIFFITH, Frances E., m. Kirtland FIELD, b. of Madison, Nov. 2, 1841, by Rev. Samuel N. Shephard	1	26
Joseph B., m. Sarah E. HILL, b. of Madison, Nov. 3, 1845, by Rev. Samuel N. Shephard	2	111
William C., d. Nov. 30, 1831, ae 54	1	175
GRIFFING, Jared, of Branford, m. Thankful STANNARD, of Guilford; Aug. 31, 1845, by Rev. George F. Kettell	2	108
Jerusha, m. Joseph PELTON, b. of Madison, June 12, 1842, by Rev. Samuel N. Shephard	2	108
Susan Amelia, of Madison, m. Albert CAHOON, of Killingworth, Feb. 1, 1846, by Rev. George F. Kettell	2	108
William L., m. Fanny M. BRADLEY, b. of Madison, July 16, 1849, by Rev. Samuel N. Shephard	2	123
GRIFFITH, [see under GRIFFETH]		
GRISWOLD, Charles E., m. Dolisca A. STONE, b. of Madison, Aug. 29, 1852, by Rev. W. W. Brown	2	144
Charles Pratt, [s. Daniel & Anne], b. Apr. 11, 1826	2	10
Clarissa, b. Jan. 7, 1791; m. Abraham Fowler SCRANTON, Nov. 22, 1810	2	27

	Vol.	Page
GRISWOLD (cont.)		
Clarissa H., of Clinton, m. James **WILCOX**, of Madison, Feb. 11, 1851, by Rev. Samuel N. Shephard	2	140
Cynthia A., m. W[illia]m C. **BUSHNELL**, b. of Madison, Oct. 11, 1837, by Rev. S. N. Shephard	1	77
Cynthia Ann, [d. Josiah & Chloe], b. Jan. 29, 1815	2	10
Cynthia S., of Madison, m. Samuel D. **BEEBE**, of Norwich, Apr. 9, 1851, by Rev. Samuel N. Shephard	2	141
Henry Josiah, [s. John & Clarissa], b. July 4, 1837	2	10
John, [s. Josiah & Chloe], b. June 13, 1809; d. Apr. 24, 1810	2	10
John, [s. Josiah & Chloe], b. July 25, 1812	2	10
John, of Madison, m. Clarrissa A. **EVARTS**, of Guilford, July 28, 1836, by Rev. S. N. Shephard	1	27
Phinehas Meigs, [s. Daniel & Anna], b. May 5, 1829	2	10
Samuel, [s. Josiah & Chloe], b. July 7, 1807	2	10
Samuel, m. Susan **GRAVE**, b. of Madison, Nov. 29, 1832, by Rev. Samuel N. Shephard	1	27
Samuel W[illia]m, [s. John & Clarrissa], b. June 19, 1840	2	10
Sarah, of Madison, m. Charles **HILLIARD**, of Killingworth, Apr. 23, 1828, by Rev. Samuel N. Shephard	1	32
HALE, Harvey, m. Mrs. Mary **DAVIS**, b. of Madison, July 5, 1829, by Rev. Samuel West	1	32
Nancy, m. Joseph A. **ROGERS**, Mar. 4, 1830, by Rev. David Smith, of Durham	1	61
Olive C., of Madison, m. Watson **DAVIS**, of Killingworth, Sept. 21, 1831, by Rev. F. W. Sizer, of Durham	1	14
HALL, [see also **HOEL** and **HULL**], Alexander W., of Wallingford, m. Matilda E. **WILCOX**, of Madison, June 17, 1830, by Rev. Samuel N. Shephard	1	33
Clarrissa M., of Madison, m. Benjamin **WILLIAMS**, Jr., of Essex, Apr. 20, 1845, by Rev. Samuel N. Shephard	2	107
Frederick W., of Guilford, m. Elizabeth M. **BUSHNELL**, of Madison, Mar. 14, 1832, by Rev. Samuel N. Shephard	1	33
Henry, m. Maretta **KELSEY**, b. of Guilford, May 9, 1852, by Rev. Samuel N. Shephard	2	143
Jeremiah A., of Wallingford, m. Jemima **FIELD**, of Madison, Nov. 1, 1835, by Rev. Stephen Hays	1	34
HALSEY, Mary Ann, m. John M. **MEIGS**, May 21, 1839	2	18
HAND, Artemesia, m. Ichabod L. **SCRANTON**, b. of Madison, Nov. 29, 1827, by Rev. Samuel N. Shephard	1	63
HARRIS, Elijah W., m. Angeline **DOUD**, b. of Madison, June 5, 1828, by Rev. Samuel N. Shephard	1	32
Mary, m. David D. **DOUD**, b. of Madison, Jan. 15, 1829, by Rev. Samuel N. Shephard	1	15

MADISON VITAL RECORDS 21

	Vol.	Page
HARRISON, Abigail, m. Jonathan **WILLARD**, b. of Madison, Sept. 16, 1845, by Rev. Samuel N. Shephard	2	110
Ann E., [d. James & Clarrissa], b. Apr. 8, 1828	2	36
Augustus Minor, [s. James & Clarrissa], b. Apr. 8, 1824	2	36
Edwin A., [s. James & Clarrissa], b. Apr. 20, 1818	2	36
Ellen L., [d. James & Clarrissa], b. Aug. 6, 1830	2	36
Ellen L., [d. James & Clarrissa], b. Nov. 9, 1832	2	36
Gustavus, [s. James & Clarrissa], b. Apr. 8, 1824	2	36
Imman, of Madison, m. Sibyl M. **NETTLETON**, of Killingworth, Feb. 23, 1843, by Rev. Lent S. Hough	2	102
James M. [s. James & Clarrissa], b. June 2, 1821	2	36
Marian J., of Madison, m. Homer H. **WELLMAN**, of New York, Oct. 7, 1851, by Rev. E. Edwin Hall, of Guilford	2	142
Marion S., [d. James & Clarrissa], b. May 17, 1826	2	36
HART, Baldwin, [s. Benjamin & Lucy], b. Mar. 12, 1815	2	11
Baldwin, of Madison, m. Charlotte Jemima **WELLES**, of Weathersfield, Dec. 23, 1841, by Rev. Joab Brace	2	11
Benjamin, [s. Benjamin & Lucy], b. Aug. 8, 1812; d. May 16, 1815	2	11
Benjamin, Dea., d. Jan. 4, 1852, ae 81 y.	2	11
Mabel, [d. Benjamin & Mary], b. Jan. 28, 1808; d. Feb. 25, 1826	2	11
Mary, [d. Benjamin & Mary], b. Mar. 31, 1805; d. Sept. 26, 1805	2	11
Mary, [d. Benjamin & Mary], b. Sept. 16, 1809; d. Mar. 13, 1810	2	11
William A., of Durham, m. Sally M. **JONES**, of Madison, June 25, 1828, by Rev. Zolva Whitmore, of Guilford	1	32
William Winthrop, [s. Benjamin & Lucy], b. Mar. 19, 1835	2	11
HAYS, Martha A., m. Samuel **NORTON**, b. of North Madison, Sept. 29, 1834, by Rev. Stephen Hays	1	56
HEALD, William L., of North Haven, m. Jane R. **DOWD**, of Madison, Mar. 26, 1845, by Rev. Samuel N. Shephard	2	109
HEMINGWAY, HEMMINGWAY, George, m. Mary E. **EVARTS**, b. of New Haven, May 5, 1852, by Rev. Samuel N. Shephard	2	143
Nicholos, of Wallingford, m. Lucy **GREEN**, of Madison, Nov. 24, 1836, by Rev. Stephen Hays	1	35
HILL, Alpha, m. James Harvey **DOUD**, Oct. 25, 1835, by Rev. David Baldwin	1	17
Betsey Ann, d. Daniel & Betsey, b. Apr. 1, 1830	1	101
Emily A., Mrs., of Madison, m. Darius **STANNARD**, of Saybrook, June 17, 1838, by Rev. Simeon Scranton	1	74
Emily M., of Madison, m. John W. **WIGGINS**, of Brooklyn, N.Y., Nov. 17, 1839, by Rev. Samuel N. Shephard	1	31
Eugene Childs, s. Samuel Butler & Hannah C., b. Mar. 14, 1845	2	11

BARBOUR COLLECTION

	Vol.	Page
HILL (cont.)		
Florilla D., of Madison, m. Lyman A. **PRATT**, of New Haven, May 29, 1842, by Rev. Samuel N. Shephard	2	100
George S., [s. Abram G. & Roxanna], b. Apr. 25, 1841	2	35
Harriet E., of Madison, m. Charles **TYLER**, of Haddam, Oct. 5, 1845, by Rev. Samuel N. Shephard	2	111
Henry S., m. Dency L. **MUNGER**, [Apr.] 21, [1850], by Rev. Reuben Torrey	2	138
Henry Sherman, s. Daniel & Betsey, b. June 4, 1827	1	101
Horace Oscar, s. Daniel & Betsey, b. Mar. 2, 1836	1	101
Ichabod, [s. Abram G. & Roxanna], b. July 16, 1828	2	35
Joel Munger, s. Daniel & Betsey, b. Sept. 21, 1833	1	101
John, of North Branford, m. Polly **WILLARD**, of Madison, Sept. 18, 1839, by Rev. Sam[ue]l N. Shephard	1	36
John A., m. Sally M. **DUDLEY**, Nov. 23, 1832, by Rev. Samuel N. Shephard	1	33
John Edward, s. John A. & Sarah M., b. Aug. 11, 1837	2	11
Joseph, d. Sept. 29, 1840, at North Madison, ae 75 y.	2	11
Joseph Hosmer, m. Emily **THOMPSON**, Aug. 14, 1831, by Rev. David Baldwin	1	33
Julius A., m. Henrietta H. **CRAMPTON**, b. of Madison, Sept. 16, 1835, by Rev. Samuel N. Shephard	1	34
Lois L., [d. Abram G. & Roxanna], b. Apr. 4, 1831	2	35
Lucy M., [d. Abram G. & Roxanna], b. June 20, 1835	2	35
Lydia Ann, [d. Abram G. & Roxanna], b. July 2, 1820	2	35
Orpha M., of Madison, m. Bridgeman G. **WHITE**, of Durham, Apr. 13, 1845, by Rev. L. S. Hough	2	106
Rosetta, [d. Abram G. & Roxanna], b. Nov. 11, 1838	2	35
Roxanna, m. William F. **CONKLING**, b. of Madison, Sept. 14, 1851, by Rev. Samuel N. Shephard	2	141
Samuel B., m. Caroline **SCRANTON**, b. of Madison, July 30, 1845, by Rev. Samuel N. Shephard	2	110
Samuel Brown, m. Orphana **KELSEY**, b. of Madison, Sept. 19, 1838, by Rev. Samuel N. Shephard	1	36
Samuel Butler, m. Hannah **COAN**, b. of Madison, Feb. 13, 1838, by Rev. Simeon Scranton	1	35
Sarah E., [d. Abram G. & Roxanna], b. Mar. 2, 1823	2	35
Sarah E., m. Joseph B. **GRIFFITH**, b. of Madison, Nov. 3, 1845, by Rev. Samuel N. Shephard	2	111
HILLIARD, Charles, of Killingworth, m. Sarah **GRISWOLD**, of Madison, Apr. 23, 1828, by Rev. Samuel N. Shephard	1	32
George B., of Killingworth, m. Harriet N. **DUDLEY**, of Madison, Nov. 28, 1833, by Rev. Samuel N. Shephard	1	34
HOEL, [see also **HOWELL**], Cynthia, m. Ellsworth **BASSETT**, Nov. 23, 1831, by Rev. Samuel N. Shephard	1	9
Philena, of Madison, m. Richard P. **CLARK**, of Saybrook, Apr. 11, 1830, by Rev. Samuel N. Shephard	1	11

	Vol.	Page
HOWELL, [see also HOEL], Nathan, m. Maria S. BASSETT, b. of Madison, Nov. 24, 1843, by Rev. Samuel N. Shephard	2	104
HOYT, Caroline, [d. Abel & Abigail], b. Jan. 30, 1801	2	10
Chlotilda, [d. Abel & Abigail], b. Aug. 2, 1807	2	10
Jonathan Samuel, [s. Abel & Abigail], b. Dec. 30, 1817	2	10
HULL, Cynthia, m. John M. BISHOP, b. of Madison, Apr. 1, 1844, by Rev. Henry Chase, at 44 Market St., New York. Recorded Aug. 18, 1890	2	115
Horace, m. Emily NORTON, b. of Madison, Oct. 26, 1836, by Rev. S. N. Shephard	1	35
Horace Augustus, [s. Horace & Emily], b. Jan. 6, 1838	2	11
Lydia, m. Charles WILLIAMS, b. of Madison, Feb. 25, 1831, by Rev. Samuel N. Shephard	1	70
Mary, [d. Horace & Emily], b. Aug. 30, 1841	2	11
Orrin, of Wallingford, m. Angenora DOWD, of Madison, [, 1839?], by Rev. Samuel N. Shephard	1	37
Susan, m. Lancellotte DUDLEY, Jan. 26, 1851, by [Rev. Geo[rge] S. Hare]	2	140
HUMISTON, Dwight, m. Mary M. CHITTENDEN, Nov. 6, 1845, by Rev. David Baldwin	2	107
ISBELL, Orland W., of Killingworth, m. Amanda DOELITTLE, of Madison, Sept. 9, 1829, by Rev. David Metcalf	1	38
IVES, Mary Ann, of Killingworth, m. Julius FIELD, of Madison, June 2, 1850, by Rev. Reuben Torrey	2	138
JOHNSON, Emily C., m. Edwin L. JONES, Jan. 1, 1838, by Rev. Stephen Hays	1	39
Luman, m. Eliza Ann FOSTER, b. of Madison, Sept. 17, 1829, by Rev. Samuel N. Shephard	1	39
Sarah, m. Bela LANE, Dec. 15, 1831, by Asa King, Killingworth	1	45
Stephen, of Haddam, m. Polly STEVENS, of Madison, June 16, 1839, by Rev. Edmund O. Bates	1	38
William H., m. Susan M. FOSTER, b. of Madison, June 6, 1841, by Rev. Judson A. Root	1	39
William H., of Guilford, m. Emily M. STEVENS, of Westbrook, Nov. 29, 1849, by Rev. Samuel N. Shephard	2	137
JONES, Augusta E., of Madison, m. Horace E. PAGE, of Guilford, Aug. 24, 1844, by Rev. L. S. Hough	2	105
Edwin L., m. Emily C. JOHNSON, Jan. 1, 1838, by Rev. Stephen Hays	1	39
Laura A., of North Madison, m. Samuel SMITH, of New York, Dec. 6, 1841, by Judson A. Root	1	60
Nathaniel C., of Mereden, m. Aplpha J. STEVENS, of Madison, Oct. 3, 1852, by Rev. W. W. Brown	2	144
Phebe Ann, m. Samuel STEAVENS, Nov. 11, 1840, by Rev. Ja[me]s H. Perry	1	74
Sally M., of Madison, m. William A. HART, of Durham, June 25, 1828, by Rev. Zolva Whitmore, of Guilford	1	32
JUDD, Betsey, w. of Maj. Eber, d. Nov. 19, 1803, ae 24 y.	2	12

	Vol.	Page
JUDD (cont.)		
Betsey B., m. Jonathan T. **LEE**, b. of Madison, Nov. 22, 1827, by Rev. Samuel N. Shephard	1	45
Betsey Barnes, d. Eber & Betsey, b. Nov. 16, 1803	2	12
Jonathan, d. Dec. 25, 1802, ae 52 y.	2	12
Mabel, wid., d. Sept. 27, 1833, ae 76	2	12
JUDSON, Charlotte M., m. Timothy V. **MEIGS**, b. of Madison, Nov. 29, 1832, by Rev. Samuel N. Shephard	1	51
Charlotte Matilda, d. Reuben & Chloe, b. Dec. 3, 1806	2	12
KELSEY, Austin, m. Maria **BRISTOL**, b. of Madison, June 19, 1836, by Rev. Stephen Hays	1	42
Benjamin, m. Roxann **GRAVE**, b. of Madison, Apr. 8, 1838, by Rev. Samuel N. Shephard	1	43
Clarrissa, of Madison, m. James **THOMAS**, of Haddam, Nov. [ ], 1826, by Rev. Samuel N. Shephard	1	60
Edward F., m. Elizabeth **WILCOX**, b. of Madison, Sept. 4, 1828, by Rev. Samuel N. Shephard	1	42
Elihu, of Saybrook, m. Catharine **SMITH**, of Madison, Mar. 28, 1848, by Rev. Samuel N. Shephard	2	115
Eliza, of Madison, m. Frederick **LANE**, of Chester, Mar. 12, 1833, by Stephen A. Loper	1	46
Francis Ashman, s. Edward F. & Elizabeth W., b. Apr. 6, 1829	1	109
Francis Ashmun, [s. Edward F. & Elizabeth], b. Apr. 6, 1829	2	13
Lois, wid., of Stephen, d. Mar. 22, 1844, ae 83	2	37
Lucy, w. of Edward, d. May 10, 1841, ae 67	2	13
Maretta, m. Henry **HALL**, b. of Guilford, May 9, 1852, by Rev. Samuel N Shephard	2	143
Mary, of Killingworth, m. David R. **MEIGS**, of Madison, July 4, 1829, by Rev. Sam[ue]l N. Shephard	1	50
Mary Elizabeth, d. Edward F. & Elizabeth W., b. Apr. 26, 1834	1	109
Mary Elizabeth, [d. Edward F. & Elizabeth], b. Apr. 26, 1834	2	13
Orphana, m. Samuel Brown **HILL**, b. of Madison, Sept. 19, 1838, by Rev. Samuel N. Shephard	1	36
Titus, m. Sarah **CONKLING**, Oct. 26, 1836, by Rev. S. N. Shephard	1	42
William, of Killingworth, m. Caroline Adah **MUNGER**, of Madison, July 8, 1838, by Rev. Harvey Bushnell	1	43
William, of Killingworth, m. Sarah M. **MUNGER**, of Madison, May 26, 1844, by Rev. L. S. Hough	2	105
KIRTLAND, Charles P., m. Sarah E. **COE**, Apr. 2, 1851, by Rev. Geo[rge] S. Hare	2	140
KNOWLES, Henry D., m. Emily A. **FOSTER**, b. of Madison, June 13, 1852, by Rev. Samuel N. Shephard	2	144
LANE, Bela, m. Sarah **JOHNSON**, Dec. 15, 1831, by Asa King, Killingworth	1	45
Frederick, of Chester, m. Eliza **KELSEY**, of Madison, Mar. 12, 1833, by Stephen A. Loper	1	46

	Vol.	Page
LANE (cont.)		
Nathan, of Killingworth, m. Emily M. **DOOLITTLE**, of Madison, June 18, 1843, by Rev. L. S. Hough	2	103
Noah, m. Betsey **STEAVENS**, b. of Madison, May 10, 1827, by Rev. Zolva Whitmore, of Guilford	1	45
LEE, Charlotte, of Madison, m. Orlando **WILCOX**, of Killingworth, Aug. 8, 1837, by S. N. Shephard	1	75
Henry, m. Rosalin **SMITH**, b. of Madison, May 6, 1840, by Rev. S. N. Shephard	1	46
Henry, m. Abigail **DUDLEY**, b. of Madison, Nov. 13, 1850, by Rev. Samuel N. Shephard	2	139
Jonathan T., m. Betsey B. **JUDD**, b. of Madison, Nov. 22, 1827, by Rev. Samuel N. Shephard	1	45
Luranda C., m. Edward M. **MEIGS**, b. of Madison, Sept. 15, 1852, by Rev. Samuel N. Shephard	2	145
Maria C., m. Edwin **BIDWELL**, b. of Madison, June 8, 1848, by Rev. Samuel N. Shephard	2	117
Timothy H., m. Lusanda C. **CHITTENDEN**, b. of Madison, Nov. 24, 1831, by Rev. Samuel N. Shephard	1	46
LEETE, Martha, m. Edwin **DeFORREST**, July 14, 1850, by [Rev. Geo[rge] S. Hare]	2	140
Mary, m. George **FIELD**, b. of Madison, Aug. 29, 1830, by Reynold Webb, J.:P.	1	24
Mary, of Guilford, m. Russsell **CRAMPTON**, of Madison, Sept. 9, 1835, by Rev. Aaron Dutton, of Guilford	1	12
LINDLEY, Rachel, b. Oct. 14, 1800; m. Henry **SCRANTON**, May 19, 1823; d. Apr. 28, 1841	2	24
LOPER, Stephen Alonzo, m. Sarah B. **MEIGS**, Apr. 11, 1827, by Rev. Samuel N. Shephard	1	45
LUCAS, John A., m. Mary A. **COX**, of Middletown, June 27, 1850, by [Rev. Geo[rge] S. Hare]	2	140
LYNDS, Benjamin, of Chester, m. Amanda **BRADLEY**, of Madison, Sept. 24, 1840, by Rev. S. N. Shephard	1	46
MAINE, Abraham, m. Alpha **FOSTER**, Jan. [ ], 1828, by Rev. Samuel N. Shephard	1	49
Alpha, m. Benjamin C. **SHELLEY**, Dec. 24, 1829, by Rev. Sam[ue]l N. Shephard	1	65
MAYNARD, Samuel W., of Durham, m. Sally Adeline **CRAMPTON**, of Madison, Aug. 4, 1841 ,by Rev. Judson A. Root	1	51
McFADDEN, John, m. Julia **DOLAN**, b. of Ireland, Nov. 10, 1851, by Rev. Samuel N. Shephard	2	142
MEIGS, Abel, d. Aug. 19, 1842, ae 77	2	37
Abigail Field, [d. John & Mary], b. May 14, 1809	2	17
Benjamin Hart, [s. Bezaleel J. & Elizabeth], b. May 15, 1832; d. Mar. 25, 1833	2	17
Charles Augustus, [s. Bezaleel J. & Elizabeth], b. Oct. 17, 1818	2	17
Charles Morrison, [s. John M. & Mary Ann H.], b. Oct. 7, 1846	2	18
Concourence, w. of Phinehas, d. Dec. 24, 1836, ae 62 y.	2	37

BARBOUR COLLECTION

	Vol.	Page
MEIGS (cont.)		
Daniel Benjamin, [s. John M. & Mary Ann H.], b .Feb. 19, 1840	2	18
David R., of Madison, m. Mary **KELSEY**, of Killingworth, July 4, 1829, by Rev. Sam[ue]l N. Shephard	1	50
David Rich, [s. John & Mary], b. Dec. 1, 1803	2	17
Edgar Courtland, [s. John M. & Mary Ann H.], b. Apr. 19, 1841	2	18
Edmond Hand, [s. Bezaleel J. & Elizabeth], b. May 4, 1823	2	17
Edward E., [twin with Ellen E., s. Edward M. & Mariette], b. June 28, 1837	2	17
Edward M., m. Marietta **WILCOX**, b. of Madison, June [ ], 1829, by Rev. Sam[ue]l N. Shephard, of Guilford	1	50
Edward M., m. Luranda C. **LEE**, b. of Madison, Sept. 15, 1852, by Rev. Samuel N. Shephard	2	145
Edward Mulford, [s. John & Mary], b. Mar. 25, 1805	2	17
Elizabeth, [d. John & Mary], b. Apr. 9, 1815	2	17
Ellen E., [twin with Edward E., d. Edward M. & Mariette], b. June 28, 1837	2	17
Emeline, [d. John & Mary], b. Mar. 8, 1811; d. Sept. 25, 1841	2	17
Frederick Dowd, s. Alfred T., b. May 7, 1852	2	40
Hannah, m. Curtis **WILCOX**, b. of Madison, July 28, 1829, by Rev. Samuel N. Shephard	1	69
Henry Josiah, [s. John & Mary], b. Oct. 29, 1823	2	17
Horace Bezaleel, [s. Bezaleel J. & Elizabeth], b. Oct. 10, 1829	2	17
Jehiel, [s. John & Mary], b. Sept. 24, 1817; d. Nov. 18, 1842	2	17
Jehiel Henry, [s. John M. & Mary Ann H.], b. Nov. 3, 1842	2	18
John, m. Mary **FIELD**, Apr. 2, 1801	2	17
John M., m. Mary Ann **HALSEY**, May 21, 1839	2	18
John Morrison, [s. John & Mary], b. Mar. 15, 1813	2	17
Louisa Maria, [d. Bezaleel J. & Elizabeth], b. Oct. 3, 1835	2	17
Lovisa, [d. John & Mary], b. Jan. 15, 1802	2	17
Mary A., of Madison, m. Lay W. **PRATT**, of Saybrook, May [ ], 1829, by Rev. Samuel N. Shephard	1	58
Mary Ann, [d. John & Mary], b. June 6, 1807	2	17
Nancy Maria, [d. Bezaleel J. & Elizabeth], b. Nov. 9, 1821; d. May 15, 1822	2	17
Rachel, m. George W. **PILGRIM**, May 30, 1831, by Rev. Sam[ue]l N. Shephard	1	58
Richard S., [s. Edward M. & Marriette], b. July 30, 1833	2	17
Samuel S., m. Mary Ann **SMITH**, Sept. 29, 1843, by Rev. Samuel N. Shephard	2	104
Sarah B., m. Stephen Alonzo **LOPER**, Apr. 11, 1827, by Rev. Samuel N. Shephard	1	45
Theodore Fordham, [s. John M. & Mary Ann H.], b. Aug. 10, 1844	2	18

MADISON VITAL RECORDS 27

	Vol.	Page
MEIGS (cont.)		
Timothy A., m. Mary L. **ALLINGTON**, b. of Madison, Oct. 24, 1841, by Rev. Samuel N. Shephard	1	52
Timothy Alfred, [s. John & Mary], b. Jan. 29, 1820	2	17
Timothy V., m. Charlotte M. **JUDSON**, b. of Madison, Nov. 29, 1832, by Rev. Samuel N. Shephard	1	51
Vincent Return, [s. Bezaleel J. & Elizabeth], b. June 23, 1838	2	17
William D., of New Haven, m. Frances M. **GRAVE**, of Madison, Sept. 27, 1849, by Rev. Samuel N. Shephard	2	124
William Dowd, [s. Bezaleel J. & Elizabeth], b. Aug. 26, 1825	2	17
-----, [child of John M. & Mary Ann H.], b. June 9, 1848	2	18
MILLER, Susan Maria, [d. Daniel W & Adeline C.], b. Apr. 22, 1841	2	18
MINOR, Ellen Sophia, [d. Charles M. & Sophia P.], b. May 1, 1837; d. Oct. 24, 1838	2	18
John Strong, [s. Charles M. & Sophia P.], b .Oct. 28, 1839; d. Apr. 18, 1841	2	18
Stephen Platts, [s. Charles M. & Sophia P.], b. Feb. 14, 1835	2	18
William Collins, [s. Charles M. & Sophia P.], b. Apr. 28, 1833	2	18
MIX, Elias C.*, m. Louisa **TRYON**, b. of Saybrook, Dec. 23, 1834, by Rev. Samuel N. Shephard (*Written "Josiah")	1	51
Josiah*, m. Louisa **TRYON**, b. of Saybrook, Dec. 23, 1834, by Rev. Samuel N. Shephard (*Should be "Elias C.")	1	51
MORGAN, Ann Elizabeth, [d. Elisha & Mary Ann], b. Mar. 29, 1843	2	19
William Henry, [s. Elisha & Mary Ann], b. Oct. 27, 1841	2	19
MOULTHROP, Joseph C., of North Branford, m. Ellen A. **DOWD**, of Madison, May 22, 1845, by Rev. Samuel N. Shephard	2	107
MUNGER, Alonzo N., of Bergen, N.Y., m. Adeline M. **WILCOX**, of Madison, Sept. 7, 1846, by Rev. Samuel N. Shephard	2	113
Ann Eliza, d. Walter P. & Eliza S., b. Feb. 27, 1836	1	113
Ann Eliza, [d. Walter S. & Eliza S.], b. Feb. 27, 1836	2	15
Caleb, of North Madison, m. Anne **FAIRFIELD**, of West Springfield, Mass., Jan. 5, 1834, by Rev. Stephen Hays	1	50
Caroline A., m. Alfred N. **WILLCOX**, b. of Madison, Nov. 5, 1845, by Rev. Samuel N. Shephard	2	111
Caroline Adah, of Madison, m. William **KELSEY**, of Killingworth, July 8, 1838, by Rev. Harvey Bushnell	1	43
Catharine L., of Madison, m. Charles L. **GAYLORD**, of Middletown, Apr. 7, 1848, by Rev. Reuben Torrey	2	116
Catharine Lucy, [d. Hubbard S. & Mabel], b. Nov. 5, 1822	2	15

BARBOUR COLLECTION

	Vol.	Page
MUNGER (cont.)		
Charles Everard, [s. Truman & Nancy], b. July 27, 1840	1	114
Cynthia, of Madison, m. Asa **BRADLEY**, of North Haven, May 4, 1830, by Rev. Samuel West	1	7
Daniel Hand, s. W[illia]m H. & Achsah, b. Oct. 17, 1818	1	112
Dency L., m. Henry S. **HILL**, [Apr.] 21, [1850], by Rev. Reuben Torrey	2	138
Dency Lucretia, [d. Hubbard S. & Mabel], b. Dec. 25, 1824	2	15
Ebenezer, d. Apr. 10, 1834, ae 79	1	187
Ebenezer, d. Apr. 10, 1834, ae 79	1	188
Eliza A., of Madison, m. Josiah B. **GLADWIN**, of Middletown, May 13, 1838, by Rev. Samuel N. Shephard	1	27
Eliza Ellen, [d. Gaylor & Dency], b. Jan. 23, 1838	2	15
Elizabeth Clark, d. W[illia]m H. & Achsah, b. Apr. 22, 1826	1	112
Esther, wid. of Wyllys, d. Mar. 12, 1846, ae 85 y. 6 m.	1	187
Esther Amelia, d. Walter P. & Eliza S., b. Mar. 17, 1834	1	113
Esther Amelia, [d. Walter S. & Eliza S.], b. Mar. 17, 1834	2	15
Fanny Ann, [d. Hubbard S. & Mabel], b. June 28, 1820	2	15
George Hubbard, [s. Gaylor & Dency], b. May 26, 1827	2	15
George W., s. Walter P. & Eliza S., b. Nov. 30, 1832	1	113
George Wyllys, [s. Walter S. & Eliza S.], b. Nov. 30, 1832	2	15
Gilbert Davis, [s. Sherman & Lucretia], b. Apr. 13, 1837	2	16
Henry Josiah, s. Josiah, Jr. & Maria, b. Feb. 4, 1829	1	114
Henry Judson, [s. Gaylor & Dency], b. Dec. 26, 1840	2	15
Jane S., m. Everett W. **DUDLEY**, b. of Madison, Apr. 23, 1848, by Rev. Reuben Torrey	2	116
Jane Submit, [d. Gaylor & Dency], b. Jan. 23, 1825	2	15
Jehiel, s. Wait & Lydia, b. Mar. 24, 1763	1	114
Joel, d. Sept. 15, 1838	2	37
Josiah, [s. Simeon & Sarah], b. Oct. 16, 1754; d. Aug. [ ], 1838	2	14
Josiah, Jr., m. Maria **FOWLER**, b. of Madison, Apr. 14, 1828, by Rev. Aaron Dutton, of Guilford	1	49
Levi Walter, s. W[illia]m H. & Sally, b. July 16, 1813; d. Sept. 19, 1821	1	112
Levi Walter, s. W[illia]m H. & Sally, d. Sept. 19, 1821, ae 8 y.	1	187
Levi Walter, s. W[illia]m H. & Achsah, b. May 22, 1824	1	112
Lucy Ann, [d. Gaylor & Dency], b. Oct. 13, 1834	2	15
Mabel, [d. Simeon & Sarah], b. Dec. 17, 1762; d. Nov. 19, 1833	2	14
Mabel Malissa, [d. Hubbard S. & Fanny], b. Dec. 16, 1828	2	15
Martha Ann, [d. Gaylor & Dency], b. Sept. 11, 1833; d. Sept. 13, 1833	2	15
Martha Hayes, [d. Hubbard S. & Fanny], b. Oct. 24, 1833	2	15
Mary, [d. Simeon & Sarah], b. Nov. 3, 1756; d. June [ ], 1840	2	14
Mary, w. of Joel, d. June 17, 1838	2	37

MADISON VITAL RECORDS

	Vol.	Page
MUNGER (cont.)		
Mary Hannah, [d. Hubbard S. & Fanny], b. Nov. 8, 1831	2	15
Mary Lucretia, [d. Sherman & Lucretia], b. May 15, 1828	2	16
Nancy Ellen, [d. Truman & Nancy], b. May 1, 1835	1	114
Parma, Mrs., of Madison, m. Minor **BRADLEY**, of Guilford, Nov. 9, 1848, by Rev. Samuel N. Shephard	2	123
Roger Sherman, [s. Sherman & Lucretia], b. Feb. 25, 1830	2	16
Roswell Gaylord, [s. Hubbard S. & Fanny], b. Mar. 18, 1827	2	15
Russell Carlton, [s. Sherman & Lucretia], b. June 11, 1832	2	16
Sally, of Madison, m. Dickinson **MURRAY**, of Guilford, Apr. 17, 1831, by Rev. David Metcalf	1	50
Sally Evarts, d. W[illia]m H. & Achsah, b. June 17, 1822	1	112
Sarah, wid. of Simeon, d. Dec. 15, 1815, ae 83 y.	1	187
Sarah M., of Madison, m. William **KELSEY**, of Killingworth, May 26, 1844, by Rev. L. S. Hough	2	105
Sarah Maria, d. Josiah & Maria, b. Mar. 10, 1831	1	114
Selden David, [s. Gaylor & Dency], b. May 29, 1831	2	15
Simeon, m. Sarah **SCRANTON**, July 3, 1751	2	14
Simeon, [s. Simeon & Sarah], b. Dec. 7, 1752; d. Oct. [ ], 1833	2	14
Simeon, [s. Wyllys & Esther], b. Dec. 18, 1787	2	14
Simeon, d. Mar. 16, 1815, ae 88	1	187
Simeon, s. Ebenezer & Susanna, b. Apr. 6, 1827, in East Guilford; d. Mar. 16, 1815, ae 88 y.	2	14
Simeon Wyllys, s. William Hand & Sally, b. Aug. 17, 1831	1	112
Truman Wallace, [s. Truman & Nancy], b. July 19, 1833	1	114
Walter Price, [s. Wyllys & Esther], b. Sept. 21, 1801; d. Sept. 4, 1851	2	14
Walter Price, of Madison, m. Eliza **SEAWARD**, of Guilford, Nov. 13, 1828, by Rev. Aaron Dutton, of Guilford	1	49
Walter Seward, s. Walter P & Eliza S., b. Dec. 31, 1829	1	113
Walter Seward, [s. Walter S. & Eliza S.], b. Dec. 31, 1829	2	15
Wellington B., m. Susan M. **NORTON**, b. of Madison, Sept. 30, 1849, by Rev. Samuel N. Shephard	2	137
William Hand, [s. Wyllys & Esther], b. Nov. 14, 1785	2	14
William Henry, [s. Sherman & Lucretia], b. Apr. 16, 1835	2	16
William Nicholas, s. W[illia]m H. & Achsah, b. July 26, 1820	1	112
Wyllys, [s. Simeon & Sarah], b. Feb. 9, 1761; d. Jan. 31, 1835	2	14
Wyllys, [s. Wyllys & Esther], b. Mar. 6, 1790	2	14
Wyllys, d. Jan. 31, 1835, ae 74	1	187
MUNSON, Mary Ann, m. Julius N. **DOWD**, b. of Madison, May 4, 1837, by Sam[ue]l N. Shephard	1	78
MURDOCK, Emeline, of Saybrook, m. Horace **NETTLETON**, of North Killingworth, Jan. 34, 1835, by Rev. Samuel N. Shephard	1	56

	Vol.	Page
MURRAY, Beulah Maria, of Guilford, m. Jared **WHITFORD**, of Brooklyn, Jan. 13, 1839, by Rev. Sam[ue]l N. Shephard	1	30
Dickinson, of Guilford, m. Sally **MUNGER**, of Madison, Apr. 17, 1831, by Rev. David Metcalf	1	50
MYERS, Abram Cannon, [s. Abram & Chloe], b. Oct. 24, 1829	2	19
Eliza, [d. Abram & Chloe], b. Oct. 4, 1825	2	19
Ezra Bradley, [s. Abram & Chloe], b. Sept. 5, 1827	2	19
James, [s. Abram & Chloe], b. Aug. 14, 1822	2	19
William Sawyer, [s. Abram & Chloe], b. May 9, 1824	2	19
NASH, Roswell, of Norwalk, m. Elizabeth M. **REDFIELD**, of Madison, June 2, 1845, by Rev. Samuel N. Shephard	2	107
NETTLETON, Horace, of North Killingworth, m. Emeline **MURDOCK**, of Saybrook, Jan. 4, 1835, by Rev. Samuel N. Shephard	1	56
Sibyl M., of Killingworth, m. Imman **HARRISON**, of Madison, Feb. 23, 1843 ,by Rev. Lent S. Hough	2	102
Sivilla, m. Joseph W. **DUDLEY**, b. of Madison, Oct. 25, 1843, by Rev. Samuel N. Shephard	2	104
NICHOLAS, Mary Roxanna, d. Mary L. **CRAMPTON**, b. Jan. 13, 1822	1	118
NORTON, Abby Maria, [d. Timothy & Abigail], b. Aug. 24, 1839	2	20
Abigail S., m. Timothy **NORTON**, Jr., Oct. 17, 1832, by Rev. Jared Andrews	1	55
Amanda, d. Eber, b. Sept. 21, 1794	2	38
Amanda, m. Austin **EVARTS**, May 15, 1822	2	38
Anson, [s. Lewis & Sarah], b. Dec. 1, 1835	2	20
Caroline, [d. Daniel & Lois], b. Nov. 21, 1803	1	117
Caroline, m. Alfred **BLATCHLEY**, May 25, 1829, by Rev. Samuel N. Shephard	1	8
Catharine, [d. Daniel & Lois], b. July 11, 1819; d. Apr. 27, 1835	1	117
Catharine, d. Daniel & Lois, d. Apr. 27, 1835, ae 15 y.	1	192
Clarrrissa, m. John A. **BUCKINGHAM**, b. of Madison, Jan. 25, 1849, by Rev. Samuel N. Shephard	2	121
Daniel, [s. Daniel & Lois], b. Apr. 13, 1808	1	117
Dinah, of Guilford, m. Edward L. **STEVENS**, of Madison, Jan. 8, 1843, by Rev. L. S. Hoyt	2	101
Eliza, [d. Daniel & Lois], b. Sept. 14, 1822; d. Jan. 18, 1836	1	117
Eliza, d. Daniel & Lois, d. Jan. 18, 1836, ae 13 y.	1	192
Emily, m. Horace **HULL**, b. of Madison, Oct. 26, 1836, by Rev. S. N. Shephard	1	35
Frederick A., m. Polly **DUDLEY**, July 3, 1842, by Rev. L. S. Hough	2	101
George Edward, [s. Jonathan Ellsworth & Eliza], b. Jan. 19, 1840	2	20
Henry Ellsworth, [s. Jonathan Ellsworth & Eliza], b. Aug. 3, 1836	2	20

MADISON VITAL RECORDS 31

	Vol.	Page
NORTON (cont.)		
Jane Eliza, [d. Jonathan Ellsworth & Eliza], b. June 14, 1830	2	20
Joel R., m. Orpha **FOSTER**, b. of Madison, Nov. 22, 1827, by Rev. Samuel N. Shephard	1	55
Joel Russell, [s. Daniel & Lois], b. Jan. 27, 1802	1	117
Jonathan Griswold, [s. Timothy & Abigail], b. May 17, 1835	2	20
Julia, m. John **SCRANTON**, Jr., May 15, 1836, by Rev. Samuel N. Shephard	1	67
Lewis, [s. Daniel & Lois], b. May 23, 1817	1	117
Lewis, d. Oct. 30, 1841	2	20
Lois, [d. Daniel & Lois], b. May 20, 1815	1	117
Mabel, [d. Daniel & Lois], b. Oct. 29, 1812	1	117
Mabel, m. Manley M. **WILCOX**, Feb. 14, 1836, by Rev. Samuel. N. Shephard	1	72
Mary, m. William Andrew **BACON**, July 2, 1827, by Rev. Samuel N. Shephard	1	7
Mary A., of Madison, m. John P. **PENNELL**, of Westbrook, Me., Aug. 22, 1852, by Rev. Stephen Hayes	2	143
Mary Augusta, [d. Jonathan Ellsworth & Eliza], b Apr. 7, 1828	2	20
Sally, Mrs., m. Bela **STANNARD**, b. of Guilford, Apr. 9, 1837, by Samuel B. C. West, J.P.	1	73
Samuel, m. Martha A. **HAYS**, b. of North Madison, Sept. 29, 1834, by Rev. Stephen Hays	1	56
Sarah, of Madison, m. William C. **STERLING**, of Salisbury, May 14, 1829, by Rev. Samuel N. Shephard	1	65
Stephen B., m. Roxanna **WILCOX**, b. of Madison, Sept. 2, 1835 ,by Rev. Samuel N. Shephard	1	56
Susan, m. Samuel **FIELD**, b. of Madison, May 10, 1832, by Rev. Samuel N. Shephard	1	25
Susan M., m. Wellington B. **MUNGER**, b. of Madison, Sept. 30, 1849, by Rev. Samuel N. Shephard	2	137
Sybel, [d. Daniel & Lois], b. Oct. 2, 1810	1	117
Timothy, Jr., m. Abigail S. **NORTON**, Oct. 17, 1832, by Rev. Jared Andrews	1	55
Zenas, [s. Daniel & Lois], b. Feb. 11, 1806	1	117
Zenas, m. Lucinda **FOSTER**, b. of Madison, Jan. 2, 1832, by Rev. Samuel N. Shephard	1	55
NOTT, Lucretia, of Saybrook, m. Theophilus **SCRANTON**, of Madison, June 24, 1848, by Rev. Samuel N. Shephard	2	118
PAGE, Horace E., of Guilford, m. Augusta E. **JONES**, of Madison, Aug. 24, 1844, by Rev. L. S. Hough	2	105
PAINE, Daniel, m. Emeline **COE**, July 22, 1834, by Rev. Samuel N. Shephard	1	59
PARDEE, Alfred Stevens, [s. James Russell & Betsey], b. Sept. 30, 1838	2	21
Axson Russell, [s. James Russell & Alma], b. Feb. 11, 1824	2	21

	Vol.	Page
PARDEE (cont.)		
Elmira, of Madison, m. Ebenezer **GOLDTHWAIT**, of Granby, Mass., Apr. 29, 1830, by Rev. Samuel West	1	27
James Elias Hobart, [s. James Russell & Betsey], b. Apr. 4, 1834	2	21
James R., d. June [ ], 1843, ae 46 y. 7 m.	2	21
Mercy Viletta, [d. James Russell & Betsey], b. Oct. 20, 1841	2	21
Polly Eliza, [d. James Russell & Betsey], b. June 1, 1832	2	21
Sally Rosena, [d. James Russell & Betsey], b. May 20, 1836	2	21
William Lewis, [s. James Russell & Alma], b. Mar. 26, 1822	2	21
PECK, Betsey J., m. Ezra S. **SMITH**, b. of Madison, Apr. 18, 1848, by Rev. Samuel N. Shephard	2	117
Joel W. S., of New Haven, m. Martha E. **BUSH**, of Madison, Oct. 22, 1851, by Rev. Samuel N. Shephard	2	142
PELTON, Joseph, m. Jerusha **GRIFFING**, b. of Madison, June 12, 1842, by Rev. Samuel N. Shephard	2	100
PENNELL, John P., of Westbrook, Me., m. Mary A. **NORTON**, of Madison, Aug. 22, 1852, by Rev. Stephen Hayes	2	143
PILGRIM, George W., m. Rachel **MEIGS**, May 30, 1831, by Rev. Sam[ue]l N. Shephard	1	58
PLATTS, Curtis, of Fair Haven, m. Catharine S. **SCRANTON**, of Madison, Apr. 2, 1844, by Rev. Samuel N. Shephard	2	106
Jemima, m. Jonathan **SCRANTON**, Oct. 30, 1834, by Rev. Samuel N. Shephard	1	67
Lydia, of Essex, m. Hezekiah P. **WILLARD**, of Madison, Feb. 5, 1844, by Rev. Samuel N. Shephard	2	105
POST, Abner, m. Eliza **SOUTHARD**, Aug. 5, 1829, by Rev. Samuel N. Shephard	1	58
Charles, of Saybrook, m. Eliza **CLANNING**, of Killingworth, July 27, 1835, by Rev. Samuel N. Shephard	1	59
PRATT, Emeline, m. Benjamin B. **COE**, Nov. 30, 1846, by Rev. Samuel N. Shephard	2	113
Lay W., of Saybrook, m. Mary A. **MEIGS**, of Madison, May [ ], 1829, by Rev. Samuel N. Shephard	1	58
Lyman A., of New Haven, m. Florilla D. **HILL**, of Madison, May 29, 1842, by Rev. Samuel N. Shephard	2	100
Mary E., of Madison, m. Wilson **STEVENS**, of Killingworth, July 31, 1843, by Rev. L. S. Hough	2	103
PRITCHARD, David, m. Wealthy F. **WILCOX**, Dec. 31, 1833, by Rev. Samuel N. Shephard	1	58
REDFIELD, Elizabeth M., of Madison, m. Roswell **NASH**, of Norwalk, June 2, 1845, by Rev. Samuel N. Shephard	2	107
Gustavus K., m. Mary **GRAVE**, b. of Madison, May 2, 1848, by Rev. Samuel N. Shephard	2	117

MADISON VITAL RECORDS 33

	Vol.	Page

REDFIELD (cont.)
Henry L., of Clinton, m. Elizabeth **COE**, of Madison,
  Oct. 27, 1839, by Rev. W[illia]m Albert Hyde, of
  Westbrook   1   62
Mary E., m. William B. **WILLARD**, b. of Madison, May
  15, 1849, by Rev. Samuel N. Shephard   2   121
Melissa, m. George A. **TOOLEY**, Mar. 24, 1850, by
  [Rev. Geo[rge] S. Hare]   2   140
Orrin, m. Sarah E. **TOOLEY**, b. of Madison, Apr. 2,
  1848, by Rev. Reuben Torrey   2   115
William, of Killingworth, m. Dency **CHITTENDEN**, of
  Madison, Nov. 26, 1835, by Rev. Stephen Hays   1   61
RICE, Richard E., m. Pamella **SCRANTON**, b. of Madison,
  Sept. 11, 1845, by Rev. Samuel N. Shephard   2   110
RICHMOND, Anstress P., [child of Dwight F. & Lucy A.], b
  .Nov. 21, 1841   2   21
Antoinette F., [d. Dwight F. & Lucy A.], b. Dec. 9, 1830   2   21
Celesta M., [d. Dwight F. & Lucy A.], b. July 8, 1836   2   21
Dolly, of Madison, m. Daniel **FRANCIS**, of
  Killingworth, Aug. 5, 1827, by Rev. Samuel West   1   24
Leander F., [s. Dwight F. & Lucy A.], b. Feb. 17, 1825   2   21
ROGERS, Charlotte Ann, [d. Joseph A. & Nancy], b. Jan. 7,
  1841   2   21
Enos Wesley, [s. Joseph A. & Nancy], b. May 10, 1838   2   21
Gilbert Leonodus, [s. Joseph A. & Nancy], b. Mar. 9,
  1836; d. Feb. 27, 1840   2   21
Harriet Matilda, [d. Joseph A. & Nancy], b. Apr. 4, 1831   2   21
Joseph A., m. Nancy **HALE**, Mar. 4, 1830, by Rev. David
  Smith, of Durham   1   61
Malichi, d. Nov. 16, 1829, ae 64 y.   2   21
Mariamme Lucretia, [d. Joseph A. & Nancy], b. A pr. 10,
  1834   2   21
ROOT, Betsey, m. Elias K. **DEE**, Nov. 25, 1829, by Reynold
  Webb, J.P.   1   14
ROSE, Franklin, m. Eliza Ann **WILCOX**, Sept. 9, 1829, by
  Reynold Webb, J.P.   1   61
Franklin, m. Abigail M. **DUDLEY**, b. of Madison, Sept.
  9, 1849 ,by Rev. E. S. Huntington   2   137
ROSS, Elizabeth L., of Saybrook, m. Daniel **DAVIS**, of
  Madison, Sept. 26, 1852, by Rev. W. W. Brown   2   144
ROSSITTER, Amelia A., of Clinton, m. William S.
  SPERRY, of New Haven, Nov. 27, 1851, by Rev.
  Samuel N. Shephard   2   142
ROWE, Amoret, m. Augustus Y. **CONKLING**, b. of Fair
  Haven, Apr. 11, 1848, by Rev. Samuel N. Shephard   2   116
SAGE, J. D., of Sandisfield, Mass., m. Ellen M. **SMITH**, of
  Madison, May 1, 1850, by Rev. Samuel N.
  Shephard   2   138
SCOTT, Mary Clarissa, [d. Ebenezer O. & Lucy Ann], b. Feb.
  19, 1841   2   26
Thomas Holt, [s. Ebenezer C.], b. July 29, 1846   2   38
William Wesley, [s. Ebenezer C.], b. Sept. [ ], 1843   2   38

	Vol.	Page
SCRANTON, Abigail, [d. Hubbard & Elizabeth H.], b. Feb. 2, 1815	2	23
Abigail, m. Austin **DOUD**, b. of Madison, Oct. 26, 1835, by Rev. Stephen Hays, of North Madison	1	17
Abraham Fowler, b. Nov. 16, 1788; m. Clarissa **GRISWOLD**, Nov. 22, 1810	2	27
Abraham Pierson, [s. Comfort O. & Elizabeth], b. Nov. 28, 1827	2	26
Abram P., m. Louisa C. **BRADLEY**, Jan. 22, 1851, by Rev. Samuel N. Shephard	2	139
Achsah, of Madison, m. Alpheas B. **BLAKE**, of North Guilford, Oct. 16, 1838, by Rev. Samuel N. Shephard	1	77
Alonzo Fowler, [s. Abraham Fowler & Clarissa], b. Feb. 22, 1828	2	27
Amelia, [d. Theophilus & Betsey], b. Apr. 10, 1818; d. Mar. 11, 1839	2	23
Caroline, of Madison, m. Levi **DEMING**, of Newington, Sept. 21, 1842, by Rev. Samuel N. Shephard	2	100
Caroline, m. Samuel B. **HILL**, b. of Madison, July 30, 1845, by Rev. Samuel N. Shephard	2	110
Caroline Elizabeth, [d. Theophilus & Betsey], b. Feb. 19, 1820	2	23
Catharine S., of Madison, m. Curtis **PLATTS**, of Fair Haven, Apr. 2, 1844, by Rev. Samuel N. Shephard	2	106
Catharine Senna, [d. Jonathan & Roxanna], b. Apr. 1, 1822	2	23
Charles, [s. Theophilus & Betsey], b. June 23, 1822	2	23
Charlotte [d. Henry & Rachel], b. Mar. 10, 1826	2	24
Charlotte Augusta, [d. Joseph A. & Susan], b. Oct. 16, 1836	2	25
Chloe Cornelia, [d. Comfort O. & Ruth], b. Sept. 7, 1821	2	26
Christopher Augustus, s. Simeon & Ann, b. July 14, 1839	2	25
Comfort Edward, [s. Comfort O. & Elizabeth], b. Dec. 17, 1833	2	26
Cynthia Ann, [d. Comfort O. & Elizaebth], b. Mar. 19, 1826	2	26
Daniel H., m. Phebe Ann **SHELLEY**, Sept. 22, 1847, by Rev. Samuel N. Shephard	2	114
Daniel Hubbard, [s. Hubbard & Elizabeth], b. Apr. 26, 1826	2	23
Edward Sereno, [s. Sereno H. & Susan R.], b. June 26, 1840	2	24
Electa, Mrs., m. Frederick W. **SCRANTON**, b. of Madison, Mar. 28, 1847, by William Case	2	114
Eliza J., m. Curtiss **STONE**, b. of Madison, Feb. 2, 1836, by Rev. Anson F. Beach	1	67
Elizabeth, m. Joseph B. **WILCOX**, of Madison, Jan. 1, 1838, by Rev. S. N. Shephard	1	75
Ellen A., of Madison, m. Frederick **FOWLER**, of Northford, Aug. 30, 1849, by Rev. Samuel N. Shephard	2	124
Ellen Augusta, [d. Henry & Rachel], b. Dec. 16, 1828	2	24

MADISON VITAL RECORDS

	Vol.	Page
SCRANTON (cont.)		
Emily Sophia, [d. Henry & Rachel], b. July 11, 1831	2	24
Erastus Clark, [s. Jonathan & Roxanna], b. Nov. 16, 1807	2	23
Ezra, [s. Erastus C. & Lydia], b. Sept. 3, 1831	2	24
Frances Amelia, [d. Joseph A. & Susan], b. Sept. 21, 1839	2	25
Frederick W., m. Mrs. Electa **SCRANTON**, b. of Madison, Mar. 28, 1847, by William Case	2	114
George Evarts, [s. Comfort O. & Elizabeth], b. Mar. 5, 1838	2	26
George Whitfield, [s. Theophilus & Betsey], b. May 23, 1811	2	23
Hamilton Wilcox, [s. Abraham Fowler & Clarissa], b. Jan. 24, 1814	2	27
Harriet, of Hamden, m. Lewis **WARNER**, Sept. 26, 1833, by Rev. Samuel N. Shephard	1	71
Harriet C., m. Alfred G. **DOUD**, b. of Madison, Nov. 28, 1833, by Rev. Samuel N. Shephard	1	16
Harriette Clarissa, [d. Abraham Fowler & Clarissa], b. Oct. 18, 1811	2	27
Henry, b. Nov. 1, 1794; m. Rachel **LINDLEY**, May 19, 1823	2	24
Henry, m. Delia A. **FITCH**, Aug. 15, 1848, by Rev. Samuel N. Shephard	2	118
Henry Lindley, [s. Henry & Rachel], b. Aug. 10, 1837; d. Oct. 23, 1838	2	24
Horatio Lee, [s. Abraham Fowler & Clarissa], b. July 4, 1818	2	27
Ichabod L., m. Artemesia **HAND**, b. of Madison, Nov. 29, 1827, by Rev. Samuel N. Shephard	1	63
James C., of Madison, m. Margaret M. **DICKINSON**, of Haddam, Jan. 3, 1836, by Rev. A. F. Beach	1	66
James Curtis, m. Rachel Emeline **STONE**, Nov. 3, 1840, by Rev. Ja[me]s H. Perry	1	74
Jane A., m. Henry **BACON**, b. of Madison, Apr. 22, 1846, by Rev. Samuel N. Shephard	2	109
Jane Ann, [d. Henry & Rachel], b. Feb. 22, 1824	2	24
Joel Griswold, [s. Abraham Fowler & Clarissa], b. Sept. 9, 1825	2	27
John, Jr., m. Julia **NORTON**, May 15, 1836, by Rev. Samuel N. Shephard	1	67
John, Jr., [s. John, Jr. & Julia], b. Sept. 12, 1845	2	25
John Hart, [s. Abraham Fowler & Clarissa], b. Nov. 8, 1822	2	27
Jonathan, m. Jemima **PLATTS**, Oct. 30, 1834, by Rev. Samuel N. Shephard	1	67
Jonathan Cornelius, [s. Jonathan & Roxanna], b. Jan. 29, 1818; d. Sept. 15, 1841	2	23
Joseph H., m. Eliza M. **WILCOX**, b. of Madison, Aug. 1, 1837, by Rev. S. N. Shephard	1	73
Joseph Hand, [s. Jonathan & Roxanna], b. Jan. 28, 1813	2	23
Joseph Samuel, [s. Abraham Fowler & Clarissa], b. June 18, 1833	2	27
Josephine Eliza, [d. Russell W. & Sylvia], b. Nov. 4, 1841	2	25

BARBOUR COLLECTION

	Vol.	Page
SCRANTON (cont.)		
Juliette, [d. Comfort O. & Elizabeth], b. Jan. 5, 1830	2	26
Leonard, m. Electa **STONE**, b. of Madison, Sept. 28, 1828, by Rev. Zolva Whitmore	1	63
Lucretia had d. Mary Ann, b. Oct. 1, 1835; father Frederick Warren	2	25
Lucretia had child Submit, b. [ ]; father Frederick Warren	2	25
Lucy Stone, [d. Comfort O. & Elizabeth], b. Mar. 2, 1836	2	26
Lydia Ellen, [d. Russell W. & Sylvia], b. Nov. 15, 1835	2	25
Mary Amelia, [d. Henry & Rachel], b. Feb. 10, 1835	2	24
Mary Ann, d. Frederick Warren & Lucretia Scranton, b. Oct. 1, 1835	2	25
Mary Eliza, [d. Erastus C. & Lydia], b. Sept. 27, 1837; d. May 3, 1841	2	24
Mary Eliza, [d. Erastus C. & Lydia], b. Sept. 23, 1840	2	24
Mary Jane, [d. John, Jr. & Julia], b. June 18, 1838	2	25
Mary R., m. Charles H. **DOUD**, Oct. 6, 1841, by Rev. Sam[ue]l N. Shephard	1	53
Mary Roxanna, [d. Jonathan & Roxanna], b. June 8, 1815; d. Sept. 28, 1816	2	23
Mary Roxanna, [d. Jonathan & Roxanna], b Apr. 2, 1820	2	23
Nancy M., of Madison, m. Joseph C. **DOAN**, of Middletown, Mar. 27, 1836, by Rev. A. F. Beach	1	17
Pamella, m. Richard E. **RICE**, b. of Madison, Sept. 11, 1845, by Rev. Samuel N. Shephard (Parnell?)	2	110
Parnell, [d. Hubbard & Elizabeth H.], b. July 2, 1819	2	23
Philemon Auger, [s. Hubbard & Elizabeth H.], b. Sept. 30, 1812	2	23
Rachel, w. of Henry, d. Apr. 28, 1841	2	24
Roxanna R., [d. Sereno H. & Susan R.], b. Sept. 4, 1834	2	24
Russell W., of Durham, m. Sylvia **WILLARD**, of Madison, Apr. 14, 1833, by Rev. Samuel N. Shephard	1	66
Ruth Elizabeth, [d. Comfort O. & Ruth], b. Aug. 20, 1818	2	26
Sally, of Madison, m. Benjamin S. **FENN**, of Canaan, May 17, 1835, by Rev. Samuel N. Shephard	1	25
Samuel R., [s. Jonathan & Roxanna], b. July 7, 1824; d. July 21, 1826	2	23
Samuel W., [s. Sereno H. & Susan R.], b. Dec. 30, 1836; d. Apr. 8, 1841	2	24
Sarah, d. Josiah & Mary, b. Jan. 26, 1733; d. Dec. 15, 1815, ae 83	2	14
Sarah, m. Simeon **MUNGER**, July 3, 1751	2	14
Sarah, m. Bela **DAVIS**, this evening, [Dec. 25, 1827], by Rev. David Smith, of Durham	1	13
Sarah A., of Madison, m. Phillip J. **TALCOTT**, of Wallingford, Dec. 28, 1851, by Rev. Samuel N. Shephard	2	143
Sarah Angeline, [d. Comfort O. & Elizabeth], b. Dec. 30, 1831	2	26
Sarah Warner, [d. Theophilus & Betsey], b. Apr. 30, 1830	2	23

MADISON VITAL RECORDS 37

	Vol.	Page

SCRANTON (cont.)

	Vol.	Page
Selden Theophilus, [s. Theophilus & Betsey], b. Oct. 15, 1814	2	23
Sereno H., m. Susan R. **DOUD**, b. of Madison, Sept. 29, 1833, by Rev. Samuel N. Shephard	1	66
Sereno Hamilton, [s. Jonathan & Roxanna], b. Mar. 1, 1811	2	23
Submit, [child of Frederick Warren & Lucretia Scranton], b. [ ]	2	25
Susan Clarissa, [d. John, Jr. & Julia], b. Feb. 10, 1840	2	25
Theophilus, m. Betsey **WARNER**, July 2, 1810	2	23
Theophilus, of Madison, m. Lucretia **NOTT**, of Saybrook, June 24, 1848, by Rev. Samuel N. Shephard	2	118
Thomas Stone, [s. Abraham Fowler & Clarissa], b. Jan. 29, 1831	2	27
Timothy, of Madison, m. Sarah **WRIGHT**, of Saybrook, Aug. 3, 1832, by Rev. F. W. Sizer	1	64
William, m. Anna **WILCOX**, b. of Madison, Dec. 23, 1832, by Rev. Samuel N. Shephard	1	66
W[illia]m Fayette, [s. Theophilus & Betsey], b. Apr. 19, 1824; d. Feb. 19, 1838	2	23

SEWARD, SEAWARD, Eliza, of Guilford, m. Walter Price **MUNGER**, of Madison, Nov. 13, 1828, by Rev. Aaron Dutton, of Guilford | 1 | 49 |
Jason, 2d, of Guilford, m. Louisa **DUDLEY**, of Madison, Nov. 6, 1828, by Rev. Aaron Dutton	1	63
Jason, Jr., of Guilford, m. Hetty Ann **DEE**, of Madison, Jan. 20, 1847, by Rev. Samuel N. Shephard	2	113
John L., of Guilford, m. Antoinette B. **CONKLING**, of Madison, Jan. 17, 1849, by Rev. Samuel N Shephard	2	120

SEYMOUR, Calista, b. July 23, 1804; m. Angus **TIBBALLS**, Oct. 25, 1832 | 2 | 28 |

SHARP, George, of New Haven, m. We[a]lthy A. **STEVENS**, of Madison, Mar. 28, 1833, by Rev. F. W .Sizer | 1 | 64 |

SHELLEY, Alice Florilla, [d. William & Sarah Ann], b. Sept. 23, 1843 | 2 | 27 |
Amelia, of Madison, m. William **BALDWIN**, of Branford, Nov. 25, 1847, by Rev. Samuel N. Shephard	2	120
Amelia Ann, [d. William & Sarah Ann], b. Jan. 18, 1830	2	27
Austin Henry, [s. William & Sarah Ann], b. Dec. 11, 1832	2	27
Benjamin C., m. Alpha **MAINE**, Dec. 24, 1829, by Rev. Sam[ue]l N. Shephard	1	65
Eliza Ann, m. Marvin **FOSTER**, b. of Madison, Sept. 5, 1831, by Rev. Samuel N. Shephard	1	25
Elizabeth Rosette, [d. William & Sarah Ann], b. Jan. 16, 1836	2	27
Florence William, [d. William & Sarah Ann], b. Sept. 21, 1840	2	27
George A., m. Georgianna **FIELD**, b. of Madison, Apr. 10, 1849, by Rev. Samuel N. Shephard	2	121

BARBOUR COLLECTION

	Vol.	Page
SHELLEY (cont.)		
Malinda F., of Madison, m. Benjamin F. **FORBES**, of Branford, Nov. 25, 1847, by Rev. Samuel N. Shephard	2	119
Malinda Frances, [d. William & Sarah Ann], b. Feb. 7, 1827	2	27
Phebe Ann, m. Daniel H. **SCRANTON**, Sept. 22, 1847, by Rev. Samuel N. Shephard	2	114
Rufus Stone, [s. William & Sarah Ann], b. Mar. 6, 1846. Enlisted in the Army; wounded Dec. 12, 1862; d. Dec. 29, 1862	2	27
Samuel Snow, [s. William & Sarah Ann], b. Feb. 24, 1825	2	27
Sarah Ann, b. Dec. 8, 1808; m. William **SHELLEY**, June 2, 1824	2	27
Sarah Arabell, [d. William & Sarah Ann], b. Sept. 19, 1849	2	27
William, b. July 7, 1802; m. Sarah Ann **SHELLEY**, June 2, 1824; d. Mar. 5, 1863 ae 61 y.	2	27
SMITH, Andrew Norton, s. Ezra & Martha, b. Jan. 24, 1828	1	122
Catharine, of Madison, m. Elihu **KELSEY**, of Saybrook, Mar. 28, 1848, by Rev. Samuel N. Shephard	2	115
Charles, of Derby, Conn., m. Lydia A. **COE**, of Madison, Mar. 3, 1844, by Rev. Nathan Tibballs	2	106
Daniel, m. Mary P. **BENTON**, b. of Guilford, Sept. 3, 1837, by Rev. S. N. Shephard	1	73
Davis Watson, [s. Junius & Amanda], b. May 8, 1840	2	26
Ellen M., of Madison, m. J. D. **SAGE**, of Sandisfield, Mass., May 1, 1850, by Rev. Samuel N. Shephard	2	138
Ezra S., m. Betsey J. **PECK**, b. of Madison, Apr. 18, 1848, by Rev. Samuel N. Shephard	2	117
Lydia, m. William **COE**, b. of Madison, Oct. 14, 1850, by Rev. Samuel N. Shephard	2	139
Mary Ann, m. Samuel S. **MEIGS**, Sept. 29, 1843, by Rev. Samuel N. Shephard	2	104
Mary C., m. Samuel **DUDLEY**, Nov. 24, 1839, by Rev. Sam[ue]l N. Shephard	1	53
Mary R., of Madison, m. Edwin **WATERHOUS[E]**, of Saybrook, Oct. 16, 1833, by Rev. Samuel N. Shephard	1	70
Rosalin, m. Henry **LEE**, b. of Madison, May 6, 1840, by Rev. S. N. Shephard	1	46
Samuel, of New York, m. Laura A. **JONES**, of North Madison, Dec. 6, 1841, by Judson A. Root	1	60
Thomas Hubbard, s. Eliza & Martha, b. Nov. 29, 1824	1	122
SNOW, Zilpha Lucretia, of Killingworth, m. John E. **WILCOX**, of Madison, July 30, 1848, by Rev. Samuel N. Shephard	2	118
SOUTHARD, Eliza, m. Abner **POST**, Aug. 5, 1829, by Rev. Samuel N. Shephard	1	58
SPENCER, Charlotte, of Madison, m. William **TAYLOR**, of Portland, July 10, 1844, by Rev. Samuel N. Shephard	2	106

MADISON VITAL RECORDS 39

	Vol.	Page

SPENCER (cont.)
Harriet, of Madison, m. Alson **TALMADGE**, of
Mereden, May 29, 1839, by Rev. Samuel N.
Shephard — 1, 231

SPERRY, William S., of New Haven, m. Amelia A.
ROSSITTER, of Clinton, Nov. 27, 1851, by Rev.
Samuel N. Shephard — 2, 142

STANNARD, Bela, of Guilford, m. Mrs. Sally **NORTON**, of
Guilford, Apr. 9, 1837, by Samuel B. C. West, J.P. — 1, 73

Darius, of Saybrook, m. Mrs. Emily A. **HILL**, of
Madison, June 17, 1838, by Rev. Simeon Scranton — 1, 74

Ely, of Clinton, m. Ann H. **TUCKER**, of North Madison,
Mar. 5, 1851, by Rev. Samuel N. Shephard — 2, 141

Joseph, of Killingworth, m. Roxanna L. **CONKLING**, of
Madison, Apr. 22, 1828, by Rev. Samuel N.
Shephard — 1, 63

Thankful, of Guilford, m. Jared **GRIFFING**, of Branford,
Aug. 31, 1845, by Rev. George F. Kettell — 2, 108

STENT, Asahel, of Brandford, m. Eliza S. **DOWD**, of
Madison, Sept. 17, 1843, by Rev. L. S. Hough — 2, 104

John, of Branford, m. Polly A. **DOWD**, of Madison, Nov.
6, 1842, by Rev. L. S. Hough — 2, 101

STERLING, William C., of Salisbury, m. Sarah **NORTON**, of
Madison, May 14, 1829, by Rev. Samuel N.
Shephard — 1, 65

STEVENS, STEAVENS, Aplpha J., of Madison, m. Nathaniel
C. **JONES**, of Mereden, Oct. 3, 1852, by Rev. W.
W. Brown — 2, 144

Asa, 2d, m. Charlotte A. **GARDNER**, b. of Madison, July
30, 1848, by Rev. Reuben Terry — 2, 119

Betsey, m. Noah **LANE**, b. of Madison, May 10, 1827, by
Rev. Zolva Whitmore, of Guilford — 1, 45

Diantha, of North Madison, m. James **BURT**, of
Springfield, Mass., Jan. 1, 1834, by Rev. Stephen
Hays, of North Madison — 1, 8

Edward L., of Madison, m. Dinah **NORTON**, of
Guilford, Jan. 8, 1843, by Rev. L. S. Hoyt — 2, 101

Edward Lewis, s. Wyllys & Betsey, b. Sept. 7, 1819 — 1, 122

Eliza J., of Clinton, m. Jonathan **WILLARD**, of Madison,
Oct. 5, 1841, by Rev. Sam[ue]l N. Shephard — 1, 31

Emeline L., m. Nelson **WILLARD**, Nov. 3, 1850, by
Rev. Burdett Hart. Int. pub. — 2, 139

Emeline Louisa, d. Wyllys & Betsey, b. July 12, 1826 — 1, 122

Emily M., of Westbrook, m. William H. **JOHNSON**, of
Guilford, Nov. 29, 1849, by Rev. Samuel N.
Shephard — 2, 137

Hiram, of Killingworth, m. Chloe R. **DOUD**, of Madison,
Apr. 24, 1834, by Stephen Hays — 1, 65

Jeremiah, Jr., of Killingworth, m. Mary Ann **STEVENS**,
d. of Simeon P., of Madison, Nov. 10, 1833, by
Samuel West — 1, 65

Julia, of Madison, m. John C. **BUELL**, of Killingworth,
Sept. 17, 1834, by Rev. Stephen Hays — 1, 76

	Vol.	Page
STEVENS, STEAVENS (cont.)		
Marriette, d. Joel & Jerusha, b. Jan. 26, 1825	2	27
Marriett, of Madison, m. David **BARTLETT**, of Enfield, Mass., Nov. 6, 1847, by Rev. James P. Terry	2	115
Mary Ann, d. of Simeon P., of Madison, m. Jeremiah **STEVENS**, Jr., of Killingworth, Nov. 10, 1833, by Samuel West	1	65
Polly, of Madison, m. Stephen **JOHNSON**, of Haddam, June 16, 1839, by Rev. Edmund O. Bates	1	38
Samuel, m. Phebe Ann **JONES**, Nov. 11, 1840, by Rev. Ja[me]s H. Perry	1	74
Samuel Wyllys, s. Wyllys & Betsey, b. Dec. 22, 1817	1	122
Sophronia, of North Madison, m. William **EVARTS**, Jr., of Guilford, May 31, 1832, by Jared Andrews	1	19
Wealthy A., of Madison, m. George **SHARP**, of New Haven, Mar. 28, 1833, by Rev. F. W. Sizer	1	64
William Henry, s. Wyllys & Betsey, b. Mar. 25, 1823	1	122
Wilson, of Killingsworth, m. Mary E. **PRATT**, of Madison, July 31, 1843, by Rev. L. S. Hough	2	103
STONE, A. E., m. C. Elvina **FIELD**, Aug. 31, 1853, by Rev. W. B. Lee, of Fair Haven	2	145
Amanda, of Madison, m. Emulous **BOARDMAN**, of Middletown, Mar. 12, 1835, by Rev. Stephen Hays	1	76
Betsey Maria, d. Stephen & Sarah, b. Oct. 31, 1804	1	123
Chloe Ann, d. Stephen & Sarah, b. Apr. 14, 1806	1	123
Curtiss, m. Eliza J. **SCRANTON**, b. of Madison, Feb. 2, 1836, by Rev .Anson F. Beach	1	67
Dolisca A., m. Charles E. **GRISWOLD**, b. of Madison, Aug. 29, 1852, by Rev. W. W. Brown	2	144
Electa, m. Leonard **SCRANTON**, b. of Madison, Sept. 28, 1828, by Rev. Zolva Whitmore	1	63
Emily Hoyt, d. Stephen & Sarah, b. Dec. 20, 1811	1	123
Heman, Jr., m. Mabel **FIELD**, b. of Madison, Nov. 6, 1828, by Rev. Zolva Whitmore, of Guilford	1	64
Henry Augustus **CLINTON**, s. Stephen & Sarah, b. Nov. 4, 1827	1	123
Jonathan Smith, s. Stephen & Sarah, b. Dec. 13, 1814	1	123
Mary Louisa, d. Stephen & Sarah, b. Jan. 20, 1808	1	123
Nancy B. J., m. James H. **BISHOP**, May 16, 1847, by Rev. David Smith	2	114
Nancy Belinda Janette, d. Stephen & Sarah, b. Nov. 26, 1822	1	123
Rachel Emeline, m. James Curtis **SCRANTON**, Nov. 3, 1840, by Rev. Ja[me]s H. Perry	1	74
Sarah Matilda, d. Stephen & Sarah, [b.] Aug. 14, 1820	1	123
Susan Munger, d. Stephen & Sarah, b. Oct. 17, 1809	1	123
Wealthy Clarissa, d. Heman, d. May 1, 1841, ae 15 y.	2	27
STORRER, John, m. Mary A. **BUSHNELL**, b. of Madison, Jan. 17, 1843, by Rev. Samuel N. Shephard	2	102
SWEET, James, m. Catharine **WALKLEY**, of Guilford, Mar. 31, 1850, by [Rev. Geo[rge] S. Hare]	2	140

MADISON VITAL RECORDS 41

	Vol.	Page
TALCOTT, Phillip J., of Wallingford, m. Sarah A. **SCRANTON**, of Madison, Dec. 28, 1851, by Rev. Samuel N. Shephard	2	143
TALMADGE, TALLMADGE, TALMAGE, Anson, of Mereden, m. Harriet **SPENCER**, of Madison, May 29, 1839, by Rev. Samuel N. Shephard	1	231
Celia A., of Madison, m. William **ATKINS**, of Berlin, Nov. 10, 1837, by Samuel B. C. West	1	5
Marilla, of Madison, m. Marcus **WAY**, of Wallingford, Oct. 30, 1836, by Samuel B. C. West, J.P.	1	72
Oswell C., m. Clara B. **BARNES**, of Branford, Nov. 4, 1849, by [Rev. Geo[rge] S. Hare]	2	140
TAYLOR, William, of Portland, m. Charlotte **SPENCER**, of Madison, July 10, 1844, by Rev. Samuel N. Shephard	2	106
W[illia]m Munroe, s. James & Rachel, b. July 27, 1840, in the Almshouse kept by Joel Stevens in Madison; d. May 9, 1842, at the house of Joel Stevens	1	134
THERYERS, Alpha, of Madison, m. Harvey **BRISTOL**, of North Killingworth, Jan. 1, 1833, by Rev. Samuel N. Shephard	1	76
THOMAS, Betsey, m. Rufus **DOWD**, of North Madison, Oct. 29, 1837, by Rev. Sam[ue]l N. Shephard	1	79
James, of Haddam, m. Clarrissa **KELSEY**, of Madison, Nov. [ ], 1826, by Rev. Samuel N. Shephard	1	60
THOMPSON, Emily, m. Joseph Hosmer **HILL**, Aug. 14, 1831, by Rev. David Baldwin	1	33
TIBBALLS, Angus, b. Nov. 19, 1805; m. Calista **SEYMOUR**, Oct. 25, 1832	2	28
Ellen, d. [Angus & Calista], b. Sept. 30, 1833	2	28
John, m. Abigail **TODD**, Nov. 4, 1849, by Rev. Samuel N. Shephard	2	137
TODD, Abigail, m. John **TIBBALLS**, Nov. 4, 1849, by Rev. Samuel N. Shephard	2	137
Jonathan, d. Feb. 10, 1819, ae 63 y.	2	29
TOOLEY, Elizabeth A., [d. Russell & Mabel], b. Mar. 7, 1840	2	28
George A., m. Melissa **REDFIELD**, Mar. 24, 1850, by [Rev. Geo[rge] S. Hare]	2	140
George Josiah, [s. Russell & Mabel], b. Feb. 13, 1830	2	28
Henry Hubbard, [s. Russell & Mabel], b. Mar. 16, 1837	2	28
Minerva, [d. Jesse & Rachel L.], b. Feb. 29, 1836	2	28
Osker, [s. Jesse & Rachel L.], b. Dec. 11, 1838	2	28
Osman Russell, [s. Russell & Mabel], b. Oct. 27, 1834	2	28
Sarah E., m. Orrin **REDFIELD**, b. of Madison, Apr. 2, 1848, by Rev. Reuben Torrey	2	115
Sarah Eliza, [d. Russell & Mabel], b. Feb. 21, 1828	2	28
-----, [child of Russell & Mabel], b. Mar. 26, 1842	2	28
TORREY, Martha E., of Madison, m. Henry G. **CROWELL**, of Boston, Mass., [Sept.] 24, [1850], by Rev. Reuben Torrey	2	138
TRACY, Daniel O. [s. John & Lucy], b. Jan. 26, 1839	2	28
John J., [s. John & Lucy], b. Feb. 27, 1837	2	28
Mary E., [d. John & Lucy], b. Apr. 18, 1835	2	28

	Vol.	Page
TRACY (cont.)		
Sarah W., [d. John & Lucy], b. Apr. 3, 1833	2	28
TREAT, Madison A., of New Milford, m. Susan R.		
BASSETT, of Madison, Aug. 11, 1849, by Rev. Geo[rge] L. Hare	2	122
TRYON, Louisa, m. Josiah **MIX**, b. of Saybrook, Dec. 23, 1834, by Rev. Samuel N. Shephard (Should be Elias C. **MIX**)	1	51
TUCKER, Albert Oscar, [s. James W. & Rhoda], b. Dec. 22, 1837	2	29
Ann H., of North Madison, m. Ely **STANNARD**, of Clinton, Mar. 5, 1851, by Rev. Samuel N. Shephard	2	141
Ann Haselton, [d. James W. & Rhoda], b. Jan. 25, 1835	2	29
J. Willis, m. Sarah E. **WILCOX**, b. of Madison, July 3, 1842, by Rev. L. S. Hough	2	101
TYLER, Charles, of Haddam, m. Harriet E. **HILL**, of Madison, Oct. 5, 1845, by Rev. Samuel N. Shephard	2	111
WALKER, Levi, of East Haven, m. Fanny L. **CONKLING**, of Madison, Oct. 22, 1846, by Rev. Samuel N. Shephard	2	113
WALKLEY, Catharine, of Guilford, m. James **SWEET**, Mar. 31, 1850, by [Rev. Geo[rge] S. Hare]	2	140
Ebenezer Silvester, s. Ebenezer & Rhoda, b. July [ ], 1829	2	35
Hannah C., of North Madison, m. James J. **COOPER**, of Wallingford, Aug. 26, 1832, by Rev. Jared Andrew, of North Madison	1	10
WARD, Elizabeth Frances, [d. Thomas C. & Frances], b. Nov. 21, 1828	2	32
Lucinda Hannah, [d. Thomas C. & Frances], b. Feb. 8, 1839	2	32
Mary Rosamond, [d. Thomas C. & Frances], b. Jan. 3, 1834	2	32
William James, [s. Thomas C. & Frances], b. Sept. 23, 1830	2	32
WARNER, Abiram A., of New Haven, m. Hannah A. **WRIGHT**, of Killingworth, Feb. 21, 1836, by Rev. Samuel N. Shephard	1	72
Betsey, m. Theophilus **SCRANTON**, July 2, 1810	2	23
Catharine E., [d. Calvin & Catharine], b. Nov. 19, 1838	2	32
Henry C., [s. Calvin & Catharine J.], b. Oct. 31, 1834	2	32
Lewis, m. Harriet **SCRANTON**, of Hamden, Sept. 26, 1833, by Rev. Samuel N. Shephard	1	71
WATROUS WATERHOUS, Daniel W., of Saybrook, m. Maryette **DUDLEY**, of Guilford, Oct. 23, 1833, by Rev. Samuel N. Shephard	1	70
Edwin, of Saybrook, m. Mary R. **SMITH**, of Madison, Oct. 16, 1833, by Rev. Sameul N. Shephard	1	70
John Newton, [s. Edwin & Mary R.], b. Oct. 11, 1838	1	137
Julian Florence, [child of Edwin & Mary R.], b. Aug. 10, 1834	1	137
Martha Frances, [d. Edwin & Mary R.], b. Mar. 20, 1836	1	137

	Vol.	Page
WAY, Jehiel P., of Chester, m. Rebecca **DUDLEY**, of Madison, June 6, 1849, by Rev. Samuel N. Shephard	2	122
Marcus, of Wallingford, m. Marilla **TALMAGE**, of Madison, Oct. 30, 1836, by Samuel B. C. West, J.P.	1	72
WEBB, Catharine M., [d. Dr. Reynold & Deborah H.], b. June 13, 1832	2	34
Daniel M., [s. Dr. Reynold & Deborah], b. Apr. 6, 1822	2	34
WELLMAN, Homer H., of New York, m. Marian J. **HARRISON**, of Madison, Oct. 7, 1851, by Rev. E. Edwin Hall, of Guilford	2	142
WELLS, Charlotte Jemima, b. Dec. 10, 1820, at Weathersfield; m. Baldwin Hart, of Madison, Dec. 23, 1841, by Rev. Joab Brace	2	11
WHEDON, Amelia Adalaide, [d Frederick L. & Mehetabel], b. Aug. 10, 1840	2	34
Betsey M., m. William B. **CRAMPTON**, b. of Madison, Oct. 16, 1844, by Rev. Samuel N. Shephard	2	109
Betsey Mehetabel, [d. Frederick L. & Mehetabel], b. Apr. 19, 1823	2	34
George Edward, [s. Frederick L. & Mehetabel], b. Jan. 6, 1838	2	34
Henry Scranton, [s. Leaman H. & Betsey], b. Nov. 20, 1839	2	34
Leverett Francis, [s. Frederick L. & Mehetabel], b. Dec. 19, 1820	2	34
Sarah Elizabeth, [d. Frederick L. & Mehetabel], b. Sept. 16, 1826	2	34
Sarah R., m. Samuel N. **COE**, b. of Madison, Sept. 1, 1846, by Rev. Samuel N. Shephard	2	112
William Frederick, [s. Frederick L. & Mehetabel], b. May 1, 1830	2	34
WHITE, Bridgeman G., of Durham, m. Orpha M. **HILL**, of Madison, Apr. 13, 1845, by Rev. L. S. Hough	2	106
WHITFORD, Jane Maria, [d. Jared & Beulah M.], b. Oct. 10, 1840	2	35
Jared, of Brooklyn, m. Beulah Maria **MURRAY** of Guilford, Jan. 13, 1839, by Rev. Samuel N. Shephard	1	30
WIGGINS, John W., of Brooklyn, N. Y., m. Emily M. **HILL**, of Madison, Nov. 17, 1839, by Rev. Samuel N. Shephard	1	31
WILCOX, WILLCOX, Adeline M., of Madison, m. Alonzo N. **MUNGER**, of Bergen, N.Y., Sept. 7, 1846, by Rev. Samuel N. Shephard	2	113
Adeline Malissa, [d. Jared & Irena], b. Jan. 18, 1823	2	32
Alfred N., m. Caroline A. **MUNGER**, b. of Madison, Nov. 5, 1845, by Rev. Samuel N. Shephard	2	111
Alfred Nelson, [s. Abel & Anna F.], b. May 14, 1823	2	30
Alvah O., m. Rachel **DOUD**, b. of Madison, Sept. 26, 1826, by Rev. Erastus Scranton, of Orange	1	68
Ann Amelia, [d. Jared & Irena], b. July 7, 1834	2	32
Ann Elizabeth, [d. Abel & Anna F.], b. Feb. 28, 1828	2	30

BARBOUR COLLECTION

	Vol.	Page
WILCOX, WILLCOX (cont.)		
Anna, m. William SCRANTON, b. of Madison, Dec. 23, 1832, by Rev. Samuel N. Shephard	1	66
Augustus C., m. Catharine Amelia CHITTENDEN, June 21, 1837, by Rev. Samuel N. Shephard	1	71
Betsey A., [d. Rebuen & Betsey], b. Nov. 16, 1835	1	138
Betsey W., m. Eber J. BISHOP, Mar. 5, 1846, by Rev. Samuel N. Shephard	2	112
Betsey Whedon, [d. Zenus & Lovisa], b. Mar. 26, 1827	2	30
Caroline Elizabeth, [d. John R. & Elizabeth C.], b. Apr. 16, 1837	2	31
Catharine Artimisia, [d. Jonathan Samuel & Chloe], b. Feb. 15, 1824	2	31
Charles E., [s. Reuben & Betsey], b. Nov. 12, 1820; d. Oct. 24, 1821	1	138
Charles E., [s. Reuben & Betsey], b. Mar. 30, 1827; d. May 20, 1843	1	138
Charles Morrison, [s. Zenus & Lovisa], b. Aug. 20, 1832	2	30
Clarrissa Nash, d. Aug[ustus] B. & Clarrissa J., b. Apr. 1, 1834	1	137
Cornelia E., [d. Joseph B. & Ruth E.], b. Oct. 25, 1841	2	30
Curtis, m. Hannah MEIGS, b. of Madison, July 28, 1829, by Rev. Samuel N. Shephard	1	69
Curtis, [s. John R. & Elizabeth C.], b. Jan. 8, 1833	2	31
Daniel Hand, [s. Jonathan Samuel & Chloe], b. May 25, 1826	2	31
Densey, Mrs., of Killingworth, m. David DOWD, of Madison, Sept. 18, 1837, by Rev. Stephen Hays	1	79
Edward, of Berlin, m. Harriet M. DOUD, of Madison, Sept. 28, 1838, by Rev. Samuel N. Shephard	1	30
Eliza Ann, m. Franklin ROSE, Sept. 9, 1829, by Reynold Webb, J.P.	1	61
Eliza Jennett, [d. Jared & Irena], b. Mar. 30, 1829	2	32
Eliza M., m. Joseph H. SCRANTON, b. of Madison, Aug. 1, 1837, by Rev. S. N. Shephard	1	73
Eliza Maria, [d. Jonathan Samuel & Chloe], b. Feb. 27, 1818; d. Aug. 3, 1841	2	31
Elizabeth, m. Edward F. KELSEY, b. of Madison, Sept. 4, 1828, by Rev. Samuel N. Shephard	1	42
Elizabeth Hannah, [d. John R. & Elizabeth C.], b. Mar. 12, 1830; d. Mar. 12, 1834	2	31
George Augustus, [s. Jonathan Samuel & Chloe], b. Sept. 20, 1830	2	31
George N., [s. Reuben & Betsey], b. Jan. 8, 1817	1	138
George N., m. Wealthy A. BISHOP, b. of Madison, Apr. 12, 1843, by Rev. L. S. Hough	2	102
Henry Beals, [s. Abel & Anna F.], b. Feb. 1, 1821	2	30
Henry Clifford, s. Henry B. & Lucetta (WOODRUFF), b. July 28, 1852	2	40
Hiram Selden, [s. Abel & Anna F.], b. Feb. 12, 1819	2	30
James, of Madison, m. Clarissa H. GRISWOLD, of Clinton, Feb. 11, 1851, by Rev. Samuel N. Shephard	2	140

	Vol.	Page
WILCOX, WILLCOX (cont.)		
James Jewell, s. Augustus B. & Clarrissa J., b. Aug. 3, 1830	1	137
Jefferson, [s. John R. & Elizabeth C.], b. May 29, 1835	2	31
Jerusha, m. Samuel K. **DOUD**, of Madison, Aug. [ ], 1827, by Rev. Samuel N. Shephard	1	13
John Augustus Hand, [s. Jonathan Samuel & Chloe], b. June 7, 1833	2	31
John E., of Madison, m. Zilpha Lucretia **SNOW**, of Killingworth, July 30, 1848, by Rev. Samuel N. Shephard	2	118
John Elliott, [s. Abel & Anna F.], b. Jan. 29, 1825	2	30
John R., m. Elizabeth **CRAMPTON**, b. of Madison, Apr. 13, 1829, by Rev. Samuel N. Shephard	1	68
John Romeo, s. Curtis & Wealthy, b. May 28, 1803	2	31
John Romeo, [s. John R. & Elizabeth C.], b. Mar. 27, 1840; d. Oct. 11, 1841	2	31
Jonathan Samuel, [s. Jonathan Samuel & Chloe], b. Feb. 28, 1820; d. Dec. 14, 1820	2	31
Jonathan Samuel, [s. Jonathan Samuel & Chloe], b. Nov. 21, 1821; d. Sept. 1, 1869	2	31
Joseph B., m. Elizabeth **SCRANTON**, b. of Madison, Jan. 1, 1838, by Rev. S. N. Shephard	1	75
Joseph Benjamin, [s. Abel & Anna F.], b. Sept. 19, 1815	2	30
Julette, m. Thomas S. **FIELD**, b. of Madison, Nov. 16, 1847, by Rev. Samuel N. Shephard	2	119
Louisa, m. George **DOUD**, b. of Madison, Feb. 1, 1831, by Rev. Samuel N. Shephard	1	16
Lucy Maria, [d. Zenus & Lovisa], b. June 8, 1830	2	30
Manfred Augustus, [s. Abel & Anna F.], b. May 15, 1830	2	30
Manley M., m. Mabel **NORTON**, Feb. 14, 1836, by Rev. Samuel N. Shephard	1	72
Marietta, m. Edward M. **MEIGS**, b. of Madison, June [ ], 1829, by Rev. Sam[ue]l N. Shephard, of Guilford	1	50
Mary E., [d. Joseph B. & Ruth E.], b. June 27, 1839	2	30
Mary S., [d. Reuben & Betsey], b. Jan. 18, 1824	1	138
Mary S., of Madison, m. Josiah B. **GLADWIN**, of Guilford, May 5, 1844, by Rev. L. S. Hough	2	105
Matilda E., of Madison, m Alexander W. **HALL**, of Wallingford, June 17, 1830, by Rev. Samuel N. Shephard	1	33
Orlando, of Killingworth, m. Charlotte **LEE**, of Madison, Aug. 3, 1837, b S. N. Shephard	1	75
Reuben Augustus, [s. Reuben & Betsey], b. Mar. 21, 1833	1	138
Rhoena, m. Amos **BISHOP**, Dec. 27, 1831, by Rev. Samuel N. Shephard	1	9
Roxanna, m. Stephen B. **NORTON**, b. of Madison, Sept. 2, 1835, by Rev. Samuel N. Shephard	1	56
Sarah E., [d. Reuben & Betsey], b. Aug. 13, 1819	1	138
Sarah E., m. J. Willis **TUCKER**, b. of Madison, July 3, 1842, by Rev. L. S. Hough	2	101
Sarah Elizabeth, [d. Jonathan Samuel & Chloe], b. June 9, 1828	2	31

	Vol.	Page
WILCOX, WILLCOX (cont.)		
Sarah Matilda, [d. Abel & Anna F.], b. June 5, 1832; d. Apr. [ ], 187[ ]	2	30
Susan, m. Achillus **DOWD**, b. of Madison, Sept. 19, 1838, by Rev. S. N. Shephard	1	80
Susan Matilda, [d. John R. & Orpha D.], b. Feb. 4, 1827; d. Feb. 19, 1827	2	31
Temperance A., [d. Reuben & Betsey], b. Aug. 17, 1830; d. Apr. 16, 1834	1	138
Timothy F., m. Lydia A. **FOSTER**, b. of Madison, Mar. 27, 1845, by Rev. Samuel N. Shephard	2	109
Timothy Field, [s. Abel & Anna F.], b. Mar. 27, 1817	2	30
Vincent Meigs, [s. Zenus & Lovisa], b. Oct. 17, 1828	2	30
Wealthy F., m. David **PRITCHARD**, Dec. 31, 1833, by Rev. Samuel N. Shephard	1	58
William Wallace, [s. Jonathan Samuel & Chloe], b. July 22, 1816; d. Jan. 27, 1841	2	31
Zinas Edwin, [s. Jared & Irena], b. May 8, 1815	2	32
-----, d. [John R. & Elizabeth C.], d. Dec. 10, 1848	2	31
WILDMAN, Albert B., of Guilford, m. Abigail G. **BENTON**, of Madison, Apr. 29, 1838, by Rev. Samuel N. Shephard	1	30
Albert B., of Guilford, m. wid. Abigail **BENTON**, of Madison, Apr. 29, 1838, by Rev. Samuel N. Shephard	1	75
WILLARD, Achilles, m. Hannah **DENISON**, b. of Madison, May [ ], 1829, by Rev. Samuel N. Shephard	1	69
Amelia Easton, [d. James & Susan], b. Feb. 22, 1832	2	33
Charles E., m. Sarah A. **COE**, b. of Madison, May 10, 1847, by Rev. Samuel N. Shephard	2	114
Charles W[illia]m, [s. Jehiel O. & Phebe], b. Dec. 5, 1826	2	33
Daniel, [s. Jehiel O. & Phebe], b. Nov. 17, 1838	2	33
Edgar Rodolphus, [s. Benjamin H. & Abigail C.], b. Nov. 22, 1835	2	33
Edward Newell, [s. James & Susan], b. Apr. 2, 1836	2	33
Emily, [d. Jehiel O. & Phebe], b. Dec. 26, 1831	2	33
Frances Delia, [child of Benjamin H. & Abigail C.], b. Jan. 12, 1839	2	33
George, [s. Lizur & Jerusha C.], b. Aug. 19, 1821	2	32
George, m. Janette R. **CAMP**, b. of Madison, May 30, 1849, by Rev. Samuel N. Shephard	2	121
George Elliott, [s. Benjamin H. & Abigail C.], b. Mar. 18, 1829	2	33
Hezekiah P., [s. Lizur & Jerusha C.], b. Feb. 27, 1818	2	32
Hezekiah P., of Madison, m. Lydia **PLATTS**, of Essex, Feb. 5, 1844, by Rev. Samuel N. Shephard	2	105
Horatio Eugene Judd, [s. Achillus & Julia], b. May 21, 1819; d. Sept. 20, 1820	2	35
Horatio Judd, [s. Achillus & Julia], b. Jan. 21, 1824	2	35
James Lawrence, [s. James & Susan], b. Oct. 15, 1823	2	33
Jared, Col., m. Julia Ann **FIELD**, b. of Madison, Nov. 8, 1835, by Rev. Stephen Hays	1	71
John Augustine, [s. James & Susan], b. Nov. 8, 1820	2	33

MADISON VITAL RECORDS 47

	Vol.	Page
WILLARD (cont.)		
John Eugene, [s. Achillus & Julia], b. Jan. 28, 1822; d. Mar. 2, 1838	2	35
Jonathan, [s. Jonathan G. & Lydia], b. May 12, 1817	2	32
Jonathan, of Madison, m. Eliza J. **STEAVENS**, of Clinton, Oct. 5, 1841, by Rev. Sam[ue]l N. Shephard	1	31
Jonathan, m. Abigail **HARRISON**, b. of Madison, Sept. 16, 1845, by Rev. Samuel N. Shephard	2	110
Julia, w. of Achillus, d. Mar. 13, 1827	2	35
Justin, [s. Jehilel O. & Phebe], b. Oct. 1, 1823	2	33
Lizur, d. Feb. 28, 1838, ae 73 y.	2	32
Marittee, of Madison, m. Albert **CAMP**, of Durham, Jan. [ ], 1828, by Rev. Samuel N. Shephard	1	10
Morriell, [s. Jehiel O. & Phebe], b. Feb. 11, 1818	2	33
Nathan Wesley, [s. Jehiel O. & Phebe], b. Nov. 5, 1835	2	33
Nelson, [s. Jehiel O. & Phebe], b. Sept. 26, 1820	2	33
Nelson, m. Emeline L. **STEVENS**, Nov. 3, 1850, by Rev. Burdett Hart. Int. pub.	2	139
Polly, of Madison, m. John **HILL**, of North Branford, Sept. 18, 1839, by Rev. Sam[ue]l N. Shephard	1	36
Ruth Ann, of Madison, m. James **FRANCIS**, of Durham, Oct. 12, 1830, by Rev. Samuel N. Shephard	1	24
Samuel F., m. Margaret B. **BRADLEY**, b. of Madison, Apr. 8, 1851, by Rev. Samuel N. Shephard	2	141
Samuel Frances, [s. James & Susan], b. Nov. 12, 1828	2	33
Sarah Augusta, [d. Jehiel O. & Phebe], b. May 18, 1829	2	33
Sophia, of Madison, m. William F. **BRADLEY**, of New Haven, July 17, 1839, by Rev. Sam[ue]l N. Shephard	1	77
Sophia W., [d. James & Susan], b. Oct. 15, 1817	2	33
Stephen, m. Maria **DUDLEY**, b. of Madison, June [ ], 1829, by Rev. Samuel N. Shephard	1	69
Sylvia, [d. Jonathan G. & Lydia], b. Mar. 8, 1815	2	32
Sylvia, of Madison, m. Russell W. **SCRANTON**, of Durham, Apr. 14, 1833, by Rev. Samuel N. Shephard	1	66
William B., m. Mary E. **REDFIELD**, b. of Madison, May 15, 1849, by Rev. Samuel N. Shephard	2	121
William Blatchley, [s. James & Susan], b. Dec. 12, 1826	2	33
William Henry, [s. Benjamin H. & Abigail C.], b. Dec. 12, 1831	2	33
WILLIAMS, Benjamin, Jr., of Essex, m. Clarrissa M. **HALL**, of Madison, Apr. 20, 1845, by Rev. Samuel N. Shephard	2	107
Charles, m. Lydia **HULL**, b. of Madison, Feb. 25, 1831, by Rev. Samuel N. Shephard	1	70
Charles, [s. Charles & Lydia], b. Oct. 20, 1832	2	34
Merriman, [s. Charles & Lydia], b. Nov. 14, 1834	2	34
Rose Ann, [d. Charles & Lydia], b. Dec. 26, 1829; d. June 10, 1830	2	34
Washington, [s. Charles & Lydia], b. Aug. 3, 1838; d. Oct. 20, 1839	2	34

	Vol.	Page
WILLIAMS (cont.)		
Washington, [s. Charles & Lydia], b. Nov. 23, 1841	2	34
WOODFORD, Benjamin B., m. Laura **BISHOP**, Aug. [ ], 1827, by Rev. Samuel N. Shephard	1	68
WRIGHT, Charlotte, of Killingsworth, m. Green **BENTON**, of Madison, Nov. 23, 1831, by Rev. Samuel N. Shephard	1	9
Hannah A., of Killingworth, m. Abiram A. **WARNER**, of New Haven, Feb. 21, 1836, by Rev. Sameul N. Shephard	1	72
Sarah, of Saybrook, m. Timothy **SCRANTON**, of Madison, Aug. 3, 1832, by Rev. F. W. Sizer	1	64
YOUNG, William Washington, s. Electa **CRAMPTON**, b. Aug. 12, 1822	1	150

MANCHESTER VITAL RECORDS
1823 – 1853

	Page
[ABBE], ABBEY, ABBY Eliza H., m. Edgar T. HALE, b. of Manchester, Aug. 22, 1848, by Rev. Benjamin C. Phelps	245
Lydia, of Manchester, m. Sheldon KILBOURN, of South Windsor, [ ], 1848, by Rev. Benjamin C. Phelps	247
Sarah, of Manchester, m. Samuel ELDRIDGE, of Manchester, Sept. 11, 1844, by Rev. P. T. Keeney	232
ABEL, Ezekiel, of Lebanon, m. Harriott BIDWELL, of Manchester, Sept. 8, 1842, by B. F. Northrop	228
ADAMS, John, of Canton, m. Lucy Ann CULVER, of Manchester, Nov. 13, 1836, by V. R. Osborn, V.D.M.	219
Lucy E., m. Francis FERGERSON, Apr. 21, 1830, by Isaac Devinel	211
ALDEN, Lucinda, m. Walter BUCKLAND, Oct. 9, 1831, by Isaac Devinel	212
ALEXANDER, Collingwood, of Manchester, m. Phyluia KEENEY, of Glastonbury, Aug. 26, 1832, by Rev. Hezekiah L. Ramsdall	214
Roxana, of East Hartford, m. William CARPENTER, of Manchester, [Nov. 27, 1834], by Rev. Salmon Hall	217
ALLEN, Hariet, m. Darias DRAKE, Aug. 15, 1825, by Elder Elisha Frink, of Tolland	203
Israel E., of East Windsor, m. Pauliana COLE, of Manchester, Jan. 1, 1829, by Enoch Burt	209
Lucy, of Manchester, m. Charles W. CLARK, of Columbia, May 1, 1853 by F. T. Perkins	265
Mariah, m. Thomas WIGGINS, Sept. [ ], 1829, by V. R. Osborn, V.D.M.	210
Martha A., m. George W. CLARK, b. of Manchester, Sept. 12, 1848, by Rev. Benjamin C. Phelps	245
Orlando, of East Windsor, m. Elmira SLATE, of Manchester, May 12, 1841, by Rev. Sanford Benton	227
Sarah, m. Benjamin A. RUSSELL, b. of Springfield, Mass., Dec. 22, 1839, by S. Benton	225
ALLICE, Thomas C., of Shipton Lower Canada, m. Julia Ann MATHER, of Manchester, July 24, 1837, by Enoch Burt	221
ANDRUS, ANDROS, Aden, Jr., m. Emeline BECKWITH, Oct. 3, 1827, by V. R. Osborn, V.D.M.	207
Elisha L., m. Clarissa DEAN, Aug. 27, 1843, by B. F. Northrop	230
Emily, of Manchester, m. Eli P. FOX, of Bolton, Jan. 15, 1828, by E. Burt	207
Mary G., of Manchester, m. Horatio N. SLOCUM, of Vernon, Aug. [ ], 1833, by B. F. Northrop	215
Sarah E., of Manchester, m. Gilbert SKINNER, of Bolton, Mar. 27, 1839, by Rev. David Bennet	223
ANNIS, ANIS, Eliza E., of Manchester, m. Horace GARDNER, of Mansfield, Nov. 24, 1831, by Rev. Ephraim Scott	212
Mary, of Manchester, m. Norman B. HALL, of Windham, Feb. 24, 1836, by Rev. S. Hall	218
ARNOLD, Ethan, of East Hartford, m. Mary THOMPSON, of Manchester, Jan. 23, 1830, by B. F. Northrop	210

	Page
ATTWOOD (?), Lucian C., of Willimansell, Mass., m. Jerusha Ann HOUSE, of East Glastonbury, Jan. 4, 1852, by Rev. John Cooper	262
AUBRIM, Oliver S., of South Windsor, m. Lucy A. GILLETT, of South Windsor, Mar. 26, 1848, by Rev. Benjamin C. Phelps	244
AUSTIN, Eleanor, of Glastenbury, m. Royal L. GAY, May 12, 1850, by Rev. B. F. Northrop	252
John, of Manchester, m. [ ] CHAMBERLIN, of Mansfield, May 28, 1840, by S. Benton	226
AVERY, Josiah B., of Boston, m. Louisa M. LYMAN, of Manchester, Nov. 1, 1836, by B. F. Northrop	219
Mary M., of Bolton, m. Clark STEEL, July 30, 1829, by V. R. Osborn, V.D.M.	210
Samuel T., of East Windsor, m. Amelia BUNCE, of Manchester, Oct. 3, 1832, by B. F. Northrop	214
BAGG, Elizabeth, of Windsor, m. Thomas G. SYMONDS, of Manchester, Jan. 10, 1852, by Rev. George W. Brewster	258
BAILEY, Mary Ann, of Manchester, m. Charles FOSTER, of East Windsor, Mar. 24, 1830, by B. F. Northrop	211
BAKER, Joanna, m. John A. RISLEY, b. of Manchester, Dec. 17, 1852, by F. T. Perkins	263
Joseph, of Murery, N.Y., m. Lucinda LANDFIER, of Manchester, Aug. 16, 1825, by Enoch Burt	204
BALL, James H., of Bristol, m. Sarah M. LUCAS, of Manchester, [ ], by Rev. M. P. Alderman	248
Ralph C., of Manchester, m. Ophilia HUBBARD, of East Hartford, Nov. 29, 1849, by Rev. M. P. Alderman	251
BARNS, William, of East Windsor, m. Lucy PERRY, of Manchester, Sept. 3, 1834, by Enoch Burt	216
William, of Lacon, Ill., m. Eunice A. HUBBARD, of Manchester, Aug. 18, 1842, by B. F. Northrop	228
BARBER, Jane, of East Hartford, m. Timothy CARROLL, of New Brunswick, [July] 19, [1847], by William Thompson	241
BASSETT, Caleb L., m. Lydia HITCHCOCK, June 5, 1828, by Enoch Burt	208
BEAM, Jacob, of New London, m. Sarah Jane GLEASON, of Manchester, Mar. 14, 1844, by B. F. Northrop	231
BECKERS, Henry, m. Cornelia Ann FOX, b. of Bolton, Jan. 28, 1846, by B. F. Northrop	236
BECKWITH, Emeline, m. Aden ANDROS, Jr., Oct. 3, 1827, by V. R. Osborn, V.D.M.	207
BEEBE, Daniel C., m. Desire PERKINS, b. of Manchester, Jan. 12, 1841, by Sanford Benton	227
BELDEN, Henry, of Hartford, m. Hannah WETHERELL, of Manchester, Oct. 7, 1835, by Bennett F. Northrop	218
BELKNAP, Charles T., of East Windsor, m. Parmelia H. PERKINS, of Manchester, Feb. 27, 1842, by Rev. R. Livesey	228
BENNETT, Ezra, m. Lucy LOOMIS, Sept. 12, 1827, by V. R. Osborn, V.D.M.	207
Phebe C., of Manchester, m. Samuel R. JONES, of New York, Mar. 31, 1852, by Rev. Lyman Leffingwell	262
BIDWELL, Abigail, of Manchester, m. Dwight DANIELS, of Ludlow, Mass., Sept. 15, 1842, by R. Livesey	228

MANCHESTER VITAL RECORDS 51

Page

BIDWELL (cont.)

Almira, m. Chester **KNOX**, b. of Chester, Dec. [ ], 1836, by B. F. Northrop	219
Ann, of Manchester, m. Gonzelo **KEENEY**, of Eastbury, Apr. 3, 1828, by Enoch Burt	208
Austin, m. Martha E. **FRENCH**, b. of Manchester, Nov. 10, 1850, by Rev. M. P. Alderman	255
Chauncy, of Manchester, m. Margaret M. **DOYL**, of Suffield, June 6, 1847, by Rev. Benjamin C. Phelps	240
Elizabeth, of Manchester, m. Edwin **HOUSE**, of Glastenbury, Nov. 3, 1841, by Rev. James A. Smith of Glastenbury	228
Emily, m. Porter **KENEY**, b. of Manchester, May 3, 1825, by Enoch Burt	203
George, of Vernon, m. Jennett **MILLARD**, of Manchester, Mar. 8, 1837, by Enoch Burt	219
Gilbert, m. Cornelia A. **KINGBURY**, Jan. 18, 1849, by Rev. B. F. Northrop	247
Harriott, of Manchester, m. Ezekiel **ABEL**, of Lebanon, Sept. 8, 1842, by B. F. Northrop	228
Hart, m. Lydia H. **BROWN**, b. of Manchester, Sept. 4, 1850, by Rev. M. F. Alderman	254
Jane, bd. May 3, 1842, ae 11. Rev. R. Livesey, Min.	335
John W., m. Sarah W. **RICH**, b. of Manchester, Oct. 16, 1851, by F. T. Perkins	257
Joseph, m. Phila **WITHERELL**, Nov. 16, 1824, by A. Benedict	202
Lucy H., of Manchester, m. Monroe **HOUSE**, of Glastenbury, Jan. 30, 1848, by Rev. B. C. Phelps	243
Maria, of Manchester, m. Theodore **WELLS**, of Farmington, Aug. 24, 1853, by F. T. Perkins	266
Martha A., of Manchester, m. Samuel M. **POTTER**, of Southington, Dec. 22, 1846, by Rev. B. F. Northrop	239
Mary Ann, of Manchester, m. William **WOODBRIDGE**, of Brooklyn, Apr. 26, 1847, by Rev. B. F. Northrop	240
Mirinda, of Manchester, m. Clement **HALE**, of Eastbury, Apr. 3, 1828, by Enoch Burt	208
BILL, John, of Middletown, m. Clarrissa **GILLMAN**, of Manchester, Nov. 12, 1823, by Rev. Frederick Wightman, of Middletown	201
BISHOP, Nelson, Rev. of Clinton, Me., m. Elizabeth **McLEAN**, of Manchester, May 1, 1833, by B. F. Northrop	214
BISSELL, BISELL, Anson N., m. Eliza **McLEAN** alias **WOODBRIDGE**, b. of Manchester, Apr. 28, 1838, by Enoch Burt	226
Charles, m. Roxey **WYLES**, Dec. 20, 1827, by E. Burt	207
David, of Colebrook, N.H., m. Clarrissa **BRYANT**, of Manchester, Nov. 9, 1823, by Enoch Burt	201
Elizabeth, of Manchester, m. George G. **ERVING**, of Hartford, Aug. 28, 1840, by Sanford Benton	226
Henry C., of Lyme, m. Elizabeth M. **HUBBARD**, of Manchester, May 5, 1846, by Rev. B. F. Northrop	237
Lewis, Maj. of St. Liewis, Mo., m. Mary Ann **WOODBRIDGE**, of Manchester, June 8, 1825, by Enoch Burt	203
Luis G,., m. Permilliar **BUKWORTH**, Apr. 18, 1824, by Isaac Devinnell	202

	Page
BISSELL, BISELL (cont.)	
Mary F., m. Charles H. **WEST**, b. of Manchester, Mar. 27, 1852, by Rev. John Cooper	260
Nancy, m. Rodolphas **LANDFIER**, Sept. 25, 1827, by E. Burt	207
Nelson, m. Percis **TOPLEFF**, Oct. 2, 1827, by V. R. Osborn, V.D.M.	207
BLINN, Martha, of Bolton, m. Albert **WHITHMORE**, of Coventry, Nov. 6, 1842, by Rev. David Bennett	229
BOUGHLIN, Seymour, of Rochester, N.Y., m. Ellen M. **VANBUGEN**, of Manchester, Apr. 29, 1847, by Rev. B. F. Northrop	240
BOWERS, BOWER, Edwin L., of Hartford, m. Mary A. **DEAN**, of Manchester, July 24, 1839, by Sanford Benton	224
Joseph B., m. Delia **BROWN**, of Manchester, May 28, 1853, by F. T. Perkins	265
Mary C., of Manchester, m. George M. **HAYDEN**, of Hartford, [Jan.] 16, 1848, by Rev. B. C. Phelps	243
Nicholes, of Vernon, m. Martha E. **POWERS**, of Vernon, Aug. 1, 1852, by Rev. George W. Brewster	261
Rosanah, of Manchester, m. Charles **WHEELER**, of Springfield, Mass., Jan. 16, 1848, by Rev. B. C. Phelps	243
BOYD, Amos H., m. Rachel P. **BUTLER**, b. of Manchester, May 5, 1829, by B. F. Northrop	209
Oliver D., of Franklin, Mass., m. Maria R. **LATHROP**, of Manchester, Aug. 28, 1826, by Enoch Burt	206
BRAGG, Calvin B., m. Orpha **FLINT**, Sept. 4, 1823, by Isaac Devinel	200
BRAINARD, Caroline, of Haddam, m. John **EMMONS**, of Haddam, Oct. 3, 1852, by Rev. George W. Brewster	263
BREWER, Sherman, of East Hartford, m. Diantha **SPENCER**, of Manchester, Oct. 3, 1838, by B. F. Northrop	223
BROCKWAY, Levie, m. George M. **WEBSTER**, b. of Hartford, Feb. [ ], 1831, by B. F. Northrop	212
BROWN, Anson M., of Bristol, m. Mary L. **MILLARD**, of Manchester, Apr. 15, 1846, by Rev. B. F. Northrop	237
Arnold C., of Stockbridge, Mass., m. Julia Ann **CHILDS**, of Manchester, Mar. 25, 1829, by V. R. Osborn, V.D.M.	210
Delia, m. Joseph B. **BOWERS**, May 29, 1853, by F. T. Perkins	265
Irene, m. Columbus **PARKER**, b. of Manchester, Dec. 31, 1839, by B. F. Northrop	225
Jane Susan, of Manchester, m. Artemus Sinds **STRONG**, of Bolton, Oct. 14, 1840, by Rev. William Reed, of Wethersfield	227
Leonora, of Manchester, m. Joseph **COMSTOCK**, of Montville, Apr. 2, 1833, by B. F. Northrop	214
Lydia H., m. Hart **BIDWELL**, b. of Manchester, Sept. 4, 1850, by Rev. M. F Alderman	254
Monroe A., m. Mary J. **FIELDING**, b. of Manchester, Oct. 12, 1851, by Rev. F. T. Perkins	257
-----, Mr. his child, bd. Mar. 15, 1842, ae 4. Rev. R. Livesey, Min.	335
BRYANT, Clarrissa, of Manchester, m. David **BISELL**, of Colebrook, N.H, Nov. 9, 1823, by Enoch Burt	201
Elizabeth F., of Manchester, m. Ralph W. **HOUGHTON**, of Hebron, Nov. 1, 1843, by Rev. Charles Noble	231
Wealthy, of Manchester, m. Elijah **FORBS**, Jr., of East Hartford, Nov. 10, 1825, by Enoch Burt	205

MANCHESTER VITAL RECORDS 53

	Page
BUCKLAND, Ann G., m. Calvin W. JACQUES, b. of Manchester, Apr. 10, 1845, by Rev. B. F. Northrop	234
Avery A., of Hartford, m. Harriet Jane HALE, of Manchester, Apr. 26, 1848, by Rev. Benjamin C. Phelps	244
Chloe W., of Manchester, m. Ralph FOSTER, of South Windsor, Apr. 2, 1851, by Rev. Theodore M. Dwight. Dated at Union Village	255
Esther, m. Mervin T. RUSSELL, b. of Manchester, Mar. 3, 1847, by Rev. B. F. Northrop	239
Francis, of Manchester, m. Olive NORMAN, of Vernon, Sept. 10, 1844, by Rev. P. T. Keeny	232
Harriet, of East Windsor, m. Benjamin STARKWEATHER, of Hartford, May 21, 1840, by S. Benton	225
Harvey, of Bolton, m. Ruth COUCH, of Manchester, Dec. 9, 1828, by Bennett F. Northrop	209
Julia, of East Hartford, m. Salmon RIDER, of Willington, July 6, 1829, by B. F. Northrop	210
Maria C., of Manchester, m. Normond FOSTER, of East Windsor, Dec. 29, 1842, by Rev. William Wright	229
Mary Ann, of Manchester, m. James B. WOOD, of East Windsor, June 5, 1844, by Rev. B. M. Walker	232
Sophia, of Manchester, m. Ebenezer W. BULL, of Hartford, Oct. 8, 1823, by Enoch Burt	200
Walter, m. Lucinda ALDEN, Oct. 9, 1831, by Isaac Devinel	212
Wells, of East Windsor, m. Samantha BUEL, of Manchester, Nov. [ ], 1833, by B. F. Northrop	215
BUCKLEY, Chauncy, m. Clarissa EDMONDS, b. of Manchester, Sept. 26, 1849, by Rev. M. P. Alderman	250
Chauncey B., of East Haddam, m. Lucy CLOUGH, of Manchester, Feb. 11, 1838, by Rev. R. W Allen	221
Susan, of Manchester, m. Henry PELTON, of East Windsor, May 27, 1845, by Rev. P. T. Keeney	235
BUELL, BUEL, Catherine, m. John Philander SLATER, Sept. [ ], 1841, by R. Livesey	228
Fanny H., m. H. H. LORD, Sept. 29, 1845, by V. R. Osborn, V.D.M.	235
Jennett B., of Manchester, m. John WARD, of Collinsville, Nov. 24, 1841, by Rev. B. F. Northrop	228
Letunna (?), of Manchester, m. Hiram CASE, of Norfolk, Nov. 30, 1837, by B. F. Northrop	221
Peter O., of Simsbury, m. Irene DEXTER, of Manchester, Sept. [ ], 1834, by B. F. Northrop	216
Samantha, of Manchester, m. Wells BUCKLAND, of East Windsor, Nov. [ ], 1833, by B. F. Northrop	215
BUKWORTH, Permilliar, m. Luis G. BISSELL, Apr. 18, 1824, by Isaac Devinnell	202
BULL, Ebenezer W., of Hartford, m. Sophia BUCKLAND, of Manchester, Oct. 8, 1823, by Enoch Burt	200
BUNCE, Amelia, of Manchester, m. Samuel T. AVERY, of East Windsor, Oct. 3, 1832, by B. F. Northrop	214
Ann, m. Daniel GRISWOLD, Oct. 30, 1828, by Enoch Burt	209
Edwin, of Manchester, m. Lucinda TRYON, of Glastenbury, Nov. 29, 1843, by Rev. Charles Noble	231
Israel, bd. Aug. 31, 1841, ae 68. Rev. R. Livesey, Min.	335

	Page
BUNCE (cont.)	
Mary Ann, m. Henry **McKINNEY**, b. of Manchester, Jan. 15, 1834, by B. F. Northrop	215
Walter, m. Emily **KENNEDY**, b. of Manchester, Nov. 23, 1852, by F. T. Perkins	263
BURKE, Emma, ae 24, m. Patrick **O'CONNOR**, ae 28, Apr. 4, 1853, by James Smythe	267
BURNS, George F., m. Julia **HEMMINGWAY**, Nov. 6, 1844, by B. F. Northrop	233
Philanda, of Manchester, m. John **DUFF**, of East Windsor, Nov. 19, 1840, by Sanford Benton	227
BURT, Martha E., m. Samuel **LOOMIS**, b. of Manchester, Apr. 8, 1835, by Enoch Burt	217
BUTLER, Rachel P., m. Amos H. **BOYD**, b. of Manchester, May 5, 1829, by B. F. Northrop	209
BUTTON, Thomas, of Hartford, m. Clarissa J. **RISLEY**, of Manchester, Apr. 15, 1840, by S Benton	225
William, of Lebanon, m. Laura **LOOMIS**, of Manchester, Jan. 23, 1838, by Rev. David Bennet	222
CABLE, Betsy, of Hartford, m. Benjamin **CULVER**, of Manchester, June 5, 1836, by S. Hull	219
CADWELL, Ellen, m. Rufus **SPENCER**, b. of Manchester, Nov. 19, 1851, by Rev. Benjamin C. Phelps, of East Hartford	262
Mathew, d. [ ]*, ae 83 years *(The date "June 9, 1893" precedes this entry)	335
CADY, Asahel, Jr., m. Catherine **HASKINS**, b. of Manchester, Oct. 20, 1836, by V. R. Osborn, V.D.M.	219
CARN, Sarah C., of Manchester, m. John S. **TAYLOR**, of Portland, Jan. 11, 1852, by Rev. George W. Brewster	258
CARPENTER, Mary B., m. Edwin **MUNSON**, Aug. 27, 1828, by Enoch Burt	209
William, of Manchester, m. Roxana **ALEXANDER**, of East Hartford, [Nov. 27, 1834], b. Rev. Salmon Hall	217
CARROLL, CARROL, Mary A., of Manchester, m. Charles **GOODALE**, of East Hartford, July 21, 1850, by Rev. M. P. Alderman	253
Timothy, of New Brunswick, m. Jane **BARBER**, of East Hartford, [July] 19, [1847], by William Thompson	241
William H., m. Jerusha E. **GRAY**, Sept. 30, 1849, by Rev. B. F. Northrop	249
CARVER, Lucinda M., of Bolton, m. William G. **FISH**, of West Windsor, Jan. 29, 1851, by Rev. M. P. Alderman	256
CASE, Ann W., bd. Oct. 24, 1841, ae 20. Rev. R. Livesey, Min.	335
Ashbel W., m. Eleanor D. **HOLLISTER**, b. of Manchester, Nov. 28, 1833, by Rev. H. L. Ramsdall	215
Austin, of East Hartford, m. Louisa E. **NORRIS**, of Manchester, Apr. 20, 1842, by Rev. E. Burk	249
Dudley, m. Lydia **COOLEY**, b. of Manchester, Feb. 7, 1836, by B. F. Northrop	218
Eliza, of Manchester, m. Hiram **MOULTON**, of East Hartford, Oct. 30, 1839, by Sanford Benton	224
Ellen A., of Manchester, m. Milton **PRIOR**, of Windsor, Nov. 3, 1851, by F. T. Perkins	257

	Page
CASE (cont.)	
Franklin M., of Hartford, m. Phebe **GRANT**, of East Windsor, Sept. 1, 1842, by B. F. Northrop	228
Hiram, of Norfolk, m. Letunna **BUEL**, of Manchester, Nov. 30, 1837, by B. F. Northrop	221
Joseph C., of Manchester, m. Nancy L. **EMERSON**, of Haddam, Jan. 6, 1850, by Rev. M. P. Alderman	251
Julia A., of Manchester, m. John B. **PHELPS**, of Glastenbury, [1845?], by Rev. B. F. Northrop	234
Mary Ann, m. Chauncey **KEENEY**, b. of Manchester, Mar. 20, 1832, by Rev. Ephraim Scott	213
Orrin, of Manchester, m. Mrs. Fanny **TRUMAINE**, of Tolland, Dec. 10, 1840, by Rev. Sanford Benton	227
CAULKINS, Henry, m. Elizabeth **HUBBARD**, b. of Hartford, Oct. [ ], 1842, by B. F. Northrop	229
CHAFFEN, Emery, of East Hartford, m. Philinda **RISLEY**, of Manchester, Apr. 28, 1847, by Levi Daggett, Jr.	240
CHAMBERLIN, -----, of Mansfield, m. John **AUSTIN**, of Manchester, May 28, 1840, by S. Benton	226
CHAPMAN, Charles, m. Harriet **PETERSON**, b. of Manchester, Oct. 10, 1852, by Rev. George W. Brewster	263
Lovina, of Portland, m. Russell **KEENEY**, of Manchester, Feb. 29, 1844, by Rev. Charles Noble	231
-----, Mr., bd. Sept. 26, 1841, ae 15. Rev. R. Livesey, Min.	335
CHARLOTTE, Lucy, ae 36, m. William R. **KEENY**, ae 29, colored, b. of Manchester, June 28, 1854, by Joseph Noyes, J.P.	266
CHENEY, CHEENEY, Calvin Nelson, [s. Calvin], b. Sept. 22, 1808	282
Charles, [s. George W.], b. Jan. 9, 1831	281
Electa, [d. Calvin], b. Apr. 9, 1815	282
Electa, of Manchester, m. Mortimer F. **HARRISON**, of New York, Aug. 8, 1842, by Rev. E. Burk	249
Electa, of Manchester, m. Richard M. **GOODMAN**, of New York City, June 18, 1845, by Rev. B. F. Northrup	235
Eliza, [d. Calvin], b. Dec. 16, 1804	282
Elisabeth, of Manchester, m. Dr. John **HUBBARD**, of Amherst, Mass., Nov. 2, 1824, by Enoch Burt	202
Emily, [d. Calvin], b. Feb. 8, 1803	282
Emely, of Manchester, m. Henry **FRANCIS**, of Hartford, May 2, 1825, by Enoch Burt	203
Emma, [d. George W.], b. Jan. 23, 1836	281
George, [s. George W.], b. Aug. 18, 1825	281
George W., m. Mary **CHENEY**, b. of Manchester, Nov. 2, 1824, by Enoch Burt	202
James, [s. George W.], b. Feb. 9, 1838	281
John, [s. George W.], b. Apr. 14, 1827	281
John, of Brownington, Vt., m. Mary Jane **LYMAN**, of Charleston, Vt., Nov. 28, 1850, by Rev. M. P. Alderman	256
Mary, [d. Calvin], b. Feb. 11, 1801	282
Mary, m. George W. **CHEENEY**, b. of Manchester, Nov. 2, 1824, by Enoch Burt	202
Mary Eliza, [d. George W.], b. Apr. 24, 1829	281
Mary Jane, m. John **WARD**, b. of Manchester, Oct. 6, 1850, by Rev. Charles R. Fisher	253

	Page
CHENEY, CHEENEY (cont.)	
Ralph, m. Jerusha **GOODWIN**, b. of Manchester, Oct. 14, 1833, by B. F. Northrup	215
Rush, of Manchester, m. Julia O. **GOODWIN**, of New York, Sept. 27, 1847, by B. F. Northrup	241
Sally Maria, [d. Calvin], b. Jan. 7, 1799	282
William, [s. George W.], b. May 21, 1833	281
William Eli, [s. Calvin], b. Oct. 7, 1806	282
CHILDS, Elisha, m. Harriet **STEDMAN**, b. of Manchester, Jan. 1, 1834, by Rev. H. L. Ramsdall	216
Julia Ann, of Manchester, m. Arnold C. **BROWN**, of Stockbridge, Mass., Mar. 25, 1829, by V. R. Osborn, V.D.M.	210
Luther, m. Catharine **VORRA**, of Hartford, July 3, 1828, by Ralph R. Phelps, J.P.	208
CLARK, Charles W., of Columbia, m. Lucy **ALLEN**, of Manchester, May 1, 1853, by F. T. Perkins	265
Ebenezer, of Manchester, m. Mary **OAKS**, of Southbridge, Sept. 3, 1837, by Rev. R. W. Allen	220
George W., m. Martha A. **ALLEN**, b. of Manchester, Sept. 12, 1848, by Rev. Benjamin C. Phelps	245
Nelson T., of Columbia, m. May A. **KEENY**, of Manchester, Sept. 16, 1849, by Rev. M. P. Alderman	250
Samuel H., of Ellington, m. Hannah M. **HARRIS**, of Manchester, May 3, 1843, by Rev. Rich[ard] Levesey	230
Vesta W., of Manchester, m. Austin **STANDISH**, of Glastenbury, Jan. 13, 1850, by Rev. B. F. Northrup	251
CLEMINS (?), Philo, of Windsor, m. Martha L. **LYMAN**, of Manchester, May 18, 1853, by F. T. Perkins	265
CLOUGH, Lucy, of Manchester, m. Chauncy B. **BUCKLEY**, of East Haddam, Feb. 11, 1838, by Rev. R. W. Allen	221
Rosella, of Manchester, m. Charles **GRANT**, of Westfield, Mass., Apr. 18, 1838, by Rev. B. W. Allen	222
COLE, Pauliana, of Manchester, m. Israel E. **ALLEN**, of East Windsor, Jan. 1, 1829, by Enoch Burt	209
COLEMAN, Simeon, m. Huldah **MILLARD**, b. of Manchester, Nov. 12, 1846, by V. R. Osborn	238
COLLINS, Roderick, of Ludlow, Mass., m. Almira **GLOVER**, of Wilbraham, Nov. 25, 1832, by B. F. Northrop	214
COMSTOCK, Joseph, of Montville, m. Leonora **BROWN**, of Manchester, Apr. 2, 1833, by B. F. Northrop	214
CONEY, Jane A., m. Simeon F. **WETHEREL**, Feb. 45, 1844, by B. F. Northrop	231
COOK, Aaron, of Ashford, m. Mabel **LYMAN**, of Manchester, June 29, 1837, by B. F. Northrop	221
Chelsia, m. Julia R. **TUCKER**, b. of Manchester, Nov. 24, 1850, by Rev. M. P. Alderman	255
Harriot, of Manchester, m. Mosley **TALCOTT**, of Marlborough, Apr. 6, 1825, by Enoch Burt	202
Harriet A., of Manchester, m. Frederick A. **LEACH**, of Coventry, May 6, 1849, by Rev. M. P. Alderman	248
John B., m. Mary **JOHNSON**, Oct. 3, 1827, by V. R. Osborn, V.D.M.	207

	Page
COOK (cont.)	
Samuel, m. Leanora **VIBBERT**, May 7, 1828, by V. R. Osborn, V.D.M.	208
Sarah, m. William **HYDE**, Aug. 25, 1846, by Rev. B. F. Northrup	238
COOLEY, Charles D., of Norwich, m. Sarah C. **FOX**, of Manchester, Jan. 2, 1853, by Rev. George M. Brewster	264
Lydia, m. Dudley **CASE**, b. of Manchester, Feb. 7, 1836, by B. F. Northrop	218
Mary, of Manchester, m. Grove **HOLLISTER**, of East Windsor, Nov. 19, 1837, by Rev. Nathan B. Benedict	221
William B., of Manchester, m. Lucy L. **HARRIS**, of Hebron, June 4, 1833, by Enoch Burt	216
COTTON, Eliza C., of Manchester, m. Halsey H. **FULLER**, of Vernon, Feb. 26, 1851, by Rev. Theodore M. Dwight	254
George, of East Hartford, m. Mary **GRISWOLD**, of Manchester, Oct. [ ], 1847, by B. F. Northrop	242
Lester, of Windsor, m. Roseanna W. **WELCH**, of Lebanon, Nov. 23, 1825, by Enoch Burt	205
COUCH, Nancy, of Manchester, m. Joel **HILLS**, of East Hartford, Sept. 17, 1826, by Ephraim V. Avery	209
Ruth, of Manchester, m. Harvey **BUCKLAND**, of Bolton, Dec. 9, 1828, by Bennett F. Northrop	209
COVEL, Mary Elizabeth, of Bolton, m. Seth **EDWARDS**, of Manchester, Sept. 3, 1843, by Rev. Ziba Loveland. Witnesses Samuel Strong & Lucy Strong	230
COWLES, Anny, m. Dudley **KENEY**, b. of Manchester, Nov. 26, 1823, by Enoch Burt	201
Eliza, of Manchester, m. Luman A. **SQUIRE**, of Bozrah, May 2, 1832, by Rev. Ephraim Scott	213
Martha, m. Henry **MUNSELL**, May 1, 1833, by Rev. Hezekiah L. Ramsdell	215
Mary, of Manchester, m. Dwight H. **KEENEY**, of East Hartford, Oct. 17, 1844, by Rev. P. T. Keeney	233
COX, Susan, of Manchester, m. Henry **HYDE**, of East Hartford, Sept. 14, 1828, by Enoch Burt	209
CROCKER, Samuel M., of Hebron, m. Cynthia **HARRINGTON**, of Manchester, Aug. 22, 1841, by Rev. Richard Liverey	227
CULVER, Benjamin, of Manchester, m. Betsy **CABLE**, of Hartford, June 5, 1836, by S. Hull	219
James N., m. Almira **PURPLE**, Nov. 7, 1826, by V. R. Osborn, V.D.M.	206
Lucy Ann, of Manchester, m. John **ADAMS**, of Canton, Nov. 13, 1836, by V. R. Osborn, V.D.M.	219
Malinda, m. John **WHECKHAM**, Nov. 19, 1823, by Isaac Devinel	201
Martha, m. Amasa C. **JOHNSON**, b. of Manchester, Jan. 13, 1828, by Joseph Noyes, J.P.	207
Mary Ann, m. Judson **McKEE**, Apr. 15, 1838, by Rev. Elias C. Scott	222
CUTLER, Clarissa, m. Joseph **WETHERELL**, b. of Manchester, Jan. 2, 1833, by B. F. Northrop	214
Joseph, m. Adaliza **WHEELER**, b. of Manchester, Nov. 11, 1838, by Rev. R. W. Allen	223
Loisa, of Manchester, m. Francis **OSBOURN**, of East Windsor, Nov. 27, 1845, by Rev. B. F. Northrop	236

BARBOUR COLLECTION

	Page
CUTLER (cont.)	
Lucius, of Manchester, m. Ruth A. **WEBSTER**, of Bolton, June 9, 1836, by S. Hull	219
DAGGETT, Hannah, m. James M. **KEITH**, b. of Manchester, May 23, 1852, by Rev. George W. Brewster	260
DALE, Ellen, of Manchester, m. George G. **STANDLY**, of West Suffield, Sept. 12, 1850, by M. F. Alderman	254
DANIELS, Aaron M., m. Betsey **DART**, b. of Manchester, June 24, 1841, by Rev. Sanford Benton	227
Aaron M., of Springfield, Mass., m. Maria G. **ENSWORTH**, of Manchester, Nov. 17, 1842, by Rev. R. Levesey	229
Betsy, bd. May 13, 1842, ae 25. Rev. R. Livesey, Min.	335
Dwight, of Ludlow, Mass., m. Abigail **BIDWELL**, of Manchester, Sept. 15, 1842, by Rev. R. Liversey	228
James A., of Woonsocket, R.I., m. Mary **WOODBRIDGE**, of Manchester, Sept. 3, 1844, by B. F. Northrop	232
DARROW, Hannah, of Vernon, m. Ely **LYMAN**, of Coventry, Nov. 18, 1835, by David Bennett	218
DART, Betsey, m. Aaron M. **DANIELS**, b. of Manchester, June 24, 1841, by Rev. Sanford Benton	227
Edna, of Manchester, m. Nelson **KEENEY**, of Bolton, Sept. 18, 1837, by Rev. R. W. Allen	220
Walter, m. Julia E. **TREAT**, Oct. 1, 1845, by V. R. Osborn, V.D.M.	235
DEAN, Ann Y., of Manchester, m. Daniel **WADSWORTH**, of Vernon, May 8, 1844, by B. F. Northrop	232
Clarissa, m. Elisha L. **ANDRUS**, Aug. 27, 1843, by B. F. Northrop	230
Mary A., of Manchester, m. Edwin L. **BOWER**, of Hartford, July 24, 1839, by Sanford Benton	224
Mary A., m. Oliver P. **WILKES**, b. of Manchester, Aug. 20, 1845, by V. R. Osborn, V.D.M.	235
Nancy, m. Sterry B. **SAVALLY**, July 1, 1830, by V. R. Osborn	211
DECKER, Harriet E., of Glastenbury, m. Austin **FLITCHER**, Oct. 10, 1847, by B. F. Northrop	241
DEMING, DEMMING, Asa, of East Glastenbury, m. Jane **SHEPHARD**, of Webster, Ma.., July 2, 1851, by Rev. George W. Brewster	256
Ebenezer, of Glastenbury, m. Jerusha **KEENEY**, of Manchester, Nov. 28, 1830, by Rev. Jeremiah Stocking	211
DEWEY, Abigail, m. W[illia]m **GREEN**, Sept. 3, 1823, by Isaac Devinel	200
DEXTER, Irene, of Manchester, m. Peter O. **BUELL**, of Simsbury, Sept. [ ], 1834, by B. F. Northrop	216
DIMOCK, DIMMOCKS, Pamelia, of Manchester, m. Lucian A. **PORTER**, of Plymouth, Sept. 7, 1846, by Rev. B. F. Northrop	238
Samuel R., m. Sarah Loisa **DIMOCK**, Nov. 23, 1849, by Rev. B. F. Northrop	252
Sarah Loisa, m. Samuel R. **DIMOCK**, Nov. 23, 1849, by Rev. B. F. Northrop	252
DOW, DOWE, Charlotte M., of Manchester, m. Robert M. **WILLSON**, of Westfield, Mass., May 5, 1841, by Rev. B. F. Northrop	227
John, m. Mary **PORTER**, Apr. 18, 1830, by V. R. Osborn, V.D.M.	211
DOYL, Margaret M., of Suffield, m. Chauncy **BIDWELL**, of Manchester, June 6, 1847, by Rev. Benjamin C. Phelps	240
DRAKE, Darias, m. Hariet **ALLEN**, Aug. 15, 1825, by Elder Elisha Frink of Tolland	203

	Page
DUFF, John, of East Windsor, .m. Philanda **BURNS**, of Manchester, Nov. 19, 1840, by Sanford Benton	227
EATON, Damaris, [d. Joseph], b. July 9, 1832	282
Mary, [d. Joseph], b. July 1, 1830	282
Mary Ann, m. James L. **SPERRY**, Sept. 14, 1851, by Rev. George E. Hill	257
EDDY, Phillip L., of Hartford, m. Sarah **PITKIN**, of Manchester, May 7, 1828, by Enoch Burt	208
EDGERLIN, John, of Vernon, m. Francis E. **KEENEY**, of Manchester, July 24, 1853, by F. T. Perkins	266
EDMONDS, Clarrissa, m. Chauncy **BUCKLEY**, b. of Manchester, Sept. 26, 1849, by Rev. M. P. Alderman	250
EDWARDS, Seth, of Manchester, m. Mary Elizabeth **COVEL**, of Bolton, Sept. 3, 1843, by Rev. Ziba Loveland. Witnesses Samuel Strong & Lucy Strong	230
-----, Mr., bd. Sept. 21, 1842, ae 24. Rev. R. Livesey, Min.	335
ELDRIDGE, Amanda, [d. Russell], b. Aug. 16, 1824	282
Daniel Haynes, [s. Russell], b. Dec. 2, 1826	282
Russell, m. Betsy **RICH**, Sept. 22, 1823, by Joseph Treson	200
Russell, [s. Russell], b. July 19, 1829	282
Samuel, of Manchester, m. Sarah **ABBEY**, of Manchester, Sept. 11, 1844, by Rev. P. T. Keeney	232
EMERSON, Nancy L., of Haddam, m. Joseph C. **CASE**, of Manchester, Jan. 6, 1850, by Rev. M. P. Alderman	251
EMMONS, John, of Haddam, m. Caroline **BRAINARD**, of Haddam, Oct. 3, 1852, by Rev. George W. Brewster	263
ENSWORTH, Maria G., of Manchester, m. Aaron M. **DANIELS**, of Springfield, Mass., Nov. 17, 1842, by Rev. R. Levesey	229
ERVING, George G., of Hartford, m. Elizabeth **BISSELL**, of Manchester, Aug. 28, 1840, by Sanford Benton	226
EVANS, EVINS, Harriet, m. Edward **PINNEY**, b. of Vernon, May 5, 1852, by Rev. George W. Brewster	259
Laura, of Manchester, m. Jacob G. **GEORGE**, of Vermont, Feb. 14, 1838, by Rev. R. W. Allen	221
Levi, m. Marilla **WYLLYS**, Mar. 25, 1824, by Isaac Devinel	201
Looisa, of Manchester, m. Davis W. **MANN**, of Coventry, June 29, 1845, by V.R. Osborn, V.D.M.	235
Moses, of Manchester, m. Tirza **KNOX**, of Stafford, Sept. 21, 1831, by R. R. Phelps, J.P.	212
Sarah, m. Chester W. **KEENEY**, Nov. 23, 1845, by V. R. Osborn, V.D.M.	236
Seth, of Manchester, m. Maria **KNOX**, of Stafford, Nov. 26, 1829, by Ralph R. Phelps, J.P.	210
FERGUSON, Francis, m. Lucy E. **ADAMS**, Apr. 21, 1830, by Isaac Devinel	211
FIELDING, Mary J., m. Monroe A. **BROWN**, b. of Manchester, Oct. 12, 1851, by Rev. F. T. Perkins	257
FISH, Hopkins, of Plainfield, m. Amelia **STOWEL**, of Boston, Sept. 3, 1827, by E. Burt	207
William G., of West Windsor, m. Lucinda M. **CARVER**, of Bolton, Jan. 29, 1851, by Rev. M. P. Alderman	256
FLINT, Joshua C., m. Electa **STEDMAN**, b. of Manchester, Aug. 22, 1827, by V. R. Osborn, V.D.M.	206

	Page
FLINT (cont.)	
Orpha, m. Calvin B. **BRAGG**, Sept. 4, 1823, by Isaac Devinel	200
FLITCHER, Austin, m. Harriet E. **DECKER**, of Glastenbury, Oct. 10, 1847, by B. F. Northrop	241
FORBES, FORBS, Elijah, Jr., of East Hartford, m. Wealthy **BRYANT**, of Manchester, Nov. 10, 1825, by Enoch Burt	205
Esther, m. Benjamin **LOOMIS**, Oct. 31, 1832, by Rev. Hezekiah L. Ramsdall	214
Jane, m. Chauncy B. **HOUSE**, Nov. 25, 1845, by V. R. Osborn, V.D.M.	236
Sidney, m. Lucy **RANDALL**, Sept. 21, 1825, by Joy H. Fairchild	204
FORD, Siloma, m. Harlow M. **FOWLER**, Mar. 4, 1846, by V. R. Osborn, V.D.M.	236
FOSTER, Charles, of East Windsor, m. Mary Ann **BAILEY**, of Manchester, Mar. 24, 1830, by B. F. Northrop	211
Elisa, of Manchester, m. Thomas **HARDING**, of East Hartford, Apr. 14, 1824, by Asahel Nettleton	201
Julia A., of Manchester, m. Edwin **SPENCER**, of East Hartford, Mar. 19, 1829, by Bennett F. Northrop	209
Normond, of East Windsor, m. Maria C. **BUCKLAND**, of Manchester, Dec. 29, 1842, by Rev. William Wright	229
Phebe A., of Manchester, m. Eli **MILLARD**, of Iowa Territory, Aug. [ ], 1838, by B. F. Northrop	222
Ralph, of South Windsor, m. Chloe W. **BUCKLAND**, of Manchester, Apr. 2, 1851, by Rev. Theodore M. Dwight. Dated at Union Village	255
FOWLER, Harlow M., m. Siloma **FORD**, Mar. 4, 1846, by V. R. Osborn, V.D.M.	236
FOX, Asa W., m. Emily **WOODBRIDGE**, b. of Manchester, Apr. 27, 1829, by Bennett F. Northrop	209
Cornelia Ann, m. Henry **BECKERS**, b. of Bolton, Jan. 28, 1846, by B. F. Northrop	236
Eleazur, m. Jerusha **SPENCER**, b. of Manchester, Sept. 4, 1845, by V. R. Osborn, V.D.M.	235
Eli P., of Bolton, m. Emily **ANDRUS**, of Manchester, Jan. 15, 1828, by E. Burt	207
Elizabeth, of Manchester, m. William C. **VIRGEN**, of Hartford, Apr. 16, 1837, by V. R. Osborn, V.D.M.	219
James, of Hillington, m. Asenath **HACKET**, of Manchester, Apr. 15, 1838, by Enoch Burt	226
Julia A., of Manchester, m. Merrit **ROOT**, of Glastenbury, Feb. 10, 1845, by Rev. P. T. Keeney	234
Laura Ann, m. Daniel **SULLIVAN**, July 5, 1846, by V. R. Osborn, V.D.M.	237
Sarah C., of Manchester, m. Charles D. **COOLEY**, of Norwich, Jan. 2, 1853, by Rev. George M. Brewster	264
Sophia, of Bolton, m. Orrin **HALE**, of Glastenbury, Apr. 9, 1833, by B. F. Northrop	214
FRANCIS, Henry, of Hartford, m. Emely **CHENEY**, of Manchester, May 2, 1825, by Enoch Burt	203
John, of Hartford, m. Lucinda C. **WHEELER**, of Manchester, June 16, 1839, by Enoch Burt	226

MANCHESTER VITAL RECORDS 61

Page

FREEMAN, Chauncy, of Hartford, m. Mary **SAUNDERS**, of Avon, Oct.
20, 1839, by B. F. Northrop — 224
Edmond, of Chickopee, Mass., m. Eliza **STOUGHTON**, of
Manchester, Apr. 16, 1849, by Rev. Benjamin Phelps — 248
FRENCH, Martha E., m. Austin **BIDWELL**, b. of Manchester, Nov. 10,
1850, by Rev. M. P. Alderman — 255
FULLER, Halsey H., of Vernon, m. Eliza C. **COTTON**, of Manchester,
Feb. 26, 1851, by Rev. Theodore M. Dwight — 254
Rufus, of Glastenbury, m. Charlotte C. **HOXIE**, of Manchester, Feb.
25, 1838, by B. F. Northrop — 221
FYLER, James H., m. Clarissa **McLEAN**, b. of Manchester, May 10,
1841, by Rev. Enoch Burt — 227
John F., of East Hartford, m. Clarissa **McLEAN**, of Vernon, Aug.
28, 1839, by Sanford Benton — 224
GARDNER, Elizabeth, of Manchester, m. Erastus **HUBBARD**, of
Hartford, Apr. 21, 1847, by Rev. B. F. Northrop — 240
Henry, m. Elizabeth **PEASE**, Oct. 5, 1845, by V. R. Osborn, V.D.M. — 236
Horace, of Mansfield, m. Eliza E. **ANNIS**, of Manchester. Nov. 24,
1831, by Rev. Ephraim Scott — 212
GAY, Royal L., m. Eleanor **AUSTIN**, of Glastenbury, May 12, 1850, by
Rev. B. F. Northrop — 252
GEERS, Benjamin F., of Williamsbury, Mass., m. Rosetta **HALE**, of
Manchester, Oct. 8, 1844, by Rev. P. T. Keeney — 233
GEORGE, Jacob G., of Vermont, m. Laura **EVANS**, of Manchester, Feb.
14, 1838, by Rev. R. W. Allen — 221
GIBSON, Ann, of Sterling, m. Noadiah **TAYLOR**, of Worthington, O.,
July 3, 1826, by Enoch Burt — 205
GILBERT, Josiah C., m. Sarah L. **POST**, b. of Hebron, Sept. 6, 1848, by
Rev. Charles Nichols — 245
GILLETT, Amanda, m. Andrew G. **KEENEY**, b. of Manchester, Dec.
31, 1851, in South Windsor, by Rev. George W. Brewster — 258
Lucy A., of South Windsor, m. Oliver S. **AUBRIM**, of South
Windsor, Mar. 26, 1848, by Rev. Benjamin C. Phelps — 244
GILLMAN, Clarrissa, of Manchester, m. John **BILL**, of Middletown,
Nov. 12, 1823, by Rev. Frederick Wightman, of Middletown — 201
GLEASON, Alfred, bd. Aug. 12, 1841, ae 22. Rev. R. Livesey, Min. — 335
Anson, of Manchester, m. Becthia W. **TRACEY**, of Lebanon, Oct.
24, 1826, by Enoch Burt — 206
Chauncy, m. Martha A. **VIBERT**, Nov. 27, 1845, by V. R. Osborn,
V.D.M. — 236
Emily, of Manchester, m. Norton C. **PECK**, of Farmington, May 2,
1847, by Benjamin C. Phelps — 240
Henry W., m. Mary **WHEELER**, b. of Manchester, Oct. 15, 1838,
by B. F. Northrop — 223
Martha, of Manchester, m. Nelson **SKINNER**, of Bolton, Nov. 10,
1844, by Rev. P. T. Keeney — 233
Sarah Jane, of Manchester, m. Jacob **BEAM**, of New London, Mar.
14, 1844, by B. F. Northrop — 231
Ward B., m. Mary M. **MATSON**, June 28, 1846, by V. R. Osborn,
V.D.M. — 237
GLOVER, Almira, of Wilbraham, Mass., m. Roderick **COLLINS**, of
Ludlow, Mass., Nov. 25, 1832, by B. F. Northrop — 214

	Page
GOODALE, Charles, of East Hartford, m. Mary A. **CARROL**, of Manchester, July 21, 1850, by Rev. M. P. Alderman	253
Cyrus, m. Mary **ROBERTS**, Oct. 8, 1823, by Joseph Treson	200
Laura, of Manchester, m. Alexander **HILLS**, of East Windsor, Nov. 13, 1842, by Rev. R. Levesey	229
GOODMAN, Richard M., of New York City, m. Electa **CHEENY**, of Manchester, June 18, 1845, by Rev. B. F. Northrop	235
GOODRICH, Henry, of Wethersfield, m. Lucretia A. **RISLEY**, of Manchester, Aug. 2, 1843, by Rev. Charles Noble	230
Margaret, m. George R. **RISLEY**, Dec. 18, 1853, by Rev. E. Burt	267
GOODWIN, Carolina Agusta, of New York, m Dr. John **SCHUR** (?), of Hartford, Nov. 16, 1848, by Rev. B. F. Northrop	245-6
Jerusha, m. Ralph **CHENEY**, b. of Manchester, Oct. 14, 1833, by B. F. Northrop	215
Julia O., of New York, m. Rush **CHENEY**, of Manchester, Sept. 27, 1847, by B. F. Northrop	241
GORDON, Orrin P., of Hartford, m Adaline **SPERRY**, of Manchester, Sept. 1, 1839, by B. F. Northrop	224
GOULD, George H., m. Almira **HOUSE**, b. of Manchester, Oct. 22, 1848, by Rev. Benjamin C. Phelps	245
GRANT, Charles, of Westfield, Mass., m. Rosella **CLOUGH**, of Manchester, Apr. 18, 1838, by Rev. B. W. Allen	222
Cornelia, m. Russell **KEENEY**, b. of Manchester, Apr. 6, 1842, by Rev. R. Livesey	228
James M., m. Julia A. **INGOLSBY**, May 10, 1850, by Rev. B. F. Northrop	252
Phebe, of East Windsor, m. Franklin M. **CASE**, of Hartford, Sept. 1, 1842, by B. F. Northrop	228
GRAVES, [see also **GROVES**], Arba, of Thompson, m. Sarah A. **SPENCER**, of Manchester, Nov. 18, 1851, by F. T. Perkins	257
GRAY, George, m. Mary M. **MARSH**, b. of Manchester, Mar. 5, 1844, by Rev. E. Burt	249
Jerusha E., m. William H. **CARROL**, Sept. 30, 1849, by Rev. B. F. Northrop	249
May E., m. James E. **LANDFEAR**, Oct. 31, 1849, by Rev. B. F. Northrop	250
Sarah A., m. Franklin B. **RISLEY**, Jan. 10, 1849, by Rev. B. F. Northrop	247
-----, Mr., bd. May 27, 1842, ae 39. Rev. R. Livesey, Min.	335
GREEN, W[illia]m, m. Abigail **DEWEY**, Sept. 3, 1823, by Isaac Devinel	200
GRISWOLD, Alfred, of Wethersfield, m. Emily **MARSH**, of Manchester, July 18, 1830, by Enoch Burt	212
Daniel, m. Ann **BUNCE**, Oct. 30, 1828, by Enoch Burt	209
Edward H., m. Harriet **WHITE**, b. of Manchester, June 10, 1847, by Rev. B. F. Northrop	241
Ethan, m. Sally **MANCHESTER**, Mar. 8, 1828, by V. R. Osborn, V.D.M.	208
Henry, m. Eliza **RUSSELL**, b. of Manchester, July 3, 1849, by Samuel Spring	248
Laura, m. William H. **JONES**, Oct. 22, 1847, by Rev. B. F. Northrop	243
Mariah Ann, of Manchester, m. Isaac **JONES**, of Hartford, Nov. 11, 1827, by V. R. Osborn, V.D.M.	207

MANCHESTER VITAL RECORDS

Page

GRISWOLD (cont.)
Mary, of Manchester, m. George **COTTON**, of East Hartford, Oct.
[ ], 1847, by B. F. Northrop — 242
GROVES, [see also **GRAVES**], Phineus, of Ellington, m. Parlynesa
PERRY, of Manchester, Nov. 24, 1834, by B. F. Northrop — 216
HACKETT, HACKET, Asenath, of Manchester, m. Daniel **PUSHAN**, of
Hartford, Mar. 7, 1830, by Lemuel White, J.P. — 210
Asenath, of Manchester, m. James **FOX**, of Hillington, Apr. 15,
1838 by Enoch Burt — 226
Marilda F., of Manchester, m. Jared **PEARL**, of Willington, Feb.
14, 1836, by B. F. Northrop — 218
HALE, Almira, of Manchester, m. Lawrence **STOUGHTON**, of East
Windsor, Dec. 25, 1826, by V. R. Osborn, V.D.M. — 206
Clement, of Eastbury, m. Mirinda **BIDWELL**, of Manchester, Apr.
3, 1828, by Enoch Burt — 208
Edgar T., m. Eliza H. **ABBY**, b. of Manchester, Aug. 22, 1848, by
Rev. Benjamin C. Phelps — 245
Harriet Jane, of Manchester, m. Avery A. **BUCKLAND**, of Hartford,
Apr. 26, 1848, by Rev. Benjamin C. Phelps — 244
John B., m. Harriet E. **KEENEY**, b. of Manchester, Nov. 14, 1838,
by Rev. R. W. Allen — 223
Orange, of Glastenbury, m. Eliza **JOHNSON**, of Manchester, May
[ ], 1834, by B. F. Northrop — 215
Orrin, of Glastenbury, m. Sophia **FOX**, of Bolton, Apr. 9, 1833, by
B. F. Northrop — 214
Rosetta, of Manchester, m. Benjamin F. **GEERS**, of Williamsbury,
Mass., Oct. 8, 1844, by Rev. P. T. Keeney — 233
Ruby, m. Dudley **PHILLIPS**, Dec. 25, 1825, by Isaac Devinel — 205
Ruba B., of Manchester, m. Alanson L. **WEIR**, of Avon, Apr. 10,
1842, by Rev. E. Burt — 249
HALEN, Phebe, m. Chester **KEENEY**, Apr. 2, 1846, by V. R. Osborn,
V.D.M. — 236
HALL, Cynthia, of Manchester, m. Azariah **WATERMAN**, of Bolton,
Sept. 16, 1835, by B. F. Northrop — 218
Martha, of Portland, m. Henry E. **ROGERS**, of Manchester, Sept. 4,
1844, by Rev. P. T. Keeney — 232
Norman B., of Windham, m. Mary **ANIS**, of Manchester, Feb. 24,
1836, by Rev. S. Hall — 218
HALLETT, Charles B., of East Hartford, m. Aurora A. **PHILLIPS**, of
Manchester, Nov. 10, 1848, by Rev. Benjamin C. Phelps — 246
HANOVER, Ira Emery, of New Hampshire, m. Elizabeth A. **IRISH**, of
Manchester, Jan. 25, 1853, by Rev. John Cooper — 264
HARDING, Thomas, of East Hartford, m. Elisa **FOSTER**, of Manchester,
Apr. 14, 1824, by Asahel Nettleton — 201
HARRINGTON, Alpheus E., m. Eliza **LEWIS**, b. of Manchester, May
[ ], 1831, by B. F. Northrop — 212
Cynthia, of Manchester, m. Samuel M. **CROCKER**, of Hebron,
Aug. 22, 1841, by Rev. Richard Liverey — 227
Louisa, m. Alvin **THAYER**, b. of Manchester, Sept. 1, 1839, by S.
Benton — 224
Sarah C., of Hebron, m. Morillo L. **PERRY**, of Manchester, Oct. 15,
1843, by Rev. Charles Noble — 231

	Page
HARRIS, Hannah M., of Manchester, m. Samuel H. CLARK, of Ellington, May 3, 1843, by Rev. Rich[ard] Levesey	230
Leviah, m. John STRONG, b. of Manchester, Aug. 1, 1841, by Rev. Richard Liverey	227
Lucy L., of Hebron, m. William B. COOLEY, of Manchester, June 4, 1833, by Enoch Burt	216
HARRISON, Mortimer F., of New York, m. Electa CHENEY, of Manchester, Aug. 8, 1842, by Rev. E. Burk	249
HARTSHORN, Marilla, of Manchester, m. Joseph HOUSE, of Glastenbury, Aug. 30, 1835, by Enoch Burt	217
HASKINS, Catherine, m. Asahel CADY, Jr., b. of Manchester, Oct. 20, 1836, by V. R. Osborn, V.D.M.	219
HAUGHTON, Lydia Clarrissa, of Hebron, m. Leonard Smith VIBBERT, of Manchester, Nov. 5, 1846, by Rev. William B. Corlyn	237
HAYDEN, George M., of Hartford, m. Mary C. BOWERS, of Manchester, [Jan.] 16, 1848, by Rev. B. C. Phelps	243
HEMMINGWAY, Julia, m. George F. BURNS, Nov. 6, 1844, by B. F. Northrop	233
HENRY, -----, of Glastonbury, m. Mary B. MINER, of Manchester, Sept. 8, 1844, by Rev. P. T. Keeney	232
HERRIC, Abigail, m. Elijah HILLS, b. of Bolton, May 17, 1836, by S. Hull	218
HILLS, HILL, Alexander, of East Windsor, m .Laura GOODALE, of Manchester, Nov. 13, 1842, by Rev. R. Levesey	229
Daniel, m. Mary Jane STEEL, b. of Manchester, Mar. 14, 1832, by Rev. Ephraim Scott	213
Elijah, m. Abigail HERRIC, b. of Bolton, May 17, 1836, by S. Hull	218
Francis A., of East Hartford, m. Sarah McLEAN, of Manchester, Aug. 11, 1846, by E. L. Goodwin, J.P.	237
Joel, of East Hartford, m. Nancy COUCH, of Manchester, Sept. 17, 1826, by Ephraim V. Avery	209
John, Jr., of East Hartford, m. Electa WETHERELL, of Manchester, [ ], by B. F. Northrop	211
Selah, of Manchester, m. Sophia HILLS, of Glastenbury, Sept. 13, 1829, by Joseph Noyes, J.P.	210
Sophia, of Glastonbury, m. Selah HILLS, of Manchester, Sept. 13, 1829, by Joseph Noyes, J.P.	210
Walter, m. Julia A. RISLEY, Oct. 23, 1845, by V. R. Osborn, V.D.M.	236
W[illia]m R., of East Hartford, m. Sybil LYMAN, of Manchester, Nov. 27, 1844, by Rev. B. F. Northrop	233
HITCHCOCK, Harriet, m. Charles LYMAN, b. of Manchester, Dec. 31, 1829, by B. F. Northrop	210
Lydia, m. Caleb L. BASSETT, June 5, 1828, by Enoch Burt	208
HOFFMAN, Edwin, m. Sophia VIBERT, b. of Manchester, Oct. 30, 1825, by Enoch Burt	204
HOLLISTER, Eleanor D., m. Ashbel W. CASE, of Manchester, Nov. 28, 1833, by Rev. H. L. Ramsdall	215
Elizabeth M., of Terrysville, m. James TERRY, Oct. 10, 1843, by B. F. Northrop	231
Grove, of East Windsor, m. Mary COOLEY, of Manchester, Nov. 19, 1837, by Rev. Nathan B. Benedict	221

	Page
HOLLISTER (cont.)	
Halsy, of Manchester, m. Mary **HOLLISTER**, of Windsor, July 2, 1848, by Rev. E. Burt	249
Levah B., of Manchester, m. John **NORTON**, of North Madison, July 3, 1833, by B. F. Northrop	215
Mary, of Manchester, m. Timothy **MUNSELL**, of East Windsor, Sept. [ ], 1838, by B. F. Northrop	223
Mary, of Windsor, m. Halsey **HOLLISTER**, of Manchester, July 2, 1848, by Rev. E. Burt	249
Mary A., m. Joseph C. **TREMAIN**, Mar. 12, 1851, by Rev. M. F. Alderman	255
Phebe, of Bolton, m. Josiah **KEENEY**, of Rome, N.Y., Nov. 27, 1837 by James Ely	220
William W., m. Maria **KEENEY**, b. of Manchester, May 19, 1835, by Rev. Salmon Hall	217
HOLMS, Henry C., of South Lee, Mass., m. Mary Cornelia **SAUNDERS**, of Manchester, Jan. 6, 1848, by Rev. Charles R. Fisher	242
HOLTON, Timothy P., of Ellington, m. Abigail **LATHROP**, of Manchester, June 2, 1829, by B. F. Northrop	209
HOPKINS, Mason B., of Foster, R.I., m. Deborah L. **PLACE**, of Manchester, June 3, 1832, by Rev. Erastus Doty, of Vernon	213
HORSMAN, Charles D., of Boston, Mass., m. Frances Ann **MORGAN**, of Springfield, Mass., Feb. 10, 1834, by George W Cheney, J.P.	215
HOSMER, Elijah B., of East Windsor, m. Clarrissa **WILSON**, of Manchester, May 7, 1845, by Rev. B. M. Walker	234
HOUGHTON, Ralph W., of Hebron, m. Elizabeth F. **BRYANT**, of Manchester, Nov. 1, 1843, by Rev. Charles Noble	231
HOUSE, Almira, m. George H. **GOULD**, b. of Manchester, Oct. 22, 1848, by Rev. Benjamin C. Phelps	245
Chauncy B., m. Jane **FORBES**, Nov. 25, 1845, by V. R. Osborn, V.D.M.	236
Edwin, of Glastenbury, m. Elizabeth **BIDWELL**, of Manchester, Nov. 3, 1841, by Rev. James A. Smith, of Glastenbury	228
Jerusha Ann, of East Glastenbury, m. Lucian C. **ATTWOOD** (?), of Willimansell, Mass., Jan. 4, 1852, by Rev. John Cooper	262
Joseph, of Glastenbury, m. Marilla **HARTSHORN**, of Manchester, Aug. 30, 1835, by Enoch Burt	217
Monroe, of Glastenbury, m. Lucy H. **BIDWELL**, of Manchester, Jan. 30, 1848, by Rev. B. C. :Phelps	243
Nelson, m. Catherine **HOWE**, b. of Glastenbury, Apr. 8, 1832, by Rev. Ephraim Scott	213
Robert, m. Clarissa **McKEE**, b. of Manchester, Apr. 27, 1826, by V. R. Osborn, Elder	205
HOWARD, Elizabeth, of Tolland, m. Roswell **WOLCOTT**, of East Windsor, Apr. 5, 1840, by S. Benton	225
Emily, of Manchester, m. Turner (?) **STEVENS**, of Webster, Mass., Dec. 11, 1849, by Rev. M. P. Alderman	250
Walter, of Perry, N.Y., m. Ruth **KEENEY**, of Manchester, May 26, 1829, by B. F. Northrop	209
HOWE, Catherine, m. Nelson **HOUSE**, b. of Glastenbury, Apr. 8, 1832, by Rev. Ephraim Scott	213
Halsey R., m. Lucretia **MORTON**, May 5, 1846, by V. R. Osborn, V.D.M.	237

BARBOUR COLLECTION

Page

HOXIE, Charlotte C., of Manchester, m. Rufus **FULLER**, of
Glastenbury, Feb. 25, 1838, by B. F. Northrop ... 221
HUBBARD, Elizabeth, m. Henry **CAULKINS**, b. of Hartford, Oct. [ ],
1842, by B. F. Northrop ... 229
Elizabeth M., of Manchester, m. Henry C. **BISSELL**, of Lyme, O.,
May 5, 1846, by Rev. B. F. Northrop ... 237
Erastus, of Hartford, m. Elizabeth **GARDNER**, of Manchester, Apr.
21, 1847, by Rev. B. F. Northrop ... 240
Eunice A., of Manchester, m. William **BARNS**, of Lacon, Ill, Aug.
18, 1842, by B. F. Northrop ... 228
Ira G., of Glastenbury, m. Maria **MILLER**, of Manchester, May [ ],
1831, by B. F. Northrop ... 212
John, Dr., of Amherst, Mass., m. Elisabeth **CHENEY**, of
Manchester, Nov. 2, 1824, by Enoch Burt ... 202
Mary E., of Glastenbury, m. John **ROBERTS**, of Grafton, N.H.,
Mar. 6, 1854, by W[illia]m M. Roberts, J.P. ... 267
Ophilia, of East Hartford, m. Ralph C. **BALL**, of Manchester, Nov.
29, 1849, by Rev. M. P. Alderman ... 251
Phila, m. Edward B. **PAYNE**, June 3, 1846, by V. R. Osborn,
V.D.M. ... 237
HUDSON, Henry W., of Oakland, m. Delia P. **OLMSTED**, of East
Hartford, Dec. 10, 1846, by Aaron F. Olmsted ... 239
HULL, Edwin S., m. Mary A. **SCOTT**, b. of Manchester, May 15, 1836,
by S. Hall ... 218
HUN, Hiram, m. Orpha **PIERCE**, Jan. 22, 1828, by V. R. Osborn, V.D.M. ... 207
HUNT, Henry L., of Bolton, m. Permelia H. **KEENEY**, of Manchester,
Nov. 27, 1839, by S. Benton ... 225
HUNTINGTON, Sarah, m. Henry **MARBLE**, Apr. 30, 1898*, by V. R.
Osborn, V. D. M. *(1828?) ... 208
HURLBURT, Stephen, Jr., m. Nancy **RISLEY**, b. of Glastenbury, Feb. 9,
1832, by Rev. Ephraim Scott ... 213
HUTCHENS, John William, s. Marcius, b. Apr. 27, 1832 ... 283
HUTCHINSON, William H., of St. Johns, N. B., m. Martha **MOORE**,
of Providence, Sept. 1, 1833, by B. F. Northrop ... 215
HYDE, Henry, of East Hartford, m. Susan **COX**, of Manchester, Sept. 14,
1828, by Enoch Burt ... 209
William, m. Sarah **COOK**, Aug. 25, 1846, b Rev. B. F. Northrop ... 238
INGALLS, Adiline M., of Manchester, m. Hiram C. **MINER**, of Bozrah,
Nov. 13, 1842, by Rev. R. Livesey ... 229
INGOLSBY, Julia A., m. James M. **GRANT**, May 10, 1850, by Rev. B.
F. Northrop ... 252
INGRAHAM, Aaron S., of Bolton, m. Sarah E. **LYMAN**, of Manchester,
Sept. 26, 1848, by Rev. B. F. Northrop ... 245
IRISH, Elizabeth A., of Manchester, m. Ira Emery **HANOVER**, of New
Hampshire, Jan. 25, 1853, by Rev. John Cooper ... 264
JACQUES, Calvin W., m. Ann G. **BUCKLAND**, b. of Manchester, Apr.
10, 1845, by Rev. B. F. Northrop ... 234
JOHNSON, Amasa C., m. Martha **CULVER**, b. of Manchester, Jan. 13,
1828, by Joseph Noyes, J.P. ... 207
Ann I., m. Benjamin M. **WATSON**, Nov. 7, 1839, by B. F. Northrop ... 224
Eliza, of Manchester, m. Orange **HALE**, of Glastenbury, May [ ],
1834, by B. F. Northrop ... 215
Mary, m. John B. **COOK**, Oct. 3, 1827, by V. R. Osborn, V.D.M. ... 207

	Page
JONES, Isaac, of Hartford, m. Mariah Ann **GRISWOLD**, Nov. 11, 1827, by V. R. Osborn, V.D.M.	207
Mary L., of Manchester, m. George M. **WELCH**, of Hartford, Sept. 29, 1847, by B. F. Northrop	241
Samuel R., of New York, m. Phebe C. **BENNETT**, of Manchester, Mar. 31, 1852, by Rev. Lyman Leffingwell	262
William H., m. Laura **GRISWOLD**, of Manchester, Oct. 22, 1847, by Rev. B. F. Northrop	243
JUCKET, Edmond B., m. Huldah M. **KEENEY**, b. of Manchester, Aug. 20, 1848, by Rev. Benjamin C Phelps	244
KEENEY, KENEY, KEENY, [see also **KENNY**], A., Col. his child bd. Oct. 7, 1842, ae 4 wks. Rev. R. Livesey	335
Almira, m. Horace **RISLEY**, b. of Manchester, Apr. 4, 1838, by B. F. Northrop	222
Andrew G., m. Amanda **GILLETT**, b. of Manchester, Dec. 31, 1851, by Rev. George W. Brewster, in South Windsor	258
Anna, Mrs., of Glastenbury, m. Russell **KEENEY**, of Manchester, May 30, 1841, by Rev. Sanford Benton	227
Atusta, of Manchester, m. Nelson **WINSLOW**, of East Hartford, June 29, 1848, by Rev. Benjamin C. Phelps	244
Charles, of Manchester, m. Caroline **SCHOFF**, of Brunswick, Conn., Nov. 25, 1847, by Rev. Benjamin C. Phelps	242
Chauncy, m. Mary Ann **CASE**, b. of Manchester, Mar. 20, 1832, by Rev. Ephraim Scott	213
Chester, m. Phebe **HALEN**, Apr. 2, 1846, by V. R. Osborn, V.D.M.	236
Chester W., m. Sarah **EVANS**, Nov. 23, 1845, by V. R. Osborn, V.D.M.	236
Dudley, m. Anny **COWLES**, b. of Manchester, Nov. 26, 1823, by Enoch Burt	201
Dwight H., of East Hartford, m. Mary **COWLES**, of Manchester, Oct. 17, 1844, by Rev. P. T. Keeney	233
Eliza, bd. Aug. 27, 1841, ae 19. Rev. R. Livesey, Min.	335
Eliza A., of East Glastenbury, m. William H. **PROUT**, of West Springfield, Nov. 27, 1851, by Rev. John Cooper	258
Elizur, m. Julia **WETHERELL**, Jan. 31, 1827, by Enoch Burt	206
Elmira, of Manchester, m. [ ] **RISLEY**, of East Hartford, Oct. 24, 1841, by Rev. R. Livesey	228
Francis, of Ellington, m. Eliza **PORTER**, of Manchester, Apr. 29, 1830, by B. F. Northrop	211
Francis E., of Manchester, m. John **EDGERLIN**, of Vernon, July 24, 1853, by F. T. Perkins	266
Francis I., m. Theodore **RISLEY**, b. of Manchester, Apr. 17, 1853, by Rev. George W. Brewster	265
Gonzelo, of Eastbury, m. Ann **BIDWELL**, of Manchester, Apr. 3, 1828, by Enoch Burt	208
Hannah, m. Josiah **LOOMIS**, b. of Manchester, Apr. 13, 1824, by Joseph Treson	202
Harriet C., of Manchester, m. Whidon **USHER**, of Coventry, Nov. 22, 1848, by Rev. L. C. Collins	247
Harriet E., m. John B. **HALE**, of Manchester, Nov. 14, 1838, by Rev. R. W. Allen	223
Henry B., m. Mary **MUNSON**, b. of Manchester, Nov. 29, 1837, by B. F. Northrop	221

BARBOUR COLLECTION

	Page
KEENEY, KENEY, KEENY (cont.)	
Huldah M., m. Edmond B. **JUCKET**, b. of Manchester, Aug. 20, 1848, by Rev. Benjamin C. Phelps	244
Ira, his child bd. June 22, 1842, ae 5 y. Rev. R. Livesey, Min.	335
Jerusha, of Manchester, m. Ebenezer **DEMING**, of Glastenbury, Nov. 28, 1830, by Rev. Jeremiah Stocking	211
John W., of Manchester, m. Elizabeth **STRONG**, of Colchester, Nov. 27, 1834, by Salmon Hall	217
Josiah, of Rome, N.Y., m. Phebe **HOLLISTER**, of Bolton, Nov. 27, 1837, by James Ely	220
Lavina, bd. Dec. 26, 1841, ae 43. Rev. R. Livesey, Min.	335
Lewis, of Glastenbury, m. Emily **TALCOTT**, of Manchester, Nov. 24, 1852, by Rev. George W. Brewster	264
Maria, m. William W. **HOLLISTER**, b. of Manchester, May 19, 1835, by Rev. Salmon Hall	217
Marinda, bd. Feb. 20, 1842, ae 42. Rev. R. Livesey, Min.	335
Marvin, m. Diantha **McKEE**, b. of Manchester, Sept. 6, 1834, by Rev. Salmon Hall	216
Mary B., m. Ethan E. **STRONG**, b. of Manchester, Apr. 10, 1839, by Rev. R. W. Allen	223
May A., of Manchester, m. Nelson T. **CLARK**, of Columbia, Sept. 16, 1849, by Rev. M. P. Alderman	250
Meloria, m. Lewis **TAYLOR**, Sept. 19, 1827, by V. R. Osborn, V.D.M.	207
Nelson, of Bolton, m. Edna **DART**, of Manchester, Sept. 18, 1837, by Rev. R. W. Allen	220
Norman, of East Glastenbury, m. Laura Jeannett **TAYLOR**, of Manchester, Mar. 31, 1847, by Rev. Sidney Dean	239
Permelia H., of Manchester, m. Henry L. **HUNT**, of Bolton, Nov. 27, 1839, by S. Benton	225
Phyluia, of Glastenbury, m. Collingwood **ALEXANDER**, of Manchester, Aug. 26, 1832, by Rev. Hezekiah L. Ramsdall	214
Porter, m. Emily **BIDWELL**, b. of Manchester, May 3, 1825, by Enoch Burt	203
Russell, of Manchester, m. Mrs. Anna **KEENEY**, of Glastenbury, May 30, 1841, by Rev. Sanford Benton	227
Russell, of Manchester, m. Cornelia **GRANT**, of Manchester, Apr. 6, 1842, by Rev. R Livesey	228
Russell, of Manchester, m. Lovina **CHAPMAN**, of Portland, Feb. 29, 1844, by Rev. Charles Noble	231
Ruth, of Manchester, m. Walter **HOWARD**, of Perry, N.Y., May 26, 1829, by B. F. Northrop	209
Sanford, of Glastenbury, m. Delia A. **TAYLOR**, of Manchester, Apr. 30, 1850, by Rev. M. P. Alderman	253
William R., ae 29, m. Lucy **CHARLOTTE**, ae 36, colored, b. of Manchester, June 28, 1854, by Joseph Noyes, J.P.	266
-----, m. Martin **WEBSTER**, Jan. 4, 1824, by Isaac Devinel	201
KEITH, James M., m. Hannah **DAGGETT**, b. of Manchester, May 23, 1852, by Rev. George W. Brewster	260
KELLOGG, Abigail, of Manchester, m. Samuel **ROSE**, of Coventry, Sept. [ ], 1834, by B. F. Northrop	216
Elizabeth, of Manchester, m. George D. **MORGAN**, of Plainfield, [ ], by B. F. Northrop	217

	Page
KENNEDY, Austin, m. Emily G. **McKEE**, b. of Manchester, May 24, 1837, by B. F. Northrop	221
Catherine A., m. Flavius A. **POST**, Nov. 23, 1851, by George E. Hill	259
Emily, m. Walter **BUNCE**, b. of Manchester, Nov. 23, 1852, by F. T. Perkins	263
KENNY, [see also **KEENEY**], John, of Hartford, m. Dolly K. **WARD**, of Manchester, Dec. 5, 1825, by Enoch Burt	205
KILBOURN, Nathan, of East Hartford, m. Hannah **SQUIRES**, of Roxbury, June 30, 1844, by Rev. Charles Noble	232
Sheldon, of South Windsor, m. Lydia **ABBY**, of Manchester, [ ], 1848, by Rev. Benjamin C. Phelps	247
KINGSBURY, KINGBURY, Cornelia A., m. Gilbert **BIDWELL**, Jan. 18, 1849, by Rev. B. F. Northrop	247
Harriet, m. Wells **WOODBRIDGE**, Dec. 27, 1847, by Rev. B. F. Northrop	243
KNOWLAND, Mary A., m. James G. **PATTEN**, b. of Manchester, Feb. 20, 1851, by Rev. Theodore M. Dwight	254
KNOX, Betsy, of Manchester, m. John G. **PARSONS**, of Hartford, May 5, 1844, by B. F. Northrop	231
Chester, m. Almira **BIDWELL**, b. of Manchester, Dec. [ ], 1836, by B. F. Northrop	219
Maria, of Stafford, m. Seth **EVINS**, of Manchester, Nov. 26, 1829, by Ralph R. Phelps, J.P.	210
Tirza, of Stafford, m. Moses **EVANS**, of Manchester, Sept. 21, 1831, by R. R. Phelps, J.P.	212
KOXEY, Phebe T., of Manchester, m. Girdon **PORTER**, of Bolton, Mar. 19, 1837, by V. R. Osborn, V.D.M.	219
LAMSON, Andrus, m. Hannah **SCOTT**, b. of Hadley, Mass., Nov. 28, 1844, by Rev. B. F. Northrop	233
LANDFEAR, LANDFIER, James E., m. May E. **GRAY**, Oct. 31, 1849, by Rev. B. F. Northrop	250
Lucinda, of Manchester, m. Joseph **BAKER**, of Murery, N.Y., Aug. 16, 1825, by Enoch Burt	204
Rodolphas, m. Nancy **BISSELL**, Sept. 25, 1827, by E. Burt	207
LATHROP, Abigail, of Manchester, m. Timothy P. **HOLTON**, of Ellington, June 2, 1829, by B. F. Northrop	209
Maria R., of Manchester, m. Oliver D. **BOYD**, of Franklin, Mass., Aug. 23, 1826, by Enoch Burt	206
LEACH, Frederick A., of Coventry, m. Harriet A. **COOK**, of Manchester, May 6, 1849, by Rev. M. P. Alderman	248
LEE, Lucy, of Vernon, m. Peter **MOORE**, of East Windsor, Aug. 14, 1825, by Enoch Burt	204
LEVALLY, Christopher W., [s. Steery B.], b. Apr. 18, 1833	283
George B., [s. Sterry B.], b. June 28, 1831	283
LEWIS, Abel, m. Fanny B. **WHEELER**, Feb. 3, 1830, by V. R. Osborn, V.D.M.	210
Eliza, m. Alpheus E. **HARRINGTON**, b. of Manchester, May [ ], 1831, by B. F. Northrop	212
Mary M., of Manchester, m. Aaron B. **LYMAN**, of Brimfield, Mass., Oct. 13, 1841, by Rev. Enoch Burt	248
Nelson, of Tolland, m. Sarah **WEAVER**, of Manchester, Apr. 12, 1835, by Salmon Hall	217
LIVESEY, William Parker, s. Richard & Jane Maria, b. Mar. 28, 1842	283

	Page
LOOMIS, Austin, of Amherst, Mass., m. Mary A. **RUSSELL**, of Manchester, June 3, 1852, by F. T. Perkins	260
Benjamin, m. Esther **FORBES**, of Manchester, Oct. 31, 1832, by Rev. Hezekiah L. Ramsdall	214
Jerijah, Jr., of Bolton, m. Mary Ann **RICE**, of Manchester, May [ ], 1834, by B. F. Northrop	215
Joseph C., of East Windsor, m. Phebe **STEEL**, of Manchester, Mar. 1, 1831, by Harman Perry	212
Joseph P., of Coventry, m. Laura **PERRY**, of Manchester, May 25, 1842, by B. F. Northrop	228
Josiah, m. Hannah **KENEY**, b. of Manchester, Apr. 13, 1824, by Joseph Treson	202
Laura, of Manchester, m. William **BUTTON**, of Lebanon, Jan. 23, 1838, by Rev. David Bennet	222
Lorin, of South Windsor, m. Emily **WETHEREL**, of Manchester, Sept. 11, 1850, by Rev. B. F. Northrop	253
Lucy, m. Ezra **BENNETT**, Sept. 12, 1827, by V. R. Osborn, V.D.M.	207
Marshall N., of Coventry, m. Mary W. **MARTIN**, of Woodstock, Feb. 7, 1829, by B. F. Northrop	223
Samuel, m. Martha E. **BURT**, b. of Manchester, Apr. 8, 1835, by Enoch Burt	217
LORD, H. H., m. Fanny H. **BUEL**, Sept. 29, 1845, by V. R. Osborn, V. D. M.	235
LOVELAND, Charlotte A., m. Emery **WILLIAMS**, of Vernon, Apr. 1, 1840, by David Averey, Rider	225
LUCAS, Sarah M., of Manchester, m. James H. **BALL**, of Bristol, [ ], by Rev. M. P. Alderman	248
LYMAN, Aaron B., of Brimfield, Mass., m. Mary M. **LEWIS**, of Manchester, Oct. 13, 1841, by Rev. Enoch Burt	248
Avis C., m. Thomas **SCOTT**, b. of Manchester, June 27, 1852, by Rev. John Cooper	260
Charles, m. Harriet **HITCHCOCK**, b. of Manchester, Dec. 31, 1829, by B. F. Northrop	210
Chester, m. Eliza **RISLEY**, b. of Manchester, Apr. 10, 1837, by James Ely	220
Ely, of Coventry, m. Hannah **DARROW**, of Vernon, Nov. 18, 1835, by David Bennett	218
Esther, of Manchester, m. William R. **PEASE**, of Ellington, Sept. 22, 1842, by B. F. Northrop	229
Louisa M., of Manchester, m. Josiah B. **AVERY**, of Bolton, Nov. 1, 1836, by B. F. Northrop	219
Mabel, of Manchester, m. Aaron **COOK**, of Ashford, June 29, 1837, by B. F. Northrop	221
Martha L., of Manchester, m. Philo **CLEMINS** (?), of Windsor, May 18, 1853, by F. T. Perkins	265
Mary A., m. Daniel B. **SMITH**, b. of Manchester, Dec. 2, 1846, by Rev. B. F. Northrop	239
Mary Bennet, of Manchester, m. Dann **RUSSELL**, of Ellington, Apr. 25, 1833, by B. F. Northrop	214
Mary Jane, of Charleston, Vt., m. John **CHENEY**, of Brownington, Vt., Nov. 28, 1850, by Rev. M. P. Alderman	256
Sarah E., of Manchester, m. Aaron S. **INGRAHAM**, of Bolton, Sept. 26, 1848, by Rev. B. F. Northrop	245

MANCHESTER VITAL RECORDS 71

Page

LYMAN (cont.)
Sybil, of Manchester, m. W[illia]m R. **HILLS**, of East Hartford,
    Nov. 27, 1844, by Rev. B. F. Northrop   233
MACK, Caroline Elizabeth, of Coventry, m. Franklin **SPALDING**, of
    Mansfield, Jan. 1, 1835, by B. F. Northrop   216
McKEE, Chester, of Glastenbury, m. Lucretia **MARSH**, of Manchester,
    Apr. 28, 1825, by Enoch Burt   203
Chester, of Glastenbury, m. Edna G. **SYMONDS**, of Manchester,
    Nov. 7, 1842, by B. F. Northrop   229
Clarissa, m. Robert **HOUSE**, b. of Manchester, Apr. 27, 1826, by V.
    R. Osborn, Elder   205
Diantha, m. Marvin **KEENEY**, b. of Manchester, Sept. 6, 1834, by
    Rev. Salmon Hall   216
Emily G., m. Austin **KENNEDY**, b. of Manchester, May 24, 1837,
    by B. F. Northrop   221
George, m. Mary **WETHERELL**, b. of Manchester, Apr. 14, 1830,
    by B. F. Northrop   211
Judson, m. Mary Ann **CULVER**, Apr. 15, 1838, by Rev. Elias C.
    Scott   222
Martin, m. Diantha **WYLLYS**, May 13, 1830, by V. R. Osborn,
    V.D.M.   211
Nancy, of Manchester, m. Erasumas B. **SELLEW**, of Glastenbury,
    June 18, 1823, by Rev. E. B. Cook   200
McKENSTIN, Harriot, m. William **McKENSTIN**, Apr. 11, 1824, by
    Isaac Devinel   201
William, m. Harriot **McKENSTIN**, Apr. 11, 1824, by Isaac Devinel   201
McKINNEY, McKINNY, Henry, m. Mary Ann **BUNCE**, b. of
    Manchester, Jan. 15, 1834, by B. F. Northrop   215
Mary Ann, m. Moses **SCOTT**, Jan. 15, 1850, by Rev. B. F.
    Northrop   251
McLEAN, Allen, m. Eliza **WOODBRIDGE**, Dec. 25, 1826, by Enoch
    Burt   206
Clarrissa, m. Simeon A. **SPENCER**, b. of Manchester, Oct. 15,
    1823, by Enoch Burt   200
Clarissa, of Vernon, m. John F. **FYLER**, of East Hartford, Aug. 28,
    1839, by Sanford Benton   224
Clarissa, m. James H. **FYLER**, b. of Manchester, May 10, 1841, by
    Rev. Enoch Burt   227
Eliza, alias **WOODBRIDGE**, m. Anson N. **BISSELL**, b. of
    Manchester, Apr. 28, 1838, by Enoch Burt   226
Elizabeth, of Manchester, m. Nelson **BISHOP** (Rev.), of Clinton,
    Me., May 1, 1833, by B. F. Northrop   214
Francis M., of Hebron, m. Miriah **SLATER**, Jan. 18, 1849, by Rev.
    B. F. Northrop   247
Mary, of Manchester, m. George D. **MORGAN**, of Plainfield, Apr.
    5, 1838, by B. F. Northrop   222
Sarah, of Manchester, m. Francis A. **HILLS**, of East Hartford, Aug.
    11, 1846, by E. L. Goodwin, J.P.   237
MANCHESTER, Sally, m. Ethan **GRISWOLD**, b. of Manchester, Mar.
    8, 1828, by V. R. Osborn, V.D.M.   208
MANN, Davis W., of Coventry, m. Loisa **EVINS**, of Manchester, June 29,
    1845, by V. R. Osborn, V.D.M.   235

	Page
MANWARING, Susan E., of Manchester, m. Horrace **SHIPMAN**, of Glastenbury, Sept. 6, 1852, by Rev. George W. Brewster	261
MARBLE, Harriet E., m. Morgan **WHITE**, b. of Manchester, Mar. 22, 1853, by Rev. George W. Brewster	264
Henry, m. Sarah **HUNTINGTON**, Apr. 30, 1898*, by V. R. Osborn, V.D.M. *("1828"?)	208
Rosannah, L., of East Hartford, m. James M. **PEERY**, of Manchester, May 24, 1843, by Rev. Rich[ard] Livesey	230
MARSH, Emily, of Manchester, m. Alfred **GRISWOLD**, of Wethersfield, July 18, 1830, by Enoch Burt	212
Lucretia, of Manchester, m. Chester **McKEE**, of Glastenbury, Apr. 28, 1825, by Enoch Burt	203
Mary M., m. George **GRAY**, b. of Manchester, Mar. 5, 1844, by Rev. E. Burt	249
MARTIN, Mary W., of Woodstock, m. Marshall N. **LOOMIS**, of Coventry, Feb. 7, 1839, by B. F. Northrop	223
MATHER, Harriot, of Manchester, m. Horace G. **VanANDEN**, of Auburn, N.Y., Apr. 28, 1838, by Enoch Burt	226
Julia Ann, of Manchester, m. Thomas C. **ALLICE**, of Shipton, Lower Canada, July 24, 1837, by Enoch Burt	221
MATSON, Mary M., m. Ward B. **GLEASON**, June 28, 1846, by V. R. Osborn, V.D.M.	237
MEEKER, Harriet, m. Ralph **WYLLYS**, b. of Manchester, May 6, 1835, by Enoch Burt	217
MERROW, Joseph B ., of Mansfield, m. Harriet **MILLARD**, of Manchester, Sept. 15, 1847, by Rev. B. F. Northrop	241
MERVIN, David H., of Westfield, Mass., m. Mrs. Matilda L. **PHELON**, of Cooperstown, N.Y., Apr. 30, 1843, by Rev. Samuel Spring, of East Hartford	230
MILLARD, Eli, of Iowa Territory, m. Phebe A. **FOSTER**, of Manchester, Aug. [ ], 1838, by B. F. Northrop	222
Harriet, of Manchester, m. Joseph B. **MERROW**, of Mansfield, Sept. 15, 1847, by Rev. B. F. Northrop	241
Huldah, m. Simeon **COLEMAN**, b. of Manchester, Nov. 12, 1846, by V. R. Osborn	238
Jennett, of Manchester, m. George **BIDWELL**, of Vernon, Mar. 8, 1837, by Enoch Burt	219
Mary L, of Manchester, m. Anson M. **BROWN**, of Bristol, Apr. 15, 1846, by Rev. B. F. Northrop	237
MILLER, Betsy, of East Hartford, m. Harvey **TUCKER**, of Vernon, May 9, 1832, by Rev. Ephraim Scott	213
Maria, of Manchester, m. Ira G. **HUBBARD**, of Glastenbury, May [ ], 1831, by B. F. Northrop	212
MINER, Hiram C., of Bozrah, m. Adiline M. **INGALLS**, of Manchester, Nov. 13, 1842, by Rev. R. Livesey	229
Martha, m. Hart **PORTER**, b. of Manchester, Jan. 12, 1837, by V. R. Osborn, V. D. M.	219
Mary B., of Manchester, m. [ ] **HENRY**, of Glastenbury, Sept. 8, 1844, by Rev. P. T. Keeney	232
MONROE, George B., bd. Mar. 10, 1842, ae 30. Rev. R. Livesey, Min.	335
MOORE, MORE, Harriet M., m. Henry P. **STAPLIN**, b. of Manchester, Mar. 8, 1848, by Benjamin C. Phelps	215

	Page
MOORE, MORE (cont.)	
Martha, of Providence, m. William H. **HUTCHINSON**, of St. Johns, N.B., Sept. 1, 1833, by B. F. Northrop	215
Peter, of East Windsor, m. Lucy **LEE**, of Vernon, Aug. 14, 1825, by Enoch Burt	204
MORGAN, Frances Ann, of Springfield, Mass., m. Charles D. **HORSMAN**, of Boston, Mass., Feb. 10, 1834, by George W. Cheney, J.P.	215
George D., of Plainfield, m. Mary **McLEAN**, of Manchester, Apr. 5, 1838, by B. F. Northrop	222
George D., of Plainfield, m. Elizabeth **KELLOGG**, of Manchester, [ ], by B. F. Northrop	217
MORTON, Lucretia, m. Halsey R. **HOWE**, May 5, 1846, by V. R. Osborn, V.D.M.	237
MOSES, W[illia]m P., of Windsor, m. Florilla M. **TALCOTT**, of Manchester, Jan. 18, 1843, by B. F. Northrop	229
MOULTON, Hiram, of East Hartford, m. Eliza **CASE**, of Manchester, Oct. 30, 1839, by Sanford Benton	224
MUNSELL, Henry, m. Martha **COWLES**, May 1, 1833, by Rev. Hezekiah L. Ramsdell	215
Timothy, of East Windsor, m. Mary **HOLLISTER**, of Manchester, Sept. [ ], 1838, by B. F. Northrop	223
MUNSON, Edwin, m. Mary B. **CARPENTER**, Aug. 27, 1828, by Enoch Burt	209
Ellen L., m. Edmund W. **SPENCER**, b. of Manchester, May 15, 1839, by B. F. Northrop	223
Mary, m. Henry B. **KEENEY**, b. of Manchester, Nov. 29, 1837, by B.F. Northrop	221
NICHOLS, Lucy M., of East Hartford, m. William C. **STRONG**, of Manchester, Nov. 24, 1839, by S. Benton	224
NORMAN, Olive, of Vernon, m. Francis **BUCKLAND**, of Manchester, Sept. 10, 1844, by Rev. P. T. Keeny	232
NORRIS, Louisa E., of Manchester, m. Austin **CASE**, of East Hartford, Apr. 20, 1842, by Rev. E Burk	249
NORTON, John, of North Madison, m. Levah B. **HOLLISTER**, of Manchester, July 3, 1833, by B. F. Northrop	215
NOYES, Henry, b. Nov. 14, 1824	282
Louisa, [d. Joseph], b. June 4, 1822	282
Mary Spencer, d. Joseph, b. Mar. 18, 1831	283
Nelson, b. Nov. 26, 1826	282
Nelson, d. Sept. 29, 1829	335
Ralph, b. Feb. 10, 1829	282
OAKS, Mary, of Southbridge, m. Ebenezer **CLARK**, of Manchester, Sept. 3, 1837, by Rev. R. W. Allen	220
O'CONNOR, Patrick, ae 23, m. Emma **BURKE**, ae 24, Apr. 4, 1853, by James Smythe	267
OLMSTED, Delia P., of East Hartford, m. Henry W. **HUDSON**, of Oakland, Dec. 10, 1846, by Aaron F. Olmsted	239
OSBOURN, Francis, of East Windsor, m. Loisa **CUTLER**, of Manchester, Nov. 27, 1845, by Rev. B. F. Northrop	236
OTIS, Catherine L., of Manchester, m. John I. **PICKET**, of New Milford, Jan. 1 ,1845, by Rev. P. T. Keeney	234

	Page
OTIS (cont.)	
John L., of Columbia, m. Catharine **PRESTON**, of Northampton, Mar. 1, 1847, by Rev. B. F. Northrop	239
Mary C., of Manchester, m. John **WALTON**, of Washington, Sept. 4, 1842, by B. F. Northrop	228
PALMER, John, m. Mary **WOODS**, b. of Manchester, Aug. 11, 1853, by F. T. Perkins	266
PARISH, Electa, m. W[illia]m **STEDMAN**, b. of Manchester, Aug. 22, 1827, by V. R. Osborn, V.D.M.	206
PARKER, Columbus, m. Irene **BROWN**, b. of Manchester, Dec. 31, 1839, by B. F. Northrop	225
Eliza, of Worcester, Mass., m. Francis T. **SLATE**, of Manchester, Sept. 11, 1842, by B. F. Northrop	228
PARKHERST, George, m. Abby **SPENCER**, b. of Manchester, Sept. 20, 1853, by Rev. Henry B. Blake	266
PARSONS, John G., of Hartford, m. Betsy **KNOX**, of Manchester, May 5, 1844, by B. F. Northrop	231
Levi, of East Windsor, m. Martha A. **PERKINS**, of Manchester, Oct. 4, 1846, by V. R. Osborn, V.D.M.	238
PATTEN, James G., m. Mary A. **KNOWLAND**, b. of Manchester, Feb. 20, 1851, by Rev. Theodore M. Dwight	254
PAYNE, Edward B., m. Phila **HUBBARD**, June 3, 1846, by V. R. Osborn, V.D.M.	237
PEARL, Jared, of Willington, m. Marilda F. **HACKET**, of Manchester, Feb. 14, 1836, by B. F. Northrop	218
PEASE, Elizabeth, m. Henry **GARDNER**, Oct. 5, 1845, by V. R. Osborn, V.D.M.	236
William R., of Ellington, m. Esther **LYMAN**, of Manchester, Sept. 22, 1842, by B. F. Northrop	229
PECK, Norton C., of Farmington, m. Emily **GLEASON**, of Manchester, May 2, 1847, by Rev. Benjamin C. Phelps	240
PELTON, Henry, of East Windsor, m. Susan **BUCKLEY**, of Manchester, May 27, 1845, by Rev. P. T. Keeney	235
Ruth D., m. Amos **SIMPSON**, b. of Chatham, July 3, 1836, by Rev. David Dorchester	219
PERKINS, Desire, m. Daniel C. **BEEBE**, b. of Manchester, Jan. 12, 1841, by Sanford Benton	227
Martha A., of Manchester, m. Levi **PARSONS**, of East Windsor, Oct. 4, 1846, by V. R. Osborn, V.D.M.	238
Parmelia H., of Manchester, m. Charles T. **BELKNAP**, of East Windsor, Feb. 27, 1842, by Rev. R. Livesey	228
PERRY, PEERY, Dewitt C., m. Celia C. **SPENCER**, b. of Manchester, Apr. 10, 1850, by Rev. Charles R. Fisher	252
James M., of Manchester, m. Rosannah L. **MARBLE**, of East Hartford, May 24, 1843, by Rev. Rich[ard] Livesey	230
Laura, of Manchester, m. Elisha **ROBERTS**, Jr., of East Hartford, Oct. 20, [1825], b Enoch Burt	204
Laura, of Manchester, m. Joseph P. **LOOMIS**, of Coventry, May 25, 1842, by B. F. Northrop	228
Lucy, of Manchester, m. William **BARNS**, of East Windsor, Sept. 3, 1834, by Enoch Burt	216
Morillo L., of Manchester, m. Sarah C. **HARRINGTON**, of Hebron, Oct. 15, 1843, by Rev. Charles Noble	231

MANCHESTER VITAL RECORDS

	Page
PERRY, PEERY (cont.)	
Parlynesa, of Manchester, m. Phineus **GROVES**, of Ellington, Nov. 24, 1834, by B. F. Northrup	216
Peter L., m. Jerusha C. **SHELDON**, of Hartford, Oct. 3, 1852, by George E. Hill	261
Sarah, of Manchester, m. William **VAN BURGEN**, of Lee, Mass., Sept. 29, 1825, by Enoch Burt	204
PETERSON, Harriet, m. Charles **CHAPMAN**, b. of Manchester, Oct. 10, 1852, by Rev. George W. Brewster	263
PHELON, Matilda L., Mrs. of Cooperstown, N.Y., m. David H. **MERVIN**, of Westfield, Mass., Apr. 30, 1843, by Rev. Samuel Spring, of East Hartford	230
PHELPS, John B., of Glastenbury, m. Julia A. **CASE**, of Manchester, [ ], by Rev. B. F. Northrup	234
PHILLIPS, Alonzo D., m. Mary **STEDMAN**, May 7, 1828, by V. R. Osborn, V.D.M.	208
Aurora A., of Manchester, m. Charles B. **HALLETT**, of East Hartford, Nov. 10, 1848, by Rev. Benjamin C. Phelps	246
Dudley, m. Ruby **HALE**, Dec. 25, 1825, by Isaac Devinel	205
PICKET, John L., of New Milford, m. Catherine L. **OTIS**, of Manchester, Jan. 1, 1845, by Rev. P. T. Keeney	234
PIERCE, Orpha, m. Hiram **HUN**, Jan. 22, 1828, by V. R. Osborn, V.D.M.	207
PIERSON, Daniel of Glastenbury, m. Anna S. **POST**, of Manchester, Dec. [ ], 1836, by B. F. Northrop	219
PINNEY, Edward, of Vernon, m. Harriet **EVINS**, of Vernon, May 5, 1852, by Rev. George W. Brewster	259
PITKIN, Eli, m. Hannah M. **TORREY**, b. of Manchester, Mar. 25, 1827, by V. R. Osborn, V.D.M.	206
Hannah, m. George C. **SKINNER**, Sept. 16, 1823, by Joy H. Fairchild	200
Hannah M., w. E[-----], bd. Sept. 28, 1842, ae 38. Rev. R. Livesey, Min.	335
Mary H., m. Owen **SPENCER**, b. of Manchester, Jan. 15, 1840, by S. Benton	225
Sarah of Manchester, m. Phillip L. **EDDY**, of Hartford, May 7, 1828, by Enoch Burt	208
W[illiam] C., of East Hartford, m. Harriet K. **RISLEY**, of Manchester, Jan. 18, 1843, by B. F. Northrop	229
PLACE, Deborah L., of Manchester, m. Mason B. **HOPKINS**, of Foster, R.I., June 3, 1832, by Rev. Erastus Doty, of Vernon	213
PORT*, Electa C., of Manchester, m Albert **ROCKWELL**, of South Windsor, Sept. 30, 1846, by Rev. B. F. Northrop *(**POST**?)	238
PORTER, Eliza, of Manchester, m. Francis **KEENEY**, of Ellington, Apr. 29, 1830, by B. F. Northrop	211
Girdon, of Bolton, m. Phebe T. **KOXEY**, of Manchester, Mar. 19, 1837, by V. R. Osborn, V.D.M.	219
Hart, m. Martha **MINER**, b. of Manchester, Jan. 12, 1837, by V. R. Osborn, V.D.M.	219
Lucian A., of Plymouth, m. Pamelia **DIMMOCKS**, of Manchester, Sept. 7, 1846, by Rev. B. F. Northrop	238
Mary, m. John **DOW**, Apr. 18, 1830, by V. R. Osborn, V.D.M.	211
POST, Anna S., of Manchester, m. Daniel **PIERSON**, of Glastenbury, Dec. [ ], 1836, by B. F. Northrop	219

	Page
POST (cont.)	
Electa C.*, of Manchester, m. Albert **ROCKWELL**, of South Windsor, Sept. 30, 1846, by Rev. B. F. Northrop *(**PORT**?)	238
Flavius A., m. Catherine A. **KENNEDY**, Nov. 23, 1851, by George E. Hill	259
Sarah L., m. Josiah C. **GILBERT**, b. of Hebron, Sept. 6, 1848, by Rev. Charles Nichols	245
POTTER, Martha A., of Manchester, m. David P. **WOODRUFF**, of Southington, June 22, 1851, by Rev. F. T. Perkins	256
Samuel M., of Southington, m. Martha A. **BIDWELL**, of Manchester, Dec. 22, 1846, by Rev. B. F. Northrop	239
POWERS, Martha E., m. Nicholas **BOWERS**, b. of Vernon, Aug. 1, 1852, by Rev. George W. Brewster	261
PRESTON, Catharine, of Northampton, m. John L. **OTIS**, of Columbia, Mar. 1, 1847, by Rev. B. F. Northrop	239
PRIOR, Milton, of Windsor, m. Ellen A. **CASE**, of Manchester, Nov. 3, 1851, by F. T. Perkins	257
PROUT, William H., of West Springfield, m. Eliza A. **KEENEY**, of East Glastenbury, Nov. 27, 1851, by Rev. John Cooper	258
PURPLE, Almira, m. James N. **CULVER**, Nov. 7, 1826, by V. R. Osborn, V.D.M.	206
PUSHAN, Daniel, of Hartford, m. Asenath **HACKETT**, of Manchester, Mar. 7, 1830, by Lemuel White, J.P.	210
RANDALL, Lucy, m. Sidney **FORBES**, Sept. 21, 1825, by Joy H. Fairchild	204
RICE, Mary Ann, of Manchester, m. Jerijah **LOOMIS**, Jr., of Bolton, May [ ], 1834, by B. F. Northrop	215
RICH, Betsy, m. Russell **ELDRIDGE**, Sept. 22, 1823, by Joseph Treson	200
George, m. Ann **SLATE**, Apr. 13, 1826, by Enoch Burt	205
Sarah W., m. John W. **BIDWELL**, b. of Manchester, Oct. 16, 1851, by F. T. Perkins	257
RIDER, Salmon, of Willington, m. Julia **BUCKLAND**, of East Hartford, July 6, 1829, by B. F. Northrop	210
RILEY, Horace F., of East Windsor, m. Mary A. **THOMPSON**, of Manchester, Nov. 25, 1847, by Rev. Benjamin C. Phelps	242
RISLEY, Clarissa J., of Manchester, m. Thomas **BUTTON**, of Hartford, Apr. 15, 1840, by S. Benton	225
Dorothy W., of Hebron, m. Nehimiah **WILLIAMS**, of Manchester, Oct. 13, 1844, by Rev. B. F. Northrop	233
Elisha B., m. Sarah L. **WHITE**, of Bolton, Oct. 31, 1848, by Rev. B. F. Northrop	245
Eliza, m. Chester **LYMAN**, b. of Manchester, Apr. 10, 1837, by James Ely	220
Franklin B., m. Sarah A. **GRAY**, Jan. 10, 1849, by Rev. B. F. Northrop	247
George H., of Glastenbury, m. Marilda **SIMONDS**, of Manchester, Jan. 14, 1852, by F. T. Perkins	259
George R., m. Margaret **GOODRICH**, Dec. 18, 1853, by Rev. E. Burt	267
Harriet K., of Manchester, m. W[illia]m C. **PITKIN**, of East Hartford, Jan. 18, 1843, by B. F. Northrop	229
Horace, m. Almira **KEENEY**, b. of Manchester, Apr. 4, 1838, by B. F. Northrop	222

	Page
RISLEY (cont.)	
John A., m. Joanna BAKER, b. of Manchester, Dec. 17, 1852, by F. T. Perkins	263
Julia A., m. Walter HILLS, Oct. 23, 1845, by V. R. Osborn, V.D.M.	236
Lucretia A., of Manchester, m. Henry GOODRICH, of Wethersfield, Aug. 2, 1843, by Rev. Charles Noble	230
Nancy, m. Stephen HURLBURT, Jr., b. of Glastenbury, Feb. 9, 1832, by Rev. Ephraim Scott	213
Otis B., m. Electa WOODWORTH, b. of Manchester, Dec. 9, 1824, by Rev. Moses Fifield	202
Philinda, of Manchester, m. Emery CHAFFEN, of East Hartford, Apr. 28, 1847, by Levi Daggett, Jr.	240
Theodore, m. Francis I. KEENEY, b. of Manchester, Apr. 17, 1853, by Rev. George W Brewster	265
-----, of East Hartford, m. Elmira KEENEY, of Manchester, Oct. 24, 1841, by Rev. R. Livesey	228
ROBERTS, Elisha, Jr., of East Hartford, m. Laura PERRY, of Manchester, Oct. 20, [1825], by Enoch Burt	204
James L., m. Mary C. ROGERS, b. of Manchester, Sept. 22, 1852, by F. T. Perkins	262
John, of Grafton, N.H., m. Mary E. HUBBARD, of Glastenbury, Mar. 6, 1854, by W[illia]m M. Roberts, J.P.	267
Mary, m. Cyrus GOODALE, Oct. 8, 1823, by Joseph Treson	200
ROCKWELL, Albert, of South Windsor, m. Electa C. PORT*, of Manchester, Sept. 30, 1846, by Rev. B. F. Northrop *(POST?)	238
Samuel S., m. Mary Ann STARKS, b. of East Windsor, Apr. 24, 1845, by Rev. P. T. Keeney	234
RODMAN, Ellen M., of Manchester, m. Wellington SEAGROVE, of South Coventry, June 6, 1847, by Rev. Benjamin C. Phelps	240
ROGERS, Henry E., of Manchester, m. Martha HALL, of Portland, Sept. 4, 1844, by Rev. P. T. Keeney	232
Mary C., m. James L. ROBERTS, b. of Manchester, Sept. 22, 1852, by F. T. Perkins	262
Peter, bd. Aug. 14, 1841, ae 45. Rev. R. Livesey, Min.	335
ROOT, Lucinda, of Manchester, m. Edward WOLCOTT, of East Windsor, Oct. 26, 1840, by Sanford Benton	226
Merrit, of Glastenbury, m. Julia A. FOX, of Manchester, Feb. 10, 1845, by Rev. P. T. Keeney	234
ROSE, Mary, of East Hartford, m. Chauncey SPENCER, of Manchester, Oct. 10, [1825], by Enoch Burt	204
Samuel, of Coventry, m. Abigail KELLOGG, of Manchester, Sept. [ ], 1834, by B. F. Northrop	216
RUSSELL, Benjamin A., m. Sarah ALLEN, b. of Springfield, Mass., Dec. 22, 1839, by S. Benton	225
Dann, of Ellington, m. Mary Bennet LYMAN, of Manchester, Apr. 25, 1833, by B. F. Northrop	214
Eliza, m. Henry GRISWOLD, b. of Manchester, July 3, 1849, by Samuel Spring	248
Mary A., of Manchester, m. Austin LOOMIS, of Amhurst, Mass., June 3, 1852, by F. T. Perkins	260
Mervin T., m. Esther BUCKLAND, b. of Manchester, Mar. 3, 1847, by Rev. B. F. Northrop	239

	Page
SAUNDERS, Amanda, m. Edwin **WILSON**, b. of Manchester, May 5, 1846, by V. R. Osborn, V.D.M.	237
Mary, of Avon, m. Chauncy **FREEMAN**, of Hartford, Oct. 20, 1839, by B. F. Northrop	224
Mary A., of Manchester, m. George E. **SEARL**, of Hartford, Jan. 2, 1853, by Rev. George W. Brewster	264
Mary Cornelia, of Manchester, m. Henry C. **HOLMS**, of South Lee, Mass., Jan. 6, 1848, by Rev. Charles R. Fisher	242
SAVALLY, Sterry B., m. Nancy **DEAN**, July 1, 1830, by V. R. Osborn	211
SCHOFF, Caroline, of Brunswick, Conn., m. Charles **KEENEY**, of Manchester, Nov. 25, 1847, by Rev. Benjamin C. Phelps	242
SHUR (?), John, Dr., of Hartford, m. Carolina Agusta **GOODWIN**, of New York, Nov. 16, 1848, by Rev. B. F. Northrop	245-6
SCOTT, Hannah, m. Andrus **LAMSON**, b. of Hadley, Mass., Nov. 28, 1844, by Rev. B. F. Northrop	218
Mary A., m. Edwin S. **HULL**, b. of Manchester, May 15, 1836, by S. Hall	218
Moses, m. Mary Ann **McKINNY**, Jan. 15, 1850, by Rev. B. F. Northrop	251
Thomas, m. Avis O. **LYMAN**, b. of Manchester, June 27, 1852, by Rev. John Cooper	260
SEAGROVE, Wellington, of South Coventry, m. Ellen M. **RODMAN**, of Manchester, June 6, 1847, by Rev. Benjamin C. Phelps	240
SEARL, George E., of Hartford, m. Mary A. **SAUNDERS**, of Manchester, Jan. 2, 1853, by Rev. George W. Brewster	264
SELLEW, Erasumas B., of Glastenbury, m. Nancy **McKEE**, of Manchester, June 18, 1823, by Rev. E. B. Cook	200
SHELDON, Jerusha C., of Hartford, m. Peter L. **PERRY**, Oct. 3, 1852, by George E. Hill	261
SHEPHARD, Jane, of Webster, Mass., m. Asa **DEMMING**, of East Glastenbury, July 2, 1851, by Rev. George W. Brewster	256
SHIPMAN, Horrace, of Glastenbury, m. Susan E. **MANWARING**, of Manchester, Sept. 6, 1852, by Rev. George W. Brewster	261
SIMONS, SYMONDS, Cicero, of Springfield, m. Harriet **WINTER**, of Manchester, Nov. 5, 1846, by Rev. B. F. Northrop	238
Edna G., of Manchester, m. Chester **McKEE**, of Glastenbury, Nov. 7, 1842, by B. F. Northrop	229
Marilda, of Manchester, m. George H. **RISLEY**, of Glastenbury, Jan. 14, 1852, by F. T. Perkins	259
Thomas G., of Manchester, m. Elizabeth **BAGG**, of Windsor, Jan. 10, 1852, by Rev. George W. Brewster	258
SIMPSON, Amos, m. Ruth D. **PELTON**, b. of Chatham, July 3, 1836, by Rev. David Dorchester	219
David, m. Ann **TENNE** (?), b. of England, Oct. 26, 1853, by Ralph Cheney, J.P.	266
SKINNER, George, s. George C. & Hannah, b. May 13, 1825	282
George C., m. Hannah **PITKIN**, Sept. 16, 1823, by Joy H. Fairchild	200
Gilbert, of Bolton, m. Sarah E. **ANDRUS**, of Manchester, Mar. 27, 1839, by Rev. David Bennet	223
Nelson, of Bolton, m. Martha **GLEASON**, of Manchester, Nov. 10, 1844, by Rev. P. T. Keeney	233
Orrin, of East Windsor, m. Laura **STRONG**, of Bolton, Dec. 25, 1834, by B. F. Northrop	216

	Page
SLATE, Ann, m. George **RICH**, Apr. 13, 1826, by Enoch Burt205	205
Elmira, of Manchester, m. Orlando **ALLEN**, of East Windsor, May 12, 1841, by Rev. Sanford Benton	227
Francis T., of Manchester, m. Eliza **PARKER**, of Worcester, Mass., Sept. 11, 1842, by B. F. Northrop	228
SLATER, John Philander, m. Catherine **BUELL**, Sept. [ ], 1841, by R. Livesey	228
Miriah, m. Francis M. **McLEAN**, of Hebron, Jan. 18, 1849, by Rev. B. F. Northrop	247
SLOCUM, Horatio N., of Vernon, m. Mary G. **ANDRUS**, of Manchester, Aug. [ ], 1833, by B. F. Northrop	215
SMITH, Daniel B., m. Mary A. **LYMAN**, b. of Manchester, Dec. 2, 1846, by Rev. B. F. Northrop	239
Jane E., m. Oliver B. **TAYLOR**, b. of Manchester, Apr. 21, 1852, by F. T. Perkins	259
Martin, m. Sarah **WYLES**, Nov. 26, 1829, by V. R. Osborn, V.D.M.	210
SNOW, Azel G., of East Haddam, m. Elisabeth **WETHERELL**, of Manchester, Apr. 26, 1843, by B. F. Northrop	230
SPALDING, Franklin, of Mansfield, m. Caroline Elizabeth **MACK**, of Coventry, Jan. 1 ,1835, by B. F. Northrop	216
SPARKS, Annett, of Vernon, m. William O. **WEAVER**, of Manchester, Aug. 1, 1852, by Rev. George W. Brewster	260
SPENCER, Abby, m. George **PARKHERST**, b. of Manchester, Sept. 20, 1853, by Rev. Henry B. Blake	266
Celia C., m. Dewitt C. **PERRY**, b. of Manchester, Apr. 10, 1850, by Rev. Charles R Fisher	252
Chauncey, of Manchester, m. Mary **ROSE**, of East Hartford, Oct. 10, [1825], by Enoch Burt	204
Diantha, of Manchester, m. Sherman **BREWER**, of East Hartford, Oct. 3, 1838, by B. F. Northrop	223
Dwight, m. Mary Fitch **WHITE**, b. of Manchester, Sept. 21, 1853, by [ ]	265
Edmund W., m. Ellen L. **MUNSON**, b. of Manchester, May 15, 1839, by B. F. Northrop	223
Edwin, of East Hartford, m. Julia A. **FOSTER**, of Manchester, May. 19, 1829, by Bennett F. Northrop	209
Francis H., bd. Mar. 30, 1842, ae 1. Rev. R. Livesey, Min.	335
Hester, of Manchester, m. Austin **STRICKLAND**, of Glastenbury, Oct. 30, 1831, by Rev. Ephraim Scott	212
Jerusha, m. Eleazur **FOX**, b. of Manchester, Sept. 4, 1845, by V. R. Osborn, V.D.M.	235
Jesse, m. Jerusha **VALNO**, b. of Manchester, May 10, 1826, by V. R. Osborn, Elder	205
Joseph G., m. Harriet **WILLIAMS**, Feb. 4, 1852, by Rev. George E. Hill	259
Norman, of Manchester, m. Hannah M. **WHEELER**, of Columbia, Sept. 8, 1835, by Enoch Burt	218
Normon G., bd. Mar. 20, 1842, ae 31. Rev. R. Livesey, Min.	335
Owen, m. Mary H. **PITKIN**, b. of Manchester, Jan. 15, 1840, by S. Benton	225
Rufus, m. Ellen **CADWELL**, b. of Manchester, Nov. 19, 1851, by Rev. Benjamin C. Phelps, of East Hartford	262

	Page
SPENCER (cont.)	
Sally C., m. James **WETHERELL**, b. of Manchester, Jan. 13, 1831, by B. F. Northrop	211
Sarah A., of Manchester, m. Arba **GRAVES**, of Thompson, Nov. 18, 1851, by F. T. Perkins	257
Simeon A., m. Clarrissa **McLEAN**, b. of Manchester, Oct. 15, 1823, by Enoch Burt	200
Wealthy M., of Manchester, m. Sanford E. **WALDO**, of Ellington, Nov. 27, 1834, by Salmon Hall	217
SPERRY, Adaline, of Manchester, m. Orrin P. **GORDON**, of Hartford, Sept. 1, 1839, by B. F. Northrop	224
James L., m. Mary Ann **EATON**, Sept. 14, 1851, by Rev. George E. Hill	257
SPRAGUE, James L., of Hampton, m. Juliett D. **WHITE**, of Bolton, Mar. 28, 1838, by B. F. Northrop	222
SQUIRES, SQUIRE, Hannah, of Roxbury, m. Nathan **KILBOURN** of East Hartford, June 30, 1844, by Rev. Charles Noble	232
Luman A., of Bozrah, m. Eliza **COWLES**, of Manchester, May 2, 1832, by Rev. Ephraim Scott	213
STANDISH, Austin, of Glastenbury, m. Vesta W. **CLARK**, of Manchester, Jan. 13, 1850, by Rev. B. F. Northrop	251
STANDLY, George G., of West Suffield, m. Ellen **DALE**, of Manchester, Sept. 12, 1850, by M. F. Alderman	254
STAPLIN, Henry P., m. Harriet M. **MORE**, b. of Manchester, May. 8, 1848, by Benjamin C. Phelps	243
STARKS, Mary Ann, m. Samuel S. **ROCKWELL**, b. of East Windsor, Apr. 24, 1845, by Rev. P. T. Keeney	234
STARKWEATHER, Benjamin, of Hartford, m. Harriet **BUCKLAND**, of East Windsor, May 21, 1840, by S. Benton	225
STEDMAN, Electa, m. Joshua C. **FLINT**, b. of Manchester, Aug. 22, 1827, by V. R. Osborn, V.D.M.	206
Emily, of Manchester, m. Alden **TALCOTT**, of Vernon, Sept. 4, 1825, by Enoch Burt	204
Harriet, m. Elisha **CHILDS**, of Manchester, Jan. 1, 1834, by Rev. H. L. Ramsdall	216
Mary, m. Alonzo D. **PHILLIPS**, May 7, 1828, by V. R. Osborn, V.D.M.	208
W[illia]m, m. Electa **PARISH**, b. of Manchester, Aug. 22, 1827, by V. R. Osborn, V.D.M.	206
STEEL, Clark, m. Mary M. **AVERY**, of Bolton, July 30, 1829, by V. R. Osborn, V.D.M.	210
Mary Jane, m. Daniel **HILL**, b. of Manchester, Mar. 14, 1832, by Rev. Ephraim Scott	213
Phebe, of Manchester, m. Joseph C. **LOOMIS**, of East Windsor, Mar. 1, 1831, by Herman Perry	212
STEVENS, Turner (?), of Webster, Mass., m. Emily **HOWARD**, of Manchester, Dec. 11, 1849, by Rev. M. P. Alderman	250
STOUGHTON, Eliza, of Manchester, m. Edmond **FREEMAN**, of Chickopee, Mass., Apr. 16, 1849, by Rev. Benjamin Phelps	248
Lawrence, of East Windsor, m. Almira **HALE**, of Manchester, Dec. 25, 1826, by V. R. Osborn, V.D.M.	206
STOWEL, Amelia, of Boston, m. Hopkins **FISH**, of Plainfield, Sept. 3, 1827, by E. Burt	207

MANCHESTER VITAL RECORDS 81

	Page
STRICKLAND, Austin, of Glastenbury, m. Hester **SPENCER**, of Manchester, Oct. 30, 1831, by Rev. Ephraim Scott	212
STRONG, Artemus Sinds, of Bolton, m Jane Susan **BROWN**, of Manchester, Oct. 14, 1840, by Rev. William Reed, of Wethersfield	227
Cornelia I., of Manchester, m. Ralph B. **TREAT**, of Hartford, May 25, 1845, by Rev. P. T. Keeney	234
Elizabeth, of Colchester, m. John W. **KEENEY**, of Manchester, Nov. 27, 1834, by Salmon Hall	217
Ethan E., m. Mary B. **KEENEY**, b. of Manchester, Apr. 10, 1839, by Rev. R. W. Allen	223
John, m. Leviah **HARRIS**, b. of Manchester, Aug. 1, 1841, by Rev. Richard Liverey	227
Laura, of Bolton, m. Orrin **SKINNER**, of East Windsor, Dec. 25, 1834, by B. F. Northrop	216
Samantha A., m. Charles **TREAT**, b. of Manchester, Oct. 3, 1847, by Rev. Benjamin C. Phelps	242
Samuel H., of Bolton, m. Lucinda E. **THOMPSON**, of Manchester, July 5, 1842, by Rev. R. Liversey	228
William C., of Manchester, m. Lucy M. **NICHOLS**, of East Hartford, Nov. 24, 1839, by S. Benton	224
SULLIVAN, Daniel, m. Laura Ann **FOX**, July 5, 1846, by V. R. Osborn, V.D.M.	237
SWEETLAND, Mirza, of Manchester, m. Eli G. **TURNEY**, of Woodbury, Nov. 10, 1840, by Rev. David Bennett	226
TALCOTT, Alden, of Vernon, m. Emily **STEDMAN**, of Manchester, Sept. 4, 1825, by Enoch Burt	204
Emily, of Manchester, m. Lewis **KEENEY**, of Glastenbury, Nov. 24, 1852, by Rev. George W. Brewster	264
Florilla M., of Manchester, m. W[illia]m P. **MOSES**, of Windsor, Jan. 18, 1843, by B. F. Northrop	229
Mosley, of Marlborough, m. Harriot **COOK**, of Manchester, Apr. 6, 1825, by Enoch Burt	202
TAYLOR, Delia A., of Manchester, m. Sanford **KEENEY**, of Glastenbury, Apr. 30, 1850, by Rev. M. P. Alderman	253
John S., of Portland, m. Sarah C. **CARN**, of Manchester, Jan. 11, 1852, by Rev. George W. Brewster	258
Laura Jeannett, of Manchester, m. Norman **KEENEY**, of East Glastenbury, Mar. 31, 1847, by Rev. Sidney Dean	239
Lewis, m. Meloria **KEENEY**, Sept. 19, 1827, by V. R. Osborn, V.D.M.	207
Noadiah, of Worthington, O., m. Ann **GIBSON**, of Sterling, July 3, 1826, by Enoch Burt	205
Oliver B., m. Jane E. **SMITH**, b. of Manchester, Apr. 21, 1852, by F. T. Perkins	259
Pitkin, of Manchester, m. Celia F. **WARREN**, of East Hartford, Apr. 22, 1849, by Rev. E. Burt	249
-----, his child bd. Sept. 27, 1842, ae 8 m. Rev. R. Livesey, Min.	335
TENNE (?), Ann, m. David **SIMPSON**, b. of England, Oct. 26, 1853, by Ralph Cheney, J.P.	266
TERRY, James, m. Elizabeth M. **HOLLISTER**, of Terrysville, Oct. 10, 1843, by B. F. Northrop	231

	Page
THAYER, Alvin, m. Louisa **HARRINGTON**, b. of Manchester, Sept. 1, 1839, by S. Benton	224
THOMPSON, THOMSON, Joseph G., of Manchester, m. Eunice C. **WALLBRIDGE**, of Stafford, Apr. 13, 1838, by B. F. Northrop	222
Lucinda E., of Manchester, m. Samuel H. **STRONG**, of Bolton, July 5, 1842, by Rev. R. Liversey	228
Mary, of Manchester, m. Ethan **ARNOLD**, of East Hartford, Jan. 23, 1830, by B. F. Northrop	210
Mary A., of Manchester, m. Horace F. **RILEY**, of East Windsor, Nov. 25, 1847, by Rev. Benjamin C. Phelps	242
-----, his child bd. Aug. 26, 1841, ae 1. Rev. Livesey, Min.	335
TOPLEFF, Percis, m. Nelson **BISSELL**, Oct. 2, 1827, by V. R. Osborn, V.D.M.	207
TORREY, Hannah M., m. Eli **PITKIN**, b. of Manchester, Mar. 25, 1827, by V. R. Osborn, V.D.M.	206
TRACEY, Becthia W., of Lebanon, m. Anson **GLEASON**, of Manchester, Oct. 24, 1826, by Enoch Burt	206
TREAT, Charles, m. Samantha A. **STRONG**, b. of Manchester, Oct. 3, 1847, by Rev. Benjamin C. Phelps	242
Julia E., m. Walter **DART**, Oct. 1, 1845, by V. R. Osborn, V.D.M.	235
Ralph B., of Hartford, m. Cornelia I. **STRONG**, of Manchester, May 25, 1845, by Rev. P. T. Keeney	234
TREMAIN, TRUMAINE, Fanny, Mrs. of Tolland, m. Orrin **CASE**, of Manchester, Dec. 10, 1840, by Rev. Sanford Benton	227
Joseph C., m. Mary A. **HOLLISTER**, Mar. 12, 1851, by Rev. M. F. Alderman	255
TRYON, Lucinda, of Glastenbury, m. Edwin **BUNCE**, of Manchester, Nov. 29, 1843, by Rev. Charles Noble	231
Sophronia, m. George **WYLLYS**, July 13, 1852, by W[illia]m Roberts, J.P.	261
TUCKER, Harvey, of Vernon, m. Betsy **MILLER**, of East Hartford, May 9, 1832, by Rev. Ephraim Scott	213
Julia R., m. Chelsia **COOK**, b. of Manchester, Nov. 24, 1850, by Rev. M. P. Alderman	255
TURNEY, Eli G., of Woodbury, m. Mirza **SWEETLAND**, of Manchester, Nov. 10, 1840, by Rev. David Bennett	226
USHER, Whidon, of Coventry, m. Harriet C. **KEENEY**, of Manchester, Nov. 22, 1848, by Rev. L. C. Collins	247
VALNO, Jerusha, m. Jesse **SPENCER**, b. of Manchester, May 10, 1826, by V. R. Osborn, Elder	205
VAN ANDEN, Horace G., of Auburn, N.Y., m. Harriot **MATHER**, of Manchester, Apr. 28, 1838, by Enoch Burt	226
VAN BUGEN, Ellen M., of Manchester, m. Seymour **BOUGHLIN**, of Rochester, N.Y., Apr. 29, 1847, by Rev. B. F. Northrop	240
VAN BURGEN, William, of Lee, Mass., m. Sarah **PERRY**, of Manchester, Sept. 29, 1825, by Enoch Burt	204
VIBBERT, VIBERT, Leanora, m. Samuel **COOK**, May 7, 1828, by V. R. Osborn, V.D.M.	208
Leonard Smith, of Manchester, m. Lydia Clarrissa **HAUGHTON**, of Hebron, Nov. 5, 1846, by Rev. William B. Corlyn	237
Martha A., m. Chauncy **GLEASON**, Nov. 27, 1845, by V. R. Osborn, V.D.M.	236

	Page
VIBBERT, VIBERT (cont.)	
Sophia, m. Edwin **HOFFMAN**, b. of Manchester, Oct. 30, 1825, by Enoch Burt	204
VIRGEN, William C., of Hartford, m Elizabeth **FOX**, of Manchester, Apr. 16, 1837, by V. R. Osborn, V.D.M.	219
VORRA, Catharine, of Hartford, m. Luther **CHILDS**, July 3, 1828, by Ralph R. Phelps, J.P.	208
WADSWORTH, Daniel, of Vernon, m. Ann Y. **DEAN**, of Manchester, May 8, 1844, by B. F. Northrop	232
WALDO, Sanford, E., of Ellington, m. Wealthy M. **SPENCER**, of Manchester, Nov. 27, 1834, by Salmon Hall	217
WALLBRIDGE, Eunice C., of Stafford, m. Joseph G. **THOMSON**, of Manchester, Apr. 13, 1838, by B. F. Northrop	222
WALTON, John, of Washington, m. Mary C. **OTIS**, of Manchester, Sept. 4, 1842, by B. F. Northrop	228
WARD, Dolly K., of Manchester, m. John **KENNY**, of Hartford, Dec. 5, 1825, by Enoch Burt	205
John, of Collinsville, m. Jennett B. **BUEL**, of Manchester, Nov. 24, 1841, by Rev. B. F. Northrop	228
John, m. Mary Jane **CHENEY**, b. of Manchester, Oct. 6, 1850, by Rev. Charles R Fisher	253
WARREN, Celia F., of East Hartford, m. Pitkin **TAYLOR**, of Manchester, Apr. 22, 1849, by Rev. E. Burt	249
WATERMAN, Azariah, of Bolton, m. Cynthia **HALL**, of Manchester, Sept. 16, 1835, by B. F. Northrop	218
WATSON, Benjamin M., m. Ann I. **JOHNSON**, Nov. 7, 1839, by B. F. Northrop	224
WEAVER, Sarah, of Manchester, m. Nelson **LEWIS**, of Tolland, Apr. 12, 1835, by Salmon Hall	217
William O., of Manchester, m. Annett **SPARKS**, of Vernon, Aug. 1, 1852, by Rev. George W. Brewster	260
WEBSTER, George M., m. Levie **BROCKWAY**, b. of Hartford, Feb. [ ], 1831, by B. F. Northrop	212
Martin, m. [ ] **KENEY**, Jan. 4, 1824, by Isaac Devinel	201
Ruth A., of Bolton, m. Lucius **CUTLER**, of Manchester, June 9, 1836, by S. Hull	219
WEIR, Alanson L., of Avon, m. Ruba B. **HALE**, of Manchester, Apr. 10, 1842, by Rev. E. Burt	249
WELCH, George M., of Hartford, m. Mary L. **JONES**, of Manchester, Sept. 29, 1847, by B. F. Northrop	241
Roseanna W., of Lebanon, m. Lester **COTTON**, of Windsor, Nov. 23, 1825, by Enoch Burt	205
WELLS, Theodore, of Farmington, m. Maria **BIDWELL**, of Manchester, Aug. 24, 1853, by F. T. Perkins	266
WEST, Charles H., m. Mary F. **BISSELL**, b. of Manchester, Mar. 27, 1852, by Rev. John Cooper	260
Eliza, m. James **WETHERELL**, Jr., b. of Manchester, Oct. 8, 1839, by B. F. Northrop	224
WETHERELL, WITHERELL, WETHEREL, Electa, of Manchester, m. John **HILLS**, Jr., of East Hartford, [ ], by B. F. Northrop	211
Elizabeth, of Manchester, m. Azel G. **SNOW**, of East Haddam, Apr. 26, 1843, by B. F . Northrop	230

	Page
WETHERELL, WITHERELL, WETHEREL (cont.)	
Emily, of Manchester, m. Lorin **LOOMIS**, of South Windsor, Sept. 11, 1850, by Rev. B. F. Northrop	253
Hannah, of Manchester, m. Henry **BELDEN**, of Hartford, Oct. 7, 1835, by Bennett F. Northrop	218
James, m. Sally C. **SPENCER**, b. of Manchester, Jan. 13, 1831, by B. F. Northrop	211
James, Jr., m. Eliza **WEST**, b. of Manchester, Oct. 8, 1839, by B. F. Northrop	224
Joseph, m. Clarissa **CUTLER**, b. of Manchester, Jan. 2, 1833, by B. F. Northrop	214
Julia, m. Elizur **KENEY**, Jan. 31, 1827, by Enoch Burt	206
Mary, m. George **McKEE**, b. of Manchester, Apr. 14, 1830, by B. F. Northrop	211
Phila, m. Joseph **BIDWELL**, Nov. 16, 1824, by A. Benedict	202
Simeon F., m. Jane A. **CONEY**, Feb. 4, 1844, by B. F. Northrop	231
WHEELER, Adaliza, m. Joseph **CUTLER**, b. of Manchester, Nov. 11, 1838, by Rev. R. W. Allen	223
Charles, of Springfield, Mass., m. Rosanah **BOWER**, of Manchester, Jan. 16, 1848, by Rev. B. C. :Phelps	243
Fanny B., m. Abel **LEWIS** Feb. 3, 1830, by V. R. Osborn, V.D.M.	210
Govenour, bd. Sept. 5, 1841, ae 20. Rev. R. Livesey, Min.	335
Hannah M., of Columbia, m. Norman **SPENCER**, of Manchester, Sept. 8, 1835, by Enoch Burt	218
Lucinda C., of Manchester, m. John **FRANCIS**, of Hartford, June 16, 1839, by Enoch Burt	226
Mary, m. Henry W. **GLEASON**, b. of Manchester, Oct. 15, 1838, by B. F. Northrop	223
WHECKHAM, John, m. Malinda **CULVER**, Nov. 19, 1823, by Isaac Devinel	201
WHITE, Harriet, m. Edward H. **GRISWOLD**, b. of Manchester, June 10, 1847, by Rev. B. F. Northrop	241
Juliett D., of Bolton, m. James L. **SPRAGUE**, of Hampton, Mar. 28, 1838, by B. F. Northrop	222
Mary Fitch, m. Dwight **SPENCER**, b. of Manchester, Sept. 21, 1853, by [ ]	265
Morgan, m. Harriet E. **MARBLE**, b. of Manchester, Mar. 22, 1853, by Rev. George W. Brewster	264
Sarah L., of Bolton, m. Elisha B. **RISLEY**, Oct. 31, 1848, by Rev. B. F. Northrop	245
WHITHMORE, Albert, of Coventry, m. Martha **BLINN**, of Bolton, Nov. 6, 1842, by Rev. David Bennett	229
WIGGINS, Thomas, m. Mariah **ALLEN**, Sept. [ ], 1829, by V. R. Osborn, V.D.M.	210
WILKES, Oliver P., m. Mary A. **DEAN**, b. of Manchester, Aug. 20, 1845, by V. R. Osborn, V.D.M.	235
WILLIAMS, Aaron, bd. Dec. 14, 1841, ae 82. Rev. R. Livesey, Min.	335
Emery, of Vernon, m. Charlotte A. **LOVELAND**, Apr. 1, 1840, by David Averey, Elder	225
George W., m. Martha **WOODBRIDGE**, b. of Manchester, Sept. 1, 1842, by B. F. Northrop	228
Harriet, m. Joseph G. **SPENCER**, Feb. 4, 1852, by Rev. George E. Hill	259

MANCHESTER VITAL RECORDS

WILLIAMS (cont.)

	Page
Nehimiah, of Manchester, m. Dorothy W. **RISLEY**, of Hebron, Oct. 13, 1844, by Rev. B. F. Northrop	233
-----, Mr. his child, bd. June 22, 1842, ae 8 m. Rev. R. Livesey, Min.	335

WILSON, WILLSON, Clarrissa, of Manchester, m. Elijah B. **HOSMER**, of East Windsor, May 7, 1845, by Rev. B. M. Walker — 234

Edwin, m. Amanda **SAUNDERS**, b. of Manchester, May 5, 1846, by V. R. Osborn, V.D.M. — 237

John W., of Manchester, m. Rachel E. **WILSON**, of Marlboro, Conn., Dec. 29, 1849, by Rev. M. P. Alderman — 251

Rachel E., of Marlboro, m. John W. **WILLSON**, of Manchester, Dec. 29, 1849, by Rev. M. P. Alderman — 251

Robert M., of Westfield, Mass., m. Charlotte M. **DOWE**, of Manchester, May 5, 1841, by Rev. B. F. Northrop — 227

WINSLOW, Nelson, of East Hartford, m Atusta **KEENEY**, of Manchester, June 29, 1848, by Rev. Benjamin C. Phelps — 244

WINTER, Harriet, of Manchester, m. Cicero **SIMONS**, of Springfield, Nov. 5, 1846, by Rev. B. F. Northrop — 238

WOLCOTT, Edward, of East Windsor, m. Lucinda **ROOT**, of Manchester, Oct. 26, 1840, by Sanford Benton — 226

Roswell, of East Windsor, m. Elizabeth **HOWARD**, of Tolland, Sept. 5, 1840, by S. Benton — 225

WOOD, WOODS, James B., of East Windsor, m. Mary Ann **BUCKLAND**, of Manchester, June 5, 1844, by Rev. B. M. Walker — 232

Mary, m. John **PALMER**, b. of Manchester, Aug. 11, 1853, by F. T. Perkins — 266

WOODBRIDGE, Charles, [s. Dudley & Betsy], b. Mar. 10, 1819 — 281

Charles Dudley, [s. Dudley & Betsy], b. Apr. 21, 1823 — 281

Christopher, [s. Dudley & Betsy], b. Nov. 20, 1817 — 281

Eliza, [d. Dudley & Betsy], b. Mar. 18, 1809 — 281

Eliza, m. Allen **McLEAN**, Dec. 25, 1826, by Enoch Burt — 206

Eliza, see Eliza **McLEAN** — 226

Emily, [d. Dudley & Betsy], b. June 16, 1811 — 281

Emily, m. Asa W. **FOX**, b. of Manchester, Apr. 27, 1829, by Bennett F. Northrop — 209

Esther Wells, [d. Dudley & Betsy], b. May 11, 1820 — 281

Francis, [s. Dudley & Betsy], b. Aug. 16, 1804 — 281

Frederick, [s. Dudley & Betsy], b. Feb. 8, 1801 — 281

Henry Chester, [s. Dudley & Betsy], b. Mar. 20, 1814 — 281

Horace, [s. Dudley & Betsy], b. Sept. 21, 1802 — 281

Martha, m. George W. **WILLIAMS**, b. of Manchester, Sept. 1, 1842, by B. F. Northrop — 228

Mary, of Manchester, m. James A. **DANIELS**, of Woonsocket, R.I., Sept. 3, 1844, by B. F. Northrop — 232

Mary Ann, [d. Dudley & Betsy], b. Jan. 25, 1807 — 281

Mary Ann, of Manchester, m. Maj. Lewis **BISSELL**, of St. Louis, Mo., June 8, 1825, by Enoch Burt — 203

Wells, m. Harriet **KINGSBURY**, Dec. 27, 1847, by Rev. B. F. Northrop — 243

William, of Brooklyn, m. Mary Ann **BIDWELL**, of Manchester, Apr. 26, 1847, by Rev. B. F. Northrop — 240

BARBOUR COLLECTION

	Page
WOODRUFF, David P., of Southington, m. Martha A. **POTTER**, of Manchester, June 22, 1851, by Rev. F. T. Perkins	256
WOODWORTH, Electa, m. Otis B. **RISLEY**, b. of Manchester, Dec. 9, 1824, by Rev. Moses Fifield	202
WYLES, [see under **WYLLYS**]	
WYLLYS, WYLES, Diantha, m. Martin **McKEE**, May 13, 1830, by V. R. Osborn, V.D.M.	211
George, m. Sophronia **TRYON**, July 13, 1852, by W[illia]m Roberts, J. P.	261
Marilla, m. Levi **EVINS**, Mar. 25, 1824, by Isaac Devinel	201
Ralph, m. Harriet **MEEKER**, b. of Manchester, May 6, 1835, by Enoch Burt	217
Roxey, m. Charles **BISSELL**, Dec. 20, 1827, by E. Burt	207
Sarah, m. Martin **SMITH**, Nov. 26, 1829, by V. R. Osborn, V.D.M.	210

MARLBOROUGH VITAL RECORDS
1803 – 1852

This volume contains a list alphabetically arranged of all the vital records of the town of Marlborough from its incorporation to about 1852. The entire record of the town prior to 1852 is found in one volume.

This list was taken from a set of cards based on a copy of the Marlborough Vital Records made in 1912 by Mr. James N. Arnold, of Providence, R.I. The Arnold Copy, now in the possession of the Connecticut State Library, has not been compared with the original and doubtless errors exist. It is hoped that as errors or omissions are found notes will be entered in this volume and on the cards which are included in the General Index of Connecticut Vital Records also in the possession of The Connecticut State Library.

Hartford, Connecticut, January, 1925

	Page
ACKLEY, Hannah, m. William WILLSON, Dec. 25, 1843, by Oliver Northam, J. P.	229
Harry, of Chatham, m. Mary DICKINSON, of Marlborough, Nov. 16, [1834], by Elder Geo[rge] W. Appleton	223
ADAMS, Frances H., farmer, ae 32, b. in Colchester, res. Marlborough, m. Lucy DICKINSON ae 29, Apr. 2, 1851, by Rev. W. C. Fiske	83-4
Frances H., of Chatham, m. Lucy DICKINSON, of Marlborough, Apr. 2, 1851, by Rev. Warren C. Fiske	238
Mary, b. Aug. 30, 1753; m. Samuel ISHAM, Jan. 18, 1775	14
ALBEE, Clark C., m. Mrs. Sarah YOUNG, b. of Mansfield, Mar. 1, 1852, by Rev. L. D. Bentley	239
ANDREWS, Amelia, m. Edward ROOT, June 1, 1823, by Sam[ue]l F. Jones, J.P.	208
Emily T., of Marlborough, m. Ralph C. GOODRICH, of Portland, Nov. 22, 1846, by Rev. Hiram Bell	233
ASHLEY, Nathaniel, m. Hannah WATROUS, Apr. 23, 1826, by Rev. David B. Ripley	210
BAILEY, Hannah, of Marlborough, m. William DeWOLF, of Salem, Aug. 12, [1821], by Rev. David B. Ripley	206
BANCROFT, Hannah, m. [Nathan] DICKINSON, June 12, 1771	11
BARBER, George W., of Hebron, m. Parthenia BRADFORD, of Marlborough, Apr. 17, 1843, by Rev. Charles Nichols	228
BASSETT, Reitenia, m. Henry JEWETT, res. Springfield, Sept. [ ], 1849, by Asa Day	77-8
BEERS, Beckwith, laborer, b. in Waterford, Conn., d. June 5, 1849; ae 78 y.	75-6
BELL, Charles H., s. Hiram, Clergyman, ae 41 & Mary E., ae 38, b. Apr. 4, 1849	71-2

	Page
BELL (cont.)	
Edward Welles, [s. Rev. Hiram], b. Dec. 23, 1841	56
Hiram, m. Mary E. **WELLES**, July 1, 1840, in the state of New York	227
Margaret Ann, [twin with Mary Jane, d. Rev. Hiram], b. Sept. 4, 1843	56
Mary Jane, [twin with Margaret Ann, d. Rev. Hiram], b. Sept. 4, 1843; d. Sept. 4, 1843	56
Sarah E., d. Hiram, Minister, ae 40 & Mary E. ae 37, b. Sept. 4, 1847	65-6
Sarah Elizabeth, [d. Rev. Hiram], b. Sept. 4, 1847	56
BENNET, Charles, Farmer, b. in Chatham, res. Marlborough, m. Frances **INGRAHAM**, July [ ], 1850, by [ ]	77-8
BIGELOW, Abigail, d. [John D. & Sarah], b. May 23, 1804	61
Ann, m. Rev. John A. **HEMSTEAD**, June 14, 1837, by Rev. W. F Vaill	224
Ann, w. Seth G., d. Apr. 24, 1842	50
Anna, d. [John D. & Sarah], b. Sept. 28, 1808	61
Betsey, m. Daniel **HEMSTEAD**, b. of Marlborough, Feb. 11, 1827, by Rev. David B. Ripley	211
Dan, s. [John D. & Sarah], b. Nov. 19, 1801	61
Dan, s. [John D. & Sarah], d. Apr. 14, 1814	61
Elizabeth, d. [John D. & Sarah], b. May 29, 1806	61
Elizabeth, Teacher, ae 44, m. Denel* **HIGGINS**, Farmer, ae 58, b. in Glastonbury, res. Glastonbury, Feb. 17, 1850, by Warren C. Fiske *(Daniel?)	83-4
Elizabeth, of Marlborough, m. Dea. Daniel **HIGGINS**, of Glastonbury, [Feb.] 17, [1851], by Rev. W. C .Fiske	238
Esther, m. William **BUEL**, Jr., Oct. 4, 1804	2
Euphratia, d. [John D. & Sarah], b. Jan. 6, 1817	61
Euphratia, m. Edmund **WEST**, Jr., Jan. 19, 1842	39
Euphrasia, m. Edmund **WEST**, Jr., Jan. 19, 1842, by Rev. Hiram Bell	227
Frances F., of Marlborough, m. Austin **LORD**, of North Haven, Aug. 21, 1850, by Rev. Hiram Bell	237
Francis F., ae 22, m. Austin **LORD**, Physician, ae 24, b. in Coventry, res. North Haven, Aug. 25, 1850, by Rev. Hiram Bell	83-4
Isaac, m. Margaret **FOOTE**, Dec. 25, 1806	19
Jemima, w. of a Farmer, b. in Hebron, d. Oct. 18, 1848; ae 63	75-6
John, m. Abigail **KELLOG**, b. of Marlborough, Nov. 12, 1823, by Rev. David B. Ripley	208
John D., m. Sarah **BUELL**, Sept. 25, 1796	61
John D., s. [John D. & Sarah], b. Nov. 20, 1797	61
John D., m. Jemima **CARRIER**, Feb. 25, 1835	61
John D., m. Jemima **CARRIER**, Feb. 25, 1835, by Rev. Chauncey Lee	222
Jonathan G., m. Hope **SKINNER**, Sept. 13, 1827, by Rev. Charles Nichols	212
Mariam, d. [Seth G. & Ann], b. Dec. 27, 1836	50
Russell, m. Roxana **LORD**, b. of Marlborough, Nov. 6, 1826, by Rev. David B. Ripley	210
Sarah, d. [John D. & Sarah], b. Oct. 8, 1799	61
Sarah, m. David **PHELPS**, Feb. 1, 1831	32

	Page
BIGELOW (cont.)	
Sarah, m David **PHELPS**, b. of Marlborough, Feb. 1, 1831, by Rev. Chauncey Lee	216
Sarah, w. John D., d. May 20, 1832	61
Seth G., m. Ann **JONES**, Feb. 14, 1836	50
Seth G., of Chatham, m. Ann **JONES**, of Marlborough, Feb. 14, 1836, by Elder Jeremiah Stocking	223
BILLINGS, George, of Hartford, m. Arulia **KELLOGG**, of Marlborough, Feb. 11, 1844, by Rev. Hiram Bell	230
BIRGE, Mary Ann, m. Josiah **WATROUS**, Oct. 10, 1830, by Rev. Alpheas Geer	215
BISSEL, Abigail, m. William **PALMER**, May 29, 1831, by Rev. Chauncey Lee	216
BLISH, Alice Maria, d. [Chauncey & Esther M.], b. July 15, 1844	58
Amelia, [d. Roger & Demis], b. June 14, 1797	62
Amelia, m. Henry **BRAINARD**, Feb. 24, 1819	43
Anson H., [s. Roger & Demis], b. Nov. 3, 1803	62
Augustus, [s. Roger & Demis], b. Aug. 20, 1801	62
Augustus, m. Delight **BUEL**, Jan. 21, 1828, by Rev. Charles Nichols	212
Chauncey, [s. Roger & Demis], b. Dec. 4, 1807	62
Chauncey, m. Esther M. **SLATE**, Mar. 2, 1834	58
Daniel, [s. Roger & Demis], b. Oct. 28, 1817	62
Edmund, m. Betsey **HILLS**, Mar. 24, 1829, by Oliver Phelps, J.P.	213
Esther Jane, d. Chauncey, Farmer, ae 42 & Esther M., ae 35, b. May 23, 1851	85-6
Harriet, [d. Roger & Demis], b. July 7, 1795	62
Harriet, [d. Roger & Demis], b. Sept. 21, 1803	62
Harriet, [d. Roger & Demis], b. Aug. 9, 1812	62
Harriet E., m. William **CARRIER**, b. of Marlborough, May 2, 1838, by Rev. Lyman Strong	226
Helen Eliza, d. Chancy, Farmer, ae 42 & Esther, ae 35, b. Jan. 25, [1849]	71-2
Mary, [d. Roger & Demis], b. Sept. 25, 1810	62
Mary L., m. George T. **LORD**, Oct. 17, 1832, by Rev. Chauncey Lee	217
Mary Tallcott, d. [Chauncey & Esther M.], b. Oct. 31, 1842	58
Prudence, [d. Roger & Demis], b. Apr. 5, 1799	62
Prudence, m. Howell **ROOT**, Farmer, June 5, 1850, by Rev. Hiram Bell	77-8
Prudence H., m. Howell **ROOT**, June 5, 1850, by Rev. Hiram Bell	236
Roger, m. Demis **HOSFORD**, Sept. [ ], 1794	62
Zeruiah, [d. Roger & Demis], b. July 17, 1814	62
Zeruiah, m. Isaac Bigelow **BUELL**, Jan. 11, 1837, by Rev. Charles Nichols	224
Zeruiah, d. [Chauncey & Esther M.], b. Oct. 30, 1838	58
Zeriah Ann, b. July 17, 1814; m. Isaac Bigelow **BUELL**, Jan. 11, 1837	57
BLYTHE, Arthur, s. John, Manufacturer, ae 23 & Mary A. ae 22, b. Dec. 25, 1850	85-6
Charles, s. James, Manufacturer, ae 28 & Sarah M., ae 24, b. Nov. 18, 1847	65-6
Edward, s. John, Laborer, ae 21 & Mary A., ae 20, b. Feb. 18, 1849	71-2
Gilbert F., d. Oct. 3, 1848; ae 4 [y.], 11 [m.]	75-6

	Page
BLYTHE (cont.)	
John, Manufacturer, ae 20, m. Mary A. **WARREN**, ae 18, Apr. 30, 1848*, by Rev. Hiram Bell *(Arnold Copy has 1841)	67-8
John, m. Mary A. **WARREN**, b. of Marlborough, Apr. 30, 1848, by Rev. Hiram Bell	234
Mary, Laborer, m. Henry **SHERMAN**, Laborer, Sept. [ ], 1849, by Rev. John Cooper	77-8
Mary, m. William Henry **SHERMAN**, b. of Marlborough, Sept. 16, 1849, by Rev. John Cooper, Easthampton	235
-----, s. W[illia]m, Manufacturer, ae 30 & Charlotte, b. June 23, 1851	85-6
-----, d. July 3, 1851; ae 11 d.	79-80
BOLLES, Alice Estell, [d. Horatio & Phebe A.], b. July 13, 1849	44
Charles Kittredge, [s. Horatio & Phebe A.], b. May 1, 1847	44
Elisha, s. [Roswell & Lois], b. Feb. 14, 1804	40
Ellen Augusta, d. [Horatio & Phebe A.], b. July 13, 1839	44
Ellen Augusta, [d. Horatio & Phebe A.], d. Nov. 25, 1842	44
Florence E., [d. Horatio & Phebe A.], b. July 3, 1845	44
Horatio, s. [Roswell & Lois], b. July 12, 1807	40
Horatio, m. Phebe A. **MACK** [ ]	44
Isadore, d. Horatio, House Joiner, ae 42 & Phebe A., ae 38, b. July 13, 1849	71-2
Mary, d. [Roswell & Lois], b. June 26, 1811	40
Mary, m. William **BUELL**, Jr., Jan. 4, 1843	57
Mary, m. William **BUELL**, Jr., b. of Marlborough, Jan. 4, 1843, by Hiram Bell	227
Sarah Walker, d. [Horatio & Phebe A.], b. Jan. 3, 1842	44
Watson, s. [Roswell & Lois], b. Feb. 2, 1816; d. Aug. 14, 1818	40
William, s. [Roswell & Lois], b. Aug. 10, 1800	40
William Watson, s. [Horatio & Phebe A.], b. Oct. 6, 1843	44
BOWEN, Mary E., m. Edwin C. **WARNER**, b. of Marlborough, Nov. 30, 1843, by Rev. Hiram Bell	229
BRADFORD, Parthenia, of Marlborough, m. George W. **BARBER**, of Hebron, Apr. 17, 1843, by Rev. Charles Nichols	228
BRAINARD, Harriet Eliza, d. [Henry & Amelia], b. Jan. 13, 1829	43
Henry, m. Amelia **BLISH**, Feb. 24, 1819	43
Henry, [s. Henry & Amelia], b. Aug. 28, 1824	43
Lewis, s. [Henry & Amelia], b. Feb. 5, 1832	43
Mary A., d. [Henry & Amelia], b. Sept. 28, 1821	43
Mary A., of Marlborough, m. Alpheas **WILLIAMS**, of Chatham, Aug. 6, 1844, by Rev. Hiram Bell	230
Oliver, of St. Louis, Mo., m. Mercy **CARRIER**, of Marlborough, Feb. 1, 1827, by Rev. David B Ripley	211
Sarah Ann, [d. Henry & Amelia], b. Mar. 29, 1823	43
Sarah C., of Marlborough, m. Reuben **SMITH**, of Chatham, Mar. 26, 1843, by Rev. B. M. Walker	228
BRIGHAM, Anna E., d. Daniel H., Merchant, ae 28 & Abby E., ae 24, b. Nov. 30, 1848	71-2
BROCKWAY, Alice, m. Aaron **SKINNER**, Nov. 24, 1802	5
BROOKS, John E., m .Harriet A. **ROOD**, Mar. 20, 1843, by Rev. Hiram Bell	228
BROWN, Almon Vallet, s. [William B. & Mariette], b. Dec. 28, 1843	37
Almon Vallet, s. [William B. & Mariette], d. Feb. 11, 1844	37

	Page
BROWN (cont.)	
Daniel, m. Esther Y. **PHELPS**, b. of Marlborough, May 28, 1849, by Rev. Hiram Bell	236
David, of Chatham, m. Loiza **WARNER**, of Marlborough, Aug. 9, 1835, by Jeremiah Stocking, Elder	222
Elias, of Windham, m. Sylvina **DICKINSON**, of Marlborough, Nov. 5, 1837, by Elder Jeremiah Stocking	225
Henriett Miranda, d. [William B. & Mariette], b. July 9, 1840	37
Joshua L., m. Jane **CURTIS**, May 16, 1821, by Rev. David B. Ripley	206
Leander Phelps, s. [William B. & Mariette], b. Nov. 23, 1838	37
Leander Phelps, s. [William B. & Mariette], d. Dec. 22, 1840	37
Leander Phelps, s. [William B. & Mariette], b. Mar. 7, 1842	37
Lydia, of Marlborough, m. Oliver **WELLS**, of Chatham, Dec. 8, 1826, by Rev. David B. Ripley	210
Mary A., m. Henry **DICKERSON**, b. of Marlborough, Dec. 22, 1844, by Rev. Hiram Bell	231
Polly, of Marlborough, m. Chester **SAUNDERS**, of Hebron, Jan. 26, 1826, by Rev. David B. Ripley	209
William B., m. Mariette **PHELPS**, Mar. 28, 1836	37
William B., of Colchester, m. Harriet **PHELPS**, of Marlborough, Mar. 28, 1836, by Rev. David Bennett	223
BUCK, Mahitable, m. [Nathan] **DICKINSON**, Nov. 20, 1762	11
BUEL, BUELL, Abigail, wid. [Capt. William], d. Apr. 8, 1819	26
Abigail, [w. Capt. William], d. Apr. 8, 1819	50
Abagail, d. [William, Jr. & Esther], b. May 19, 1827	2
Abigail, d. Sept. 9, 1849, ae 22	79-80
Aphelia* Theresa, d. [Daniel & Betsey], b. Sept. 6, 1810 *(Orphelia?)	24
Aphelia, see also Orphelia	
Asahel Lord, s. [Daniel & Betsey], b. Aug. 17, 1816	24
Charles, s. [Daniel & Betsey], b. Feb. 17, 1823	24
Daniel, b. Apr. 12, 1781	24
Daniel, m. Betsey **LORD**, Dec. 28, 1807	24
Daniel, d. May 7, 1840	24
David, s. [William, Jr. & Esther], b. June 23, 1819	2
Delight, w. William, [Jr.], d. Oct. 18, 1803	2
Delight, d. [William, Jr. & Esther], b. June 24, 1805	2
Delight, m. Augustus **BLISH**, Jan. 21, 1828, by Rev. Charles Nichols	212
Elihu P., of Hebron, m. Lucy **KELLOGG**, of Marlborough, [Feb.] 20, [1833], by Rev. Tertius D. Southworth	218
Elizabeth J., of Marlborough, m. Elihu M. **DAY**, of Colchester, May 29, 1833, by Rev. Charles Nichols	219
Elizabeth Jane, d. [William, Jr. & Esther], b. Feb. 21, 1814	2
Esther, d. [William, Jr. & Esther], b. May 23, 1808	2
Esther, d. Sept. 12, 1849, ae 67	79-80
Harriet, d. Oct. 27, 1849, ae 27	79-80
Harriet Adalaide, [d. William, Jr. & Mary], b. Dec. 19, 1849	57
Harriet Ann, d. [William, Jr. & Esther], b. Jan. 27, 1822	2
Isaac Bigelow, s. [William, Jr. & Esther], b. Mar. 18, 1812	2
Isaac Bigelow, b. Mar. 18, 1812; m. Zeriah Ann **BLISH**, Jan. 11, 1837	57

	Page
BUEL, BUELL (cont.)	
Isaac Bigelow, m. Zeruiah **BLISH**, Jan. 11, 1837, by Rev. Charles Nichols	224
Lucian, [s. William, Jr. & Mary], b. Aug. 29, 1846	57
Mary, m. John Bulkley **LORD**, Dec. 10, 1778	15
Mary, Farming, d. Mar. 4, 1851; ae 58	79-80
Orphelia T., b. Sept. 6, 1810; m. Sherman C. **LORD**, Nov. 29, 1832	51
Ophelia Theresa, m. Sherman C. **LORD**, Nov. 29, 1832, by Rev. Chauncey Lee	218
Roland Osmus, s. [Isaac Bigelow & Zeriah Ann], b. Jan. 29, 1841	57
Sarah, m. John D. **BIGELOW**, Sept. 25, 1796	61
Sophia, d. [William, Jr. & Esther], b. Mar. 15, 1816	2
Theron, s. [William, Jr. & Mary], b. July 25, 1844	57
William, Jr., of Hebron, m. Delight **FINLEY**, of Colchester, Nov. 6, 1800	2
William, s. [William, Jr. & Delight], b. Aug. 19, 1801; d. Jan. 20, 1802	2
William, Jr., m. Esther **BIGELOW**, Oct. 4, 1804	2
William, s. [William, Jr. & Esther], b. June 5, 1810	2
William, Capt. d. Mar. 6, 1819	26
William, Capt., d. Mar. 6, 1819	50
William, Jr., m. Mary **BOLLES**, Jan. 4, 1843	57
William, Jr., m. Mary **BOLLES**, b. of Marlborough, Jan. 4, 1843, by Hiram Bell	227
William, d. Sept. 3, 1849, ae 71	79-80
-----, d. [William, Jr. & Delight], b. Oct. 6, 1803; d. Oct. 19, 1803	2
BULKELEY, BULKLEY, Betsey, m. Noble E. **LORD**, Dec. 14, 1834, by Rev. Chauncey Lee	222
Eunice, m. Roger **FOOTE**, May 26, 1790	27
Lois, m. Eliphalet **LORD**, Nov. 7, 1826	43
BURNHAM, William, m. Pamelia **WYLLYS**, Nov. 2, 1828, by Oliver Phelps, J. P.	213
BURR, Courtland, Manufacturer, res. East Haddam, m. Harriet **SISSON**, Nov. 4, 1849, by Asa Day	77-8
CAMERON, William, m. Eunice **CURTISS**, b. of Attleborough, July 4, 1830, by Oliver Phelps, J.P.	215
CARRIER, Ann, of Marlborough, m. Elijah K. **GILBERT**, of Hamilton, N.Y., Jan. 21, 1827, by Rev. David B. Ripley	211
David, s. Thomas, d. Aug. 14, 1807, in the 37th y. of his age	4
Ebenezer, s. Thomas, 2nd, d. Apr. 23, 1810	30
Emily, m. Bishop **ROOT**, Mar. 27, 1825, by Sam[ue]l F. Jones, J.P.	208
Eunice, b. Mar. 17, 1774; m. Joseph **INGRAHAM**, Jr., Dec. 28, 1803	42
Harriet, of Marlborough, m. Daniel **PRATT**, of West Chester, Sept. 18, 1828, by Rev. Chauncey Lee	212
Harriet Eliza, w. [William], d. Jan. 29, 1839	52
Harriet Louisa, [twin with Helen Eliza, d. [William & Harriet Eliza], b. Jan. 8, 1839	52
Helen Eliza, [twin with Harriet Louisa, d. [William & Harriet Eliza], b. Jan. 8, 1839	52
Hiram, m. Elizabeth **WEST**, Dec. 15, 1831, by Rev. Chauncey Lee	216
Jemima, m. John D. **BIGELOW**, Feb. 25, 1835	61

MARLBOROUGH VITAL RECORDS 93

Page

CARRIER (cont.)
Jemima, m. John D. **BIGELOW**, Feb. 25, 1835, by Rev. Chauncey Lee — 222
Joseph, m. Chelsea **HUXFORD**, Sept. 5, 1827, by Oliver Phelps, J.P. — 212
Julia, of Marlborough, m. Timothy **WATROUS**, of Colchester, Dec. 25, 1826, by David B Ripley — 210
Lois Day, d. [William], b. Feb. 13, 1845 — 52
Mercy, of Marlborough, m. Oliver **BRAINARD**, of St. Louis, Mo., Feb. 1, 1827, by Rev. David B. Ripley — 211
Olive, ae 22, b. in East Haddam, m. Joseph **WASHBURN**, ae 22, b. in Clinton, N.Y., res. Clinton, N.Y., Aug. 21, 1850, by Rev. H. Bell — 83-4
Olive S., of Marlborough, m. Joseph W. **HUBBARD**, of Clinton, N.Y., Aug. 21, 1850, by Rev. Hiram Bell — 237
Philena, of Marlborough, m. Alfred **KELLOGG**, of Chatham, Apr. 29, 1830, by Rev. Chauncey Lee — 215
Rebecca, wid. Andrew, d. Sept. 20, 1807 — 22
Roderick, m. Eliza **SAUNDERS**, Nov. 27, 1834, by Rev. Chauncey Lee — 221
Sarah Emeline, d. [William], b. Oct. 11, 1846 — 52
William, m. Harriet E. **BLISH**, b. of Marlborough, May 2, 1838, by Rev. Lyman Strong — 226
W[illia]m, m. Emeline **PHELPS**, b. of Marlborough, Aug. 17, 1840, by Hiram Bell — 226
William G., of Colchester, m. Sarah Ann **WARNER**, of Marlborough, June 7, 1847, by Rev. J. B. Gould — 233
CARTER, Asa. [s. Charles], b. May 8, 1818 — 49
Charles, s. [Charles], b. Dec. 9, 1830 — 49
David, s. [Charles], b. Feb. 20, 1822 — 49
Eleazer, m. Sarah **CURTIS**, Nov. 28, 1821, by David B. Ripley — 207
Eliza, d. [Charles], b. Sept. 17, 1819 — 49
Eunice, m. Sylvester **GILBERT**, Nov. 26, 1805 — 38
Franes, d. [Charles], b. Mar. 22, 1828 — 49
Jerusha, m. Asa **FOOTE**, Apr. 26, 1752 — 9
Laura Ann, d. [Charles], b. Jan. 14, 1824 — 49
CASE, Josephine, factory worker, res. Marlborough, m. Joseph C.
  GILBERT, Saddler, b. in Hebron, res. Hebron, Mar. 15, 1848, by Rev. Hiram Bell — 67-8
  Josephine, of Marlborough, m. Joseph C. **GILBERT**, of Manchester, Mar. 15, 1848, by Rev. Hiram Bell — 234
CHAPMAN, Ansel, of Glastonbury, m. Hannah **HUXFORD**, of Marlborough, Jan. 15, 1823, by Rev. David B. Ripley — 207
Charles, of Glastonbury, m. Matilda **HUBBARD**, of Marlborough, May 7, 1845, by Rev. Hiram Bell — 231
CLARK, Edwin A., of Hartford, m. Ann S. **PERKINS**, of Marlborough, Apr. 15, 1841, by Hiram Bell — 226
COLEMAN, Asa, m. Mary **DEMING**, Aug. 15, 1826, by Sam[uel] F. Jones, J.P. — 209
Eliza, m. Robert H. **WILBUR** Feb. 20, 1843, by Rev. Hiram Bell — 227
Enos, m. Julianna **FOX**, Dec. 9, 1824, by Sam[uel] F. Jones, J.P. — 208
Ephraim, of Marlborough, m. Anna **WATROUS**, Feb. 23, 1826, by Sam[uel] F. Jones, J.P. — 209

COLEMAN (cont.)

	Page
Huldah, ae 19, res. Marlborough, m. Noah L. **SNOW**, Farmer, ae 26, b. in Columbia, res. Marlborough, Mar. 18, 1849, by Rev. Hiram Bell	73-4
Huldah, m. Noah L. **SNOW**, b. of Marlborough, Mar. 18, 1849, by Rev. Hiram Bell	235
Maria, d. Asa, Farmer, ae 43 & Mary, ae 41, b. Oct. 24, 1847	65-6
Mary A., ae 17, m. Benj[amn] D. **WILBUR**, Farmer, ae 23, Oct. 20, 1850, by Rev. H. Leffingwell	83-4
Mary A., m. Benjamin R. K. **WILBUR**, b. of Marlborough, Oct. 20, 1850, by Rev. Marvin Leffingwell	237
Mary E., m. Hiram L. **MAINE**, Mar. 11, 1838, by Rev. W[illia]m F. Vaill	225
Ruth, m. Ogden **WILSON**, Jan. 15, 1827, by Sam[ue]l F. Jones, J.P.	210

COLES, [see under **COWLES**]

COOK, Sylvester E., Farmer, b. in Chatham, m. 2nd w. Emeline **JACKSON**, b. in Marlborough, Jan. 27, 1850, by Asa Day — 77-8

COTTON, Francis, m. Nancy **HILLS**, Nov. 29, 1832, by Oliver Phelps, J.P. — 218

COWLES, COLES, Sherman H., of Norfolk, m. Caroline **LORD**, of Marlborough, May 1, 1842, by Hiram Bell — 227

W[illia]m, Farmer, ae 28, b. in Norfolk, res. Canton, m. Abigail P[atience] **LORD**, ae 27, Mar. 6, 1851, by Rev. Warren C. Fiske — 83-4

W[illia]m*, of Canton, m. Abigail P. **LORD**, of Marlborough, Apr. 16, 1851, by Rev. Warren C. Fiske *(**COWLES**, of Norfolk) — 238

CROCKER, Caroline, m. George **LORD**, Jan. 8, 1809 — 31

CROUCH, Joseph, Farmer, b. in Glastonbury, res. Marlborough, m. Betsey E. **RILEY**, Factory worker, b. in Glastonbury, res. Marlborough, Aug. 28, 1847, by Daniel Phelps, J.P. — 67-8

Joseph, m. Betsey E. **RILEY**, b. of Marlborough, Aug. 28, 1847, by David Phelps, J.P. — 234

CULLUMS, COLUMS, Emily E., m. Jedediah L. **THOMPSON**, b. of Marlborough, Aug. 2, 1846, by Rev. Hiram Bell — 232

Samuel G., Farmer, d. Mar. 11, [1848], ae 39 — 69-70

CULVER, Amanda, Housekeeper, d. Dec. 29, 1847, ae 19, in East Windsor — 69-70

Harriet, of Marlborough, m. Andrew **FLOOD**, of East Hampton, Apr. 29, 1849, by Rev. Hiram Bell — 235

Harriet, ae 22, b. in Manchester, res. Marlborough, m. Andrew **FLOOD**, Farmer, ae 33, b. in East Haddam, res. Chatham, Apr. 30, 1849, by Rev. Hiram Bell — 73-4

CURTIS, CURTISS, Charles Cotesworth Pinckney, s. [Joseph], b. July 30, 1802 — 4

Eliza, d. [Joseph], b. Oct. 11, 1800 — 4

Eliza, m. Norman P. **WARNER**, b. of Marlborough, Jan. 1, 1844, by Rev. Hiram Bell — 229

Eunice, m. William **CAMERON**, b. of Attleborough, July 4, 1830, by Oliver Phelps, J.P. — 215

Francess, d. [Joseph], b. Nov. 11, 1798 — 206

Jane, m. Joshua L. **BROWN**, May 16, 1821, by Rev. David B. Ripley — 206

	Page
CURTIS, CURTISS (cont.)	
Nathaniel, m. Lovina **WELDON**, b. of Marlborough, Feb. 22, 1824, by Rev. David B. Ripley	208
Reuben, m. Mrs. Joanna **MARKALL**, Apr. 17, 1809, by Joel Foote, J.P.	29
Sarah, m. Eleazer **CARTER**, Nov. 28, 1821, by David B. Ripley	207
DARBY, Eliza, of Marlborough, m. Benjamin **ROUND**, of Providence, R.I., Feb. 28, 1830, by Joel Foote, J.P.	214
DAY, Asa, of Colchester, m. Charlotte P. **JONES**, of Marlborough, Dec. 31, 1834, by Rev. Leonard B Griffing	222
Asa W., [s. Asa], b. May 6, 1844	55
Elihu M., of Colchester, m. Elizabeth J. **BUELL**, of Marlborough, May 29, 1833, by Rev. Charles Nichols	219
John W., [s. Asa], b. Mar. 9, 1836	55
Samuel Jones, [s. Asa], b. Nov. 5, 1840	55
DEAN, Abner, b. Aug. 25, 1729; m. Jane **ISHAM**, Jan. [ ], 1752	34
Amos, m. Marsilva **INGHAM**, Nov. 5, 1795	26
Jane, [w. Abner], d. July 10, 1813	34
Silva, Mrs., d. [ ]; ae 91	79-80
DEMING, Mary, m. Asa **COLEMAN**, Aug. 15, 1826, by Sam[uel] F. Jones, J.P.	209
DERBE, Mary Maria, m. Horace **WELLES**, Aug. 31, 1824, by Rev. David B. Ripley	208
DeWOLF, William, of Salem, m. Hannah **BAILEY**, of Marlborough, Aug. 12, [1821], by Rev. David B. Ripley	206
DEXTER, Jonathan, of Killingly, m. Sophia **FOOTE**, of Marlborough, Jan. 31, 1827, by Rev. David B. Ripley	211
DICKERSON, [see also **DICKINSON**], Henry, m. Mary A. **BROWN**, b. of Marlborough, Dec. 22, 1844, by Rev. Hiram Bell	231
Maria, m. Samuel F. J. **ROOT**, b. of Marlborough, Oct. 20, 1844, by Rev. Hiram Bell	230
DICKINSON, [see also **DICKERSON**], Abner, s. [Nathan & Hannah], b. Oct. 8, 1782	11
Ann, m. David **FINLEY**, 2nd, Jan. 1, 1829, by Isaac Dwinel	213
Betty, d. [Nathan & Mahitable], b. May 28, 1765	11
Deborah, d. [Nathan & Deborah], b. June 30, 1760	11
Deborah, w. [Nathan], d. Mar. 10, 1762	11
Emela, of Marlborough, m. Charles **HURLBURT**, of Chatham, June 20, 1827, by Jeremiah Stocking, J.P.	211
Emma H., d. James N., Farmer, ae 31 & Harriet, ae 19, b. Dec. 1, 1847	65-6
Eveline, of Marlborough, m. Selden P. **SEARS**, of Chatham, Nov. 30, 1843, by Rev. Hiram Bell	229
Hannah, d. [Nathan & Hannah], b. Jan. 21, 1773	11
Jerusha, m. Harvey **LOVELAND**, Nov. 7, 1827, by Oliver Phelps, J.P.	212
Jesse, s. [Nathan & Hannah], b. July 19, 1774	11
Lucy, ae 29, m. Frances H. **ADAMS**, Farmer, ae 32, in Colchester, res. Marlborough, Apr. 2, 1851, by Rev. W. C. Fiske	83-4
Lucy, of Marlborough, m. Frances H. **ADAMS**, of Chatham, Apr. 2, 1851, by Rev. Warren C. Fiske	238
Mahitable, d. [Nathan & Mahitable], b. Aug. 10, 1763	11
Mahitable, w. [Nathan], d. Nov. 8, 1770	11

BARBOUR COLLECTION

	Page
DICKINSON (cont.)	
Mary, m. Harvey **TRYON**, May 27, 1829, by Isaac Dwinel	213
Mary, of Marlborough, m. Harry **ACKLEY**, of Chatham, Nov. 16, [1834], by Elder Geo[rge] W. Appleton	223
Nathan, b. Jan. 21, 1737	11
Nathan, m. Deborah **SKINNER**, Nov. 18, 1758	11
[Nathan], m. Mahitable **BUCK**, Nov. 20, 1762	11
Nathan, s. [Nathan & Mahitable], b. Mar. 10, 1767	11
[Nathan], m .Hannah **BANCROFT**, June 12, 1771	11
Orrin, m. Mary **RODMAN**, Sept. 16, 1833, by Oliver Phelps, J.P.	219
Sarah, d. [Nathan & Mahitable], b. Oct. 8, 1768	11
Seth, s. [Nathan & Hannah], b. Nov. 4, 1779	11
Sylvina, of Marlborough, m. Elias **BROWN**, of Windham, Nov. 5, 1837, by Elder Jeremiah Stocking	225
Wolcott, s. [Nathan & Hannah], b. Oct. 7, 1777	11
-----, ch. of Oren, Farmer, ae 45 & Mary, ae 39, b. Mar. 22, 1848	65-6
-----, s. Nathan R., Farmer, ae 25 & Mary A., ae 20, b. Apr. 22, 1849	71-2
-----, d. J. Munroe, Farmer & Harriet, b. Jan. [ ], 1850	81-2
-----d. Orrin, Farmer & Mary, b. July 10, 1850	81-2
DIXON, Alvinzia, s. [Henry C. & Salome], b. Jan. 7, 1813	8
Henry, s. [Henry C. & Salome], b. July 10, 1825	8
DOAN, Seth, m. Jemima **HALING**, May 13, 1807	21
DOYLE, Elizabeth, d. Alexander, Machinist, ae 35 & Elizabeth ae 34, b. May 24, 1851	85-6
DUNHAM, Anna, wid., d. June 28, 1844	48
Asa C., s. [Asa], b. Aug. 13, 1821	46
Daniel E., [s. Sylvester C.], b. June 11, 1814	48
Delia A., [d. Sylvester C.], b. Feb. 20, 1817	48
Delia A., Tailoress, ae 33, m. Geo[rge] H. **LATHROP**, Carpenter, ae 45, b. in Franklin, res. Franklin, Dec. 29, 1850, by Rev. W. C. Fiske	83-4
Delia A., of Marlborough, m. George H. **LATHROP**, of Franklin, Dec. 29, 1850, by Rev. W. C. Fiske	238
Florilla, [d. Sylvester C.], b. Feb. 18, 1822; d. Feb. 20, 1824	48
Henry M., [s. Asa], b. Jan. 14, 1824	46
James E., [s. Asa], b. Oct. 24, 1831	46
John E., [s. Sylvester C.], b. Nov. 12, 1819	48
John E., Farmer, ae 28, m. Elvira A. **SOCKET**, Factory Worker, ae 35, b. in Vernon, res. Marlborough, Aug. 22, 1848, by Rev. Hiram Bell	73-4
John E., m. Mrs. Eliza **SOCKET**, b. of Marlborough, Aug. 22, 1848, by Rev. Hiram Bell	235
Lewis E., [s. Asa], b. Nov. 19, 1826	46
Lucy A., [d. Sylvester C.], b. Mar. 5, 1810	48
Moses, Farmer, d. May 1, 1850, ae 21 y.	79-80
Moses C., [s. Asa], b. July 12, 1829	46
Oren, m. Sophia **RANN**, of Marlborough, Oct. 4, 1826, by Rev. David B. Ripley	209
Rachel M., [d. Sylvester C.], b. Mar. 21, 1808	48
Rachel M., m. Solomon B. **EDWARDS**, Jan. 13, 1833, by Rev. Chancey Lee	218
Sylvester C., Jr., [s. Sylvester C.], b. Mar. 6, 1812	48
-----, d. John E., Farmer, ae 28 & Elvia A., ae 35, b. May 31, 1849	71-2

	Page
DUTTON, William G., Shoemaker, d. June 12, [1848], ae 44, in Glastonbury	69-70
EASTON, Azis, of East Hartford, m. Mary **GOODWIN**, of Marlborough, Sept. 23, 1830, by Rev. Chauncey Lee	215
EDWARDS, Solomon B., m. Rachel M. **DUNHAM**, Jan. 13, 1833, by Rev. Chancey Lee	218
EMILY, Charles, s. Joseph, Manufacturer, ae 35, & Damon, ae 35, b. Oct. 9, 1850	85-6
Sarah Ann, d. Joseph, Mule Spinner, ae 32 & Tamer, ae 32, b. Nov. 14, 1847	65-6
EMMONS, Elizabeth, ae 19, m. W[illia]m **PHELPS**, Farmer, ae 38, b. in Colchester, Oct. 25, 1850, by Rev. S. D. Jewett	83-4
EVANS, Julius, of Marlborough, m. Harriet **THOMAS**, of Hartford, July 31, 1825, by Rev. David B. Ripley	209
EVERETT, EVERITT, EVERETTE, Abigail, m. George **LORD**, Apr. 27, 1812	31
Elisha H., Farmer, b. in Marlborough, res. Nantucket, m. Mary E. **SKINNER**, res. Marlborough, Sept. 27, 1847, by Rev. Hiram Bell	67-8
Elisha H., of New Bedford, Mass., m. Mary E. **SKINNER**, of Marlborough, Sept. 27, 1847, by Rev. Edgar J. Doolittle, Hebron	234
Eunice Amelia, m. Gardiner **LORD**, Sept. [ ], 1817	58
FIELDING, Frederick A., m. Mary B. **OVERTON**, b. of Marlborough, Oct. 3, 1830, by Rev. Chauncey Lee	215
Inis, s. H. A., Machinist, ae 47 & Mary B., ae 40, b. Mar. 30, 1851	85-6
Sarah A., Factory worker, ae 16, m. Nehemiah G. **SHERMAN**, Warper in Factory, ae 21, b. in Chatham, res. Marlborough, Nov. 30, 1848, by Rev. Hiram Bell	73-4
Sarah A., m. Nehemiah G. **SHERMAN**, b. of Marlborough, Nov. 30, 1848, by Rev. Hiram Bell	235
FINLEY, Daniel Barbridge, s. [William & Abby A.], b. Apr. 10, 1844	13
David, b. Aug. 27, 1761; m. Lucy **PHELPS**, Jan. 22, 1784	13
David, m. Polly **HOSFORD**, Apr. 16, 1800	13
David, d. Nov. 29, 1840	13
David, 2nd, m. Ann **DICKINSON**, Jan. 1, 1829, by Isaac Dwinel	213
Delight, of Colchester, m. William **BUEL**, Jr., of Hebron, Nov. 6, 1800	2
Dilight, of Marlborough, m. John H. **POST**, of Coventry, Chenange Cty., N.Y., June 29, 1834, by Jeremiah Stocking, Elder	220
Dennison, s. [William & Abby A.], b. June 27, 1849	13
Emeline, m. Andrew **INGRAHAM**, Dec. 13, 1833, by Rev. Chauncey Lee	218
Esther Ann, d. Samuel, Farmer, ae 40 & Eliza R., ae 35, b. Sept. 12, 1847	65-6
Hannah, d. [David & Lucy], b. July 20, 1785; d. Jan. 14, 1787	13
Hannah, d. [David & Lucy], b. June 26, 1789	13
James, s. [David & Lucy], b. Sept. 6, 1787; d. Apr. 27, 1791	13
James, s. [David & Lucy], b. Nov. 17, 1794	13
James, Farmer, d. Oct. 20, 1847; ae 53	69-70
John W., m. Sophronia **ROOT**, b. of Marlborough, June 6, 1833, by Jeremiah Stocking, Elder	219
Lucy, d. [David & Lucy], b. Apr. 19, 1797	13

BARBOUR COLLECTION

	Page
FINLEY (cont.)	
Lucy, w. David, d. Oct. 10, 1799	13
Lydia, d. [David & Lucy], b. May 10, 1792	13
William, [s. David & Polly], b. July 19, 1807	13
William, m. Abby A. **HEMPSTEAD**, Aug. 27, 1838	13
William, m. Abby Ann **HEMPSTEAD**, Aug. 27, 1838, by Rev. Charles Nichols	226
FLOOD, Andrew, Farmer, ae 33, b. in East Haddam, res. Chatham, 2nd m. Harriet **CULVER**, ae 22, b. in Manchester, res. Marlborough, Apr. 30, 1849, by Rev. Hiram Bell	73-4
Andrew, of East Hampton, m. Harriet **CULVER**, of Marlborough, Apr. 29, 1849, by Rev. Hiram Bell	235
Harriet, ae 23, m. 2nd h. David D. **PENHARLOW**, Farmer, ae 23, b. in Mansfield, Oct. 9, 1850, by Rev. H. Leffingwell	83-4
Harriet, of Marlborough, m. David D. **PENHARLOW**, of Mansfield, Oct. 9, 1850, by Rev. Marvin Leffingwell	237
FOOTE, Abigail, d. [Joel & Abigail Robins], b. Dec. 15, 1792	10
Abigail L., d. [George & Rachel Caroline], b. Apr. 30, 1836	39
Abigail Robbins Lord, w. [Joel], d. Jan. 8, 1795	10
Albert, s. [Elijah & Lois], b. Sept. 19, 1825	28
Amelia, d. [Roger & Eunice], b. July 15, 1801	27
Arba, of Chester, Mass., m. Ann H. **NORTHAM**, of Marlborough, Mar. 16, 1834, by Rev. Chauncey Lee	220
Asa, m. Jerusha **CARTER**, Apr. 26, 1752	9
Asa, s. [Asa & Jerusha], b. May 1, 1753	9
Asa, s. [Asa ;& Jerusha], d. June 8, 1781	9
Asa, s. [Joel & Abigail Robins], b. Apr. 26, 1791; d. Nov. 24, 1791	10
Asa, s. [Joel & Rachel], b. Mar. 20. 1798	10
Asa, Sr., d. May 11, 1799	9
Asa, m. Caroline **HALE**, Oct. [ ], 1832	60
Betsey, d. [Israel & Elizabeth], b. May 2, 1786	18
Betsey, [w. Elijah], d. Apr. 7, 1810	28
Caroline, d. [Roger & Eunice], b. Sept. 7, 1806	27
Caroline, of Marlborough, m. Luke **RISLEY**, of St. Louis, Mo., Dec. 31, 1829, by Rev. William Jarvis	214
Caroline, d. [Asa & Caroline], b. Aug. 6, 1844	60
Carter, s. [Roger & Eunice], b. June 10, 1804	27
Charles, s. [Roger & Eunice], b. July 1, 1817	27
David, s. [Asa ;& Jerusha], b. Oct. 5, 1760	9
David, s. [Asa & Jerusha], d. Aug. 1, 1793	9
David, s. [Roger & Eunice], b. Aug. 13, 1809	27
Dolly Olmstead, d. [Roger & Eunice], b. Mar. 3, 1797	27
Edwin, s. [Joel & Rachel], b. Nov. 15, 1799	10
Eleazer Hale, [s. Asa & Caroline], b. May 12, 1842	60
Elijah, s. [Israel & Elizabeth], b. Sept. 24, 1784	18
Elijah, m. Betsey **STRONG**, Apr. 15, 1809	28
Elijah, m. Lois **WORTHINGTON**, of Colchester, Feb. 15, 1811	28
Elizabeth, w. Israel, d. Apr. 6, 1795	18
Elizabeth, of Marlborough, m. John **HOLLISTER**, of Hanover, O., July 19, 1826, by Rev David B Ripley	210
Emily, d. [Joel & Rachel], b. Apr. 25, 1805	10
Emily, m. Royal **KINGSBURY**, b. of Marlborough, Apr. 20, 1828, by Rev. George C. Shepard, of Hebron	212

MARLBOROUGH VITAL RECORDS

Page

FOOTE (cont.)

Emily, Mrs., b. in East Haddam, d. Nov. 1, 1848, ae 41 1/2 yrs.	75-6
Emily Hale*, [d. Asa & Caroline], d. Jan. 15, 1844 *(Perhaps Eleazer Hale Foote)	60
Erastus, s. [Israel & Elizabeth], b. Feb. 28, 1788	18
Eunice, d. [Roger & Eunice], b. May 12, 1791	27
Ezra, s. [Asa & Jerusha], b. Aug. 22, 1757	9
Ezra, s. [Asa & Jerusha], d. May 16, 1780	9
Ezra, s. [Roger & Eunice], b. Oct. 30, 1792; d. July 29, 1793	27
Ezra, s. [Roger & Eunice], b. Jan. 7, 1795	27
Frances E., d. [George & Rachel Caroline], b. Jan. 7, 1830	39
Francis Edward, s. [Elijah & Lois], b. June 28, 1814	28
Frances Edwards, s. [Elijah & Lois], d. Oct. 27, 1825	28
George, s. [Joel & Rachel], b. Oct. 5, 1801; d. Oct. 7, 1801	10
George, s. [Joel & Rachel], b. Oct. 22, 1802	10
George, s. [Elijah & Lois], b. Aug. 13, 1818	28
George, m. Rachel Caroline **JONES**, Sept. 5, 1824	39
Horace, s. [Roger & Eunice], b. Mar. 21, 1799	27
Israel, 2nd, m Sarah **OTIS**, Nov. 5, 1778	18
Israel, m. Elizabeth **WORTHINGTON**, Mar. 17, 1782	18
Israel, s. [Israel & Elizabeth], b. Jan. 19, 1783	18
Israel, m. Prudence **HALE**, Feb. 1, 1797	18
Israel, d. May 18, 1826	18
Jerusha, d. [Asa & Jerusha], b. Feb. 24, 1755	9
Jerusha, w. [Asa], d. May 15, 1770	9
Jerusha, d. [Joel & Abigail Robins], b. Jan. 4, 1789	10
Jerusha, d. [Asa & Jerusha], d. May 30, 1793	9
Joel, s. [Asa & Jerusha], b. June 26, 1763	9
Joel, m. Abigail Robins **LORD**, Oct. 28, 1787	10
Joel, m. Rachel **LORD**, of East Haddam, Nov. 15, 1796	10
Joel, s. [Asa & Caroline], b. Apr. 10, 1840	60
Joel, [s. Asa & Caroline], d. Jan. 14, 1844	60
Joel Worthington, s. [Elijah & Lois], b. May 25, 1822	28
Justin, s. [Israel & Elizabeth], b. Apr. 1, 1790	18
Justin Henry, s. [Elijah & Betsey], b. Apr. 3, 1810	28
Linus, s. [Roger & Eunice], b. July 12, 1813	27
Margaret, m. Isaac **BIGELOW**, Dec. 25, 1806	19
Marina, d. [Roger & Eunice], b. Jan. 16, 1812; d. Apr. 16, 1812	27
Mary Jane, d. [George & Rachel Caroline], b. Nov. 30, 1832	39
Polly, d. [Israel & Prudence], b. Mar. 25, 1798	18
Rachel, w. Joel, d. Oct. 6, 1843	10
Rachel Caroline, d. [George & Rachel Caroline], b. June 22, 1825	39
Rachel Lord, d. [Joel & Rachel], b. Jan. 25, 1809; d. May 5, 1809	10
Robbins, d. [Joel & Abigail Robins], b. Jan. 4, 1795	10
Robbins, d. [Joel & Abigail Robbins], d. Jan. 12, 1795	10
Roger, s. [Asa & Jerusha], b. June 9, 1765	9
Roger, m. Eunice **BULKLEY**, May 26, 1790	27
Samuel Edwin, s. [Elijah & Lois], b. June 23, 1815	28
Samuel Philips Lord, s. [Joel & Rachel], b. Aug. 10, 1801; d. Sept. 20, 1812	10
Sarah, d. [Israel, 2nd & Sarah], b. Aug. 2, 1779	18
Sarah w. Israel, d. Feb. 1, 1781	18
Sarah, d. Israel, m. Roger **HALE**, Dec. 24, 1801	18

100 BARBOUR COLLECTION

	Page
FOOTE (cont.)	
Sophia, d. [Israel & Prudence], b. Nov. 9, 1800	18
Sophia, of Marlborough, m. Jonathan **DEXTER**, of Killingly, Jan. 31, 1827, by Rev. David B. Ripley	211
William L., s. [Joel & Rachel], b. Mar. 27, 1807	10
William Worthington, s. [Elijah & Lois], b. Jan. 8, 1812	28
-----, s. [Israel & Elizabeth], b. Mar. 23, [1795]; d. Mar. 27, 1795	18
-----, d. Oct. 28, 1848, ae 1 d.	75-6
FOX, Julianna, m. Enos **COLEMAN**, Dec. 9, 1824, by Sam[uel] F. Jones, J.P.	208
Mercy, m. James **LOVELAND**, of Glastonbury, [ ], 28, 1822, by Sam[ue]l F. Jones, J.P.	207
FREEMAN, David, of Hebron, m. Mary **ROBINSON**, of Marlborough, July 30, 1820, by Rev. Nathan B. Burgess, Glastonbury	206
Jane, [m. Absolom **THOMAS**,]	34
John, of Hebron, m. Caroline **PHELPS**, of Marlborough, Nov. 4, 1840, by Sylvester Selden	226
FRITH, Mary, Factory worker, d. July 9, 1848; ae 28, in Philadelphia	69-70
FULLER, Asahel, of Colchester, m. Nancy **INGRAHAM**, of Marlborough, Oct. 16, 1825, by Rev. David B. Ripley	209
Charles R., of Columbia, m. Sophia **SAUNDERS**, of Marlborough, Sept. 11, 1834, by Rev. Chauncey Lee	220
Eleanor Frances, d. Joel, Farmer & Emeline, b. Jan. [ ], 1850	81-2
Emeline, m. Julius **WELCH**, Nov. 16, 1826, by Sam[uel] F. Jones, J.P.	210
James, Farmer, ae 22, b. in Salisbury, res. Marlborough, m. Adalaide **SEARS**, ae 30, b. in Chatham, Mar. 29, 1849, by Rev. Hiram Bell (1850?)	77-8
James, of Marlborough, m. [ ] **SEARS**, of East Hampton, Mar. 29, 1850, by Rev. Hiram Bell	236
-----, d. James, Laborer, ae 21 & Adaline, ae 22, Middle Haddam, b. Nov. 14, 1850	85-6
-----, d. Jan. 2, 1851; ae 5 w.	79-80
GELSTON, Matilda W., ae 23, res. Marlborough, m. Daniel H. **READ**, Tanner, ae 23, b. in Middletown, res. Coventry, Mar. 19, 1849, by Rev. Solomon G. Hitchcock	73-4
GILBERT, Eleazer Carter, [s. Sylvester & Eunice], d. Dec. 23, 1829	38
Elijah K., of Hamilton, N.Y., m. Ann **CARRIER**, of Marlborough, Jan. 21, 1827, by Rev. David B. Ripley	211
Eunice, d. [Sylvester & Eunice], b. May 30, 1817	38
Eunice, m. Lucius W. **McINTOSH**, Apr. 5, 1836, by Rev. Chauncey Lee	224
Jerusha, d. [Sylvester & Eunice], b. June 7, 1810	38
Jerusha, d. [Sylvester & Eunice], d. Dec. 28, 1830	38
Joseph C., Saddler, b. in Hebron, res. Hebron, m. Josephine **CASE**, Factory worker, res. Marlborough, Mar. 15, 1848, by Rev. Hiram Bell	67-8
Joseph C., of Manchester, m. Josephine **CASE**, of Marlborough, Mar. 15, 1848, by Rev. Hiram Bell	234
Sylvester, m. Eunice **CARTER**, Nov. 26, 1805	38
Sylvester Carter, s. [Sylvester & Eunice], b. Apr. 18, 1824* *(Probably 1807)	38
Sylvester Carter, s. [Sylvester & Eunice], d. Dec. 31, 1830	38

	Page
GILDERSLEEVE, Henry, of Portland, m. Emily F. **NORTHAM**, of Marlborough, May 25, 1843, by Alpheas Geer, Minister, in Hebron	228
GILLETT, GILLETTE, David, twin with Dianna, s. Nathan, sawyer, & Abby, b. Sept. 8, 1849	81-2
Dianna, twin with David, d. Nathan, sawyer, & Abby, b. Sept. 8, 1849	81-2
Ellen, d. Nathan, Miller, ae 26 & Abigail, ae 33, b. May 13, 18348	65-6
GILMAN, Franklin, Trackman, b. in Burlington, Vt., res. Springfield, Mass., m. Calista J. **RATHBURN**, Milliner, ae 26, b. in Vernon, res. Marlborough, Feb. 4, 1849, by Rev. Rob[er]t McGonegal	73-4
GOODRICH, Ralph C., of Portland, m. Emily T. **ANDREWS**, of Marlborough, Nov. 22, 1846, by Rev. Hiram Bell	233
GOODWIN, Mary, of Marlborough, m. Azis **EASTON**, of East Hartford, Sept. 23, 1830, by Rev. Chauncey Lee	215
GRIFFIN, Emily S., of Marlborough, m. W[illia]m H. **TREAT**, of Middletown, Aug. 11, 1845, by L. C. Collins	232
HADING, Lucinda, m. Julius Hollister **SPENCER**, b. of Marlborough, Apr. 3, 1831, by Chauncey Lee	216
HALE, Anson, s. Anson, Farmer, ae 40 & Hannah, b. Apr. [ ], 1851	85-6
Caroline, m. Asa **FOOTE**, Oct. [ ], 1832	60
Israel Foote, s. Roger & Sarah, b. Apr. 21, 1804	18
Prudence, m. Israel **FOOTE**, Feb. 1, 1797	18
Roger, m. Sarah **FOOTE**, d. of Israel, Dec. 24, 1801	18
Sarah, w. Roger, d. Apr. 25, 1804	18
Titus, s. Roger & Sarah, b. Oct. 14, 1802	18
HALING, Alfred Watrous, s. Alfred, Mule Spinner, ae 34 & Sarah, ae 28, b. June 11, 1848	65-6
Jemima, m. Seth **DOAN**, May 13, 1807	21
Laura, of Marlborough, m. Isaac **MORLEY**, of Glastonbury, Oct. 22, 1833, by Rev. Chauncey Lee	219
HALL, Charles, [s. Gustavus], b. May 27, 1833	54
Charlotte Electa, [d. Gustavus], b. Sept. 27, 1841	54
Daniel, [twin with David Skinner, s. Gustavus], b. Aug. 18, 1851	54
David, of Hebron, m. Martha C. **NORTHAM**, of Marlborough, May 16, 1826, by Rev. David B Ripley	209
David Skinner, s. Gustavus, Farmer, ae 40 & Louisa, ae 40, b. Apr. 18, 1850	85-6
David Skinner, [twin with Daniel, s. Gustavus], b. Aug. 18, 1851	54
Elizabeth, [d. Gustavus], b. Aug. 27, 1847	54
Ezra, [s. Gustavus], b. May 11, 1835	54
Ezra, b. in Hebron, d. Feb. 25, 1850, ae 68	79-80
Gustavus, m. Louisa **SKINNER**, Dec. 15, 1831, by Rev. Chauncey Lee	216
Gustavus E., [s. Ezra], b. Feb. 13, 1810	53
Joel, [s. Gustavus], b. Aug. 1, 1845	54
Martin, [s. Gustavus], b. June 14, 1837	54
Martin, [s. Gustavus], b. Sept. 18, 1852	54
Mary, [d. Gustvus], b. Aug. 16, 1843	54
-----, d. Aug. 20, 1850, ae 2 d.	79-80
HASKELL Philo, d. Sept. 17, 1847, ae 2 m.	69-70

	Page
HEMPSTEAD, HEMSTEAD, Abby A., m. William **FINLEY**, Aug. 27, 1838	13
Abby Ann, m. William **FINLEY**, Aug. 27, 1838, by Rev. Charles Nichols	226
Daniel, m. Betsey **BIGELOW**, b. of Marlborough, Feb. 11, 1827, by Rev. David B. Ripley	211
John A., Rev., m. Ann **BIGELOW**, June 14, 1837, by Rev. W. F. Vaill	224
HERVEY, Alfred, m. Dolly **KNEELAND**, Apr. 27, [1836], by Rev. Chauncey Lee	224
HEYDEN, Miriam, of Marlborough, m. Ottenill **WARRELL**, Jr.*, of Woonsocket, Aug. 6, 1837, by Rev. W[illia]m F. Vaill. Int. Pub. July 30, 1837, Woonsocket, by Joseph Smith *(Perhaps "Othniel **WARREN**, Jr.?")	225
HIGGINS, Daniel, Dea., of Glastonbury, m. Elizabeth **BIGELOW**, of Marlborough, [Feb.] 17, [1851], by Rev. W. C Fiske	238
Deuel*, Farmer, ae 58, b. in Glastonbury, res. Glastonbury, m. 2nd w. Elizabeth **BIGELOW**, Teacher, ae 44, Feb. 17, 1851, by Warren C. Fiske *(Probably "Daniel")	83-4
HILLS, Asahel, [s. Ephraim], b. June 6, 1812	45
Betsey, [d. Ephraim], b. June 21, 1806	45
Betsey, m. Edmund **BLISH**, Mar. 24, 1829, by Oliver Phelps, J.P.	213
Britta Curtis, [ch. of Ephraim], b. Sept. 23, 1798	45
Cornelia, [d. Ephraim], b. June 22, 1820	45
Cynthia Ann, [d. Ephraim], b. Apr. 10, 1824	45
David, [s. Ephraim], b. Dec. 20, 1804	45
Ephraim, Farmer & Shoemaker, d. Apr. 26, [1848]; ae 71	69-70
Erskine, of Enfield, m. Julia **WRISLEY**, of Marlborough, Mar. 22, 1837, by Elder Jeremiah Stocking	224
Horace, of Hartford, m. Lucy **RISLEY**, of Marlborough, May 1, 1833, by Jeremiah Stocking, Elder	218
J. B., s. Lyman, Teamster, ae 35 & Alvira, ae 34, b. Jan. 1, 1851	85-6
Lyman, [s. Ephraim], b. May 22, 1817	45
Nancy, [d. Ephraim], b. June 17, 1810	45
Nancy, m. Francis **COTTON**, Nov. 29, 1832, by Oliver Phelps, J.P.	218
Philo, [s. Ephraim], b. May 30, 1808	45
Sherman, [s. Ephraim], b. Dec. 8, 1814	45
HILTON, Lydia, m. Brewster C. **HUXFORD**, b. of Marlborough, May 8, 1825, by Rev. David B. Ripley	209
HINKLEY, Phelena, of Lebanon, m. Abraham **TILLOTSON**, of Marlborough, Nov. 22, 1846, by Rev. Hiram Bell	233
HODGE, Elisha, of Hebron, m. Mary L. **ROOTE**, of Marlborough, Apr. 5, 1843, by Hiram Bell	228
HOLCOMB, George, of Simsbury, m. Martha **RODMAN**, of Marlborough, Feb. 20, 1827, by Rev. David B. Ripley	211
HOLLISTER, Alpheas, of Sagratus, N.Y., m. Mary **PALMER**, of Marlborough, June 8, 1820, by Rev. David B. Ripley	206
John, of Hanover, O., m. Elizabeth **FOOTE**, of Marlborough, July 19, 1826, by Rev. David B. Ripley	210
HOOD, -----, d. [ ]	79-80
HOSFORD [see also **HUXFORD**], Demis, m. Roger **BLISH**, Sept. [ ], 1794	62
Hope, b. Jan. 6, 1772; m. Ashbel **PHELPS**, Jr., May 16, 1793	32

	Page
HOSFORD (cont.)	
Lucy, m. John S. **JONES**, b. of Marlborough, May 1, 1833, by Jeremiah Stocking, Elder	218
Lydia, m. Joel **WASHBURN**, Nov. 16, 1807	25
Mindwell, m. Moses **PELTON**, May 14, 1791	8
Polly, m. David **FINLEY**, Apr. 16, 1800	13
Sarah J., m. John S. **JONES**, b. of Marlborough, Oct. 6, 1823, by Jeremiah Stocking, J.P.	208
HOUER*, Austin, Farmer, ae 25, b. in Tolland, res. Tolland, m. Jane **WILBUR**, Farming, ae 17, b. in Marlborough, Nov. 11, [1850], by Asa Day *(**HOUSE** (?))	77-8
HUBBARD, Edwin, m. Lucy **PHELPS**, Nov. 25, 1834, by Rev. Chauncey Lee	221
Joseph W., of Clinton, N.Y., m. Olive S. **CARRIER**, of Marlborough, Aug. 21, 1850, by Rev. Hiram Bell	237
Matilda, of Marlborough, m. Charles **CHAPMAN**, of Glastonbury, May 7, 1845, by Rev. Hiram Bell	231
HURLBUT, Charles, of Chatham, m. Emela **DICKINSON**, of Marlborough, June 20, 1827, by Jeremiah Stocking, J.P.	211
HUXFORD, [see also **HOSFORD**], Brewster C., m. Lydia **HILTON**, b. of Marlborough, May 8, 1825, by Rev. David B. Ripley	209
Chelsea, m. Joseph **CARRIER**, Sept. 5, 1827, by Oliver Phelps, J.P.	212
Hannah, of Marlborough, m. Ansel **CHAPMAN**, of Glastonbury, Jan. 15, 1823, by Rev. David B. Ripley (**HOSFORD**?)	207
INGHAM, [see also **INGRAHAM**], Marsilva, m. Amos **DEAN**, Nov. 5, 1795	26
INGRAHAM, INGRAM, [see also **INGHAM**], Andrew, s. [Joseph, Jr. & Eunice], b. Sept. 3, 1807	42
Andrew, m. Emeline **FINLEY**, Dec. 13, 1833, by Rev. Chauncey Lee	218
Ansel McIntosh, s. [Elisha & Sarah], b. Mar. 9, 1816	35
Celinda Penelope, d. [Elisha & Sarah], b. Feb. 19, 1815	35
Eleanor, d. [Elisha & Sarah], b. Sept. 25, 1813	35
Elias, s. [Joseph, Jr. & Eunice], b. Oct. 1, 1805	42
Elisha, m. Sarah **INGRAM**, Apr. 15, 1813	35
Esther, m. Joshua **ROOT**, Jr., Nov. 8, 1811	36
Frances, m. Charles **BENNET**, farmer, b. in Chatham, res. Marlborough, July [ ], 1850], by [ ]	77-8
Joseph, Jr., b. July 8, 1776; m. Eunice **CARRIER**, Dec. 28, 1803	42
Nancy, of Marlborough, m. Asahel **FULLER**, of Colchester, Oct. 16, 1825, by Rev. David B Ripley	209
Sarah m. Elisha **INGRAM**, Apr. 15, 1813	35
William Henry, s. [Elisha & Sarah], b. Dec. 30, 1817	35
ISHAM, Charles, s. [Samuel & Mary], b. Aug. 20, 1784	14
Giles, s. [Samuel & Mary], b. Sept. 25, 1789	14
Jane, b. Feb. 13, 1734; m. Abner **DEAN**, Jan. [ ], 1752; d. July 10, 1813	34
Lucy, d. [Samuel & Mary], b. Sept. 22, 1780	14
Mary, see Mary **KING**	14
Polly, d. [Samuel & Mary], b. Feb. 19, 1776	14
Sally, [d. Samuel & Mary], b. Mar. 13, 1778	14
Samuel, b. Dec. 19, 1752; m. Mary **ADAMS**, Jan. 18, 1775	14
Waitstill, d. [Samuel & Mary], b. Oct. 23, 1786	14

BARBOUR COLLECTION

	Page
JACKSON, Emeline, b. in Marlborough, m. 2nd h. Sylvester E. COOK, Farmer, b. in Chatham, Jan. 27, 1850, by Asa Day	77-8
JEWETT, Henry, res. Springfield, m. Reitenia BASSETT, Sept. [ ], 1849, by Asa Day	77-8
JOHNSON, Persia*, Farmer, ae 57, b. Lyme, m. 2nd w. Philenah TILLOTSON, ae 58, b. Lebanon, Sept. 19, 1847, by Asa Day, J.P. *(Pierce?)	67-8
Pierce, of Columbia, m. Phileman TILLOTSON, of Marlborough, Sept. 19, 1847, by Asa Day, J.P.	234
JONES, Ann, of Marlborough, m. Seth G. BIGELOW, of Chatham, Feb. 14, 1836, by Elder Jeremiah Stocking	223
Ann, m. Seth G. BIGELOW, Feb. 14, 1836; d. Apr. 24, 1842	50
Anna, d. [Samuel Finley & Anna], b. May 25, 1806	12
Celecta*, m. David LORD 2nd, Apr. 29, 1829, by Rev. Chauncey Lee *(Electa?)	213
Charlotte, d. [Samuel Finley & Anna], b. Jan. 4 ,1817	12
Charlotte P., of Marlborough, m. Asa DAY, of Colchester, Dec. 31, 1834, by Rev. Leonard B Griffing	222
Eleazer, ae 23, m Elizabeth KELLOGG, ae 47, Mar. 19, 1851, by Amos B.Latham	83-4
Eleazer, m. Elizabeth KELLOGG, Mar. 19, 1851, by Amos B. Latham, J.P.	238
Electa, d. [Samuel Finley & Anna], b. Apr. 29 ,1809	12
Electa, see also Celecta	
John, s. [Samuel Finley & Anna], b. Jan. 11, 1799; d. Mar. 13, 1801	12
John S., m. Sarah J. HOSFORD, b. of Marlborough, Oct. 6, 1823, by Jeremiah Stocking, J.P.	208
John S., m. Lucy HOSFORD, b. of Marlborough, May 1, 1833, by Jeremiah Stocking, Elder	218
John Samuel, s. [Samuel Finley & Anna], b. Feb. 4, 1802	12
Mary M., of Marlborough, m. Calvin D. PERKINS, of South Glastonbury, Apr. 1, 1838, by Elder Thomas Jones	225
Rachel Caroline, m. George FOOTE, Sept. 5, 1824	39
Samuel, s. [John S .], b. Aug. 4, 1826	36
Samuel Finley, m. Anna STRONG, Sept. 10, 1797	12
Sarah, [w. John S .], d. Mar. 10, 1831	36
William E., m. Emily RICHMOND, b. of Marlborough, Nov. 2, 1846, by Rev. Moses Chace	233
KELLOGG, KELLOG, Abigail, m. John BIGELOW, b. of Marlborough, Nov. 12, 1823, by Rev. David B. Ripley	208
Alfred, of Chatham, m. Philena CARRIER, of Marlborough, Apr. 29, 1830, by Rev. Chauncey Lee	215
Arulia, of Marlborough, m. George BILLINGS, of Hartford, Feb. 11, 1844, by Rev. Hiram Bell	230
Elizabeth, ae 47, m. 2nd h. Eleazer JONES, ae 23, Mar. 19, 1851, by Amos B. Latham	83-4
Elizabeth, m. Eleazer JONES, Mar. 19, 1851, by Amos B. Latham, J.P.	238
Jane K., of East Hampton, m. Asa C. SHAYLOR, of Westchester, Mar. 4, 1851, by Rev. W. C. Fiske	238
Jane K., ae 22, b. in Chatham, m. Asa C. SHALER, Farmer, ae 26, b. in Colchester, res. Colchester, Mar. 6, 1851, by Rev. W. C. Fiske	83-4

MARLBOROUGH VITAL RECORDS

	Page
KELLOGG, KELLOG (cont.)	
Lucy, of Marlborough, m. Elihu P. BUELL, of Hebron, [Feb.] 20, [1833], by Rev. Tertius D. Southworth	218
KENEY, Lydia C., of Newark, Vt., m. David **MOULTON**, of Brookfield, Mass., Nov. 30, 1845, by L. C. Collins	232
KILBORN, Celinda, d. [David, Jr. & Lydia], b. Apr. 17, 1796	7
David, Jr., m. Lydia **WELLES**, b. of Colchester, Mar. 13, 1793	7
David, s. [David, Jr. & Lydia], b. Apr. 12, 1803	7
David Welles, s. [David, Jr. & Lydia], b. July 7, 1800; d. Feb. 20, 1802	7
Edward, s. [David, Jr. & Lydia], b. [ ], 1813	7
Lydia, d. [David, Jr. & Lydia], b. July 12, 1794	7
Marian, d. [David, Jr. & Lydia], b. Aug. 19, 1804	7
Sally, d. [David, Jr. & Lydia], b. Jan. 27, 1798	7
KING, Mary, (**ISHAM**), w. Rev. Solomon & d. of Samuel & Mary **ISHAM**, d. Jan. 1, 1807	14
Mary, see also Polly **ISHAM**	
KINGSBURY, Royal, m. Emily **FOOTE**, b. of Marlborough, Apr. 20, 1828, by Rev. George C Shepard. of Hebron	212
Sabrina, of Tolland, m. Moseley **TALCOTT**, of Marlborough, Nov. 10, 1803	6
KNEELAND, Dolly, m. Alfred **HERVEY**, Apr. 27, [1836], b. Rev. Chauncey Lee	224
Erastus, m. Percy **LORD**, Jan. 7, 1829, by Rev. Chauncey Lee	213
LATHAM, Amos B., b. June 1, 1816, in Hebron; m. Caroline M. [**LOOMIS**], Sept. 5, 1837	52
Amos B., m. Eliza A. **McEVER**, [ ]	52
Amos M., [s. Amos B.], b. Dec. 27, 1846	52
Betsey M., [d. Amos B.], b. Oct. 12, 1840, in Hebron	52
Elizabeth, wid. of a Farmer, b. in Preston, d. Feb. 12, 1849; ae 79	75-6
Harriet J., [d. Amos B. & Caroline M.], b. Dec. 6, 1838, in Hebron	52
Imogene C., [d. Amos B.], b. Apr. 9, 1849	52
Imogene C., d. Amos B. Farmer, ae 29 & Caroline M., ae 33, b. Apr. 9, [1849]	71-2
Joel E., [s. Amos B.], b. Jan. 4, 1845	52
William E., [s. Amos B.], b. Sept. 28, 1842	52
LATHROP, Geo[rge] H., Carpenter, ae 45, b. in Franklin, res. Franklin, m. Delia A. **DUNHAM**, Tailoress, ae 33, Dec. 29, 1850, by Rev. W. C. Fiske	83-4
George H., of Franklin, m. Delia A. **DUNHAM**, of Marlborough, Dec. 29, 1850, by Rev. W. C. Fiske	238
LEWIS, Emily S., d. Daniel C., Farmer & Sophronia, b. Dec. 7, 1849	81-2
LOOMIS, Caroline M., b. Sept. 23, 1820, in Colchester; m. Amos B. **LATHAM**, Sept. 5, 1837	52
LORD, Abigail, d. [Elisha, Jr. & Barsheba], b. Sept. 13, 1801	17
Abigail, of Marlborough, m. Sophron **USHER**, of Chatham, Nov. 8, 1826, by Rev. David B. Ripley	210
Abigail P., of Marlborough, m. W[illia]m **COLES** *, of Canton, Apr. 16, 1851, by Rev. Warren C. Fiske *("**COWLES**", of Norfolk)	238
Abigail P[atience], ae 27, m. W[illia]m **COLES***, Farmer, ae 28, b. in Norfolk, res. Canton, Mar. 6 ,1851, by Rev. Warren C. Fiske *note says, "**COWLES**"	83-4

BARBOUR COLLECTION

	Page
LORD (cont.)	
Abigail Putnam, [d. George & Abigail], b. Nov. 14, 1820	31
Abigail Robbins, see Abigail Robbins Lord **FOOTE**	10
Abigail Rob[b]ins, m. Joel **FOOTE**, Oct. 28, 1787	10
Asahel, s. [Ichabod & Elizabeth], b. July 17, 1787	3
Asahel, s. [Ichabod & Elizabeth], d. Sept. 14, 1814	3
Austin, Physician, ae 24, b. in Coventry, res. North Haven, m. Francis F. **BIGELOW**, ae 22, Aug. 25, 1850, by Rev. Hiram Bell	83-4
Austin, of North Haven, m. Frances F. **BIGELOW**, of Marlborough, Aug. 21, 1850, by Rev. Hiram Bell	237
Authur, [s. Gardiner & Eunice Amelia], b. June 28, 1821	58
Betsey, m. Daniel **BUEL**, Dec. 28, 1807	24
Bulkley, s. [Ichabod & Elizabeth], b. Nov. 21, 1798	3
Caroline, d. [Ichabod & Elizabeth], b. Dec. 10, 1783	3
Caroline, [w. George], d. Apr. 1,1810	31
Caroline, d. [George & Abigail], b. Feb. 11, 1818	31
Caroline, of Marlborough, m. Sherman H. **COWLES**, of Norfolk, May 1, 1842, by Hiram Bell	227
Charles H., [s. Epaphras], b. Apr. 27, 1813	43
Daniel, [s. Epaphras], b. Mar. 4, 1811	43
Daniel, m. Prudence M. **SMITH**, b. of Marlborough Apr. 28, 1844, by Rev. Hiram Bell	230
David, 2nd, m. Celecta **JONES**, Apr. 29, 1829, by Rev. Chauncey Lee	213
David Miller, m. Prude **TALCOTT**, June 27, 1799	15
David Miller, [s. David Miller & Prude], b. Feb. 2, 1804	15
David Miller, d. Jan. 28, 1846	15
Electa Jane, d. [George T.], b. July 24, 1838	29
Eliphalet, [s. Epaphras], b. Feb 9, 1804	43
Eliphalet, m. Lois **BULKELEY**, Nov. 7, 1826	43
Elisha, Jr., m. Barsheba **SELLEW**, Nov.6, 1800	17
Elizabeth, w. Ichabod, b. Oct. 27, 1761	3
Elizabeth, d. [Ichabod & Elizbeth], b. Dec. 25, 1781	3
Elizabeth, w. [Ichabod], d. Aug. 11, 1842	3
Epaphrus, d. May 6 ,1819	31
Frances, d. [Eliphalet & Lois], b. Jan. 24, 1834	43
Gardiner, m. Eunice Amelia **EVERITT**, Sept. [ ], 1817	58
George, m. Caroline **CROCKER**, Jan. 8, 1809	31
George, m. Abigail **EVERETT**, Apr. 27, 1812	31
George Hinman, [s. George & Abigail], b. July 15, 1815	31
George T., m. Mary L. **BLISH**, Oct. 17, 1832, by Rev. Chauncey Lee	217
George Tallcott, s. [David Miller & Prude], b. Mar. 23, 1806	15
Harriet Strong, [d. George & Abigail], b. May 17, 1824	31
Henry, [s. Gardiner & Eunice Amelia], b. Feb. 14, 1823	58
Henry Sherman, [s. Sherman C. & Orphelia T.], b. Oct. 11, 1842	51
Horace, s. [Gardiner & Eunice Amelia], b. Nov. 11, 1818	58
Howel, s. [Ichabod & Elizabeth], b. Mar. 24, 1795	3
Ichabod, b. June 12, 1762; m. Elizabeth [ ], June 14, 1781	3
Ichabod, [s. Ichabod & Elizabeth], b. Oct. 5, 1785	3
Ichabod, d. Feb. 11, 1840	3
John, s. [George T.], b. July 10, 1834	29

	Page
LORD (cont.)	
John Bulkley, m. Mary **BUEL**, Dec. 10, 1778	15
John Bulkeley, s. [David Miller & Prude], b. July 9, 1800	15
Joshua B., [s. Epaphras], b. Mar. 6, 1809	43
Louisa A., d. [Gardiner & Eunice Amelia], b. Apr. 28, 1825	58
Lucius, s. [George T.], b. Mar. 13, 1833	29
Lucius Orlando, s. [David Miller & Prude], b. May 24, 1808	15
Lucius Orlando [s. David Miller & Prude], d. June 14, 1826	15
Lucretia, d. [Ichabod & Elizabeth], b. Jan. 11, 1797	3
Lucretia, [d. Ichabod & Elizabeth], d. Feb. 8, 1839	3
Lucy, d. [Ichabod & Elizabeth], b. Jan. 27, 1801; d. Apr. 13, 1801	3
Lucy, d. [Ichabod & Elizabeth], b. July 12, 1802	3
Mary Buel, d. [David Miller & Prude], b. Feb. 2, 1802	15
Mary Caroline, d. [Sherman C. & Orphelia T.], b. June 26, 1835	51
Noble E., m. Betsey **BULKELEY**, Dec. 14, 1834, by Rev. Chauncey Lee	222
Noble Everitt, s. [George & Abigail], b. Aug. 4, 1813	31
Ogden, s. [Elisha, Jr. & Barsheba], b. Dec. 9, 1802	17
Patience, w. [Epaphras], d. Feb. 26, 1836	31
Piercey, [twin with Prissella, d. Elisha, Jr. & Barsheba], b. Aug. 30, 1804	17
Percy, m. Erastus **KNEELAND**, Jan. 7, 1829, by Rev. Chauncey Lee	213
Phyla, d. [Ichabod & Elizabeth], b. Mar. 25, 1790	3
Prissella, [twin with Piercey, d. Elisha, Jr. & Barsheba], b. Aug. 30, 1804	17
Prudence Ann, d. [David H., Jr.], b. June 21, 1830	30
Rachel, of East Haddam, m. Joel **FOOTE**, Nov. 15, 1796	10
Roger B., [s. George T.], b. Oct. 26, 1844	29
Roxana, d. [Ichabod & Elizabeth], b. Nov. 11, 1792	3
Roxana, m. Russell **BIGELOW**, b. of Marlborough, Nov. 6, 1826, by Rev. David B. Ripley	210
Sarah, d. [Epaphras & Patience], d. Feb. 11, 1826	31
Sherman C., b. Dec. 8, 1809; m. Orphelia T. **BUELL**, Nov. 29, 1832	51
Sherman C., m. Ophelia Theresa **BUELL**, Nov. 29, 1832, by Rev. Chauncey Lee	218
Sherman Crocker, s. [George & Caroline], b. Dec. 8, 1809	31
William C., [s. Epaphras], b. May 6, 1806	43
William Everett, s. [Gardiner & Eunice Amelia], b. Dec. 18, 1827	58
LOVELAND, Harvey, m. Jerusha **DICKINSON**, Nov. 7, 1827, by Oliver Phelps, J.P.	212
James, of Glastonbury, m. Mercy **FOX**, [ ] 28, 1822, by Sam[uel] F. Jones, J.P.	207
LYMAN, Betsey A., ae 20, m. Dudley A. **WRIGHT**, Paper Maker, ae 30, Mar. 12, 1848, by Amos B. Latham, J.P.	67-8
Betsey A., m. Dudley A. **WRIGHT**, Mar. 12, 1848, by Amos B. Latham, J.P.	234
McEVER, Eliza A., m. Amos B. **[LATHAM]**, [ ]	52
McINTOSH, Lucius W., m. Eunice **GILBERT**, Apr. 5, 1836, by Rev. Chauncey Lee	224
MACK, Josiah, m. Hannah **ROOT**, Dec. 3, [1820], by Samuel T. Jones, J.P.	206
Phebe A., m. Horatio **BOLLES**, [ ]	44

	Page
MAINE, Hiram L., m. Mary E. COLEMAN, Mar. 11, 1838, by Rev. W[illia]m F. Vaill	225
MANWARING, Charles, [s. Samuel C.], b. Apr. 13, 1838; d. Feb. 25, 1844	14
Susan C., [d. Samuel C.], b. July 13, 1832	14
MARKALL, Joanna, Mrs., m. Reuben CURTIS, Apr. 17, 1809, by Joel Foote, J.P.	29
MATHEWSON, Joseph, Farmer, b., S. Coventry, res. S. Coventry, m. Sophia P. RATHBURN, ae 42, b. in Vernon, res. Marlborough, Aug. 22, 1848, by Rev. Rob[er]t McGonegal	73-4
MILLER, David, Capt., d. Apr. 11, 1803	26
Lucy, m. Amos STAPLES, of Hampton, Nov. 27, 1835, by Elder Thomas Jones	223
Sarah, w. [Capt. David], d. Oct. 26, 1833	26
MINER, Clarissa, m. Hiram WILSON, Sept. 25, 1834, by Rev. Leonard B Griffing	221
Joseph, m. Adaline WILSON, Sept. 25, 1834, by Rev. Leonard B Griffing	221
MITCHELL, Warren, of East Haddam, m. Angeline MORGAN, of Marlborough, Apr. 16, 1824, by Rev. David B. Ripley	208
MITTSON, Harley T., Farmer, d. Sept. 15, 1847; ae 6 [ ] (Perhaps "TILLOTSON"?)	69-70
MORGAN, Angeline, of Marlborough, m. Warren MITCHELL, of East Haddam, Apr. 16, 1824, by Rev. David B. Ripley	208
Thaddeus B., of Marlborough, m. Betsey STRONG, of Bolton, Oct. 27, 1822, by Rev. David B. Ripley	207
MORLEY, Isaac, of Glastonbury, m. Laura HALING, of Marlborough, Oct. 22, 1833, by Rev. Chauncey Lee	219
MOULTON, David, of Brookfield, Mass., m. Lydia C. KENEY, of Newark, Vt., Nov. 30, 1845, by L. C. Collins	232
MURRY, -----, d. Patrick, Laborer & Mary, b. June [ ], 1850	81-2
NICHOLS, Hannah Octavia, d. [Orry & Hannah], b. Sept. 10, 1808	5
John Benjamin, s. [Orry & Hannah], b. Feb. 6, 1807	5
Phebe Permela, d. Orry & Hannah, b. Oct. 24, 1806	5
NORTHAM, Ann H., of Marlborough, m. Arba FOOTE, of Chester, Mass., Mar. 16, 1834, by Rev. Chauncey Lee	220
Emily F., [d. Oliver], b. Sept. 27, 1819	47
Emily F., of Marlborough, m. Henry GILDERSLEVE, of Portland, May 25, 1843, by Rev. Alpheas Geer, of Hebron	228
Martha C., of Marlborough, m. David HALL, of Hebron, May 16, 1826, by Rev. David B Ripley	209
Ralph, [s. Oliver], b. Aug. 3, 1823	47
Sophia, of Marlborough, m. Ebenezer B. PELTON, of Chatham, Sept. 28, 1834, by Rev. Chauncey Lee	220
NORTON, -----, ch. of William, Machinist & Sophia, b. May [ ], 1850	81-2
OTIS, Sarah, m. Israel FOOTE, 2nd, Nov. 5, 1778	18
OVERTON, Mary B., m. Frederick A. FIELDING, b. of Marlborough, Oct. 3, 1830, by Rev. Chauncey Lee	215
PALMER, Clarissa, of Marlborough, m. Avery TENANT, of Chatham, Jan. 9, 1822, by David B Ripley	207
Mary, of Marlborough, m. Alpheas HOLLISTER, of Sagratus, N.Y., June 8, 1820, by Rev. David B. Ripley	206

	Page
PALMER (cont.)	
William, m. Abigail **BISSEL**, May 29, 1831, by Chauncey Lee, Minister	216
PAYSON, Betsey, m. David B. **RIPLEY**, Jan. 1, 1807	23
PELTON, David Miller, s. [Moses & Mindwell], b. Dec. 7, 1800	8
Ebenezer B., of Chatham, m. Sophia **NORTHAM**, of Marlborough, Sept. 28, 1834, by Rev. Chauncey Lee	220
Elisha, s. [Moses & Mindwell], b. Apr. 26, 1795	8
Frederick, s. [Moses & Mindwell], b. Jan. 17, 1797	8
Moses, m. Mindwell **HOSFORD**, May 14, 1791	8
Susanna, d. [Moses & Mindwell], b. Mar. 30, 1793	8
PENHARLOW, Amanda Ann, d. David D., Laborer, ae 24 & Harriet, ae 23, b. July 22, 1851	85-6
David D., Farmer, ae 23, b. in Mansfield, m. Harriet **FLOOD**, ae 23, Oct. 9, 1850, by Rev. H. Leffingwell	83-4
David D., of Mansfield, m. Harriet **FLOOD**, of Marlborough, Oct. 9, 1850, by Rev. Marvin Leffingwell	237
PERKINS, Ann S., of Marlborough, m. Edwin A. **CLARK**, of Hartford, Apr. 15, 1841, by Hiram Bell	226
Calvin D., of South Glastonbury, m. Mary M. **JONES**, of Marlborough, Apr. 1, 1838, by Elder Thomas Jones	225
John A., s. Hezekiah, Laborer, ae 56 & Elizabeth N., ae 45, b. Aug. 12, 1848	71-2
PETERS, Amelia C., d. Apr. 12, 1848; ae 1 m.	69-70
PHELPS, Aaron, b. Oct. 26, 1781; m. Polly **PHELPS**, Aug. 5, 1805	37
Aaron Root, s. [Aaron & Polly], b. Sept. [ ], 1806	37
Aaron Root, [s. Aaron & Polly], d. Apr. 2, 1810	37
Ashbel, Jr., b. Aug. 23, 1767; m. Hope **HOSFORD**, May 16, 1793	32
Ashbel, Jr., d. Jan. [ ], 1829	32
Ashbel Hosford, s. [Ashbel, Jr. & Hope], b. May 3, 1794	32
Augustus, twin with Erastus, s. [Frederick & Bethiah], b. June 11, 1806	16
Augustus, m. Julia **SKINNER**, Dec. 15, 1831, by Rev. Chauncey Lee	217
Caroline, d. [Oliver], b. Jan. 10, 1815	41
Caroline, of Marlborough, m. John **FREEMAN**, of Hebron, Nov. 4, 1840, by Sylvester Selden	226
Charles H., s. Williamiam, Farmer, ae 35 & Martha, ae 28, b. Feb. 12, 1848	65-6
Cyrus, s. [Oliver], b. Feb. 17, 1799	41
David, s. [Ashbel, Jr. & Hope], b. Apr. 29, 1799	32
David, s. [Frederick & Bethiah], b. May 25, 1800	16
David, s. [Oliver], b. Aug. 31, 1810	41
David, m. Sarah **BIGELOW**, Feb. 1, 1831	32
David, m. Sarah **BIGELOW**, b. of Marlborough, Feb. 1, 1831, by Rev. Chauncey Lee	216
Emeline, d. [Oliver], b. Mar. 11, 1813	41
Emeline, m. W[illia]m **CARRIER**, b. of Marlborough, Aug. 17, 1840, by Hiram Bell	226
Epaphrus, s. [Frederick & Bethiah], b. [ ]	16
Epaphras, [s. Frederick & Bethiah], d. Feb. 16, 1844	16
Erastus, s. [Frederick & Bethiah], b. July 5, 1802; d. Apr. 27 1806	16

PHELPS (cont.)

	Page
Erastus, twin with Augustus, s. [Frederick & Bethiah], b. June 11, 1806	16
Esther, d. [Ashbel, Jr. & Hope], b. Oct. 18, 1809	32
Esther Y., m. Daniel **BROWN**, b. of Marlborough, May 28, 1849, by Rev. Hiram Bell	236
Frederick, m. Bethiah **STOW**, Aug. 25, 1798	16
Frederick, d. Mar. 15, 1842	16
Harriet, of Marlborough, m. William B. **BROWN**, of Colchester, Mar. 28, 1836, by Rev. David Bennett	223
Hope, d. [Ashbel, Jr. & Hope], b. Apr. 4, 1807	32
Hope, w. [Ashbel, Jr.], d. Feb. [ ], 1835	32
Hope H., m. Hiram **WEST**, Dec. 9, 1829	35
Hope H., m. Hiram **WEST**, Dec. 9, 1829, by Rev. Chauncey Lee	214
Jerusha, d. [Ashbel, Jr. & Hope], b. Mar. 19, 1801	32
Jerusha, m. Howell **ROOT**, July 4, 1822	59
Jerusha, m. Joel **ROOT**, b. of Marlborough, July 4, 1822, by Rev. David B. Ripley	207
Lucy, m. David **FINLEY**, Jan. 22, 1784	13
Lucy, d. [Frederick & Bethiah], b. Apr. 5, 1799; d. May 9, 1799	16
Lucy, d. [Frederick & Bethiah], b. Mar. 13 ,1804	16
Lucy, m. Edwin **HUBBARD**, Nov. 25, 1834, by Rev. Chauncey Lee	221
Maryetta, d. [Aaron & Polly], b. July 29, 1810	37
Mariette, m. William B. **BROWN**, Mar. 28, 1836	37
Martha, b. in Hebron, d. Sept. 29, 1849, ae 29	79-80
Oliver, s. [Oliver], b. Oct. 18, 1800	41
Oliver, s. [Oliver], d. July 16, 1801	41
Oliver, s. [Oliver], b. Jan. 23, 1803	41
Oliver, Jr., m. Lucy Ann **WEST**, Nov. 4, 1829, by Rev. Chauncey Lee	214
Polly, b. Aug. 14, 1788; m. Aaron **PHELPS**, Aug. 5, 1805	37
Sarah, d. [Oliver], b. Oct. 23, 1795	41
Sarah Ann, d. [David & Sarah], b. Oct. 16, 1833	32
Sophia, d. [Frederick & Bethiah], b. Mar. 17, 1811	16
Timothy, s. [Oliver], b. Mar. 26, 1806	41
William, s. [Frederick & Bethiah], b. Dec. 22, 1812	16
W[illia]m, Farmer, ae 38, b. in Colchester, m. 2nd w. Elizabeth **EMMONS**, ae 19, Oct. 25, 1850, by Rev. S. D. Jewett	83-4
-----, s. David, Farmer & Hannah, b. July 14, 1850	81-2
POOLE, William, s. Elijah & Mary, b. Jan.2, 1809	30
PORTER, Sally, m. Eben **STRONG**, Mar. 17, 1807	20
POST, John H., of Coventry, Chenango Cty., N.Y., m. Dilight **FINLEY**, of Marboroough, June 29, 1834, by Jeremiah Stocking, Elder	220
PRATT, Daniel, of West Chester, m. Harriet **CARRIER**, of Marlborough, Sept. 18, 1828, by Rev. Chauncey Lee	212
RANDS, Sophia Maria, b. Feb. 14, 1807	25
RANN, Sophia, m. Oren **DUNHAM**, Oct. 4, 1826, by Rev. David B Ripley	209
RATHBURN, Calista J., Milliner, ae 26, b. in Vernon, res. Marlborough, m. Franklin **GILMAN**, Trackman, b. in Burlington, Vt., res. Springfield, Mass., Feb. 4, 1849, by Rev. Rob[er]t McGonegal	73-4

MARLBOROUGH VITAL RECORDS

Page

RATHBURN (cont.)
   Sophia P., ae 42, b. in Vernon, res. Marlborough, m. Joseph
      MATHEWSON, Farmer, b. in S. Coventry, res. S. Coventry,
      Aug. 22, 1848, by Rev. Rob[er]t McGonegal   73-4
READ, REED, Collins, of East Windsor, m. Malenda **WYLLYS**, of
   Marlborough, Nov. 8, 1829, by Rev. Chauncey Lee   214
   Daniel H., Tanner, ae 23, b. in Middletown, res. Coventry, m.
      Matilda W. **GELSTON**, ae 23, res. Marlborough, Mar. 19,
      1849, by Rev. Solomon G. Hitchcock   73-4
RICH, Harriet, of Marlborough, m. John R. **WHEELER**, of Willimantic,
   Aug. 26, 1849, by Rev. Hiram Bell   236
RICHMOND, Albert W., [s. William W.], b. June 30, 1831   44
   Emily, m. William E. **JONES**, b. of Marlborough, Nov. 2, 1846, by
      Rev. Moses Chace   233
   Emily F., [d. William W.], b. Nov.17, 1826   44
   Frances A., [ch. of William W.], b. May 1, 1828   44
   Harriet K., [d. William W.], b. Dec. 31, 1823   44
   William H., [s. William W.], b. Oct. 23, 1821   44
RILEY, Betsey E., Factory worker, b. in Glastonbury, res.
   Marlborough, m. Joseph **CROUCH**, Farmer, b. in Glastonbury,
   res. Marlborough, Aug. 28, 1847, by Daniel Phelps, J.P.   67-8
   Betsey E., m. Joseph **CROUCH**, b. of Marlborough, Aug. 28,
      1847, by David Phelps, J.P.   234
RIPLEY, Caroline, d. [David & Betsey], b. May 22, [1812]; d. Aug. 5,
   1812   23
   Caroline, d. [David B. & Betsey], b. Aug. 9, 1813   23
   Catharine, [d. David B. & Betsey], b. Jan. 6, 1823   23
   Cynthia Williston, d. [David B. & Betsey], b. June 29, 1816   23
   David B., m. Betsey **PAYSON**, Jan. 1, 1807   23
   David Elliott, [s. David B. & Betsey], b. Aug. 16, 1819   23
   Elizabeth, d. [David B. & Betsey], b. Feb. 23, 1810   23
   Mary, d. [David & Betsey], b. Oct. 10, 1825   23
RISLEY, Lucy, of Marlborough, m. Horace **HILLS**, of Hartford, May 1,
   1833, by Jeremiah Stocking, Elder   218
   Luke, of St. Louis, Mo., m. Caroline **FOOTE**, of Marlborough,
      Dec. 31, 1829, by Rev. William Jarvis   214
ROBINSON, Mary, of Marlborough, m. David **FREEMAN**, of Hebron,
   July 30, 1820, by Rev. Nathan B. Burgess, Glastonbury   206
RODMAN, Martha, of Marlborough, m. George **HOLCOMB**, of
   Simsbury, Feb. 20, 1827, by Rev. David B. Ripley   211
   Mary, m. Orrin **DICKINSON**, Sept. 16, 1833, by Oliver Phelps, J.P.   219
ROGERS, Eunice, of Chatham, m. John S. **WHITNEY**, of Marlborough,
   Nov. 5, 1820, by Rev. David B. Ripley   206
ROOD, Harriet A., m. John E. **BROOKS**, Mar. 20, 1843, by Rev. Hiram
   Bell   228
ROOT, ROOTE, Antoinett, d. [Howell & Jerusha], b. May 26, 1826   59
   Aristarchus Smith, s. [Edward & Thankful], b. Apr. 14, 1804   33
   Bishop, m. Emily **CARRIER**, Mar. 27, 1825, by Sam[ue]l F. Jones,
      J.P.   208
   Chauncey Langdon, s. [Edward & Thankful], b. May 26, 1802   33
   Cynthia, d. [Edward & Thankful], b. Apr. 14, 1806   33
   Delia L., [d. Elisha], b. May 14, 1816   63

	Page
ROOT, ROOTE (cont.)	
Edward, b. Nov. 4, 1772; m. Thankful **SHATTUCK**, Sept. 19, 1796	33
Edward, s. [Edward & Thankful], b. July 24, 1798	33
Edward, of Marlborough, m. Amelia **ANDREWS**, June 1, 1823, by Sam[ue]l F. Jones, J.P.	208
Eliza, d. [Joshua, Jr. & Esther], b. Sept. 7, 1813	36
Ezekiel, s. [Edward & Thankful], b. June 18, 1808	33
Gustavus, s. [Elisha], b. Mar. 19, 1823	63
Hannah, d. [Edward & Thankful], b. July 8, 1800	33
Hannah, m. Josiah **MACK**, Dec. 3, [1820], by Samuel T. Jones, J.P.	206
Hoel, m. Jerusha **PHELPS**, b. of Marlborough, July 4, 1822, by Rev. David B Ripley	207
Howell, m. Jerusha **PHELPS**, July 4, 1822	59
Howell, Farmer, ae [ ], m. 2nd w. Prudence **BLISH**, June 5, 1850, by Rev. Hiram Bell	77-8
Howell, m. Prudence H. **BLISH**, June 5, 1850, by Rev. Hiram Bell	236
Jane E., of Marlborough, m. Cyres **WELCH**, of Chatham, Sept. 11, 1842, by Rev. Lorrene Pierce	227
Joshua, Jr., m. Esther **INGRAHAM**, Nov. 8, 1811	36
Laura S., [d. Elisha], b. May 21, 1820	63
Laura S., of Marlborough, m. Thomas N. **WILLIAMS**, of Chatham, Apr. 15, 1846, by Rev. Hiram Bell	232
Laurett, d. [Howell & Jerusha], b. Dec. 17, 1822	59
Mary L., d. [Elisha], b. Aug. 17, 1813	63
Mary L., of Marlborough, m. Elisha **HODGE**, of Hebron, Apr. 5, 1843, by Hiram Bell	228
Ralph, m. Elizabeth **STAPLES**, Feb. 25, 1821, by Rev. David B. Ripley	206
Randall Augustus, s. [Edward & Thankful], b. Aug. 8, 1811	33
Samuel F. J., m. Maria **DICKERSON**, b. of Marlborough, Oct. 20, 1844, by Hiram Bell	230
Sherman E., s. [Elisha], b. July 7, 1810	63
Sophronia, m. John W. **FINLEY**, b. of Marlborough, June 6, 1833, by Jeremiah Stocking, Elder	219
Stephen, s. [Joshua, Jr. & Esther], b. Mar. 12, 1812	36
ROUND, Benjamin, of Providence, R.I., m Eliza **DARBY**, of Marlborough, Feb. 28, 1830, by Joel Foote, J.P.	214
RUSSELL, Benjamin, m. Olive **RUSSELL**, Mar. 2, 1832, by Oliver Phelps, J.P.	217
Olive, m. Benjamin **RUSSELL**, Mar. 2, 1832, by Oliver Phelps, J.P.	217
Oliver, m. Eliza [ ], b. of Marlborough, Jan. 17, 1837, by Rev. Calvin Chapin, of Rocky Hill	226
SAUNDERS, Chester, of Hebron, m. Polly **BROWN**, of Marlborough, Jan. 26, 1826, by Rev. David B. Ripley	209
Delight, Mrs., m. Josiah **WATROUS**, Mar. 29, 1840, by Hiram Bell	226
Eliza, m. Roderick **CARRIER**, Nov. 27, 1834, by Rev. Chauncey Lee	221
Sophia, of Marlborough, m. Charles R. **FULLER**, of Columbis, Sept. 11, 1834, by Rev. Chauncey Lee	220
SEARS, Adalaide, ae 30, b. in Chatham, m. James Fuller, Farmer, ae 22, b. in Salisbury, res. Marlborough, Mar. 29, 1849, by Rev. Hiram Bell	77-8

	Page
SEARS (cont.)	
Selden P., of Chatham, m. Eveline **DICKINSON**, of Marlborough, Nov. 30, 1843, by Rev. Hiram Bell	229
-----, of East Hampton, m. James **FULLER**, of Marlborough, Mar. 29, 1850, by Rev. Hiram Bell	236
SELLEW, Barsheba, m. Elisha **LORD**, Jr., Nov. 6, 1800	17
SHALER, [see under **SHAYLOR**]	
SHATTUCK, Thankful, b. Oct. 14, 1777; m. Edward **ROOT**, Sept. 19, 1796	33
SHAYLOR, SHALER, Asa C., of Westchester, m. Jane K. **KELLOGG**, of East Hampton, Mar. 4, 1851, by Rev. W. C Fiske	238
Asa C., Farmer, ae 26, b. in Colchester, res. Colchester, m. Jane K. **KELLOGG**, ae 22, b. in Chatham, Mar. 6, 1851, by Rev. W. C. Fiske	83-4
SHEPARD, Charles Lord, s. [Cornelius & Sarah], b. Mar. 24, 1806	1
Chauncey Knowles, s. [Cornelius & Sarah], b. Feb. 20, 1804	1
Cornelius, m. Sarah **SKINNER**, Nov. 10, 1790	1
Cornelius, s. [Cornelius & Sarah], b. Dec. 1, 1794	1
David, s. [Cornelius & Sarah], b. Apr. 19, 1791	1
Ely, [s. Cornelius & Sarah], b. Jan. 19, 1799	1
Jerusha, d. [Cornelius & Sarah], b. Nov. 22, 1796	1
Pamela, d. [Cornelius & Sarah], b. Oct. 11, 1801	1
Sally, d. [Cornelius & Sarah], b. Nov. 21, 1792	1
SHERMAN, Henry, Laborer, m. Mary **BLYTHE**, Laborer, Sept. [ ], 1849, by Rev. John Cooper	77-8
Nehemiah G., Warper in Factory, ae 21, b. in Chatham, res. Marlborough, m. Sarah A. **FIELDING**, Factory worker, ae 16, Nov. 30, 1848, by Rev. Hiram Bell	73-4
Nehemiah G., m. Sarah A. **FIELDING**, b. of Marlborough, Nov. 30, 1848, by Rev. Hiram Bell	235
William Henry, m. Mary **BLYTHE**, b. of Marlborough, Sept. 16, 1849, by Rev. John Cooper, East Hampton	235
-----, d. Nov. 21, 1849, ae 10 w.	79-80
SHERWOOD, Josephine, b. in England, d. Feb. 24, 1849, ae 6 w.	75-6
SISSON, Harriet, m Courtland **BURR**, Manufacturer, res. East Haddam, Nov. 4, 1849, by Asa Day	77-8
SKINNER, Aaron, m. Alice **BROCKWAY**, Nov. 24, 1802	5
Aaron Lathrop, s. [Aaron & Alice], b. Nov. 29, 1803	5
David, d. Nov. [ ], 1850; ae 82	79-80
Deborah, m. Nathan **DICKINSON**, Nov. 18, 1758	11
Elizabeth, d. [Benjamin], b. Mar. 7, 1825	40
Harriet A., [d. Benjamin], b. Oct. 15, 1822	40
Hope, m. Jonathan G. **BIGELOW**, Sept. 13, 1827, by Rev. Charles Nichols	212
Julia, m. Augustus **PHELPS**, Dec. 15, 1831, by Rev. Chauncey Lee	217
Louisa, m. Gustavus **HALL**, Dec. 15, 1831, by Rev. Chauncey Lee	216
Mary E., res. Marlborough, m. Elisha H. **EVERETT**, Farmer, b. in Marlborough, res. Nantucket, Sept. 27, 1847, by Rev. Hiram Bell	67-8
Mary E., of Marlborough, m. Elisha H. **EVERETTE**, of New Bedford, Mass., Sept. 27, 1847, by Rev. Edgar J. Doolittle, Hebron	234
Samantha M., d. [Benjamin], b Sept. 30, 1826	40

	Page
SKINNER (cont.)	
Sarah, m. Cornelius **SHEPARD**, Nov. 10, 1790	1
SLATE, Esther M., m. Chauncey **BLISH**, Mar. 2, 1834	58
SMITH, Prudence M., m. Daniel **LORD**, b. of Marlborough, Apr. 28, 1844, by Rev. Hiram Bell	230
Reuben, of Chatham, m. Sarah C. **BRAINARD**, of Marlborough, Mar. 26, 1843, by Rev. B. M. Walker	228
SNOW, Noah L., Farmer, ae 26, b. in Columbia, res. Marlborough, m. Huldah **COLEMAN**, ae 19, res. Marlborough, Mar. 18, 1849, by Rev. Hiram Bell	73-4
Noah L., m. Huldah **COLEMAN**, b. of Marlborough, Mar. 18, 1849, by Rev. Hiram Bell	235
-----, d. N. Lester, Farmer & Huldah, b. [Jan.] 13, [1850]	81-2
SOCKET, Eliza, Mrs. m. John E. **DUNHAM**, b. of Marlborough, Aug. 22, 1848, by Rev. Hiram Bell	235
Elvira A., Factory worker, ae 35, b. in Vernon, res. Marlborough, m. 2nd John E. **DUNHAM**, Farmer, ae 28, Aug. 22, 1848, by Rev. Hiram Bell	73-4
SPENCER, Julius Hollister, m. Lucinda **HADING**, b. of Marlborough, Apr. 3, 1831, by Chauncey Lee	216
STAPLES, Amos, of Hampton, m. Lucy **MILLER**, Nov. 27, 1835, by Elder Thomas Jones	223
Elizabeth, m. Ralph **ROOT**, Feb. 25, 1821, by Rev. David B. Ripley	206
Sarah, b. in Colchester, d. Dec. 19, 1848; ae 8 y.	75-6
Sarah, d. Amos, Blacksmith, ae 40 & Lucy, ae 36, res. Glastonbury, b. Feb. 28, 1849	71-2
STEVENS, Frances Nelson, ch. of Elisha, Teamster, ae 21, & Emma, ae 23, Hartford, b. Dec. 28, 1847	65-6
STODDARD, Edward, twin with Edwin, s. Joseph, Farmer, ae 33 & Catharine, ae 30, b. Dec. 26, 1848	71-2
Edwin, twin with Edward, s. Joseph, Farmer, ae 33 & Catharine, ae 30, b Dec. 26, 1848	71-2
Edwin, d. Jan. 11, 1849, ae 16 d.	75-6
Mary E., d. Mar. 21, 1848, ae 6 m., in Glastonbury	69-70
-----, s. Joseph, Laborer, ae 30 & Caroline, ae 28, Middle Haddam, b. Mar. 24, 1851	85-6
STOW, Bethiah, m. Frederick **PHELPS**, Aug. 25, 1798	16
STRONG, Anna, m. Samuel Finley **JONES**, Sept. 10, 1797	12
Betsey, m. Elijah **FOOTE**, Apr. 15, 1809	28
Betsey, of Bolton, m. Thaddeus B. **MORGAN**, of Marlborough, Oct. 27, 1822, by Rev. David B Ripley	207
Charles, s. Charles, Teamster, ae 30 & Amanda M., ae 29, b. Oct. 8, 1847	65-6
Eben, m. Sally **PORTER**, Mar. 17, 1807	20
Eben Russell, s. [Eben & Sally], b. Sept. 4, 1812	20
Giles Porter, s. [Eben & Sally], b. Jan. 29, 1810	20
Giles Porter, [s. Eben & Sally], d. Dec. 27, 1831	20
Jerusha Ann, d. [Eben & Sally], b. Dec. 20, 1817	20
Mary Ann, d. [Eben & Sally], b. June 19, 1820	20
Sally Maria, d. [Eben & Sally], b. Dec. 20, 1807	20
-----, s. Cha[rle]s, Farmer & Maria, b. Oct. [ ], 1849	81-2
TALCOTT, TALLCOTT, Abigail, [d. Moseley & Harriet], b. Dec. 22, 1832	6

	Page
TALCOTT, TALLCOTT (cont.)	
Cook, [s. Moseley & Harriet], b .Aug. 11, 1826	6
Harriet, w. Moseley, d. Nov. 13, 1834	6
Hart, s. Moseley [& Harriet], b. Aug. 19, 1834	6
Lee, [s. Moseley & Harriet], b. Dec. 24, 1828; d. Oct. 21, 1833, ae 4 y. 10 m.	6
Moseley, of Marlborough, m. Sabrina **KINGSBURY**, of Tolland, Nov. 10, 1803	6
Prude, m. David Miller **LORD**, June 27, 1799	15
Sabrina, w. Moseley, d. Sept. 8, 1822, ae 43 y.	6
TENANT, Avery, of Chatham, m. Clarissa **PALMER**, of Marlborough, Jan. 9, 1822, by David B Ripley	207
THOMAS, Absolom, [m. Jane **FREEMAN**,]	34
Emily Jane, [d. Absolom & Jane], b. Jan. 18, 1811	34
Griswold, [s. Absolom & Jane], b. Oct. 24, 1807	34
Harriet, of Hartford, m. Julius **EVANS**, of Marlborough, July 31, 1825, by Rev. David B. Ripley	209
Luther, [s. Absolom & Jane], b. Nov. 3, 1805	34
THOMPSON, Alphonzo, s. Jedediah L., Mule Spinner, ae 24 & Emily, ae 25, b. Mar. 31, 1838	65-6
Jedediah L., m. Emily E. **CULLUMS**, b. of Marlborough, Aug. 2, 1846, by Rev. Hiram Bell	232
Sarah A., of East Haddam, m. John W. **WILBUR**, of Marlborough, May 4, 1845, by Rev. Hiram Bell	231
TILLOTSON, Abraham, of Marlborough, m. Phelena **HINCKLEY**, of Lebanon, Nov. 22, 1846, by Rev. Hiram Bell	233
Abraham, Farmer, d. Aug. 15, 1847, ae 50	69-70
Harley, farmer, d. Sept. 15, 1847, ae 6	69-70
Philenah, ae 58, b. Lebanon, m. Persia **JOHNSON**, Farmer, ae 57, b. Lyme, Sept. 19, 1847, by Asa Day	67-8
Philemah, of Marlborough, m. Pierce **JOHNSON**, of Columbia, Sept. 19, 1847, by Asa Day, J.P.	234
TREAT, W[illia]m H., of Middletown, m. Emily S. **GRIFFIN**, of Marlborough, Aug. 11, 1845, by L. C. Collins	232
TRYON, Harvey, m. Mary **DICKINSON**, May 27, 1829, by Isaac Dwinel	213
TURNER, William W., of Glastonbury, m. Bathsheba B. **WRISLEY**, of Marlborough, Oct. 1, 1822, by Rev. David B. Ripley	207
USHER, Elisha L., [s. Sophron], b. Aug. 23, 1835	49
Sophron, of Chatham, m. Abigail **LORD**, of Marlborough, Nov. 8, 1826, by Rev. David B. Ripley	210
WARNER, Edwin C., m. Mary E. **BOWEN**, b. of Marlborough, Nov. 30, 1843, by Rev. Hiram Bell	229
John B., m. Elizabeth F. **WHITE**, June 7, 1847, by Rev. Hiram Bell	233
Loiza, of Marlborough, m. David **BROWN**, of Chatham, Aug. 9, 1835, by Jeremiah Stocking, Elder	222
Norman P., m. Eliza **CURTIS**, b. of Marlborough, Jan. 1, 1844, by Rev. Hiram Bell	229
Sarah Ann, of Marlborough, m. William G. **CARRIER**, of Colchester, June 7, 1847, by Rev. J. B. Gould	233
-----, ch. of John B., Blacksmith, ae 25 & Elizabeth T., ae 21, b. July 4, 1848	65-6

	Page
WARRELL, Ottenill, Jr., of Woonsocket, m. Miriam **HEYDEN**, of Marlborough, Aug. 6, 1837, by Rev. W[illia]m F. Vaill. Int. Pub. July 30, 1837, Woonsocket, by Joseph Smith (Perhaps "Othniel Warren, Jr.")	225
WARREN, Mary A., ae 18, m. John **BLYTHE**, Manufacturer, ae 20, Apr. 30, 1841, by Rev. Hiram Bell	67-8
Mary A., m. John **BLYTHE**, b. of Marlborough, Apr. 30, 1848, by Rev. Hiram Bell	234
WASHBURN, Joel, m. Lydia **HOSFORD**, Nov. 16, 1807	25
Joseph, Teacher, ae 22, b. in Clinton, N.Y., res. Clinton, N.Y., m. Olive **CARRIER**, ae 22, b. in East Haddam, Aug. 21, 1850, by Rev. H. Bell	83-4
WATERS, Hannah, m. William **WILSON**, Apr. 22, 1832, by Samuel F. Jones, J.P.	217
WATROUS, Anna, m. Ephraim **COLEMAN**, Feb. 23, 1826, by Sam[ue]l F. Jones, J.P.	209
George, m. Lucy **WILSON**, Dec. 12, 1834, by Rev. Leonard B. Griffing	222
Geo[rge], Laborer, d. July 21, 1851; ae 19	79-80
Hannah, m. Nathaniel **ASHLEY**, Apr. 23, 1826, by Rev. David B Ripley	210
Josiah, m. Mary Ann **BIRGE**, Oct. 10, 1830, by Rev. Alpheas Geer	215
Josiah, m. Mrs. Delight **SAUNDERS**, Mar. 29, 1840, by Hiram Bell	226
Timothy, of Colchester, m. Julia **CARRIER**, of Marlborough, Dec. 25, 1826, by David B. Ripley	210
WELCH, Cyres, of Chatham, m. Jane E. **ROOTE**, of Marlborough, Sept. 11, 1842, b Rev. Lorrene Pierce	227
Julius, m. Emeline **FULLER**, Nov. 16, 1826, by Sam[uel] F. Jones, J.P.	210
WELDON, Lovina, m. Nathaniel **CURTIS**, b. of Marlborough, Feb. 22, 1824, by Rev. David B. Ripley	208
WELLES, WELLS, Horace, m. Mary Maria **DERBE**, Aug. 31, 1824, by Rev. David B. Ripley	208
Lydia, m. David **KILBORN**, Jr., b. of Colchester, Mar. 13, 1793	7
Mary E., m. Hiram **BELL**, July 1, 1840, in the state of New York	227
Oliver, of Chatham, m. Lydia **BROWN**, of Marlborough, Dec. 8, 1826, by Rev. David B. Ripley	210
WEST, Addison L., s. [Hiram & Hope H.], b. May 4, 1844	35
Albert J., d. Dec. 12, 1848, ae 15 m.	75-6
Amasa, [s. Edmund], b. Apr. 7, 1810	33
Chauncey B., s. [Edmund, Jr. & Emphratia], b .Jan. 3, 1843	39
Cyrus, [s. Edmund], b. Feb. 28, 1812	33
Edmund, Jr., [s. Edmund], b. May 5, 1815	33
Edmund, Jr., m. Emphratia **BIGELOW**, Jan. 19, 1842	39
Edmund, Jr., m. Euphrasia **BIGELOW**, Jan. 19, 1842, by Rev. Hiram Bell	227
Elizabeth, m. Hiram **CARRIER**, Dec. 15, 1831, by Rev. Chauncey Lee	216
Elizabeth B., [d. Edmund], b. Nov. 7, 1807	33
Frances L., d. [Hiram & Hope H.], b. July 9, 1831	35
Gustavus, [s. Edmund], b. Jan. 11, 1818	33
Henry, [s. Edmund], b. July 2, 1821	33
Hiram, [s. Edmund], b. Jan. 22, 1803	33

	Page
WEST (cont.)	
Hiram, m. Hope H. **PHELPS**, Dec. 9, 1829	35
Hiram, m. Hope H. **PHELPS**, Dec. 9, 1829, by Rev. Chauncey Lee	214
Lucy, [d. Edmund], b. Apr. 4, 1805	33
Lucy Ann, m. Oliver **PHELPS**, Jr., Nov. 4, 1829, by Rev. Chauncey Lee	214
Lucy L., [d. Hiram & Hope H.], b. Mar. 31, 1837	35
WHEELER, John R., of Willimantic, m. Harriet **RICH**, of Marlborough, Aug. 26, 1849, by Rev. Hiram Bell	236
WHITE, Elizabeth F., m. John B. **WARNER**, June 7, 1847, by Rev. Hiram Bell	233
WHITNEY, John S., of Marlborough, m. Eunice **ROGERS**, of Chatham, Nov. 5, 1820, by Rev. David B. Ripley	206
WILBUR, Benjamin R. K., m. Mary A. **COLEMAN**, b. of Marlborough, Oct. 20, 1850, by Rev. Marvin Leffingwell	237
Benj[amin] K., Farmer, ae 23, m. Mary A. **COLEMAN**, ae 17, Oct. 20, 1850, by Rev. H. Leffingwell	83-4
Flora, d. Sept. 23, 1848; ae 18 m.	75-6
Jane, Farming, ae 17, b. in Marlborough, m Austin **HOUER** (?)*, Farmer, ae 25, b. in Tolland, res. Tolland, Nov. 11, [1850], by Asa Day *(Perhaps "HOUSE"?)	77-8
John W., of Marlborough, m. Sarah A. **THOMPSON**, of East Haddam, May 4, 1845, by Rev. Hiram Bell	231
Robert H., m. Eliza **COLEMAN**, Feb. 20, 1843, by Rev. Hiram Bell	227
-----, ch. [of] John, Wagon maker, ae 25 & Sarah Ann, ae 23, b. Aug. 15, 1847	65-6
-----, d. John W., Wagon maker, ae 28 & Mary Ann, ae 26, b. Mar. 25, 1851	85-6
WILLIAMS, Alpheas, of Chatham, m. Mary A. **BRAINARD**, of Marlborough, Aug. 6, 1844, by Rev. Hiram Bell	230
Thomas N., of Chatham, m. Laura S. **ROOT**, of Marlborough, Apr. 15, 1846, by Rev. Hiram Bell	232
WILSON, WILLSON, Adaline, m. Joseph **MINER**, Sept. 25, 1834, by Rev. Leonard B. Griffing	221
Hiram, m. Clarissa **MINER**, Sept. 25, 1834, by Rev. Leonard B. Griffing	221
Lucy, m. George **WATROUS**, Dec. 12, 1834, by Rev. Leonard B. Griffing	222
Ogden, m. Ruth **COLEMAN**, Jan. 15, 1827, by Sam[uel] F. Jones, J.P.	210
William, m. Hannah **WATERS**, Apr. 22, 1832, by Samuel Jones, J.P.	217
William, m. Hannah **ACKLEY**, Dec. 25, 1843, by Oliver Northam, J.P.	229
WOOD, -----, d. Hood, Farmer & Harriet, b. Jan. [ ], 1850	81-2
WORTHINGTON, Elizabeth, m. Israel **FOOTE**, Mar. 17, 1782	18
Lois, of Colchester, m. Elijah **FOOTE**, Feb. 15, 1811	28
WRIGHT, Dudley A., Paper Maker, ae 30, m. Betsey A. **LYMAN**, ae 20, Mar. 12, 1848, by Amos B. Latham, J.P.	67-8
Dudley A., m. Betsey A. **LYMAN**, Mar. 12, 1848, by Amos B. Latham, J.P.	234
WRISLEY, Bathsheba B., of Marlborough, m. William W. **TURNER**, of Glastonbury, Oct. 1, 1822, by Rev. David B. Ripley	207

BARBOUR COLLECTION

	Page
WRISLEY (cont.)	
Julia, of Marlborough, m. Erskine **HILLS**, of Enfield, Mar. 22, 1839, by Elder Jeremiah Stocking	224
WYLLYS, Abba M., d. [William], b. Apr. 28, 1806	21
Caroline, d. [William], b. May 9, 1821; d. Sept. 8, 1825	21
Cynthia, d. [William], b. Sept. 4, [1811]; d. [Sept.] 21, 1811	21
Jane, d. [William], b. Oct. 14, 1818	21
John, s. [William], b. Dec. 2, 1814	21
Joseph H., [s. William], b. Jan. 13, 1810	21
Malenda, of Marlborough, m. Collins **REED**, of East Windsor, Nov. 8, 1829, by Rev. Chauncey Lee	214
Pamelia, m. William **BURNHAM**, Nov. 2, 1828, by Oliver Phelps, J.P.	213
Permelia, d. [William], b. Apr. 22, 1808	21
Reuben, s. [William], b. Mar. 7, 1823	21
Sophronia, d. [William], b. Oct. 5, 1812	21
Susanna, d. [William], b. Dec. 22, 1816	21
William, s. [William], b. Apr. 6, 1805	21
W[illia]m, d. Jan. 9, 1828	21
YOUNG, Sarah, Mrs., m. Clark C. **ALBEE**, b. of Mansfield, Mar. 1, 1852, by Rev. L. D. Bentley	239
NO SURNAME, Eliza, m. Oliver **RUSSELL**, b. of Marlborough, Jan. 17, 1837, by Rev. Calvin Chapin, of Rocky Hill	226
Elizabeth, b. Oct. 27, 1761; m. Ichabod **LORD**, June 14, 1781	3
-----, d. Aug. 28, 1848; ae 3 w.	69-70
-----, s. Hiram S., Laborer, ae 49 & Emily, ae 41 1/2, b. Oct. 27, 1848	71-2
-----, negro, Laborer, d. Mar. 19, 1850	79-80

MERIDEN VITAL RECORDS
1806-1853

This volume contains a list alphabetically arranged of all the vital records of the town of Meriden from its incorporation to about 1853. The entire record of the town prior to 1853 is found in one volume. This list was taken from a set of cards based on a copy of the Meriden Vital Records made in 1915 by Miss Ethel L. Scofield, of New Haven, Conn. The Scofield Copy, now in the possession of the Connecticut State Library, has not been compared with the original and doubtless errors exist. It is hoped that as errors or omissions are found notes will be entered in this volume and on the cards which are included in the General Index of Connecticut Vital Records also in the possession of the Connecticut State Library.

Hartford, Conn., January, 1925

	Page
ABBOT, John, of Middlebury, m. Laury Ann BISHOP, of North Haven, [ ], [1830?], by Charles J. Hinsdale	37
ADAMS, Belinda A., of Meriden, m. Charles A. ROBERTS, of Middletown, Nov. 24, 1853, by Rev. Harvey Miller	121
Frances H., of Weathersfield, m. Walter W. WEBB, of Meriden, Mar. 31, 1852, by Rev. G. W. Perkins	110
ALCOTT, Ambrose V., m. Ann .V. UPSON, b. of Wolcott, Sept. 4, 1845, by Rev. C. Munson	85
ALLEN, Jennet, of Meriden, m. Erastus COLTON, of Cheshire, Sept. 13, 1838, by Arthur Granger	60
ANDREWS, Abigail, d. Oliver & Hannah, b. Jan 5, 1800	7
Abigail, of Meriden, m. Marcus Miles TA[L]MAGE, of New Haven, Nov. 11, 1824, by James Keeler	26
Almon, s. Marvel & Sally, b. Feb. 11, 1808	9
Ann Eliza, of Southington, m. Byron TWISS, of Southington, Oct. 21, 1849, by Rev. Harvey Miller	99
Arza, m. Harriet HART, b. of Meriden, July 24, 1837, by Arthur Granger	56
Caroline Ann, d. Benajah & Elizabeth, b. Mar. 28, 1811	12
Caroline Ann, d. [Benajah & Elizabeth], d. Sept. 6, 1821	22
Caroline Ann, 2nd, d. [Benajah & Elizabeth], b. Jan. 22, 1822	22
Caroline M., of Cheshire, m. Horace YALE, of Meriden, May 29, 1853, by Rev. Harvey Miller	116
Catharine J., of Meriden, m. Ephraim A. KELSEY, of Westbrook, Apr. 5, 1847, by Rev. G. W. Perkins	89
Dan, m. Elizabeth HOUGH, Feb. 25, 1807	2
Emmily, d. Dan & Elizabeth, b. July 3, 1807	11
Emily, m. Samuel M. PARSONS, b. of Meriden, Sept. 3, 1828, by Rev. James Keeler	33

BARBOUR COLLECTION

	Page
ANDREWS (cont.)	
Hannah, d. Marvel & Sally, b. Feb. 26, 1810	11
Hannah, of Meriden, m. Sylvester B. **LINDSLEY**, of East Haddam, Oct. 3, 1830, by Rev. James [Keeler]	40
Henry Ogden, s. Benajah & Elizabeth, b. Feb. 15, 1815	22
Huldah E., w. Marvel, d. Nov. 20, 1819	67
Isaac, s. [Benajah & Elizabeth], b. Nov. 25, 1819	22
John M., of Simsbury, m. Caroline A. **HALL**, of Wallingford, May 12, 1836, by Rev. Robert A .Hallam	57
John R., of Canton, m. Jane **BALDWIN**, of Meriden, June 14, 1848, by Rev. Harvey Miller	93
Julius, s. Marvel & Huldah E., b. Nov. 20, 1819	67
Laura, m. Jacob **HALL**, b. of Meriden, Sept. 2, 1835, by Rev. Edward Ingersoll	51
Laura A., of Meriden, m. W[illia]m F. **LOGAN**, of New Haven, Oct. 12, 1853, by Rev. G. H. Deshon	122
Levina, d. Oliver & Hannah, b. May 24, 1803	7
Levina, see also Luvinna	
Lucy A., m. Henry B. **CHAFFEE**, Dec. 27, 1852, by Rev. Giles H. Deshon	114
Luvinna, d. Marvel & Sally, b. June 26, 1812	14
Luvinna, see also Levina	
Martha M., of Cheshire, m. Stephen L. **PARKER**, of Meriden, Nov. 23, 1845, by Rev. John Parker	83
Marvel, m. Esther **HALL**, b. of Meriden, Jan. 24, 1822, by Samuel Miller	20
Mary A., of Meriden, m. Jared H. **CANFIELD**, of New Haven, May 19, 1840, by Harvey Miller	62
Mary Augusta, d. Benajah & Elizabeth, b. Mar. 26, 1813	15
Mary E., m. Orrin **COWLES**, b. of Meriden, Oct. 13, 1830, by Rev. James [Keeler]	40
Mary Elizabeth, d. Dan & Elizabeth, b. Aug. 25, 1809	11
Mehitable, of Hamden, m. Alfred **COOPER**, of North Haven, Dec. 24, 1850, by Harvey Miller	104
Nathaniel, Jr., of Wallingford, m. Ann **COUCH**, of Meriden, Sept. 13, 1821, by Sam[ue]ll Miller	20
Oliver, m. Hannah **CURTIS**, Dec. 27, 1796	7
Polly, m. Samuel **CURTIS**, Nov. 20, 1805	10
Reuben, s. Oliver & Hannah, b. Aug. 4, 1801	7
Sally, w. Marvel, d. Oct. 30, 1816	67
Seth, s. Oliver & Hannah, b. June 12, 1805	7
Sherlock, s. Oliver & Hannah, b. Feb. 1, 1798	7
William Henry, s. Oliver & Hannah, b. Apr. 22, 1807	7
ANTHONY, Lemuel Orrison, s. Samuel & Sybil, b. Dec. 21, 1825	49
M., m. Freeman G. **HALL**, of Wallingford, Oct. 16, 1853, by Rev. Harvey Miller	120
Philemon, m. Eunice **PERKINS**, Nov. 24, 1825, by Titus Ives	28
Samuel Hall, s. Samuel & Sybel, b. Jan. 4, 1819	18
ARNOLD, John, m. Harriet **MILLER**, b. of New Haven, July 2, 1840, by Rev. Harvey Miller	62
ATKINS, Alonzo S., of New Hartford, m. Mary A. **JOHNSON**, of Meriden, Sept. 24, 1848, by Rev. Albert Nash	97

	Page
ATKINS (cont.)	
Asahel R., of Meriden, m. Rebecca M. **HULL**, of Wallingford, Jan. 9, 1842, by Rev. Harvey Miller	69
Betsey C., of Meriden, m. Orren **SCOVELL**, of Lewis County, New York, June 2, 1845, by Rev. C. Munson	82
Maria, of Meriden, m. Elisa **BRADLEY**, of Branford, Nov. 30, 1843, by Rev. H. Miller	75
ATWATER, Esther T., m. John **BUTLER**, Jr., b. of Meriden, Mar. 11, 1849, by Rev. N. S Wheaton	96
-----, Dea. of Hamden, m. Mrs. Jane **HUBBARD**, of Meriden, Mar. 21, 1821, by Rev. Erastus Ripley	19
ATWELL, Sophronia S., of Meriden, m. Edward E. **BOWEN**, of Woodstock, June 15, 1836, by George B. Atwell	54
AUGER, Julius S., of New Haven, m. Lavinia D. **MERRIAM**, of Meriden, Aug. 11, 1835, by Charles J. Hinsdale	50
AUSTIN, Abigail, [d. Amos & Sarah], b. Mar. 16, 1818	36
Amos, m. Sarah **HULL**, Oct. 29, 1807	8
Amos, Jr., s. Amos & Sarah, b. Mar. 27, 1813	36
Eli, [s. Amos & Sarah], b. Sept. 28, 1815	36
Emily, [d. Amos & Sarah], b. Feb. 15, 1824	36
Emily, of Meriden, m. Charles **BLANCHARD**, of Springfield, Vt., Nov. 1, 1846, by Rev. G. W. Perkins	88
Esther, of Meriden, m. Joseph **LONDON**, of Wallingford, May 26, 1844, by Rev. H. Miller	75
Harriet, m. Edwin **WILCOX**, Sept. 23, 1827, by Charles J. Hinsdale	32
Hiram, s. Amos & Sarah, b. Sept. 5, 1808	14
John P., m. Rebecca **REED**, b. of Meriden, [Apr.] 30, [1835], by Rev. George B. Atwell	50
Lois, b. May 11, 1764; m. Joseph **TWISS**, Oct. 11, 1786	17
Lucretia, m. Benjamin **MERRIAM**, July 4, 1799	15
Meriah, [d. Amos & Sarah], b. Mar. 13, 1823; d. Mar. 17, [1823]	36
Phebe, d. [Amos & Sarah], b. Mar. 19, 1811	14
Sarah, of Meriden, m. Timothy **PHELPS**, of Marlboro, Nov. 17, 1831, by Rev. Russell Jennings	43
AYRES, David J., m. Sarah A. **SEARLES**, b. of Poundridge, N.Y., May 7, 1848, by Rev. John E. Searles	93
BABLE, Peter, of Westbrook, Me., m. Mrs. Lucena **SHEPHERD**, of Southington, Conn., Jan. 9, 1852, by Rev. William W. Hurd	110
BACON, Isaac, of Middletown, m. Chloe **BALDWIN**, of Meriden, Sept. 18, 1823, by Samuel Miller	23
Samuel, 2nd, of Middletown, m. Lydia C. **REMINGTON**, Oct. 19, 1853, by Rev. Harvey Miller	121
BAGG, Isaac C., m. Lucretia **NEWTON**, May 19, 1850, by Rev. Giles H. Deshon	104
BAILEY, Eliphalet, of Haddam, m. Maria **BALDWIN**, of Meriden, Apr. 10, 1823, by Samuel Miller	23
Lavinia, b. Dec. 5, 1816; m. Edwin **BIRDSEY**, Apr. 12, 1837	59
Prudence, m. Chester **RICE**, Aug. 31, 1812	68
Sarah A., m. Charles **PARMELEE**, b. of Meriden, Oct. 9, 1851, by Rev. G. W. Perkins	108
Theodore, F., m. Emily F. **ROBERTS**, Sept. 25, 1853, by Rev. A. A. Stevens	120
BALDWIN, Alma, [ch. of Moses & Eda], b. June 27, 1816	45

BALDWIN (cont.)

	Page
Alma, of Meriden, m. Jared **COTTON**, of Middletown, Oct. 23, 1843, by Rev. Levi H. Wakeman, of Westfield	72
Augusta Ann, d. [Ransom & Sarah], b. Aug. 29, 1834	68
Augusta Ann, d. [Ransom & Sarah], d. June 1, 1837	68
Charlotte, d. Samuel, Jr. & Achseh, b. Mar. 12, 1805	7
Chloe, of Meriden, m. Isaac **BACON**, of Middletown, Sept. 18, 1823, by Samuel Miller	23
Clarenda, d. Samuel, Jr. & Achseh, b. June 3, 1807	7
Clarinda, m. James **BALDWIN**, b. of Meriden, Mar. 26, 1829, by Samuel Miller	34
Emily C., of Meriden, m. James C. **FARRINGTON**, of New York, May 9, 1833, by Iranus Atkins	47
Frederick, [s. Moses & Eda], b. Aug. 3, 1818	45
George C., of Litchfield, m. Francis A. **GEAR**, of Meriden, Apr. 13, 1851, by Rev. Harvey Miller	105
George N., of Meriden, b. Cornelia D. **RICE**, of Wallingford, Oct. 12, 1845, by Rev. H. Miller	83
Henry, s. Joseph C. & Rosetta, b. Aug. 23, 1806	1
Henry, [s. Moses & Eda], b. Jan. 10, 1821	45
Henry L., m. Eliza Ann **HALL**, Sept. 2 ,1846, by Rev. H. Miller	87
Hiram, s. Ransom & Sarah, b. Feb. 17, 1825	68
Hiram, s. [Ransom & Sarah], d. Feb. 25, 1827	68
Isaac, s. Samuel, Jr. & Achsah, b. Apr. 3, 1803	7
James, [twin with Jane, s. Moses & Eda], b. Dec. 5, 1825	45
James, m. Clarinda **BALDWIN**, b. of Meriden, Mar. 26, 1829, by Samuel Miller	34
Jane, [twin with James, d. Moses & Eda], b. Dec. 5, 1825	45
Jane, of Meriden, m. John R. **ANDREWS**, of Canton, June 14, 1848, by Rev. Harvey Miller	93
Jesse G., of Oxford, m. Lydia **RICE**, of Meriden, Apr. 15, 1830, by Charles J .Hinsdale	37
Joseph C., m. Rosetta **GRISWOLD**, Oct. 24, 1805	1
Linius, [s. Moses & Eda], b. May 19, 1832	45
Lois Augusta, d. [Ransom & Sarah], b. Sept. 1, 1829	68
Lois Augusta, d. [Ransom & Sarah], d. Apr. 20, 1840	68
Maria, of Meriden, m. Eliphalet **BAILEY**, of Haddam, Apr. 10, 1823, by Samuel Miller	23
Mary, d. [Ransom & Sarah], b. Jan. 10, 1838	68
Mary J., m. William S. [ ], b. of Meriden, Feb. 3, 1831, by Rev. Russell Jennings	41
Moses, m. Eda **LYMAN**, Apr. 19, 1816	45
Rachel, m. Robert **WILLIAMS**, b. of Meriden, July 22, 1827, by Samuel Miller	31
Ransom, m. Sarah **TWISS**, b. of Meriden, Nov. 20, 1823, by Samuel Miller	24
Ransom, s. [Ransom & Sarah], b. May 28, 1836	68
Rosina E., of Meriden, m. Alonzo H. **GALLUP**, of Norwich, Sept. 9, 1849, by Rev. Albert Nash	98
Roxana, d. [Ransom & Sarah], b. Dec. 17, 1840	68
Samuel, m. Hannah **TAYLOR**, Sept. 22, 1774	7
Samuel, Jr., m. Achsah **HALE**, Feb. 15, 1801	7

	Page
BALDWIN (cont.)	
Samuel, m. Elizabeth **HALL**, b. of Meriden, May 31, 1829, by Rev. Daniel Burrows	35
Sarah Maria, d. [Ransom & Sarah], b. Feb. 12, 1831	68
Sophronia, [d. Moses & Eda], b. Oct. 22, 1819	45
Sophronia, of Meriden, m. Alvenzo E. **WILCOX**, of Middletown, Oct. 3, 1837, by Leland Howard	56
Sylvanus, s. Joseph C. & Rosetta, b. Aug. 28, 1808	10
Thomas T., of Meriden, m. Harriet **WILLIAMS**, of Middletown, Aug. 6, 1831, by Rev. Nathan E. Shailer, of Berlin	42
Vincy Ann, d. [Ransom & Sarah], b. Apr. 20, 1827	68
Vincy Ann, d. [Ransom & Sarah], d. Apr. 20, 1833	68
William A., of North Haven, m. Lucy Lucina **MERRIAM**, of Meriden, Apr. 14, 1836, by Rev. Edward Ingersoll	52
BANCROFT, Dewit C., of Rome, N.Y., m. Francis D. **BULL**, of Meriden, Mar. 31, 1845, by Rev. G. W. Perkins	80
BARBOUR, Joseph, m. Harriet **CONKLIN**, b. of Meriden, Oct. 22, 1852, by Rev. A. A. Stevens	113
BARKER, Benjamin, of Branford, m. Mabel **BOOTH**, of Meriden, Jan. 2, 1842, by Rev. Harvey Miller	69
Hannah, m. Lucius **CURTISS**, of Meriden, May 15, 1853, by Rev. George W. Perkins	117
BARNES, BARNS, Augustus, of Southington, m. Lucy Ann **HARRISON**, of Meriden, Dec. 18, 1842, by Rev. Harvey Miller	71
Benjamin, of Southington, m. Sarah **BENNER**, of Meriden, Nov. 18, 1845, by Rev. John E. Searles	91
Daggett, of Southington, m. Martha **BLINN**, of Meriden, Apr. 27, 1845, by Rev. G. W. Perkins	81
Henry R., of New Haven, m. Elizabeth B. **CLARK**, of Meriden, Aug. 11, 1846, by Rev. Saul Clark	86
Jane M., m. John **HOWD**, b. of Southington, Sept. 3, 1851, by Rev. G. W. Perkins	108
Mary, of Meriden, m. Abijah **HALL**, of Leydin, N.Y., Feb. 23, 1823, by Samuel Miller	22
Sarah A., of Southington, m. Franklin B. **EMMONS**, of Meriden, July 1, 1851, by Rev. G. W. Perkins	107
Sylvia, of Southington, m. Anson **BRADLEY**, Oct. 9, 1836, by Rev. Stephen Topliff	54
BARTHOLOMEW, George B., of Sheffield, Mass., m. Caroline **STEWART**, of Meriden, Mar. 10, 1831, by Rev. Russell Jennings	41
Joel, Jr., of Wallingford, m. Hulda **LYMAN**, of Meriden, Sept. 19, 1824, by Samuel Miller	25
Luzern, of Wallingford, m. Betsey **YALE**, of Meriden, July 20, 1836, by Arthur Granger	54
Sarah J., m. Morris C. **CLARK**, May 31, 1852, by Rev. Harvey Miller. Witnesses, Geo[rge] H. Andrews, Roxanna Andrews. Affidavit made Feb. 14, 1868, to John H. Barie, Notary Public	110
BARTLETT, John A., of Providence, R.I., m. Aurelia **SIBLEY**, of Meriden, July 2, 1840, by Rev. Harvey Miller	62
BEACH, George, of North Haven, m. Lydia G. **REDFIELD**, of Guilford, Aug. 7, 1845, by Rev. Harvey Miller	82

	Page
BEACH (cont.)	
Horace G., of Meriden, m. Esther L. **LUCAS**, of Middletown, July 7, 1847, by Rev. G. W. Perkins	91
Warren P., of Meriden, m. Juliette **BECKLEY**, of Berlin, May 11, 1842, by Rev. G. W. Perkins	70
BEARDSLEY, Maria, m. Morris **HITCHCOCK**, b. of Meriden, June 28, 1835, by Nathan Booth, J.P.	50
BECKLEY, Chester, of Berlin, m. Mary E. **BELDEN**, of Meriden, June 20, 1847, by Rev. Harvey Miller	91
Everton*, of Berlin, m. Elizabeth Ann **FARRINGTON**, of Meriden, July 8, 1832, by Horatio Potter *("Evelyn" written in margin in pencil)	44
George, m. Maria M. **LEWIS**, b. of Meriden, Nov. 30, 1842, by Alexander Miller, minister	76
John, of Berlin, m. Mary H. **CURTISS**, of Meriden, Nov. 17, 1850, by Rev. Harvey Miller	102
Juliette, of Berlin, m. Warren P. **BEACH**, of Meriden, May 11, 1842, by Rev. G. W. Perkins	70
Laura A., of Berlin, m. Jonathan **MORLEY**, Dec. 12, 1852, by Rev. Harvey Miller	114
Ralph H., m. Mrs. Abigail **FOSTER**, May 1, 1836, by Arthur Granger	53
BEECHER, Julia, m. Timothy **KENNEDY**, b. of Southington, Mar. 28, 1837, by Rev. J. Goodwin	55
BELDEN, Edwin, m. Betsey A. **RECOR**, b. of New Britain, Sept. 16, 1841, by Rev. G. W. Perkins	65
Grace, m. George **MECOMEZ**, b. of Meriden, Sept. 9, 1852, by Rev. Francis Bolton	113
Mary A., m. Erastus **HIGLEY**, b. of Meriden, Apr. 18, 1867*, by Rev. John E. Searles (*1847?)	91
Mary E., of Meriden, m. Chester **BECKLEY**, of Berlin, June 20, 1847, by Rev. Harvey Miller	91
Orrin, m. Mary **LEWIS**, b. of Meriden, Dec. 24, 1823, by Reuben Ives	24
Sarah I., m. Burdett C. **BOOTH**, May 12, 1851, by Rev. Harvey Miller	106
BEMENT, Joseph, m. Malinda **LUNG**, Apr. 4, 1833, by Daniel Wildman	47
BENEDICK, Eliphalet H., of Southington, m. Caroline **HALL**, of Meriden, Aug. 15, 1853, by Rev. Harvey Miller	119
BENHAM, Aurelia, m. Edwin E. **CURTIS**, Dec. 24, 1826, by Rev. Nathaniel T. Bruce, in St. Andrews Church	29
Darius, m. Cynthia **CONE**, Aug. 3, 1806	2
Darius, m. Eunice **CURTISS**, [May] 4, [1836], by George B Atwell	53
Edward W., of Cheshire, m. Grace A. **HIGBY**, of Meriden, May 6, 1849, by Rev. Albert Nash	98
Samuel, m. Polly Samantha **DOUGLASS**, Oct. 13, 1825, by Charles J. Hinsdale	27
Susan J., m. James A. **FRARY**, Dec. 25, 1832, by Rev. Robert A. Hallum	45
BENNER, Sarah, of Meriden, m. Benjamin **BARNES**, of Southington, Nov. 18, 1846, by Rev. John E. Searles	91
BENNETT, BENNET, Alonzo, m. Mary A. **YALE**, b. of Meriden, Nov. 25, 1847, by Rev. John E. Searles	92

	Page
BENNETT, BENNET (cont.)	
Laura, m. Zeno **REDFIELD**, b. of Meriden, Jan. 2, 1848, by Rev. John E. Searles	93
Susan, m. Samuel **WAY**, Jr., b. of Meriden, Sept. 1, 1823, by Elijah Willard	23
BIGELOW, Edward, of Amania, m. Mary Ann **BOIES**, of Blanford, June 27, 1853, by Rev. G. W. Perkins	119
BINGHOFF, Eustina Dorethea, m. Charles August Gootlieb **RAVEN**, b. of Germany, Aug. 31, 1851, by Rev. G. W. Perkins	107
BIRDSEY, Alanson, b. Nov. 26, 1805; m. Clarissa **WILCOX**, Aug. 10, 1829	59
Alina, d. Eli C. & Rebecca C., b. Sept. 25, 1826	50
Alma, d. [Eli C. & Rebecca C.], b. Sept. 25, 1826	59
Almond, m. Aurilla **THARP**, Nov. 25, 1832, by Rev. Seth Higby	45
Andrew J., s. [Edwin & Lavinia], b. Apr. 29, 1838; d. Nov. 13, 1839	59
Delia, b. Mar. 8, 1810; m. Orsanius **CROCKER**, Sept. 2, 1830	59
Delia, m. Orsanius **CROCKER**, Sept. 2, 1830, by Rev. Russell Jennings	39
Edwin, b. Apr. 3, 1816; m. Lavinia **BAILEY**, Apr. 12, 1837	59
Eli Andrew, s. [Edwin & Lavinia], b. Jan. 24, 1841; d. May 11, 1843	59
Eli C., b. Dec. 21, 1799; m. Rebecca C. **WILCOX**, June 3, 1824	59
Eli C., s. Eli C. & Rebecca C., b. Feb. 16, 1843	72
Eli C ., s. [Eli C. & Rebecca C.], b .May 16, 1843	59
Eli C., d. Oct. 9, 1843	72
Elizabeth, d. [Alanson & Clarissa], b. Feb. 10, 1830	59
Elizabeth, m. Walter **BOOTH**, Jr., b. of Meriden, July 5, 1848, by Rev. Harvey Miller	93
Gershom, s. [Alanson & Clarissa], b. May 5, 1832	59
Linus, s. [Eli C. & Rebecca C.], b. Apr. 13, 1825	59
Linus, s. Eli C. & Rebecca C., b. Apr. 13, 1835 (Probably 1825)	50
Lucy J., m. William J. **IVES**, b. of Meriden, Sept. 1, 1841, by Rev. Harvey Miller	65
Lucy Maria, d. [Edwin & Lavinia], b. Sept. 12, 1839	59
Mary Jane, d. [Alanson & Clarissa], b. [ ], 1841	59
Russel, s. [Alanson & Clarissa], b. Apr. 12, 1837; d. Mar. 6, 1839	59
BISHOP, Austin, m. Savelia **MERRIAM**, b. of Meriden, Nov. 20, 1834, by Charles P Hinsdale	49
Laury Ann, of North Haven, m. John **ABBOT**, of Middlebury, [ ], [1830?], by Charles J. Hinsdale	37
Lavinia, b. Aug. 5, 1795; m. Hubbard **MERRIAM**, Oct. 15, 1823	67
Lavinia, m. Hubbard **MERRIAM**, Oct. 16, 1823, by Reuben Ives	23
Martin, of North Haven, m. Sylvinia **BRADLEY**, of Meriden, Jan. 1, 1826, by Samuel Miller	28
BIVINS, Alvin E., of Southington, m. Lua **CLINTON**, of Meriden, Nov. 24, 1831, by Charles J. Hinsdale	43
BLACKSTONE, Phebe, m. Ezra **RUTTY**, b. of Meriden, Jan. 23, 1851, by Rev. Harvey Miller	104
BLAKE, Elizabeth, m. Wooster Y. **IVES**, b. of Meriden, [Jan.] 25, [1837], by Geo[rge] B. Atwell	55
Harriet, of Meriden, m. Edward A. **PARKER**, of Cheshire, Sept. 1, 1845, by Rev. Harvey Miller	83
John S., m. Eliza **POMEROY**, Oct. 17, 1832, by Rev. John Boyden	45

BARBOUR COLLECTION

	Page
BLAKE (cont.)	
Sarah M., m. William **FORDRED**, b. of New York City, Nov. 27, 1836, by Jonathan Goodwin	55
BLAKESLEE, BLAKESLY, BLAKSLEY, Aaron Chatterton, s. Oliver & Harriet, b. July 26, 1841	81
Oliver, of Wallingford, m. Harriet **WARNER**, of Middletown, Oct. 1, 1840, by Rev. Harvey Miller	63
Oliver Dutton, [s. Oliver & Harriet], b. June 7, 1843	81
Walter, m. Charlotte **WEBBER**, Feb. 17, 1828, by Charles J. Hinsdale	33
BLANCHARD, Charles, of Springfield, Vt., m. Emily **AUSTIN**, of Meriden, Nov. 1, 1846, by Rev. G. W. Perkins	88
BLINN, Martha, of Meriden, m. Daggett **BARNES**, of Southington, Apr. 27, 1845, by Rev. G. W. Perkins	81
BLISS, George W., of Springfield, Mass., m. Lydia A. **HAYDEN**, of Westbrook, Conn., June 9, 1850, by Rev. Harvey Miller	102
BLODGETT, Caroline M., m. Edward S. **SANDERSON**, of Middletown, Oct. 30, 1853, by Rev. A. S. Cheesbrough	121
Marana A., now of Meriden, m. Samuel J. **BUCKINGHAM**, of Oxford, June 15, 1851, by Rev. G. W. Perkins	106
BOARDMAN, Luther, of Rocky Hill, m. Lydia Ann **FRARY**, of Meriden, Oct. 18, 1838, by Rev. John Marshall Guion	60
BOIES, Mary Ann, of Blanford, m. Edward **BIGELOW**, of Amenia, June 27, 1853, by Rev. G. W. Perkins	119
BONFOEY, Phebe, of Meriden, m. Horace **CLARK**, of Chatham, Sept. 21, 1835, by Rev. Edward Ingersoll	51
BOOTH, Burdett C., m. Sarah I. **BELDEN**, May 12, 1851, by Rev. Harvey Miller	106
Cyrenius, m. Almena **HOUGH**, Oct. 22, 1826, by Charles J. Hinsdale	29
Elisa, of Meriden, m. Philip **SAGE**, of Middletown, Nov. 16, 1843, by Rev. H. Miller	72
Elizabeth B., m. Albert J. **FORBES**, Feb. 16, 1851, by Rev. Giles H. Deshon	104
Friend C., m. Mary A. **PERKINS**, b. of Meriden, May 10, 1853, by Rev. Harvey Miller	116
Harriet N., b. Apr. 13, 1816	25
Harriet Newel, d. [Walter & Laura], b. Apr. 13, 1816	16
Henry D., of New York, m. Eliza Ann **CURTIS**, of Meriden, Aug. 29, 1831, by Rev. James Keeler	42
Laura L., b. Mar. 1, [1818]; d. Mar. 17, 1818	25
Laura M., b. July 15, 1822	25
Lucy, of Wallingford, m. Abel **YALE**, of Meriden, Aug. 29, 1841, by Rev. Harvey Miller	65
Lydia, m. George P. **CATLIN**, of Amenia, Nov. 23, 1853, by Rev. G. W. Perkins	122
Mabel, of Meriden, m. Benjamin **BARKER**, of Branford, Jan. 2, 1842, by Rev. Harvey Miller	69
Mary R., m. Isaac I. **TIBBALS**, b. of Meriden, May 14, 1834, by Charles J. Hinsdale	48
Mary Rebeckah, d. [Walter & Laura], b. Mar. 15, 1811	14
Sarah, b. July 24, [1819]; d. Aug. 2 ,1819	25
Walter, m. Laura **MITCHEL**, Jan. 1, 1810	14

	Page
BOOTH (cont.)	
Walter, Jr., m. Elizabeth **BIRDSEY**, of Meriden, July 5, 1848, by Rev. Harvey Miller	93
-----, s. [Walter & Laura], b. Feb. 4, 1813; d. Feb. 18, 1813	14
-----, d. Walter & Laura, b. Dec. 23, 1813; d. Dec. 27, 1813	16
BOTSFORD, Ezra, of Martinsburgh, N.Y., m. Betsey **WAY**, of Meriden, Sept. 10, 1832, by Charles J. Hinsdale	44
Lucy, of Berlin, m. Samuel S. **ANDERSON**, of Cheshire, Sept. 10, 1832, by Charles J. Hinsdale	44
BOULER, Mary Ann., m. John **KENWORTHY**, b. of England, Jan. 10, 1853, by Rev. Francis Bottom	118
BOWEN, Edward E., of Woodstock, m. Sophornia S. **ATWELL**, of Meriden, June 15, 1836, by George B Atwell	54
BRACKENRIDGE, Josiah C., of Ware, Mass., m. Francis A. **BRADLEY**, of Meriden, Nov. 20, 1844, by Rev. C. Munson	79
BRACKETT, John B., m. Mary A. **TUTTLE**, b. of New Haven, Apr. 22, 1850, by Rev. A. A. Stephens	102
BRADLEY, Abby A., m. Walter **HUBBARD**, Oct. 13, 1852, by Rev. George W. Perkins	117
Andrew A., of Meriden, now of Dorchester, Mass., m. Harriet **BUTLER**, of Meriden, June 4, 1845, by Rev. G. W. Perkins	81
Anson, m. Sylvia **BARNES**, of Southington, Oct. 9, 1836, by Rev. Stephen Topliff	54
Charles W., of Middletown, m. Rebecca M. **HUMPHREY**, of Southington, Dec. 8, 1850, by Rev. Harvey Miller	103
Eliza, m. Harrison **CURTIS**, b. of Meriden, Oct. 17, 1838, by Harvey Miller	57
Elisa, of Branford, m. Maria **ATKINS**, of Meriden, Nov. 30, 1843, by Rev. H. Miller	75
Francis A., of Meriden, m. Josiah C. **BRACKENRIDGE**, of Ware, Mass., Nov. 20, 1844, by Rev. C .Munson	79
Harriet A., of Meriden, m. W[illia]m F. **HARRISON**, of Southington, Dec. 15, 1844, by Rev. Harvey Miller	79
Hiram, m. Susan A. **ELLIOTT**, b. of Meriden, Sept. 18, 1831, by Rev. Russell Jennings	42
Isabella, of Meriden, m. George **DUNHAM**, of Southington, May 3, 1853, by Rev. F. Bolton	116
Jane S., of Meriden, m. Samuel A. **FLAGG**, of Middletown, Mar. 12, 1851, by Rev. A. A. Stevens	105
Jennet, m. Edmund **PARKER**, b. of Meriden, Sept. 3, 1834, by Rev. Simon Shailer, of Wallingford	49
Mary, of Cheshire ,m. Sheldon **LEWIS**, of Bristol, Sept. 30, 1850, by Rev. A. A. Stevens	102
Roxanna, m. Luther E. **WEBB**, b. of Meriden, Dec. 2, 1846, by Rev. G. W. Perkins	89
Sarah, Mrs. m. Lewis **HOTCHKISS**, Mar. 31, 1823, by Charles J. Hinsdale	24
Sylvinia, of Meriden, m. Martin **BISHOP**, of North Haven, Jan. 1, 1826, by Samuel Miller	28
Warren S., of Branford, m. Mary M. **DOUGLASS**, of Meriden, May 11, 1842, by Rev. G. W. Perkins	69
William L., m. Frances **COE**, Nov. 7, 1848, by Rev. Harvey Miller	96

	Page
BRAGDON, Susan N., m. John O. **BUTLER**, b. of Meriden, Aug. 29, 1852, by Rev. Harvey Miller	112
William H., m. Harriet **FILES**, Feb. 13, 1851, by Rev. Harvey Miller	104
BRAINARD, Asahel S., of Haddam, m. Lucyett **LANDERS**, of Redfield, N.Y., Jan. 1, 1849, by Rev. Albert Nash	97
Joseph B., of Haddam, m. Sarah Ann **DIMOCK**, of Meriden, May 5, 1833, by Rev. Robert A. Hallum	47
Sarah, of Haddam, m. Asaph **HUBBARD**, Apr. 9, 1843, by Harvey Miller	71
BRAY, Anson, of Southbury, m. Betsey H. **PLANT**, of Meriden, Jan. 18, 1826, by Samuel Miller	28
BREWSTER, Samuel, m. Mary **PATERSON**, Aug. 6, 1848, by Rev. [ ] Wheaton	93
BRISTOL, Benedict, m. Nancy Ann **PARKER**, b. of Cheshire, Jan. 2, 1848, by Rev. John E. Searles	92
George, of Cheshire, m. Lucy Jane **CASTELON**, of Berlin, Feb. 17, 1853, by Rev. Francis Bottom	118
Julius, of Southington, m. Fanny **HITCHCOCK**, of Cheshire, Dec. 29, 1852, by Rev. Harvey Miller	115
BRONSON, Eliza, m. Franklin **GRISWOLD**, b. of Meriden, Nov. 22, 1829, by Rev. James Keeler	36
Zenas, m. Sally **MITCHELL**, Oct. 3, 1824, by Charles J. Hinsdale	25
BROOKS, BROOK, Alfred, m. Sarah H. **UPSON**, b. of Meriden, May 13, 1838, by Arthur Granger	57
Eliza C., of Waterbury, m. Samuel A. **MERRIAM**, of Meriden, Jan. 1, 1833, by Rev. Robert A. Hallum	46
Enos, of Farmington, m. Eunice **HALL**, of Meriden, Oct. 2, 1822, by Rev. Josiah Graves, of Middletown	22
Fidelia, of Wallingford, m. Douglass **CHAPMAN**, of Meriden, Dec. 25, 1848, by Rev. N. S. Wheaton	95
James S., m. Melicent A. **CLARK**, b. of Meriden, Aug. 31, 1823, by Reuben Ives	23
Laura, m. Roswell **COWLES**, Jan. 19, 1805	2
Laura A., m. Richard W. **FOWLER**, Dec. 26, 1853, by Rev. G. W. Perkins	123
William, m. Mary Ann **SIZER**, May 21, 1836, by George B Atwell	53
BROWN, Anne O., of Meriden, m. Israel A. **SHERMAN**, of Freedonia, N.Y., July 20, 1830, by Charles J. Hinsdale	38
Elizur, of Canton, Conn., m. Maria **CLINTON**, of Meriden, Apr. 15, 1841, by Rev. G. W. Perkins	64
Eunice W., of Windsor, m. Philander **STEVENS**, of Meriden, Sept. 17, 1848, by Rev. Albert Nash	97
Harriet C., m. Roderick **BROWN**, b. of Meriden, May 6, 1849, by Rev. A. A. Stephens	100
Roderick, m. Harriet C. **BROWN**, b. of Meriden, May 6, 1849, by Rev. A. A .Stephens	100
Sarah Jane, m. James **RYAN**, b. of Meriden, Mar. 31, 1850, by Rev. George W. Perkins	103
BUCKINGHAM, Samuel J., of Oxford, m. Marana A. **BLODGETT**, now of Meriden, June 15, 1851, by Rev. G. W. Perkins	106
BUCKLEY, Benjamin J., m. Emily A. **CLARK**, b. of Meriden, Dec. 30, 1838, by Rev. John M. Guion	60
BULL, Edwin Y., s. [William & Ruth], b. Feb. 19, 1823	69

	Page
BULL (cont.)	
Francis D., of Meriden, m. Dewit C. **BANCROFT**, of Rome, N.Y., Mar. 31, 1845, by Rev. G. W. Perkins	80
George W., s. William & Ruth, b. May 9, 1809	69
George W., m. Julia A. **COOK**, b. of Meriden, Sept. 2, 1841, by Rev. Harvey Miller	65
William H., s. [William & Ruth], b. Dec. 21, 1818	69

BUNNELL, BUNNEL, Jesse H., m. Ruth Ann **PARKER**, of Meriden, Oct. 14, 1835, by Rev. Simon Shailer, of Wallingford — 52

Sarah A., m. Isaac C. **RICHMOND**, Oct. 23, 1853, by Rev. Harvey Miller — 121

BURGHOFF, Fredericka, of Wallingford, late of Hanover, Germany, m. Charles Schneeman, Nov. 4, 1852, by Rev. Harvey Miller — 114

BURNS, Catherine, m. Michal **COLLINS**, b. of Meriden, Sept. 10, 1848, by Rev. G. W. Perkins — 95

BURR, Asa, of Haddam, m. Mrs. Rachel **MORGAN**, Sept. 4, 1853, by Rev. A. S. Cheesbrough — 119

Esther, m. Edward **SPARKS**, Nov. 27, 1823, by Charles J. Hinsdale — 24

Martha M., of Haddam., m. Frederick W. **HOTCHKISS**, of New Britain, Dec. 18, 1853, by [Rev. N. Mead] — 123

BURRITT, Lucretia, of Meriden, m. Joseph **LOISELLE**, of Montreal, Canada, Oct. 21, 1849, by Rev. Harvey Miller — 99

BUSH, Eunice K., m. Patrick J. **CLARK**, Sept. 2, 1840, by Rev. Edwin R. Gilbert — 63

BUTLER, Albert, b. Nov. 8, 1801 — 66

Charles D., m. Harriet **IVES**, b. of Pittsfield, Mass., Feb. 17, 1829, by Sam[ue]l Miller — 34

Harriet, of Meriden, m. Andrew A. **BRADLEY**, formerly of Meriden, now of Dorchester, Mass., June 4, 1845, by Rev. G. W. Perkins — 81

Henry, b. Nov. 6, 1807 — 66

Henry C., b. Nov. 6, 1807; [m. Sophronia **HOTCHKISS**,] — 66

Henry C., of Meriden, m. Sophronia **HOTCHKISS**, of Meriden, Jan. 12, 1832, by Charles J. Hinsdale — 43

Henry C., m. Elizabeth **FOSTER**, Nov. 25, 1841, by Rev. G. W. Perkins — 68

Isaac, b. Oct. 20, 1824 — 66

Isaac, m. Sarah I **SHIPMAN**, b. of Meriden, Sept. 22, 1851, by Rev. A. A. Stevens — 108

Joel J., m. Maryann **NORTON**, [Aug.] 27, [1835], by George B Atwell — 51

John, b. Sept. 15, 1770; [m. Ruth **PARKER**,] — 66

John, Jr., b. Nov. 27, 1816 — 66

John, m. Ann **REDFIELD**, b. of Meriden, Aug. 20, 1839, by Rev. Melancthon Hoyt — 61

John, Jr., m. Esther T. **ATWATER**, b. of Meriden, Mar. 11, 1849, by Rev. N. S Wheaton — 96

John Hotchkiss, s. [Henry C. & Sophronia], b. July 27, 1839 — 66

John O., m. Susan N. **BRAGDON**, b. of Meriden, Aug. 29, 1852, by Rev. Harvey Miller — 112

Julia, [d. John & Ruth], b. Dec. 17, 1798; d. Oct. 2, 1799 — 66

Justus, m. Fanny **GRISWOLD**, b. of Meriden, Apr. 26, 1829, by Rev. James Keeler — 35

BARBOUR COLLECTION

	Page
BUTLER (cont.)	
Laura, m. Moses **LYMAN**, Oct. 26, 1820, by Erastus Ripley	19
Levi, b. June 19 ,1819	66
Lucetta, of Meriden, m. Jason **PARKER**, of Cheshire, Mar. 29, 1821, by James Noyes	20
Lucy A., of Meriden, m. Lorenzo **SMITH**, of Westbrook Apr. 4, 1847, by Rev. C. Munson	90
Lucy Cowles, d. [Henry C. & Sophronia], b. May 5, 1833	66
Lyman, b. July 29, 1814	66
Lyman, m. Mary Ann **CLARK**, Jan. 8, 1840, by Harvey Miller	58
Mary M., of Middletown, m. Loomis L. **PERKINS**, of Hitchcockville, Oct. 8, 1848, by Rev. Albert Nash	97
Mary Philomela, d. [Henry C. & Sophronia], b. Aug. 10, 1835	66
Philomela, w. [ ], d. Mar. 20, 1809	66
Philomela, b. Feb. 22, 1812	66
Philomela, b. [ ], d. July 17, 1814	66
Ruth, w. John, d. Sept 30, 1799	66
Ruth A., b. Nov. 28, 1804	66
Ruth A., m. Morris **STEPHENS**, of Durham, Jan. 14, 1830, by Charles J. Hinsdale	36
Sophronia, w. Henry C., d. Apr. 17, 1841	66
Susan, b. Jan. 1, 1822	66
Susan, m. Sidney P. **HALL**, Apr. 2, 1843, by Rev. J. F. Cushing	87
Susannah, m. Aaron **CURTIS**, Oct. 13, 1793	13
Uriah, of Meriden, m. Jennet Minerva **LEWIS**, of Bristol, Sept. 24, 1826, by Samuel Miller	29
William Kirtland, s. Levi & Harriet M., b. Oct. 31, 1844	82
BUTTON, Bedotha P., of North Haven, m. Lemuel J. **CURTISS**, of Meriden, Dec. 24, 1835, by Rev. Edward Ingersoll	52
BYINGTON, Robert A., of Wallingford, m. Lovisa **MILLER**, of Meriden, Sept. 5, 1830, by Rev. Russell Jennings	39
CAMP, Phoebe E., d. of Elah, of Meriden, m. F. E. **HINMAN**, of Kinderhook, N.Y., Sept. 26, 1843, by G. W. Perkins	75
CANFIELD, Jared H., of New Haven, m. Mary A. **ANDREWS**, of Meriden, May 19, 1840, by Harvey Miller	62
CANNON, Burdett, of Wallingford, m. Juliett **MERRIAM**, of Meriden, [Apr.] 25, [1839], by Rev. Edwin R. Gilbert, of Wallingford	60
CARRINGTON, Edwin O., of Ohio, m. Emily **YALE**, of Meriden, July 12, 1842, by Rev. G. W. Perkins	70
CARTER, Lewis, m. Maria **PARKER**, b. of Wallingford, Oct. 15, 1823, by Samuel Miller	23
CASTELON, [see also **KESTEREN**], Lucy Jane, of Berlin, m. George **BRISTOL**, of Cheshire, Feb. 17, 1853, by Rev. Francis Bottom	118
CATLIN, George P., of Amenia, m. Lydia **BOOTH**, Nov. 23, 1853, by Rev. G. W. Perkins	122
CHAFFEE, Henry R., m. Lucy A. **ANDREWS**, Dec. 27, 1852, by Rev. Giles H. Deshon	114
CHAPMAN, [see also **CHIPMAN**], Douglass, of Meriden, m. Fidelia **BROOKS**, of Wallingford, Dec. 25, 1848, by Rev. N. S. Wheaton	95
Eliphalet H., m. Antonette Y. **ISBELL**, of Meriden, Nov. 22, 1846, by Rev. H. Miller	88

	Page
CHAPMAN (cont.)	
Samuel, of Hartford, m. wid. Mary K. **WEIGHT**, of Meriden, Dec. 20, 1846, by Rev. John Parker	89
CHILDS, Ralph P., of Chatham, m. Chloe **HULL**, of Cheshire, Jan. 4, 1846, by Rev. H. Miller	84
CHIPMAN, [see also **CHAPMAN**], Elizabeth, m. Enos **GRANNISS**, Nov. 24, 1803	14
CHURCH, Henry J., m. Elizabeth A. **FOSKETT**, b. of Meriden, May 12, 1853, by Rev. Harvey Miller	116
CHURCHILL, William E., m. Sarah M. **COWLES**, b. of Meriden, July 24, 1832, by Charles J. Hinsdale	46
CLARK, CLARKE, Abel D., of Pittsfield, m. Jerusha **HART**, of Meriden, Sept. 12, 1822, by Samuel Miller	21
Charles, s. Charles & Hannah, b. Nov. 4, 1815	16
Charles, Jr., m. Emma **PEARSON**, Oct. 21, 1853, by Rev. Giles H. Deshon	122
Charles H., m. Jennette **CURTIS**, d. of Asahel, b. of Meriden, Dec. 25, 1836, by Rev. John Marshall Guion	55
Chaunc[e]y, m. Mary **SMITH**, Dec. 22, 1824, by Charles J. Hinsdale	26
Cordelia Sophia, m. Ezra **IVES**, Dec. 9, 1845, by Rev. Saul Clark	83
Edwin B., of Chester, m. Harriet B. **NEWTON**, of Meriden, June 3, 1844, by Rev. G. W. Perkins	76
Elizabeth B. of Meriden, m. Henry R. **BARNES**, of New Haven, Aug. 11, 1846, by Rev. Saul Clark	86
Emeline S., of Meriden, m. Henry **STEDMAN**, of Berlin, Aug. 13, 1828, by Rev. James Keeler	33
Emily A., m. Benjamin J. **BUCKLEY**, b. of Meriden, Dec. 30, 1838, by Rev. John M. Guion	60
Gertrude A., of Meriden, m. James B. **MERRIAM**, of Wallingford, Feb. 3, 1850, by Rev. H. Miller	101
Harriet R., of Meriden, m. Rev. John T. **PETTEE**, of Winchendon, Mass., Oct. 26, 1843, by Rev. John Parker	72
Horace, of Chatham, m. Phebe **BONFOEY**, of Meriden, Sept. 21, 1835, by Rev. Edward Ingersoll	51
Lavinia, m. Russel **PACKARD**, b. of Pittsfield, Mass., Feb. 17, 1829, by Samuel Miller	34
Lydia Ann, d. [Patrick & Lydia], b. Mar. 22, 1810	16
Lydia Ann, d. [Patrick & Lydia], b. May 7, 1813; d. [ ]	16
Lydia Ann, d. [Patrick & Lydia], d. Aug. 10, 1813	16
Lydia Ann, d. [Patrick & Lydia], d. Sept. 15, 1814	16
Marcy Ann Smith, d. [Patrick & Lydia], b. Nov. 28, 1816	16
Mary Ann, m. Lyman **BUTLER**, Jan. 8, 1840, by Harvey Miller	58
Millicent, d. [Patrick & Lydia], b. June 6, 1802	16
Melicent A., m. James S. **BROOKS**, b. of Meriden, Aug. 31, 1823, by Reuben Ives	23
Morris C., m. Sarah J. **BARTHOLOMEW**, May 31, 1852, by Rev. Harvey Miller. Witnesses Geo[rge] H. Andrews, Roxanna Andrews. Affidavit made Feb. 14, 1868, to John H. Bari, Notary Public.	110
Nancy, of Meriden, m. Philemon **PIERPOINT**, of North Haven, Dec. 18, 1842, by C. W. Everest	70
Nancy, m. Philemon **PIERPOINT**, Dec. 18, 1842, by Rev. C. W. Everest	87

	Page
CLARK, CLARKE (cont.)	
Patrick, m. Lydia **TAYLOR**, Aug. 22, 1801	16
Patrick J., m. Eunice K. **BUSH**, of Meriden, Sept. 2, 1840, by Rev. Edwin R. Gilbert	63
Patrick Jeremiah, s. [Patrick & Lydia], b. Jan. 18, 1815	16
Remic, m. Sarah **WHITE**, Dec. 11, 1825, by Charles J .Hinsdale	27
Remick K., m. Abigail **REDFIELD**, b. of Meriden, Jan. 12, 1841, by Rev. Harvey Miller	63
Remeck Knowl[e]s, s. [Patrick & Lydia], b. Sept. 20, 1803	16
Roxanna Barns, d. [Patrick & Lydia], b. Oct. 3, 1811	16
Roxanna Barns, d. [Patrick & Lydia], d. July 24, 1813	16
Samuel S., m. Jane M. **COE**, b. of Meriden, Feb. 4, 1847, by Rev. G. W. Perkins	89
Susan F., m. Phineas A. **SPENCER**, b. of Meriden, Mar. 31, 1850, by Rev. Albert Nash	101
Tiresa, d. [Patrick & Lydia], b. July 20, 1805	16
Tiresa, d. [Patrick & Lydia], d. Aug. 16, 1806	16
Tiresa Emeline, d. [Patrick & Lydia], b. June 7, 1807	16
CLINTON, Lua, of Meriden, m. Alvin E. **BIVINS**, of Southington, Nov. 24, 1831, by Charles J. Hinsdale	43
Maria, of Meriden, m. Elizur **BROWN**, of Canton, Conn., Apr. 15, 1841, by Rev. G. W. Perkins	64
COAN, [see also **CONE**], William Y., m. Jane A. **UPSON**, of Meriden, Nov. 8, 1841, by Rev. G. W. Perkins	66
COE, Andrew, of Middletown, m. Caroline E. **COE**, of Meriden, [May 5, 1841], by Rev. John Moore, of Hartford	64
Caroline E., of Meriden, m. Andrew **COE**, of Middletown, [May 5, 1841], by Rev. John Moore, of Hartford	64
Frances, m. William L. **BRADLEY**, Nov. 7, 1848, by Rev. Harvey Miller	96
Harriet L. Mrs., of Meriden, m. Hezekiah **HALL**, of Wallingford, May 5, 1841, by Rev. John Moore, of Hartford	64
Jane M., m. Samuel S. **CLARK**, b. of Meriden, Feb. 4, 1847, by Rev. G. W. Perkins	89
Timothy J., of Middletown, m. Lavinia A. **HALL**, of Meriden, May 3, 1846, by Rev. Hervey Miller	86
William W., of Middletown, m. Dency **MARKHAM**, of Middle Haddam, Apr. 27, 1851, by Rev. Harvey Miller	106
COLE, [see also **COWLES**], Lucy, m. Pomeroy **STACK**, Nov. 15, 1826, by Charles J. Hinsdale	29
Urban, m. Mary L. **GRAHAM**, of Berlin, Sept. 15, 1844, by Rev. H. Miller	78
COLLINS, Aaron L., m. Sylvia A. **WHITE**, Mar. 26, 1851, by Rev. G. W. Perkins	106
Betsey, m. Stephen **SEYMOUR**, Nov. 27, 1823, by Charles J. Hinsdale	24
Edward J., of Meriden, m. Marion **PATRICK**, of Berlin, Aug. 25, 1846, by Rev. G. W. Perkins	86
Huldah, of Meriden, m. Jesse M. **MORRIS**, of Ohio, Nov. 21, 1822, by Rev. Stephen Hays, of Middletown	22
Keziah, m. Curtis L. **NORTH**, b. of Meriden, Aug. 26, 1841, by Rev. G W. Perkins	65
Lament, m. Brenton **HALL**, Feb. 18, 1762	5

	Page
COLLINS (cont.)	
Michal, m. Catherine **BURNS**, b. of Meriden, Sept. 10, 1848, by Rev. G. W. Perkins	95
Nancy, m. Asaph **MERRIAM**, b. of Meriden, Mar. 28, 1833, by Charles J. Hinsdale	46
Susan, m. William T. **RICE**, b. of Meriden, Nov. 7, 1841, by Rev. G. W. Perkins	65
COLTON, Erastus, of Cheshire, m. Jennet **ALLEN**, of Meriden, Sept. 13, 1838, by Arthur Granger	60
CONE, [see also **COAN**], Cynthia, m. Darius **BENHAM**, Aug. 3, 1806	2
Hannah, m. Thaddeus **IVES**, Nov. 4, 1807	9
Sylvanus J., of Meriden, m. Eveline E. **STONE**, of Middletown, May 15, 1845, by Rev. B. H. Miller	81
Sylvanus J., of Meriden, m. Louisa **STOWE**, of Middletown, Nov. 4, 1849, by Rev. Harvey Miller	99
CONKLIN, Harriet, m. Joseph **BARBOUR**, b. of Meriden, Oct. 22, 1852, by Rev. A. A. Stevens	113
CONLEY, Melitta, m. Elias **HOLT**, b. of Meriden, Apr. 18, 1822, by Samuel Miller	21
COOK, Alexander, m. Betsey **COOK**, of Wallingford, Oct. 10, 1836, by Arthur Granger	54
Betsey, of Wallingford, m. Alexander **COOK**, Oct. 10, 1836, by Arthur Granger	54
George W., m. Electa C. **PERKINS**, b. of Meriden, Apr. 18, 1853, by Rev. Harvey Miller	115
Henry W., m. Lydia A. **MARKHAM**, June 23, 1853, by Rev. Harvey Miller	117
Julia A., m. George W. **BULL**, b. of Meriden, Sept. 2, 1841, by Rev. Harvey Miller	65
Loisa, m. Edward **WALDING**, b. of Wallingford, July 30, 1832, by Charles J. Hinsdale	46
Lucius J., of Durham, m. Jane C. **MERRIAM**, Mar. 8, 1846, by Rev. C. Munson	85
Marvin L., of Middletown, m. Mary Jane **CURTIS**, of Berlin, Oct. 13, 1851, by Rev. Daniel S Rodman, of Cheshire	108
Porter, of Wallingford, m. Emeline **DAYTON**, of Meriden, Sept. 16, 1838, by Harvey Miller	57
COOPER, Alfred, of North Haven, m. Mehitabel **ANDREWS**, of Hamden, Dec. 24, 1850, by Harvey Miller	104
CORNWELL, Lester, of Middletown, m. Betsey **MIX**, of Wallingford, Oct. 6, 1827, by Sam[ue]l Miller	32
COTTON, Jared, of Middletown, m. Alma **BALDWIN**, of Meriden, Oct. 23, 1843, by Rev. Levi H. Wakeman, of Westfield	72
COUCH, Ann, of Meriden, m. Nathaniel **ANDREWS**, Jr., of Wallingford, Sept. 13, 1821, by Sam[ue]ll Miller	20
Beri, of Meriden, m. Marria **REDFIELD**, of Killingworth, Apr. 28, 1823, by Samuel Miller	23
Ira, m. Lucy Cordelia **TRACY**, b. of Meriden, Sept. 25, 1828, by Rev. James Keeler	34
John, Capt., d. Apr. 11, 1806	4
Lucy Ann, m. Francis W. **SMITH**, b. of Meriden, Dec. 15, 1852, by Rev. Giles H. Deshon	114

	Page
COUCH (cont.)	
Maria, m. Benjamin **TWISS**, Apr. 14, 1830, by Rev. William Bentley	37
Rosetta, m. Nelson **MERRIAM**, b. of Meriden, Mar. 28, 1833, by Charles J. Hinsdale	46
Susan M., m. Henry S. **WHITE**, b. of Meriden, Oct. 17, 1844, by Rev. Robert A. Hallam, of New London	78
COWLES, [see also **COLE**], Caroline B., of Meriden, m. Henry S. **DURAND**, of Berlin, Oct. 15, 1838, by Arthur Granger	60
Caroline R., [d. Roswell & Laura], b. Dec. 27, 1817	31
Elisha Allin, [s. Roswell & Laura], b. Dec. 20, 1809	31
George, [s. Roswell & Laura], b. Apr. 25, 1814	31
Gilbert, s. Roswell & Laura, b. Sept. 5, 1807	8
Gilbert, s. Roswell & Laura, b. Sept. 5, 1807	31
Lucy, m. Isaac I. **TIBBALS**, b. of Meriden, Sept. 1, 1831, by Charles J. Hinsdale	43
Mary Ann, d. Roswell & Laura, b. Dec. 8, 1805	2
Orrin, m. Mary E. **ANDREWS**, b. of Meriden, Oct. 13, 1830, by Rev. James [Keeler]	40
Philomela, b. Mar. 25, 1777	66
Rebecca, d. May 13, 1811	12
Roswell, m. Laura **BROOKS**, Jan. 19, 1805	2
Samuel, [s. Roswell & Laura], b. Nov. 14, 1821	31
Sarah M., m. William E. **CHURCHILL**, b. of Meriden, July 24, 1832, by Charles J. Hinsdale	46
Sophia, m. Erastus **HALL**, Oct. 13, 1830, by Rev. James Keeler	40
William, [s. Roswell & Laura], b. Feb. 8, 1812	31
COYLE, Catharine E., m. David **ELLIS**, Nov. 5, 1848, by Rev. Harvey Miller	95
CRANDALL, Cornelia, of Middletown, m. Darius **PEARCE**, July 4, 1839, by Harvey Miller	61
CROCKER, Edwin Russel, s. [Orsanius & Julia Ann], b. Aug. 20, 1834	59
Julia Ann, d. [Orsanius & Delia], b. Sept. 21, 1831	59
Orsanius, b. Dec. 4, 1804; m. Delia **BIRDSEY**, Sept. 2, 1830	59
Orsanius, m. Delia **BIRDSEY**, Sept. 2, 1830, by Rev. Russell Jennings	39
Sarah Delia, d. [Orsanius & Julia Ann], b. Nov. 10, 1836	59
CROSBY, Nancy C., m. Ezekiel R. **MERRIAM**, b. of Meriden, Apr. 30, 1851, by Rev. G. W. Perkins	106
CROWELL, Mary C., of Middletown, m. Truman S. **STILES**, of Southbury, Apr. 12, 1851, by Rev. Harvey Miller	105
CUMMINS, Eunice, m. Roswell **CURTIS**, July 30, [1809], by Ephraim Cook, J.P.	11
CURTIS, CURTISS, Aaron, m. Susannah **BUTLER**, Oct. 13, 1793	13
Abagail, w. Elisha, d. Feb. 28, 1826	29
Alanson, s. Elisha, b. Oct. 27, 1818	25
Alanson, s. Elisha & Abigail, b. Oct. 27, 1818	29
Alfred, s. [Levi & Sarah], b. Jan. 1, 1798	13
Alfred P., m. Sarah M. **HITCHCOCK**, b. of Meriden, Oct. 15, 1851, by Rev. Giles H. Deshon	109
Alfred Pierpont, [s. Samuel & Polly], b. July 4, 1817	32
Amasa Horatio Nelson, s. Roswell & Eunice, b. Jan. 30, 1810	11
Amelia, d. Amos & Polly, b. Sept. 7, 1804	4

	Page
CURTIS, CURTISS (cont.)	
Amelia, of Meriden, m. David Barber **GILBERT**, of Tolland, Nov. 30, 1824, by Rev. Ashbil Baldwin	26
Amelia, [d. Amos], d. July 15, 1829	31
Amos, b. Apr. 14, 1779; d. Sept. 25, 1857	31
Amos, m. Polly **CURTIS**, Mar. 18, 1802	4
Amos, m. Louisa **JOHNSON**, Dec. 6, 1818	31
Asahel, m. Mehetabel **REDFIELD**, Nov. 8, 1812	14
Asahel, Jr., [s. Asahel & Mahitable], b. Feb. 25, 1821	35
Asahel, Jr., m. Ann E. **WILCOX**, Feb. 29, 1844, by Rev. J. F Cushing	87
Asahel Benham, s. [Aaron & Susannah], b. Jan. 10, 1797	13
Asahel H., m. Juliett **YALE**, b. of Meriden, Sept. 12, 1841, by Rev. C. W. Everest	65
Augusta Loisa, d. [Homer & Julia Ann], b. June 29, 1840	67
Benjamin Upson, [s. Asahel & Mahitable], b. July 20, 1817	35
Caroline, m. Edward N. **HALL**, b. of Meriden, Jan. 1, 1843, by Harvey Miller	71
Charles Augustus, s. Ivah & Hannah, b. Aug. 17, 1807	9
Clarissa, m. Ezra **RUTTY**, b. of Meriden, Sept. 16, 1832, by Rev. Russell Jennings	46
Daniel Reed, s. [Aaron & Susannah], b. Apr. 24, 1800	13
Edmond B., of Meriden, m. Hannah L. **LANE**, of Wallingford, Feb. 15, 1852, by Rev. Harvey Miller	110
Edwin, s. Elisha & Abigail, b. Sept. 1, 1805	7
Edwin E., m. Aurelia **BENHAM**, Dec. 24, 1826, by Rev. Nathaniel T. Bruce, in St. Andrews Church	29
Eli E., m. Louisa **CURTISS**, b. of Meriden, Feb. 27, 1825, by Samuel Miller	29
Eli E., m. July A. **CURTIS**, Aug. 30, 1820, by Rev. Russell Jennings	39
Eli Elisha, s. Elisha & Abigail, b. Feb. 27, 1804	7
Elisha, m. Abigail **HALL**, Feb. 18, 1796	7
Eliza, d. Samuel & Polly, b. mar. 4, 1807	10
Eliza Ann, of Meriden, m. Henry D. **BOOTH**, of New York, Aug. 29, 1831, by Rev. James Keeler	42
Elizabeth, of Meriden, m. Edwin L. **LINES**, of Baltimore, Md., Aug. 13, 1832, by Charles J. Hinsdale	46
Elizabeth Collins, d. Homer & Julia Ann, b. Sept. 14, 1836	67
Emeline, d. Samuel & Polly, b. Sept. 12, 1808	10
Emeline, m. Lewis A. **GREEN**, Apr. 19, 1827, by Nathaniel T Bruce	30
Emila Emilesa, d. Iva & Hannah, b. Dec. 25, 1809	14
Enos Hall, s. Elisha & Abigail, b. Sept. 12, 1796	7
Eunice, m. Darius **BENHAM**, [May] 4, [1836], by George B Atwell	53
George Redfield, [s. Asahel & Mahitable], b. Dec. 25, 1825	35
Hannah, m. Oliver **ANDREWS**, Dec. 27, 1796	7
Hannah, m. Rev. John Turner **CUSHING**, Sept. 15, 1847, by Rev. Cyrus Munson	92
Harley, s. [Levi & Sarah], b. Mar. 2, 1801	13
Harrison, m. Eliza **BRADLEY**, b. of Meriden, Oct. 17, 1838, by Harvey Miller	57
James Harrison, s. Elisha & Abigail, b. Mar. 5, 1817	17
James Harrison, s. Elisha & Abagail, d. Mar. 2, 1819	29
Jennett, d. Asahel & Mahitable, b. Mar. 14, 1814	35

	Page
CURTIS, CURTISS (cont.)	
Jennette, d. Asahel, m. Charles H. **CLARK**, b. of Meriden, Dec. 25, 1836, by Rev. John Marshall Guion	55
Jery, s. [Levi & Sarah], b. Feb. 24, 1796	13
Jesse, m. Beulah W. **JOHNSON**, Dec. 31, 1849, by Rev. Harvey Miller	100
July A., m. Eli E. **CURTIS**, Aug. 30, 1830, by Rev. Russell Jennings	39
Kelsey, of Wallingford, m. Eliza R. **SUTLIFF**, of Meriden, Apr. 11, 1847, by Rev. Harvey Miller	90
Laurettta, d. Roswell & Eunice, b. Sept. 3 ,1812	15
Lemuel, s. Eli E. & Julia A., b. Aug. 17, 1830	43
Lemuel J., of Meriden, m. Bedotha P. **BUTTON**, of North Haven, Dec. 24, 1835, by Rev. Edward Ingersoll	52
Lemuel Johnson, s. Elisha & Abigail, b. Jan. 15, 1814	15
Leonard, s. [Levi & Sarah], b. June 15, 1805	13
Levi, m. Lucy **HALL**, Mar. 28, 1790	13
Levi, [s. Levi & Lucy], b. May 12, 1791	13
Levi, m. Sarah **FRANCES**, Dec. 5, 1792	13
Louisa, m. Eli E. **CURTISS**, b. of Meriden, Feb. 27, 1825, by Samuel Miller	27
Lucius, m. Hannah **BARKER**, b. of Meriden, May 15, 1853, by Rev. George W. Perkins	117
Lucy, w. Levi, d. May 12, 1791	5
Lucy, d. [Levi & Sarah], b. May 24, 1794	13
Lucy, d. Elisha & Abigail, b Apr. 14, 1800	7
Lucy, m. Horace **REDFIELD**, Dec. 25, 1817	31
Lucy M., [d. Amos & Louisa], b. Jan. 16, 1820	31
Lucy Maria, of Meriden, m. Edgar **MUNSON**, of Bradford, N.Y., June 15, 1852, by Rev. Robert A. Hallam, of New London	113
Maria, d. Amos & Polly, b. July 16, 1806	4
Mary, of Meriden, m. Samuel **ROBERTS**, of Berlin, May 5 ,1829, by Charles J. Hinsdale	35
Mary H. ,of Meriden, m. John **BECKLEY**, of Berlin, Nov. 17, 1850, by Rev. Harvey Miller	102
Mary Jane, of Berlin, m. Marvin L. **COOK**, of Middletown, Oct. 13, 1851, by Rev. Daniel S. Rodman, of Cheshire	108
Mary Rice, d. Iva & Hannah, b Apr. 9, 1812	14
Oliver Bronson, [s. Aaron & Susannah], b. Aug. 9, 1794	13
Patty, d. [Levi & Sarah], b. Oct. 24, 1800	13
Phebe, m. Sidney **MERRIAM**, Oct. 8 ,1807	6
Phebe Ann, [d. Asahel & Mahitable], b. June 21, 1815	35
Phebe Ann, m. Robert A. **HALLAM**, b. of Meriden, Nov. 4, 1834, by Rev. William H. Walter, of Milford	49
Polly, m. Amos **CURTIS**, Mar. 18 ,1802	4
Polly, [d. Amos], b. Mar. 16, 1812; d. Apr. 10, 1826	31
Polly Samantha, d. Samuel & Polly, b. Jan. 18 ,1812	32
Polly Samantha, of Meriden, m. W[illia]m H. **GREEN**, of New Haven, Nov. 14, 1830, by Rev. James Keeler	41
Roswell, m. Eunice **CUMMINS**, July 30, [1809], by Ephraim Cook, J.P.	11
Ruth, m. Silas **RICE**, Aug. 4 ,1796	8
Ruth, [d. Amos], b. Mar. 14, 1809; d. Dec. 3, 1812	31
Samuel, m. Polly **ANDREWS** Nov. 20 ,1805	10

MERIDEN VITAL RECORDS 137

Page

CURTIS, CURTISS (cont.)
   Samuel T., m. Rebecca T. **HOUGH**, b. of Meriden, Oct. 3, 1832 ,by
      Charles J. Hinsdale   45
   Sylvester J., [s. Amos & Louisa], b. Sept. 30, 1826   31
   William A., [s. Amos], b. May 26, 1816   31
CUSHING, John Turner, Rev. m. Hannah **CURTIS**, Sept. 15, 1847, by
   Rev. Cyrus Munson   92
CUTLER, William D., of Meriden, m. Ann **DAVIDSON**, of Brooklyn,
   [July], 18, [1830], by Rev. Russell Jennings   39
DANIELS, Charles, of Lyme, m. Emily L. **LESTER**, of Meriden, May 2,
   1847, by Rev. Harvey Miller   90
   Nathan A., of Norwich, m. Sarah Jane **STEWART**, of Meriden, Jan.
      2, 1837, by Geo[rge] B. Atwell   55
   Seth J., m. Rebecca C. **WOOD**, b. of Southwick, Mass., May 3,
      1851, by Tilton C. Doolittle, J.P.   107
DARROW, Porter, m. Elizabeth **DURAND** Apr. 6, 1852, by Rev. A. A.
   Stevens   111
DAVIDSON, Ann, of Brooklyn, m. William D. **CUTLER**, of Meriden,
   [July] 18, [1830], by Rev Russell Jennings   39
DAYTON, Darling, m. Asenath **THOMPSON**, May 13, 1814   15
   Decatur, s. [Darling & Asenath], b. Oct. 31, 1815   15
   Emeline, of Meriden, m. Porter **COOK**, of Wallingford, Sept. 16,
      1838, by Harvey Miller   57
   Jane Wright, d. Darling & Asenath, b. Aug. 5, 1823   23
   Lydia Emeline, d. Darling & Asenath, b. Apr. 9, 1820   18
   Mary Ann, m. John **SUTLIFF**, Nov .22, 1827, by Charles J.
      Hinsdale   32
   Merriam* Bedotha, d. Darling & Asenath, b. May 22, 1817
      *(Mariann)   17
   Sally, m. James P. **REDFIELD**, Mar. 19, 1826, by Charles J.
      Hinsdale   28
DeWOLF, Sylvia, m. Hiram **UPSON**, Sept. 25, 1828, by Charles J.
   Hinsdale   34
DICKINSON, Harriet E., of New Haven, m. Edwin **REDFIELD**, of
   Meriden, Dec. 24, 1848, by Rev. N. S. Wheaton   95
DIMOCK, Sarah Ann, of Meriden, m. Joseph B. **BRAINARD**, of
   Haddam, May 5, 1833, by Rev Robert A. Hallum   47
DIXON, Eliza, of Montreal, L.C., m. Charles **PAGE**, of East Haven, Apr.
   13, 1847, by Rev. Harvey Miller   90
DOOLITTLE, Eliza, m. Jonas **STANLEY**, Mar. 20, 1808   8
   Mary J., of Meriden, m. Andrew J. **SMITH**, of Bristol, Jan. 14, 1851,
      by Rev. Harvey Miller   104
DORMAN, Harriet, m. Rufus **WARNER**, Mar. 11, 1832, by Charles J.
   Hinsdale   43
DOUGLASS, Eliza H., of New Haven, m. Benjamin H. **ROBERTS**, of
   Middletown, Apr. 4, 1852, by Rev. G. W. Perkins   110
   John Ballard, d. June 22, 1814   15
   Julia A., of Cheshire, m. Newton W. **DOWNS**, of New Haven, Sept.
      16, 1849, by Rev. Harvey Miller   99
   Julia Ann, m. Jeremiah **HILL**, July 2, 1826, by Charles J. Hinsdale   29
   Julia Ann, of Meriden, m. Alva **MERRIAM**, of Coventry, O., Jan.
      18, 1846, by Rev. E Cushman   83-4

	Page
DOUGLASS (cont.)	
Lemuel L., of Meriden, m. Mary A. **IVES**, of North Haven, May 11, 1842, by Rev. G. W. Perkins	69
Louisa Antoineete, d. [Thomas & Hannah], b. Feb. 13, 1816	16
Mary M., of Meriden, m. Warren S. **BRADLEY**, of Branford, May 11, 1842, by Rev. G. W .Perkins	69
Polly Samantha, m. Samuel **BENHAM**, Oct. 13, 1825, by Charles J. Hinsdale	27
Reuben H., m. Zeruah **MILES**, of Southington, Jan. 4, 1853, by Rev. A. A. Stevens	115
Thomas, m. Hannah **SANFORD**, Sept. 26, 1814	16
DOWD, Delia M., m. Ossian L. **HATCH**, b. of Meriden, Oct. 13, 1852, by Rev. G. W .Perkins	117
DOWNS, Newton W., of New Haven, m. Julia A. **DOUGLASS**, of Cheshire, Sept. 16, 1849, by Rev. Harvey Miller	99
DUNHAM, George, of Southington, m. Isabella **BRADLEY**, of Meriden, May 3, 1853, by Rev. F. Bolton	116
Samuel, m. Susan **FOSTER**, Apr. 16, 1853, by Rev. George W. Perkins	117
DURAND, Abigail, of Cheshire, m. James **LEWIS**, of Meriden, Oct. 13, 1844, by Rev George W. Perkins	78
Cornelia, of Meriden, m. Edwin S. **JONES**, of New Haven, Nov. 24, 1846, by Rev. G. W. Perkins	89
Elizabeth, m. Porter **DARROW**, Apr. 6, 1852, by Rev. A. A. Stevens	111
Eunice, Mrs., m. Eli **THRALL**, Nov. 23, 1851, by Rev. A A Stevens	109
Henry S., of Berlin, m. Caroline B. **COWLES**, of Meriden, Oct. 16, 1838, by Arthur Granger	60
Sarah H., of Berlin, m. Gamaliel F. **SNOW**, of Meriden, Feb. 2, 1847, by Rev. G. W. Perkins	89
DUTTON, Orrin J., of Southington, m. Irena **RICE**, of Meriden, Oct. 30, 1833, by Charles J. Hinsdale	48
EAGES, Elizabeth, of Meriden, m. George W. **OSBORN**, of New Haven, June 30, 1851, by Rev. G. W. Perkins	107
EATON, Edwin, m. Sarah **HAYDEN**, Dec. 1, 1840, by Erastus Ripley	63
Julia Ann, of Meriden, m. Jesse W. Perkins, of Woodbury, Nov. 29, 1846, by Rev. G. W. Perkins	89
Zerad, of Ellington, m. Emma **HAYDEN**, of Berlin, Mar. 10, 1846, by Rev. H. Miller	85
ELLIOTT, Susan A., m. Hiram **BRADLEY**, b. of Meriden, Sept. 18, 1831, by Rev. Russell Jennings	42
ELLIS, David, m. Catharine E. **COYLE**, of Meriden, Nov. 5, 1848, by Rev. Harvey Miller	95
ELTON, Caroline E., m. Allen L. **PECK**, b. of Berlin, Dec. 29, 1852, by Rev. Harvey Miller	115
ELWELL, Charles W., of Saccarappa, Me., m. Charlotte A. **HANSON**, of Portland, Me., Aug. 1, 1852, by Rev. Harvey Miller	118
EMMONS, Franklin B., of Meriden, m. Sarah A. **BARNES**, of Southington, July 1, 1851, by Rev. G. W. Perkins	107
ENSIGN, Caroline E., of Meriden, m. Jason **MILDRUM**, of Middletown, Aug. 15, 1841, by Rev. Harvey Miller	64
EVARTS, EVERTS, Betsey, of Guilford, m. Joel B. **MERRIAM**, of Meriden, May 18, 1834, by Rev. Robert A. Hallam	48

	Page
EVARTS, EVERTS (cont.)	
Eunice, m. Philo Hart, b. of Meriden, May 7, 1848, by Rev. John E. Searles	93
EVERTS [see under **EVARTS**]	
FARNSWORTH, John F., of Fleming, N.Y., m. Mary **SHORNERS**, of Meriden, Sept. 18, 1853, by Rev. Harvey Miller	120
FARRINGTON, Betsey Ann, [d. Joseph & Tryphena], b. Nov. 28, 1811	21
Elizabeth Ann, of Meriden, m. Everton **BECKLEY**, of Berlin, July 8, 1832, by Horatio Potter	44
James C., of New York, m. Emily C. **BALDWIN**, of Meriden, May 9, 1833, by Iranus Atkins	47
Jennet C., of Meriden, m. Samuel W. **McCAMLEY**, of New York, July 1, 1832, by Horatio Potter	44
Jennet Caroline, [d. Joseph & Tryphena], b. Apr. 13, 1808	21
Joseph, [s. Joseph & Tryphena], b. June 25, 1772	21
Joseph, m. Tryphena **PERKINS**, Oct. 13, 1804	21
Lavinia M., of Meriden, m. Luther **PARMELEE**, of Guilford, Apr. 7, 1836, by Rev. Edward Ingersoll	52
Lavinia Maria, [d. Joseph & Tryphena], b. Mar. 26, 1806	21
Mary, m. James P. **REDFIELD**, July 9, 1809	10
FELLOWS, John, m. Maria **NOBLE**, June 17, 1838, by Erastus Ripley	57
FILES, Harriet, m. William H. **BRAGDON**, Feb. 13, 1851, by Rev. Harvey Miller	104
FINLEY, Cornelia J., of Clinton, m. John **SHELLY**, of Durham, Oct. 24, 1847, by Rev. John E. Searles	92
FLAGG, Samuel A., of Middletown, m. Jane S. **BRADLEY**, of Meriden, Mar. 12, 1851, by Rev. A. A. Stevens	105
FORBES, Albert J., m. Elizabeth B. **BOOTH**, Feb. 16, 1851, by Rev. Giles H. Deshon	104
FORDRED, William, m. Sarah M. **BLAKE**, b. of New York City, Nov. 27, 1836, by Jonathan Goodwin	55
FOSKETT, Elizabeth A., m. Henry J. **CHURCH**, b. of Meriden, May 12, 1853, by Rev. Harvey Miller	116
FOSTER, Abigail, Mrs., m. Ralph H. **BECKLEY**, May 1, 1836, by Arthur Granger	53
Albert, of Meriden, m. Adah **SAVAGE**, of Berlin, June 22, 1853, by Rev. George W. Perkins	119
Amos, m. Ruth [**IVES**], Dec. 10, 1795	9
Amos, [s. Amos & Ruth], b. May 17, 1806	9
Eli, m. Lucina **MERIAM**, Aug. 12, 1824, by Charles J. Hinsdale	25
Elisabeth, m. Bethuel **LUSK**, Feb. 15, 1798	4
Elizabeth, m. Henry C. **BUTLER**, Nov. 25, 1841, by Rev. G. W Perkins	68
Eunice, m. Abner **WAY**, Dec. 28, 1780	3
George, of Haddam, m. Hannah **YALE**, of Meriden, June 5, 1824, by Samuel Miller	25
Homer, s. Matthew & Charlotte, b. Apr. 12, 1806	1
Julia, [d. Amos & Ruth], b. Sept. 10. 1796; d. Oct. 2, 1796	9
Julia, [d. Amos & Ruth], b. Aug. 26, 1804	9
Martin, [s. Amos & Ruth], b. Jan. 24, 1808	9
Percy, [s. Amos & Ruth], b. Jan. 2, 1801	9
Polly, [d. Amos & Ruth], b. Oct. 26, 1797	9
Sarah, d. Levi & Sarah, b. Aug. 30, 1807	2

	Page
FOSTER (cont.)	
Sarah, m. Zina K. **MURDOCK**, b. of Meriden, Sept. 11, 1834, by Charles J. Hinsdale	48
Susan, m. Samuel **DUNHAM**, Apr. 16, 1853, by Rev. George W. Perkins	117
Thomas, d. Oct. 7, 1806	1
Uri, s. Levi & Sarah, b. June 27, 1809	11
William, [s. Amos & Ruth], b. Mar. 11, 1799	9
FOWLER, Richard W., m. Laura A. **BROOKS**, Dec. 26, 1853, by Rev. G. W. Perkins	123
FRANCIS, FRANCES, Frederick, of Berlin, m. Maria J. **HALL**, of Meriden, Aug. 23, 1830, by Charles J. Hinsdale	38
Hannah, m. Joseph **HALL**, Nov. 3, 1803	6
Harriet C., of Meriden, m. William H. **POWERS**, of Abington, Mass., Oct. 8, 1848, by Rev. Harvey Miller	94
Sarah, m. Levi **CURTIS**, Dec. 6, 1792	13
FRARY, James A., m. Susan J. **BENHAM**, Dec. 25, 1832, by Rev. Robert A. Hallum	45
James H., m. Ellen A. **PECK**, Dec. 22, 1852, by Rev. Giles H. Deshon	114
Lydia Ann, of Meriden, m. Luther **BOARDMAN**, of Rocky Hill, Oct. 18, 1838, by Rev. John Marshall Guion	60
Roxanna G., m. W[illia]m W. **LYMAN**, Sept. 5, 1844, by Rev. C. Munson	77
FREEMAN, Greene, m. Emeline **RICE**, July 7, 1842, by Rev. J. F. Cushing	86
FREMELLA, Julia, m. James **STEVENS**, b. of Cheshire, Dec. 20, 1849, by Rev. Albert Nash	100
FRENCH, Cook, of Bethany, m. Lucretia **HALL**, of Meriden, Dec. 6, 1835, by George B. Atwell	52
FRISBIE, Y. Whittemore, of Guiilford, m. Jane C. **LAWRENCE** (?), of Meriden, July 24, 1853, by Rev. Lester Lewis, of Bristol	119
FULLER, Sarah, m. Elihu **WATROUS**, Sept. 10, 1812	33
FURGERSON, Ira, m. Julia **GOODRICH**, May 15, 1853, by Rev. Harvey Miller	116
GALE, Francis A., of Lenox, Mass., m. Mary J. **YALE**, of Meriden, Oct. 10, 1825, by Samuel Miller	27
GALLUP, Alonzo H., of Norwich, m. Rosina E. **BALDWIN**, of Meriden, Sept. 9, 1849, by Rev. Albert Nash	98
GARFIELD, John C., of Tyringham, Mass., m. Sarah M. **RICE**, of Meriden, Dec. 25, 1841, by Rev. C. W. Everest	68
GAYLORD, Elias, Jr., of Cheshire, m. Mary Ann **YALE**, of Meriden, Apr. 18, 1830, by Charles J. Hinsdale	37
GEAR, Francis A., of Meriden, m. George C. **BALDWIN**, of Litchfield, Apr. 13, 1851, by Rev. Harvey Miller	105
GERALDS, Thomas, Rev., of the New York Conference of the Methodist E. Church, m. Betsey **PARKER**, of Meriden, June 17, 1844, by Rev. John Parker	75
GILBERT, David Barber, of Tolland, m. Amelia **CURTISS**, of Meriden, Nov. 30, 1824, by Rev. Ashbil Baldwin	26
Rebecca, of Ludlow, Vt., m. Alonzo B. **HOUGH**, of Meriden, Feb. 28, 1833, by Charles J. Hinsdale	46

	Page
GLADWIN, Silas, of Haddam, m. Thankful B. REMINGTON, of Meriden, Sept. 2, 1846, by Rev. H. Miller	87
GOFF, Lucinda T., of Haddam, m. Henry SEDGEWICK, of Meriden, Mar. 15, 1849, by Rev. Harvey Miller	96
GONEAU, Celia, m. Francis [ ], of Quebec, Canada, Sept. 4, 1852, by Rev. Harvey Miller	112
GOODRICH, Alfred N., of Middletown, m. Ellen A. YALE, of Meriden, Nov. 12, 1848, by Rev. Harvey Miller	96
Julia, m. Ira FURGERSON, May 15, 1853, by Rev. Harvey Miller	116
Martha E., of Meriden, m. Isaac SMITH, of Wallingford, Mar. 18, 1849, by Rev. Harvey Miller	96
Nathan T., m. Evelina TODD, Dec. 6 ,1826, by Charles J. Hinsdale	29
GOODWILL, William, m. Elizabeth MERRIAM, b. of Meriden, May 4, 1841, by Rev. G. W. Perkins	64
GRAHAM, Mary L., of Berlin, m. Urban COLE, Sept. 15, 1844, by Rev. H. Miller	78
GRANNIS, Ann Chipman, d. [Enos & Elizabeth], b. Apr. 20, 1808	14
Elizabeth, d. [Enos & Elizabeth], b. June 2, 1806	14
Enos, m. Elizabeth CHIPMAN, Nov. 24, 1803	14
Enos, s. [Enos & Elizabeth], b. Sept. 6, 1804	14
William Edward, s. [Enos & Elizabeth], b. Dec. 31, 1811	14
GREEN, GREENE, Eliza A., of Meriden, m. Minor G. PAGE, of Willimantic, Oct. 15, 1851, by Rev. G. W. Perkins	108
Lewis A., m. Emeline CURTIS, Apr. 19, 1827, by Nathaniel T. Bruce	30
W[illia]m H., of New Haven, m. Polly Samantha CURTIS, of Meriden, Nov. 14, 1830, by Rev. James Keeler	41
GRIFFIN, Nancy J., m. John H. HOLLAND, Oct. 12, 1853, by Rev. A. A. Stevens* *(First written "by Rev. G. H. Deshon")	122
GRISWOLD, Abner, m. Olive PARKER, Sept. 14, 1802	3
Amanda, d. Giles O. & Lucy, b. July 17, 1800	2
Amanda, m. Sherlock PERKINS, Nov. 6, 1823, by Reuben Ives	24
Calvin, s. Abner & Olive, b. Nov. 9, 1806	3
Caroline, m. Lucius B. SMITH, b. of Meriden, Oct. 30, 1839, by Rev. E. E. Beardsley, of Cheshire	58
Cyrus, s. Abner & Olive, b. Mar. 15, 1805	3
Fanny, m. Justus BUTLER, b. of Meriden, Apr. 26, 1829, by Rev. James Keeler	35
Franklin, s. Giles O. & Lucy, b. Apr. 26, 1803	2
Franklin, m. Eliza BRONSON, b. of Meriden, Nov. 22, 1829, by Rev. James Keeler	36
George, s. Abner & Olive, b. June 27, 1803	3
Harry, m. Maria J. RICE, b. of Meriden, May 31, 1835, by Rev. Edward Ingersoll	50
Ira, s. Giles O. & Lucy, b. Apr. 15, 1805	3
Lucy, w. Giles O., d. Feb. 22, 1822, ae 43	21
Rosetta, m. Joseph C. BALDWIN, Oct. 24, 1805	1
GUILD, Delila F., m. James Y. POMEROY, b. of Meriden, Sept. 17, 1848, by Rev. Harvey Miller	94
GUY, Abigail, m. Branton HALL, May 18, 1784	5
Anna, d. Jan. 11, 1789	5
Esther R., d. Orchard & Lois, b. Sept. 15, 1819	30
George Washington, s. Orchard & Lois, b. Sept. 21, 1813	15

BARBOUR COLLECTION

	Page
GUY (cont.)	
Joel H., of Meriden, m. Jemima **WETMORE**, of Middletown, Nov. 9, 1828, by Charles J. Hinsdale	34
Joel Hall, s. Orchard & Lois, b. June 12, 1804	7
Orchard, m. Lois **HALL**, May 29, 1794	6
Rebeckah, m. Collins **HALL**, Mar. 17, 1795	4
HALE, [see also **HALL** & **HULL**], Achseh, m. Samuel **BALDWIN**, Jr. Feb. 15, 1801	7
Ephraim, of Glastenbury, m. Mary E. **HALL**, of Wallingford, Jan. 27, 1850, by Rev. Albert Nash	101
Frances A., of Meriden, m. Edwin H. **LOOMIS**, of Coventry, Dec. 5, 1853, by Rev. Harvey Miller	122
Harriet, of Meriden, m. Sherman **WILCOX**, of Berlin, Dec. 2, 1843, by Rev. Alexander Miller	76
William, of Middletown, m. Phebe Ann **IVES**, of Meriden, Apr. 30. 1833, by Charles J. Hinsdale	47
HALL, [see also **HALE** & **HULL**], Abigail, m. Elisha **CURTIS**, Feb. 18, 1796	7
Abigail, d. Collins & Rebeckah, b. Nov. 25, 1796	4
Abijah, of Leydin, N.Y., m. Mary **BARNS**, of Meriden, Feb. 23, 1823, by Samuel Miller	22
Alma, d. Collins & Rebeckah, b. Oct. 5 ,1799	4
Alma, of Meriden, m. James **HOUGH**, of Meriden, May 29, 1831, by Charles J. Hinsdale	41
Almer, of Wallingford, m. Fanny **IVES**, of Martinsburgh, N.Y., Dec. 6, 1827, by Samuel Miller	32
Almon, m. Jemima **LOVELAND**, Sept. 15, 1839, by Rev. Harvey Miller	62
Ann Eliza, d. Hiram & Lucy Ann, b. Sept. 20, 1838	60
Anna Guy, d. Brenton & Abigail, b. June 22, 1792	5
Augustus, s. Brenton & Abigail, b. July 5, 1785	5
Augustus, s. Collins & Rebeckah, b. Oct. 30, 1806	6
Augustus, m. Mary **PRESTON**, Nov. 27, 1806	6
Avery, [s. John W. & Polly], b. Mar. 14, 1822	26
Beri, [s. John W. & Polly], b. Feb. 20, 1813	26
Brenton, m. Lament **COLLINS**, Feb. 18, 1762	5
Brenton, m. Abigail **GUY**, May 18, 1784	5
Caroline, of Meriden, m. Eliphalet H. **BENEDICK**, of Southington, Aug. 15, 1853, by Rev. Harvey Miller	119
Caroline A., of Wallingford, m. John M. **ANDREWS**, of Simsbury, May 12, 1836, by Rev. Robert A. Hallam	57
Casper, s. Brenton & Abigail, b. Apr. 5, 1790	5
Charlotte, m. Walter **WILLIAMS**, Mar. 27, 1823, by Charles J. Hinsdale	24
Clarrissa, [d. John W. & Polly], b. Jan. 8, 1820	26
Collens, s. Brenton & Lament, b. Jan. 10, 1766	5
Collins, m. Rebeckah **GUY**, Mar. 17, 1795	4
Cornelia, d. [Russel & Sally], b. Aug. 29, 1810	15
Edward N., m. Caroline **CURTIS**, b. of Meriden, Jan. 1, 1843, by Harvey Miller	71
Elisha, s. Collins & Rebeckah, b. May 1, 1803	4
Eliza, d. Theophilus & Bethia, b. June 17, 1806	3

	Page
HALL (cont.)	
Eliza Ann, m. Henry L. **BALDWIN**, Sept. 2, 1846, by Rev. H. Miller	87
Eliza E., m. Leyden **RICHARDSON**, Apr. 5, 1825, by Charles J. Hinsdale	27
Elisabeth, m. Seth D. **PLUM**, Dec. 10, 1803	3
Elizabeth, m. Samuel **BALDWIN**, b. of Meriden, May 31, 1829, by Rev. Daniel Burrows	35
Elvira, m. Silas Y. **IVES**, Sept. [23, 1835], by Geo[rge] B Atwell;	51
Emily, of Meriden, m. Darius **ROBBERTS**, of Middletown, Dec. 25, 1827, by Samuel Miller	32
Erastus, m. Sophia **COWLES**, Oct. 13, 1830, by Rev. James Keeler	40
Erastus C., s. Collins & Rebeckah, b. Jan. 2 ,1805	4
Esther, m. Marvel **ANDREWS**, b. of Meriden, Jan. 24, 1822, by Samuel Miller	20
Eunice, of Meriden, m. Enos **BROOKS**, of Farmington, Oct. 2, 1822, by Rev. Josiah Graves, of Middletown	22
Freeman G., of Wallingford, m. M. **ANTHONY**, Oct. 16, 1853, by Rev. Harvey Miller	120
George Preston, s. Augustus & Mary, b. Sept. 27, 1807	9
George William, s. [Russel & Sally], b. May 8, 1812	15
Hannah, m. Joel **HULL**, Oct. 6, 1818	18
Hannah, Mrs., m. John **HALL**, b. of Meriden, Dec. 15, 1836, by Geo[rge] B Atwell	55
Harry William, s. Theophilus & Bethiah, b. July 21, 1804	3
Harry William, s. Theophilus & Bethiah, d. Sept. 30, 1807	3
Hezekiah, of Wallingford, m. Mrs. Harriet L. **COE**, of Meriden, May 5, 1841, by Rev. John Moore, of Hartford	64
Hiram, m. Lucy Ann **OLES**, b. of Meriden, Nov. 30, 1837, by Leland Howard	56
Ira, s. Brenton & Abigail, b. Dec. 27, 1787	5
Jacob, m. Laura **ANDREWS**, b. of Meriden, Sept.2, 1835, by Rev. Edward Ingersoll	51
James, m. Harriet W. **WAY**, b. of Meriden, Nov. 3, 1846, by Rev. G. W. Perkins	88
James Willard, [s. John W. & Polly], b. Oct. 7, 1824	26
Jennett, m. Samuel C. **PADDOCK**, b. of Meriden, Mar. 19, 1837, by Geo[rge] B. Atwell	56
Jen[n]ett, of Wallingford, m. Amasa B. **IVES**, of Meriden, Jan. 6, 1845, by Rev. Harvey Miller	80
Joab, s. Brenton & Lament, b. Jan. 12, 1781	5
John, m. Ruth **HALL**, Dec. 12, 1798	6
John, m. Mrs. Hannah **BELL**, b. of Meriden, Dec. 15 ,1836, by Geo[rge] B. Atwell	55
John W., m. Polly **TODD**, Mar. 26, 1812	26
Joseph, m. Hannah **FRANCES**, Nov. 3, 1803	6
Josephine Butler, d. Sidney P. & Susan, b. Nov 21, 1845	88
Lament, d. Brenton & Lament, b. July 12, 1776	5
Lament, w. Brenton, d. Nov. 31, 1782	5
Lavinia A., of Meriden, m. Timothy J. **COE**, of Middletown, May 3, 1846, by Rev. Harvey Miller	86
Levi, m. Elisabeth Williams, June 1, 1800	6
Levi Yale, s. Phineas & Agness, b. Jan. 24, 1781	6

	Page
HALL (cont.)	
Lois, m. Orchard **GUY**, May 29, 1794	6
Lucien, m. Lavinia **PECK**, Aug.2, 1842, by Rev. Harvey Miller	69
Lucretia, of Meriden, m. Cook **FRENCH**, of Bethany, Dec. 6, 1835, by George B Atwell	52
Lucy, d. Brenton & Lament, b. Mar. 13, 1771	5
Lucy, m. Levi **CURTIS** Mar. 28, 1790	13
Luther, s. Augustus & Polly, b. Aug. 26, 1809	12
Maria J., of Meriden, m. Frederick **FRANCIS**, of Berlin, Aug. 23, 1830, by Charles J. Hinsdale	38
Mariette, m. Stephen **IVES**, b. of Meriden, Apr. 6, 1843, by Harvey Miller	71
Mary, d. Phineas & Agness, b. July 24, 1775	6
Mary Ann, [d. John W. & Polly]. b. Sept. 18, 1818	26
Mary E., of Wallingford, m. Ephraim **HALE**, of Glastenbury, Jan. 27, 1850, by Rev. Albert Nash	101
Mary L., m. Anson M. **WILLIAMS**, b. of Meriden, Sept. 12, 1847, by Rev. John E. Searles	92
Nancy M., m. John **YALE**, b. of Meriden, Oct. 30, 1833, by Charles J. Hinsdale	43
Noah, s. Phineas & Agness, b. Nov. 9, 1786	6
Noah, m. Harriet **HOTCHKISS**, Nov. 8, 1807	6
Norman O., of Middletown, m. Harriet E. **REDFIELD**, of Guilford, Nov. 14, 1853, by Rev. A. A. Stevens	122
Oliver, s. Brenton & Lament, b. Dec. 12, 1779	5
Phinehas, m. Agness **YALE**, Nov. 8, 1774	6
Rebecca G., m. Joseph B. **TWISS**, b. of Meriden, Sept. 14, [1831], by Rev. Russell Jennings	42
Rebec[c]a Guy, d. Augustus, 2nd & Polly, b. Sept. 5, 1811	12
Russel, m. Sally **IVES**, Oct. 12, 1809	15
Ruth, m. John **HALL**, Dec. 12 ,1798	6
Sally, m. Gordon **HARVEY**, Jan. 16 ,1826, by Charles J .Hinsdale	28
Samuel, s. Brenton & Lament, b. June 10, 1768	5
Samuel, d. Mar. 11, 1795	5
Sarah, d. Brenton & Lament, b. Jan. 15, 1774	5
Sarah, w. Benjamin A., d. Mar. 17, 1792	5
Sherman, s. Joseph & Hannah, b. Apr. 26, 1806	6
Sidney P., m. Susan **BUTLER**, Apr. 2, 1843, by Rev. J. F. Cushing	87
Silas Hill, s. Elijah & Sarah, b. Jan. 14, 1787	10
Theophilus, 2nd, m. Bethiah **MERRIAM**, Mar. 24, 1803	3
Theophilus, d. May 17, 1804	4
William, [s. John W. & Polly], b. Sept. 2, 1816	26
William Brenton, s. Brenton & Lament, b. May 31, 1764	5
HALLAM, Robert A., m. Phebe Ann **CURTISS**, b. of Meriden, Nov. 4, 1834, by Rev. William H. Walter, of Milford	49
HANSON, Charlotte A., of Portland, Me., m. Charles W. **ELWELL**, of Saccarappa, Me., Aug. 1, 1852, by Rev. Harvey Miller	112
HARRIS, Lucy A., of Middletown, m. Samuel D. **PUFFER**, of Meriden, Dec. 2, 1850, by Rev. A. A. Stevens	102
HARRISON, Lucy Ann, of Meriden, m. Augustus **BARNS**, of Southington, Dec. 18, 1842, by Rev. Harvey Miller	71
Mary C., m. George H. **ROBINSON**, Apr. 29, 1844, by Rev Alexander Miller	76

MERIDEN VITAL RECORDS 145

Page

HARRISON (cont.)
Roswell, of Litchfield, m. Serviah **HULL**, of Meriden, Feb. 21,
  1821, by Erastus Ripley — 19
Silva, of Southington, m. Henry **JOHNSON**, of Meriden, Aug. 22,
  1832, by Charles J. Hinsdale — 43
W[illia]m F., of Southington, m. Harriet A. **BRADLEY**, of Meriden,
  Dec. 15, 1844, by Rev. Harvey Miller — 79
HARSHAW, Mary, of Chatham, m. Charles **LANGDON**, of Cheshire,
  Aug. 8, 1841, by Harvey Miller — 64
HART, Cyprian, of Bristol, m. Eliza A. **PERDEW**, of Meriden, Apr. 4,
  1852, by Rev. Harvey Miller — 111
  Daniel, s. Samuel I. & Abagail, b. June 19, 1815 — 44
  Daniel H., of Meriden, m. Harriet G. **MILLER**, of Middletown, May
    14, 1840, by Harvey Miller — 58
  Edmund B., s. [Daniel & Harriet G.], b. Dec. 31, 1845 — 94
  Elizabeth, [twin with Jerusha, d. Samuel I. & Abagail], b. Aug. 22,
    1822 — 44
  Elizabeth, of Meriden, m. Edward B. **MILLER**, of New Haven, Oct.
    24, 1852, by Rev. Harvey Miller — 113
  Ellen D., d. [Daniel & Harriet G.], b. Nov 23, 1842 — 94
  Emily, of Meriden, m. John **PROFFIT**, of Hartford, Apr. 13, 1845,
    by Rev. John Parker — 80
  Harriet, m. Arza **ANDREWS**, b. of Meriden, July 24, 1837, by
    Arthur Granger — 56
  Henry F., of New Britain, m. wid. Abby C. **LEACH**, of Meriden,
    July 8, 1849, by Rev. George W. Perkins — 98
  Ives W., s. Daniel & Harriet G., b. Oct. 4, 1841 — 94
  Jerusha, [twin with Elizabeth, d. Samuel I. & Abagail], b. Aug. 22,
    1822 — 44
  Jerusha, of Meriden, m. Abel D. **CLARK**, of Pittsfield, Sept. 12,
    1822, by Samuel Miller — 21
  Jerusha, m. Horace **PRATT**, May 5, 1844, by Rev. H. Miller — 75
  Joseph C., m. Margaret **LANE**, of Canton, May 20, 1852, by Rev.
    John Parker — 111
  Maria, of New Britain, m. Allen **STACY**, of Penn, Sept. 12, 1847, by
    Rev. John E. Searles — 91
  Philo, m. Eunice **EVERTS**, b. of Meriden, May 7, 1848, by Rev.
    John E. Searles — 93
HARTSHORN, [see also **HARTSON**], Merritt, m. Emeline **YALE**, of
  Meriden, Nov. 29, 1838, by Harvey Miller — 60
HARTSON, [see also **HARTSHORN**], Caroline, m. Ira H. **SMITH**, Dec.
  24, 1838, by Rev. Melancthon Hoyt — 60
HARVEY, Allen W., m. Mary E. **MORGAN**, b. of Meriden, June 6,
  1853, by Rev. George W. Perkins — 119
  Gordon, m. Sally **HALL**, Jan. 16, 1826, by Charles J. Hinsdale — 28
HATCH, Ossian L., m. Delia M. **DOWD**, b. of Meriden, Oct. 13, 1852,
  by Rev. G. W. Perkins — 117
HAYDEN, Emma, of Berlin, m. Zerad **EATON**, of Ellington, Mar. 10,
  1846, by Rev. H. Miller — 85
  Lydia A., of Westbrook, Conn., m. George W. **BLISS**, of
    Springfield, Mass., June 9, 1850, by Rev. Harvey Miller — 102
  Sarah, m. Edwin **EATON**, Dec. 1, 1840, by Erastus Ripley — 63

	Page
HEMINGWAY, William, of New York, m. Ann A. **HUGEN**, of Meriden, Jan. 6, 1851, by Rev. George W. Perkins	103
HIBBARD, Marg[ar]et, of Burlington, Vt., m. Jonathan J. **SPENCER**, of Meriden, Jan. 27, 1850, by Rev. Abner Nash	101
HIGBY, Caroline L., m. James H. **WILLIAMS**, b. of Meriden, Apr. 21, 1850, by Rev. John Parker	102
Grace A., of Meriden, m. Edward W. **BENHAM**, of Cheshire, May 6, 1849, by Rev. Albert Nash	98
HIGLEY, Erastus, m. Mary A. **BELDEN**, b. of Meriden, Apr. 18, 1867*, by Rev. John E. Searles (*1847?)	91
HILL, George, m. Almira **STARR**, b. of Middletown, July 22, 1827, by Samuel Miller	31
Jeremiah, m. Julia Ann **DOUGLASS**, July 2, 1826, by Charles J. Hinsdale	29
HINMAN, F. E., of Kinderhook, N.Y., m. Pheobe E. **CAMP**, d. of Elah, of Meriden, Sept. 26, 1843, by G. W. Perkins	75
HITCHCOCK, Fanny, of Cheshire m. Julius **BRISTOL**, of Southington, Dec. 29, 1852, by Rev. Harvey Miller	115
Morris, m. Maria **BEARDSLEY**, b. of Meriden, June 28, 1835, by Nathan Booth, J.P.	50
Polly A., m. Wyllys **MATTHEWS**, b. of Meriden, Dec. 26, 1821, by Samuel Miller	20
Sarah M., m. Alfred P. **CURTISS**, b. of Meriden, Oct. 15, 1851, by Rev. Giles H. Deshon	109
HOLLAND, Charles B., m. Frances A. **SHERMAN**, b. of Meriden, Oct. 19, 1848, by Rev. G. W. Perkins	95
John H., m. Nancy J. **GRIFFIN**, Oct. 12, 1853, by Rev. A. A. Stevens* *(First written "by Rev. G. H. Deshon")	122
HOLT, Elias, m. Melitta **CONLEY**, b. of Meriden, Apr. 18, 1822, by Samuel Miller	21
HORNELL, Charles, m. Delia Maria **YALE**, b. of Meriden, Dec. 26, 1852, by Rev. Harvey Miller	114
HORTON, Sampson, of South Glastenbury, m. Emily **TILBURY**, of Kensington, Apr. 21, 1849, by Rev. C. Munson	90
HOTCHKISS, Fred[e]rick W., of New Britain, m. Martha M. **BURR**, of Haddam, Dec. 18, 1853, by [Rev. N. Mead]	123
Hannah C., m. Isaac P. **LEWIS**, May 22, [1853(?)], by Rev. Harvey Miller	116
Harriet, m. Noah **HALL**, Nov. 8, 1807	6
Lewis, m. Mrs. Sarah **BRADLEY**, Mar. 31, 1823, by Charles J. Hinsdale	24
Sarah A., m. Edward P. **YALE**, May 2, 1852, by Rev. A. A. Stevens	111
Sophronia, b. July 15, 1807; m. Henry C. **BUTLER**, [ ]; d. Apr. 17, 1841	66
Sophronia, of Meriden, m. Henry C. **BUTLER**, of Meriden, Jan. 12, 1832, by Charles J. Hinsdale	43
HOUGH, Almena, m. Cyrenius **BOOTH**, Oct. 22, 1826, by Charles J. Hinsdale	29
Alonzo B., of Meriden, m. Rebecca **GILBERT**, of Ludlow, Vt., Feb. 28, 1833, by Charles J. Hinsdale	46
Avery, m. Almira **RICE**, Dec. 20, 1821, by Erastus Ripley	20
Charlotte, m. Eli **WAY**, Dec. 19, 1821, by Erastus Ripley	20
David, m. Phebe **MATHEW**, Aug. 30, 1805	13

MERIDEN VITAL RECORDS 147

	Page
HOUGH (cont.)	
David Norman, [s. David & Phebe], b. Nov. 4, 1811	13
Elizabeth, m. Dan **ANDREWS**, Feb. 25, 1807	2
Frances, m. Ruel H. **PERKINS**, Dec. 26, 1853, by Rev. Giles H. Deshon	123
James, s. James A. & Sarah, b. Dec. 28, 1807	10
James, of Meriden, m. Alma **HALL**, of Meriden, May 29, 1831, by Charles J. Hinsdale	41
Joel, of Wallingford, m. Mary **ROYCE**, of Meriden, June [ ], 1836, by Arthur Granger	53
Lois Thankfull, [d. David & Phebe], b. Oct. 30, 1809	13
Polly Burritt, [d. David & Phebe], b. May 25, 1806	13
Rebecca T., m. Samuel T. **CURTIS**, b. of Meriden, Oct. 3, 1832, by Charles J. Hinsdale	45
Sally, m. Ira **PRESTON**, Nov. 24, 1825, by Charles J. Hinsdale	27
Sally, m Asaph **MERRIAM**, b. of Meriden, Nov. 20, 1828, by Rev. Charles Hinsdale	34
William C., of Meriden, m. Isabella G. **THORP**, of West Springfield, Mass., Jan. 20, 1831, by Charles J. Hinsdale	41
William Ogden, [s. David & Phebe], b. Nov. 25, 1807	13
HOWD, John, m. Jane M. **BARNES**, b. of Southington, Sept. 3, 1851, by Rev. G. W. Perkins	108
HUBBARD, Alma, m. Jonathan **YALE**, 2nd, Nov. 28, 1816	18
Almira, had s. James Hervey **YALE**, b. Oct. 1, 1819; reputed f. Jonathan Yale, 2nd	23
Asaph, m. Sarah **BRAINARD**, of Haddam, Apr. 9, 1843, by Harvey Miller	71
Guy H., of Claremont, N.H., m. Clarissa A. **RICE**, of Meriden, Oct. 21, 1851, by Rev. Giles H. Deshon	109
Jane, of Meriden, m. Dea. [ ] **ATWATER**, of Hamden, Mar. 21, 1821, by Rev. Erastus Ripley	19
Rebeckah, m. Silas **RICE**, Mar. 18, 1802	8
T. S., of Upper Middletown, m. Jance C. **WOODRUFF**, of Meriden, Nov. 14, 1849, by Rev. A. A. Stephens	100
Walter, m. Abby A. **BRADLEY**, Oct. 13, 1852, by Rev. George W. Perkins	117
HUGEN, Ann A., of Meriden, m. William **HEMINGWAY**, of New York, Jan. 6, 1851, by Rev. George W. Perkins	103
HUGHES, Partrick, m. Ellen **TOPPING**, b. of Meriden, Sept. 12, 1852, by Ward Coe, J.P.	120
HULL, [see also HALE & HALL], Anna, of Cheshire, m. Henry **WAY**, of Meriden, Oct. 1, 1840, by Rev. Harvey Miller	63
Charles J., m. Louisa W. **LANDON**, Jan. 14, 1850, by Rev. Harvey Miller	100
Chloe, of Cheshire, m. Ralph P. **CHILDS**, of Chatham, Jan. 4, 1846, by Rev. H. Miller	84
Cornelius, m. Polly A. **ROGERS**, Nov. 29, 1827, by Charles J. Hinsdale	32
Hannah, of Cheshire, m. Amasa **SIZER**, Jr., of New London, Dec. 18, 1842, by Rev. Harvey Miller	71
Isaac Chauncey, s. Joel & Hannah, b. Oct. 31, 1819	18
Joel, m. Hannah **HALL**, Oct. 6, 1818	18
John, s. Joel & Hannah, b. June 26, 1822	22

148   BARBOUR COLLECTION

	Page
HULL (cont.)	
Mary A., m. Selden **IVES**, b. of Meriden, Mar. 31, 1843, by Rev. Alexander Miller	76
Mary Maria, m. Partrick **LEWIS**, b. of Meriden, Jan. 28, 1824, by Reuben Ives	24
Nancy, m. Horace **WOOD**, Mar. 16, 1837, by Geo[rge] B. Atwell	55
Rachel, m. Edward **JOHNSON**, Nov. 7, 1805	11
Rebecca M., of Wallingford, m. Asahel R. **ATKINS**, of Meriden, Jan. 9, 1842, by Rev. Harvey Miller	69
Sarah, m. Amos **AUSTIN**, Oct. 29, 1807	8
Serviah, of Meriden, m. Roswell **HARRISON**, of Litchfield, Feb. 21, 1821, by Erastus Ripley	19
Susan, wid., b. Jan. 15, 1781	66
Zerviah, see under Serviah	
HUMPHREY, Rebecca M., of Southington, m. Charles W. **BRADLEY**, of Middletown, Dec. 8, 1850, by Rev. Harvey Miller	103
HURLBURT, HULBERT, George, of Hartford, m. Clarissa M. **LANGDON**, of Cheshire, Mar. 3, 1850, by Rev. Albert Nash	101
Hannah, m. Timothy **IVES**, Jr., Sept. 30, 1802	4
ISBELL, Antonette Y., m. Eliphalet H. **CHAPMAN**, Nov. 22, 1846, by Rev. H. Miller	88
Emily J., b. Mar. 13, 1829	67
Eveline T., of West Meriden, m. Sylvester J. **SHERMAN**, of Branford, Sept. 24, 1848, by Rev. Harvey Miller	94
Henry L., b. May 31, 1839	67
Isaac H., b. Aug. 7, 1841	67
John C., b. Apr. 3, 1837	67
Mary L, b. May 17, 1835	67
Sarah C., b. Dec. 22, 1830; d. Oct. 2, 1831	67
Sarah C., b. July 4, 1832	67
Sarah C., d. Apr. 15, 1837	67
IVES, Aaron W., of Meriden, m. Sarah L. **UPSON**, of Cheshire, Apr. 5, 1846, by Rev. H. Miller	85
Aaron Watrous, [s. Watrous & Polly], b. May 25, 1817	17
Abigail, d. Timothy, Jr. & Hannah, b. Sept. 18, 1808	4
Amasa B., of Meriden, m. Jenett **HALL**, of Wallingford, Jan. 6, 1845, by Rev. Harvey Miller	80
Betsey, d. Ichabod & Mary, b. June 14, 1786	9
Betsey, m. John **YALE**, Mar. 12, 1803	9
Edgar Van Buren [s. Silas Y. & Elvira], b. Oct. 18, 1839	79
Eli, m. Gelina Ann **POMEROY**, b. of Meriden, Sept. 30, 1830, by Rev. Russell Jennings	39
Elias N., s. Silas Y. & Elvira, b. Jan. 14, 1837	79
Elias Y., m. Cornelia **POMEROY**, b. of Meriden, Aug. 22, 1827, by Samuel Miller	31
Eliza, d. Timothy & Hannah, b. Feb. 8, 1806	15
Elisa, m. Edwin R. **YALE**, b. of Meriden, Mar. 14, 1824, by Samuel Miller	25
Ezra, m. Cordelia Sophia **CLARKE**, Dec. 9, 1845, by Rev. Saul Clark	83
Fanny, of Martinsburgh, N.Y., m. Almer **HALL**, of Wallingford, Dec. 6, 1827, by Samuel Miller	32
Franklin T., [s. Titus & Lodema], b. Aug. 19, 1828	38

	Page
IVES (cont.)	
Hannah, of Meriden, m. Jefferson **MILLER**, of Granville, Mass., Oct. 11, 1820, by Samuel Miller	19
Harriet, m. Charles D. **BUTLER**, b. of Pittsfield, Mass., Feb. 17, 1829, by Sam[ue]l Miller	34
Isabel, m. Levi **RICE**, Mar. 13, 1806	2
Jerusha, m. Albert B. **POTTER**, b. of Meriden, Nov. 18, 1830, by Charles J. Hinsdale	41
Jotham, s. Jesse & Marilla, b. Sept. 7, 1808	11
Lucinda, m. Lee **RICE**, Oct. 11, 1810	14
Lucy, d. Timothy & Hannah, b. May 5, 1810	15
Maria H., [d. Titus & Lodema], b. July 12, 1813	38
Mary A., of North Haven, m. Lemuel L. **DOUGLASS**, of Meriden, May 11, 1842, by Rev. G. W. Perkins	69
Nathaniel Y., [s. Titus & Lodema], b. Nov. 11, 1815	38
Nelson Hall, [s. Silas Y. & Elvira], b. Nov. 16, 1841	79
Phebe Ann, [d. Watrous & Polly], b. July 28, 1813	17
Phebe Ann, of Meriden, m. William **HALE**, of Middletown, Apr. 30, 1833, by Charles J. Hinsdale	47
Russell J., m. Flora Ann **WHITE**, b. of Meriden, Sept. 18, 1853, by Rev. Harvey Miller	120
Ruth, m. Amos **FOSTER**, Dec. 10, 1795	9
Sally, m. Russel **HALL**, Oct. 12, 1809	15
Sarah R., m. Harvey **MILLER**, b. of Meriden, May 21, 1839, by Alfred Bennet	60
Selden, m. Mary A. **HULL**, b. of Meriden, Mar. 31, 1843, by Rev. Alexander Miller	76
Silas Y., [s. Titus & Lodema], b. Sept. 23 ,1811	38
Silas Y., m. Elvira **HALL**, Sept. 23, 1835, by Geo[rge] B. Atwell	51
Stephen, m. Mariette **HALL**, b. of Meriden, Apr. 6, 1843, by Harvey Miller	71
Susan L., [d. Titus & Lodema], b. May 19, 1821	38
Thaddeus, m. Hannah **CONE**, Nov. 4, 1807	9
Timothy, Jr., m. Hannah **HULBERT**, Sept. 30, 1802	4
Titus, m. Lodama **YALE**, Oct. 18, 1808	9
Watrous, m. Polly **YALE**, Sept. 15, 1809	17
William J., m. Lucy J. **BIRDSEY**, b. of Meriden, Sept. 1, 1841, by Rev. Harvey Miller	65
William Jackson, [s. Watrous & Polly], b. July 29, 1815	17
Wooster Y., m. Elizabeth **BLAKE**, b. of Meriden, [Jan.] 25, [1837], by Geo[rge] B. Atwell	55
Wo[o]ster Yale, [s. Watrous & Polly], b. July 8, 1810	17
JANES, William W., m. Nancy **WEBB**, June 14, 1836, by Arthur Granger	53
JENNINGS, Charles Russell, s. Russell & Maria, b. July 19, 1830	42
JOHNSON, Alfred, of Wallingford, m. Lucy **LAWRENCE**, of Meriden, Feb. 19, 1826, by Rev. Ashbil Baldwin	28
Betsey A., m. Aaron **PRATT**, Nov. 27, 1832, by Charles J. Hinsdale	45
Beulah W., m. Jesse **CURTISS**, Dec. 31, 1849, by Rev. Harvey Miller	100
Edward, m. Rachel **HULL**, Nov. 7, 1805	11
Edward, s. [Edward & Rachel], b. Aug. 1, 1808	11
Elim L., of Meriden, m. Lucy M. **WARNER**, of Middletown, May 22, 1839, by Harvey Miller	60-1

BARBOUR COLLECTION

Page

JOHNSON (cont.)

Elizabeth, of Meriden, m. William **LANE**, of Westville, Mass., Dec. 2, 1851, by Rev. G. W. Perkins   109

Geo[rge] William, s. [Edward & Rachel], b. June 6, 1810   11

George William, s. Edward & Rachel, b. Dec. 19, 1811   13

Henry, of Meriden, m. Silva **HARRISON**, of Southington, Aug. 22, 1832, by Charles J. Hinsdale   43

Jonathan B., of Wallingford, m. Sarah J. **TOOKER**, of Meriden, Oct. 10, 1852, by Rev. Harvey Miller   113

Louisa, m. Amos **CURTIS**, Dec. 6, 1818   31

Mary, m. William **JOHNSON***, Nov. 20, 1803   *(YALE)   3

Mary A., of Meriden, m. Alonzo S. **ATKINS**, of New Hartford, Sept. 24, 1848, by Rev. Albert Nash   97

Matilda d., m. Joel W. **STUTTER**, b. of Meriden, July 3, 1851, by Rev. Giles H. Deshon   108

Sarah, d. [Edward & Rachel], b. Nov. 14, 1806   11

Sarah, of Worcester, Mass., m. William **SAVAGE**, Sept. 18, 1844, by Rev. Harvey Miller   78

William*, m. Mary **JOHNSON**, Nov. 20, 1803   *(Johnson overwritten to read "YALE")   3

JOLIN, Caroline, m. Michael **MULLEN**, b. of Germany, May 30, 1853, by Rev. George W. Perkins   118

JONES, Edwin S., of New Haven, m. Cornelia **DURAND**, of Meriden, Nov. 24, 1846, by Rev. G. W. Perkins   89

Henry, m. Harriet **YALE**, b. of Meriden, Dec. 19, 1839, by Harvey Miller   58

JUDD, William M., of Kent, m. Betsey **RICE**, of Meriden, Dec. 3, 1840, by Rev. E. Colton   63

KELLOGG, C. Vincent, m. Emma J. **WARNER**, Nov 21, 1853, by Rev. G. W. Perkins   121

KELSEY, Ephraim A., of Westbrook, m. Catharine J. **ANDREWS**, of Meriden, Apr. 5, 1847, by Rev. G. W Perkins   89

Ephraim A., m. Delia **MARVIN**, of Meriden, Sept. 5, 1852, by Rev. Harvey Miller   112-3

Harvey S., of New Haven, m. Mary **LEFFINGWELL**, of Clinton, Oct. 9, 1844, by Rev. C. Munson   77

KENNEDY, Timothy, m. Julia **BEECHER**, b. of Southington, Mar. 28, 1837, by Rev. J. Goodwin   55

KENT, Mary Ann, of Middletown, m. Charles **WOOD**, of Shelburne Falls, Mass., Oct. 16, 1853, by Rev. Harvey Miller   120

KENWORTHY, John, m. Mary Ann **BOULER**, b. of England, Jan. 10, 1853, by Rev. Francis Bottom   118

KESTEREN, [see also **CASTELON**], Ann, m. Adam **SAUNDERS**, Oct. 4, 1852 ,by Rev. J. H. Deshon   113

KILBOURN, Henry, of Bristol, m. Lucretia **MACORNEY**, of Meriden, May 4, 1840, by Harvey Miller   58

KIRKLAND, Martha P., m. William **LEWIS**, Jr., b. of Meriden, Sept. 10, 1833, by Charles J. Hinsdale   47

KIRTLAND, Asa, of Saybrook, m. Elizabeth C. **SANFORD**, of Meriden, Nov. 1, 1849, by Rev. A. A. Stephens   100

LANDERS, Lucyett, of Redfield, N.Y., m. Asahel S. **BRAINARD**, of Haddam, Jan. 1, 1849, by Rev. Albert Nash   97

LANDON, [see under **LANGDON**]

MERIDEN VITAL RECORDS

	Page
LANE, Emily of Killingworth, m. Henry **ROYCE**, of Meriden, June 10, 1847, by Rev. G. W. Perkins	90
Hannah L., of Wallingford, m. Edmond B. **CURTISS**, of Meriden, Feb. 15, 1852, by Rev. Harvey Miller	110
Henry, of Farmington, m. Lucy Ann **TUTTLE**, of Meriden, Apr. 15, 1849, by Rev. George W. Perkins	98
Margaret, of Canton, m. Joseph C. **HART**, May 20, 1852, by Rev. John Parker	111
William, of Westville, Mass., m. Elizabeth **JOHNSON**, of Meriden, Dec. 2, 1851, by Rev. G. W. Perkins	109
LANGDON, LANDON, Charles, of Cheshire, m. Mary **HARSHAW**, of Chatham, Aug. 8, 1841, by Harvey Miller	64
Clarissa M., of Cheshire, m. George **HURLBURT**, of Hartford, Mar. 3, 1850, by Rev. Albert Nash	101
Louisa W., m. Charles J. **HULL**, Jan. 14, 1850, by Rev. Harvey Miller	100
LAWRENCE, Asahel A., m. Roxana **MERRIAM**, Nov. 13, 1834, by Rev. William R. Curtiss	49
Caroline, of Meriden, m. Almeron **MILES**, of Cheshire, Sept. 12, 1833, by Rev. Simon Shailor, of Wallingford	48
Jane C., of Meriden, m. Y. Whittemore **FRISBIE**, of Guilford, July 24, 1853, by Rev. Lester Lewis, of Bristol	119
Lucy, of Meriden, m. Alfred **JOHNSON**, of Wallingford, Feb. 19, 1826, by Rev. Ashbil Baldwin	28
LEACH, Abby C., wid. of Meriden, m. Henry F. **HART**, of New Britain, July 8, 1849, by Rev. George W. Perkins	98
Peter G., m. wid. Abby C. **SNOW**, b. of Meriden, Apr. 15, 1844, by Rev. G. W. Perkins	76
LEE, Amos, of Geneva, N.Y., m. Cloe **MERRIMAN**, of Meriden, Oct. 17, 1831, by Charles J. Hinsdale	43
LEFFINGWELL, Mary, of Clinton, m. Harvey S. **KELSEY**, of New Haven, Oct. 9, 1844, by Rev. C. Munson	77
LEGAN, W[illia]m F., of New Haven, m. Laura A. **ANDREWS**, of Meriden, Oct. 12, 1853, by Rev. G. S. Deshon	122
LEONARD, Benjamin, of Kent, m. Catharine E. **PERKINS**, of Meriden, Apr. 7, 1840, by Harvey Miller	58
Maria E., of Meriden, m. William L. **THOMPSON**, of New Orleans, La., Sept. 23, 1846, by Rev. G. W. Perkins	88
LESTER, Chalsotte, A., Mrs. m. Anthony **MOWREY**, b. of Meriden, June 8, 1851, by Rev. [ ], of the Center Cong. Church	107
Emily L., of Meriden, m. Charles **DANIELS**, of Lyme, May 2, 1847, by Rev. Harvey Miller	90
Henry M., of Meriden, m. Maria A. **WOLCOTT**, of Weathersfield, Apr. 5, 1852, by Rev. Harvey Miller	111
LEWIS, Amelia, d. Isaac & Esther, b. June 22, 1807	2
Amelia, of Meriden, m. Samuel **YALE**, of Wallingford, Feb. 11, 1824, by Reuben Ives	24
Charles Henry, s. Jared & Mehitable L., b Apr. 5, 1834	49
Charlotte Elizabeth, d. Jared & Mehitable L., b. Aug. 20, 1832	49
Esther, d. Isaac & Esther, b. June 25, 1816	16
Esther, m. Frederick **NEWTON**, Feb. 17, 1734, by Rev. Robert A. Hallam	48

	Page
LEWIS, (cont.)	
Francis E., of Meriden, m. Edgar J. **MILES**, of Cheshire, May 4, 1845, by Rev. B. H. Miller	81
Frances Esther, d. Partrick & Mary M., b. Jan. 10, 1829	40
Isaac, d. May 13, 1823	29
Isaac, m. Harriet **POMEROY**, b. of Meriden, May 11, 1836, by William A. Hickney	53
Isaac Chauncey, s. Isaac & Esther, b. Oct. 19, 1812	13
Isaac P., m. Hannah C. **HOTCHKISS**, May 22, [1853 (?)], by Rev. Harvey Miller	116
Isaac Partrick, [s. Partrick & Mary M.], b. Oct. 18, 1830	40
James, of Meriden, m. Abigail **DURAND**, of Cheshire, Oct. 13, 1844, by Rev. George W. Perkins	78
Jared, s. Isaac & Esther, b. Jan. 27, 1811	12
Jared, of Meriden, m. Mehitabel L. **PADDOCK**, of Meriden, Jan. 1, 1832, by Charles J. Hinsdale	43
Jennet Minerva, of Bristol, m. Uriah **BUTLER**, of Meriden, Sept. 24, 1826, by Samuel Miller	29
Josephine W., of Meriden, m. Joseph H. **REED**, of Worcester, Mass., Nov. 27, 1851, by Rev. Harvey Miller	109
Julia, d. Isaac & Esther, b. Mar. 12, 1809	11
Julia, of Meriden, m. Timothy **LOOMIS**, of Middletown, June 9, 1831, by Rev. James Keeler	42
Maria, d. Partrick & Mary, b. Dec. 10, 1824	29
Maria M., m. George **BECKLEY**, b. of Meriden, Nov. 30, 1842, by Rev. Alexander Miller	76
Mary, m. Orrin **BELDEN**, b. of Meriden, Dec. 24, 1823, by Reuben Ives	24
Partrick, m. Mary Maria **HULL**, b. of Meriden, Jan. 28, 1824, by Reuben Ives	24
Samuel, s. Isaac & Esther, b. Mar. 30, 1814	15
Sheldon, of Bristol, m. Mary **BRADLEY**, of Cheshire, Sept. 30, 1850, by Rev. A. A .Stevens	102
Susan, d. Partrick & Marcy, b. Mar. 8, 1827	30
Susan, of Meriden, m. Richard **STRONG**, of East Windsor, June 24, 1845, by Rev. Harvey Miller	82
William, Jr., m. Martha P. **KIRKLAND**, b. of Meriden, Sept. 10, 1833, by Charles J. Hinsdale	47
LINDSLEY, LINSLEY, Hannah, of Meriden, m. Lester **PARIS** (?), of Warehouse Point, June 5, 1837, by Rev. John Marshall Guion	56
Noah, s. William A. & Abiga[i]l T., b. Aug. 6, 1807	2
Sarah Hillard, d. Randolph & Jennet, b. Apr. 21, 1836	67
Sylvester B., of East Haddam, m. Hannah **ANDREWS**, of Meriden, Oct. 3, 1830, by Rev. James [Keeler]	40
William A., m. Abigail T. **TYLER**, Oct. 5, 1806, by Rev. Mathew Noyes, of Branford	2
LINES, Edwin L., of Baltimore, Md., m. Elizabeth **CURTIS**, of Meriden, Aug. 13, 1832, by Charles J .Hinsdale	46
LINSLEY, [see under **LINDSLEY**]	
LITTLE, Mary E., of Meriden, m. James H. **TREADWAY**, of Middletown, July 2, 1829, by Rev. James Keeler	35
LOISELLE, Joseph, of Montreal, Canada, m. Lucretia **BURRITT**, of Meriden, Oct. 21, 1849, by Rev. Harvey Miller	99

MERIDEN VITAL RECORDS

	Page
LONDON, Joseph, of Wallingford, m. Esther AUSTIN, of Meriden, May 26, 1844, by Rev. H. Miller	75
LONG, Walter R., of Troy, N.Y., m. Harriet M. PRATT, of Meriden, Sept. 13, 1842, by Rev. G. W. Perkins	70
LOOMIS, Edwin H., of Coventry, m. Frances A. HALE, of Meriden, Dec. 5, 1853, by Rev. Harvey Miller	122
Timothy, of Middletown, m. Julia LEWIS, of Meriden, June 9, 1831, by Rev. James Keeler	42
LOVELAND, Jemima, m. Almon HALL, Sept. 15, 1839, by Rev. Harvey Miller	62
LUCAS, Benjamin, of Middletown, m. Sarah MOORE, of Berlin, Aug. 10, 1845, by Rev. Harvey Miller	82
Esther L., of Middletown, m. Horace G. BEACH, of Meriden, July 7, 1847, by Rev. G. W. Perkins	91
LUNG, Anna, m. William LUNG, b. of Meriden, Apr. 3 ,1832, by Charles J. Hinsdale	44
Malinda, m. Joseph BEMENT, Apr. 4, 1833, by Daniel Wildman	47
William, m. Anna LUNG, b. of Meriden, Apr. 3, 1832, by Charles J. Hinsdale	44
LUSK, Bethuel, m. Elisabeth FOSTER, Feb. 15, 1798	4
George Wyllys, s. Bethuel & Elisabeth, b. May 11, 1807	4
Hiram, s. Bethuel & Elisabeth, b. Sept. 5, 1798	4
LYMAN, Eda, m. Moses BALDWIN, Apr. 19, 1816	45
Hulda, of Meriden, m. Joel BARTHOLOMEW, Jr., of Wallingford, Sept. 19, 1824, by Samuel Miller	25
Mary, of Meriden, m. Chaunc[e]y TAYLOR, of Glastenbury, Mar. 27, 1825, by Samuel Miller	27
Moses, m. Laura BUTLER, Oct. 26, 1820, by Erastus Ripley	19
W[illia]m W., m. Roxanna G. FRARY, Sept. 5, 1844, by Rev. C. Munson	77
McCAMLEY, Samuel W., of New York, m. Jennet C. FARRINGTON, of Meriden, July 1, 1832, by Horatio Potter	44
McGALL, James P., m. Mary MARTIAL, b. of Meriden, Mar. 21, 1847, by Rev. John E. Searles	91
McGINN, Mary G., of Middletown, m. Walter WARNER, of Hamden, May 14, 1837, by Rev. Ransom Johnson	77
McGUION, Mary G., of Middletown, m. Walter WARNER, of Hamden, May 14, 1837, by Ransom Johnson	56
MACORNEY, Lucretia, of Meriden, m. Henry KILBOURN, of Bristol, May 4, 1840, by Harvey Miller	58
MARBLE, John, m. Lydia STARR, b. of Middletown, July 31, 1825, by Samuel Miller	27
MARKHAM, Dency, of Middle Haddam, m. William W. COE, of Middletown, Apr. 27, 1851, by Rev. Harvey Miller	106
Lydia A., m. Henry W. COOK, June 23, 1853, by Rev. Harvey Miller	117
MARTIAL, Mary, m. James P. McGALL, b. of Meriden, Mar. 21, 1847, by Rev. John E. Searles	91
MARTIN, Achsah, d. Lyman & Charlotte, b. Feb. 3, 1826	36
Francis, s. [Lyman & Charlotte], b. Jan. 18, 1828	36
Mary E., of Meriden, m. Sylvester RANDOLL, of Hartford, Mar. 27, 1847, by Rev. G. W. Perkins	89
Samuel, Jr., m. Lucy YEOMANS, Sept. 26, 1822, by Samuel Miller	21

154 BARBOUR COLLECTION

	Page
MARVIN, Delia, m. Ephraim A. **KELSEY**, Sept. 5, 1852, by Rev. Harvey Miller	112-3
James, of Colebrook, m. Mary A. **WOOD**, of Meriden, May 9, 1833, by Rev. Stephen Topliff, of Middletown	47
MATTHEWS, MATHEW, Phebe, m. David **HOUGH**, Aug. 30, 1805	13
Wyllys, m. Polly A. **HITCHCOCK**, b. of Meriden, Dec. 26, 1821, by Samuel Miller	20
MATTOON, Polly, of Meriden, m. Samuel **REED**, of Durham, May 2, 1821, by Elijah Willard	20
MECOMEZ, George, m. Grace **BELDEN**, b. of Meriden, Sept. 9, 1852, by Rev. Francis Bolton	113
MERRIAM, MERIAM, [see also **MERRIMAN**], Ahira, [ch. of Benjamin & Lucretia], b. Mar. 28, 1806	15
Alva, of Coventry, O., m. Julia Ann **DOUGLASS**, of Meriden, Jan. 18, 1846, by Rev. E. Cushman	83-4
Ann Eliza, [d. Asahel & Elizabeth], b. Feb. 1, 1803	21
Ann Eliza, m. William **MERRIAM**, b. of Meriden, Dec. 25, 1820, by Reuben Ives	20
Asahel, m. Elizabeth [ ], Jan. 11, 1802	21
Asahel, [s. Asahel & Elizabeth], b. Sept. 5, 1814; d. Oct. 27, 1814	21
Asaph, m. Sally **HOUGH**, b. of Meriden, Nov. 20, 1828, by Rev. Charles Hinsdale	34
Asaph, m. Nancy **COLLINS**, b. of Meriden, Mar. 28, 1833, by Charles J. Hinsdale	46
Benjamin, m. Lucretia **AUSTIN**, July 4, 1799	15
Benjamin Ely, [s. Benjamin & Lucretia], b. Dec. 6, 1801	15
Bethiah, m. Theophilus **HALL**, Mar. 24, 1803	3
Elizabeth, m. William **GOODWILL**, b. of Meriden, May 4, 1841, by Rev. G. W. Perkins	64
Elizur, [s. Benjamin & Lucretia], b. Nov. 10, 1804	15
Ezekiel R., m. Nancy C. **CROSBY**, b. of Meriden, Apr. 30, 1851, by Rev. G. W. Perkins	106
Harriet E., d. [Hubbard & Lavinia], b. Aug. 9, 1830	67
Hubbard, b. Feb. 4, 1799; m. Lavinia **BISHOP**, Oct. 15, 1823	67
Hubbard, m. Lavinia **BISHOP**, Oct. 16, 1823, by Reuben Ives	23
Isaac H., s. [Hubbard & Lavinia], b. Apr. 20, 1825	67
James B., of Wallingford, m. Gertrude A. **CLARKE**, of Meriden, Feb. 3, 1850, by Rev. H. Miller	101
Jane C., m. Lucius J. **COOK**, of Durham, Mar. 8, 1846, by Rev. C .Munson	85
Joel B., of Meriden, m. Betsey **EVARTS**, of Guilford, May 18, 1834, by Rev. Robert A. Hallam	48
Joel Bani, [s. Asahel & Elizabeth], b. Sept. 19, 1809	21
Joseph B., s. [Hubbard & Lavinia], b. Nov. 2, 1831	67
Joseph B., of Meriden, m. Caroline A. **TALMADGE**, of Franklin, N.Y., Dec. 25, 1853, by Rev. N. Mead	123
Julia, [d. Benjamin & Lucretia], b. Sept. 29, 1800	15
Juliett, of Meriden, m. Burdett **CANNON**, of Wallingford, [Apr.] 25, [1839], by Rev. Edwin R. Gilbert, of Wallingford	60
Laura Ann M., d. [Hubbard & Lavinia], b. Jan. 3, 1827	67
Lavinia D., of Meriden, m. Julius S. Auger, of New Haven, Aug. 11, 1835, by Charles J. Hinsdale	50
Lucina, m. Eli Foster, Aug. 12, 1824, by Charles J. Hinsdale	25

	Page
MERRIAM, MERIAM (cont.)	
Lucy Lucina, [d. Asahel & Elizabeth], b. July 19, 1818	21
Lucy Lucina, of Meriden, m. William A. **BALDWIN**, of North Haven, Apr. 14, 1835, by Rev. Edward Ingersoll	52
Nelson, m. Rosetta **COUCH**, b. of Meriden, Mar. 28, 1833, by Charles J. Hinsdale	46
Roxana, m. Asahel S. **LAWRENCE**, Nov. 13, 1834, by Rev. William R. Curtiss	49
Ruth Mariah, [d. Asahel & Elizabeth], b. Sept. 16, 1812	21
Salmon, m. Minerva **RICE**, Feb. 15, 1826, by Charles J. Hinsdale	28
Samuel A., of Meriden, m. Eliza C. **BROOKS**, of Waterbury, Jan. 1, 1833, by Rev. Robert A. Hallum	46
Sarah E., of Meriden, m. Benjamin **PAGE**, of North Branford, Oct. 20, 1836, by Rev. John Marshall Guion	54
Sarah Elizabeth [d. Asahel & Elizabeth], b. Feb. 8, 1816	21
Selden, of Meriden, m. Cynthia C. **RUSSELL**, of Bristol, Mar. 15, 1832, by Charles J. Hinsdale	43
Sevelia, m. Austin **BISHOP**, b. of Meriden, Nov. 20, 1834, by Charles P. Hinsdale	49
Sidney, m. Phebe **CURTIS**, Oct. 8, 1807	6
Stephen B., of Coventry, O., m. Eunice **TIBBALS**, of Meriden, July 31, 1836, by Rev. Stephen Beach, of East Haddam	54
Sylvia M., d. Salmon, of Meriden, m. Henry S. **MERWIN**, of Durham, May 16, 1848, by Rev. G. W. Perkins	95
William, m. Ann Eliza **MERRIAM**, b. of Meriden, Dec. 25, 1820, by Reuben Ives	20
MERRICK, Levnie Deming, d. Miner & Sally, b. July 3, 1816	16
MERRIL, Ruth, m. Horace **MERRIMAN**, Sept. 19, 1808	11
MERRIMAN, [see also **MERRIAM**], Cloe, of Meriden, m. Amos **LEE**, of Geneva, N.Y., Oct. 17, 1831, by Charles H. Hinsdale	43
Eli Barnes, s. Horace & Ruth, b. Aug. 22, 1809	11
Eliza, of Berlin, m. Luther **ROBBINS**, of Waterbury, Jan. 22, 1851, by Rev. G. W. Perkins	103
Horace, m. Ruth **MERRIL**, Sept. 19, 1808	11
Iram, s. Elisha & Chloe, b. July 9, 1800	10
Joel, m. Harriet **YALE**, b. of Meriden, Apr. 8, 1830, by Charles J. Hinsdale	37
MERWIN, Henry S., of Durham, m. Sylvia M. **MERRIAM**, d. of Salmon, of Meriden, May 16, 1848, by Rev. G. W. Perkins	95
MILDRUM, Jason, of Middletown, m. Caroline E. **ENSIGN**, of Meriden, Aug. 15, 1841, by Rev. Harvey Miller	64
MILES, Almeron, of Cheshire, m. Caroline **LAWRENCE**, of Meriden, Sept. 12, 1838, by Rev. Simon Shailor, of Wallingford	48
Edgar J., of Cheshire, m. Francis E. **LEWIS**, of Meriden, May 4, 1845, by Rev. B. H. Miller	81
Zeruah, of Southington, m. Reuben H. **DOUGLASS**, Jan. 4, 1853, by Rev. A. A. Stevens	115
MILLER, Almond, of Meriden, m. Catharine A. **ROGERS**, of New Haven, Dec. 25, 1845, by Rev. H. Miller	84
Edward, of Meriden, m. Caroline M. **NEAL**, of Southington, Aug. 30, 1848, by Rev. Harvey Miller	94
Edward B., of New Haven, m. Elizabeth **HART**, of Meriden, Oct. 24, 1853, by Rev. Harvey Miller	113

	Page
MILLER (cont.)	
Elisha, m. Abigail **THARP**, May 6, 1827, by Charles J. Hinsdale	30
Griswold P., m. Harriet **WOODRUFF**, of Southington, Apr. 22, 1851, by Rev. Harvey Miller	108
Harriet, m. John **ARNOLD**, b. of New Haven, July 2, 1840, by Rev. Harvey Miller	62
Harriet G., of Middletown, m. Daniel H. **HART**, of Meriden, May 14, 1840, by Harvey Miller	58
Harvey, m. Sarah R. **IVES**, b. of Meriden, May 21, 1839, by Alfred Bennet	60
Jefferson, of Granville, Mass., m. Hannah **IVES**, of Meriden, Oct. 11, 1820, by Samuel Miller	19
Joel, of Wallingford, m. Clarisa **PLUM**, of Meriden, Mar. 13, 1823, by Sedgewick Rice	22
Lovisa, of Meriden, m. Robert A. **BYINGTON**, of Wallingford, Sept. 5, 1830, by Rev. Russell Jennings	39
MITCHELL, MITCHEL, Aaron, d. June 15, 1811	12
Abigail, d. Dec. 1, 1805	6
Charles Henry, s. Zenas & Abigail, b. Apr. 3, 1805	6
Laura, m. Walter **BOOTH**, Jan. 1, 1810	14
Moses, d. July 4, 1811	12
Rebecca, w. Jotham, d. Mar 15, 1811	12
Sally, m. Zenas **BRONSON**, Oct. 3, 1824, by Charles J. Hinsdale	25
Sylvinah, d. Dec. 24, 1805	6
Titus Meriman, s. Zenas & Abigail, b. July 16, 1801	6
MIX, Amanda, w. Titus, d. July 14, 1829	38
Betsey, of Wallingford, m. Lester **CORNWELL**, of Middletown, Oct. 6, 1827, by Sam[ue]l Miller	32
Charles, s. Jairus B. & Lucy, b. July 3, 1805	10
Elihu J., s. Titus & Amanda, b. Aug. 2, 1807	38
Eliza, d. Titus & Amanda, b. Apr. 17, 1809	38
Ervin, s. Titus & Amanda, b. Oct. 9, 1820	38
Louisa, d. Jairus B. & Lucy, b. Nov. 27, 1807	10
Mira, d. Titus & Amanda, b. Dec. 11, 1814	38
Orvel, d. Titus & Amanda, b. Apr. 25, 1811	38
Titus, s. Titus & Amanda, b. Aug. 15, 1812	38
MOFFIT, Henry A., m. Julia M. **WILCOX**, Jan. 6, 1853, by Rev. Francis Bottom	118
MOORE, Sarah, of Berlin, m. Benjamin **LUCAS**, of Middletown, Aug. 10, 1845, by Rev. Harvey Miller	82
MORGAN, Anna, m. David **ROBBERTS**, May [ ], 1794	8
Mary E., m. Allen W. **HARVEY**, b. of Meriden, June 6, 1853, by Rev. George W. Perkins	119
Rachel, m. Asa **BURR**, of Haddam, Sept. 4, 1853, by Rev. A. S. Cheesbrough	119
MORLEY, Jonathan, m. Laura A. **BECKLEY**, of Berlin, Dec. 12, 1852, by Rev. Harvey Miller	114
MORRIS, Jesse M., of Ohio, m. Huldah **COLLINS**, of Meriden, Nov. 21, 1822, by Rev. Stephen Hays, of Middletown	22
MORSE, [see also **MOSS**], Lois, of Wallingford, m. Jacob **WETMORE**, of Meriden, Oct. 7, 1825, by Samuel Miller	27
Mirca, m. John **YEOMANS**, Jr., Jan. 30, 1822	28

MERIDEN VITAL RECORDS 157

	Page
MORSE (cont.)	
Vincy, of Wallingford, m. Oliver **REMINGTON**, of Coventry, R.I., Sept. 14, 1826, by Samuel Miller	29
MOSES, Jane A., of Middletown, m. Luther C. **WHITE**, Nov. 28, 1844, by Bishop Harvey Miller	79
MOSS, [see also **MORSE**], Jared, of Cheshire, m. Clarissa **SMITH**, of Meriden, Nov. 30, 1820, by Erastus Ripley	19
Mary Ann, of Meriden, m. Nathaniel **PECK**, of Columbia, Cheshire, July 23, 1820, by Rev. Elijah Willard	18
MOWREY, Anthony, m. Mrs. Chalsotte A. **LESTER**, b. of Meriden, June 8, 1851, by Rev. [ ], of Center Cong. Church	107
MULLEN, Michael, m. Caroline **JOLIN**, b. of Germany, May 30, 1853, by Rev. George W. Perkins	118
MUNSON, Edgar, of Bradford, N.Y., m. Lucy Maria **CURTISS**, of Meriden, June 15, 1852, by Rev. Robert A. Hallam, of New London	118
Nancy, of Southington, m. Hensdale S. **ROYCE**, of Meriden, Aug. 5, 1845, by Rev. G. W. Perkins	86
MURDOCK, Zina D., m. Sarah **FOSTER**, b. of Meriden, Sept. 11, 1834, by Charles J. Hinsdale	48
NEAL, Caroline M., of Southington, m. Edward **MILLER**, of Meriden, Aug. 30, 1848, by Rev. Harvey Miller	94
Rollin H., of South Boston, m. Melissa D. **YALE**, of Meriden, Sept. 26, 1833, by Nathaniel Hervey	48
NETTLETON, Nelson, of Killingworth, m. Har[r]iet **NORTON**, of Meriden, Mar. 2 ,1830, by Jesse Baker, Elder	37
NEWTON, Frederick, m. Esther **LEWIS**, Feb. 17, 1834, by Rev. Robert A. Hallam	48
Harriet B., of Meriden, m. Edwin B. **CLARK**, of Chester, June 3, 1844, by Rev. G. W. Perkins	76
Lucretia, m. Isaac C. **BAGG**, May 19, 1850, by Rev. Giles H. Deshon	104
NOBLE, Maria, m. John **FELLOWS**, June 17, 1838, by Erastus Ripley	57
NORTH, Curtis L., m. Keziah **COLLINS**, b. of Meriden, Aug. 26, 1841, by Rev. G. W. Perkins	65
NORTON, Har[r]iet, of Meriden, m. Nelson **NETTLETON**, of Killingworth, Mar. 2, 1830, by Jesse Baker, Elder	37
Henry C., of Berlin, m. Lucy O. **WOODRUFF**, of Waitsfield, Vt., May 12, 1851, by Rev. Harvey Miller	106
Maryann, m. Joel J. **BUTLER**, [Aug.] 27, [1835], by George B Atwell	51
OLDS, Cordelia, b. Sept. 22, 1816	30
Daniel, b. Mar. 30, 1807	30
Elizabeth, b. July 29, 1813	30
Frederick A., b. Nov. 10, 1804	30
Harriet N., of Meriden, m. Dudley P. **ROSS**, of Clinton, May 2, 1847, by Rev. G. W. Perkins	90
Lemuel, b. Nov. 4, 1800	30
Livenius, b. Oct. 17, 1797	30
Mary, b. Apr. 27, 1811	30
Russel, b. Dec. 10, 1798	30
Samuel, b. Jan. 8, 1809	30
Sarah L., b. Sept. 30, 1802	30

	Page
OLDS (cont.)	
William P., b. Apr. 27, 1796	30
OLES, Lucy Ann, m. Hiram **HALL**, b. of Meriden, Nov. 30, 1837, by Leland Howard	56
OSBORN, George W., of New Haven, m. Elizabeth **EAGES**, of Meriden, June 30, 1851, by Rev. G. W. Perkins	107
PACKARD, Russel, m. Lavinia **CLARK**, b. of Pittsfield, Mass., Feb. 17, 1829, by Samuel Miller	34
PADDOCK, Mariann, m. Asa **YALE**, b. of Meriden, June 19, 1828, by Samuel Miller	33
Mehitabel L., m. Jared **LEWIS**, b. of Meriden, Jan. 1, 1832, by Charles J. Hinsdale	43
PADDOCK, Samuel, Jr., m. Charlotte **YALE**, b. of Meriden, Jan. 22, 1823, by Samuel Miller	22
Samuel, C., m. Jennett **HALL**, b. of Meriden, Mar. 19, 1837, by Geo[rge] B. Atwell	56
PAGE, Benjamin, of North Branford, m. Sarah E. **MERRIAM**, of Meriden, Oct. 20, 1836, by Rev. John Marshall Guion	54
Charles, of East Haven, m. Eliza **DIXON**, of Montreal, L.C., Apr. 13, 1847, by Rev. Harvey Miller	90
Minor G., of Willimantic, m. Eliza A. **GREENE**, of Meriden, Oct. 15, 1851, by Rev. G. W. Perkins	108
PARIS (?), Lester, of Warehouse Point, m. Hannah **LINSLEY**, of Meriden, June 5, 1837, by Rev .John Marshall Guion	56
PARKER, Betsey, of Meriden, m. Rev. Thomas **GERALDS**, of the New York Conference of the Methodist E. Church, June 17, 1844, by Rev. John Parker	75
Betsey H., m. William W. **WHITE**, of Derby, Nov. 12, 1846, by Rev. H. Miller	88
Edmund, m. Jennet **BRADLEY**, b. of Meriden, Sept. 3, 1834, by Rev. Simon Shailer, of Wallingford	49
Edward A., of Cheshire, m. Harriet **BLAKE**, of Meriden, Sept. 1 1845, by Rev. Harvey Miller	83
Emily W., d. John, b. Nov. 2, 1842; d. Dec. 17, 1843	72
Fanny, m. Simeon **PERKINS**, May 13, 1807	11
George White, s. John, b. Sept. 19, 1846	88
Harriet, of Meriden, m. Samuel **PRATT**, of Southington, Aug. 28, 1833, by Rev. Simon Shalor, of Wallingford	47
Harriet M., m. Seymour H. **PATTERSON**, b. of Wallingford, [ ], by Tilton E. Doolittle, J.P.	103
Jason, of Cheshire, m. Lucetta **BUTLER**, of Meriden, Mar. 29, 1821, by James Noyes	20
Maria, m. Lewis **CARTER**, b. of Wallingford, Oct. 15, 1823, by Samuel Miller	23
Nancy Ann, m. Benedict **BRISTOL**, b. of Cheshire, Jan. 2, 1848, by Rev. John E. Searles	92
Olive, m. Abner **GRISWOLD**, Sept. 14, 1802	3
Ruth, b. Aug. 24, 1777; [m. John **BUTLER**,]	66
Ruth Ann, m. Jesse H. **BUNNEL**, b. of Meriden, Oct. 14, 1835, by Rev. Simon Shailer, of Wallingford	52
Sarah, m. George **TIBBALS**, Dec. 4, 1845, by Rev. Hervey Miller	83
Stephen L., of Meriden, m. Martha M. **ANDREWS**, of Cheshire, Nov. 23, 1845, by Rev. John Parker	83

	Page
PARMELEE, Charles, m. Sarah A. BAILEY, b. of Meriden, Oct. 9, 1851, by Rev. G. W. Perkins	108
Erastus P., m. Laura SMITH, of Meriden, Nov. 29, 1827, by Charles J. Hinsdale	32
Luther, of Guilford, m. Lavinia M. FARRINGTON, of Meriden, Apr. 7, 1836, by Rev. Edward Ingersoll	52
Mary C., m. Ira J. PRESTON, b. of Meriden, Apr. 18, 1852, by Rev. A. A. Stevens	111
PARSONS, Charles H., of Elyria, O., m. Sarah RICE, of Meriden, Jan. 5, 1852, by Rev. G. W. Perkins	110
Elizabeth, d. Samuel M. & Emily, b. Mar. 10, 1830	40
Samuel M., m. Emily ANDREWS, b. of Meriden, Sept. 3, 1828, by Rev. James Keeler	33
PATRICK, Marion, of Berlin, m. Edward J. COLLINS, of Meriden, Aug. 25, 1846, by Rev. G. W. Perkins	86
PATTERSON, PATERSON, Mary, m. Samuel BREWSTER, Aug. 6, 1848, by Rev. [ ] Wheaton	93
Seymour H., m. Harriet M. PARKER, b. of Wallingford, [ ], by Tilton E. Doolittle, J.P.	103
PEARCE, Darius, m. Cornelia CRANDALL, of Middletown, July 4, 1839, by Harvey Miller	61
PEARSON, Emma, m. Charles CLARK, Jr., Oct. 21, 1853, by Rev. Giles H. Deshon	122
PEASE, John H., of Wilbraham, Mass., m. Harriet A. SANDERSON, of Meriden, June 15, 1851, by Rev. A. A Stevens	107
PECK, Alden, m. Elizabeth W. STEWART, b. of Meriden, Aug. 2, 1853, by Rev. N. Mead	119
Allen L., m. Caroline E. ELTON, b. of Berlin, Dec. 29, 1852, by Rev. Harvey Miller	115
Ellen A., m. James H. FRARY, Dec. 22, 1852, by Rev. Giles H. Deshon	114
Harriet, of Berlin, Conn., m. Charles WRIGHT, of Mass., Oct. 3, 1830, by Rev. James [Keeler]	40
Henry, m. Harriet PERKINS, b. of Meriden, July 23, 1829, by Rev. James Keeler	36
Lavinia, m. Lucien HALL, Aug. 2, 1842, by Rev. Harvey Miller	69
Mary E., m. Dennis C. WILCOX, Dec. 23, 1852, by Rev. George W Perkins	117
Nathaniel, of Columbia, Cheshire, m. Mary Ann MOSS, of Meriden, July 23, 1820, by Rev. Elijah Willard	18
PEELER, David L., of Springfield, m. Sophia S. SKINNER, of Hartford, June 3, 1848, by Rev. G. W .Perkins. Int. pub. in Hartford, by Rev. Horace Bushnell	94
PEIOR*, George F., m. Mary B. RICHARDSON, b. of Middletown, [, 1846?], by Rev. W. G. Howard, of Middletown, *(Perhaps "PRIOR")	87
PERDEW, Eliza A., of Meriden, m. Cyprian HART, of Bristol, Apr. 4, 1852, by Rev. Harvey Miller	111
PERKINS, Anna, twin with Fanny, d. Simeon & Fanny, b. Aug. 20, 1810	12
Benjamin, b. Aug. 29, 1785; m. Polly B. WILSON, July 23, 1807	9
Catharine E., of Meriden, m. Benjamin LEONARD, of Kent, Apr. 7, 1840, by Harvey Miller	58

Page

PERKINS (cont.)
Electa C., m. George W. **COOK**, b. of Meriden, Apr. 18, 1853, by
 Rev. Harvey Miller   115
Eunice, m. Philemon **ANTHONY**, Nov. 24, 1825, by Titus Ives   28
Fanny, twin with Anna, d. Simeon & Fanny, b. Aug. 20, 1810   12
Harriet, m. Henry **PECK**, b. of Meriden, July 23, 1829, by Rev.
 James Keeler   36
Harriet Pluymert, d. Simeon & Fanny, b. Oct. 3, 1808   11
Jesse W., of Woodbury, m. Julia Ann **EATON**, of Meriden, Nov. 29,
 1846, by Rev. G. W. Perkins   89
Loomis L., of Hitchcockville, m. Mary M. **BUTLER**, of
 Middletown, Oct. 8, 1848, by Rev. Albert Nash   97
Mary A., m. Friend C. **BOOTH**, b. of Meriden, May 10, 1853, by
 Rev. Harvey Miller   116
Orson N., of Franklin, m. Lucretia C. **SCOTT**, of Prattsville, N.Y.,
 Oct. 7, 1849, by Rev. Harvey Miller   98
Ruel H., of Meriden, m. Frances **HOUGH**, Dec. 26, 1853, by Rev.
 Giles H. Deshon   123
Sarah Maria, m. James **TURNER**, Apr. 6, 1836, by Arthur Granger   53
Sherlock, m. Amanda **GRISWOLD**, Nov. 6, 1823, by Reuben Ives   24
Simeon, m. Fanny **PARKER**, May 13, 1807   11
Tryphena, m. Joseph **FARRINGTON**, Oct. 13, 1804   21
Tryphosa, of Meriden, m. Salmon **READ**, of Wallingford, Sept. 3,
 1820, by Rev. Elijah Willard   18
William Sherlock, s. Simeon & Fanny, b. July 29, 1812   14
PERSIS, Urilla P., of Readsborough, Vt., m. Bennet **SEARLES**, of
 Wallingford, Nov. 28, 1847, by Rev. John E. Searles   92
PETTEE, John T., of Winchendon, Mass., m. Harriet R. **CLARK**, of
 Meriden, Oct. 26, 1843, by Rev. John Parker   72
PETTIT, Mary, d. [Samuel & Rebecca], b. Sept. 21, 1813   12
Narcissa, d. Samuel & Rebecca, b. May 30, 1811   12
Susanna, d. Samuel & Rebeckah, b. Mar. 14, 1809   12
PHELPS, Timothy, of Marlboro, m. Sarah **AUSTIN**, of Meriden, Nov.
 17, 1831, by Rev. Russell Jennings   43
[**PIERCE**], [see under **PEARCE**]
PIERPOINT, Philemon, of North Haven, m. Nancy **CLARK**, of Meriden,
 Dec. 18, 1842, by C. W. Everest   70
Philemon, m. Nancy **CLARK**, Dec. 18, 1842, by Rev. C. W. Everest   87
PLANT, Betsey H., of Meriden, m. Anson **BRAY**, of Southbury, Jan. 18,
 1826, by Samuel Miller   28
PLUM, Clarissa, d. Seth D. & Elizabeth, b. Jan. 23, 1805   3
Claris[s]a, of Meriden, m. Joel **MILLER**, of Wallingford, Mar. 13,
 1823, by Sedgewick Rice   22
James M., of Berlin, m. Jennet F. **YALE**, of Meriden, June 8, 1830,
 by Rev. William Bently   38
Russel Harison, s. Seth D. & Elisabeth, b. July 21, 1813; d. Jan. 22,
 1816   15
Seth D., m. Elisabeth **HALL**, Dec. 10, 1803   3
Seth Otis, s. Seth D. & Elizabeth, b. June 22, 1820; d. May 15, 1822   21
PLUYMERT, Amelia, of Meriden, m. Joseph **WARNER**, of
 Middletown, Feb. 5, 1821, by Samuel Miller   19
POMEROY, Charles, [s. Noah & Nancy], b. Sept, 3, 1825   30

MERIDEN VITAL RECORDS

	Page
POMEROY (cont.)	
Cornelia, m. Elias Y. **IVES**, b. of Meriden, Aug. 22, 1827, by Samuel Miller	31
Eliza, m. John S. **BLAKE**, Oct. 17, 1832, by Rev. John Boyden	45
Eugenia, [s. Noah & Nancy], b. July 13, 1821	30
Gelina Ann, m. Eli **IVES**, b. of Meriden, Sept. 30, 1830, by Rev. Russell Jennings	39
Harriet, d. Noah & Nancy, b. Dec. 27, 1817	30
Harriet, m. Isaac **LEWIS**, b. of Meriden, May 11, 1836, by William A. Hickney	53
James Y., m. Delila F. **GUILD**, b. of Meriden, Sept. 17, 1848, by Rev. Harvey Miller	94
Nancy, [d. Noah & Nancy], b. Mar. 23, 1823	30
Norman, [s. Noah & Nancy], b. Sept. 22, 1819	30
POTTER, Albert B., of Meriden, m. Jerusha **IVES**, of Meriden, Nov. 18, 1830, by Charles J. Hinsdale	41
Sariah Mariah, d. Albert R. & Jerusha, b. June 12, 1833	49
POWERS, William H., of Abington, Mass., m. Harriet C. **FRANCIS**, of Meriden, Oct. 8, 1848, by Rev .Harvey Miller	94
PRATT, Aaron, m. Betsey A. **JOHNSON**, Nov. 27, 1832, by Charles J Hinsdale	45
Aaron J., s. Aaron & Betsey A., b. Sept. 29, 1843. Copied Jan. 27, 1868, from a record made at the time of birth	73
Elizabeth B., of Meriden, m. Matthew **ROGERS**, of Bethany, N.Y., Oct. 22, 1846, by Rev. G. W. Perkins	88
Harriet M., of Meriden, m. Walter R. **LONG**, of Troy, N.Y., Sept. 13, 1842, by Rev. G. W. Perkins	70
Horace, m. Jerusha **HART**, May 5, 1844, by Rev. H. Miller	75
Samuel, of Southington, m. Harriet **PARKER**, of Meriden, Aug. 28, 1833, by Rev. Simon Sha[i]lor, of Wallingford	47
PRESTON, Almena, of Meridan, m. George A. **SAWYER**, of Middletown, Nov. 17, 1842, by G. W. Perkins	71
Ira, m. Sally **HOUGH**, Nov. 24, 1825, by Charles J. Hinsdale	27
Ira J., m. Mary C. **PARMELEE**, b. of Meriden, Apr. 18, 1852, by Rev. A. A. Stevens	111
Mary, m. Augustus **HALL**, Nov. 27, 1806	6
PRITCHARD, Eliza Jane, of Waterbury, m. Joseph W. **TURNER**, of Middletown, Sept. 8, 1845, by Rev. Harvey Miller	83
PROFFIT, John, of Hartford, m. Emily **HART**, of Meriden, Apr. 13, 1845, by Rev. John Parker	80
PUFFER, Bathsheba, of Meriden, m. Joel **TUCKER**, of Monson, Mass., Apr. 19, 1853, by Rev. A. A. Stevens	115
Samuel D., of Meriden, m. Lucy A. **HARRIS**, of Middletown, Dec. 2, 1850, by Rev. A. A Stevens	102
RANDOLL, Sylvester, of Hartford, m. Mary E. **MARTIN**, of Meriden, Mar. 27, 1847, by Rev. G. W. Perkins	89
RAVEN, Charles August **GOOTLIEB**, m. Eustina Dorethea **BINGHOFF**, b. of Germany, Aug. 31, 1851, by Rev. G. W. Perkins	107
READ, REED, Joseph H., of Worcester, Mass., m. Josephine W. **LEWIS**, of Meriden, Nov. 27, 1851, by Rev. Harvey Miller	109
Rebecca, m. John P. **AUSTIN**, b. of Meriden, [Apr.] 30, [1835], by Rev. George B. Atwell	50

	Page
READ, REED (cont.)	
Salmon, of Wallingford, m. Tryphosa **PERKINS**, of Meriden, Sept. 3, 1820, by Rev. Elijah Willard	18
Samuel, of Durham, m. Polly **MATTOON**, of Meriden, May 2, 1821, by Elijah Willard	20
Thomas H., of Lisbon, Conn., m. Sarah C. **SHERMAN**, of Wallingford, July 27, 1852, by Rev. Harvey Miller	112
RECOR, Betsey A., m. Edwin **BELDEN**, b. of New Britain, Sept. 16, 1841, by Rev. G. W. Perkins	65
REDFIELD, Abigail, [d. Horace & Lucy], b. Feb. 1, 1823	31
Abigail ,m. Remick K. **CLARK**, b. of Meriden, Jan. 12, 1841, by Rev. Harvey Miller	63
Ann, [d. Horace & Lucy], b. Mar. 3, 1819	31
Ann, m. John **BUTLER**, b. of Meriden, Aug. 20, 1839, by Rev. Melancthon Hoyt	61
Chloe E., of Meriden, m. George **REDFIELD**, of Clinton, Sept. 13, 1846, by Rev. H. Miller	87
Edwin, [s. Horace & Lucy], b. Mar. 17, 1825	31
Edwin, of Meriden, m. Harriet E. **DICKINSON**, of New Haven, Dec. 24, 1848, by Rev. N. S. Wheaton	95
Elisha K., s. James P. & Polly, b. July 16, 1812	33
George, of Clinton, m. Chloe E. **REDFIELD**, of Meriden, Sept. 13, 1846, by Rev. H. Miller	87
Harriet E., of Guilford, m. Norman C. **HALL**, of Middletown, Nov. 14, 1853, by Rev. A. A. Stevens	122
Horace, m. Lucy **CURTIS**, Dec. 25, 1817	31
Horace, [s. Horace & Lucy], b. Apr. 24, 1821	31
James P., m. Mary **FARRINGTON**, July 9, 1809	10
James P., m. Sally **DAYTON**, Mar. 19, 1826, by Charles J. Hinsdale	28
Lucy, [d. Horace & Lucy], b. Aug. 20, 1827	31
Lucy A., m. Samuel P. **STANNARD**, Aug. 6, 1848, by Rev. Albert Nash	96
Lydia G., of Guilford, m. George **BEACH**, of North Haven, Aug. 7, 1845, by Rev. Harvey Miller	82
Marris, of Killingworth, m. Beri **COUCH**, of Meriden, Apr. 28, 1823, by Samuel Miller	23
Mary Emaline, d. James P. & Polly, b. Aug. 19, 1810	13
Mehetabel, m. Asahel **CURTIS**, Nov. 8, 1812	14
Zeno, m. Laura **BENNETT**, b. of Meriden, Jan. 2, 1843, by Rev. John E. Searles	93
REED, [see under **READ**]	
REMINGTON, Henry E., [s Oliver T. & [E]unicy], b. Mar. 16, 1832	44
Hiram, s. Oliver T. & [E]unicy, b. Dec. 31, 1822?	44
Hiram M., of Meriden, m. Harriet **ROBERTS**, of Westfield, Aug. 2, 1847, by Rev. Harvey Miller	91
Lydia C., m. Samuel **BACON**, 2nd, of Middletown, Oct. 19, 1853, by Rev. Harvey Miller	121
Lydia E., [d. Oliver T. & [E]unicy], b. July 30, 1830	44
Mary E., d. Oliver F., b. Feb. 17, 1841	64
Oliver, of Coventry, R.I., m. Vincy **MORSE**, of Wallingford, Sept. 14, 1826, by Samuel Miller	29
Sarah L., d. Oliver & Vincy, b. Nov. 11, 1837	61
Susan V., d. Oliver & Vincy, b. May 5, 1836	53

MERIDEN VITAL RECORDS 163

	Page
REMINGTON (cont.)	
Thankfull B., [d. Oliver T. & [E]unicy], b. Dec. 22, 1827	44
Thankful B., of Meriden, m. Silas **GLADWIN**, of Haddam, Sept. 2, 1846, by Rev. H. Miller	87
Thomas F., of Meriden, m. Eunice **ROGERS**, of Wallingford, Nov. 6, 1842, by Rev. Harvey Miller	70
William L., s. Oliver T. & Vincy, b. Aug. 24, 1845	83
RICE, Almira, d. Silas & Ruth, b. May 24, 1797	8
Almira, m. Avery **HOUGH**, Dec. 20, 1821, by Erastus Ripley	20
Ashbel B., s. [Chester & Prudence], b. June 26, 1827	68
Betsey, of Meriden, m. William M. **JUDD**, of Kent, Dec. 3, 1840, by Rev. E. Colton	63
Chester, m. Prudence **BAILEY**, Aug. 31, 1812	68
Clarrisa, m. Elias **SMITH**, Nov. 10, 1797	7
Clarissa A., d. [Chester & Prudence], b. Nov. 17, 1824	68
Clarissa A., of Meriden, m. Guy H. **HUBBARD**, of Claremont, N.H., Oct. 21, 1851, by Rev. Giles H. Deshon	109
Cornelia D., of Wallingford, m. George N. **BALDWIN**, of Meriden, Oct. 12, 1845, by Rev. H. Miller	83
Diana, m. Isaac **YALE**, Dec. 30, 1807	10
Emeline, m. Greene **FREEMAN**, July 7, 1842, by Rev. J. F. Cushing	86
Emeline L., d. [Chester & Prudence], b. Feb. 15, 1816	68
Gelina, m. John **YEOMANS**, Jr., Feb. 9, 1815	28
Harriet J., d. [Chester & Prudence], b. Jan. 11, 1822	68
Hiram H., s. [Chester & Prudence], b. Feb. 9, 1819	68
Irena, of Meriden, m. Orrin J. **DUTTON**, of Southington, Oct. 30, 1833, by Charles J. Hinsdale	48
Jane, d. Silas & Rebeckah, b. July 1, 1805	8
John, of Wallingford, m. Olive **SEDGEWICK**, of Meriden, Aug. 12, 1822, by Sedgewick Rice	21
Lee, m. Lucinda **IVES**, Oct. 11, 1810	14
Levi, m. Isabel **IVES**, Mar. 13, 1805	2
Lucinda Ann, d. [Lee & Lucinda], b. May 8, 1812	14
Lucy, m. Joel **YALE**, Sept. 27, 1804	8
Lydia, of Meriden, m. Jesse G. **BALDWIN**, of Oxford, Apr. 15, 1830, by Charles J. Hinsdale	37
Maria J., d. [Chester & Prudence], b. June 14, 1813	68
Maria J., m. Harry **GRISWOLD**, b. of Meriden, May 31, 1835, by Rev. Edward Ingersoll	50
Mary J., of Meriden, m. Elisha **STEVENS**, of Watertown, Mar. 1, 1824, by Rev. Sedgewick Rice, of Wallingford	25
Minerva, m. Salmon **MERRIAM**, Feb. 15, 1826, by Charles J. Hinsdale	28
Phebe, d. Silas & Ruth, b. Feb. 23, 1799	8
Reuben J., of Wallingford, m. Jane H. **TUCKER**, of New Hartford, Sept. 17, 1848, by Rev. Albert Nash	97
Ruth, w. Silas, d. Mar. 30, 1801	8
Ruth Curtis, d. Silas & Rebeckah, b. Oct. 14, 1803	8
Sarah, of Meriden, m. Charles H. **PARSONS**, of Elyria, O., Jan. 5, 1852, by Rev. G. W. Perkins	110
Sarah M., of Meriden, m. John C. **GARFIELD**, of Tyringham, Mass., Dec. 25, 1841, by Rev. C. W. Everest	68
Silas, m. Ruth **CURTIS**, Aug. 4, 1796	8

BARBOUR COLLECTION

	Page
RICE (cont.)	
Silas, m. Rebeckah **HUBBARD**, Mar. 18, 1802	8
Susannah, m. Elisha **TAYLOR**, Aug. 25, 1811	19
William T., m. Susan **COLLINS**, b. of Meriden, Nov. 7, 1841, by Rev. G. W. Perkins	65
RICHARDSON, Leyden, m. Eliza E. **HALL**, Apr. 5, 1825, by Charles J. Hinsdale	27
Mary B., m. George F. **PEIOR***, b. of Middletown, [, 1846?], by Rev. W. G. Howard, of Middletown *(**PRIOR**)	87
RICHMOND, Horace, m. Amelia **WATROUS**, b. of Meriden, July 27, 1842, by Rev. John Parker	69
Isaac C., m. Sarah A. **BUNNELL**, Oct. 23, 1853, by Rev. Harvey Miller	121
Susan M., of Meriden, m. Hiram B. **TALMAGE**, of New Haven, Apr. 29, 1849, by Rev. Albert Nash	97
ROBBINS, Luther, of Waterbury, m. Eliza **MERRIMAN**, of Berlin, Jan. 22, 1851, by Rev. G. W. Perkins	103
ROBERTS, ROBBERTS, Benjamin H., of Middletown, m. Eliza H. **DOUGLASS**, of New Haven, Apr. 4, 1852, by Rev. G. W. Perkins	110
Charles A., of Middletown, m. Belinda A. **ADAMS**, of Meriden, Nov. 24, 1853, by Rev. Harvey Miller	121
Darius, of Middletown, m. Emily **HALL**, of Meriden, Dec. 25, 1827, by Samuel Miller	32
David, m. Anna **MORGAN**, May [ ], 1794	8
Emily F., m. Theodore F. **BAILEY**, Sept. 25, 1853, by Rev. A. A. Stevens	120
Ephraim, [s. David & Anna], b. July 17, 1800	8
Hannah, m. William **ROGERS**, Jan. 1, 1843, by Rev. Alexander Miller	76
Harriet, of Westfield, m. Hiram M. **REMINGTON**, of Meriden, Aug. 2, 1847, by Rev. Harvey Miller	91
Josiah, [s. David & Anna], b. Sept. 20, 1791	8
Martha S., of Litchfield, m. Mark **TUCKER**, of Woodbridge, May 14, 1843, by G. W. Perkins	72
Mercy Minerva, [d. David & Anna], b. July 17, 1804	8
Micha Whitfield, [s. David & Anna], b. July 21, 1802	8
Orsemus, [ch. of David & Anna], b. June 21, 1797	8
Rebeckah, [d. David & Anna], b. Mar. 22, 1795	8
Rebeckah, [d. David & Anna], b. July 31, 1807	8
Russel, [s. David & Anna], b. Sept. 11, 1787	8
Sally, [d. David & Anna], b. Feb. 16, 1790	8
Samuel, of Berlin, m. Mary **CURTIS**, of Meriden, May 5, 1829, by Charles J. Hinsdale	35
ROBINSON, George H., m. Mary C. **HARRISON**, Apr. 29, 1844, by Rev. Alexander Miller	76
ROGERS, Catharine A., of New Haven, m. Almond **MILLER**, of Meriden, Dec. 25, 1845, by Rev. H. Miller	84
Eunice, of Wallingford, m. Thomas F. **REMINGTON**, of Meriden, Nov. 6, 1842, by Rev. Harvey Miller	70
Matthew, of Bethany, N.Y., m. Elizabeth B. **PRATT**, of Meriden, Oct. 22, 1846, by Rev. G. W. Perkins	88

MERIDEN VITAL RECORDS 165

	Page
ROGERS (cont.)	
Polly A., m. Cornelius **HULL**, Nov. 29, 1827, by Charles J. Hinsdale	32
William, m. Hannah **ROBERTS**, Jan. 1, 1843, by Rev. Alexander Miller	76
ROSS, Dudley P., of Clinton, m. Harriet N. **OLDS**, of Meriden, May 2, 1847, by Rev. G. W. Perkins	90
ROYCE, Henry, of Meriden, m. Emily **LANE**, of Killingworth, June 10, 1847, by Rev. G. W. Perkins	90
Hensdale S., of Meriden, m. Nancy **MUNSON**, of Southington, Aug. 5, 1846, by Rev. G. W. Perkins	86
Mary, of Meriden, m. Joel **HOUGH**, of Wallingford, June [ ], 1836, by Arthur Granger	53
RUSSELL, Cynthia C., of Bristol, m. Selden **MERRIAM**, of Meriden, Mar. 15, 1832, by Charles J. Hinsdale	43
Phebe, of Meriden, m. Samuel **WILFORD**, of Branford, Jan. 6, 1850, by Rev. Albert Nash	101
RUTTY, Ezra, m. Clarissa **CURTIS**, b. of Meriden, Sept. 16, 1832, by Rev. Russell Jennings	46
Ezra, m. Phebe **BLACKSTONE**, b. of Meriden, Jan. 23, 1851, by Rev. Harvey Miller	104
RYAN, James, m. Sarah Jane **BROWN**, b. of Meriden, Mar. 31, 1850, by Rev. George W. Perkins	103
SAGE, Barzilla D., of Middletown, m. Elizabeth P. **YALE**, of Meriden, Mar. 20, 1831, by Rev. Russell Jennings	41
Philip, of Middletown, m. Elisa **BOOTH**, of Meriden, Nov. 16, 1843, by Rev. H. Miller	72
SANDERSON, Edward S., of Middletown, m. Caroline M. **BLODGETT**, Oct. 30, 1853, by Rev. A. S. Cheesbrough	121
Harriet A., of Meriden, m. John H. **PEASE**, of Wilbraham, Mass., June 15, 1851, by Rev. A. A. Stevens	107
Samuel S., of Cheshire, m. Lucy **BOTSFORD**, of Berlin, Sept. 10, 1832, by Charles J. Hinsdale	44
SANFORD, Elizabeth C., of Meriden, m. Asa **KIRTLAND**, of Saybrook, Nov. 1, 1849, by Rev. A. A. Stephens	100
Hannah, m. Thomas **DOUGLASS**, Sept. 26, 1814	16
SAUNDERS, Adam, m. Ann **KESTEREN**, Oct. 4, 1852, by Rev. J. H. Deshon	113
SAVAGE, Adah, of Berlin, m. Albert **FOSTER**, of Meriden, June 22, 1853, by Rev George W. Perkins	119
William, m. Sarah **JOHNSON**, of Worcester, Mass., Sept. 18, 1844, by Rev. Harvey Miller	78
SAWYER, George A., of Middletown, m. Almena **PRESTON**, of Meriden, Nov. 17, 1842, by G. W. Perkins	71
SCHNEEMAN, Charles, m. Fredericka **BURGHOFF**, of Wallingford, late of Hanover, Germany, Nov. 4, 1852, by Rev. Harvey Miller	114
SCOTT, Lucretia C., of Prattsville, N.Y., m. Orson N. **PERKINS**, of Franklin, Oct. 7, 1849, by Rev. Harvey Miller	98
SCOVIL, **SCOVELL**, Eleazer, m. Elizabeth **WHITE**, Sept. 11, 1808	10
Elizabeth W., m. Henry **WILCOX**, May 9, 1832, by Rev. John R. Crane, of Middletown	46
Jane J., m. John F. **TOWNER**, Sept. 22, 1835, by Rev. John R. Crane, of Middletown	51

BARBOUR COLLECTION

Page

SCOVIL, SCOVELL (cont.)
    Orren, of Lewis County, New York, m. Betsey C. **ATKINS**, of Meriden, June 2, 1845, by Rev. C .Munson   82
SEARLES, Bennet, of Wallingford, m. Urilla P. **PERSIS**, of Readsborough, Vt., Nov. 28, 1847, by Rev. John E. Searles   92
    Sarah A., m. David J. **AYRES**, b. of Poundridge, N.Y., May 7, 1848, by Rev. John E. Searles   93
SEDGEWICK, Henry, of Meriden, m. Lucinda T. **GOFF**, of Haddam, Mar. 15, 1849, by Rev. Harvey Miller   96
    Olive, of Meriden, m. John **RICE**, of Wallingford, Aug. 12, 1822, by Sedgewick Rice   21
SELLEW, Anson R., m. Alma **YALE**, Nov. 16, 1845, by Rev. Hervey Miller   83
SEYMOUR, Stephen, m. Betsey **COLLINS**, Nov. 27, 1823, by Charles J. Hinsdale   24
    William Henry, s. Stephen & Electa, b. July 4, 1817   22
SHELLY, John, of Durham, m. Cornelia J. **FINLEY**, of Clinton, Oct. 24, 1847, by Rev. John E. Searles   92
SHEPHERD, Lucena, Mrs. of Southington, Conn., m. Peter **BABLE**, of Westbrook, Me. Jan. 9, 1852, by Rev. William W. Hurd   110
SHERMAN, Frances A., m. Charles B. **HOLLAND**, b. of Meriden, Oct. 19, 1848, by Rev. G. W. Perkins   95
    Israel A., of Freedonia, N.Y., m. Anne O. **BROWN**, of Meriden, July 20, 1830, by Charles J. Hinsdale   38
    Jane A., of Wallingford, m. Alanson **WATROUS**, of Chester, Oct. 29, 1843, by G. W. Perkins   75
    Sarah C., of Wallingford, m. Thomas H. **READ**, of Lisbon, Conn., July 27, 1852, by Rev. Harvey Miller   112
    Sylvester J., of Branford, m. Eveline T. **ISBELL**, of West Meriden, Sept. 24, 1848, by Rev. Harvey Miller   94
SHIELS, Margaret A., of New Haven, m. Henry **SLATTER**, of Meriden, Apr. 24, 1851, by Rev. Harvey Miller   105
SHIPMAN, Sarah I., m. Isaac **BUTLER**, b. of Meriden, Sept. 22, 1851, by Rev. A. A. Stevens   108
SHORNERS, Mary, of Meriden, m. John F. **FARNSWORTH**, of Fleming, N.Y., Sept. 18, 1853, by Rev. Harvey Miller   120
SIBLEY, Aurelia, of Meriden, m. John A. **BARTLETT**, of Providence, R.I., July 1840, by Rev. Harvey Miller   62
    Caroline, of Westfield, Mass., m. Solomon **YEOMANS**, of Meriden, Aug. 26, 1830, by Rev. Jesse Baker   38-9
SIZER, Amasa, Jr., of New London, m. Hannah **HULL**, of Cheshire, Dec. 18, 1842, by Rev. Harvey Miller   71
    Mary Ann, m. William **BROOKS**, May 21, 1836, by George B Atwell   53
SKINNER, Sophia S., of Hartford, m. David L. **PEELER**, of Springfield, June 3, 1848, by Rev. G. W. Perkins. Int. pub. in Hartford, by Rev .Horace Bushnell   94
SLATTER, Henry, of Meriden, m. Margaret A. **SHIELS**, of New Haven, Apr. 24, 1851, by Rev. Harvey Miller   105
SMITH, Andrew J. , of Bristol, m. Mary J. **DOOLITTLE**, of Meriden, Jan. 14, 1851, by Rev. Harvey Miller   104
    Charles C., of Conway, Mass., m. Dorothy **THAYER**, of Chesterfield, Mass., Oct. 19, 1851, by Rev. Harvey Miller   109

MERIDEN VITAL RECORDS

Page

SMITH (cont.)
Clarissa, of Meriden, m. Jared **MOSS**, of Cheshire, Nov. 20, 1820,
   by Erastus Ripley   19
Elias, m. Clarrisa **RICE**, Nov. 10, 1797   7
Elias, s. Elias & Clarisa, b. July 10, 1798   7
Francis W., m. Lucy Ann **COUCH**, b. of Meriden, Dec. 15, 1852, by
   Rev. Giles H. Deshon   114
Ira H., m. Caroline **HARTSON**, Dec. 24, 1838, by Rev. Melancthon
   Hoyt   60
Isaac, of Wallingford, m. Martha E. **GOODRICH**, of Meriden, Mar.
   18, 1849, by Rev. Harvey Miller   96
Laura, m. Erastus P. **PARMELEE**, Nov. 29, 1827, by Charles J.
   Hinsdale   32
Lorenzo, of Westbrook, m. Lucy A. **BUTLER**, of Meriden, Apr. 4,
   1847, by Rev. C. Munson   90
Lucius B., m. Caroline **GRISWOLD**, b. of Meriden, Oct. 30, 1839,
   by Rev .E. E. Beardsley, of Cheshire   58
Mary, m. Chaunc[e]y **CLARK**, Dec. 22, 1824, by Charles J.
   Hinsdale   26
Sophia, of Westfield, m. John [   ], of Newton, L.I., Aug. 12, 1840
   by Rev. S. S. Stocking   62
SNOW, Abby C., wid. m. Peter G. **LEACH**, b. of Meriden, Apr. 15, 1844,
   by Rev. G. W. Perkins   76
Gamaliel F., of Meriden, m. Sarah H. **DURAND**, of Berlin, Feb. 2,
   1847, by Rev. G. W. Perkins   89
SOUTHWORTH, Rechelsia T., m. John L. **TOMLINSON**, Mar. 22,
   1853, by Rev. Harvey Miller   115
SPARKS, Edward, m. Esther **BURR**, Nov. 27, 1823, by Charles J.
   Hinsdale   24
SPENCER, SPENSER, Jonathan J., of Meriden, m. Marg[ar]et, of
   Burlington, Vt., Jan. 27, 1850, by Rev. Abner Nash   101
Martha, Mrs. of Haddam, m. Guilbert **STOWE**, of Meriden, Sept.28,
   1824, by Rev. Josiah Graves, of Middletown   26
Phineas A., m. Susan F. **CLARK**, b. of Meriden, Mar. 31, 1850, by
   Rev. Albert Nash   101
SPERRY, Henry B., of Meriden, m. Charlotta **WARNER**, of
   Wethersfield, Jan. 20, 1848, by Rev. John E. Searles   93
Lewis L., m. Sarah **WATSON**, b. of Meriden, Mar. 2, 1845, by Rev
   Samuel W. Smith   80
STACK, Pomeroy, m. Lucy **COLE**, Nov. 15, 1826, by Charles J.
   Hinsdale   29
STACY, Allen, of Penn., m. Maria **HART**, of New Britain, Sept. 1, 1847,
   by Rev. John E. Searles   91
STANLEY, Jonas, m. Eliza **DOOLITTLE**, Mar. 20, 1808   8
STANNARD, Samuel P., m. Lucy A. **REDFIELD**, Aug. 6, 1848, by Rev.
   Albert Nash   96
STARR, Almira, m. George **HILL**, b. of Middletown, July 22, 1827, by
   Samuel Miller   31
Lydia, m. John **MARBLE**, b. of Middletown, July 31, 1825, by
   Samuel Miller   27
STEDMAN, Henry, of Berlin, m. Emeline S. **CLARK**, of Meriden, Aug.
   13, 1828, by Rev. James Keeler   33

	Page
STEVENS, STEPHENS, Elisha, of Watertown, m. Mary J. **RICE**, of Meriden, Mar. 1, 1824, by Rev. Sedgewick Rice, of Wallingford	25
James, m. Julia **FREMELIA**, b. of Cheshire, Dec. 20, 1849, by Rev. Albert Nash	100
Morris, of Durham, m. Ruth A. **BUTLER**, Jan. 14, 1830, by Charles J. Hinsdale	36
Philander, of Meriden, m. Eunice W. **BROWN**, of Windsor, Sept. 17, 1848, by Rev. Albert Nash	97
STEWART, Caroline, of Meriden, m. George B. **BARTHOLOMEW**, of Sheffield, Mass., Mar. 10, 1831, by Rev. Russell Jennings	41
Elizabeth W., m. Alden **PECK**, b. of Meriden, Aug. 2, 1853, by Rev. N. Mead	119
Sarah Jane, of Meriden, m. Nathan A. **DANIELS**, of Norwich, Jan. 2, 1837, by Geo[rge] B. Atwell	55
STILES, Dorus A., of West Springfield, Mass., m. Betsey Ann **WARNER**, d. of John P., of Meriden, July 5, 1847, by Rev. G. W. Perkins	90
Truman S., of Southbury, m. Mary C. **CROWELL**, of Middletown, Apr. 12, 1851, by Rev. Harvey Miller	105
STONE, Eveline E., of Middletown, m. Sylvanus J. **CONE**, of Meriden, May 15, 1845, by Rev. B. H. Miller	81
STOWE, Guilbert, of Meriden, m. Mrs. Martha **SPENSER**, of Haddam, Sept. 28, 1824, by Rev. Josiah Graves, of Middletown	26
Louisa, of Middletown, m. Sylvanus J. **CONE**, of Meriden, Nov. 4, 1849, by Rev. Harvey Miller	99
STRONG, Richard, of East Windsor, m. Susan **LEWIS**, of Meriden, June 24, 1845, by Rev. Harvey Miller	82
STUTTER, Joel W., m. Matilda D. **JOHNSON**, b. of Meriden, July 3, 1851, by Rev. Giles H. Deshon	108
SUTLIFF, Eliza R., of Meriden, m. Kelsey **CURTIS**, of Wallingford, Apr. 11, 1847, by Rev. Harvey Miller	90
Eliza Rebecca, [d. Anson & Mehitabel], b. Oct. 29, 1823	86
Harriet Atwood, d. Anson & Mehitabel, b. Sept. 16, 1821	86
John, m. Mary Ann **DAYTON**, Nov. 22, 1827, by Charles J. Hinsdale	32
Samuel Anson, s. [Anson & Mehitabel], b. Aug. 17, 1825	86
William Albert, s. [Anson & Mehitabel], b. Sept. 23, 1829	86
TALMADGE, TALMAGE, TAMAGE, Caroline A., of Franklin, N.Y., m. Joseph B. **MERRIAM**, of Meriden, Dec. 25, 1853, by Rev. N. Mead	123
Hiram B., of New Haven, m. Susan M. **RICHMOND**, of Meriden, Apr. 29, 1849, by Rev. Albert Nash	97
Marcus Miles, of New Haven, m. Abagail **ANDREWS**, of Meriden, Nov. 11, 1824, by James Keeler	26
TANNER, Mary Alenah, d. Lewis H. & Sarah D., b. Oct. 25, 1842	71
William Lewis, b. May 3, 1844	76
TAYLOR, Chaunc[e]y, of Glastenbury, m. Mary **LYMAN**, of Meriden, Mar. 27, 1825, by Samuel Miller	27
Elisha, m. Susannah **RICE**, Aug. 25, 1811	19
Hannah, m. Samuel **BALDWIN**, Sept. 22, 1774	7
Lois Louisa, d. [Elisha & Susannah], b. July 4, 1812	19
Lydia, m. Patrick **CLARK**, Aug. 22, 1801	16

MERIDEN VITAL RECORDS

	Page
TENANT, Henry J., m. Sarah A. YALE, Sept. 22, 1839, by Harvey Miller	61
THARP, [see under THORPE]	
THAYER Dorothy, of Chesterfield, Mass., m. Charles O. SMITH, of Conway, Mass., Oct. 19, 1851, by Rev. Harvey Miller	109
THOMPSON, Asenath, m. Darling DAYTON, May 13, 1814	15
William L., of New Orleans, La., m. Maria E. LEONARD, of Meriden, Sept. 23, 1846, by Rev. G. W. Perkins	88
THORP[E], THARP, Abigail, m. Elisha MILLER, May 6, 1827, by Charles J. Hinsdale	30
Aurilla ,m. Almond BIRDSEY, Nov. 25, 1832, by Rev. Seth Higby	45
Isabella G., of West Springfield, Mass., m. William C. HOUGH, of Meriden, Jan. 20, 1831, by Charles J. Hinsdale	41
THRALL, Eli, m. Mrs. Eunice DURAND, Nov. 23, 1851, by Rev. A. A. Stevens	109
TIBBALS, Eunice, of Meriden, m. Stephen B. MERRIAM, of Coventry, O., July 31, 1836, by Rev. Stephen Beach, of East Haddam	54
George m. Sarah PARKER, Dec. 4, 1845, by Rev .Hervey Miller	83
Isaac I., m. Lucy COWLES, b. of Meriden, Sept. 1, 1831, by Charles J. Hinsdale	43
Isaac I., m. Mary R. BOOTH, b. of Meriden, May 14, 1834, by Charles J. Hinsdale	48
Sarah, of Meriden, m. Stephen M. WEIR, of Glastenbury, Nov. 1, 1853, by Rev. Harvey Miller	121
TILBURY, Emily, of Kensington, m. Sampson HORTON, of South Glastenbury, Apr. 21, 1849, by Rev. C. Munson	90
TODD, Evelina, m. Nathan T. GOODRICH, Dec. 6, 1826, by Charles J. Hinsdale	29
Polly, m. John W. HALL, Mar. 26, 1812	26
TOMLINSON, John L., m. Rechelsia T. SOUTHWORTH, Mar. 22, 1853, by Rev. Harvey Miller	115
TOOKER, Sarah J., of Meriden, m. Jonathan B. JOHNSON, of Wallingford, Oct. 10, 1852, by Rev. Harvey Miller	113
TOPPING, Ellen, m. Partrick HUGHES, b. of Meriden, Sept. 12, 1853, by Ward Coe, J.P.	120
TOWNER, John F., m. Jane J. SCOVIL, Sept. 22, 1835, by Rev. John R. Crane, of Middletown	51
TRACY, Lucy Cordelia, m. Ira COUCH, b. of Meriden, Sept. 25, 1828, by Rev. James Keeler	34
TREADWAY, James H., of Middletown, m. Mary E. LITTLE, of Meriden, July 2, 1829, by Rev. James Keeler	35
TREAT, Mary, m. Lauren P. TUTTLE, Sept. 4, 1839, by Rev. Harvey Miller	62
TUCKER, Jane R., of New Hartford, m. Reuben J. RICE, of Wallingford, Sept. 17, 1848, by Rev. Albert Nash	97
Joel, of Monson, Mass., m. Bathsheba PUFFER, of Meriden, Apr. 19, 1853, by Rev. A. A. Stevens	115
Mark, of Woodbridge, m. Martha S. ROBERTS, of Litchfield, May 14, 1843, by G. W. Perkins	72
TURNER, James, m. Sarah Maria PERKINS, Apr. 6, 1836, by Arthur Granger	53
Joseph W., of Middletown, m. Aliza Jane PRITCHARD, of Waterbury, Sept. 8, 1845, by Rev. Harvey Miller	83

	Page
TUTTLE, Lauren P., m. Mary TREAT, Sept. 4, 1839, by Rev. Harvey Miller	62
Lucy Ann, of Meriden, m. Henry LANE, of Farmington, Apr. 15, 1849, by Rev. George W. Perkins	98
Mary A., m. John B. BRACKETT, b. of New Haven, Apr. 22, 1850, by Rev. A. A. Stephens	102
TWISS, Abigail, d. [Joseph & Lois], b. Aug. 15, 1788	17
Abigail, d. [Joseph & Lois], d. Jan. 24, 1789	17
Abigail, [d. Joseph & Lois], b. Aug. 21, 1792	17
Abigail, 2nd, d. [Joseph & Lois], d. Aug. 28, 1793	17
Abigail, [d. Joseph & Lois], b. May 10, 1795	17
Abigail, d. Joseph & Lois, d. June 2, 1819, ae 24 y.	18
Austin, [s. Joseph & Lois], b. Apr. 29, 1790	17
Austin, d. May 18, 1826	72
Benjamin, [s. Joseph & Lois], b. Oct. 31, 1798	17
Benjamin, m. Maria COUCH, Apr. 14, 1830, by Rev. William Bentley	37
Byron, s. Hiram & Caroline, b. Oct. 17, 1828	38
Byron, of Southington, m. Ann Eliza ANDREWS, of Southington, Oct. 21, 1849, by Rev. Harvey Miller	99
Hiram, [s. Joseph & Lois], b. Apr. 2, 1805	17
Ira, [s. Joseph & Lois], b. Apr. 17, 1797	17
Joseph, b. Apr. 13, 1761; m. Lois AUSTIN, Oct. 11, 1786	17
Joseph, [s. Joseph & Lois], b. May 17, 1791	17
Joseph, s. [Joseph & Lois], b. Apr. 3, 1799	17
Joseph, d. May 15, 1842	72
Joseph B., [twin with Joshua A., s. Joseph & Lois], b. May 6, 1803	17
Joseph B., m. Rebecca G. HALL, b. of Meriden, Sept. 14, [1831], by Rev. Russell Jennings	42
Joshua A., [twin with Joseph B., s. Joseph & Lois], b. May 6, 1803	17
Joshua A., d. May 29, 1829	72
Lois, [d. Joseph & Lois], b. Mar. 3, 1794	17
Lois, d. Joseph & Lois, d. Dec. 20, 1822	72
Russel, [s. Joseph & Lois], b. Sept. 4, 1807	17
Sarah, [d. Joseph & Lois], b. Jan. 9, 1801	17
Sarah, m. Ransom BALDWIN, b. of Meriden, Nov. 20, 1823, by Samuel Miller	24
Susan M., w. Benjamin, d. July 3, 1831	56
TYLER, Abigail T., m. William A. LINDSLEY, Oct. 5, 1806, by Rev. Mathew Noyes, of Branford	2
Thomas, of Haverhill, Mass., m. Mahitable YALE, of Meriden, Jan. 1, 1828, by Samuel Miller	32
UPSON, Ann V., m. Ambrose V. ALCOTT, b. of Wolcott, Sept. 4, 1845, by Rev. C. Munson	85
Hiram, m. Sylvia D[e]WOLF, Sept. 25, 1828, by Charles J. Hinsdale	34
Jane A., m. William Y. COAN, b. of Meriden, Nov. 8, 1841, by Rev. G. W. Perkins	66
Sarah H. m. Alfred BROOK, b. of Meriden, May 13, 1838, by Arthur Granger	57
Sarah L., of Cheshire, m. Aaron W. IVES, of Meriden, Apr. 5, 1846, by Rev. H. Miller	85
WALDING, Edward, of Wallingford, m. Loisa COOK, of Wallingford, July 30, 1832, by Charles J. Hinsdale	46

	Page
WALKER, Susan Isabella, d. Daniel A. & Ann D., b. Mar. 15, 1834	49
WARNER, Betsey Ann, d. of John P., of Meriden, m. Dorus A. **STILES**, of West Springfield, Mass., July 5, 1847, by Rev. G. W. Perkins	90
Charlotte, of Wethersfield, m. Henry B. **SPERRY**, of Meriden, Jan. 20, 1848, by Rev. John E. Searles	93
Emma J., m. C. Vincent **KELLOGG**, Nov. 21, 1853, by Rev. G. W. Perkins	121
Harriet, of Middletown, m. Oliver **BLAKESL[E]Y**, of Wallingford, Oct. 1, 1840, by Rev. Harvey Miller	63
Joseph, of Middletown, m. Amelia **PLUYMERT**, of Meriden, Feb. 5, 1821, by Samuel Miller	19
Lucy M., of Middletown, m. Elim L. **JOHNSON**, of Meriden, May 22, 1839, by Harvey Miller	60-1
Rufus, m. Harriet **DORMAN**, Mar. 11, 1832, by Charles J. Hinsdale	43
Walter, of Hamden, m. Mary G. **McGUION**, of Middletown, May 14, 1837, by Ransom Johnson	56
Walter, of Hamden, m. Mary G. **McGINN***, of Middletown, May 14, 1837, by Rev. Ransom Johnson *(McGUION)	77
WATROUS, Alanson, of Chester, m. Jane A. **SHERMAN**, of Wallingford, Oct. 29, 1843, by G. W. Perkins	75
Amelia, d. [Elihu & Sarah], b. Nov. 8, 1817	33
Amelia, m. Horace **RICHMOND**, b. of Meriden, July 27, 1842, by Rev. John Parker	69
Elihu, m. Sarah **FULLER**, Sept. 10, 1812	33
Lydia Ann, d. [Elihu & Sarah], b. Dec. 21, 1814	33
Sarah Jane, [d. Elihu & Sarah], b. May 26, 1816	33
William, s. [Elihu & Sarah], b. Apr. 26, 1819	33
WATSON, Sarah, m. Lewis L. **SPERRY**, b. of Meriden, Mar. 2, 1845, by Rev. Samuel W. Smith	80
WAY, Abner, m. Eunice **FOSTER**, Dec. 28, 1780	3
Betsey, d. Samuel & Betsey, b. Mar. 31, 1806	1
Betsey, of Meriden, m. Ezra **BOTSFORD**, of Martinsburgh, N.Y., Sept. 10, 1832, by Charles J. Hinsdale	44
Eli, m. Charlotte **HOUGH**, Dec. 19, 1821, by Erastus Ripley	20
Fidelia Susan, d. [Samuel & Susan], b. Jan. 11, 1839	85
Harriet W., m. James **HALL**, b. of Meriden, Nov. 3, 1846, by Rev. G. W. Perkins	88
Harriet Williams, d. [Samuel & Susan], b. Mar. 5, 1826	85
Henry, of Meriden, m. Anna **HULL**, of Cheshire, Oct. 1, 1840, by Rev. Harvey Miller	63
Hervey Ellsworth, s. [Samuel & Susan], b. Jan. 17, 1828	85
Julius, s. Samuel & Betsey, b. Oct. 11, 1810	12
Justus, s. [Samuel & Susan], b. Oct. 20, 1832	85
Lucius Eldridge, s. Samuel & Susan, b. May 31, 1824	85
Mary Amelia, d. [Samuel & Susan], b. May 23, 1830	85
Mary Rice, d. Samuel & Betsey, b. Sept. 10, 1807	2
Samuel, Jr., m. Susan **BENNET**, b. of Meriden, Sept. 1, 1823, by Elijah Willard	23
Sarah, of Meriden, m. James D. **WEBBER**, of Martinsburg, N.Y., Oct. 11, 1842, by Rev. G. W. Perkins	70
Sherman, s. Samuel & Betsey, b. Mar. 3, 1809	11

BARBOUR COLLECTION

	Page
WEBB, George, m. Eliza Ann **WHITE**, Nov. 7, 1824, by Charles J. Hinsdale	26
John Barrett, b. Jan. 25, 1833	67
Luther E., b. Apr. 22, 1827	67
Luther E., m. Roxanna **BRADLEY**, b. of Meriden, Dec. 2, 1846, by Rev. G. W. Perkins	89
Mary Anna, b. Jan. 14, 1841	67
Nancy, m. William W. **JANES**, June 14, 1836, by Arthur Granger	53
Walter W., of Meriden, m. Frances H. **ADAMS**, of Weathersfield, Mar. 31, 1852, by Rev. G. W. Perkins	110
Walter W[illia]m, b. Nov. 7, 1830	67
WEBBER, Charlotte, m. Walter **BLAKSLEY**, Feb. 17, 1828, by Charles J. Hinsdale	33
James D., of Martinsburg, N.Y., m. Sarah **WAY**, of Meriden, Oct. 11, 1842, by Rev. G. W. Perkins	70
WEIGHT, Mary K., wid, of Meriden, m. Samuel **CHAPMAN**, of Hartford, Dec. 20, 1846, by Rev. John Parker	89
WEIR, Stephen M., of Glastenbury, m. Sarah **TIBBALS**, of Meriden, Nov. 1, 1853, by Rev. Harvey Miller	121
WETMORE, **WHETMORE**, Abner C., m. Abigail **WILCOX**, Feb. 15, 1844, by Rev. Harvey Miller	75
Fra[n]ces I., s. Jacob F. & Lois, b. Dec. 10, 1827; d. Feb. 18, 1828	37
Frances, [s. Jacob F. & Lois], b. Apr. 17, 1829	37
Jacob, of Meriden, m. Lois **MORSE**, of Wallingford, Oct. 7, 1825, by Samuel Miller	27
Jemima, of Middletown, m. Joel H. **GUY**, of Meriden, Nov. 9, 1828, by Charles J. Hinsdale	34
WHETMORE, [see under **WETMORE**]	
WHITE, Eliza Ann, d. Amos & Hannah, b. Nov. 8, 1800	1
Eliza Ann, m. George **WEBB**, Nov. 7, 1824, by Charles J. Hinsdale	26
Elizabeth, m. Eleazer **SCOVIL**, Sept. 11, 1808	10
Flora Ann, m. Russell J. **IVES**, b. of Meriden, Sept. 18, 1853, by Rev. Harvey Miller	120
Frederick A., s. Amos & Hannah, b. May 18, 1802	1
Henry S., m. Susan M. **COUCH**, b. of Meriden, Oct. 17, 1844, by Rev. Robert A. Hallam, of New London	78
Luther C., m. Jane A. **MOSES**, of Middletown, Nov. 28, 1844, by Bishop Harvey Miller	79
Sarah, m. Remic **CLARK**, Dec. 11, 1825, by Charles J. Hinsdale	27
Sarah G., d. Amos & Hannah, b. Feb. 10, 1804	1
Sylvia A., m. Aaron L. **COLLINS**, Mar. 26, 1851, by Rev. G. W. Perkins	106
William W., of Derby, m. Betsey H. **PARKER**, Nov. 12, 1846, by Rev. H. Miller	88
WILCOX, **WILLCOX**, Abigail, m. Abner C. **WETMORE**, Feb. 15, 1844, by Rev. Harvey Miller	75
Alvenzo E., of Middletown, m. Sophronia **BALDWIN**, of Meriden, Oct. 3, 1837, by Leland Howard	56
Ann E., m. Asahel **CURTISS**, Jr., Feb. 29, 1844, by Rev. J. F. Cushing	87
Clarissa, b. June 5, 1809; m. Alanson **BIRDSEY**, Aug. 10, 1829	59
Dennis C., m. Mary E. **PECK**, Dec. 23, 1852, by Rev. George W. Perkins	117

MERIDEN VITAL RECORDS

	Page
WILCOX, WILLCOX (cont.)	
Edwin, m. Harriet **AUSTIN**, Sept. 23, 1827, by Charles J. Hinsdale	32
Henry, m. Elizabeth W. **SCOVIL**, May 9, 1832, by Rev. John R. Crane, of Middletown	46
Julia M., m. Henry A. **MOFFITT**, Jan. 6, 1853, by Rev. Francis Bottom	118
Polly, of Westfield, m. Julius **YALE**, of Meriden, Nov. 8, 1827, by Charles J. Hinsdale	32
Rebecca C., b. Aug. 21, 1805; m. Eli C. **BIRDSEY**, June 3, 1824	59
Sherman, of Berlin, m. Harriet **HALE**, of Meriden, Dec. 2, 1843, by Rev. Alexander Miller	76
WILFORD, Samuel, of Branford, m. Phebe **RUSSELL**, of Meriden, Jan. 6, 1850, by Rev. Albert Nash	101
WILLARD, Albert, s. Elijah & Thankfull, b. Apr. 6, 1819	18
WILLIAMS, Anson M., m. Mary L. **HALL**, b. of Meriden, Sept. 12, 1847, by Rev. John E. Searles	92
Elisabeth, m. Levi **HALL**, June 1, 1800	6
Hannah, of Meriden, m. Henry M. **WINSLOW**, of Waterbury, Feb. 4, 1852, by Rev. Harvey Miller	110
Harriet, of Middletown, m. Thomas T. **BALDWIN**, of Meriden, Aug. 6, 1831, by Rev. Nathan E. Shailer, of Berlin	42
James H., m. Caroline L. **HIGBY**, b. of Meriden, Apr. 21, 1850, by Rev. John Parker	102
Robert, m. Rachel **BALDWIN**, b. of Meriden, July 22, 1827, by Samuel Miller	31
Walter, m. Charlotte **HALL**, Mar. 27, 1823, by Charles J. Hinsdale	24
WILSON, Polly B., m. Benjamin **PERKINS**, July 23, 1807	9
WINSLOW, Henry M., of Waterbury, m. Hannah **WILLIAMS**, of Meriden, Feb. 4, 1852, by Rev. Harvey Miller	110
WOLCOTT, Maria A., of Weathersfield, m. Henry M. **LESTER**, of Meriden, Apr. 5, 1852, by Rev. Harvey Miller	111
WOOD, Charles, of Shelburne Falls, Mass., m. Mary Ann **KENT**, of Middletown, Oct. 16, 1853, by Rev. Harvey Miller	120
Horace, m. Nancy **HULL**, Mar. 16, 1837, by Geo[rge] B. Atwell	55
Mary A., of Meriden, m. James **MARVIN**, of Colebrook, May 9, 1833, by Rev. Stephen Topliff, of Middletown	47
Rebecca D., m. Seth J. **DANIELS**, b. of Southwick, Mass., May 3, 1851, by Tilton C. Doolittle, J.P.	107
WOODRUFF, Harriet, of Southington, m. Griswold P. **MILLER**, Apr. 22, 1851, by Rev. Harvey Miller	105
Jance C., of Meriden, m. T. S. **HUBBARD**, of Upper Middletown, Nov. 14, 1849, by Rev. A. A. Stephens	100
Jane Eliza, d. Wyllys & Mary, b. Jan. 14, 1832	45
Lucy O., of Waitsfield, Vt., m. Henry C. **NORTON**, of Berlin, May 12, 1851, by Rev. Harvey Miller	106
Mary, [d. Wyllys & Mary], b. Mar. 8, 1832?	45
WRIGHT, Charles, of Mass., m. Harriet **PECK**, of Berlin, Conn., Oct. 3, 1830, by Rev. James [Keeler]	40
YALE, Abel, of Meriden, m. Lucy **BOOTH**, of Wallingford, Aug. 29, 1841, by Rev. Harvey Miller	65
Agness, m. Phinehas **HALL**, Nov. 8, 1774	6
Alma, m. Anson R. **SELLEW**, Nov. 16, 1845, by Rev. Hervey Miller	83

YALE (cont.)

	Page
Alma Agusta, [d. Jonathan & Alma], b. June 5, 1826	42
Anna, d. John & Bets[e]y, b. May 9, 1807	9
Asa, m. Mariann **PADDOCK**, b. of Meriden, June 19, 1828, by Samuel Miller	33
Asahel, [s. Asahel], b. Dec. 4, 1788	12
Betsey, of Meriden, m. Luzern **BARTHOLOMEW**, of Wallingford, July 20, 1836, by Arthur Granger	54
Charlotte, m. Samuel **PADDOCK**, Jr., b. of Meriden, Jan. 22, 1823, by Samuel Miller	22
Delia Maria, m. Charles **HORNELL**, b. of Meriden, Dec. 26, 1852, by Rev. Harvey Miller	114
Edward P., m. Sarah A. **HOTCHKISS**, May 2, 1852, by Rev. A. A. Stevens	111
Edwin R. ,m. Eliza **IVES**, b. of Meriden, Mar. 14, 1824, by Samuel Miller	25
Edwin Rodolphus, s. William & Mary, b. Aug. 8, 1804	3
Elizabeth P., of Meriden, m. Barzilla D. **SAGE**, of Middletown, Mar. 20, 1831, by Rev. Russell Jennings	41
Ellen A., of Meriden, m. Alfred N. **GOODRICH**, of Middletown, Nov. 12, 1848, by Rev. Harvey Miller	96
Elvira, [d. Jonathan & Alma], b. Sept. 29, 1830	42
Emeline, m. Merritt **HARTSHORN**, b. of Meriden, Nov. 29, 1838, by Harvey Miller	60
Emily, of Meriden, m. Edwin O. **CARRINGTON**, of Ohio, July 12, 1842, by Rev. G. W. Perkins	70
Hannah, of Meriden, m. George **FOSTER**, of Haddam, June 5, 1824, by Samuel Miller	25
Hannah S., m. Ira N. **YALE**, b. of Meriden, May 2, 1838, by Rev. John Marshall Guion	57
Harriet, m. Joel **MERRIMAN**, b. of Meriden, Apr. 8, 1830, by Charles J. Hinsdale	37
Harriet, m. Henry **JONES**, b. of Meriden, Dec. 19, 1839, by Harvey Miller	58
Horace, of Meriden, m. Caroline M. **ANDREWS**, of Cheshire, May 29, 1853, by Rev. Harvey Miller	116
Ira N., m. Hannah S. **YALE**, b. of Meriden, May 2, 1838, by Rev. John Marshall Guion	57
Isaac, m. Diana **RICE**, Dec. 30, 1807	10
James Hervey, m. Jonathan, 2nd & Almira **HUBBARD**, b. Oct. 1, 1819	23
James Monroe, s. Jonathan & Alma, b. Oct. 1, 1819	42
Jediah Hubbard, [s. Jonathan & Alma], b. Feb. 28, 1824	42
Jennet F., of Meriden, m. James M. **PLUM**, of Berlin, June 8, 1830, by Rev. William Bently	38
Joel, m. Lucy **RICE**, Sept. 27, 1804	8
Joel, d. Dec. 14, 1805	1
Joel Hiram, [s. Asahel], b. Jan. 14, 1808	12
John, m. Betsey **IVES**, Mar. 12, 1803	9
John, m. Nancy M. **HALL**, b. of Meriden, Oct. 30, 1833, by Charles J. Hinsdale	48
Jonathan, 2nd, m. Alma **HUBBARD**, Nov. 28, 1816	18

	Page
YALE (cont.)	
Juliett, m. Asahel H. **CURTIS**, b. of Meriden, Sept. 12, 1841, by Rev. C. W. Everest	65
Julius, of Meriden, m. Polly **WILLCOX**, of Westfield, Nov. 8, 1827, by Charles J. Hinsdale	32
Keturah, [d. Asahel], b. Feb. 9 1803	12
Levi, m. Polly **YALE**, Nov. 24, 1808	10
Lodama, m. Titus **IVES**, Oct. 18, 1808	9
Lucy, d. Joel & Lucy, b. Apr. 7, 1806	8
Mariah, [d. Asahel], b. Mar. 2, 1800	12
Mary, d. John & Betsey, b. Mar. 26, 1804	9
Mary, d. William & Mary, b. Jan. 16, 1808	3
Mary A., m. Alonzo **BENNETT**, b. of Meriden, Nov. 25, 1847, by Rev. John E. Searles	92
Mary Ann, of Meriden, m. Elias **GAYLORD**, Jr., of Cheshire, Apr. 18, 1830, by Charles J. Hinsdale	37
Mary J., of Meriden, m. Francis A. **GALE**, of Lenox, Mass., Oct. 10, 1825, by Samuel Miller	27
Mahitable, of Meriden, m. Thomas **TYLER**, of Haverhill, Mass., Jan. 1, 1828, by Samuel Miller	32
Melissa D., of Meriden, m. Rollin H. **NEAL**, of South Boston, Sept. 26, 1833, by Nathaniel Hervey	48
Noah, [s. Asahel], b. Mar. 4, 1791	12
Polly, m. Levi **YALE**, Nov. 24, 1808	10
Polly, m. Watrous **IVES**, Sept. 15, 1809	17
Rebeckah, [d. Asahel], b. Feb. 13, 1787	12
Sally, [d. Asahel], b. Dec. 8, 1794	12
Samuel, of Wallingford, m. Amelia **LEWIS**, of Meriden, Feb. 11, 1824, by Reuben Ives	24
Sarah A., m. Henry J. **TENANT**, Sept. 22, 1839, by Harvey Miller	61
Saphronia Mary, d. Joel & Lucy, b. Apr. 14, 1812	14
William, m. Mary **JOHNSON**, Nov. 20, 1803 (Yale first written "**JOHNSON**")	3
William Hubbard, s. [Jonathan, 2nd & Alma], b. Nov. 23, 1817	18
William Rodolphus, s. Edwin R. & Eliza, b. Sept. 22, 1828	34
YEOMANS, Eunice, d. John & Gelina, b. Sept. 25, 1816	28
Eunice, d. John & Gelina, d. Feb. 16, 1817	28
Gelina, [w. John], d. Oct. 11, 1820	28
John, Jr., m. Gelina **RICE**, Feb. 9, 1815	28
John, Jr., m. Mirca **MORSE**, Jan. 20, 1822	28
Laura, d. John & Gelina, b. Sept .16, 1819	28
Lucy, m. Samuel **MARTIN**, Jr., Sept. 26, 1822, by Samuel Miller	21
Solomon, of Meriden, m. Caroline **SIBLEY**, of Westfield, Mass., Aug. 26, 1830, by Rev. Jesse Baker	38-9
NO SURNAME	
Elizabeth, m. Asahel **MERRIAM**, Jan. 11, 1802	21
Francis, of Quebec, Canada, m. Celia **GONEAU**, Sept. 4, 1852, by Rev. Harvey Miller	112
John, of Newton, L.I., m. Sophia **SMITH**, of Westfield, Aug. 12, 1840, by Rev. S. S. Stocking	62
William S., m. Mary J. **BALDWIN**, b. of Meriden, Feb. 3, 1831, by Rev. Russell Jennings	41
-----, d. [ ], b. Dec. 23, [1813], d. Dec. 27, 1813	25

MIDDLEBURY VITAL RECORDS
1807 – 1850

	Page
ABBOTT, Anna, m. Aaron **TUTTLE**, Jr., Nov. 21, 1822, by Frederick Holcomb	111
Anna, of Northfield, m. John **HOTCHKISS**, of Middlebury, Oct. 12, 1834, by Rev. Jason Atwater	123
Emma, m. Henry **TOWNSEND**, b. of Middlebury, Nov. 21, 1827, by Rev. Alpheas Geer, in Waterbury	115
Justina, m. William **ELLIS**, b. of Middlebury, Mar. 30, 1835*, by Rev. J. Atwater *(Probably 1845)	133
Lydia Ann, of Middlebury, m. Edwin S. **DUNBAR**, of Camden, N.Y., Nov. 30, 1837, by Rev. Oliver Hopson	126
Philo, m. Elizabeth Ann **WOOSTER**, Nov. 5, 1822, by Frederick Holcomb	110
Philomela, m. George F. **SMITH**, Nov. 23, 1825, by Frederick Holcomb	113
Ruth, m. Anson **PLATT**, b. of Middlebury, Apr. 5, 1831, by Jason Atwater	120
Sarah, m. Hawkins W. **MONSON**, b. of Middlebury, Apr. 10, 1839, by Rev. E Washburn	128
ADAMS, Alvira, m. James **TUTTLE**, b. of Middlebury, Oct. 6, 1848, by F. W. Sizer	147
Alvira, m. James **TUTTLE**, b. of Middlebury, Oct. 6, 1848, by Rev. F. W. Sizer	66
ALDEN, Henry P., of Windsor, N.Y., m. Sophronia M. **McKEE**, of Middlebury, Dec. 29, [1852], by Rev. W[illia]m H. Bangs	33
Henry P., of Windsor, N.Y., m. Sophronia **McKEE**, of Middlebury, Dec. 29, 1852, by Rev. W[illia]m H. Bangs	67
ALLEN, Ezra, m. Abigail A. **WILMOT**, Oct. 12, 1834, by Daniel Wooster	123
Sarah, of Waterbury, m. Sylvester R. **BACON**, of Middlebury, Sept. 18, 1836, by Rev. J. Atwater	125
W[illia]m, of Woodbridge, res. Naugatuck, m. Maria **STODDARD**, of Naugatuck, Aug. 29, 1841, by Rev. Jason Atwater	130
ATWOOD, Chloe S., of Woodbury, m. Nelson J. **HAYES**, of Middlebury, June 3, 1846, by Rev. Ebenezer C. Beers	135
Erasmus H., of Waterbury, m. Thirza **SAXTON**, May 20, 1832, by Rev. J. Atwater	121
Joel H., [s.] of Henry S., b. June 16, 1851	63
Jos[eph] Wheeler, [s.] Henry S., b. Sept. 8, 1849	62
Sally, m. Harvie **NORTHROP**, Mar. 12, 1823, by Fred Holcomb	111
-----, [ch.] of Henry S., farmer, ae 29, b. Watertown & Maria, ae 25, b. Southbury, b. Feb. 27, 1853	64
AYRES, Adna, of Starkey, N.Y., m. Martha M. **THOMPSON**, d. Eli, of Middlebury, Oct. 26, 1842, by Rev. J. Atwater	130
BACON, Sylvester R., of Middlebury, m. Sarah **ALLEN**, of Waterbury, Sept. 18, 1836, by Rev. J. Atwater	125
Timothy C., of Woodbury, m. Catharine S. **CAMP**, of Middlebury, Nov. 5, 1845, by Rev. J. Atwater	134

… 178 BARBOUR COLLECTION

	Page
BALDWIN, Alfred, b. Aug. 22, 1809	2
Amos, of Middlebury, m. Eliza HAWKINS, of Derby, Feb. 19, 1823, by Rev. Mark Mead	111
Harvey, Farmer, d .Oct. 15, 1848; ae 14	58-9
Ira F., of Middlebury, m. Susan F. MERRILL, of Naugatuck, [ ], [1853?], by Rev. J. R. Arnold	215
Isaac M.., of Middlebury, m. Ann HAWKINS, of Derby, Jan. 18, 1835, by Rev. J. Atwater	124
Lewis W., m. Martha M. BRONSON, June 6, 1844, by Rev. J. Atwater	132
Lucy M., d. Lewis W., b Aug. 18, 1848	62
Maria, of Middlebury, m. Samuel BALDWIN, of Milford, Feb. 27, 1822, by Rev. Mark Mead	76
Melinda, m. Jonas BRONSON, Aug. 10, 1806	27
Merritt C., m. Nancy A. STONE, b. of Middlebury, Apr. 22, 1846, by Rev. J. Atwater	134
Nancy A., of Middlebury, m. Jonathan STILES, of Southbury, Nov. 13, 1831, by James D. Wooster, J.P.	120
Riley, of Derby, m. Olive BENHAM, of Middlebury, May 5, 1825, by Rev. Mark Mead	112
Samuel, of Milford, m. Maria BALDWIN, of Middlebury, Feb. 27, 1822, by Rev. Mark Mead	76
BARLOW, Mary Jane, of Middlebury, m. Henry CLARK, of Burlington, Jan. 7, 1849, by Geo[rge] P. Prudden	137
BARNES, Myra W., of Canaan, m. Esther RIGGS, d. Samuel, May 27, 1832, by Rev. J. Atwater	121
BARTHOLOMEW, Sally, Mrs., of Tallmadge, O., m. Titus S. BRONSON, of Anarborer*, Mich., Jan. 18, 1827, by Rev. Mark Mead *(Ann Arbor)	114
Sereno, of Wallingford, m. Sarah A. BENHAM, of Middlebury, Sept. 30, 1847, by Rev. Geo[rge] P. Prudden	56
Sereno, of Wallingford, m. Sarah A. BENHAM, of Middlebury, Sept. 30, 1847, by Geo[rge] P. Prudden	136
BARTIS, Elizabeth, b. in New Hampshire, wid., d. May 3, 1848; ae 87	57
BEAVENS, [see under BEVENS]	
BEERS, Henry P., [s.] Sidney, b. May 21, 1849	62
BENEDICT, Esther, m. Jacob LINSLEY, b. of Middlebury, Oct. 20, 1829, by Rev. Mark Mead	117
BENHAM, Amos, d. Apr. 11, 1850; ae 79	58-9
George S., m. Olive FENN, Nov. 3, 1825, by Rev. Mark Mead	113
John, m. Lydia A. TREAT, b. of Middlebury, June 30, 1841, by Rev. J. Atwater	130
Julius H., of Woodbridge, m. Mary S. THOMPSON, of Middlebury, Apr. 24, 1845, by Rev. J. Atwater	134
Maria L., of Middlebury, m. Joel CURTISS, of Plymouth, June 13, 1852, by Rev. Joel R. Arnold	149
Olive, of Middlebury, m. Riley BALDWIN, of Derby, May 5, 1825, by Rev. Mark Mead	112
Olive, d. Oct. 20, 1851; ae 53	60-1
Polly T., of Middlebury, m. Nichols WAKELEY, of Huntington, Nov. 24, 1831, by Rev. J. Atwater	120
Sarah A., of Middlebury, m. Sereno BARTHOLOMEW, of Wallingford, Sept. 30, 1847, by Rev. Geo[rge] P. Prudden	56

MIDDLEBURY VITAL RECORDS 179

	Page
BENHAM (cont.)	
Sarah A., of Middlebury, m. Sereno **BARTHOLOMEW**, of Wallingford, Sept. 30, 1847, by Geo[rge] P. Prudden	136
-----, [ch.] Lockwood P., b. Nov. 27, 1850	63
BENNET, Truman, of Oxford, m. Mrs. Anna **HOTCHKISS**, Feb. 12, 1838, by Rev. J. Atwater	127
BERRY, Lucy, m. Moses **RIGGS**, b. of Derby, Aug. 1, 1821, by Rev. Mark Mead	75
BEVENS, BEAVENS, Ann M., [d.] David C., carriage maker, b. Aug. 23, 1847	55
Charles, [s.], David C., b. Nov. 29, 1849	62
Julia Ann, of Middlebury, m. Cyrus **BOTCHFORD**, of Derby, Dec. 28, 1847, by F. W. Sizer	147
BLACKMAN, Hannah, wid., d. June 7, 1850, ae 85	58-9
Mary E., [d.] Isaac, farmer, of Woodbury, b. Sept. 17, 1847	55
-----, [ch.] of John E., farmer, ae 28, Middlebury & Hannah S., ae 28, Woodbury, b. Oct. 3, 1852	64
BLAKELEY, Merinda, of Middlebury, m. David **KETCHUM**, of Welton, Saratoga County, N.Y., May 4, 1829, by Daniel Wooster	117
BOOTH, Clarissa, m. Simeon L. **BRISTOL**, of Milford, Sept. 11, 1839, by Rev. J. Atwater	128
Cornelia, m. W[illia]m R. **TUCKER**, b. of Middlebury, Dec. 16, 1840, by Rev. Jason Atwater	129
Emmeline, m. George **LUM**, of Oxford, Oct. 18, 1830, by Rev. Jason Atwater	119
Henry, [s.] Silas L., b. May 3, 1850	62
Maria, m. Horatio N. **SMITH**, b. of Middlebury, Oct. 9, 1837, by Rev. Oliver Hopson	126
-----, [ch.] of Silas L., b. Mar. 22, 1852	63
BOTCHFORD, Cyrus, of Derby, m. Julia Ann **BEVENS**, of Middlebury, Dec. 28, 1847, by F. W. Sizer	147
BOUGHTON, Charles, of Waterbury, m. Melinda **PORTER**, [Mar.] 24, [1830], by Rev. Mark Mead	118
BOWEN, Michael, Jr., m. Almira **STONE**, b. of Middlebury, Mar. 14, 1821, by Rev. Mark Mead	75
BOWERS, Michael, m. Electa **MANUIL**, b. of Middlebury, May 7, 1827, by Rev. Mark Mead	115
Nancy, of Middlebury, m. Adam **LUM**, of Southbury, last evening, [Apr. 27, 1828], by Rev. Mark Mead	115
BOWLER, Mary Jane, m. Henry **CLARK**, of Burlington, Jan. 7, 1849, by Rev. G. P. Prudden	66
BRACE, Clarissa, of Middlebury, m. Walter H. **DAVIS**, of New Boston, Mass., Oct. 24, 1835, by Rev. J. Atwater	125
Luce, of Middlebury, m. Amasa **ROBERTS**, of Waterbury, Nov. 9, 1822, by Rev. Samuel Potter, of Woodbridge & Salem	110
BRADLEY, Anna, of Middlebury, m. Emaluel **MOSS**, of Cheshire, Nov. 18, 1830, by Rev. Rodney Bossetee, of Monroe	119
Anna, of Middlebury, m. Emaluel **MOSS**, of Cheshire, Nov. 18, 1830, by Rev. Rodney Rossiter, of Monroe	120
Elizabeth J., m. David **WOOSTER**, Nov. 9, 1826, by Rev. Mark Mead	114
Ellenor, [d.], W[illia]m, b. [ ]	62

BRADLEY (cont.)
	Page
James Henry, [s.] of Noyes, dec. & Sarah B., b Feb. 3, 1851	63
John, m. Martha **TREAT**, b. of Middlebury, Apr. 8, 1830, by Rev. Mark Mead	118
Martha, of Middlebury, m. Thomas **SOLLY**, of Southbury, Feb. 8, 1835, by H. Humphries	124
Nancy, m. Thomas A. **WOOSTER**, b. of Middlebury, Sept. 27, 1840, by George L. Fuller	129
Noyes, of Middlebury, m. Sarah **TWITCHELL**, of Middlebury, Sept. 22, 1850, by Rev. Joseph Scott	66
Noyes, m. Sarah **TWITCHELL**, b. of Middlebury, Sept. 22, 1850, by Rev. Joseph Scott, of Naugatuck	138
Noyes, farmer, b. in Oxford, d. Oct. 1, 1850, ae 56	58-9
Sarah, wid., d. Mar. 13, 1849; ae 78	58-9
Walter D., [s.] J. Nelson, b. July 15, 1849	62
Wealthy, m. Jason **STODDARD**, b. of Middlebury, May 26, 1822, by Rev. Mark Mead	76
-----, [ch.] William, b. Dec. 9, 1850	63
-----, [ch.], of Noble, b. Sept. 28, 1851	63
-----, s. Noble, d. Oct. 5, 1851; ae 6 d.	60-1
-----, [ch.], of William, farmer, ae 31, b. Middlebury & Elizabeth S., ae 34, b. in Waterbury, b. Dec. 30, 1852	64
BRIGGS, Mary, b. in Ireland, d. Oct. 23, 1850; ae 36	58-9
BRISTOL, George E., m. Martha **PORTER**, Apr. 5, 1835, by Rev. Joel R. Arnold, of Waterbury	124
Henry, s. Sheldon, of Oxford, m. Maria **MANVILL**, d. Horace, of Middlebury, Sept. 22, 1841, by Rev. J. Atwater	130
Maria E., Mrs. of Middlebury, m. Jason **CURTIS**, of Southbury, Mar. 29, 1851, by Rev. Stephen Topliff	66
Maria E., of Middlebury, m. Jason **CURTISS**, of Southbury, [Mar.] 19, [1851], by Rev. Stephen Topliff	147
Simeon L., of Milford, m. Clarissa **BOOTH**, Sept. 11, 1839, by Rev. J. Atwater	128
BROADWILL, Luther, of Derby, m. Jane **TWITCHELL**, of Oxford, Jan. 22, 1831, by Daniel Wooster	119
BROCKET, Mary, b. Feb. 22, 1734	2
Mary, m. Isaac **BRONSON**, Feb. 13, 1755	27
BRONSON, [see also **BUNSON**], Alfred, m. Esther **CURTISS**, Nov. 14, 1832, by Rev. J. Atwater	122
Almy, m. Lyman **CAMP**, b. of Middlebury, Jan. 24, 1821, by Rev. Mark Mead	75
Anna, w. Julius, b. in Waterbury, d. Mar. 13, 1848; ae 39	57
Asahel, farmer, b. in Waterbury, d. Apr. 23, 1850; ae 90	58-9
Caroline, d. Horace, of Middlebury, m. Albert **MANVEL**, of Woodbury, Sept. 2, 1844, by Rev. J. Atwater	133
Catharine, b. Apr. 28, 1823	2
Catharine, [d.] Aug. 23, 1825	54
Catharine J., of Middlebury, m. Judson B. **GALPIN**, of New Haven, May 16, 1841, by Rev. J. Atwater	129
Chauncey, b. Nov. 30, 1767	2
Chauncey, s. [Isaac & Mary], d. May 16, 1768	54
Chester B., [s.] of Lester, b. June 7, 1851	63
Cleora, b. July 31, 1809	2

	Page
BRONSON (cont.)	
Edward, b. Jan. 18, 1828	2
Edward L., of Waterbury, m. Cornelia S. **TOWNSEND**, of Middlebury, Oct. 22, 1851, by George F. Bronson	143
Eliza, d. Horace, m. Albert **MANVILL**, of Elizabeth Port, N.Y., June 27, 1838, by Rev. J. Atwater	127
Emma, of Middlebury, m. W[illia]m A. **CHAMBERLAIN**, of Woodstock, Nov. 17, 1847, by Rev. Geo[rge] P. Prudden	56
Emma, of Middlebury, m. W[illia]m A. **CHAMBERLAIN**, of Woodstock, Nov. 17, 1847, by Geo[rge] P .Prudden	136
Esther, of Middlebury, m. John **HINE**, of Waterbury, Oct. 10, 1822, by Rev. Mark Mead	76
Esther, (Asahel), b. in Waterbury; d. Dec. 26, 1848; ae 87	57
Ethel, b. July 22, 1765	2
Eunice, b. Dec. 4, 1755	2
Eunice, d. Isaac & Mary, d. June 30, 1776	54
Frances Eliza, [d.] Lester, b. Aug. 5, 1849	62
George Cook, b. Sept. 17, 1807	2
George Franklin, b. Jan. 21, 1821	2
Hannah, b. May 1, 1769	2
Hannah, b. Nov. 10, 1774	2
Hannah, m. Ezekiel **STONE**, Oct. 26, 1794	43
Hannah, single, d. Mar. 22, 1851; ae 60	58-9
Harriet L., d. Alfred, of Middlebury, m. George W. **PORTER**, of Watertown, Nov. 1, 1838, by Rev. J. Atwater	127
Isaac, s. Isaac, b. Oct. 4, 1736	2
Isaac, m. Mary **BROOKET**, Feb .13, 1755	27
Isaac, b. Mar. 10, 1760	2
Isaac, m. Rebecca **THOMPSON**, Nov. 4, 1810	27
Isaac, b. May 22, 1826	2
Jane, of Middlebury, m. John H. **WOODRUFF**, of Watertown, Nov. 2, 1841, by Rev. N. S. Richardson	130
Jared, m. Lydia **MALLORY**, Dec. 29, 1813	27
Jared, m. Anna **MALLORY**, Oct. 13, 1830, by Rev. Jason Atwater	119
Jonas, m. Melinda **BALDWIN**, Aug. 10, 1806	27
Julia, m. Larmon G. **TOWNSEND**, b. of Middlebury, Nov. 12, [1827], by Rev. Mark Mead	115
Julia Maria, b. Jan. 12, 1820	2
Julius, m. H. Augusta **RADFORD**, b. of Middlebury, Jan. 3, 1849, by Rev. G. P. Prudden	66
Julius, m. Helen Augusta **RADFORD**, b. of Middlebury, Jan. 3, 1849, by Geo[rge] P. Prudden	137
Laban, b. Feb. 15, 1762	2
Laban, s. [Isaac & Mary], d. Nov. 28, 1801	54
Leonard, b. June 24, 1797	2
Leonard, m. Nancy **PLATT**, Apr. 14, 1819	27
Lester, b. Jan. 24, 1815	2
Louisa, of Middlebury, m. David **WARREN**, of Watertown, Mar. 24, 1847, by Rev. Geo[rge] P. Prudden	136
Marcia, m. Lucius A. **THOMPSON**, Nov. 1, 1843, by Rev. J. Atwater	132
Martha M., m. Lewis W. **BALDWIN**, June 6, 1844, by Rev. J. Atwater	132

182 BARBOUR COLLECTION

	Page
BRONSON (cont.)	
Mary, b. Sept. 15, 1757	2
Mary, w. Isaac, d. Aug. [ ], 1810	54
Mary, m. Merret **PLATT**, b. of Middlebury, Nov. 25, 1838, by Rev. Abraham Browne, at Elizabeth Port, N.J.	127
Mary Jane, eldest d. Garry, of Middlebury, m. Reuben **HUNGERFORD**, of Watertown, Apr. 15, 1840, by Rev. J. Atwater	128
Sarah, b. Mar. 21, 1775	2
Sarah, d. [Isaac & Mary], d. Oct. 10, 1777	54
Sarah, m. Franklin **HINE**, Nov. 17, 1846, by Rev. George P. Prudden	135
Sylvester, m. Emily Eunice **HAMLIN**, Oct. 17, 1836, by Rev. J. Atwater	126
Titus, b. Oct. [ ], 1751	2
Titus [d.] May 26, 1820	54
Titus, b. in Middlebury, res. Ill., d. Jan. 6, 1853; ae 64	60-1
Titus S., of Anarborer*, Mich., m. Mrs. Sally **BARTHOLOMEW**, of Tallmadge, O., Jan. 18, 1827, by Rev. Mark Mead *(Ann Arbor)	114
Virtue, b. Mar. 23, 1778	2
BROWN, W[illia]m, of Waterbury, m. Rachel V. **FENN**, of Middlebury, Mar. 25, 1844, by Rev. J. Atwater	132
BRUSH, Jane, m. David T. **MEIGS**, b. of Oxford, [, 1848 (?)], by Rev. G. P. Prudden	66
Jane, of Middlebury, m. David F. **MEIGS**, of Oxford, Dec. 31, 1848, by Geo[rge] P. Prudden	137
BRYANT, Delia, m. William **McGUIRE**, of Oxford, July 18, 1830, by Rev. Jason Atwater	119
BUCKINGHAM, Belinda C., of Middlebury, m. Andrew T. **HOTCHKISS**, of Bethany, Nov 29, 1849, by W[illia]m H. Bangs	139
Caroline, of Middlebury, m. Rollo S. **MARSH**, b. in New Milford, res. Waterbury, Jan. 24, 1848, by Rev. F W. Sezer	56
Cornelia A., of Middlebury, m. Rollo S. **MARSH**, of New Milford, Jan. 24, 1848, by F. W. Sizer	147
Harriet L., m. Frederick **POPE**, b. of Middlebury, Oct. 13, 1850, by Geo[rge] P. Prudden	138
Harriet S., of Middlebury, m. Frederick **POPE**, of Oxford, Oct. 13, 1850, by Rev. G. P. Prudden	66
Sarah, tailoress, ae 43, b. Vermont, res. Middlebury, m. 2nd h. Stephen **KEELER**, shoemaker, ae 42, b. Redding, res. Bridgeport, Nov. 25, 1852, by Rev. J. R. Arnold	67
Sarah, Mrs. of Middlebury, m. Stephen **KEELER**, of Bridgeport, Nov. 25, 1852, by Rev. J. R. Arnold	149
BUNSON, [see also **BRONSON**], Robert, of Prospect, m. Mary **HINE**, of Middlebury, Apr. 7, 1830, by Rev. Mark Mead	118
CAIN, CANE, Emily G., m. Lucius **GUNN**, b. of Middlebury, Sept. 29, 1828, by Rev. Mark Mead	116
Lewis O., of Bethany, m. Matilda H. **WOOSTER**, of Naugatuck, Jan. 15, 1852, by Rev. William Gay	148
-----, [s.] Charles, laborer, ae 22, b. Bethlem, colored, & Betsey Ann, ae 20, b. Washington, s.b. Jan. 19, 1853	64

MIDDLEBURY VITAL RECORDS 183

	Page
CAMP, Calvin, m. Salome **STONE**, b. of Middlebury, Nov. 5, 1823, by Rev. Mark Mead	111
Catharine S., of Middlebury, m. Timothy C. **BACON**, of Woodbury, Nov. 5, 1845, by Rev. J. Atwater	134
Clarissa, m. Timothy Dwight **NORTHROP**, Apr. 11, 1833, by Rev. J. Atwater	122
Lyman, m. Almy **BRONSON**, b. of Middlebury, Jan. 24, 1821, by Rev. Mark Mead	75
Mehitable, m. David **STONE**, b. of Middlebury, Apr. 27, 1824, by Rev. Mark Mead	112
Symon, d. July 18, 1848; ae 50	57
CANE, [see under **CAIN**]	
CARDON, -----, [ch.] of Michael L., b. Nov. 24, 1851	63
CARGILL, Edward, [s.] W[illia]m B., b. Aug. 12, 1849	62
Mary Foster, [d.] Foster M., b. Feb. 8, 1849	62
CASTLE, Angelina, of Waterbury, m. Rev. Daniel **SMITH**, of Derby, Dec. 9, 1832, by Rev. Heman Bangs	122
CHAMBERLAIN, W[illia]m A., of Woodstock, m. Emma **BRONSON**, of Middlebury, Nov. 17, 1847, by Rev. Geo[rge] P. Prudden	56
W[illia]m A., of Woodstock, m. Emma **BRONSON**, of Middlebury, Nov. 17, 1847, by Geo[rge] P. Prudden	136
CLARKE, CLARK, Almon, of Milford, m. Susan **CLARK**, of Middlebury, Nov. 8, 1821, by Rev. Mark Mead	76
Amelia Esther, m. Heman **GAYLORD**, b. of Middlebury, Nov. 29, 1847, by F. W. Sizer	147
Amy, d. Nov. 25, 1851; ae 55	60-1
Arteson S., [s.] Gould S., b. Oct. 5, 1849	62
Charlotte, b. in Milford, d. Nov. 18, 1851; ae 35	60-1
Daniel, d. Aug. 29, 1847; ae 88	57
Dwight, m. Julia M. **RICHARDSON**, b. of Middlebury, Nov. 15, 1848, by Geo[rge] P. Prudden	137
Dwight, m. Julia M. **RICHARDSON**, b. of Middlebury, Nov. 16, 1848, by Rev. G. P. Prudden	66
Edward, of Waterbury, m. Maria P. **STONE**, Dec. 6, 1837, by Rev. J. Atwater	127
Esther A., m. Heman **GAYLORD**, b. of Middlebury, Nov. 29, 1847, by Rev. F. W. Sezer	56
Henry, of Burlington, m. Mary Jane **BOWLER**, Jan. 7, 1849, by Rev. G. P. Prudden	66
Henry, of Burlington, m. Mary Jane **BARLOW**, of Middlebury, Jan. 7, 1849, by Geo[rge] P. Prudden	137
James, of Waterbury, m. Sarah M. **SILLIMAN**, of Monroe, Jan. 14, 1841, by J. Atwater	129
Joseph D., [s.] of Dwight, b. May 11, 1851	63
Julia A., m. Charles A. **TOMLINSON**, of Oxford, Dec. 26, 1839, by Rev. J. Atwater	128
Martha A., d Daniel, 2nd, m. Hawley **LANDERS**, of Southbury, Oct. 15, 1840, by Rev. J. Atwater	129
Mary, m. Caleb **NETTLETON**, b. of Middlebury, Mar. 2, 1845, by Rev. J. Atwater	133
Susan, of Middlebury, m. Almon **CLARK**, of Milford, Nov. 8, 1821, by Rev. Mark Mead	76

                                                                    Page
CLARK, CLARKE (cont.)
Therolow J., m. Clarissa **STODDARD**, b. of Middlebury, May 6,
   1824, by Rev. Mark Mead   112
William, of Derby, m. Emma **UNDERWOOD**, of New York, Nov.
   3, 1850, by Rev. Ira Abbott   66
William, of Bermingham, m. Emma **UNDERWOOD**, of New York,
   Nov. 3, 1850, by Rev. Ira Abbott   139
-----, s. Dwight, d. Mar. 2, 1852; ae 10 m.   60-1
COOK, Harriet, of Humphrysville, m. W[illia]m **ROBERTS**, of
   Middlebury, Sept. 8, 1844, by Rev. J. Atwater   133
COOPER, -----, [ch.] of Timothy, b. [   ]   63
COTTINGHAM, Jane. H., b. in New Haven, d. Sept. 16, 1848, in New
   Haven; ae 20 m.   58-9
CRANE, Robert F., [s.] Dr. Robert, b. May 8, 1850   62
-----, [d.] Robert, b. May 7, 1849   62
-----, infant, d. Dr. R.[   ], d. May 13, 1849; ae 6 d. 58-9
CULVER, John W., [s.] W[illia]m, stone mason, b. Dec. 25, 1847   55
CURTISS, CURTIS, Anna, m. David **PORTER**, Jr., b. of Middlebury,
   Mar. 25, 1823 ,by Rev. Mark Mead   111
Benjamin, of Southbury, m. Lucy **MONSON**, of Middlebury, Sept.
   30, 1839, by Rev. E. Washburn   128
Chester, m. Rebecca **THOMPSON**, b. of Middlebury, Sept. 10,
   1843, by Rev. J. Atwater   132
Esther, m. Alfred **BRONSON**, Nov. 14, 1832, by Rev. J. Atwater   122
Ira, m. Lois **HAYDEN**, b. of Waterbury, Nov. 9, 1822, by Cyrus
   Silliman, Elder   110
Jason, of Southbury, m. Lydia **PECK**, Dec. 21, 1836, by Rev. J.
   Atwater   126
Jason, of Southbury, m. Mrs. Maria E. **BRISTOL**, of Middlebury,
   [Mar.] 19, [1851], by Rev. Stephen Topliff   147
Jason, of Southbury, m. Mrs. Maria E. **BRISTOL**, of Middlebury,
   Mar. 29, 1851, by Rev. Stephen Topliff   66
Joel, of Plymouth, m. Maria L. **BENHAM**, of Middlebury, June 13,
   1852, by Rev. Joel R. Arnold   149
Levey*, of Middlebury, m. David **GOODWIN**, of Litchfield,
   [   ], [1828], by Rev. Mark Mead. Recorded June 19,
   1828 *(Lucy?)   115
Mary A., m. Charles E. **RICHARDSON**, of New Haven, May 26,
   1844, by Rev. J. Atwater   132
Phebe, m. Benjamin **FENN**, b. of Middlebury, Feb. 1, 1835, by
   Daniel Wooster   124
Sherman, farmer, b. in Southbury, d. Oct. 4, 1848; ae 68   58-9
William, of Southbury, m. Hannah **PECK**, of Middlebury, Apr. 25,
   1822, by Rev. Mark Mead   76
DASCOM, Mary E., m. Calvin **SMITH**, b. of Woodbury, Mar. 3 ,1847,
   by Geo[rge] P. Prudden   135
DAVIS, Alexander G., of Waterbury, m. Elisa M. **TUTTLE**, of
   Middlebury, May 5, 1835, by Rev. J. Atwater   125
Benjamin, of Rutland, N.Y., m. Melissa **JOHNSON**, of Middlebury,
   [Jan.] 6, [1822], by James D. Wooster, J.P.   75
Walter H., of New Boston, Mass., m. Clarissa **BRACE**, of
   Middlebury, Oct. 24, 1835, by Rev J. Atwater   125

MIDDLEBURY VITAL RECORDS 185

	Page
DAYTON, Truman, of Watertown, m. Harriet TYLER, of Middlebury, Dec. 11, 1822, by Horace Hooker	110
DOWNER, John C., of Bozrah, m. Julia A. C. LINSLEY, of Middlebury, Feb. 12, 1845, by Rev. J. Atwater	131
DRAKE, W[illia]m M., of Waterbury, m. Harriet P. NORTHROP, of Watertown, Oct. 2, 1847, by F. W. Sizer	147
DRIVER, Mary, of Torrington, m. Samuel PORTER, Oct. 18, 1836, by Rev. J. Atwater	126
DUNBAR, Edwin S., of Camden, N.Y., m. Lydia Ann ABBOTT, of Middlebury, Nov. 30, 1837, by Rev. Oliver Hopson	126
ELLIOTT, Asa, b. in Stonington, single, d. June 13, or 14, 1851; ae 91	58-9
ELLIS, Adelaide, [d.] W[illia]m, b. Oct. 2, 1848	62
Adella Euginea, [d.] of Geo[rge] C., b. May [ ], 1851	63
Ellenor Francis, [d.] W[illia]m, b. June 30, 1850	62
Eugenia D., [ch. of] Geo[rge] C., b. Oct. 10, 1848	62
Eugenia D., d. G. C., d. Sept. 6, 1850; ae 23 m.	58-9
Frances, d. W[illia]m, d. Oct. 5, 1850; ae 4	58-9
Geo[rge]*, b. in Mass., d. Mar. 1, 1850; ae 72 *(Perhaps "Mrs. George")	58-9
Imogene, [d. G. C.], d. Oct. 1, 1850; ae 7 y.	58-9
William, m. Justina ABBOTT, b. of Middlebury, Mar. 30, 1835*, by Rev. J. Atwater *(Probably 1845)	133
-----, Mrs., d. May 15, 1852; ae 83	60-1
EVANS, Cha[rle]s, of New Milford, m. Elizabeth H. RADFORD, of Middlebury, Jan. 15, 1850, by Rev. W[illia]m H. Bangs	66
Cha[rle]s, of New Milford, m. Elizabeth RADFORD, of Middlebury, Jan. 15, 1850, by W[illia]m H. Bangs	139
FAIRCLOUGH, John, of Waterbury, m. Levinia OSBORN, of Middlebury, Feb. 17, 1844, by Rev. Geo[rge] Waterbury	132
FELLOWS, Eleazer, of New York State, m. Phebe ROBERTS, Aug. 28, 1831, by Leonard Bronson, J.P.	120
FENN, Amelia, of Middlebury, m. Alanson H. HICKCOX, of Watertown, Dec. 4, 1828, by Rev. Mark Mead	116
Benjamin, m. Phebe CURTISS, b. of Middlebury, Feb. 1, 1835, by Daniel Wooster	124
Benjamin, b. in Milford, d. Dec. 11, 1851; ae 97	60-1
Bennet, m. Sarah MANVIL, Apr. 28, 1833, by Rev. J. Atwater	122
Currence, b. in Woodbury, w. Sam[ue]l, d. Apr. 18, 1848; ae 77	57
David M., m. Tabitha TUTTLE, Nov. 26, 1832, by Rev. J. Atwater	121
Lafayette A., [s.] Leonard, b. Jan. 17, 1849	62
Olive, m. George S. BENHAM, Nov. 3, 1825, by Rev. Mark Mead	113
Rachel V., of Middlebury, m. W[illia]m BROWN, of Waterbury, Mar. 25, 1844, by Rev. J. Atwater	132
Sam[ue]l, of Waterbury, m. Caroline M. SMITH, of Bristol, June 9, 1850, by Rev. G. P. Prudden	66
Samuel, of Middlebury, m. Caroline M. SMITH, of Bristol, June 9, 1850, by Geo[rge] P. Prudden	138
Samuel, b. in Watertown, d. Mar. 14, 1852; ae 85	60-1
Sherman, of Middlebury, m. Eliza A. MORRIS, of Waterbury, Oct. 4, 1843, by Rev. J. Atwater	132
Susan, m. Henry W. SCOTT, of Southbury, Oct. 10, 1837, by Rev. J. Atwater	127

186 BARBOUR COLLECTION

	Page
FITCH, Orville L., of Canaan, m. Sophronia HURLBURT, of Middlebury, Nov. 27, 1842, by Rev. J. Atwater	131
FOOT, William D., of Middlebury, m. Sally HAWKINS, of Derby, Mar. 5, 1827, by Eli Barnett, Elder	114
FOX, Alma, m Charles E. MANSFIELD, b. of Woodbury, Mar. 27, 1839, by Rev. J. Atwater	127
Emily, of Middlebury, m. Charles PATTERSON, of Naugatuck, Aug. 3, 1851, by Rev. Ja[me]s R. Mushon	66
Henry, [s.] Marcus, b. Feb. 3, 1849	62
Mary A., b. in Woodbury, res. Middlebury, m. Albert E. STILES, b. in Oxford, res. Middlebury, July 3, 1848, by Rev. John Churchill	56
William, of Woodbury, m. Roxy PAINTER, of Watertown, Sept. 13, 1835, by Rev. J. Atwater	125
FRENCH, David, of Trumbull, m. Hannah M. STONE, May 23, 1844, by Rev. J. Atwater	132
FULLER, Elizab eth W., [d.] Nelson, farmer, b. Apr. 15, 1848	55
Ellen, of Middlebury, m. Edwin W. HORTON, of Naugatuck, Apr. 4, 1852, by Rev. Joel R. Arnold	149
GALPIN, Eliza, m. Ebenezer SMITH, Feb. 2, 1834, by Rev. J. Atwater	123
Elizabeth A., b. in Southbury, d. Aug. 13, 1847; ae 68	57
Judson B., of New Haven, m. Catharine J. BRONSON, of Middlebury, May 16, 1841, by Rev. J. Atwater	129
GAY, Mary, d. Dec. 26, 1851; ae 3	60-1
GAYLORD, Amasa, d. Dec. 21, 1851; ae 73	60-1
George, s. Heman, b. Dec. 23, 1848	62
Giles, [s.] Heman, b. Mar. 4, 1850	62
Heman, m. Amelia Esther CLARK, b. of Middlebury, Nov. 29, 1847, by F. W. Sizer	147
Heman, m. Esther A. CLARK, b. of Middlebury, Nov. 29, 1847, by Rev. F. W. Sezer	56
Lucy Ann, of Middlebury, m. Giles ST. JOHN, of Walton, Deleware Co., N.Y., June 12, 1839, by Rev. J. Atwater	128
William, of Middlebury, m. Harriet L. TUTTLE, of New Haven, [Jan.] 26, [1835], by Rev. J. Atwater	124
GIDNEY, Elisha W., grandson of Elisha WHEELER, of Oxford, m. Nancy SMITH, of Middlebury, Dec. 23, 1844, by Rev. J. Atwater	133
GILBERT, Joseph, shoemaker, b. in Berlin, d. May 3, 1850; ae 70	58-9
GOODWIN, David, of Litchfield, m. Levey* CURTISS, of Middlebury, [ ], [1828(?)], by Rev. Mark Mead. Recorded June 19, 1828 *(Lucy?)	115
GRILLEY, Mariett, m. Jerome NEWTON, b. of Waterbury, Sept. 10, 1843, by Rev. Geo[rge] Waterbury	131
-----, [ch.] Henry, b. [ ]	62
GUNN, Amelia, b. Aug. 5, 1780	7
Amelia, of Middlebury, m. Dr. Alfred STARR, of New Town, Apr. 6, 1845, by Rev. Geo[rge] Waterbury	133
Charles G., of Middlebury, m. Augusta M. WARNER, of Middlebury, Sept. 29, 1845, by Rev. E. C. Beers	134
Charles Gilbert, b. Nov. 7, 1823	7
Elizabeth Amelia, b. Oct. 10, 1827	7
Johannah, b. Nov. 1, 1809	7

	Page
GUNN (cont.)	
John, b. Dec. 24, 1774	7
John, m. Amelia **HULL**, Oct. 2, 1800	32
Lucius, b. Oct. 29, 1805	7
Lucius, m. Emily G. **CAIN**, b. of Middlebury, Sept. 29, 1828, by Rev. Mark Mead	116
Marcus, b. Nov. 4, 1801	7
Sidney Columbus, b. Jan. 25, 1831	7
William, b. Jan. 22, 1803	7
HALL, Harry, of Sandisfield, Mass., m. Martha M. **JOHNSON**, of Naugatuck, Jan. 18, 1852, by Rev. Joel R. Arnold	148
HAMLIN, Daniel D., of Farmington, m. Julia A. **MALLORY**, of Middlebury, Jan. 15, 1832, by Rev. Jason Atwater	121
Emily Eunice, m. Sylvester **BRONSON**, Oct. 17, 1836, by Rev. J. Atwater	126
HAWKINS, Ann, of Derby, m. Isaac M. **BALDWIN**, of Middlebury, Jan. 18, 1835, by Rev. J. Atwater	124
Eliza, of Derby, m. Amos **BALDWIN**, of Middlebury, Feb. 19, 1823, by Rev. Mark Mead	111
Sally, of Derby, m. William D. **FOOT**, of Middlebury, Mar. 5, 1827, by Eli Barnett, Elder	114
HAWLEY, Charity, b. Aug. 2, 1795	8
David, b. Mar. 31, 1810	8
Elisha N., m. Susan A. **TYLER**, b. of Middlebury, June 3, 1829, by Rev. Mark Mead	117
John, b. Dec. 14, 1806	8
Levit, b. Jan. 8, 1792	8
Mary, b. Dec. 18, 1790	8
Samuel, b. Dec. 3, 1803	8
Stephen, b. May 20, 1817	8
HAYDEN, Lois, m. Ira **CURTISS**, b. of Waterbury, Nov. 9, 1822, by Cyrus Silliman, Elder	110
HAYES, Nelson J., of Middlebury, m. Chloe S. **ATWOOD**, of Woodbury, June 3, 1846, by Rev. Ebenezer C. Beers	135
HICKCOX, Alanson H., of Watertown, m. Amelia **FENN**, of Middlebury, Dec. 4, 1828, by Rev. Mark Mead	116
Mary M., of Waterbury, m. Elijah **WOOSTER**, of Middlebury, Feb. 11, 1838, by E. F. Merrill, J.P.	126
HINE, Anthony D., [s.] Dwight, b. Jan. 23, 1851	62
Clara S., [d.] Rev. Sylvester, b. Nov. 16, 1849	62
Franklin, m. Sarah **BRONSON**, Nov. 17, 1846, by Rev. George P. Prudden	135
John, of Waterbury, m. Esther **BRONSON**, of Middlebury, Oct. 10, 1822, by Rev. Mark Mead	76
John, of Waterbury, m. Hannah M. **TUCKER**, of Middlebury, Sept. 6, 1835, by Rev. J. Atwater	125
Mary, of Middlebury, m. Robert **BUNSON**, of Prospect, Apr. 7, 1830, by Rev. Mark Mead	118
Wesley D., d. Mar. 10, 1852; ae 6 y.	60-1
HORTON, Edwin W., of Naugatuck, m. Ellen **FULLER**, of Middlebury, Apr. 4, 1852, by Rev. Joel R. Arnold	149
HOTCHKISS, Andrew T., of Bethany, m. Belinda C. **BUCKINGHAM**, of Middlebury, Nov. 29, 1849, by W[illia]m H. Bangs	139

	Page
HOTCHKISS (cont.)	
Anna, Mrs., m. Truman **BENNET**, of Oxford, Feb. 12, 1838, by Rev. J. Atwater	127
John, of Middlebury, m. Anna **ABBOTT**, of Northfield, Oct. 12, 1834, by Rev. Jason Atwater	123
HULL, Amelia, m. John **GUNN**, Oct. 2, 1800	32
Cha[rle]s, b. in Naugatuck, s. Geo[rge], d. Aug. 13, 1849, in New Haven; ae 4 y.	58-9
George W., of Naugatuck, m. Esther M. **NICHOLS**, of Middlebury, June 18, 1843, by Rev. Daniel Wooster	131
Lawrence S., of Salem Bridge, m. Lucretia G. **PORTER**, of Middlebury, Mar. 18, 1830, by Rev. Amos Pettingill, of Salem Bridge	118
HUNGERFORD, Reuben, of Watertown, m. Mary Jane **BRONSON**, eldest d. Garry, of Middlebury, Apr. 15, 1840, by Rev. J. Atwater	128
HURLBURT, Amanda M., m. Monroe **SMITH**, May 8, 1844, by Rev. J. Atwater	132
Sophronia, of Middlebury, m. Orville L. **FITCH**, of Canaan, Nov. 27, 1842, by Rev. J. Atwater	131
JACKSON, Esther, of Middlebury, m. Henry N. **LAW**, of Oxford, Feb. 18, 1850, by Rev. G. P. Prudden	66
Esther, m. Henry N. **LOW**, of Middlebury, Feb. 18, 1850, by Geo[rge] P. Prudden	138
JOHNSON, Harry F., m. Mary **TREAT**, b. of Middlebury, May 26, 1825, by Rev. Alpheas Geer, of Waterbury	113
Levant D., of Wolcott, m. Nancy E. **JOHNSON**, of Oxford, May 13, 1841, by Rev. J. Atwater	129
Lora Eliza, of Oxford, m. Horace R. **ROBERTS**, of Middletown, Oct. 14, 1835, by James D. Wooster, J.P.	125
Martha M., m. Elisha C. **JONES**, b. of Middlebury, Feb. 3, 1851, by Rev. G. P. Prudden	66
Martha M., m. Elisha C. **JONES**, b. of Middlebury, Feb. 3, 1851, by Rev. Geo[rge] P. Prudden	147
Martha M., of Naugatuck, m. Harry **HALL**, of Sandisfield, Mass., Jan. 18, 1852, by Rev. Joel R. Arnold	148
Melissa, of Middlebury, m. Benjamin **DAVIS**, of Rutland, N.Y., [Jan.] 6, [1822], by James D. Wooster, J.P.	75
Nancy E., of Oxford, m. Levant D. **JOHNSON**, of Wolcott, May 13, 1841, by Rev. J. Atwater	129
Theodore, s. Henry, d. Apr. 19, 1851; ae 16 (colored)	58-9
William, m. Mrs. Betsey **NICHOLS**, Sept. 15, 1833, by James D. Wooster, J.P.	123
JONES, Elisha C., m. Martha M. **JOHNSON**, b. of Middlebury, Feb. 3, 1851, by Rev. G. P. Prudden	66
Elisha C., m. Martha M. **JOHNSON**, b. of Middlebury, Feb. 3, 1851, by Rev. Geo[rge] P. Prudden	147
JUDD, Henry S. B., [s.] Spencer, b. June 29, 1849	62
-----, s. Spencer, d. Sept. 25, 1848; ae 4	57
JUDSON, Ransom, of Woodbury, m. Lucy **TUTTLE**, of Middlebury, Mar. 27, 1822, by Rev. Alpheas Geer, of Waterbury & Salem	76

KEELER, Stephen, shoemaker, ae 42, b. Redding, res. Bridgeport, m. 2nd
  w. Sarah BUCKINGHAM, tailoress, ae 43, b. Vermont, res.
  Middlebury, Nov. 25, 1852, by Rev. J. R. Arnold   67
  Stephen, of Bridgeport, m. Mrs. Sarah BUCKINGHAM, of
  Middlebury, Nov. 25, 1852, by Rev. J. R. Arnold   149
KELLEY, -----, [ch.] of Patrick, b. Jan. 1 ,1852   63
KELSEY, Norton, of North Granby, m. Elizabeth L. WOOSTER, of
  Middlebury, Nov. 16, 1848, by Rev. G. P. Prudden   66
  Norton, of North Granby, m. Elizabeth L. WOOSTER, of
  Middlebury, Nov. 16, 1848, by Geo[rge] P. Prudden   137
KETCHUM, David, of Welton Saratoga County, N.Y., m. Merinda
  BLAKELEY, of Middlebury, May 4, 1829, by Daniel Wooster   117
LANDERS, Hawley, of Southbury, m. Martha A. CLARK, d. Daniel,
  2nd, Oct. 15, 1840, by Rev. J. Atwater   129
LAW, Henry N., of Oxford, m. Esther JACKSON, of Middlebury, Feb.
  18 ,1850, by Rev. G. P. Prudden   66
LEWIS, Aaron, of Southbury, m. Ruth A. WOOSTER, of Middlebury,
  Apr. 9, 1843, by Philip L. Hoyt   131
  Laura, of Wolcott, m. John W. WILMOT, of New Haven, Oct. 27,
  [1842], by Rev. J. Atwater   131
LINSLEY, Jacob, m. Esther BENEDICT, b. of Middlebury, Oct. 20,
  1829, by Rev. Mark Mead   117
  Jacob, Physician, b. in Branford, d. Feb. 6, 1849; ae 57   58-9
  Julia A. C., of Middlebury, m. John C. DOWNER, of Bozrah, Feb.
  12, 1845, by Rev. J. Atwater   131
LOW, Henry N., m. Esther JACKSON, b. of Middlebury, Feb. 18, 1850,
  by Geo[rge] P. Prudden   138
  -----, [ch.] of Henry, b. Aug. 29, 1851   63
LUM, Adam, of Southbury, m. Nancy BOWERS, of Middlebury, last
  evening, [Apr. 27, 1828], by Rev. Mark Mead   115
  George, of Oxford, m. Emmeline BOOTH, Oct. 18, 1830, by Rev.
  Jason Atwater   119
McGEE, [see also McKEE], Mary ,of Middlebury, m. Larmon L.
  WOOSTER, of New Haven, Sept. 16, 1849, by W[illia]m H.
  Bangs   139
McGUIRE, William, of Oxford, m. Delia BRYANT, July 18, 1830, by
  Rev. Jason Atwater   119
McKEE, [see also McGEE], Sophronia, of Middlebury, m. Henry P.
  ALDEN, of Windsor, N.Y., Dec. 29, 1852, by Rev. W[illia]m
  H. Bangs   67
  Sophronia M., of Middlebury, m. Henry P. ALDEN, of Windsor,
  N.Y., Dec. 29, [1852], by Rev. W[illia]m H. Bangs   33
MALLORY, MALLERY, Anna, m. Jared BRONSON, Oct. 13, 1830 by
  Rev. Jason Atwater   119
  David Jr., m. Electa MANSON, b. of Middlebury, Nov. 27, 1822, by
  Rev. Alpheas Geer, of Waterbury   110
  Delia, d. Charles, farmer, ae 40 & Lucy Ann, ae 37, b. in Sherman,
  Aug. 29, 1852   64
  Henrietta, m. Charles TREAT, Nov. 24, 1831, by Rev. J. Atwater   120
  Julia A., of Middlebury, m. Daniel D. HAMLIN, of Farmington,
  Jan. 15, 1832, by Rev. Jason Atwater   121
  Lydia, m. Jared BRONSON, Dec. 29, 1813   27

MALLORY, MALLERY (cont.)

	Page
Maria E., m. Stephen **STONE**, b. of Middlebury, Mar. 30, 1829, by Rev. Mark Mead	117
Rosette, of Middlebury, m. Elisha M. **STEVENS**, of Waterbury, Jan. 1, 1835, by Rev. J. Atwater	124
Thomas, farmer, d. Jan. 30, 1849; ae 84	58-9

MANSFIELD, Charles E., m. Alma **FOX**, b. of Woodbury, Mar. 27, 1839, by Rev. J. Atwater — 127

MANVILL, MANUIL, MANVEL, MANVIL, MANVILLE, Albert, of Elizabeth Port, N.J., m. Eliza **BRONSON**, d. Horace, June 27, 1838, by Rev. J. Atwater — 127

Albert, of Woodbury, m. Caroline **BRONSON**, d. Horace, of Middlebury, Sept. 2, 1844, by Rev. J. Atwater — 133

Burrit, m. Augusta **WINMAN**, of New Milford, Nov. 6, 1836, by Rev. J. Atwater — 126

Electa, m. Michael **BOWERS**, b. of Middlebury, May 7, 1827, by Rev. Mark Mead — 115

Emeret, m. William **TUTTLE**, Oct. 17, 1830, by Rev. Jason Atwater — 119

Jennett, [d.] of Bennet, b. Oct. 20, 1851 — 63

Joseph, [twin with Josephine, s.] Burritt, b. Sept. 2, 1850 — 63

Josephine, [twin with Joseph, d.] Burritt, b. Sept. 2, 1850 — 63

Maria, d. Horace, of Middlebury, m. Henry **BRISTOL**, s. Sheldon, of Oxford, Sept. 22, 1841, by Rev. J. Atwater — 130

Mary Ann, d. Uri, of Middlebury, m. John D. **MINDER**, of Woodbury, Oct. 20, 1844, by Rev. J. Atwater — 133

Sarah, m. Bennet **FENN**, Apr. 28, 1833, by Rev. J. Atwater — 122

MARSH, Rollo S., b. in New Milford, res. Waterbury, m. Caroline **BUCKINGHAM**, of Middlebury, Jan. 24, 1848, by Rev. F. I. Sezer — 56

Rollo S., of New Milford, m. Cornelia A. **BUCKINGHAM**, of Middlebury, Jan. 24, 1848, by F. W. Sizer — 147

MEIGS, David F., of Oxford, m. Jane **BRUSH**, of Middlebury, Dec. 31, 1848, by Geo[rge] P. Prudden — 137

David T., m. Jane **BRUSH**, b. of Oxford, [, 1848], by Rev. G. P. Prudden — 66

MERRILL, MARRELL, MARRILL, Susan F., of Naugatuck, m. Ira F. **BALDWIN**, of Middlebury, [, 1853 (?)], by Rev. J. R. Arnold — 215

-----, [ch.] of Burnett, cooper, b. July 5, 1848 — 55

-----, infant of B[   ],. d. July 5, 1848; ae 1 d. — 57

MILES, Catharine, b. in Woodbury, d. Mar. 30, 1849; ae 78 — 58-9

Sally, d. Jan. 13, 1850; ae 80 — 58-9

MINDER, John D., of Woodbury, m. Mary Ann **MANVIL**, d. Uri, of Middlebury, Oct. 20, 1844, by Rev. J. Atwater — 133

MITCHELL, Amos, of Southbury, m. Esther Maria **TYLER**, of Middlebury, May 29, 1850, by Geo[rge] P. Prudden — 138

MORRIS, Eliza A., of Waterbury, m. Sherman **FENN**, of Middlebury, Oct. 4, 1843, by Rev. J. Atwater — 132

Elizabeth, of Southbury, m. David **SEGAR**, of Newtown, June 4, 1820, by Daniel Wooster, J.P., at Julius Morris — 75

MOSES, Celina, b. Nov. 2, 1810 — 12

Joshua Orasmus, b. Sept. 7, 1797 — 12

Levitta, b. Mar. 15, 1801 — 12

MIDDLEBURY VITAL RECORDS 191

	Page
MOSES (cont.)	
Nelson Lee, b. Dec. 26, 1807	12
MOSS, Anna, w. Emaleel, d. June 7, 1851; ae 71	58-9
Emaluel, of Cheshire, m Anna **BRADLEY**, of Middlebury, Nov. 18, 1830, by Rev. Rodney Rossetee, of Monroe	119
Emaluel, of Cheshire, m. Anna **BRADLEY**, of Middlebury, Nov. 18, 1830, by Rev. Rodney Rossiter, of Monroe	120
MUNSON, MONSON, MANSON, Electa, m. David **MALLORY**, Jr., b. of Middlebury, Nov. 27, 1822, by Rev. Alpheas Geer, of Waterbury	110
Electa Ann, m. William J. **NICKERSON**, b. of Middlebury, July 16, 1843, by Rev. Geo[rge] Waterbury	131
Hawkins W., m. Sarah **ABBOTT**, b. of Middlebury, Apr. 10, 1839, by Rev. E. Washburn	128
Lucy, of Middlebury, m. Benjamin **CURTISS**, of Southbury, Sept. 30, 1839, by Rev. E. Washburn	128
Stiles F., m. Harriet N. **STONE**, d. Stephen, Nov. 13, 1838, by Rev. Jason Atwater	127
-----, [ch.] of Stiles F., b. July 8, 1851	63
NETTLETON, Caleb, m. Mary **CLARKE**, b. of Middlebury, Mar. 2, 1845, by Rev. J. Atwater	133
NEWTON, Jerome, m. Mariett **GRILLEY**, b. of Waterbury, Sept. 10, 1843, by Rev. Geo[rge] Waterbury	131
Nathan F., of Waterbury, m. Esther **TREAT**, of Middlebury, Dec. 18, 1828, by Rev. Alpheas Geer, of Waterbury	116
Nathan F., wagon maker, b. in Waterbury, d. Dec. 26, 1850, ae 44	58-9
NICHOLS, Betsey, Mrs., m. William **JOHNSON**, Sept. 15, 1833, by James D. Wooster, J.P.	123
Caroline S., [d.] of Isaac, b. Sept. 10, 1850	63
Ellen, of Middlebury, m. W[illia]m W. **PERKINS**, of New Haven, May 19, 1850, by Rev. W[illia]m H. Bangs	66
Ellen A., of Middlebury, m. William W. **PERKINS**, of Plymouth, May 19, 1850, by W[illia]m H. Bangs	139
Esther M., of Middlebury, m. George W. **HULL**, of Naugatuck, June 18, 1843, by Rev. Daniel Wooster	131
Jane, b. in Mass., d. Apr. 13, 1848, ae 23	57
Lester, [s.] Joel S., b. Feb. 16, 1849	62
Patty, w. Peter, d. Jan. 30, 1850; ae 75	58-9
-----, [ch.] of Charles L., b. Apr. 25, 1848	55
-----, ch. of Edward, b. Aug. 16, 1848	62
NICKERSON, William J., m. Electa Ann **MUNSON**, b. of Middlebury, July 16, 1843, by Rev. Geo[rge] Waterbury	131
NORTHROP, Harriet P., of Watertown, m. W[illia]m M. **DRAKE**, of Waterbury, Oct. 2, 1847, by F. W. Sizer	147
Harvie, m. Sally **ATWOOD**, Mar. 12, 1823, by Fred Holcomb	111
Mary, d. Dec. 18, 1851, ae 77	60-1
Milan P., m. Almira L. **STRICTLAND**, b. of Watertown, Sept. 12, 1834, by Rev. J. Atwater	123
Timothy Dwight, m. Clarissa **CAMP**, Apr. 11, 1833, by Rev. J. Atwater	122
NORTON, -----, [ch.] of Friend, farmer, b. Mar. 16, 1848	55
OSBORN, Abraham, m. Mary Ann **WOOSTER**, Dec. 6, 1831, by Rev. Chauncey Prindle	121

BARBOUR COLLECTION

Page

OSBORN (cont.)
Elam P., of Camden, N.Y., m. H[ ] **PLATT**, of Middlebury, May 4, 1845, by Rev. J. Atwater — 134
Horace B., of Watertown, m. Sarah J. **TUTTLE**, of Middlebury, Mar. 4, 1849, by Rev. G. P. Prudden — 66
Horace B., of Watertown, m. Sarah J. **TUTTLE**, of Middlebury, Mar. 4, 1849, by Geo[rge] P. Prudden — 137
Levinia, of Middlebury, m. John **FAIRCLOUGH**, of Waterbury, Feb. 17, 1844, by Rev. Geo[rge] Waterbury — 132
Lucian, m. Sarah **SCARRETT**, b. of Naugatuc, Aug. 11, 1844, by Rev. J. Atwater — 133
Noah A., m. Mary A. **WASHBURN**, b. of Middlebury, Mar. 30, 1851, by Rev. Geo[rge] P. Prudden — 148

PAGE, Silas Ives, of Philadelphia, m. Sophia **STONE**, d. David, of Middlebury, Aug. 16, 1848, by Rev. J. Atwater — 137
Silas Meredith, [s.] Silas J., b. Sept. 1, 1849 — 62

PAINTER, Roxy, of Watertown, m. William **FOX**, of Woodbury, Sept. 13, 1835, by Rev. J. Atwater — 125

PATCHEN, Melissa, of Westport, m. Bennet **SAXTON**, of Middlebury, Feb. 15, 1847, by Rev. George P. Prudden — 135

PATTERSON, Charles, of Naugatuck, m. Emily **FOX**, of Middlebury, Aug. 3, 1851, by Rev. Ja[me]s R. Mushon — 66

PECK, Cornelia, [d.] Jay, painter, b. Apr. 25, 1848 — 55
Hannah, of Middlebury, m. William **CURTISS**, of Southbury, Apr. 25, 1822, by Rev. Mark Mead — 76
Lucy, m. Charles **TOWNSEND**, Nov. 28, 1826, by Rev. Alpheas Geer, of Waterbury — 114
Lydia, m. Jason **CURTISS**, of Southbury, Dec. 21, 1836, by Rev. J. Atwater — 126

PENNY, Theodora S., [ch.] William, b. Oct. 9, 1850 — 63

PERKINS, W[illia]m W., of New Haven, m. Ellen **NICHOLS**, of Middlebury, May 19, 1850, by Rev. W[illia]m H. Bangs — 66
William W., of Plymouth, m. Ellen A. **NICHOLS**, of Middlebury, May 19, 1850, by W[illia]m H. Bangs — 139
-----, [ch.] of William W., b. Mar. 22, 1851 — 63

PLATT, Anson, b. June 5, 1810 — 15
Anson, m. Ruth **ABBOTT**, b. of Middlebury, Apr. 5, 1831, by Jason Atwater — 120
Arthur, [s.] Joseph P., b. Aug. 21, 1849 — 62
Frederick, [s.] Luther S., b. Oct. 8, 1848 — 62
Gideon Lucian, b. July 20, 1813 — 15
H-----, of Middlebury, m. Elam P. **OSBORN**, of Camden, N.Y., May 4, 1845, by Rev. J. Atwater — 134
Joseph P., m. Meheteble A. **THOMPSON**, b. of Middlebury, Apr. 28, 1830, by Rev. Mark Mead — 118
Joseph Perkins, b. Nov. 16, 1808 — 15
Luther G., m. Diantha **THOMPSON**, b. of Middlebury, Dec. 13, 1847, by Geo[rge] P. Prudden — 136
Luther S., m. Diantha **THOMPSON**, b. of Middlebury, Dec. 13, 1847, by Rev. Geo[rge] P. Prudden — 56
Marvin B., of Waterbury, m. Nancy R. **SMITH**, of Middlebury, Nov. 2, 1848, by Rev. Geo[rge] P. Prudden — 66

MIDDLEBURY VITAL RECORDS 193

	Page
PLATT (cont.)	
Marvin B., of Waterbury, m. Nancy R. **SMITH**, of Middlebury, Nov. 12, 1848, by Geo[rge] P. Prudden	137
Merret, m. Mary **BRONSON**, b. of Middlebury, Nov. 25, 1838, by Rev. Abraham Browne, of Elizabeth Port, N.J.	127
Merret S., of South Britain, m. Maria **SMITH**, of Middlebury, Nov. 23, 1853, by Rev. J. R. Arnold	215
Nancy, m. Leonard **BRONSON**, Apr. 14, 1819	27
-----, ch. of L. S., d. Apr. 25, 1852, ae 4. w.	60-1
POPE, Frederick, [s.] Augustus F., blacksmith, of Wolcottville, b. Sept. 4, 1847	55
Frederick, of Oxford, m. Harriet S. **BUCKINGHAM**, of Middlebury, Oct. 13, 1850, by Rev. G. P. Prudden	66
Frederick m. Harriet L. **BUCKINGHAM**, b. of Middlebury, Oct. 13, 1850, by Geo[rge] P. Prudden	138
-----, [ch.] of Frederick, b. Oct. 20, 1851	63
PORTER, Clarinda, d. Mar. 12, 1848, ae [ ]	57
David Jr., m. Anna **CURTISS**, b. of Middlebury, Mar. 25, 1823, by Rev. Mark Mead	111
David, d. Mar. 25, 1852, ae 69	60-1
George W., of Watertown, m. Harriet L. **BRONSON**, d. Alfred, of Middlebury, Nov. 1, 1838, by Rev. J. Atwater	127
Lucretia G., of Middlebury, m. Lawrence S. **HULL**, of Salem Bridge, Mar. 18, 1830, by Rev. Amos Pettingill, of Salem Bridge	118
Martha, m. George E. **BRISTOL**, Apr. 5, 1835, by Rev. Joel R. Arnold, of Waterbury	124
Melinda, m. Charles **BOUGHTON**, of Waterbury, [Mar.] 24, [1830], by Rev. Mark Mead	118
Samuel, m. Mary **DRIVER**, of Torrington, Oct. 18, 1836, by Rev. J. Atwater	126
PRINDLE, Josephine A., [d.] Francis, b. Mar. 10, 1849	62
PRUDDEN, Theophilus, [s.] Rev. Geo[rge] P., b. July 7, 1849	62
RADFORD, Elizabeth, of Middlebury, m. Cha[rle]s **EVANS**, of New Milford, Jan. 15, 1850, by W[illia]m H. Bangs	139
Elizabeth H., of Middlebury, m. Cha[rle]s **EVANS**, of New Milford, Jan. 15, 1850, by Rev. W[illia]m H. Bangs	66
H. Augusta, m. Julius **BRONSON**, b. of Middlebury, Jan. 3, 1849, by Rev. G. P. Prudden	66
Helen Augusta, m. Julius **BRONSON**, b. of Middlebury, Jan. 3, 1849, by Geo[rge] P. Prudden	137
REAFREE, Maria, twin with Mary, [d.] of Alfred, b. Sept. 24, 1851	63
Mary, twin with Maria, [d.] of Alfred, b. Sept. 24, 1851	63
RICE, Mary, of Woodbridge, m. Ebenezer **WELTON**, of Waterbury, Mary 24, 1827, by Rev. Mark Mead	115
Sally, of Middlebury, m. Luther H. **TOWNE**, of Rutland, N.Y., [ ], [1821(?)], by Rev. Mark Mead. Recorded Feb. 9, 1821	75
RICHARDSON, Betsey, m. Mary **WOOSTER**, Jan. 11, 1827, by Rev. Mark Mead [Both female names in Arnold Copy]	114
Charles E., of New Haven, m. Mary A. **CURTISS**, May 26, 1844, by Rev. J. Atwater	132
Ellen, (colored), [b.] [ ]	17

	Page
RICHARDSON (cont.)	
Geo[rge] Nathan, [s.] Geo[rge] F., farmer, ae 22, Middlebury & Jane, ae 20, Middlebury, b. Sept. 25, 1852	64
Julia M., m. Dwight **CLARK**, b. of Middlebury, Nov. 15, 1848, by Geo[rge] P. Prudden	137
Julia M., m. Dwight **CLARK**, b. of Middlebury, Nov. 16, 1848, by Rev. G. P. Prudden	66
Polly, of Middlebury, m. Ransom **STEVENS**, of Lowville, N.Y., Jan. 28, 1823, by Rev. Mark Mead	111
-----, [ch.] James, b. Oct. 13, 1850	63
RIGGS, Esther, d. Samuel, m. Myra W. **BARNES**, of Canaan, May 27, 1832, by Rev. J. Atwater	121
Moses, m. Lucy **BERRY**, b. of Derby, Aug. 1, 1821, by Rev. Mark Mead	75
Polly, of Middlebury, m. Henry S. **WHEELER**, of Southbury, Oct. 22, 1828, by Rev. Mark Mead	116
ROBERTS, ROBBERTS, Amasa, of Waterbury, m. Luce **BRACE**, of Middlebury, Nov. 9, 1822, by rEv. Samuel Potter, of Woodbridge & Salem	110
Amasa, blacksmith, b. in Waterbury, d. Sept. 20, 1848, ae 79	58-9
Geo[rge] Washington, [s.] W[illia]m J., b. May 15, 1849	62
Horace R., of Middletowon, m. Lora Eliza **JOHNSON**, of Oxford, Oct. 14, 1835, by James D. Wooster, J.P.	125
Mary, [d.] William, shoemaker, b. May 2, 1848	55
Nancy E., of Waterbury, m. Harmon W. **STODDARD**, of Woodbury, Dec. 28, 1845, by Rev. E. C. Beers	134
Phebe, m. Eleazer **FELLOWS**, of New York State, Aug. 28, 1831, by Leonard Bronson, J.P.	120
W[illia]m, of Middlebury, m. Harriet **COOK**, of Humphrysville, Sept. 8, 1844, by Rev. J. Atwater	133
-----, [ch.] of William J., b. Apr. 19, 1851	63
ROSE, -----, [ch.] of Bela, of Waterbury, b. June 21, 1850	52
SACKET, Henry, of Oxford, m. Almira **SCOVILL**, of Middlebury, Feb. 14, 1842, by Rev. Daniel Wooster	130
ST. JOHN, Giles, of Walton Delaware Co., N.Y., m. Lucy Ann **GAYLORD**, of Middlebury, June 12, 1839, by Rev. J. Atwater	128
SAXTON, Bennet, of Middlebury, m. Melissa **PATCHEN**, of Westport, Feb. 15, 1847, by Rev. George P. Prudden	135
Thirza, m. Erasmus H. **ATWOOD**, of Waterbury, May 20, 1832, by Rev. J. Atwater	121
SCARRETT, Sarah, m. Lucian **OSBORN**, b. of Naugatuc, Aug. 11, 1844, by Rev. J. Atwater	133
SCOTT, Garry, of Woodbury, m. Sally **TUTTLE**, of Middlebury, Mar. 12, 1826, by Grove L. Brownell	113
Henry W., of Southbury, m. Susan **FENN**, Oct. 10, 1837, by Rev. J. Atwater	127
Josiah S., farmer, d. Mar. 21, 1850; ae 80	58-9
Josiah T., of Cornwall, Vt., m. Mehitable **TYLER**, of Middlebury, Aug. 25, 1822, by Rev. Samuel Rich, of Columbia	76
Mary E., d. Jan. 28, 1851, ae 22	58-9
SCOVILL, SCOVILLE, Almira, of Middlebury, m. Henry **SACKET**, of Oxford, Feb. 14, 1842, by Rev. Daniel Wooster	130

MIDDLEBURY VITAL RECORDS 195

	Page
SCOVILL, SCOVILLE (cont.)	
James C., of Waterbury, m. Marcia **SMITH**, of Middlebury, Nov. 20, 1850, by Rev. G. P. Prudden	
James C., of Waterbury, m. Marcia **SMITH**, of Middlebury, Nov. 20, 1850, by Geo[rge] P. Prudden	139
SEGAR, David, of Newtown, m. Elizabeth **MORRIS**, of Southbury, June 4, 1820, by Daniel Wooster, J.P., at Julius Morris, in Middlebury	75
SIKES, Rebecca D., of Suffield, m. Lorenzo J. **THOMAS**, of Bethlem, May 2, 1852, by Rev. J. R. Arnold	149
SILLIMAN, Sarah M., of Monroe, m. James **CLARK**, of Waterbury, Jan. 14, 1841, by J. Atwater	129
SMITH, SMYTH, Calvin, m. Mary E. **DASCOM**, b. of Woodbury, Mar. 3, 1847, by Geo[rge] P. Prudden	135
Caroline M., of Bristol, m. Sam[ue]l **FENN**, of Waterbury, June 9, 1850, by Rev. G. P. Prudden	66
Caroline M., of Bristol, m. Samuel **FENN**, of Middlebury, June 9, 1850, by Geo[rge] P. Prudden	138
Daniel, Jr., m. Anna **STONE**, b. of Middlebury, June 21, 1826, by Rev. Mark Mead	113
Daniel, Rev., of Derby, m. Angelina **CASTLE**, of Waterbury, Dec. 9, 1832, by Rev. Heman Bangs	122
Daniel, farmer, d. Mar. 1, 1849, ae 90	58-9
Ebenezer, m. Eliza **GALPIN**, Feb. 2, 1834, by Rev. J. Atwater	123
Fred[eric]k A., [s.] John, miller, of Naugatuck, b. Mar. 2, 1848	55
George F., m. Philomela **ABBOTT**, Nov. 23, 1825, by Frederick Holcomb	113
Horatio N., m. Maria **BOOTH**, b. of Middlebury, Oct. 9, 1837, by Rev. Oliver Hopson	126
Horatio N., [s.] of Nelson, b. June 22, 1851	63
Marcia, of Middlebury, m. James C. **SCOVILLE**, of Waterbury, Nov. 20, 1850, by Rev. G. P. Prudden	66
Marcia, of Middlebury, m. James C. **SCOVILLE**, of Waterbury, Nov. 20, 1850, by Geo[rge] P. Prudden	139
Maria, of Middlebury, m. Merret S. **PLATT**, of South Britain, Nov. 23, 1853, by Rev. J. B. Arnold	215
Mary Jane, d. W[illia]m H., d. Aug. 10, 1848, ae 14 m.	58-9
Mehetebel, of Middlebury, m. Curtiss **WHEELER**, of Southbury, Jan. 1, 1829, by Rev. Mark Mead	117
Monroe, m. Amanda M. **HURLBURT**, May 8, 1844, by Rev. J. Atwater	132
Nancy, of Middlebury, m. Elisha W. **GIDNEY**, grandson of Elisha **WHEELER**, of Oxford, Dec. 23, 1844, by Rev. J. Atwater	133
Nancy R., of Middlebury, m. Marvin B. **PLATT**, of Waterbury, Nov. 2, 1848, by Rev. Geo[rge] P. Prudden	66
Nancy R., of Middlebury, m. Marvin B. **PLATT**, of Waterbury, Nov. 12, 1848, by Geo[rge] P. Prudden	137
William, of Washington, m. Julia **STONE**, of Middlebury, Feb. 24, 1825, by Rev. Mark Mead	112
William H., m. Emmeline **THOMPSON**, June 9, 1834, by Rev. J. Atwater	123
-----, wid. Ebenezer, d. Oct. 4, 1849, ae 84	58-9

	Page
SMITH (cont.)	
-----, [ch.] of Davis S., farmer, ae 33 & Jane M., ae 29, b. Feb. 20, 1853	64
SOLLY, Thomas, of Southbury, m. Martha **BRADLEY**, of Middlebury, Feb. 8, 1835, by H. Humphries	124
SPLANN, -----, [ch.] of Cornelius, laborer, ae 35, b. Ireland & Mary, ae 34, b. Ireland, b. Jan. 31, 1853	64
STARR, Alfred, Dr., of New Town, m. Amelia **GUNN**, of Middlebury, Apr. 6, 1845, by Rev. Geo[rge] Waterbury	133
STEVENS, Elisha M., of Waterbury, m. Rosette **MALLORY**, of Middlebury, Jan. 1, 1835, by Rev. J. Atwater	124
Ransom, of Lowville, N.Y., m. Polly **RICHARDSON**, of Middlebury, Jan. 28, 1823, by Rev. Mark Mead	111
STILES, Albert E., b. in Oxford, res. Middlebury, m. Mary A. **FOX**, b. in Woodbury, res. Middlebury, July 3, 1848, by Rev. John Churchill	56
Henry W., [s.] Albert E., b. Feb. 10, 1850	62
Jonathan, of Southbury, m. Nancy A. **BALDWIN**, of Middlebury, Nov. 13, 1831, by James D. Wooster, J.P.	120
-----, [ch.] of Albert E., b. Nov. 19, 1851	63
STODDARD, Clarissa, m. Therolow J. **CLARK**, b. of Middlebury, May 6, 1824, by Rev. Mark Mead	112
Harmon W., of Woodbury, m. Nancy E. **ROBERTS**, of Waterbury, Dec. 28, 1845, by Rev. E. C. Beers	134
Jason, m. Wealthy **BRADLEY**, b. of Middlebury, May 26, 1822, by Rev. Mark Mead	76
Maria, of Naugatuck, m. W[illia]m **ALLEN**, of Woodbridge, now res. Naugatuck, Aug. 29, 1841, by Rev. Jason Atwater	130
STONE, Almira, m. Michael **BOWEN**, Jr., b. of Middlebury, Mar. 14, 1821, by Rev. Mark Mead	75
Anna, m. Daniel **SMITH**, Jr., b. of Middlebury, June 21, 1826, by Rev. Mark Mead	113
Anne, b. Sept. 10, 1803	18
Charles Beacher, b. July 22, 1807	18
Chester, b. July 13, 1795	18
David, b. Apr. 14, 1799	18
David, m. Mehitable **CAMP**, b. of Middlebury, Apr. 27, 1824, by Rev. Mark Mead	112
Ezekiel, b. Feb. 11, 1771	18
Ezekiel, m. Hannah **BRONSON**, Oct. 26, 1794	43
Ezekiel, m. Susannah **STRONG**, May 8, 1805	43
Hannah, d. Oct. 5, 1804	68
Hannah M., m. David **FRENCH**, of Trumbull, May 23, 1844, by Rev. J. Atwater	132
Harriet N., d. Stephen, m. Stiles F. **MUNSON**, Nov. 13, 1838, by Rev. Jason Atwater	127
Julia, b. Apr. 11, 1801	18
Julia, of Middlebury, m. William **SMITH**, of Washington, Feb. 24, 1825, by Rev. Mark Mead	112
Maria P., m. Edward **CLARK**, of Waterbury, Dec. 6, 1837, by Rev. J. Atwater	127
Nancy A., m. Merritt C. **BALDWIN**, b. of Middlebury, Apr. 22, 1846, by Rev. J. Atwater	134

	Page
STONE (cont.)	
Nancy B., [d.] Elley G., b. Aug. 20, 1848	62
Salome, m. Calvin **CAMP**, b. of Middlebury, Nov. 5, 1823, by Rev. Mark Mead	111
Samuel Mansfield, b. May 8, 1797	18
Sophia, d. David, of Middlebury, m. Silas Ives **PAGE**, of Philadelphia, Aug. 16, 1848, by Rev. J. Atwater	137
Sophia Susan, b. Mar. 27, 1806	18
Stephen, m. Maria E. **MALLORY**, b. of Middlebury, Mar. 30, 1829, by Rev. Mark Mead	117
William Ezekiel, b. Nov. 2, 1808	18
-----, b. in Southbury, w. Ez[ekiel], d. Dec. 31, 1851; ae 74	60-1
-----, [ch.] of Charles B., b. May 29, 1852	63
STRICTLAND, Almira L., m. Milan P. **NORTHROP**, b. of Watertown, Sept. 12, 1834, by Rev. J. Atwater	123
STRONG, Susannah, m. Ezekiel **STONE**, May 8, 1805	43
THOMAS, Lorenzo J., of Bethlem, Conn., m. Rebecca D. **SIKES**, of Suffield, May 2, 1852, by Rev. J. R. Arnold	149
Ransom, of Woodbridge, m. Clarissa **WOODRUFF**, of Middlebury, Feb. 3, 1825, by Rev. Mark Mead	112
THOMPSON, Ann, of Bethlem, m. Wheeler **TUTTLE**, of Southbury, Jan. 27, 1836, by Daniel Wooster	125
Diantha, m. Luther S. **PLATT**, b. of Middlebury, Dec. 13, 1847, by Rev. Geo[rge] P. Prudden	56
Diantha, m. Luther G. **PLATT**, b. of Middlebury, Dec. 13, 1847, by Geo[rge] P. Prudden	136
Emmeline, m. William H. **SMITH**, June 9, 1834, by Rev. J. Atwater	123
Lucius A., m. Marcia **BRONSON**, Nov. 1, 1843, by Rev. J. Atwater	132
Martha M., d. Eli, of Middlebury, m. Adna **AYRES**, of Starkey, N.Y., Oct. 26, 1842, by Rev. J. Atwater	130
Mary S., of Middlebury, m. Julius H. **BENHAM**, of Woodbridge, Apr. 24, 1845, by Rev. J. Atwater	134
Meheteble A., m. Joseph P. **PLATT**, b. of Middlebury, Apr. 28, 1830, by Rev. Mark Mead	118
Olive, of Woodbury, m. Alvin **TUTTLE**, of Middlebury, Nov. 9, [1828], by Rev. Mark Mead	116
Rebecca, m. Isaac **BRONSON**, Nov. 4, 1810	27
Rebecca, m. Chester **CURTISS**, b. of Middlebury, Sept. 10, 1843, by Rev. J. Atwater	132
TOMLINSON, Charles A., of Oxford, m. Julia A. **CLARK**, Dec. 26, 1839, by Rev. J. Atwater	128
TOWNE, Luther H., of Rutland, N.Y., m. Sally **RICE**, of Middlebury, [ ], [1821(?)], by Rev. Mark Mead. Recorded Feb. 9, 1821	75
TOWNSEND, Charles, m. Lucy **PECK**, Nov. 28, 1826, by Rev. Alpheas Geer, of Waterbury	114
Cornelia S., of Middlebury, m. Edward L. **BRONSON**, of Waterbury, Oct. 22, 1851, by George F. Bronson	148
Grace H., b. Jan. 2, 1840	19
Henry, m. Emma **ABBOTT**, b. of Middlebury, Nov. 21, 1827, by Rev. Alpheas Geer, in Waterbury	115
Julia P., [d.] Cha[rle]s, farmer, b. Feb. 10, 1848	55

	Page
TOWNSEND (cont.)	
Larmon G., m. Julia **BRONSON**, b. of Middlebury, Nov. 12, [1827], by Rev. Mark Mead	115
Susan, d. Charles, d. Jan. 22, 1851, ae 15	58-9
TREAT, Charles, m. Henrietta **MALLORY**, Nov. 24, 1831, by Rev. J. Atwater	120
Esther, of Middlebury, m. Nathan F. **NEWTON**, of Waterbury, Dec. 18, 1828, by Rev. Alpheas Geer, of Waterbury	116
Lydia A., m. John **BENHAM**, b. of Middlebury, June 30, 1841, by Rev. J. Atwater	130
Martha, m. John **BRADLEY**, b. of Middlebury, Apr. 8, 1830, by Rev. Mark Mead	118
Mary, m. Harry F. **JOHNSON**, b. of Middlebury, May 26, 1825, by Rev. Alpheas Geer, of Waterbury	113
Sam[ue]l W., m. Betsey **TUTTLE**, Dec. 4, 1822, by Frederick Holcomb	110
-----, [ch.] Philo, b. Mar. 6, 1849	62
-----, [ch.] Philo, b. Mar. 10, 1851	63
TUCKER, Hannah M., of Middlebury, m. John **HINE**, of Waterbury, Sept. 6, 1835, by Rev. J. Atwater	125
William H., of Oxford, m. Clarissa J. **TUTTLE**, Apr. 24, 1833, by Rev. J. Atwater	122
W[illia]m R., m. Cornelia **BOOTH**, b. of Middlebury, Dec. 16, 1840, by Rev. Jason Atwater	129
TUTTLE, Aaron, Jr., m. Anna **ABBOTT**, Nov. 21, 1822, by Frederick Holcomb	111
Alvin, of Middlebury, m. Olive **THOMPSON**, of Woodbury, Nov. 9, [1828], by Rev. Mark Mead	116
Betsey, m. Sam[ue]l W. **TREAT**, Dec. 4, 1822, by Frederick Holcomb	110
Burton, s. Truman, d. Mar. 10, 1851, ae 9	58-9
Clarissa J., m. William H. **TUCKER**, of Oxford, Apr. 24, 1833, by Rev. J. Atwater	122
Elisa M., of Middlebury, m. Alexander G. **DAVIS**, of Waterbury, May 5, 1835, by Rev. J. Atwater	125
Harriet L., of New Haven, m. William **GAYLORD**, of Middlebury, [Jan.] 26, [1835], by Rev. J. Atwater	124
James, m. Elvira **ADAMS**, b. of Middlebury, Oct. 6, 1848, by Rev. F. W. Sizer	66
James, m. Alvira **ADAMS**, b. of Middlebury, Oct. 6, 1848, by F. W. Sizer	147
James Leroy, [s.] James, b. Feb. 7, 1850	62
Lucy, of Middlebury, m. Ransom **JUDSON**, of Woodbury, Mar. 27, 1822, by Rev. Alpheas Geer, of Waterbury & Salem	76
Mary Ellen, [d.] Silas T., b. Jan. 10, 1851	63
Sally, of Middlebury, m. Garry **SCOTT**, of Woodbury, Mar. 12, 1826, by Grove L. Brownell	113
Sarah J., of Middlebury, m. Horace B. **OSBORN**, of Watertown, Mar. 4, 1849, by Rev. G. P. Prudden	66
Sarah J., of Middlebury, m. Horace B. **OSBORN**, of Watertown, Mar. 4, 1849, by Geo[rge] P. Prudden	137
Tabitha, m. David F. **FENN**, Nov. 26, 1832, by Rev. J. Atwater	121

	Page
TUTTLE (cont.)	
Wheeler, of Southbury, m. Ann **THOMPSON**, of Bethlem, Jan. 27, 1836, by Daniel Wooster	125
William, m. Emeret **MANVILLE**, Oct. 17, 1830, by Rev. Jason Atwater	119
-----, [ch.] of James, b. Jan. 14, 1852	63
-----, d. J[ ], d. Feb. 11, 1852; ae 4 w.	60-1
TWITCHELL, Jane, of Oxford, m. Luther **BROADWILL**, of Derby, Jan. 22, 1831, by Daniel Wooster	119
Sarah, m. Noyes **BRADLEY**, b. of Middlebury, Sept. 22, 1850, by Rev. Joseph Scott	66
Sarah, m. Noyes **BRADLEY**, b. of Middlebury, Sept. 22, 1850, by Rev. Joseph Scott, of Naugatuck	138
TYLER, Augusta Jane, [d.] Enos B., b. Oct. 12, 1850	63
Bennet E. [s.] Edwin, b. June 9, 1850	62
Cha[rle]s Bayler, [s.] of Edwin C., farmer, Oxford & Betsey A., Washington, b. Dec. 29, 1852	64
Ellsworth J., [s.] Ja[me]s A., b. July 10, 1849	62
Esther Maria, of Middlebury, m. Amos **MITCHELL**, of Southbury, May 29, 1850, by Geo[rge] P. Prudden	138
Franklyn A., [s.] Enos B., b. Apr. 10, 1849	62
Harriet, of Middlebury, m. Truman **DAYTON**, of Watertown, Dec. 11, 1822, by Horace Hooker	110
Mehitable, of Middlebury, m. Josiah T. **SCOTT**, of Cornwall, Vt., Aug. 25, 1822, by Rev. Samuel Rich, of Columbia	76
Susan A., m. Elisha N. **HAWLEY**, b. of Middlebury, June 3, 1829, by Rev. Mark Mead	117
-----, s. Edwin, d. Feb. 10, 1852, ae 20 m.	60-1
-----, [ch.] of Enos B., b. July 19, 1852	63
TYRRELL, Rufus, [s.] Alvah M., b. Mar. 10, 1849	62
-----, [ch.] of George, b. June 23, 1851	63
-----, [ch.] of Alvah M., b. Aug. 28, 1851	63
UNDERWOOD, Emma, of New York, m. William **CLARK**, of Derby, Nov. 3, 1850, by Rev. Ira Abbott	66
Emma, of New York, m. William **CLARK**, of Bermingham, Nov. 3, 1850, by Rev. Ira Abbott	139
WAKELEY, WAKELEE, Geo[rge], of Southbury, m. Fanny Jane **WOOSTER**, of Middlebury, Nov. 28, 1850, by Rev. W[illia]m H. Bangs	66
George, of Southbury, m. Fanny Jane **WOOSTER**, of Middlebury, Nov. 28, 1850, by W[illiam] H. Bangs	139
Nichols, of Huntington, m. Polly T. **BENHAM**, of Middlebury, Nov. 24, 1831, by Rev. J. Atwater	120
WARNER, Augusta M., m. Charles G. **GUNN**, b. of Middlebury, Sept. 29, 1845, by Rev. E. C. Beers	134
WARREN, David, of Watertown, m. Louisa **BRONSON**, of Middlebury, Mar. 24, 1847, by Rev. Geo[rge] P. Prudden	136
WASHBURN, Mary A., m. Noah A. **OSBORN**, b. of Middlebury, Mar. 30, 1851, by Rev. Geo[rge] P. Prudden	148
WELTON, Ebenezer, of Waterbury, m. Mary **RICE**, of Woodbridge, May 24, 1827, by Rev. Mark Mead	115
WHEELER, Curtiss, of Southbury, m. Mehetebel **SMITH**, of Middlebury, Jan. 1, 1829, by Rev. Mark Mead	117

	Page
WHEELER (cont.)	
Elisha, see Elisha W. **GIDNEY**	133
Henry S., of Southbury, m. Polly **RIGGS**, of Middlebury, Oct. 22, 1828, by Rev. Mark Mead	116
WHITNEY, -----, [ch.] of Freeman, laborer, b. Feb. 13, 1848	55
WILDMAN, Anna, b. in Kent, d. June 25, 1848; ae 54	57
WILMOT, Abigail A., m. Ezra **ALLEN**, Oct. 12, 1834, by Daniel Wooster	123
John L., of New Haven, m. Laura **LEWIS**, of Wolcott, Oct. 27, [1842], by Rev. J. Atwater	131
WINMAN, Augusta, of New Milford, m. Burrit **MANVIL**, Nov. 6, 1836, by Rev. J. Atwater	126
WOODRUFF, Clarissa, of Middlebury, m. Ransom **THOMAS**, of Woodbridge, Feb. 3, 1825, by Rev. Mark Mead	112
John H., of Watertown, m. Jane **BRONSON**, of Middlebury, Nov. 2, 1841, by Rev. N. S. Richardson	130
WOOSTER, David, m. Elizabeth J. **BRADLEY**, Nov. 9, 1826, by Rev. Mark Mead	114
Elijah, of Middlebury, m. Mary M. **HICKCOX**, of Waterbury, Feb. 11, 1838, by E. F. Merrill, J.P.	126
Elizabeth Ann, m. Philo **ABBOTT**, Nov. 5, 1822, by Frederick Holcomb	110
Elizabeth L., of Middlebury, m. Norton **KELSEY**, of North Granby, Nov. 16, 1848, by Rev. G. P. Prudden	66
Elizabeth L., of Middlebury, m. Norton **KELSEY**, of North Granby, Nov. 16, 1848, by Geo[rge] P. Prudden	137
Fanny Jane, of Middlebury, m. Geo[rge] **WAKELEE**, of Southbury, Nov. 28, 1850, by Rev. W[illia]m H. Bangs	66
Fanny Jane, of Middlebury, m. George **WAKELEE**, of Southbury, Nov. 28, 1850, by W[illiam] H. Bangs	139
Larmon L., of New Haven, m. Mary **McGEE**, of Middlebury, Sept. 16, 1849, by W[illia]m H. Bangs	139
Mary, m. Betsey **RICHARDSON**, Jan. 11, 1827, by Rev. Mark Mead (Both female names in Arnold Copy)	114
Mary Ann, m. Abraham **OSBORN**, Dec. 6, 1831, by Rev. Chauncey Prindle	121
Matilda H., of Naugatuck, m. Lewis O. **CAIN**, of Bethany, Jan. 15, 1852, by Rev. William Gay	148
Ruth A., of Middlebury, m. Aaron **LEWIS**, of Southbury, Apr. 9, 1843, by Philip L. Hoyt	131
Sylvester P., [s.] Ebenezer, farmer, b. Mar. 1, 1848	55
Thomas A., m. Nancy **BRADLEY**, b. of Middlebury, Sept. 27, 1840, by George L. Fuller	129

MONROE VITAL RECORDS
1823 – 1854

This volume contains a list alphabetically arranged of all the vital records of the town of Monroe from its incorporation to about 1854. The entire record of the town prior to 1854 is found in one volume. This list was taken from a set of cards based on a copy of the Monroe Vital Records made in 1917 by James N. Arnold, of Providence, R.I. The Arnold Copy, now in the possession of the Connecticut State Library, has not been compared with the original and doubtless errors exist. It is hoped that as errors or omissions are found notes will be entered in this volume and on the cards which are included in the General Index of Connecticut Vital Records also in the possession of the Connecticut State Library.

Hartford, Conn., May, 1926

	Page
ADAMS, Mary E., of Monroe, m. John C. SMITH, of New Milford, this day, [June 8, 1843], by Rodney Rossiter	86
ATWATER, Lucius, Rev. of Danbury, m. Mrs. Hannah S. BEARDSLEY, of Monroe, Sept. 17, 1850, by Rev. Levi H. Wakeman	99
BABBITT, Julia Ann, of Monroe, m. John Dimond ZIMMERMAN, of Fairfield, Nov. 28, 1833, by Daniel Jones	69
BAKER, Maria, of Monroe, m. Lyman WATERS, of Huntington, this day, [Sept. 8, 1840], by Rodney Rossiter	81
BALDWIN, Alonzo, of Derby, m. Rebecca R. LEWIS, of Monroe, this day, [Aug. 7, 1842], by Rodney Rossiter	84
Jane, of Huntington, m. Russell L. HUBBELL, of Monroe, this day, [June 1, 1851], by Ephraim Leach, J.P.	101
Sarah Jane, m. John Holbrook CHATFIELD, b. of Oxford, Oct. 31, 1847, by Rev. John Hobert Betts	94
BARLOW, Francis B., of Brookfield, m. Tressa Ann PULFORD, of Newtown, Sept. 23, 1829, by Rev. John Lovejoy	62
BEACH, Amelia, of Monroe, m. William SEYMOUR, of Watertown, this day [Sept. 26, 1842], by Rodney Rossiter	85
Charles, of Trumbull, m. Elizabeth E. BEARDSLEE, of Monroe, this day, [Oct. 21, 1829], by Rodney Rossiter	62
Cornelia, of Monroe, m. Edward HILL, of Weston, this day, [Mar. 16, 1836], by Rodney Rossiter	72
David, m. Hepsa FRENCH, b. of Monroe, Nov. 19, 1831, by Daniel Jones	66
William, m. Sarah CURTISS, b. of Monroe, June 20, 1825, by Rev. Menzies Raynor	54

BARBOUR COLLECTION

Page

BEACH (cont.)
William, Jr., m. Lucy Ann **NICHOLS**, this day [Mar. 5, 1843], by
Rodney Rossiter — 86
BEARD, James, of Huntington, m. Phebe **BEARDSLEE**, of Monroe,
Sept. 24, 1826, by Rev. Menzies Raynor — 57
Simeon, m. Anna **HUBBELL**, Dec. 5, 1827, by William H. Lewis — 59
BEARDSLEY, BEARDSLEE, Ann, m. Edwin C. **HURD**, Jan. 6, 1853
[sic], by Rev. George L. Foote [Probably 1850] — 97
Ann Jennett, of New Milford, m. George **LYON**, of Trumbull, Oct.
30, 1831, by Rev. Charles Sherman — 65
Christie Ann, of Monroe, m. Cyrannus **CURTISS**, of New Town,
this day, [May 16, 1838], by Rev. W[illia]m Denison — 75
Eli D., of Sherman, m. Caroline A. **BLACKMAN**, of Huntington,
this day, [July 2, 1838], by Rodney Rossiter — 76
Elizabeth E., of Monroe, m. Charles **BEACH**, of Trumbull, this day,
[Oct. 21, 1829], by Rodney Rossiter — 62
Frances Eliza, d. Ezra & Eliza, m. Orville Burton **SHERWOOD**,
Sept. 10, 1848, by Rev. John Herbert Betts — 95
Hannah S., Mrs. of Monroe, m. Rev. Lucius **ATWATER**, of
Danbury, Sept. 17, 1850, by Rev. Levi H. Wakeman — 99
Harriet, m. Starr **SHERMAN**, this day [Oct. 1, 1840], by Rodney
Rossiter — 81
Henry C., M.D., m. Harriet **HAWLEY**, b. of Monroe, Apr. 25, 1833,
by Daniel Jones — 68
James Smith, m. Rebecca **NICHOLS**, June 18, 1834, by Rev.
Nathan Wildman — 70
John G., m. Mary **NICHOLS**, b. of Monroe, this day [May 2, 1836],
by Rev. William Denison — 73
Joseph D., m. Amelia A. **COGSWELL**, b. of Monroe, June 12,
1842, by Rev. John H. Waterbury — 84
Malissa, of Monroe, m. Hiram **OWEN**, of Kalamazoo, Mich., Oct. 6,
1836, by Rev. James Kent — 73
Maryette, of Monroe, m. William A. **JUDSON**, of Fairfield, this day
[Feb. 21, 1836], by Rodney Rossiter — 72
Nancy, of Monroe, m. Abraham A. **DARLING**, of Reading, Mar. 10,
1830, by Daniel Jones — 63
Phebe, of Monroe, m. James **BEARD**, of Huntington, Sept. 24,
1826, by Rev. Menzies Raynor — 57
Polly Betsey, of Monroe, m. Nelson **SHERMAN**, of Trumbull, Aug.
14, 1823, by Rev. Menzies Raynor — 50
Rufus, m. Betsey A. **NICHOLS**, b. of Monroe, June 17, 1849, by
Rev. E. E. Beardsley, of New Haven — 97
Sally, of Monroe, m. Eli **BLACKMAN**, of Huntington, Nov. 2,
1826, by Rev. Menzies Raynor — 57
Sarah Garrett, of Monroe, m. George **BENEDICT**, of Norwalk, Oct.
12, 1828, by Daniel Jones — 60
Sylvia, of Monroe, m. Lucius B. **BURROUGHS**, of Trumbull, this
day [May 27, 1832], by Rodney Rossiter — 67
William, of Bridgeport, m. Nancy Janette **NICHOLS**, of Monroe,
this day, [Jan. 9, 1837], by Rev. David G. Tomlinson, of
Trumbull — 74
BEEBE, Polly J., of Oxford, m. Charles G. **TUCKER**, of Monroe, this
day [Mar. 27, 1834], by Rodney Rossiter — 69

MONROE VITAL RECORDS

	Page
BEERS, Ebenezer, of Newtown, m. Maria DIKEMAN, of Monroe, Nov. 3, 1850, by John Hoffman	100
Esther, m. Daniel H. BENNITT, b. of Monroe, Apr. 7, 1829, by Stephen Middlebrooks, J.P.	61
LeGrand G., of Trumbull, m. Hepsa A. EDWARDS, of Monroe, Apr. 7, 1845, by Rev. William White Bronson	89
Lewis, of Trumbull, m. Jane CABLE, of Monroe, Nov. 27, 1844, by Rev. George L. Fuller	89
Noah, of Weston, m. Mary OLMSTEAD, of Monroe, this day [Oct. 30, 1838], by Rev. W[illia]m Denison	77
Ruthanna, of Monroe, m. Daniel C. GORE, of Fishkill, N.Y., Jan. 30, 1831, by Daniel Jones	63
Simeon E., of Newtown, m. Ann Eliza McEWEN, of Monroe, this day, [Sept. 5, 1831], by Rodney Rossiter	65
BELDEN, David P., m. Emeline JANE, Feb. 1, 1847, by Rev. George L. Fuller	93
Mary Ann, of Monroe, m. Reuben MILLER, of Bridgeport, Aug. 28, 1836, by Rev. James Kent	73
Sally, of Monroe, m. Timothy MILLER, of Bridgeport, this day, [Apr. 17, 1836], by Rodney Rossiter	72
BENEDICT, George, of Norwalk, m. Sarah Garrett BEARDSLEE, of Monroe, Oct. 12, 1828, by Daniel Jones	60
Luke, m. Mary PORTER, b. of Monroe, Jan. 26, 1844, by Rev. George L. Fuller	89
Ralph, of Monroe, m. Phebe A. CORNING, of Monroe, Oct. 1, 1846, by Rev. Samuel W. Smith, Int. Pub.	93
BENNETT, BENNITT, Charles L., m. Elizabeth Ann HURD, this day [Nov. 14, 1839], by Rodney Rossiter	79
Daniel H., m. Esther BEERS, b. of Monroe, Apr. 7, 1829, by Stephen Middlebrooks, J.P.	61
Eli G., m. Minerva SHERMAN, this day [Feb. 10, 1850], by Rev. R. D. Gardner	98
Elizabeth, m. Wells W. LEWIS, this day [Dec. 2, 1849], by Rev. R. D. Gardner	98
Harry, of Trumbull, m. Laura HUBBELL, this day [Apr. 15, 1844], by Rev. R. D. Gardner	88
James H., m. Sylvia M. HURD, b. of Monroe, Oct. 14, 1849, by Rev. James Mallery, of Stepney	98
Judson, m. Jenette JUDSON, this day [June 28, 1840], by Rodney Rossiter	80
Smith, of Monroe, m. Susan SNOW, of Ashford, Oct. 9, 1836, by Rev. David Bennett	74
William, of Newtown, m. Anna NICHOLS, of Monroe, Mar. 12, 1826, by Rev. David Bennett	55
BETTS, John H., Rev., of New Hartford, m. Mary BOTSFORD, of Monroe, Oct. [ ], 1850, by John Hoffman	100
BEVANS, BEAVENS, Eliza, m. Mortimer Delville HAWLEY, b. of Monroe, Apr. 22, 1827, by David Hawley, J.P.	58
Minerva S., of Trumbull, m. James H. LINNE, of Monroe, this day [Feb. 7, 1847], by Rev. R. D. Gardner	93
BIGELOW, Benjamin M., of Reading, m. Mary S. PRINDLE, of Monroe, Oct. 3, 1853, by Rev. Alva Gregory	103

BARBOUR COLLECTION

	Page
BISCO, Julia, of New Town, m. Burton HAWLEY, of Monroe, Aug. 6, 1834, by Rev. Nathan Wildman	70
BISHOP, Francis G., of New York, m. Mrs. Phebe M. CURLY, of Monroe, June 17, 1849, by Rev. Nathan C. Lewis	98
BLACKMAN, [see also BLAKEMAN], Caroline A., of Huntington, m. Eli D. BEARDSLEE, of Sherman, this day [July 2, 1838], by Rodney Rossiter	76
Eli, of Huntington, m. Sally BEARDSLEE, of Monroe, Nov. 2, 1826, by Rev. Menzies Raynor	57
Isaac, of New Town, m. Sarah OLMSTED, of Weston, this day [Nov. 24, 1833], by Rodney Rossiter	68
Lawrence Belden, of Huntington, m. Nancy HAWLEY, of Monroe, this day, [Mar. 31, 1839], by Rodney Rossiter	78
Sarah A., m. Charles EDWARDS, b. of Monroe, Oct. 21, 1849, by Rev. N. C. Lewis	97
Stephen R., of Danbury, m. Cornelia THOMPSON, of Monroe, Dec. 8, 1850, by Ephraim Leach, J.P.	101
BLAKEMAN, [see also BLACKMAN], Betsey, of Monroe, m. Daniel LYON, of Weston, Apr. 5, 1829, by Stephen Middlebrook, J.P.	61
Betsey, m. Asa HAYES, b. of Monroe, this day, [Sept. 20, 1843], by Rev. William Denison	87
Jane, of Monroe, m. Eugene BOTSFORD, of New Town, Oct. 15, 1854, by Rev. Alva Gregory	103
BLISS, Horace N., of Bozrah, m. Henrietta TUCKER, of Monroe, Jan. 7, 1849, by Judson G. Lyman	95
BOOTH, Ann Jennette, of Monroe, m. Truman JACKSON, of Hamden, this day, [Sept. 9, 1837], by Rodney Rossiter	75
Ann T., of Monroe, m. Horace CABLE, of Oxford, this day, [June 18, 1845], by Rev. R. D. Gardner	90
Anna, of Monroe, m. Daniel MOREHOUSE, of New Town, this day [Mar. 24, 1833], by Truman Peck, J.P.	67
Beach, m. Phebe LEWIS, b. of Monroe, Aug. 21, 1825, by Israel A. Beardslee, J.P.	55
David L., of Huntington, m. Julia M. LEWIS, of Monroe, Oct. 16, 1850, by Rev. Nathaniel C. Lewis	99
Edgar, m. Ann Eliza RUSSELL, b. of Huntington, Nov. 24, 1850, in East Village Church, by Rev. N. C. Lewis	100
Elisha, m. Susan JUDSON, this day [Oct. 11, 1846], by Rev. R. D. Gardner	92
Elmer, of Newtown, m. Ann T. CURTISS, of Monroe, July 1, 1832, by Daniel Jones	67
Margaret Ann, m. William C. PRUDEN, of Orange, this day [July 4, 1841], by Rodney Rossiter	82
Maria, see Maria BRADLEY	88
Mariah, m. David B. LANE, this day [July 28, 1839], by Rodney Rossiter	78
Mary, m. Ambrose WHEELER, this day [July 6, 1834], by Rodney Rossiter	70
Orvil, m. Jenett TOMLINSON, b. of Monroe, Apr. 9, 1831, by Rev. Horace Bartlett	64
Ruth Ann Hubbell, m. Mark HUBBELL, June 10, 1850, by Rev. Levi H. Wakeman	98

	Page
BOOTH (cont.)	
Sally, m. W[illia]m **TURNEY**, Dec. 3, 1823, by Chauncey G. Lee. Int. Pub. at Brookfield	50
Seline, of Stratford, m. Eliza **SHELTON**, of Monroe, this day [Sept. 3, 1834], by Rodney Rossiter	70
William, m. Pamelia **SHERWOOD**, b. of Monroe, Dec. 25, [1823], by Rev. Menzies Raynor	50
BOSTWICK, Betsey, m. Roswell B. **CURTISS**, this day [Feb. 21, 1836], by Rodney Rossiter	72
Jane M., m. Charles E. **HAWLEY**, this day [Mar. 4, 1844], by Rodney Rossiter	87
Mary Ann, of Monroe, m. Jothan **SHERMAN**, of New Town, this day [Feb. 11, 1834], by Rodney Rossiter	69
Polly A., of Monroe, m. Samuel **LYON**, of Trumbull, Oct. 11, 1846, by Rev. W[illia]m Denison	92
BOTSFORD, Elizabeth, m. William **THAIR**, b. of Seymour, Jan. 18, 1852, by Rev. H. H. Morgan	102
Elizabeth A., of Monroe, m. Rufus W. **WATSON**, of Coxsackie, N.Y., this day [Nov. 13, 1838], by Rodney Rossiter	77
Eugene, of New Town, m. Jane **BLAKEMAN**, of Monroe, Oct. 15, 1854, by Rev. Alva Gregory	103
Henry, of Newtown, m. Rebecca **JOHNSON**, of Monroe, Oct. 18, 1847, by Rev. S. W. Smith, Int. Pub.	93
Mary, of Monroe, m. Rev. John H. **BETTS**, of New Hartford, Oct. [ ], 1850, by John Hoffman	100
Mary A., of Newtown, m. John **CURTISS**, of Monroe, Nov. 16, 1847, by Rev. John Hobert Betts	94
BRADLEY, Henry, of New Town, m. Sylvina **HAWLEY**, of Monroe, this day [Aug. 20, 1837], by Rodney Rossiter	74
Maria, d. Eden Booth, of Monroe, m. Wales **WHEELER**, of Huntington, Mar. 8, 1844, by Rodney Rossiter	88
Polly, of Newtown, m. Charles L. **DAYTON**, of Monroe, Dec. 9, 1827, by Rev. Amos Bassett	59
BRISCO, [see also **BRISTO**], Amanda, m. Peter W. **VREDENBURGH**, b. of Monroe, July 15, 1850, by Rev. S. W. Smith, Int. Pub.	99
James, of Newtown, m. Harriet **CLARK**, of Monroe, Nov. 23, 1828, by Ashbel Steele, of Trumbull	60
John, of New Town, m. Amarillus **MALLETT**, of Monroe, Mar. 16, 1836, by Levi Edwards, J.P.	73
BRISTO, [see also **BRISCO**], Catharine, m. James P. **BURTON**, this day [Dec. 3, 1848], by Rev. L. D. Nickerson, of Stepney	95
BRYAN, Betsey A., of Monroe, m. William **BURWELL**, of New Jersey, this day, [Nov. 7, 1841], by Rodney Rossiter	82
BULKLEY, Nancy L., of Monroe, m. John **DEACON**, of Waterbury, this day [Dec. 20, 1848], by Rev. R. D. Gardner	95
BUNDY, Benjamin, m. Thurzy **PRAY**, June 13, 1825, by Samuel Wheeler, J.P. Int. Pub.	53
BURR, Antha, of Monroe, m. Edwin **DAVIS**, of Bridgeport, Apr. 14, 1824, by Menzies Raynor	50
Benjamin, m. Ruamy **HUBBLE**, b. of Monroe, this day [Mar. 19, 1840], by Rev. William Denison	79
Rosilla A., m. Charles **STAPLES**, this day [Nov. 29, 1838], by Rodney Rossiter	77

	Page
BURRITT, Charity, m. Benjamin W. **LANPHEAR**, this day [June 8, 1840], by Rodney Rossiter	80
Charlotte, m. John **CRAIN**, b. of Newtown, Oct. 28, 1827, by Rev. Menzies Raynor	59
George, m. Susan R. **HUBBELL**, b. of Monroe, this day [Nov. 9, 1842], by Rev. William Denison	86
Nancy, m. George **TYRRELL**, this day [Dec. 31, 1835], by Rodney Rossiter	71
BURROUGHS, Lucius B., of Trumbull, m. Sylvia **BEARDSLEE**, of Monroe, this day, [May 27, 1832], by Rodney Rossiter	67
BURT, Elisha B., of Trumbull, m. Nancy **SHERMAN**, of Monroe, this day [Sept. 26, 1830], by Rodney Rossiter	63
BURTON, James P., m. Catharine **BRISTO**, of Monroe, this day [Dec. 3, 1848], by Rev. L. D. Nickerson, of Stepney	95
BURWELL, William, of New Jersey, m. Betsey A. **BRYAN**, of Monroe, this day, [Nov. 7, 1841], by Rodney Rossiter	82
CABLE, Horace, of Oxford, m. Ann T. **BOOTH**, of Monroe, this day [June 18, 1845], by Rev. R. D. Gardner	90
Jane, of Monroe, m. Lewis **BEERS**, of Trumbull, Nov. 27, 1844, by Rev. George L. Fuller	89
CAIN, Charles, of Huntington, m. Harriet **COE**, of Monroe, Dec. 17, 1827, by Donald Judson, J.P.	59
CANN (?), Nancy, m. John B. **VOSE**, Nov. 4, 1839, by Asa Hays	79
CARGILL, Foster M., of New Town, m. Jane **RIKER**, of Monroe, this day, [Aug. 4, 1833], by Rodney Rossiter	68
Lucretia Caroline, m. Taylor **MORGAN**, of Danbury, this day [Dec. 2, 1844], by Rev. R. D. Gardner	89
Lucretia Caroline, m. Taylor **MORGAN**, of Danbury, this day [Dec. 2, 1844], by Rev. R. D. Gardner	91
CHAPMAN, Amelia, m. Alfred **TURNEY**, Jan. 29, 1824, by Cyrus H. Beardslee, J.P.	50
CHATFIELD, John Holbrook, m. Sarah Jane **BALDWIN**, b. of Oxford, Oct. 31, 1847, by Rev. John Hobert Betts	94
CLARK, CLARKE, Andrew, m. Eliza **PECK**, b. of Monroe, Feb. 11, 1829, by Daniel Jones	61
Ann Mariah, of Monroe, m. Russell **CLARKE**, of Mt. Vernon, O., this day, [Sept. 6, 1835], by Rodney Rossiter	71
Charles C., m. Augusta **THOMPSON**, this day [Nov. 27, 1844], by Rodney Rossiter	88
Eliza, of Monroe, m. Dr. Mortimer N. **SHELTON**, of Huntington, May 1, 1827, by Rev. Menzies Raynor	58
Emeline, m. Daniel **LEWIS**, b. of Monroe, last evening, [Dec. 11, 1825], by Chauncey G. Lee	56
Harriet, of Monroe, m. James **BRISCO**, of Newtown, Nov. 23, 1828, by Ashbel Steele, of Trumbull	60
Harriet Ann, of Monroe, m. Levi T. **SQUIER**, of Roxbury, this day [May 12, 1844], by Rodney Rossiter	88
Herman, m. Maria **CURTISS**, b. of Monroe, July 28, 1825, by Rev. Menzies Raynor	54
John, m. Lucy Ann **SHERWOOD**, this day [Apr. 17, 1834], by Rodney Rossiter	69
John, of Monroe, m. Mary **CURTISS**, of New Town, this day, [Oct. 23, 1836], by Rodney Rossiter	73

MONROE VITAL RECORDS 207

Page

CLARK, CLARKE (cont.)
John, m. Sarah M. **FRENCH**, this day [Oct. 17, 1842], by Rodney
Rossiter ... 85
Leman, m. Sally Malilda **SHERWOOD**, this day [Sept. 20, 1840],
by Rodney Rossiter ... 81
Lucy R., of Monroe, m. Edward H. **ROSE**, of Harrison, O., May 20,
1825, by C. G. Lee ... 53
Lidia, m. Nathan N. **WHEELER**, b. of Monroe, Sept. 7, 1828, by
Daniel Jones ... 60
Phelena, m. Julius **LEWIS**, this day [June 13, 1830], by Rodney
Rossiter ... 63
Russell, of Mt. Vernon, O., m. Ann Mariah **CLARKE**, of Monroe,
this day, [Sept. 6, 1835], by Rodney Rossiter ... 71
Susan Ann, of Huntington, m. Edwin **TOMLINSON**, of Monroe,
this day [Jan. 3, 1836], by Rodney Rossiter ... 71
William, of New Town, m. Elizabeth **LEWIS**, of Monroe, this day
[Dec. 31, 1838], by Rodney Rossiter ... 77
CLEMENT, Eliza, m. Harvey **ELLS**, b. of Milford, Aug. 5, 1827, by
Rev. Andrew Fowler, of Trumbull ... 58
COE, George M., of Danbury, m. Eliza **FRENCH**, of Monroe, this day
[Feb. 25, 1846], by Rodney Rossiter ... 92
Harriet, of Monroe, m. Charles **CAIN**, of Huntington, Dec. 18, 1827,
by Donald Judson, J.P. ... 59
COGSWELL, Amelia A., m. Joseph D. **BEARDSLEE**, b. of Monroe,
June 12, 1842, by Rev. John H. Waterbury ... 84
Sarah, of Monroe, m. Thomas **EATON**, of Mantivus, N.Y., this day
[June 12, 1842], by Rev. John H. Waterbury ... 84
COLEMAN, Esther, m. David **TAYLOR**, May 16, 1824, by Roswell
Hawkes ... 51
CONGO, Elijah, of Sherman, m. Hannah **MANN**, of Monroe, Dec. 26,
1824, by Isreal A. Beardslee, J.P. ... 52
Elijah, of Sherman, m. Hannah **MANN**, of Monroe, Feb. 17, 1825,
by Israel A. Beardslee, J.P. ... 53
CORNING, Charles, m. Caroline **HUBBELL**, b. of Monroe, this day
[Feb. 2, 1845], by Rev. William Denison ... 91
Phebe A., of Monroe, m. Ralph **BENEDICT**, of Monroe, Oct. 1,
1846, by Rev. Samuel W. Smith, Int. Pub. ... 93
CRAFTON, William M., m. Jane **WHEELER**, Nov. 15, [1835], by
Matthew Batchelor ... 71
CRAIN, John, m. Charlotte **BURRITT**, b. of Newtown, Oct. 28, 1827, by
Rev. Menzies Raynor ... 59
CROFOOT, Clarinda, of New Town, m. Seth W. **DREW**, of Reading,
this day [Dec. 24, 1836], by Rodney Rossiter ... 74
CURLY, Phebe M., Mrs., of Monroe, m. Francis G. **BISHOP**, of New
York, June 17, 1849, by Rev. Nathan C. Lewis ... 98
CURTISS, Ame E., of Monroe, m. Albert **WILCOXSON**, of Stratford,
Nov. 23, 1852, by J. W. Hoffman ... 102
Ami S., of Trumbull, m. Julia Ann **PECK**, of Monroe, Mar. 26,
1840, by Rev. J. Hitchcock, of Newtown ... 80
Ann T., of Monroe, m. Elmer **BOOTH**, of Newtown, July 1, 1832,
by Daniel Jones ... 67
Catharine M., m. Henry **PLUMB**, this day [   ], by Rev. R.
D. Gardner. Recorded Oct. 6, 1851. ... 101

CURTISS (cont.)

	Page
Charles, of Monroe, m. Rebecca **TURNEY**, of Trumbull, Jan. 13, 1828, by Rev. Amos Bassett	60
Charles W., of Trumbull, m. Rebecca **SHERMAN**, of Monroe, this day [Apr. 8, 1851], by Rev. R. D. Gardner	101
Charlotte, of Monroe, m. Daniel **HILL**, of Weston, this day [Sept. 28, 1831], by Rodney Rossiter	65
Cyrenus, of New Town, m. Christie Ann **BEARDSLEE**, of Monroe, this day, [May 16, 1838], by Rev. W[illia]m Denison	75
Dan C., of Brookfield, m. Frances A. **FRENCH**, of Monroe, this day [ ], by Rev. R. D. Gardner. Recorded Aug. 11, 1847	94
Eliza M., of Monroe, m. Stepney **SILLIMAN**, of Bridgeport, this day, [Feb. 25, 1850], by Rev. R. D. Gardner	98
Harriet, m. Willis **TURNEY**, this day [Jan. 7, 1830], by Rodney Rossiter	62
Henry T., m. Mary E. H. **WHEELER**, this day [Aug. 6, 1844], by Rev. R. D. Gardner	88
Hepsey, m. Nathaniel **SHERMAN**, Apr. 18, 1831, by Stephen Middlebrooks, J.P.	64
Jane, Mrs., m. Eli J. **PECK**, b. of Monroe, July 24, 1842, by Levi Edwards, J.P.	84
John, of Monroe, m. Mary A. **BOTSFORD**, of Newtown, Nov. 16, 1847, by Rev. John Hobert Betts	94
Judson, of Trumbull, m. Sylvia **EDWARDS**, of Monroe, this day [Feb. 26, 1835], by Rodney Rossiter	70
Lewis, m. Hannah E. **PECK**, b. of Monroe, Sept. 3, 1843, by George L. Fuller	87
Maria, m. Herman **CLARKE**, b. of Monroe, July 28, 1825, by Rev. Menzies Raynor	54
Mary, of New Town, m. John **CLARKE**, of Monroe, this day [Oct. 23, 1836], by Rodney Rossiter	73
Mary A., m. James W. **HAWLEY**, b. of Monroe, Nov. 24, 1833, by Rev. Nathan Wildman	69
Mary Ann, of Monroe, m. Luther C. **DARLING**, of Brookhaven, L.I., this day [Jan. 1, 1843], by Rodney Rossiter	85
Robert, of Monroe, m. Mrs. Clarissa **DAVIS**, of Sherman, July 26, 1838, by Levi Edwards, J.P.	76
Roswell B., m Betsey **BOSTWICK**, this day [Feb. 21, 1836], by Rodney Rossiter	72
Sarah, m. William **BEACH**, b. of Monroe, June 20, 1825, by Rev. Menzies Raynor	54
Susan, of Trumbull, m. Henry **LYON**, of Monroe, June 30, 1848, by Rev. Samuel W. Smith, Int. Pub.	96
W[illia]m Henry, m. Nancy Mariah **HAWLEY**, this day [Sept. 10, 1839], by Rodney Rossiter	79

DARLING

Abraham A., of Reading, m. Nancy **BEADSLEE**, of Monroe, Mar. 10, 1830, by Daniel Jones	63
Luther C., of Brookhaven, L.I., m. Mary Ann **CURTIS**, of Monroe, this day [Jan. 1, 1843], by Rodney Rossiter	85

DART

John, m. Lucy Ann **ROBERTS**, b. of Monroe, Nov. 24, 1831, by Daniel Jones	66

MONROE VITAL RECORDS

Page

DART (cont.)
Levi, of Huntington, m. Betsey Mariah **SHARP**, of Monroe, Aug.
23, 1829, by Elijah Middlebrooks, J.P. — 62
William, of Huntington, m. Molly B. **SHARP**, of Monroe, July 6,
1826, by Rev. Menzies Raynor — 56
DAVIS, Betsey, of Monroe, m. David W. **GILBERT**, of Weston, Nov. 8,
1837, by Levi Edwards, J.P. — 75
Clarissa, Mrs. of Sherman, m. Robert **CURTISS**, of Monroe, July
26, 1838, by Levi Edwards, J.P. — 76
Edwin, of Bridgeport, m. Antha **BURR**, of Monroe, Apr. 14, 1824,
by Menzies Raynor — 50
Lauina, of Monroe, m. Noah **LAKE**, of Sherman, Oct. 6, 1833, by
Truman Peck, J.P. — 68
Sarah C., m. Ebenezer **JOICE**, Dec. 2, 1838, by Rodney Rossiter — 77
Solomon, of North Canaan, m. Belinda **WOLSA**, of Monroe, Nov. 3,
1844, by Henry Lewis, J.P. — 89
Thankfull, of Monroe, m. George **LAKE**, of Sherman, June 12,
1838, by Levi Edwards, J.P. — 76
DAWES, Eliza, or Eliza Hurd, m. Isaac **LAKE**, b. of Monroe, July 4,
1825, by Samuel Wheeler, J.P. — 55
DAYTON, Charles L., of Monroe, m. Polly **BRADLEY**, of Newtown,
Dec. 9, 1827, by Rev. Amos Bassett — 59
Polly, m. Nehemiah **SELEY**, Oct. 18, 1841, by George P. Curtis, J.P. — 83
DEACON, John, of Waterbury, m. Nancy L. **BULKLEY**, of Monroe, this
day [Dec. 20, 1848], by Rev. R. D. Gardner — 95
DeFOND, Joseph W., of Newark, N.J., m. Ann Eliza **PAYNE**, of Monroe,
Apr. 22, 1849, by Rev. James Mallory, of Stepney — 97
DEMINGS, Charles, of Bridgeport, m. Roxey F. **ROBINS**, of Monroe,
Sept. 23, 1831, by Daniel Jones — 65
DICKERMAN, Burr, m. Flora **HINMAN**, Nov. 26, [1835], by Matthew
Batchelor — 71
DICKINSON, Charles, m. Harriet **FRANKLIN**, this day [Feb. 6, 1831],
by Rodney Rossiter — 64
DIKEMAN, Maria, of Monroe, m. Ebenezer **BEERS**, of Newtown, Nov.
3, 1850, by John Hoffman — 100
DODD, Frederick, m. Mary **JOICE**, b. of Monroe, Jan. 29, 1842, by
Henry Lewis, J.P. — 84
DOWNS, Jane, of Monroe, m. Nichols B. **HUBBELL**, of Huntington, this
day [Jan. 19, 1840], by Rodney Rossiter — 79
DREW, Charity Mariah, of Monroe, m. Nelson **TOMLINSON**, of
Huntington, Nov. 8, 1842, by Rev. John H. Waterbury — 85
Phebe Ann, of Monroe, m. Nathan Bennett **NICHOLS**, of
Huntington, this day [Dec. 25, 1841], by Rev William
Denison — 83
Seth W., of Reading, m. Clarinda **CROFOOT**, of New Town, this
day [Dec. 24, 1836], by Rodney Rossiter — 74
DUNNING, Elizabeth A., of Monroe, m. Eli Gilbert **JONES**, of
Huntington, Feb. 9, 1824, by Chauncy G. Lee — 50
DURAND, DURAN, Jenett, m. John **GILBERT**, this day [Feb. 6, 1834],
by Rodney Rossiter — 69
Lockwood, of Birmingham, m. Jennett **TUCKER**, of Monroe, this
day [Sept. 20, 1846], by Rodney Rossiter — 92

                                                                    Page
DURAND, DURAN (cont.)
  Polly, of Monroe, m. William **TAYLOR**, of Watertown, May 15,
    1845, by Rev. Stephen J. Stebbins   90
EATON, Thomas, of Mantivus, N.Y., m. Sarah **COGSWELL**, of
    Monroe, this day [June 12, 1842], by Rev. John H. Waterbury   84
EDWARDS, Agar, m. Fidelia **MILLEN** (?), b. of Monroe, this day [Jan.
    13, 1839], by Rev. Eli Brunson   78
  Charles, m. Sarah A. **BLACKMAN**, b. of Monroe, Oct. 21, 1849, by
    Rev. N. C. Lewis   97
  George T., m. Hannah **HEMMINGWAY**, b. of Monroe, July 14,
    1839, by Rev. Nathaniel Mead   78
  Hepsa A., of Monroe, m. LeGrand G. **BEERS**, of Trumbull, Apr. 7,
    1845, by Rev. William White Bronson   89
  Jane, m. William **PENFIELD**, b. of Fairfield, Nov. 3, 1830, by Rev.
    Horace Bartlett   64
  Sarah R., m. Burr S. **HUBBELL**, b. of Monroe, this day [Mar. 26,
    1839], by Rev. W[illia]m Denison   78
  Sylvia, of Monroe, m. Judson **CURTISS**, of Trumbull, this day [Feb.
    26, 1835], by Rodney Rossiter   70
ELLS, Harvey, m. Eliza **CLEMENT**, b. of Milford, Aug. 5, 1827, by
    Rev. Andrew Fowler, of Trumbull   58
FAIRCHILD, Harriet Catharine, of Monroe, m. John Blackman
    NICHOLS, of New Town, Sept. 12, 1847, by Rev. John
    Hobert Betts   94
  Sarah, of Monroe, m. Lazarus **GILBERT**, of Huntington, July 4,
    1852, by J. W. Hoffman   102
FAIRWEATHER, [see under **FAYERWEATHER**]
FARNAM, [see also **FARHAM**], Phebe Ann, of Newtown, m. Harvey
    LATTIN, of Monroe, this day [Jan. 22, 1832], by Rodney
    Rossiter   66
FARHAM, [see also **FARNAM**], Rebecca E., of New Town, m. Horace
    B. **LATTIN**, of Dover, N.Y., July 31, 1836, by Levi Edwards,
    J.P.   73
FAYERWEATHER, FAIRWEATHER, Ruth Ann, of Monroe, m.
    William **HAYS**, of Newtown, Nov. 8, 1826, by Rev. William
    Mitchell, of Newtown   57
  Susan, of Trumbull, m. Asa **HUBBELL**, of Monroe, Sept. 4, 1825,
    by Levi Edwards, J.P.   54
FENN, William, of Middlebury, m. Sally **JUDSON**, of Monroe, June 9,
    1824, by C. G. Lee   51
FERRISS, George, of Newtown, m. Abigail **RICHARDS**, of Monroe,
    May 5, 1829, by Daniel Jones   62
FINCH, Peter, of Monroe, m. Mary **SMITH**, of Newtown, Jan. 31, 1847,
    by Asa Hayes, J.P.   93
FOUNTAIN, John F., of Fairfield, m. Delia **GILBERT**, of Monroe, Mar.
    12, 1837, by Rodney Rossiter   74
FRANKLIN, Harriet, m. Charles **DICKINSON**, this day [Feb. 6, 1831],
    by Rodney Rossiter   64
FREEMAN, Joanna, m. Titus **FREEMAN**, b. of Fairfield, Aug. 29, 1824,
    by C. G. Lee   51
  Monson, of Monroe, m. Jane **MORRIS**, of Huntington, this day
    [Oct. 2, 1842], by Rodney Rossiter   85

	Page
FREEMAN (cont.)	
Titus, m. Joanna **FREEMAN**, b. of Fairfield, Aug. 29, 1824, by C. G. Lee	51
FRENCH, Alfred L., of Seymour, m. Mary B. **LANE**, of Monroe, June 1, 1851, by Rev. John Hoffman	101
Benjamin M., m. Julia **ROWELL**, b. of Monroe, Feb. 15, [1829], by Daniel Jones	61
Eliza, m. Lucius **PENFIELD**, b. of Monroe, Jan. 18, 1826, by Chauncey G. Lee	55
Eliza, of Monroe, m. George M. **COE**, of Danbury, this day [Feb. 25, 1846], by Rodney Rossiter	92
Frances A., of Monroe, m. Dan C. **CURTISS**, of Brookfield, this day, [ ], by Rev. R. D. Gardner. Recorded Aug. 11, 1847	94
Hepsa, m. David **BEACH**, b. of Monroe, Nov. 19, 1831, by Daniel Jones	66
Hoyt, m. Jennett **HEMINGWAY**, this day [Dec. 23, 1832], by Rodney Rossiter	67
Julia, of Monroe, m. Thompson **JUDSON**, of Stratford, this day [Apr. 12, 1840], by Rev. Abel Nichols, of Bridgewater, Conn.	80
Julia A., m. Henry E. **SEARS**, b. of Monroe, this day [Nov. 24, 1850], by Rev. W[illia]m Denison, of Humphreyville	100
Louisa, of New Town, m. Levi P. **PECK**, of Monroe, May 29, 1838, by Asa Hays	76
Sarah M., m. John **CLARKE**, this day [Oct. 17, 1842], by Rodney Rossiter	85
Sherman, of New York, m. Laury **TURNEY**, of Monroe, Aug. 3, 1828, by Levi Edwards, J.P.	60
Sterling, m. Mariah **HEMINGWAY**, this day [Nov. 28, 1832], by Rodney Rossiter	67
GERMAN, [see also **SHERMAN**], Susan, m. Charles **JOHNSON**, Mar. 28, 1849, by Rev. Lorenzo D. Nickerson, of Stepney	96
GIBSON, Roxany, m. Rant **PEAS**, Aug. 24, 1824, by Samuel Wheeler, J.P.	51
GILBERT, Alonzo, m. Abby **LYON**, Dec. 21, 1823, by Israel A. Beardslee, J.P.	50
David W., of Weston, m. Betsey **DAVIS**, of Monroe, Nov. 8, 1837, by Levi Edwards, J.P.	75
Delia, of Monroe, m. John F. **FOUNTAIN**, of Fairfield, Mar. 12, 1837, by Rodney Rossiter	74
John, m. Jenett **DURAND**, this day [Feb. 6, 1834], by Rodney Rossiter	69
Lazarus, of Huntington, m. Sarah **FAIRCHILD**, of Monroe, July 4, 1852, by J. W. Hoffman	102
Sally, m. Alonzo **ROWEL**, b. of Monroe, July 8, 1829, by Daniel Jones	62
Walter, m. Elizabeth **HAWLEY**, b. of Monroe, June 11, 1848, by Rev. Samuel W. Smith, Int. Pub.	96
Wanzer S., of Weston, m. Malinda **SOMERS**, of Weston, Aug. 29, 1841, by Rev. Stephen S. Stebbins	82
GLOVER, Andrew B., of Newtown, m. Sarah H. **WILCOXSON**, of Monroe, Jan. 26, 1825, at the house of the late John Wilcoxson, by Rev. Ebenezer Platt, of Darien	52

	Page
GOODSELL, Betsey, of Monroe, m. Nelson B. **PATTERSON**, of Easton, this day, [June 4, 1851], by Rev. R. D. Gardner	101
Jonathan, of New Town, m. Anna **PATTERSON**, of Monroe, Apr. 21, 1835, by Jacob Beers, J.P.	71
GOODYEAR, Jesse F., of Hamden, m. Nancy **LANE**, of Monroe, this day [Mar. 12, 1837], by Rev. Mr. Clarke	74
GORE, Daniel C., of Fishkill, N.Y., m. Ruthanna **BEERS**, of Monroe, Jan. 30, 1831, by Daniel Jones	63
GRAY, Beebe M., of Trumbull, m. Mary **SHERMAN**, of Monroe, May 28, 1826, by Rev. Menzies Raynor	56
HAIDERSTECK, Frederic, m. Martha **MATTHEWS**, b. foreigners, Mar. 10, 1850, by John Hoffman	99
HALL, Mariah, m. Minot **PECK**, Sept. 1, 1833, by Rev. Luther Mead	68
HARRIS, Sylvester, of Southbury, m. Mary Ann **JOHNSON**, of Oxford, June 4, 1843, at East Village, by Rev. George L. Fuller	87
HAWLEY, Burton, of Monroe, m. Julia **BISCO**, of New Town, Aug. 6, 1834, by Rev. Nathan Wildman	70
Charles E., m. Jane M. **BOSTWICK**, this day [Mar. 4, 1844], by Rodney Rossiter	87
Elizabeth, m. Walter **GILBERT**, b. of Monroe, June 11, 1848, by Rev. Samuel W. Smith, Int. Pub.	96
Harriet, m. Underhill **NELSON**, b. of Danbury, Nov. 13, 1831, by Rev. John Lovejoy	94
Harriet, m. Henry C. **BEARDSLEE**, M. D., b. of Monroe, Apr. 25, 1833, by Daniel Jones	68
James W., m. Mary A. **CURTISS**, b. of Monroe, Nov. 24, 1833, by Rev. Nathan Wildman	69
Jane E., of Monroe, m. Nathaniel **WHEELER**, of Huntington, this day [Mar. 12, 1843], by Rev. R. D. Gardner	86
Jane E., of Monroe, m. Aaron B. **MALLET**, of Trumbull, Nov. 1, 1843, by Rev. W[illia]m White Bronson, of Trumbull	88
John S., of Monroe, m. Amarillus **PECK**, of Brookfield, Sept. 21, 1828, by Levi Edwards, J.P.	60
Marette, of Monroe, m. Silvanus P. **SHELTON**, of Huntington, this day, [Jan. 4, 1843], by Rodney Rossiter	85
Maria, m. Wate **PLUMB**, b. of Monroe, this day [Apr. 26, 1843], by Rev. R. D. Gardner	86
Mortimer Delville, m. Eliza **BEAVENS**, b. of Monroe, Apr. 22, 1827, by David Hawley, J.P.	58
Nancy, of Monroe, m. Lawrence Belden **BLACKMAN**, of Huntington, this day [Mar. 31, 1839], by Rodney Rossiter	78
Nancy Mariah, m. W[illia]m Henry **CURTISS**, this day [Sept. 20, 1839], by Rodney Rossiter	79
Plumb, of Trumbull, m. Anthey **PAYNE**, of Monroe, Apr. 5, 1840, by Rev. Nathaniel Mead	80
Rozilla A., of Monroe, m. Lewis **TURNEY**, of Trumbull, June 1, 1824, by Rev. Beardslee Northrop, of Trumbull	51
Susan, m. Ebenezer M. **OSBORN**, this day [Nov. 24, 1839], by Rev. W[illia]m Denison	79
Sylvanus, of Monroe, m. Maria **SHERMAN**, of Monroe, Jan. 27, 1825, by Rev. Beardslee Northrop, of Trumbull	53
Sylvanus, of Monroe, m. Maria **SHERMAN**, of Monroe, Jan. 27, 1825, by Rev. Beardslee Northrop, of Trumbull	54

	Page
HAWLEY (cont.)	
Sylvina, of Monroe, m. Henry **BRADLEY**, of New Town, this day [Aug. 20, 1837], by Rodney Rossiter	74
HAYES, HAYS, Asa, m. Betsey **BLAKEMAN**, b. of Monroe, this day [Sept. 20, 1843], by Rev. William Denison	87
Hannah, m. John T. **LAMPHEAR**, Apr. 20, 1834, by Rev. Nathan Wildman	70
Nancy, of Monroe, m. David **TOMLINSON**, of Oxford, Sept. 24, 1825, by Samuel Wheeler, J.P.	55
Phebe E., of Monroe, m. George **KNAPP**, of Weston, this day [Mar. 2, 1845], by Rev. William Denison	90
William, of Newtown, m. Ruth Ann **FAIRWEATHER**, of Monroe, Nov. 8, 1826, by Rev. William Mitchell, of Newtown	57
HEMINGWAY, HEMMINGWAY, Hannah, m. George T. **EDWARDS**. b, of Monroe, July 14, 1839, by Rev. Nathaniel Mead	78
Jennett, m. Hoyt **FRENCH**, this day [Dec. 23, 1832], by Rodney Rossiter	67
Mariah, m. Sterling **FRENCH**, this day [Nov. 28, 1832], by Rodney Rossiter	67
-----, m,. Allen **PLATT**, b. of Monroe, Oct. 9, 1844, by Rev. Aaron S. Hill	90
HIGGINS, Lacey, of New Town, m. Priscilla **SILLAMAN**, of Monroe, this day, [Nov. 18, 1840], by Rodney Rossiter	81
HILL, Daniel, of Weston, m. Charlotte **CURTIS**, of Monroe, this day, Sept. 28, 1831, by Rodney Rossiter	65
Edward, of Weston, m. Cornelia **BEACH**, of Monroe, this day [Mar. 16, 1836], by Rodney Rossiter	72
HINMAN, Flora, m. Burr **DICKERMAN**, Nov. 26, [1835], by Matthew Batchelor	71
HOFFMAN, John W., Rev., m. Julia A. **WHEELER**, of Monroe, May 17, 1853, by Rev. W[illia]m White Bronson, of Danbury	102
HOIT, W[illia]m W., m. Lomena **NICHOLS**, b. of Monroe, this day [Nov. 15, 1846], by W[illia]m Denison	92
HUBBELL, HUBBLE, HUBBEL, Adaline, of Monroe, m. George **SHERWOOD**, of Readding, this day [Dec. 25, 1833], by Rodney Rossiter	68
Ann E., of Monroe, m. John H. **WHEELER**, of Danbury, Nov. 13, 1850, by Rev. Levi H. Wakeman	99
Anna, m. Simeon **BEARD**, Dec. 5, 1827, by William H. Lewis	59
Asa, of Monroe, m. Susan **FAYERWEATHER**, of Trumbull, Sept. 4, 1825, by Levi Edwards, J.P.	54
Burr S., m. Sarah R. **EDWARDS**, b. of Monroe, this day [Mar. 26, 1839], by Rev. W[illia]m Denison	78
Caroline, m. Alson **SEELEY**, Jr., this day [Nov. 26, 1835], by Rodney Rossiter	71
Caroline, m. Charles **CORNING**, b. of Monroe, this day [Feb. 2, 1845], by Rev. William Denison	91
Charles, m. Charlotte A. **SHELTON**, Sept. 10, 1848, by Judson G. Lyman	95
Elihu, m. Sally **LYON**, b. of Monroe, Apr. 3, 1825, by Levi Edwards, J.P.	52
Jane, m. William **TURNEY**, Dec. 16, 1825, by Rev. Ashbel Baldwin, of Trumbull	58

HUBBELL, HUBBLE, HUBBEL (cont.)

	Page
Laura, m. Harry **BENNETT**, of Trumbull, this day [Apr. 15, 1844], by Rev. R. D. Gardner	88
Margaret, of Monroe, m. Moses **SHERWOOD**, of Reading, this day, [Dec. 24, 1834], by Rodney Rossiter	70
Mark, m. Ruth Ann Hubbell **BOOTH**, June 10, 1850, by Rev. Levi H. Wakeman	98
Mary Jane, of Monroe, m. George R. **TURNEY**, of Trumbull, this day, [Apr. 12, 1846], by Rodney Rossiter	91
Mary Jane, of Huntington, m. Bennett **SHERMAN**, of Newtown, June 20, 1852, by Rev. H. H. Morgan	102
Nichols B., of Huntington, m. Jane **DOWNS**, of Monroe, this day, [Jan. 19, 1840], by Rodney Rossiter	79
Rebecca, of Monroe, m. Harvy **PLUMB**, of Plymouth, Oct. 25, 1826, by Levi Edwards, J.P.	57
Rebecca, of Monroe, m. Daniel **LYON**, of Reading, this day, [Aug. 24, 1831], by Rodney Rossiter	65
Ruamy, m. Benjamin **BURR**, b. of Monroe, this day [Mar. 19, 1840], by Rev. William Denison	79
Rufus, m. Eliza **TUCKER**, Sept. 11, 1842, by Rev. Geo[rge] L. Foote	84
Russell L., of Monroe, m. Jane **BALDWIN**, of Huntington, this day, [June 1, 1851], by Ephraim Leach, J.P.	101
Sheldon, m. Lydia **POPE**, Mar. 28, 1841, by Rev. David Bennett	81
Susan R., m. George **BURRITT**, b. of Monroe, this day [Nov. 9, 1842], by Rev. William Denison	86
William, m. Jane Eliza **WINTON**, Aug. 20, 1840, by Rev. David G. Tomlinson, of Trumbull	81

HUGGINS, James H., of New Haven, m. Mary A. **SUMMERS**, of Monroe, this day, [Nov. 14, 1850], by Rev. R. D. Gardner — 100

HURD, Charles G., of Monroe, m. Sarah A. **TOMLINSON**, of Huntington, Apr. 8, 1852, by Rev. J. W. Hoffman — 102

Edwin C., m. Ann **BEARDSLEE**, Jan. 6, 1853 [sic], by Rev. George L. Foote [Probably 1850]	97
Eliza, see Eliza Dawes	55
Elizabeth Ann, m. Charles L. **BENNETT**, this day [Nov. 14, 1839], by Rodney Rossiter	79
Ezra A., m. Mary E. **WELLS**, this day [Feb. 26, 1839], by Rodney Rossiter	78
Henry, of Huntington, m. Mrs. Melissa **OWEN**, of Monroe, Nov. 16, 1845, by Rev. Aaron S. Hill	91
Hiram, m. Jerusha **SHERMAN**, b. of Monroe, Nov. 15, 1829, by Daniel Jones	62
James R., of Monroe, m. Delia **LANE**, of Huntington, Oct. 31, 1841, by Rev. Stephen S. Stebbins	83
Julia Maria, m. Alden **SEELEY**, this day [June 11, 1843], by Rodney Rossiter	86
Nancy, of Monroe, m. Dwight **SHERMAN**, of Newtown, Oct. 25, 1847, by Rev. Samuel W. Smith, Int. Pub.	96
Sylvia M., m. James H. **BENNETT**, b. of Monroe, Oct. 14, 1849, by Rev. James Mallory, of Stepney	98

IVES, Joel, of Cheshire, m. Julia E. **MORS[E]**, of Middlebury, this day [Jan. 14, 1839], by Rodney Rossiter — 77

MONROE VITAL RECORDS 215

Page

IVES (cont.)
Joel, Jr., of Cheshire, m. Rebecca **MOSS**, of Middlebury, this day,
[Sept. 3, 1840], by Rodney Rossiter ... 81
JACKSON, Moses, of Oxford, m. Eliza **JUDSON**, of Monroe, Feb. 23,
1825, by Newton Tuttle. Witnesses Ezekiel Curtiss & Stiles
Judson ... 52
Truman, of Hamden, m. Ann Jennette **BOOTH**, of Monroe, this
day, [Sept. 9, 1837], by Rodney Rossiter ... 75
JANE, Emeline, m. David P. **BELDEN**, Feb. 1, 1847, by Rev. George L.
Fuller ... 93
JENKINS, Nathan, m. Aurilla **PATTERSON**, b. of Monroe, Oct. 14,
1827, by Rev. Menzies Raynor ... 59
JENNEY, Eliza, m. Lyman **SEARS**, this day [Jan. 2, 1848], by Rev. R. D.
Gardner ... 95
JENNINGS, Elvira, m. Frederick **SHERMAN**, this day [Feb. 19, 1843],
by Rodney Rossiter ... 85
JOHNSON, Albert, m. Mary L. **WHEELER**, b. of Monroe, Apr. 10,
1832, by Rev. Samuel Bassett ... 66
Charles, m. Susan **GERMAN**, Mar. 28, 1849, by Rev. Lorenzo D.
Nickerson, of Stepney ... 96
Delia, m. George **MOREHOUSE**, b. of Monroe, Jan. 17, 1833, by
Rev. Stephen Martindale ... 67
Harry, of White Plains, N.Y., m. Nancy **PETTS**, of Monroe,
(colored), Oct. 14, 1827, by Rev. Menzies Raynor ... 59
Mary Ann, of Oxford, m. Sylvester **HARRIS**, of Southbury, June 4,
1843, at East Village, by Rev. George L. Fuller ... 87
Mary Ann, m. Patrick **LYNCH**, b. of Monroe, Sept. 28, 1853, by
Rev. Alva Gregory ... 103
Rebecca, of Monroe, m. Henry **BOTSFORD**, of Newtown, Oct. 18,
1847, by Rev. S. W. Smith, Int. Pub. ... 93
Sylvia, m. J. Botsford **PORTER**, b. of Monroe, Oct. 19, 1847, by
Rev. Samuel W. Smith, Int. Pub. ... 96
JOICE, Ebenezer, m. Sarah C. **DAVIS**, Dec. 2, 1838, by Rodney Rossiter ... 77
Mary, m. Frederick **DODD**, b. of Monroe, Jan. 29, 1842, by Henry
Lewis, J.P. ... 84
Sarah, m. Phineas **LOBDELL**, this day [Aug. 4, 1845], by Rev. B.
D. Gardner ... 90
JONES, Daniel, Rev., of Monroe, m. Eliza Ann **LOCKWOOD**, of York
Town, N.Y., Mar. 28, 1834, by Rev. James Kent, of Trumbull ... 70
Eli Gilbert, of Huntington, m. Elizabeth A. **DUNNING**, of Monroe,
Feb. 9, 1824, by Chauncey G. Lee ... 50
JONI (?), Sarah S., of Huntington, m. George W. **ROOT**, of Oxford, Sept.
3, 1827, by Rev. Menzies Raynor ... 58
JORDAN, Lewis, of New Town, m. Jane **TOMLINSON**, of Oxford, this
day, [Oct. 18, 1838], by Rodney Rossiter ... 77
JUDD, Charles S., of Bethel, m. Cornelia **JUDSON**, of Monroe, this day,
[ ], by Rev. R. D. Gardner. Recorded Dec. 4, 1850 ... 100
JUDSON, Cornelia, of Monroe, m. Charles S. **JUDD**, of Bethel, this day,
[ ], by Rev. R. D. Gardner. Recorded Dec. 4, 1850 ... 100
Eliza, of Monroe, m. Moses **JACKSON**, of Oxford, Feb. 23, 1825,
by Newton Tuttle. Witnesses Ezekiel Curtiss & Stiles Judson ... 52
James, m. Charity **PANE**, Apr. 16, 1826, by Israel A. Beardslee, J.P. ... 55

	Page
JUDSON (cont.)	
Jenette, m. Judson **BENNETT**, this day [June 28, 1840], by Rodney Rossiter	80
John E., of Monroe, m. Pamela **STURGES**, of Wilton, this day [Dec. 27, 1846], by Rev. R. D. Gardner	93
Sally, of Monroe, m. William **FENN**, of Middlebury, June 9, 1824, by C. G. Lee	51
Sally, of Monroe, m. Rilander **NICHOLS**, of Trumbull, Jan. 12, 1825, by Chauncey G. Lee	52
Susan, m. Elisha **BOOTH**, this day [Oct. 11, 1846], by Rev. R. D. Gardner	92
Thompson, of Stratford, m. Julia **FRENCH**, of Monroe, this day, [Apr. 12, 1840], by Rev. Abel Nichols, of Bridgewater, Conn.	80
William A., of Fairfield, m. Maryette **BEARDSLEE**, of Monroe, this day, [Feb. 21, 1836], by Rodney Rossiter	72
KNAPP, George, of Weston, m. Phebe E. **HAYES**, of Monroe, this day, [Mar. 2, 1845], by Rev. William Denison	90
LAKE, George, of Sherman, m. Thankfull **DAVIS**, of Monroe, June 12, 1838, by Levi Edwards, J.P.	76
Isaac, m. Eliza **DAWES**, or Eliza **HURD**, b. of Monroe, July 4, 1825, by Samuel Wheeler, J.P.	55
Noah, of Sherman, m. Lauina **DAVIS**, of Monroe, Oct. 6, 1833, by Truman Peck, J.P.	68
LAM, Esther, of Monroe, m. Joseph **WILLCOX**, of Newtown, Mar. 30, 1825, by Rev. Menzies Raynor	53
LAMBERSON, Amy, of Monroe, m. Edmond **LEAVENWORTH**, of Huntington, Oct. 26, [1823], by Rev. Menzies Raynor	50
LAMPHEAR, LANPHEAR, Benjamin W., m. Charity **BURRITT**, this day [June 8, 1840], by Rodney Rossiter	80
Hannah, m. Agar **NICHOLS**, b. of Monroe, Sept. 3, 1831, by Jacob Beers, J.P.	66
John T., m. Hannah **HAYES**, Apr. 20, 1834, by Rev. Nathan Wildman	70
Sylvia, of Easton, m. John **SEARS**, of Monroe, May 27, 1849, by Rev. James Mallory, of Stepney	97
LAMPKIN, Louisa, of Monroe, m. John **POWELL**, Jr., of Huntington, this day, [Apr. 16, 1834], by Rodney Rossiter	69
LANE, Curtis, m. Mary Ann **LEWIS**, b. of Huntington, Sept. 11, 1825, by Rev. Julius Field	53
David B., m. Mariah **BOOTH**, this day [July 28, 1839], by Rodney Rossiter	78
Delia, of Huntington, m. James R. **HURD**, of Monroe, Oct. 31, 1841, by Rev. Stephen S. Stebbins	83
Esther Cornelia, of Monroe, m. Joseph **WILLCOXSON**, of Newtown, Mar. 30, 1825, by Rev .Menzies Raynor	54
Laura, m. Chauncy **WHEELER**, b. of Monroe, Oct. 16, 1825, by Donald Judson, J.P.	54
Mary B., of Monroe, m. Alfred L. **FRENCH**, of Seymour, June 1, 1851, by Rev. John Hoffman	101
Nancy, of Monroe, m. Jesse F. **GOODYEAR**, of Hamden, this day, [Mar. 12, 1837], by Rev. Mr. Clarke	74
LARABEE*, Sidney R., m. Lydia A. **WAKELEY**, Apr. 30, 1854, by Rev. Alva Gregory *(Written "**SABAREE**")	103

	Page
LATTIN, Harvey, of Monroe, m. Phebe Ann **FARNAM**, of Newtown, this day, [Jan. 22, 1832], by Rodney Rossiter	66
Horace B., of Dover, N.Y., m. Rebecca E. **FARNAM**, of New Town, July 31, 1836, by Levi Edwards, J.P.	73
Lyman, of New Town, m. Lovisa **OLMSTED**, of Monroe, this day, [Jan. 18, 1836], by Rev. William Denison	72
LEACH, David K., [s. Ephraim & Sarah], b. Mar. 10, 1837	10
Isaac K., [s. Ephraim & Sarah], b. Jan. 21, 1839	10
Levi E., [s. Ephraim & Sarah], b. Oct. 20, 1843	10
LEAVENWORTH, Edmond, of Huntington, m. Amy **LAMBERSON**, of Monroe, Oct. 26, [1823], by Rev. Menzies Raynor	50
Eli, of Monroe, m. Sarah A. **LORD**, of Weston, Nov. 24, 1833, by Rev. Nathan Wildman	69
Lorenzo W., of New Milford, m. Sarah Eliza **TYRRELL**, of Monroe, Jan. 18, 1843, by Rev. David G. Tomlinson, of Trumbull	86
Mark, m. Emeline **PECK**, this day [July 10, 1831], by Rodney Rossiter	64
Sarah M., of Monroe, m. Samuel **WAKELEE**, of Easton, this day, [Sept. 10, 1845], by Rev. William Denison	91
LEWIS, Charles, of Trumbull, m. Julia A. **OLMSTEAD**, of Monroe, this day, [Oct. 24, 1843], by Rev. W[illia]m Denison, of Weston	87
Daniel, m. Emeline **CLARKE**, b. of Monroe, last evening, [Dec. 11, 1825], by Chauncey G. Lee	56
Elizabeth, of Monroe, m. William **CLARKE**, of New Town, this day, [Dec. 31, 1838], by Rodney Rossiter	77
Julia M., of Monroe, m. David L. **BOOTH**, of Huntington, Oct. 16, 1850, by Rev. Nathaniel C. Lewis	99
Julius, m. Phelena **CLARK**, this day [June 13, 1830], by Rodney Rossiter	63
Mary Ann, m. Curtis **LANE**, b. of Huntington, Sept. 11, 1825, by Rev. Julius Field	53
Mary E., of Monroe, m. David **PIERCE**, of Roxbury, Dec. 20, 1843, by Rev. G. L. Fuller	87
Phebe, m. Beach **BOOTH**, b. of Monroe, Aug. 21, 1825, by Israel A. Beardslee, J.P.	55
Rebecca R., of Monroe, m. Alonzo **BALDWIN**, of Derby, this day, [Aug. 7, 1842], by Rodney Rossiter	84
Silas C., of Weston, m. Eliza **WAKELEY**, of Monroe, Sept. 12, 1841, by Rev. George Waterbury	82
Sylvia C., of Monroe, m. Abraham H. **YOUNG**, of Bridgeport, this day, [May 12, 1833], by Rodney Rossiter	68
Wells W., m. Elizabeth **BENNETT**, this day [Dec. 2, 1849], by Rev. R. D. Gardner	98
LINNE (?), James H., of Monroe, m. Minerva S. **BEVANS**, of Trumbull, this day, [Feb. 7, 1847], by Rev. R. D. Gardner	93
LOBDELL, Phineas, m. Sarah **JOICE**, this day [Aug. 4, 1845], by Rev. R. D. Gardner	90
LOCKWOOD, Eliza Ann, of York Town, N.Y., m. Daniel **JONES** (Rev.), of Monroe, Mar. 28, 1834, by Rev. James Kent, of Trumbull	70
LORD, Sarah A., of Weston, m. Eli **LEAVENWORTH**, of Monroe, Nov. 24, 1833, by Rev. Nathan Wildman	69

BARBOUR COLLECTION

	Page
LUM (?), Polly J., m. Zalmon S. **PECK**, of New Town, this day [Apr. 7, 1833], by Rodney Rossiter	67
LUTHER, Granville, m. Jane E. **SEERS**, this day [Nov. 22, 1831], by Rodney Rossiter	66
LYNCH, Patrick m. Mary Ann **JOHNSON**, b. of Monroe, Sept. 28, 1853, by Rev. Alva Gregory	103
LYON, Abby, m. Alonzo **GILBERT**, Dec. 21, 1823, by Israel A. Beardslee, J.P.	50
Daniel, of Weston, m. Betsey **BLAKEMAN**, of Monroe, Apr. 5, 1829, by Stephen Middlebrook, J.P.	61
Daniel, of Reading, m. Rebecca **HUBBELL**, of Monroe, this day [Aug. 24, 1831], by Rodney Rossiter	65
George, of Trumbull, m. Ann Jenett **BEARDSLEE**, of New Milford, Oct. 30, 1831, by Rev. Charles Sherman	65
Henry, of Monroe, m. Susan **CURTISS**, of Trumbull, June 30, 1848, by Rev. Samuel W. Smith, Int. Pub.	96
Sally, m. Elihu **HUBBELL**, b. of Monroe, Apr. 3, 1825, by Levi Edwards, J.P.	52
Samuel, of Trumbull, m. Polly A. **BOSTWICK**, of Monroe, Oct. 11, 1846, by Rev. W[illia]m Denison	92
McEWEN, Ann Eliza, of Monroe, m. Simeon N. **BEERS**, of Newtown, this day, [Sept. 5, 1831], by Rodney Rossiter	65
Charles, m. Sarah **SUMMERS**, this day [Dec. 1, 1841], by Rev. R. D. Gardner	83
MALLETT, MALLET, Aaron, of Trumbull, m. Lydia A. **SHERMAN**, of Monroe, Dec. 22, 1851, by Rev. J. G. Downing, of Trumbull	102
Aaron B., of Trumbull, m. Jane E. **HAWLEY**, of Monroe, Nov. 1, 1843, by Rev. W[illia]m White Bronson, of Trumbull	88
Abel, m. Amarillus **TOWSEY**, b. of Monroe, Jan. 17, 1829, by Stephen Middlebrook, J.P.	61
Amarillus, of Monroe, m. John **BRISCO**, of Newtown, Mar. 16, 1836, by Levi Edwards, J.P.	73
Esther Jane, of Monroe, m. Burton **WAYLAND**, of Trumbull, this day, [Jan. 31, 1838], by Rodney Rossiter	75
Frances F., m. Homer F. **TILFORD**, of New York, Dec. 25, 1850, by John Hoffman	101
Mahala, m. Ephraim Lee **WOODIN**, this day [Oct. 19, 1841], by Rodney Rossiter	82
Stephen S., of Trumbull, m. Flora M. **SHERMAN**, of Monroe, this day, [May 17, 1843], by Rodney Rossiter	86
MANN, Hannah, of Monore, m. Elijah **CONGO**, of Sherman, Dec. 26, 1824, by Israel A. Beardslee, J.P.	52
Hannah, of Monroe, m. Elijah **CONGO**, of Sherman, Feb. 17, 1825, by Israel A. Beardslee, J.P.	53
MARTHER, Alexander, of Bridgeport, m. Fanny **POPE**, of Monroe, [Nov.] 27, [1828], by Daniel Jones	61
MATTHEWS, Martha, m. Frederick **HAIDERSTECK**, b. foreigners, Mar. 10, 1850, by John Hoffman	99
MILLEN (?), Fidelia, m. Agar **EDWARDS**, b. of Monroe, this day [Jan. 13, 1839], by Rev. Eli Brunson	78
MILLER, Reuben, of Bridgeport, m. Mary Ann **BELDEN**, of Monroe, Aug. 28, 1836, by Rev. James Kent	73

	Page
MILLER (cont.)	
Timothy, of Bridgeport, m. Sally **BELDEN**, of Monroe, this day, [Apr. 17, 1836], by Rodney Rossiter	72
MINES, Maria Jenette, m. Winthrop **PECK**, b. of Newtown, this day, [Apr. 2, 1845], by Rodney Rossiter	89
MOREHOUSE, Daniel, of New Town, m. Anna **BOOTH**, of Monroe, this day, [Mar. 24, 1833], by Truman Peck, J.P.	67
George, m. Delia **JOHNSON**, b. of Monroe, Jan. 17, 1833, by Rev. Stephen Martindale	67
John B., of New Town, m. Laura Ann **OSBORN**, of Monroe, this day, [Jan. 8, 1834], by Rodney Rossiter	69
MORGAN, Taylor, of Danbury, m. Lucretia Caroline **CARGILL**, this day, [Dec. 2, 1844], by Rev. R. D. Gardner	89
Tayler, of Danbury, m. Lucretia Caroline **CARGILL**, this day, [Dec. 2, 1844], by Rev. R. D. Gardner	91
Urbin D., m. Laura A. **TAYLOR**, b. of Bridgeport, Nov. 24, 1853, by Rev. Alva Gregory	103
MORRIS, Jane, of Huntington, m. Monson **FREEMAN**, of Monroe, this day, [Oct. 2, 1842], by Rodney Rossiter	85
MORS[E], MOSS, Julia E., of Middlebury, m. Joel **IVES**, of Cheshire, this day, [Jan. 14, 1839], by Rodney Rossiter	77
Rebecca, of Middlebury, m. Joel **IVES**, Jr., of Cheshire, this day, [Sept. 3, 1840], by Rodney Rossiter	81
NELSON, Underhill, of Danbury, m. Harriet **HAWLEY**, of Danbury, Nov. 13, 1831, by Rev. John Lovejoy	94
NICHOLS, Agar, m. Hannah **LANPHEAR**, b. of Monroe, Sept. 3, 1831, by Jacob Beers, J.P.	66
Anna, of Monroe, m. William **BENNETT**, of Newtown, Mar. 12, 1826, by Rev. David Bennett	55
Betsey A., m. Rufus **BEARDSLEE**, b. of Monroe, June 17, 1849, by Rev. E. E. Beardsley, of New Haven	97
David P., of Trumbull, m. Harriet **SHERMAN**, of Monroe, this day, [Jan. 4, 1842], by Rev. R. D. Gardner	83
J. Spencer, m. Caroline **WHEELER**, b. of Monroe, this day, [Sept. 20, 1846], by Rev. W[illia]m Denison	92
James R., of Trumbull, m. Elizabeth **SEELEY**, of Monroe, this day, [Aug. 25, 1846], by Rodney Rossiter	92
John, of Monroe, m. Delia **WHEELER**, of Trumbull, this day, [Mar. 15, 1840], by Rodney Rossiter	79
John Blackman, of New Town, m. Harriet Catharine **FAIRCHILD**, of Monroe, Sept. 12, 1847, by Rev. John Hobert Betts	94
Lomena, m. W[illia]m W. **HOIT**, b. of Monroe, this day [Nov. 15, 1846], by W[illia]m Denison	92
Lucy Ann, m. William **BEACH**, Jr., this day [Mar. 5, 1843], by Rodney Rossiter	86
Maria Amelia, m. Asa **WHITE**, b. of New Town, Nov. 9, 1844, by Rev. Aaron S. Hill	90
Mary, m. John G. **BEARDSLEE**, b. of Monroe, this day [May 2, 1836], by Rev. William Denison	73
Nancy Janette, of Monroe, m. William **BEARDSLEY**, of Bridgeport, this day [Jan. 9, 1837], by Rev. David G. Tomlinson, of Trumbull	74

	Page
NICHOLS (cont.)	
Nathan Bennett, of Huntington, m. Phebe Ann **DREW**, of Monroe, this day, [Dec. 26, 1841], by Rev. William Denison	83
Rebecca, m. James Smith **BEARDSLEE**, June 18, 1834, by Rev. Nathan Wildman	70
Rilander, of Trumbull, m. Sally **JUDSON**, of Monroe, Jan. 12, 1825, by Chauncey G. Lee	52
Roswell V., m. Jane E. **SILLIMAN**, b. of Monroe, Feb. 15, 1844, by Rev. R. D. Gardner	87
NICKERSON, Cynthia M., m. Jay **PECK**, b. of Monroe, Sept. 30, 1838, by Rev. Cyrus Silliman	76
NOBLE, Isaac, m. Polly **WHEELER**, b. of Monroe, Apr. 6, 1829, by Samuel Wheeler, J.P.	61
NORTHROP, Charles W., of Washington, m. Harriet **TYLER**, of Huntington, July 5, 1840, by Henry Lewis, J.P.	80
ODLE, Manervy, m. [ ] **TREADWELL**, b. of Weston, Jan. 7, 1827, by Levi Edwards, J.P.	58
OLMSTEAD, OLMSTED, John, Jr., m. Juliaette **SHERMAN**, b. of Monroe, this day, [Dec. 17, 1835], by Rev. William Denison	71
Julia A., of Monroe, m. Charles **LEWIS**, of Trumbull, this day, [Oct. 24, 1843], by Rev. W[illia]m Denison, of Weston	87
Lovisa, of Monroe, m. Lyman **LATTIN**, of New Town, this day, [Jan. 18, 1836], by Rev. William Denison	72
Mary, of Monroe, m. Noah **BEERS**, of Weston, this day [Oct. 30, 1838], by Rev. W[illia]m Denison	77
Sarah, of Weston, m. Isaac **BLACKMAN**, of New Town, this day, [Nov. 24, 1833], by Rodney Rossiter	68
OSBORN, OSBOURNE, Annis, Mrs., m. Nehemiah Terrell **RANE**, Dec. 18, 1825, by Rev. E. J. Ives, of Trumbull	56
Daniel, m. Mary **SINCLAIR**, Apr. 1, 1849, by Rev. Lorenzo D. Nickerson, of Stepney	96
Ebenezer M., m. Susan **HAWLEY**, this day [Nov. 24, 1839], by Rev. W[illia]m Denison	79
Laura Ann, of Monroe, m. John B. **MOREHOUSE**, of New Town, this day, [Jan. 8, 1834], by Rodney Rossiter	69
Laura J., of Monroe, m. William S. **WARRINER**, of New York, [ ], by Rev. William Denison, of Weston. Recorded Apr. 8, 1847	93
Sally, of Waterbury, m. LeGrand **SHARP**, this day [Aug. 13, 1837], by Rodney Rossiter	74
Sarah Ann, of Monroe, m. Orrin O. **TAYLOR**, of Trumbull, this day, [May 17, 1847], by Rev. W[illia]m Denison	94
OWEN, Hiram, of Kalamazo, Mich., m. Malissa **BEARDSLEY**, of Monroe, Oct. 6, 1836, by Rev. James Kent	73
Melissa, Mrs. of Monroe, m. Henry **HURD**, of Huntington, Nov. 16, 1845, by Rev. Aaron S. Hill	91
PARMELEE, Marcus M., m. Rebecca **STAPLES**, Nov. 7, 1830, by Stephen Middlebrooks, J.P.	63
PATTERSON, Anna, of Monroe, m. Jonathan **GOODSELL**, of New Town, Apr. 21, 1835, by Jacob Beers, J.P.	71
Aurilla, m. Nathan **JENKINS**, b. of Monroe, Oct. 14, 1827, by Rev. Menzies Raynor	59

MONROE VITAL RECORDS

PATTERSON (cont.)
Nelson B., of Easton, m. Betsey **GOODSELL**, of Monroe, this day, [June 4, 1851], by Rev. R. D. Gardner — 101
PAYNE, PANE, Ann Eliza, of Monroe, m. Joseph W. **DeFOND**, of Newark, N.J., Apr. 22, 1849, by Rev. James Mallory, of Stepney — 97
Anthey, of Monroe, m. Plumb **HAWLEY**, of Trumbull, Apr. 5, 1840, by Rev. Nathaniel Mead — 80
Armina, m. Henry **SMITH**, b. of Monroe, Apr. 14, 1840, by Jacob Beers, J.P. — 80
Charity, m. James **JUDSON**, Apr. 16, 1826, by Israel A. Beardslee, J.P. — 55
Louisa, of Trumbull, m. Abell **PECK**, of Monroe, June 29, 1825, by Rev. Edward J. Ives — 56
PEAS, Rant, m. Roxany **GIBSON**, Aug. 24, 1824, by Samuel Wheeler, J.P. — 51
PECK, Abell, of Monroe, m. Louisa **PAYNE**, of Trumbull, June 29, 1825, by Rev. Edward J. Ives — 56
Amarillus, of Brookfield, m. John S. **HAWLEY**, of Monroe, Sept. 21, 1828, by Levi Edwards, J.P. — 60
Eli J., m. Mrs. Jane **CURTISS**, b. of Monroe, July 24, 1842, by Levi Edwards, J.P. — 84
Eliza, m. Andrew **CLARK**, b. of Monroe, Feb. 11, 1829, by Daniel Jones — 61
Emeline, m. Mark **LEAVENWORTH**, this day, [July 10, 1831], by Rodney Rossiter — 64
George, m. Polly **PECK**, b. of Monroe, Dec. 30, 1823, by Rev. Menzies Raynor — 50
Hannah E., m. Lewis **CURTISS**, b. of Monroe, Sept. 3, 1843, by George L. Fuller — 87
Jay, m. Cynthia M. **NICKERSON**, b. of Monroe, Sept. 30, 1838, by Rev. Cyrus Silliman — 76
Julia Ann, of Monroe, m. Ami S. **CURTISS**, of Trumbull, Mar. 26, 1840, by Rev. J. Hitchcock, of Newtown — 80
Levi P., of Monroe, m. Louisa **FRENCH**, of New Town, May 29, 1838, by Asa Hays — 76
Mary J., of Monroe, m. William G. **PRINDLE**, of Newtown, Jan. 2, 1845, by Jacob Beers, J.P. — 88
Minot, m. Mariah **HALL**, Sept. 1, 1833, by Rev. Luther Mead — 68
Nancy M., m. Joseph **PLUMB**, Nov. 4, 1832, by Stephen Middlebrooks, J.P. — 67
Polly, m. George **PECK**, b. of Monroe, Dec. 30, 1823, by Rev. Menzies Raynor — 50
Winthrop, m. Maria Jenette **MINES**, b. of Newtown, this day, [Apr. 2, 1845], by Rodney Rossiter — 89
Zalmon S., of New Town, m. Polly J. **LUM**, (?), this day [Apr. 7, 1833], by Rodney Rossiter — 67
PENFIELD, Lucius, m. Eliza **FRENCH**, b. of Monroe, Jan. 18, 1826, by Chauncey G. Lee — 55
William, of Fairfield, m. Jane **EDWARDS**, of Fairfield, Nov. 3, 1830, by Rev. Horace Bartlett — 64
PERKINS, Lucinda, of Derby, m. Smith **SHELTON**, of Huntington, Sept. 13, 1826, by Samuel Wheeler, J.P. — 57

	Page
PETTS, Nancy, of Monroe, m. Harry JOHNSON, of White Plains, N.Y., (colored), Oct. 14, 1827, by Rev .Menzies Raynor	59
PIERCE, David, of Roxbury, m. Mary E. LEWIS, of Monroe, Dec. 20, 1843, by Rev. G. L. Fuller	87
PITTS, Roxey, m. George WILSON, b. of Monroe, Aug. 5, 1831, by Daniel Jones	65
PLATT, Allen, m. [ ] HEMINGWAY, b. of Monroe, Oct. 9, 1844, by Rev. Aaron S. Hill	90
Huldah J., m. W[illia]m H. STEBBINS, Jan. 10, 1850, by Rev. Stephen J. Stebbins	97
PLUMB, Charles L., of New Town, m. Julia A. SEARS, of Monroe, this day, [Sept. 24, 1837], by Rodney Rossiter	75
Harvy, of Plymouth, m. Rebecca HUBBELL, of Monroe, Oct. 25, 1826, by Levi Edwards, J.P.	57
Henry, m. Catharine M. CURTISS, this day [ ], by Rev. R. D. Gardner. Recorded Oct. 6, 1851	101
Joseph, m. Nancy M. PECK, Nov. 4, 1832, by Stephen Middlebrooks, J.P.	67
Wate, m. Maria HAWLEY, b. of Monroe, this day [Apr. 26, 1843], by Rev. R. D. Gardner	86
POPE, Fanny, of Monroe, m. Alexander MARTHER, of Bridgeport, [Nov.] 27, [1828], by Daniel Jones	61
Lydia, m. Sheldon HUBBEL, Mar 28, 1841, by Rev. David Bennett	81
PORTER, J. Botsford, m. Sylvia JOHNSON, b. of Monroe, Oct. 19, 1847, by Rev. Samuel W. Smith, Int. Pub.	96
Mary, m. Luke BENEDICT, b. of Monroe, Jan. 26, 1844, by Rev. George L. Fuller	89
POWELL, John, Jr., of Huntington, m. Louisa LAMPKIN, of Monroe, this day, [Apr. 16, 1834], by Rodney Rossiter	69
PRAY, Thurzy, m. Benjamin BUNDY, June 13, 1825, by Samuel Wheeler, J.P. Int. Pub.	53
PRINDLE, Charles, m. Eliza STODDARD, this day [Aug. 15, 1838], by Rodney Rossiter	76
Mary S., of Monroe, m. Benjamin M. BIGELOW, of Reading, Oct. 3, 1853, by Rev. Alva Gregory	103
William G., of Newtown, m. Mary J. PECK, of Monroe, Jan. 2, 1845, by Jacob Beers, J.P.	88
PRUDEN, William C., of Orange, m. Margaret Ann BOOTH, this day [July 4, 1841], by Rodney Rossiter	82
PULFORD, Hannah Maria, of Monroe, m. Addison RICHARD, of Cornwall, this day, [Oct. 8, 1837], by Rodney Rossiter	75
Tressa Ann, of Newtown, m. Francis B. BARLOW, of Brookfield, Sept. 23, 1829, by Rev. John Lovejoy	62
RANE, Nehemiah Terrell, m. Mrs. Annis OSBORN, Dec. 18, 1825, by Rev. E. J. Ives, of Trumbull	56
RICHARDS, RICHARD, Abigail, of Monroe, m. George FERRISS, of Newtown, May 5, 1829, by Daniel Jones	62
Addison, of Cornwall, m. Hannah Maria PULFORD, of Monroe, this day [Oct. 8, 1837], by Rodney Rossiter	75
RICKER, [see also RIKER], Charles, of Monroe, m. Elizabeth A. SPERRY, of New Haven, May 5, 1845, by Rev. William B. Knapp	91

	Page
RIKER, [see also **RICKER**], Jane, of Monroe, m. Foster M. **CARGILL**, of New town, this day[Aug. 4, 1833], by Rodney Rossiter	68
ROBBINS, ROBINS, Roxey F., of Monroe, m. Charles **DEMINGS**, of Bridgeport, Sept. 23, 1831, by Daniel Jones	65
ROBERTS, Emeline, m. William **SIRNNE***, this day [Dec. 22, 1844], by Rodney Rossiter *(Uncertain)	89
John W., of Fairfield, m. Annis **SHARP**, of Monroe, Mar. 13, 1824, by Hawley Sanford, Elder	51
Lucy Ann, m. John **DART**, b. of Monroe, Nov. 24, 1831, by Daniel Jones	66
Paulina, of Monroe, m. David **TOUSEY**, Jr., of New Town, Apr. 17, 1836, by Rev. James Kent	72
Sydney, m. Sarah Ann **ROWEL**, b. of Monroe, May 16, 1830, by Daniel Jones	63
ROOT, George W., of Oxford, m. Sarah S. **JONI**(?), of Huntington, Sept. 3, 1827, by Rev. Menzies Raynor	58
ROSE, Edward H., of Harrison, O., m. Lucy R. **CLARKE**, of Monroe, May 20, 1825, by C. G. Lee	53
ROWELL, ROWEL, Alonzo, m. Sally **GILBERT**, b. of Monroe, July 8, 1829, by Daniel Jones	62
Julia, m. Benjamin W. **FRENCH**, b. of Monroe, Feb. 15, [1829], by Daniel Jones	61
Sarah Ann, m. Sydney **ROBERTS**, b. of Monroe, May 16, 1830, by Daniel Jones	63
RUSSELL, Ann Eliza, m. Edgar **BOOTH**, b. of Huntington, Nov. 24, 1850, in East Village Church, by Rev. N. C. Lewis	100
SABAREE, Sidney R., see under Sidney R. **LARABEE**	
SEARS, SEERS, Henry E., m. Julia A. **FRENCH**, b. of Monroe, this day, [Nov. 24, 1850], by Rev. W[illia]m Denison, of Humphreyville	100
Jane E., m. Granville **LUTHER**, this day [Nov. 22, 1831], by Rodney Rossiter	66
John, of Monroe, m. Sylvia **LANPHEAR**, of Easton, May 27, 1849, by Rev. James Mallory, of Stepney	97
Julia A., of Monroe, m. Charles L. **PLUMB**, of New Town, this day, [Sept. 24, 1837], by Rodney Rossiter	75
Lyman, m. Eliza **JENNEY**, this day [Jan. 2, 1848], by Rev. R. D. Gardner	95
Maria, m. John A. **TOMLINSON**, this day [Apr. 20, 1834], by Rodney Rossiter	70
Mary R., m. Henry B. **SHERMAN**, this day [Jan. 21, 1849], by Rev. R. D. Gardner	95
William, m. Druscilla **TURNEY**, this day [Dec. 12, 1830], by Rodney Rossiter	63
SEELEY, SELEY, Alden, m. Julia Maria **HURD**, this day [June 11, 1843], by Rodney Rossiter	86
Alson, Jr., m. Caroline **HUBBELL**, this day, [Nov. 26, 1835], by Rodney Rossiter	71
Elizabeth, of Monroe, m. James R. **NICHOLS**, of Trumbull, this day, [Aug. 25, 1846], by Rodney Rossiter	92
Nehemiah, m. Polly **DAYTON**, Oct. 18, 1841, by George P Curtis, J.P.	83
SEYMOUR, William, of Watertown, m. Amelia **BEACH**, of Monroe, this day, [Sept. 26, 1842], by Rodney Rossiter	85

224 BARBOUR COLLECTION

	Page
SHARP, Abigail E., of Monroe, m. Salam G. **STANNALL**, of Essex, Mass., [ ], 1854, by Thomas Judd	103
Annis, of Monroe, m. John W. **ROBERTS**, of Fairfield, Mar. 13, 1824, by Hawley Sanford, Elder	51
Betsey Mariah, of Monroe, m. Levi **DART**, of Huntington, Aug. 23, 1829, by Elijah Middlebrooks, J.P.	62
LeGrand, m. Sally **OSBOURNE**, of Waterbury, this day [Aug. 13, 1837], by Rodney Rossiter	74
Molly B., of Monroe, m. William **DART**, of Huntington, July 6, 1826, by Rev. Menzies Raynor	56
SHELTON, Charlotte A., m. Charles **HUBBELL**, Sept. 10, 1848, by Judson G. Lyman	95
Eliza, of Monroe, m. Seline **BOOTH**, of Stratford, this day [Sept. 3, 1834], by Rodney Rossiter	70
Mortimer N., Dr. of Huntington, m. Eliza **CLARK**, of Monroe, May 1, 1827, by Rev. Menzies Raynor	58
Silvanus P., of Huntington, m. Marette **HAWLEY**, of Monroe, this day, [Jan. 4, 1843], by Rodney Rossiter	85
Smith, of Huntington, m. Lucinda **PERKINS**, of Derby, Sept. 13, 1826, by Samuel Wheeler, J.P.	57
SHERMAN, [see also **GERMAN**], Bennett, of Newtown, m. Mary Jane **HUBBELL**, of Huntington, June 20, 1852, by Rev. H. H. Morgan	102
Deaclamy, of Monroe, m. John B. **VARSE**, of Newtown, Apr. 9, 1831, by Rev. Horace Bartlett	64
Dwight, of Newtown, m. Nancy **HURD**, of Monroe, Oct. 25, 1847, by Rev. Samuel W Smith. Int. Pub.	96
Eliza, of Monroe, m. Curtiss **WARNER**, of Southbury, Feb. 25, 1838, by Rev. James Kent	75
Flora M., of Monroe, m. Stephen S. **MALLETT**, of Trumbull, this day, [May 17, 1843], by Rodney Rossiter	86
Frederick, m. Elvira **JENNINGS**, this day [Feb. 19, 1843], by Rodney Rossiter	85
Harriet, of Monroe, m. David P. **NICHOLS**, of Trumbull, this day, [Jan. 4, 1842], by Rev. R. D. Gardner	83
Henry B., m. Mary R. **SEARS**, this day [Jan. 21, 1849], by Rev. R. D. Gardner	95
Jerusha, m. Hiram **HURD**, b. of Monroe, Nov. 15, 1829, by Daniel Jones	62
Jothan, of New Town, m. Mary Ann **BOSTWICK**, of Monroe, this day [Feb. 11, 1834], by Rodney Rossiter	69
Juliaette, m. John **OLMSTEAD**, b. of Monroe, this day [Dec. 17, 1835], by Rev. William Denison	71
Lydia A., of Monroe, m. Aaron **MALLET**, of Trumbull, Dec. 22, 1851, by Rev. J. G. Downing, of Trumbull	102
Maria, m. Sylvanus **HAWLEY**, b. of Monroe, Jan. 27, 1825, by Rev. Beardslee Northrop, of Trumbull	53
Maria, of Monroe, m. Sylvanus **HAWLEY**, of Monroe, Jan. 27, 1825, by Rev. Beardslee Northrop, of Trumbull	54
Mary, of Monroe, m. Beebe M. **GRAY**, of Trumbull, May 28, 1826, by Rev. Menzies Raynor	56
Mary E., of Monroe, m. John **STILLSON**, of Newtown, Oct. 10, 1849, by Rev. James Mallory, of Stepney	97

MONROE VITAL RECORDS 225

Page

SHERMAN (cont.)
Minerva, m. Eli G. **BENNETT**, this day [Feb. 10, 1850], by Rev. R.
D. Gardner 98
Nancy, of Monroe, m. Elisha B. **BURT**, of Trumbull, this day, [Sept.
26, 1830], by Rodney Rossiter 63
Nathaniel, m. Hepsey **CURTISS**, Apr. 18, 1831, by Stephen
Middlebrooks, J.P. 64
Nelson, of Trumbull, m. Polly Betsey **BEARDSLEE**, of Monroe,
Aug. 14, 1823, by Rev. Menzies Raynor 50
Rebecca, of Monroe, m. Charles W. **CURTISS**, of Trumbull, this
day, [Apr. 8, 1851], by Rev. R. D. Gardner 101
Starr, m. Harriet **BEARDSLEY**, this day [Oct. 1, 1840], by Rodney
Rossiter 81
SHERWOOD, Betsey Ann, of Monroe, m. Robert **TURNEY**, of
Trumbull, Nov. 20, 1828, by Daniel Jones 61
George, of Readding, m. Adaline **HUBBELL**, of Monroe, this day,
[Dec. 25, 1833], by Rodney Rossiter 68
Lucy Ann, m. John **CLARKE**, this day [Apr. 17, 1834], by Rodney
Rossiter 69
Moses, of Reading, m. Margaret **HUBBELL**, of Monroe, this day,
[Dec. 24, 1834], by Rodney Rossiter 70
Nathan C., of Easton, m. Clarissa **TERRELLS**, of Monroe, Oct. 6,
1850, by Rev. Levi Smith, Int. Pub. 99
Orville Burton, m. Frances Eliza **BEARDSLEE**, d. Ezra & Eliza,
Sept. 10, 1848, by Rev. John Herbert Betts 95
Pamela, m. William **BOOTH**, b. of Monroe, Dec. 25, [1823], by
Rev. Menzies Raynor 50
Sally Malilda, m. Leman **CLARK**, this day [Sept. 20, 1840], by
Rodney Rossiter 81
SILLIMAN, SILLAMAN, Jane E., m. Roswell V. **NICHOLS**, b. of
Monroe, Feb. 15, 1844, by Rev. R. D. Gardner 87
Priscilla, of Monroe, m. Lacey **HIGGINS**, of New Town, this day,
[Nov. 18, 1840], by Rodney Rossiter 81
Stepney, of Bridgeport, m. Eliza M. **CURTISS**, of Monroe, this day,
[Feb. 25, 1850], by R. D. Gardner 98
SINCLAIR, Mary, m. Daniel **OSBORN**, Apr. 1, 1849, by Rev. Lorenzo
D. Nickerson, of Stepney 96
SIRNNE (?), William, m. Emeline **ROBERTS**, this day [Dec. 22, 1844],
by Rodney Rossiter 89
SMITH, Caroline, m. Burr **WATKINS**, b. of Monroe, Dec. 24, 1826, by
Levi Edwards, T. C. 57
Henry, m. Armina **PAYNE**, b. of Monroe, Apr. 14, 1840, by Jacob
Beers, J.P. 80
John C., of New Milford, m. Mary E. **ADAMS**, of Monroe, this day,
[June 8, 1843], by Rodney Rossiter 86
Mary, of Newtown, m. Peter **FINCH**, of Monroe, Jan. 31, 1847, by
Asa Hayes, J.P. 93
Mary E., of Derby, m. Harmon **WHITLOCK**, of Monroe, Dec. 24,
1849, by Rev. James Mallory, of Stepney 98
Wakeman, of Newtown, m. Betsey **WHEELER**, of Monroe, Oct. 21,
1827, by Amos Bassett 59
SNOW, Susan, of Ashford, m. Smith **BENNETT**, of Monroe, Oct. 9,
1836, by Rev. David Bennett 74

	Page
SOMERS, Malinda, of Weston, m. Wanzer S. GILBERT, of Weston, Aug. 29, 1841, by Rev Stephen S. Stebbins	82
SPERRY, Elizabeth A., of New Haven, m. Charles RICKER, of Monroe, May 5, 1845, by Rev. William B. Knapp	91
SQUIER, Levi T., of Roxbury, m. Harriet Ann CLARK, of Monroe, this day, [May 12, 1844], by Rodney Rossiter	88
STANNALL, Salam G., of Essex, Mass., m. Abigail E. SHARP, of Monroe, [ ], 1854, by Thomas Judd	103
STAPLES, Charles, m. Rosilla A. BURR, this day [Nov. 29, 1838], by Rodney Rossiter	77
Rebecca, m. Marcus M. PARMELEE, Nov. 7, 1830, by Stephen Middlebrooks, J.P.	63
STEBBINS, W[illia]m H., m. Huldah J. PLATT, Jan. 10, 1850, by Rev. Stephen J. Stebbins	97
STILLSON, John, of Newtown, m. Mary E. SHERMAN, of Monroe, Oct. 10, 1849, by Rev. James Mallory, of Stepney	97
STODDARD, Eliza, m. Charles PRINDLE, this day [Aug. 15, 1838], by Rodney Rossiter	76
STURGES, Pamela, of Wilton, m. John E. JUDSON, of Monroe, this day, [Dec. 27, 1846], by Rev. R. D. Gardner	93
SUMMERS, Mary A., of Monroe, m. James H. HUGGINS, of New Haven, this day, [Nov. 14, 1850], by Rev. R. D. Gardner	100
Sarah, m. Charles McEWEN, this day [Dec. 1, 1841], by Rev. R. D. Gardner	83
TAYLOR, David, m. Esther COLEMAN, May 16, 1824, by Roswell Hawkes	51
Laura A., m. Urbin D. MORGAN, b. of Bridgeport, Nov. 24, 1853, by Rev. Alva Gregory	103
Orrin C., of Trumbull, m. Sarah Ann OSBORN, of Monroe, this day, [May 17, 1847], by Rev. W[illia]m Denison	94
Wealthy M., of Monroe, m. Charles B. WHITTLESEY, of Huntington, this day, [Mar. 31, 1836], by Rodney Rossiter	72
William, of Watertown, m. Polly DURAN, of Monroe, May 15, 1845, by Rev. Stephen J Stebbins	90
TERRELLS, [see also TYRRELL], Clarissa, of Monroe, m. Nathan C. SHERWOOD, of Easton, Oct. 6, 1850, by Rev. Levi Smith, Int. Pub.	99
THAIR, William, m. Elizabeth BOTSFORD, b. of Seymour, Jan. 18, 1852, by Rev. H. H. Morgan	102
THOMPSON, Augusta, m. Charles C. CLARKE, this day [Nov. 27, 1844], by Rodney Rossiter	88
Cornelia, of Monroe, m. Stephen R. BLACKMAN, of Danbury, Dec. 8, 1850, by Ephraim Leach, J.P.	101
TILFORD, Homer F., of New York, m. Frances F. MALLETT, Dec. 25, 1850, by John Hoffman	101
TOMLINSON, Burke, of Oxford, m. Sarah Abigail WHEELER, of Monroe, this day, [Jan. 27, 1834], by Rodney Rossiter	68
David, of Oxford, m. Nancy HAYES, of Monroe, Sept. 24, 1825, by Samuel Wheeler, J.P.	55
Edwin, of Monroe, m. Susan Ann CLARKE, of Huntington, this day, [Jan. 3, 1836], by Rodney Rossiter	71
Jane, of Oxford, m. Lewis JORDAN, of New Town, this day, [Oct. 18, 1838], by Rodney Rossiter	77

MONROE VITAL RECORDS 227

Page

TOMLINSON (cont.)
Jenett, m. Orvil **BOOTH**, b. of Monroe, Apr. 9, 1831, by Rev.
Horace Bartlett — 64
John A., m. Maria **SEARS**, this day [Apr. 20, 1834], by Rodney
Rossiter — 70
Nelson, of Huntington, m. Charity Mariah **DREW**, of Monroe, Nov.
8, 1842, by Rev. John H. Waterbury — 85
Sarah A., of Huntington, m. Charles G. **HURD**, of Monroe, Apr. 8,
1852, by Rev. J. W. Hoffman — 102
TOUSEY, TOWSEY, Amarillus, m. Abel **MALLETT**, b. of Monroe,
Jan. 17, 1829, by Stephen Middlebrook, J.P. — 61
David, Jr., of New Town, m. Paulina **ROBERTS**, of Monroe, Apr.
17, 1836, by Rev. James Kent — 72
TREADWELL, -----, m. Manervy **ODLE**, b. of Weston, Jan. 7, 1827, by
Levi Edwards, J.P. — 58
TUCKER, Charles G., of Monroe, m. Polly J. **BEEBE**, of Oxford, this
day, [Mar. 27, 1834], by Rodney Rossiter — 69
Eliza, m. Rufus **HUBBELL**, Sept. 11, 1842, by Rev. Geo[rge] L.
Foote — 84
Henrietta, of Monroe, m. Horace N. **BLISS**, of Bozrah, Jan. 7, 1849,
by Judson H. Lyman — 95
Jennett, of Monroe, m. Lockwood **DURAND**, of Birmingham, this
day, [Sept. 20, 1846], by Rodney Rossiter — 92
TURNEY, Albert, Dea., of Easton, m. Mrs. Lucretia **WALKER**, of
Monroe, June 16, 1850, by Rev. C. T. Printice — 100
Alfred, m. Amelia **CHAPMAN**, Jan. 29, 1824, by Cyrus H.
Beardslee, J.P. — 50
Drusilla, m. William **SEARS**, this day [Dec. 12, 1830], by Rodney
Rossiter — 63
George R., of Trumbull, m. Mary Jane **HUBBELL**, of Monroe, this
day, [Apr. 12, 1846], by Rodney Rossiter — 91
Laury, of Monroe, m. Sherman **FRENCH**, of New York, Aug. 3,
1828, by Levi Edwards, J.P. — 60
Lewis, of Trumbull, m. Rozilla A. **HAWLEY**, of Monroe, June 1,
1824, by Rev. Beardslee Northrop, of Trumbull — 51
Rebecca, of Trumbull, m. Charles **CURTISS**, of Monroe, Jan. 13,
1828, by Rev. Amos Bassett — 60
Robert, of Trumbull, m. Betsey Ann **SHERWOOD**, of Monroe,
Nov. 20, 1828, by Daniel Jones — 61
W[illia]m, m. Sally **BOOTH**, Dec. 3, 1823, by Chauncey G. Lee.
Int. Pub. at Brookfield — 50
William, m. Jane **HUBBELL**, Dec. 16, 1826, by Rev. Ashbel
Baldwin, of Trumbull — 58
Willis, m .Harriet **CURTISS**, this day [Jan. 7, 1830], by Rodney
Rossiter — 62
TYLER, Harriet, of Huntington, m. Charles W. Northrop, of Washington,
July 5, 1840, by Henry Lewis, J.P. — 80
TYRRELL, [see also **TERRELLS**], George, m. Nancy **BURRITT**, this
day [Dec.31, 1835], by Rodney Rossiter — 71
Sarah Eliza, of Monroe, m. Lorenzo W. **LEAVENWORTH**, of New
Milford, Jan. 18, 1843, by Rev. David G. Tomlinson, of
Trumbull — 86

	Page
VARSE, [see also **VOSE**], John B., of Newtown, m. Deaclamy **SHERMAN**, of Monroe, Apr. 9, 1831, by Rev. Horace Bartlett	64
VOSE, [see also **VARSE**], John B., m. Nancy **CANN** (?), Nov. 4, 1839, by Asa Hays	79
VREDENBURGH, Peter H., m. Amanda **BRISCO**, b. of Monroe, July 15, 1850, by Rev. S. W. Smith. Int. Pub.	99
WAKELEY, WAKELEE, Eliza, of Monroe, m. Silas C. **LEWIS**, of Weston, Sept. 12, 1841, by Rev. George Waterbury	82
Lydia A., m. Sidney R. **LABAREE**, Apr. 30, 1854, by Rev. Alva Gregory	103
Samuel B., of Easton, m. Sarah M. **LEAVENWORTH**, of Monroe, this day, [Sept. 10, 1845], by Rev. William Denison	91
WALKER, Lucretia, Mrs. of Monroe, m. Dea. Albert **TURNEY**, of Easton, June 16, 1850, by Rev. C. T. Printice	100
WARNER, Curtiss, of Southbury, m. Eliza **SHERMAN**, of Monroe, Feb. 26, 1838, by Rev. James Kent	75
WARRINER, William S., of New York, m. Laura J. **OSBORN**, of Monroe, [ ], by Rev. William Denison, of Weston. Recorded Apr. 8, 1847	93
WATERS, Lyman, of Huntington, m. Maria **BAKER**, of Monroe, this day, [Sept. 8, 1840], by Rodney Rossiter	81
WATKINS, Burr, m. Caroline **SMITH**, b. of Monroe, Dec. 24, 1826, by Levi Edwards, T.C.	57
WATSON, Rufus W., of Coxsackie, N.Y., m. Elizabeth A. **BOTSFORD**, of Monroe, this day [Nov. 13, 1838], by Rodney Rossiter	77
WAYLAND, Burton, of Trumbull, m. Esther Jane **MALLETT**, of Monroe, this day [Jan. 31, 1838], by Rodney Rossiter	75
WELLS, Mary E., m. Ezra A. **HURD**, this day [Feb. 26, 1839], by Rodney Rossiter	78
WHEELER, Ambrose, m. Mary **BOOTH**, this day [July 6, 1834], by Rodney Rossiter	70
Betsey, of Monroe, m. Wakeman **SMITH**, of Newtown, Oct. 21, 1827, by Rev. Amos Bassett	59
Caroline, m. J. Spencer **NICHOLS**, b. of Monroe, this day [Sept. 20, 1846], by Rev. W[illia]m Denison	92
Chauncy, m. Laura **LANE**, b. of Monroe, Oct. 16, 1825, by Donald Judson, J.P.	54
Delia, of Trumbull, m. John **NICHOLS**, of Monroe, this day, [Mar. 15, 1840], by Rodney Rossiter	79
Jane, m. William M. **CRAFTON**, Nov. 15, [1835], by Matthew Batchelor	71
John H., of Danbury, m. Ann E. **HUBBELL**, of Monroe, Nov. 13, 1850, by Rev. Levi H. Wakeman	99
Julia A., of Monroe, m. John W. **HOFFMAN** (Rev.), May 17, 1853, by Rev. W[illia]m White Bronson, of Danbury	102
Mary E. H., m. Henry T. **CURTISS**, this day [Aug. 6, 1844], by Rev. R. D. Gardner	88
Mary L, m. Albert **JOHNSON**, b. of Monroe, Apr. 10, 1832, by Rev. Samuel Bassett	66
Nathan N., m. Lidia **CLARK**, b. of Monroe, Sept. 7, 1828, by Daniel Jones	60
Nathaniel, of Huntington, m. Jane E. **HAWLEY**, of Monroe, this day, [Mar. 12, 1843], by Rev. R. D. Gardner	86

MONROE VITAL RECORDS 229

Page

WHEELER (cont.)
Polly, m. Isaac **NOBLE**, b. of Monroe, Apr. 6, 1829, by Samuel
    Wheeler, J.P.   61
Sarah Abigail, of Monroe, m. Burke **TOMLINSON**, of Oxford, this
    day, [Jan. 27, 1834], by Rodney Rossiter   68
Wales, of Huntington, m. Maria **BRADLEY**, d. Eden **BOOTH**, of
    Monroe, Mar. 8, 1844, by Rodney Rossiter   88
WHITE, Asa, m. Maria Amelia **NICHOLS**, b. of New Town, Nov. 9,
    1844, by Rev. Aaron S. Hill   90
WHITLOCK, Harmon, of Monroe, m. Mary E. **SMITH**, of Derby, Dec.
    24, 1849, by Rev. James Mallory, of Stepney   98
WHITTLESEY, Charles B., of Huntington, m. Wealthy M. **TAYLOR**, of
    Monore, this day [Mar. 31, 1836], by Rodney Rossiter   72
[**WILCOX**], **WILLCOX**, Joseph, of Newtown, m. Esther **LAM**, of
    Monroe, Mar. 30, 1825, by Rev. Menzies Raynor   53
WILCOXSON, **WILLCOXSON**, Albert, of Stratford, m. Ame E.
    CURTISS, of Monroe, Nov. 23, 1852, by J. W. Hoffman   102
Joseph, of Newtown, m. Esther Cornelia **LANE**, of Monroe, Mar.
    30, 1825, by Rev. Menzies Raynor   54
Sarah H., of Monroe, m. Andrew B. **GLOVER**, of Newtown, Jan.
    26, 1825, at the house of the late John Willcoxson, by Rev.
    Ebenezer Platt, of Darien   52
WILSON, George, m. Roxey **PITTS**, b. of Monroe, Aug. 5, 1831, by
    Daniel Jones   65
WINTON, Jane Eliza, m. William **HUBBELL**, Aug. 20 ,1840, by Rev.
    David G. Tomlinson, of Trumbull   81
WOLSA, Belinda, of Monroe, m. Solomon **DAVIS**, of North Canaan,
    Nov. 3, 1844, by Henry Lewis, J.P.   89
WOODIN, Ephraim Lee, m. Mahala **MALLETT**, this day [Oct. 19,
    1841], by Rodney Rossiter   82
YOUNG, Abraham H., of Bridgeport, m. Sylvia C. **LEWIS**, of Monroe,
    this day, [May 12, 1833], by Rodney Rossiter   68
ZIMMERMAN, John Dimond, of Fairfield, m. Julia Ann **BABBITT**, of
    Monroe, Nov. 28, 1833, by Daniel Jones   69

MONTVILLE VITAL RECORDS
1786 – 1850

This volume contains a list alphabetically arranged of the vital records of Montville earlier than 1852.

In 1896 Henry A. Baker, for a number of years Town Clerk of Montville, published his "History of Montville, Connecticut, 1640-1896" and many vital records appear therein. For the past few years the originals, on which this history was probably based, have been lost. In the fall of 1925 a book of records, with the cover and pages 1 and 2 missing, was found and a year later was copied.

This list was taken from a set of cards based on the manuscript copy which is now in the possession of the Connecticut State Library. This copy has not been compared with the original and doubtless errors exist. It is hoped that as errors or omissions are found notes will be entered in this volume and on the cards which are included in the General Index of Connecticut Vital Records also in the possession of the Connecticut State Library.

Hartford, Conn., January, 1927

	Page
ADAMS, Hannah, m. Ebenezer **SMITH**, Jr., Oct. 10, 1793	21
ADGATE, Anna*, [d. Asahel & Sarah], b. Oct. 22, 1796 *(First written "Mary" and crossed out)	12
Asahel, m. Sarah **AVERY**, Apr. 11, 1790	12
Mary, see under Anna	
Mary H., [d. Asahel & Sarah], b. May 31, 1794	12
Ruth L., twin with Sarah M., d. [Asahel & Sarah], b. June 15, 1798	12
Sarah M., twin with Ruth L., d. [Asahel & Sarah], b. June 15, 1798	12
Thomas Avery, s. [Asahel & Sarah], b. Jan. 24, 1791	12
ALLYN, Elizabeth, b. Feb. 17, 1769; m. George **MINARD**, Mar. 17, 1791	20
Joseph K., [s. Nathan], b. Feb. 15, 1800	9
Oliver, [s. Nathan], b. Oct. 15, 1802	9
ATWELL, Samuel, d. Nov. 26, 1850	42
AVERY, Polly, m. Asa **COMSTOCK**, Feb. 28, 1801	12
Sarah, m. Asahel **ADGATE**, Apr. 11, 1790	12
BABCOCK, E., m. Esther **COBB**, d. Simeon, [ ]	15
BAILEY, BAILY, Ame Abigal, [d. Samuel & Lydia **CROCKER**], b. [ ], 1801; m. [ ] **BEAUMONT**, [ ] now living 1893* *(This entire entry supplied in a later hand)	47
Chloe, [d. Samuel & Lydia **CROCKER**], b. [ ], 1789	47
Gordon, [s. Samuel & Lydia **CROCKER**], b. [ ], 1792	47
Lydia, [d. Samuel & Lydia **CROCKER**], b. [ ], 1795	47

	Page
BAILEY, BAILY (cont.)	
Lydia, d. [Samuel & Lydia **CROCKER**], [ ], 1798	47
Samuel, m. Lydia **CROCKER**, May 6, 1787* *(Inserted in a later hand)	47
BAKER, Abigail, m. David **CONGDON**, s. John & Amy, Mar. 24, 1780; d. Feb. 11, 1781	14
Betsey, [d. Josiah], b. Oct. 6, 1793; d. Nov. 11, 1793	25
Charles, [s. Lebbeus & Polly], b. Jan. 23, 1795; d. Feb. 12, 1796	16
Charlotte, [d. Josiah], b. Nov. 10, 1783; m. Isaac **WHIPPLE**, [ ]* *(In pencil in a later hand)	25
Cyrus, [s. Jared, Jr.], b. May 29, 1804	24
Daniel, b. Nov. 7, 1770	24
Daniel, m. Sally **RAYMOND**, June 27, 1797	5
Elijah, [s. Lebbeus & Polly], b. Feb. 19, 1801	16
Elizabeth, m. Josiah **RAYMOND**, Sept. 2, 1784	50
Esther, [d. Lebbeus & Polly], b .Nov. 1, 1797	16
George Griswold, [s. Daniel & Sally], b. Dec. 19, 1798	5
James, [s. Josiah], b. Oct. 3, 1771	25
Jared, Jr., b. Jan. 5, 1774	24
John, [s. Lebbeus & Polly], b. Mar. 24, 1805	16
Josiah, b. Aug. 13, 1746; m. [ ], Nov. 15, 1770	25
Josiah, his w. [ ], b. Apr. 2, 1752	25
Josiah, [s. Josiah], b. Oct. 20, 1794; m. Delia **EDWARDS**, [ ]* *(In pencil in a later hand)	25
Lebbeus, m. Polly **CHAPEL**, Mar. 28, 1793	16
Lemuel, [s. Lebbeus & Polly], b. Dec. 23, 1793	16
Lois, b. June 15, 1775; m. David **TURNER**, Nov. 26, 1797	16
Lois, [d. Josiah], b. June 15, 1775; m. Daniel **TURNER**, [ ]* *(In pencil in a later hand)	25
Lois, m. Edward **WHITE**, Dec. 25, 1791	26
Lydia, [d. Lebbeus & Polly], b. July 5, 1796	16
Lyman, [s. Jared, Jr.], b. Mar. 11, 1794	24
Marcy*, [d. Lebbeus & Polly], b. Jan. 9, 1803 *(Perhaps "Marey")	16
Marvin, [s. Jared, Jr.], b. Aug. 19, 1801	24
Mary, [d. Josiah], b. July 13, 1781; m. James **TURNER**, [ ]* *(In pencil in a later hand)	25
Mary, b. July 13, 1781; m. James **TURNER**, July 14, 1805	40
Mary, m. Thomas **ROGERS**, Nov. 7, 1784	23
Mary, of Montville, m. James **TURNER**, of Waterford, July 14, 1805, by Moses Warren, J.P.	3
Mary Ann, [d. Daniel & Sally], b. Apr. 24, 1800	5
Nabby, [d. Josiah], b. July 26, 1789; m. James **REED**, [ ]* *(In pencil in a later hand)	25
Nabby, [d. Jared, Jr.], b. Feb. 22, 1799	24
Phebe, [d. Jared, Jr.], b. Mar. 4, 1796	24
Sarah, [d. Daniel & Sally], b. Mar. 12, 1802	5
BALOTE, Betsey, m. Benjamin **COBB**, Nov. 21, 1787	9
BECKWITH, Naomi, had s. Phamomenon, b. Feb. 13, 1794	52
Phamomenon, s. Naomi **BECKWITH**, b. Feb. 13, 1794	52
BEMISS, Berella, [d. Elijah & Sarah], b. Nov. 9, 1808	29
Elijah, b. Jan. 2, 1776, in Hebron; m. Sarah **MAYNARD**, Mar. 4, 1798	29
Elijah, [s. Elijah & Sarah], b. Mar. 21, 1799	29

MONTVILLE VITAL RECORDS 233

	Page
BEMISS (cont.)	
Isephena, [d. Elijah & Sarah], b. Dec. 3, 1804	29
John B., [s. Elijah & Sarah], b. Feb. 14, 1803, in Waterford	29
Sarah Maria, [d. Elijah & Sarah], b. Apr. 12, 1810	29
Sarah Maynard, [d. Elijah & Sarah], b. Dec. 31, 1800	29
Sarah Maynard, d. [Elijah & Sarah], d. Sept. 27, 1805, in Waterford	29
BISHOP, Clement D., m. Nancy **FITCH**, Feb. 7, 1805	10
Harriot, [d. Thomas & Eliza], b. Jan. 21, 1801	14
Lucretia, m. John **BLISS**, Dec. 19, 1802	4
Mary, m. David **CONGDON**, Jan. 29, 1784	14
Sally, [d. Thomas & Eliza], b. Apr. 22, 1805	14
Stephen, of Waterford, m. Amy **DAVIS**, of Montville, Oct. 18, 1804, by Clement Bishop, J.P.	9
Thomas, m. Eliza **STRICKLAND**, June 30, 1800	14
Thomas S., [s. Thomas & Eliza], b. Mar. 1, 1803	14
BLISS, Elisabeth, [d. Pelatiah], b. May 8, 1769	6
Giles Bishop, s. [John & Lucretia], b. Dec. 16, 1803	4
Hannah, [d. Pelatiah], b. Jan. 19, 1772	6
John, [s. Pelatiah], b. Nov. 8, 1780	6
John, m. Lucretia **BISHOP**, Dec. 19, 1802	4
Pelatiah, [s. Pelatiah], b. Mar. 17, 1774	6
BOLLES, BOLLS, Calvin, m. Hester **DARROW**, Dec. 5, 1811, by Reuben Palmer	32
Elizabeth, of New London, m. Ezra **SMITH**, of Montville, Dec. 27, 1798	49
Harriet Newell, d. Calvin & Hester, b. July 1, 1814	32
BRADFORD, Adonijah F., [s. Perez & Betty], b. Aug. 9, 1771	11
Adon F., m. Sally **DOLBEARE**, Apr. 27, 1794	11
Adonijah F., m. Sarah **DOLBEARE**, d. John, [ ]	19
Betsey Rogers, [d. Adon. F. & Sally], b. July 7, 1802	11
Jennett, [d. William & Hannah], b. Dec. 10, 1803	8
John Dolbeare, [s. Adon. F. & Sally], b. Aug. 28, 1797	11
John Dolbeare, [s. William & Hannah], b. May 7, 1806	8
Parthenia, b. Aug. 13, 1773; m. William **BRADFORD**, Jan. 24, 1796	8
Parthenia, [d. Perez & Betty], b. Aug. 13, 1773	11
Parthenia, d. [William & Parthenia], b. Dec. 4, 1796	8
Parthenia, w. William, d. Dec. 20, 1796	8
Perez, m. Betty **ROGERS**, Feb. 22, 1770	11
Perez Fitch, [s. Adon. F. & Sally], b. Feb. 23, 1795	11
Sally Sherwood, [d. Adon. F. & Sally], b. Nov. 8, 1799	11
Samuel P., [s. William & Hannah], b. Apr. 23, 1810* *(Entry in pencil in a later hand)	8
William, b. Jan. 30, 1772; m. Parthenia **BRADFORD**, Jan. 24, 1796	8
William, m. Hannah **DOLBEARE**, Jan. 30, 1803	8
William B., [s. William & Hannah], b. Feb. 1, 1808* *(Entry in pencil in a later hand)	8
BREED, Lucretia, of Stonington, m. George W. **SMITH**, of Montville, Nov. 23, 1803, by Christopher Avery	6
BULKELEY, Patience, m. David H. **JEWETT**, Aug. 10, 1769	3
CALDWELL, Sally, m. Jason **COMSTOCK**, July 11, 1781	22
CAMP, Anna, m. John **CROCKER**, May 18, 1758	47

	Page
CAPEL, [see also CHAPPELL], Asa, s. of Ezekiel*, m. Betsey CHAPMAN, d. Joseph*, Apr. 23, 1798 *(In pencil in a later hand)	5
Charles, [s. Asa & Betsey], b. Feb. 2, 1799	5
Joseph, [s. Asa & Betsey], b. Aug. 10, 1800	5
Lyman, [s. Asa & Betsey], b. May 4, 1804	5
Oliver, [s. Asa & Betsey], b. Jan. 10, 1802	5
CAULKINS, Oliver W., s. John P. & Nancy L., b. Oct. 14, 1847	45
CHAPMAN, Betsey, d. Joseph*, m. Asa CAPEL, s. of Ezekiel*, Apr. 12, 1798 *(In pencil in a later hand)	5
Charles A., [s. Joseph Lee & Phebe], b. Oct. 29, 1838* *(In pencil in a later hand)	38
Frank, [s. Joseph Lee & Phebe], b. [ ], 1827* *(In pencil in a later hand)	38
Gideon, m. Sally COOK, d. Rev. Rozel, [ ]	6
Hannan, [child of Joseph Lee & Phebe], b. June 27, 1824	38
Joseph Lee, [s. Zebulon & Anne], b. Dec. 9, 1795	50
Joseph Lee, m. Phebe WICKWIRE, Feb. 5, 1818	38
Leander, [s. Joseph Lee & Phebe], b. May 18, 1828* *(In pencil in a later hand)	38
Mary, [d. Zebulon & Anne], b. July 15, 1798	50
Mary Jane, [d. Joseph Lee & Phebe], b. [ ]* *(In pencil in a later hand)	38
Oliver Raymond, [s. Zebulon & Anne], b. May 6, 1801; d. Mar. 19, 1802, ae 10 m. 13 d.	50
Oliver Wolcott, [s. Joseph Lee & Phebe], b. Oct. 21, 1818	38
Sarah Gardner, [d. Joseph Lee & Phebe], b. Sept. 15, 1821	38
Zebulon, m. Anne LATIMER, Mar. 12, 1795	50
Zebulon, d. June 8, 1802, in the 37th y. of his age	50
[CHAPPELL], CHAPEL, [see also CAPEL], Abigail, m. Mathew TURNER, July 19, 1795	3
Betsey, [d. William & Eunice], b. Sept. 16, 1787* *(First written "May 8, 1790" and crossed out)	15
Eunice, b. Sept. 29, 1753; m. William CHAPEL, June 19, 1777	15
Eunice, [d. William & Eunice], b. July 29, 1793	15
Goddard M., [s. William & Eunice], b. Jan. 31, 1785	15
Jonathan, [s. William & Eunice], b. July 8, 1796	15
Polly, m. Lebbeus BAKER, Mar. 28, 1793	16
Polly, of Hebron, m. Amos ROGERS, of Montville, Feb. 19, 1804, by Clement Bishop, J.P.	7
Rebeckah, [d. William & Eunice], b. July 18, 1780	15
Sally, [d. William & Eunice], b. May 8, 1790	15
Simon, [s. William & Eunice], b. Oct. 8, 1782	15
William, b. Dec. 21, 1754; m. Eunice CHAPEL, June 19, 1777	15
CHESTER, Anna, d. Dea. Joseph, d. Oct. 26, 1803	18
Caroline, m. John SMITH, 2nd, Oct. 7, 1795	12
David, m. Prudy FOX, Nov. 8, 1797	18
Dorothy, m. Ephraim FELLOWS, Apr. 4, 1802, by Rev. Andrew Lee, of Lisbon	13
Eliza, d. [David & Prudy], b. Apr. 4, 1799	18
John Fox, s. [David & Prudy], b. Sept. 8, 1801	18
Mary, m. Asahel OTIS, Jan. 15, 1792	18
Sophia Maria, [d. David & Prudy], b. July 8, 1803	18

MONTVILLE VITAL RECORDS 235

	Page
CHURCH, Amy, b. Apr. 1, 1754; m. James **COMSTOCK**, Aug. 2, 1773	21
Esther, m. Joseph **ROGERS**, Feb. 15, 1785	24
Joseph, Jr.*, s. Joseph & Mary, b. Oct. 28, 1781 *(In pencil is "brother to Amos, drowned, ae 40 y., also his mother, sister to Amy Church, w. of James Comstock)"	27
CLARK, Thankfull, m. Samuel **PALMER**, Oct. 30, 1780	8
-----, m. Fanny **NEWBERY**, d. Davis, [ ]	17
COBB, Benjamin, [s. Simeon], b. May 28*, 1765 *(Perhaps "May 20")	15
Benjamin, m. Betsey **BALOTE**, Nov. 21, 1787	9
Betsey, [d. Simeon], b. Mar. 16, 1771	15
Esther, [d. Simeon], b. July 16, 1773; m. E. **BABCOCK**, [ ]* *(In pencil in a later hand)	15
Eunice, [d. Simeon], b. Oct. 16, 1785	15
Hannah, [d. Simeon], b. Jan. 14, 1780	15
Isaac, [s. Simeon], b. Mar. 28, 1775	15
Joseph, [s. Simeon], b. Apr. 7, 1762	15
Nancy, [d. Simeon], b. Apr. 20, 1778	15
Nathaniel, [s. Simeon], b. Jan. 31, 1768	15
Patty, d. [Benjamin & Betsey], b. Feb. 29, 1790	9
Simeon, [s. Simeon], b. Nov. 4, 1759	15
Stephen, [s. Simeon], b. May 6, 1789	15
COMSTOCK, Amos, [s. James & Amy], b. Aug. 14, 1791	21
Amy, [d. James & Amy], b. Oct. 28, 1776	21
Asa, m. Polly **AVERY**, Feb. 28, 1801	12
Asahel Otis, [s. Samuel & Elizabeth], b. Aug. 6, 1813	35
Betsey, [d. Jason & Sally], b. Jan. 16, 1789	22
Clarissa, [d. William A. & Mary], b. Apr. 21, 1840	44
Elisa Ann, [d. William A. & Mary], b. Apr. 15, 1837	44
Elizabeth Ann, [d. Samuel & Elizabeth], b. Jan. 2, 1817	35
Erastus, [s. Jason & Sally], b. Jan. 5, 1794	22
Esther, m. Isaac **TURNER**, s. Isaac, [ ]	25
Eunice, m. Giles **TURNER**, s. Isaac, [ ]	25
Fairbanks, [s. James & Amy], b. Jan. 1, 1779	21
Grace, m. Guy **TURNER**, Dec. 8, 1799	28
Grace, m. Guy **TURNER**, s. Isaac, [ ]	25
Hannah, [d. James & Amy], b. Aug. 3, 1784	21
Hannah M., [d. William A. & Mary], b. Aug. 20, 1834	44
Harriet, [d. James & Amy], b. Oct. 18, 1797	21
James, b. Feb. 7, 1750; m. Amy **CHURCH**, Aug. 2, 1773	21
James, [s. James & Amy], b. May 7, 1774; m. Fanny Rogers, [ ]* *(In pencil in a later hand)	21
Jason, m. Sally **CALDWELL**, July 11, 1781	22
Jemima, [d. James & Amy], b. Jan. 21, 1789	21
John, m. Nancy **NEWBERY**, d. Davis, [ ]	17
John Rusland, [s. James & Amy], b. Mar. 3, 1782	21
John Rusland, m. Sarah **WHALEY**, Dec. 25, 1813* *(In pencil in a later hand "1812" is correct)	30
Mary, [d. Jason & Sally], b. Mar. 11, 1787	22
Mary, m. Reuben **PALMER**, Jr., Mar. 17, 1805	13
Nabby, [d. Jason & Sally], b. Apr. 7, 1796	22
Olive, m. James **HOWARD**, Dec. 21, 1800	16
Prentis, [s. James & Amy], b. Sept. 5, 1795	21
Reuben, [s. Asa & Polly], b. Mar. 13, 1805	12

236 BARBOUR COLLECTION

	Page
COMSTOCK (cont.)	
Reuben P., s. Asa & Mary, d. May 28, 1837, ae 32 y.	12
Robert, [s. James & Amy], b. Oct. 31, 1786	21
Sally, [d. Jason & Sally], b. July 25, 1803	22
Samuel, [s. Jason & Sally], b. Oct. 11, 1785	22
Samuel, m. Elizabeth TURNER, Oct. 11, 1812	35
Samuel, m. Elisabeth TURNER, d. Isaac, [ ]	25
Sarah, [d. James & Amy], b. Aug. 28, 1793	21
Stephen, [s. Jason & Sally], b. Dec. 15*, 1790 *(First written "16th")	22
Washington, [s. Jason & Sally], b. Sept. 10, 1798	22
William, [s. Jason & Sally], b. Oct. 10, 1782	22
William A., [s. Asa & Polly], b. Aug. 13, 1803	12
CONGDON, Abigail, w. David, d. Feb. 11, 1781	14
Abigail, [d. David & Mary], b. Feb. 9, 1787	14
Anna, [d. David & Mary], b. May 15, 1794	14
David, s. John & Amy, b. Aug. 25, 1756; m. Abigail BAKER, Mar. 24, 1780	14
David, m. Mary BISHOP, Jan. 29, 1784	14
David, [s. David & Mary], b. May 22, 1789	14
David, d. Feb. 19, 1850, ae 93 y. 6 m.	14
Elisha, [s. David & Mary], b. Feb. 5, 1797	14
Hannah, [d. David & Mary], b. Mar. 11, 1800	14
Henry N., [s. Nicholas B. & Polly], b. Dec. 10, 1829	37
Jeremiah, s. [David & Abigail], b. Jan. 23, 1781; d. Sept. 11, 1784	14
John, [s. David & Mary], b. Dec. 21, 1784	14
Joshua, [s. David & Mary], b. Sept. 3, 1805	14
Mary, w. David, d. Apr. 24, 1813	14
Nicholas, [s. David & Mary], b. Nov. 30, 1802	14
Nicholas B., m. Polly HILL, Sept. 20, 1827	37
Samuel H., [s. Nicholas B. & Polly], b. June 20, 1828	37
Stephen, [s. David & Mary], b. Feb. 5, 1792	14
COOK, Aurilla, [d. Rev. Rozel], b. Feb. 22, 1791; m. George FOX, [ ]* *(In pencil in a later hand)	6
Clarissa, [d. Rev. Rozel], b. Dec. 14, 1794; m. Henry T. ROGERS, [ ]* *(In pencil in a later hand)	6
Ebenezer, [s. Rev. Rozel], b. Feb. 12, 1785; m. M. MARTIN, [ ]* *(In pencil in a later hand)	6
Lydia, [d. Rev. Rozel], b. Jan. 13, 1797; m. Tyler PALMER, [ ]* *(In pencil in a later hand)	6
Rosetta, [d. Rev. Rozel], b. Apr. 7, 1787; m. Christopher DOLBEARE, [ ]* *(In pencil in a later hand)	6
Sally, [d. Rev. Rozel], b. Mar. 12, 1789; m. Gideon CHAPMAN, [ ]* *(In pencil in a later hand)	6
CRANDAL, Lester, [s. Phineas], b. May 17, 1796	52
Lucinda, [d. Phineas], b. Oct. 20, 1790, at New London	52
Phineas, [s. Phineas], b. Sept. 13, 1793	52
CROCKER, Anne, [d. John & Anna], b. July 20, 1772	47
Anne, [w. John], d. Oct. 7, 1787	47
Elisabeth, [d. John & Ana], b. May 14, 1768	47
John, m. Anna CAMP, May 18, 1758	47
John, [s. John & Anna], b. Sept. 11, 1765	47
John, m. Thankful ROBBINS, June 13, 1802, by John G. Hillhouse	47

MONTVILLE VITAL RECORDS 237

	Page
CROCKER (cont.)	
Joseph, [s. John & Anna], b. Mar. 21, 1759; d. Oct. 28, 1776	47
Joseph, [s. John & Anna], b. Apr. 8, 1781	47
Lydia, [d. John & Anna], b. Oct. 27, 1761; m. Samuel **BAILEY**, May 6, 1787* *(Inserted in a later hand)	47
Malzor, [s. John & Anna], b. Aug. 6, 1763	47
Mary, [d. John & Anna], b. May 30, 1770	47
Mercy, [d. John & Anna], b. Mar. 20, 1775	47
Sarah, [d. John & Anna], b. May 31, 1777	47
DARROW, Hester, m. Calvin **BOLLES**, Dec. 5, 1811, by Reuben Palmer	32
DAVIS, Amy, of Montville, m. Stephen **BISHOP**, of Waterford, Oct. 18, 1804, by Clement Bishop, J.P.	9
DELANEY, Richard, drowned June 29, 1878, in Pequot Pond	46
DENISON, Abel P., [s. George], b. Aug. 30, 1789	18
Amy, [d. George], b. Nov. 4, 1792	18
Asa, [s. George], b. May 29, 1797	18
Sarah, [d. George], b. Feb. 22, 1801	18
DODGE, Mercy, m. Hallam **LATIMER**, Sept. 17, 1778	51
DOLBEARE, DOLBERE, Abby, [d. Samuel,]* *(In pencil in a later hand)	19
Abby Sabina, [d. Guy & Abby], b. Apr. 4, 1822	37
Benjamin, [s. John], b. Dec. 18, 1780	19
Benjamin, [s. George,]* *(In pencil in a later hand)	19
Christopher, [s. John], b. June 10, 1776; d. May 7, 1846* *(In pencil in a later hand)	19
Christopher, m. Rosetta **COOK**, d. Rev. Rozel, [ ]	6
Daniel, [s. John], b. Aug. 14, 1790	19
Eleanor, [d. John], b. July 10, 1785	19
Elisha, [s. John], b. June 23, 1778	19
George, [s. John], b. Feb. 1, 1774	19
Guy, m. Abby **HAZARD**, Feb. 18, 1816	37
Guy, d. June 17, 1823, ae 33 y.	37
Guy, [s. George,]* *(In pencil in a later hand)	19
Hannah, b. Apr. 16, 1783; m. William **BRADFORD**, Jan. 30, 1803	8
Hannah, [d. John], b. Apr. 16, 1783	19
Hannah Mumford, [d. Guy & Abby], b. Dec. 20, 1816	37
James, [s. John], b. Nov. 14, 1771	19
James Guy, [s. Guy & Abby], b. Mar. 19, 1820	37
John, [s. John], b. Sept. 14, 1788	19
John, m. Sarah **RAYMOND**, Dec. 23, [ ]* *(Entire entry crossed out)	19
John, s. George, [ ]* *(In pencil in a later hand)	19
Lemuel, [s. John], b. Feb. 13, 1793	19
Lucy, [d. George,]* *(In pencil in a later hand)	19
Marian, [d. George]* *(In pencil in a later hand)	19
Mary, [d. John], b. Dec. 25, 1791	19
Mumford, s. [Samuel,]* *(In pencil in a later hand)	19
Nabby, [d. John], b. Feb. 5, 1796	19
Sally, m. Adon. F. **BRADFORD**, Apr. 27, 1794	11
Samuel, [s. Samuel,]* *(In pencil in a later hand)	19
Sarah, [d. John], b. Jan. 21, 1770; m. Adonijah F. **BRADFORD**, [ ]* *(In pencil)	19
Susan Mary, [d. Guy & Abby], b. Oct. 30, 1818	37

	Page
EDWARDS, Delia, m. Josiah BAKER, s. Josiah, [ ]	25
FARGO, Elijah, s. Stanton & Fanny, b. Nov. 30, 1787	30
FELLOWS, FELLOWES, Ephraim, m. Dorothy CHESTER, Apr. 4, 1802, by Rev. Andrew Lee, of Lisbon	13
Francis, s. [Ephraim & Dorothy], b. Nov. 20, 1803	13
FITCH, Anne, [d. James & Abigail], b. May 7, 1800	4
James, m. Abigail FOX, May 14, 1797	4
John Gardiner, [s. James & Abigail], b. June 20, 1798	4
Nancy, m. Clement D. BISHOP, Feb. 7, 1805	10
FORD, Joseph Griswold, s. Joseph B. & Abigail, b. Oct. 22, 1812	28
FOX, Abigail, m. James FITCH, May 14, 1797	4
Eleanor, b. Feb. 16, 1802; m. Azel F. ROGERS, Oct. 18, 1821	41
Eunice G., d. [Ezekiel & Lydia], b. Apr. 25, 1804; d. Aug. 12, 1804	13
Ezekiel, b. June 18, 1781; m. Lydia LORD, June 26, 1803	13
George, m. Aurilla COOK, d. Rev. Rozel, [ ]	6
Lydia, w. Ezekiel, d. Jan. 29, 1805	13
Prudy, m. David CHESTER, Nov. 8, 1797	18
FULLER, Samuel, [s. Jesse & Hannah], b. Nov. 29, 1821	14
GALLUP, Orilla, [d. Robert], b. May 27, 1802	15
Polly, [d. Robert], b. June 13 ,1796	15
GARDNER, Amasa, [s. David], b. Nov. 1, 1776	25
Anstrus, [d. David], b. June 24, 1787	25
Artemas, [s. David], b. Jan. 15, 1792	25
Artemas, [s. Azel* & Anna], b. Oct. 24, 1814 *(Crossed out and overwritten in pencil "Erastus")	36
Azel, [s. David], b. Aug. 5, 1780	25
Sharlot*, [s. Azel & Anna], b. Feb. 4, 1821 *("Charlotte")	36
David H., [s. David], b. Aug. 2, 1778	25
Erastus, [s. David], b. July 16, 1789	25
John, [s. David], b. Feb. 1, 1786	25
John, Dr., d. Aug. [ ], 1801	10
Julian, [s. Azel & Anna], b. July 9, 1818	36
Julian, b. July 9, 1818; m. Richard RAYMOND, [ ]	43
Katharine, [d. David], b. May 17, 1773	25
Lucinda, [d. David], b. Nov. 12, 1782	25
Sally R., [d. Azel* & Anna], b. July 5, 1716 *(Crossed out and overwritten in pencil "Erastus")	36
Salmon, [s. David], b. Dec. 5, 1804	25
GATES, Elisabeth, b. Jan. 17, 1756; m. Ebenezer ROGERS, Nov. 24, 1774	26
GILBERT, Polly, m. Joseph LEWIS, Oct. 29, 1790	17
GREEN, Frances, of Bozrah, m. Clarasa WILLIAMS, Jan. 7, 1848*, by J. L. Chapman, J.P. *(Perhaps "1868")	45
HARRIS, Edmund F., m. Harriet M. MORGAN, June 4, 1848	45
HAZARD, HASARD, Abby, m. Guy DOLBEARE, Feb. 18, 1816	37
Betsey, m. Daniel WORTHINGTON, Mar. 28, 1790	49
HILL, Betsey T., b. Sept. 21, 1813; m. Nathan SCHOLFIELD, Sept. 8, 1830	42
Jonathan, Jr., s. Jonathan & Charlotte, b. Feb. 11, 1789	28
Polly, m. Nicholas B. CONGDON, Sept. 20, 1827	37
HILLHOUSE, Mary, m. Joshua RAYMOND, Sept. 28, 1809	32
HOLMES, Harriot, d. [Naomi], b. Dec. 1, 1808	31
John B., s. Seth W. & Mary, b. June 23, 1780	27

	Page
HOLMES (cont.)	
Naomi, had s. Thomas, b. June 19 ,1807 & d. Harriot, b. Dec. 1, 1808	31
Thomas, [s. Naomi], b. June 19, 1807	31
HOWARD, Amos, s. [James & Olive], b. Dec. 15, 1801	16
James, m. Olive **COMSTOCK**, Dec. 21, 1800	16
James, [s. James & Olive], b. Oct. 30, 1804	16
HUNTLEY, Elihu, m. Anna **MANWARING**, Nov.* 20, 1790 *(First written "May")	23
Erastus, [s. Elihu & Anna], b. Mar. 17, 1803	23
Ira, [s. Elihu & Anna], b. Feb. 23, 1805	23
Jemima, [d. Elihu & Anna], b. Aug. 19, 1794	23
Lydia, [d. Elihu & Anna], b. May 15, 1791	23
Marvin, [s. Elihu & Anna], b. Nov. 20, 1796	23
Oliver, [s. Elihu & Anna], b. Feb. 22, 1779	23
Stephen Gorton, [s. Elihu & Anna], b. Apr. 1, 1801	23
JEWETT, Anne, [d. David H. & Patience], b. June 1, 1774; d. Dec. [ ], 1774	3
Charles, [s. David H. & Patience], b. June 9, 1777	3
Charles Bulkeley, [s. David H. & Patience], b. Dec. [ ], 1775; d. May [ ], 1776	3
David, [s. David H. & Patience], b. June 17, 1772	3
David H., m. Patience **BULKELEY**, Aug. 10, 1769	3
David H. & Patience, had child, s. b. Apr. 20, 1779	3
Eliza, [d. David H. & Patience], b. Oct. 9, 1780	3
George, [s. David H. & Patience], b. May 22, 1785	3
Harriet, [d. D avid H. & Patience], b. Jan. 16, 1791	3
Nancy, twin with Patty, d. [David H. & Patience], b. July 6, 1787	3
Patience, [d. David H. & Patience], b. Aug. 15, 1770	3
Patty, twin with Nancy, d. [David H. & Patience], b. July 6, 1787	3
Sarah, [d. David H. & Patience], b. Oct. 8, 1782	3
[LAMPHERE], LANDPHERE, Achsah Palmer, [s. Charles F. & Lucy Ann], b. Mar. 3, 1844	39
Charles F., b. Apr. 28, 1816; m. Lucy Ann **PALMER**, Mar. 10, 1841	39
Charles Oliver, [s. Charles F. & Lucy Ann], b. June 13, 1845	39
Frances Albena, [d. Charles F. & Lucy Ann], b. Feb. 20, 1843	39
Mary Palmer, [d. Charles F. & Lucy Ann], b. Jan. 14, 1842	39
Reuben Palmer, [s. Charles F. & Lucy Ann], b. Feb. 3, 1847	39
LATIMER, Anne, m. Zebulon **CHAPMAN**, Mar. 12, 1795	50
Boradill, [d. George & Rachel], b. Aug. 31, 1786	10
Daniel Dodge, [s. Hallam & Mercy], b. June 22, 1795	51
David, s. [Hallam & Mercy], b. May 7, 1779	51
David, [s. Hallam & Mercy], d. Dec. 28, 1800	51
Frances, [child Hallam & Mercy], b. Mar. 6 ,1790	51
George, m. Rachel **SMITH**, Oct. 10, 1773	10
George G., [s. George & Rachel], b. June 5, 1791	10
Hallam, m. Mercy **DODGE**, Sept. 17, 1778	51
Lucy, [d. Hallam &Mercy], b. Aug. 16, 1787	51
Lydia, [d. George & Rachel], b. June 2, 1775	10
Marcy, [d. Hallam & Mercy], b. Dec. 3, 1781; d. Aug. 27, 1782	51
Mercy Anne, [d. Hallam & Mercy], b. Jan. 12, 1799	51
Nathan Lee Lord, [s. Hallam & Mercy], b. Feb. 9, 1793	51
Nicholas, [s. George & Rachel], b. May 4, 1798	10

	Page
LATIMER (cont.)	
Nicholas Hallam, [s. Hallam & Mercy], b. Oct. 17, 1785; d. Oct. 22, 1786	51
Patty, [d. George & Rachel], b. Jan. 30, 1781	10
Peter, [s. Hallam & Mercy], b. Aug. 1, 1783; d. May 11, 1784	51
Rachel, [d. George & Rachel], b. July 2, 1777	10
Sally, [d. George & Rachel], b. Aug. 31, 1789; d. Nov. 25, 1793	10
LEACH, Albert, [s. John], b. Oct. 20, 1808	39
Henry, [s. John], b. Nov. 4, 1804	39
Susan, [d. John], b. June 20, 1814	39
Thomas, [s. John], b. Mar. 3, 1812	39
William, [s. John] b. Aug. 20, 1817	39
LEWIS, Betsey, [d. Joseph & Polly], b. Nov. 12, 1796; d. Feb. 11, 1879; ae 82 y. 3 m.* *(In pencil in a later hand)	17
Elias, [s. Joseph & Polly], b. Nov. 24, 1798	17
Gilbert, [s. Joseph & Polly], b. Oct. 8, 1792	17
James, [s. Joseph & Polly], b. Sept. 10, 1802	17
Jonathan, [s. Joseph & Polly], b. Sept. 3, 1800	17
Joseph, m. Polly **GILBERT***, Oct. 29, 1790 *(In pencil in a later hand)	17
Joseph, Jr., [s. Joseph & Polly], b. Nov. 3, 1790	17
Polly, [d. Joseph & Polly], b. Sept. 16, 1794	17
LOOMIS, Betsey, [d. Jacob & Silina M.], b. Jan. 27, 1793	22
Ellen, m. Avery **MORGAN**, Mar. 5, 1848	43
Eloisa, [d. Jacob & Silina M.], b. Nov. 14, 1801	22
Harriet, [d. Jacob & Silina M.], b. Jan. 29, 1797	22
Hubbel, [s. Jacob & Silina M.], b. Dec. 27, 1804	22
Jacob, [s. Jacob & Silman M.], b. Apr. 19, 1795	22
Lucretia, [d. Jacob & Silman M.], b. Aug. 26, 1798	22
Mary, [d. Jacob & Silina M.], b. June 6, 1791	22
Philena, [d. Jacob & Silina M.], b. Mar. 6, 1800	22
Rachel, [d. Jacob & Silina M.], b. July 17, 1789	22
Sarah, [d. Jacob & Silina M.], b. Nov. 17, 1786	22
Selina M., [d. Jacob & Silina M.], b. Feb. 27, 1788	22
Seth W., [s. Jacob & Silina M.], b. Mar. 31, 1803	22
LORD, Lydia, b. Mar. 31, 1780; m. Ezekiel **FOX**, June 26, 1803	13
MANWARING, Anna, m. Elihu **HUNTLEY**, Nov.*, 20, 1790 *(First written "May")	23
Charles Denison, b. Nov. 22, 1791	30
MAPLES, Stephen, m. Amy **SMITH**, d. Ebenezer, Jr. & Hannah	21
MARTIN, M., m. Ebenezer **COOK**, s. Rev. Rozel, [ ]	6
MAYNARD, [see also **MINARD**], Anna C., [d. Henry], b. June 27, 1801	33
Eliza, [d. Henry], b. Feb. 22, 1800	33
Harry, [s. Henry], b. Apr. 6, 1798	33
Heneritta, [d. Henry], b. Dec. 21, 1793	33
Lyman, [s. Henry], b. Feb. 12, 1796	33
Mary L., [d. Henry], b. Feb. 23, 1810	33
Roswell, [s. Henry], b. Sept. 8, 1803	33
Sarah, b. Oct. 24, 1775, in [ ]; m. Elijah **BEMISS**, Mar. 4, 1798	29
Thomas J., [s. Henry], b. Nov. 6, 1805	33
MINARD, [see also **MAYNARD**], Betsey, [d. George & Elisabeth], b. Aug. 22, 1796	20
Caleb, [s. George & Elisabeth], b. June 27, 1798	20

MONTVILLE VITAL RECORDS 241

	Page
MINARD (cont.)	
Charlotte, [d. Lemuel], b. July 22, 1781	21
Christopher Allyn, [s. George & Elisabeth], b. Dec. 19, 1791	20
Clarissa, [d. Lemuel], b Feb. 11, 1779	21
Cynthia, [d. George & Elisabeth], b. June 13, 1793	20
George, b. Aug. 12, 1767; m. Elisabeth **ALLYN**, Mar. 17, 1791	20
George, [s. George & Elisabeth], b. Dec. 22, 1794	20
Giles, [s. George & Elisabeth], b. July 22, 1803	20
Joel, [s. George & Elisabeth], b. Apr. 29, 1800	20
Lemuel, [s. Lemuel], b. Mar. 2, 1788	21
Mary Ann, [d. George & Elisabeth], b. Feb. 21, 1810	20
Molly, [d. Lemuel], b. Dec. 5, 1783	21
Nabby Maria, [d. George & Elisabeth], b. June 25, 1805	20
Sally, [d. George & Elisabeth], b. Nov. 11 ,1807	20
Susannnah, [d. Lemuel], b. May 15, 1790	21
MINER, Albert, [twin with Alfred, s. Thomas B.], b. June 18, 1832	38
Alfred, [twin with Albert, s. Thomas B.], b. June 18, 1832	38
Josephine, [d. Thomas B.], b. Mar. 6, 1835	38
Napoleon, [s. Thomas B.], b. Oct. 31, 1830	38
MONROE, John, s. Sally **MONROE**, b. Mar. 9, 1801	27
Sally, had s. John, b. Mar. 9, 1801	27
MORGAN, Avery, m. Ellen **LOOMIS**, Mar. 5, 1848	43
Harriet M., m. Edmund F. **HARRIS**, June 4, 1848	45
NEWBURY, NEWBERY, Benjamin F., [s. David], b. Aug. 20, 1808	17
Betsey, [d. David], b. Oct. 12, 1787	17
Elkanah, [s. David], b. Oct. 13, 1789; m. Nancy [ ]* *(In pencil in a later hand)	17
Eunice, [d. Davis], b. Mar. 7, 1801	17
Fanny, [d. Davis], b. Aug. 7 ,1796; m. [ ] **CLARK**, [ ]* *(In pencil in a later hand)	17
Maria, [d. Davis], b. June 10, 1794	17
Nancy, [d. Davis], b. Dec. 9, 1785*; m. John **COMSTOCK**, [ ]* *(Perhaps "1785") *(In pencil in a later hand)	17
Sabra, [d. Davis], b. Jan. 15, 1799	17
Sally, [d. Davis], b. Apr. 23, 1792; m. Daniel **ROGERS**, [ ]* *(In pencil in a later hand)	17
Williams, [s. Davis], b. May 13, 1804	17
NOBLES, Anna, m. Adonijah **ROGERS**, Oct. 15, 1775	19
OTIS, Asahel, m. Mary **CHESTER**, Jan. 15, 1792	18
Asahel Jackson, [s. Asahel & Mary], b. Apr. 4, 1803	18
Charles, [s. Asahel & Mary], b. Oct. 4, 1795	18
Joseph, s. [Asahel & Mary], b. Sept. 24, 1792	18
Levi, [s. Asahel & Mary], b. Sept. 5, 1798	18
Maryan, [d. Asahel & Mary], b. Dec. 22, 1800	18
PALMER, Cornelia C., [d. Gideon & Mercy M.], b. Oct. 14, 1819	35
Elisha C., [s. Joshua G. & Hannah], b. Jan. 30, 1818	32
Elisha H., [s. Gideon & Mercy M.], b. June 23, 1814	35
Gideon, m. Mercy M.* **TURNER**, July 11, 1813 *(Here follows in pencil "B. June 29, 1795")	35
Gideon, [s. Gideon & Mercy M.], b. Oct. 30, 1816	35
Gideon, m. Mercy Maria **TURNER**, d. Isaac, [ ]	25

PALMER (cont.)

	Page
John, s. [Samuel & Thankfull], b. Dec. 15, 1782* *(First written "1802" and crossed out)	8
John O., [s. Joshua G. & Hannah], b. Nov. 29, 1816	32
Joseph C., [s. Gideon & Mercy M.], b. Jan. 22, 1833	35
Lucy, [d. Samuel & Thankfull], b. July 23, 1803	8
Lucy Ann, b. Oct. 28, 1816; m. Charles F. **LANDPHERE**, Mar. 10, 1841	39
Lydia, [d. Samuel & Thankfull], b. Sept. 26, 1784	8
Lydia, had s. Marvin, b. Jan. 18, 1805	8
Lydia, Mrs. m. Abel **SMITH**, Apr. 6, 1808, by Peleg Randal, Elder	29
Maria T., [d. Gideon & Mercy M.], b. July 3, 1830	35
Marvin, s. Lydia **PALMER**, b. Jan. 18, 1805	8
Matthew T., [s. Gideon & Mercy M.], b. Sept. 26, 1823	35
Nelson, [s. Samuel & Thankfull], b. Nov. 15, 1799	8
Reuben, Jr. ,m. Mary **COMSTOCK**, Mar. 17, 1805	13
Reuben T., [s. Gideon & Mercy M.], b. Sept. 24, 1825	35
Robert McKown, [s. Samuel & Thankfull], b. Mar. 29, 1787	8
Samuel, m. Thankfull **CLARK**, Oct. 30, 1780	8
Samuel Whaley, [s. Samuel & Thankfull], b. Aug. 15, 1797	8
Saryann T., [d. Gideon & Mercy M.], b. Mar. 30, 1818	35
Tyler, m. Lydia **COOK**, d. Rev. Rozel, [ ]	6
William H., [s. Gideon & Mercy M.], b. Oct. 14, 1821	35

PRENTIS, Grace, w. Samuel, b. Mar. 29, 1766 — 36
Grace, [d. Samuel & Grace], b. July 25, 1798 — 36
Jonathan, [s. Samuel & Grace], b. Aug. 21, 1796 — 36
Samuel, b. Aug. 24, 1764 — 36
Samuel, [s. Samuel & Grace], b. Nov. 20, 1805 — 36
Thomas, [s. Samuel & Grace], b. June 12, 1808 — 36
Turner, [s. Samuel & Grace], b. Aug. 7, 1800 — 36

RAYMOND, Abby Turner, [d. Mulford C. & Abby Ann], b. Dec. 28, 1832; d. Dec. 13, 1833 — 40
Edward, [s. Nathaniel L. & Louisa], b. June 23, 1792 — 48
Eliza B., w. George, Jr., d. June 17, 1834, ae 32 — 41
Eliza Rogers, [d. George, Jr. & Eliza B.], b. June 17, 1834 — 41
Elizabeth B., [d. Joshua & Mary], b. Apr. 17, 1812 — 32
Ellen Christopher, [d. Mulford C. & Abby Ann], b. May 6, 1835 — 40
Eunice, d. [Nathaniel L. & Louisa], b. Feb. 14, 1790 — 48
Frances Ann, [d. Richard & Julian], b. Dec. 13, 1839 — 43
George, Jr., b. Jan. 19, 1801; m. Eliza B. **ROGERS**, Apr. 5, 1821 — 41
Harriet Bridget, [d. Mulford C. & Abby Ann], b. Aug. 27, 1829; d. Aug. 2, 1832 — 40
Henry*, [s. Richard & Julian], b. [   ] *(In pencil) — 43
James H., [s. Joshua & mary], b. June 28, 1810 — 32
James Mulford, [s. Mulford C. & Abby Ann], b. Feb. 4, 1840 — 40
John, s. [Nathaniel L. & Louisa], b. Sept. 19, 1785 — 48
John, d. May 7, 1789 — 48
Joshua, d. Sept. 14, 1784 — 48
Joshua, 2nd, [s. Josiah & Elisabeth], b. June 13, 1785 — 50
Joshua, m. Mary **HILLHOUSE**, Sept. 28, 1809 — 32
Josiah, m. Elisabeth **BAKER**, Sept. 2, 1784 — 50
Josiah, [s. Josiah & Elisabeth], b. Nov. 24, 1791 — 50
Josiah, d. July 21, 1795 — 50

MONTVILLE VITAL RECORDS   243

                                                              Page
RAYMOND (cont.)
Josiah, [s. Joshua & Mary], b. Jan. 7, 1815   32
Julia*, [d. Richard & Julian], b. [   ] *(In pencil)   43
Laura Augusta, [d. George, Jr. & Eliza B.], b Aug. 11, 1829   41
Lemuel, [s. Nathaniel L. & Louisa], b. June 4, 1801   48
Louisa, m. Nathaniel L. **RAYMOND**, Dec. 30, 1784; b. [   ]
   1757* *(Date of birth in pencil)   48
Martha Denison, [d. George, Jr. & Eliza B.], b. Sept. 30, 1824 41
Mary Caroline, [d. George, Jr. & Eliza B.], b. July 18, 1827   41
Mercy, d. [Nathaniel L. & Louisa], b. Aug. 14, 1794   48
Mercy E.*, [d. Richard & Julian], b. [   ] *(In pencil)   43
Mulford, s. [Nathaniel L. & Louisa], b. Sept. 20, 1796   48
Mulford C., b. July 23, 1800; m. Abby Ann **TURNER**, Jan. 16, 1827 40
Mulford C., & Abby Ann, had infant s.[   ], b. Dec. 8, 1842; d. Feb.
   4, 1843   40
Nathan, b. July 11, 1781; m. Hannah **SISTARE**, Apr. 3, 1802   4
Nathaniel L., m. Louisa **RAYMOND**, Dec. 30, 1784; b. [   ],
   1757* *(Date of birth in pencil)   48
Nathaniel L., d. July 15, 1829; ae 72   48
Nathaniel Lynde, [s. Nathaniel L. & Louisa], b. Aug. 13, 1787 48
Oliver, [s. Nathaniel L. & Louisa], b. Apr. 6, 1799   48
Orlando, [s. Josiah & Elisabeth], b. Nov. 4, 1789   50
Richard, b. May 24, 1811; m. Julian **GARDNER** [   ]   43
Robert, [s. Richard & Julian], b. Feb. 10, 1837   43
Sally, m. Daniel **BAKER**, June 27, 1797   5
Sarah, m. John **DOLBEARE**, Dec. 23, [ ]* *(Entire entry
   crossed out)   19
Sherwood*, [s. Richard & Julian, b.   ] *(In pencil)   43
Theodore, [s. George, Jr. & Eliza B.], b. Oct. 13, 1822   41
William*, [s. Richard & Julian,   ] *(In pencil)   43
READ, Julia Ann, m. Willet R. **WOOD**, July 4, 1830   44
ROBBINS, Thankful, m. John **CROCKER**, June 13, 1802, by John G.
   Hilllhouse   47
ROGERS, Adonijah, m. Anna **NOBLES**, Oct. 15, 1775   19
Adonijah Benjamin, [s. Adonijah & Anna], b. Oct. 1, 1792   19
Amos, of Montville, m. Polly **CHAPEL**, of Hebron, Feb. 19, 1804,
   by Clement Bishop, J.P.   7
Andrew, [s. Adonijah & Anna], b. Aug. 5, 1785   19
Andrew, m. Elisabeth **ROGERS**, Nov. 13, 1788   7
Andrew, s. [Andrew & Elisabeth], b. Jan. 15, 1792   7
Andrew, d. Aug. 23, 1792   7
Ann Clarissa, [d. Adonijah & Anna], b. Feb. 25, 1795   19
Asenath, of Montville, d. Davis, m. Joseph **TRUMAN**, of Norway, s.
   William, Feb. 4, 1798   52
Azel F., b. Dec. 18, 1791; m. Eleanor **FOX**, Oct. 18, 1821   41
Azel F. & Eleanor, had s. [   ], b. Mar. 4, 1825; d. same day 41
Azel F., Jr., [s. Azel F. & Eleanor], b. July 25, 1826   41
Azel F., [s. Azel F. & Eleanor], d. July 17, 1830   41
Betty, m. Perez **BRADFORD**, Feb. 22, 1770   11
Betty, [d. Ebenezer & Elizabeth], b. Jan. 7, 1778   26
Betty, [d. Adonijah & Anna], b. Jan. 13, 1790   19
Caroline Worthington, [d. Azel F. & Eleanor], b. May 21, 1823; d.
   Oct. 17, 1824   41

BARBOUR COLLECTION

Page

ROGERS (cont.)

Charles, [s. Joseph & Esther], b. Mar. 31, 1796	24
Charles Lee, [s. Adonijah & Anna], b. Nov. 4, 1777	19
Clark Truman, [s. Ethan & Sally], b. June 23, 1798, in New London, Great Neck	20
Crandal, [s. Phinehas], b. Feb. 17, 1789	31
Daniel, [s. Ebenezer & Elisabeth], b. Nov. 23, 1787	26
Daniel, m. Sally **NEWBERY**, d. Davis, [　　　]	17
David, [s. Joseph & Esther], b. Apr. 11, 1801	24
Ebenezer, b. June 3, 1744; m. Elisabeth **GATES**, Nov. 24, 1774	26
Ebenezer, [s. Ebenezer & Elisabeth], b. Dec. 27, 1792	26
Elias, [s. Phinehas], b. Oct. 2 ,1806	31
Elisha Hinman, [s. Thomas & Mary], b. July 5, 1785	23
Eliza, [d. Thomas & Mary], b. July 25, 1802	23
Eliza, [d. Joseph & Esther], b. Dec. 9, 1802	24
Eliza B., b. July 25, 1802; m George **RAYMOND**, Jr.	41
Elisabeth, m. Andrew **ROGERS**, Nov. 13, 1788	7
Elisabeth, [w. Andrew], d. Apr. 6, 1793	7
Elisabeth Ann, [d. David & Mary], b. May 1, 1807	26
Ellen F., [d. Azel F. & Eleanor], b. [　　　]* *(In pencil in a later hand)	41
Emma Louisa M. S., [d. Azel F. & Eleanor], b. July 24, 1829	41
Ethan, of New London, m. Sally **TRUMAN**, of Southhold, N.Y., Dec. 25, 1794	20
Ethan, Jr., [s. Ethan & Sally], b. Apr. 11, 1796, in Southhold, L.I.	20
Fanny, m. James **COMSTOCK**, s. James & Amy, [　　　]	21
Hannah, [d. Phinehas], b. May 20, 1801	31
Harriet M., [d. Azel F. & Eleanor], b. [　　　]*　*(In pencil in a later hand)	41
Henry, [s. Phinehas], b. Sept. 19, 1792	31
Henry T., m. Clarissa **COOK**, d. Rev. Rozel, [　　　]	6
Henry Truman, [s. Thomas & Mary], b. Apr. 20, 1789	23
Hypocrates*, [s. Joseph & Esther,　　　] *(Written in pencil)	24
Jared Starr, [s. Thomas & Mary], b. Jan. 7, 1787	23
Jesse, [s. Ethan & Sally], b. June 23, 1803	20
John, [s. Joseph & Esther], b. Dec. 16, 1792	24
John Baptist, [s. Thomas & Mary], b. June 24, 1794; d. Oct. 5, 1798	23
John Randolph, [s. Azel F. & Eleanor], b. Sept. 5, 1832	41
Joseph, m. Esther **CHURCH**, Feb. 15, 1785	24
Joseph, [s. Joseph & Esther], b. Mar. 13, 1794	24
Lebbeus, s. [Andrew & Elisabeth], b. Aug. 2, 1789	7
Lemuel Douglass, [s. Phinehas], b. Oct. 16, 1794	31
Lucy, [d. Phinehas], b. Dec. 24, 1804	31
Lydia, [d. Ebenezer & Elisabeth], b. June 15, 1776	26
Mary, [d. David & Mary], b. Apr. 1, 1804	26
Mary Ann, [d. Thomas & Mary], b. Apr. 10, 1799	23
Mercy, [d. Phinehas], b. Sept. 30, 1798	31
Naomi, twin with Ruth, d. [Phinehas], b. Apr. 28, 1786	31
Nehemiah, [s. Adonijah & Anna], b. Sept. 19, 1781	19
Patty, [d. Joseph & Esther], b. May 20, 1798	24
Pelatiah, [s. Adonijah & Anna], b. July 15, 1783	19
Phineas, [s. Phinehas], b. Nov. 2, 1796	31

MONTVILLE VITAL RECORDS 245

	Page
ROGERS (cont.)	
Rebeckah, [d. Phinehas], b. Dec. 4, 1784	31
Russel, [s. David & Mary], b. May 1, 1806	26
Ruth, [twin with Naomi, d. Phinehas], b. Apr. 28, 1786	31
Sally, [d. Joseph & Esther], b. June 5, 1788	24
Samuel, s. [Andrew & Elisabeth], b. July 3, 1790	7
Sarah, [d. Adonijah & Anna], b. Oct. 27, 1787	19
Sophia, [d. Joseph, Jr. & Esther], b. Mar. 20, 1786	24
Sophia Jane, [d. Azel F. & Eleanor], b. Sept. 4, 1834	41
Susannah, [d. Ethan & Sally], b. Sept. 3, 1801	20
Susannah, [d. David & Mary], b. Feb. 26, 1810	26
Thomas, m. Mary **BAKER**, Nov. 7, 1784	23
Thomas Patterson, s. David & Mary, b. Apr. 14, 1802	26
Thomas Perkins, [s. Thomas & Mary], b. Jan. 15, 1797	23
SCHOLFIELD, Mariah, [d. Nathan & Betsey T.], b. Aug. 28, 1833	42
Nathan, b. Apr. 14, 1806; m. Betsey T. **HILL**, Sept. 8, 1830	42
Socrates, [s. Nathan & Betsey T.], b. June 12, 1831	42
SHEFFIELD, Frederick Ulysses, s. Paul & Hannah, b. July 6, 1793	28
Tabitha, d. [Paul & Hannah], b. May 4, 1796	28
SISTARE, Hannah, b. July 26, 1784; m. Nathan **RAYMOND**, Apr. 3, 1802	4
SMITH, Abel, m. Mrs. Lydia **PALMER**, Apr. 6, 1808, by Peleg Randal, Elder	29
Allen Breed, s. Abel & Lydia, b. May 6, 1811	29
Amy, [d. Ebenezer, Jr. & Hannah], b. Jan. 31, 1802; m. Stephen **MAPLES**, [ ]* *(In pencil in a later hand)	21
Amy, [d. Abel & Lydia], b. May 10, 1820	29
Asa, [s. Asa & Dezire], b. Sept. 4, 1806	29
Benjamin Alvah, [s. Abel & Lydia], b. Nov. 17, 1812	29
Ebenezer, Jr., m. Hannah **ADAMS**, Oct. 10, 1793	21
Elijah, [s. Asa & Dezire], b. May 26, 1801	29
Ezra, of Montville, m. Elizabeth **BOLLS**, of New London, Dec. 27, 1798	49
George W., of Montville, m. Lucretia **BREED**, of Stonington, Nov. 23, 1803, by Christopher Avery	6
John, 2nd, m. Caroline **CHESTER**, Oct. 7, 1795	12
Lurinda, [d. Ebenezer, Jr. & Hannah], b. Jan. 17, 1794	21
Mary, [d. Abel & Lydia], b. Aug. 27, 1817	29
Nancy, d. Asa & Dezire, b. July 3, 1797	29
Phebe*, [d. Ebenezer, Jr. & Hannah], [ ], m. Stephen **MAPLES**, [ ]* *(In pencil in a later hand)	21
Rachel, m. George **LATIMER**, Oct. 10, 1773	10
Ransford Wheeler, [s. Ebenezer, Jr. & Hannah], b. Nov. 29, 1804	21
Roxanna*, [d. Ebenezer, Jr. & Hannah,] *(In pencil in a later hand)	21
William, [s. Asa & Dezire], b. Apr. 9, 1804	29
STEBBINS, Nancy, m. Jared **TURNER**, June 7, 1810	34
Nancy, m. Jared **TURNER**, s. Isaac, [ ]	25
STRICKLAND, Eliza, m. Thomas **BISHOP**, June 30, 1800	14
[STUART], STUWARD, Jonathan Pember, s. Nathan & Drusilla, b. May 9, 1813	33
TORRY, Irena, d. Mary **WOOD**, b. Feb. 17, 1781	52

	Page
TRUMAN, Clarissa, [d. Joseph & Asenath], b. July 13, 1802* *(Entire entry added in a later hand)	52
Cynthia, [d. Joseph & Asenath], b. June 12, 1800* *(Entire entry added in a later hand)	52
Joseph, of Norway, s. William, m. Asenath **ROGERS**, of Montville, d. Davis, Feb. 4, 1798	52
Sally, of Southhold, on Long Island, N.Y., m. Ethan **ROGERS**, of New London, Dec. 25, 1794	20
TURNER, Abby Ann, b. Aug. 29, 1808; m. Mulford C. **RAYMOND**, Jan. 16, 1827	40
Abby Ann, [d. James & Mary], b. Aug. 29, 1808	40
Almira, [d. Giles & Eunice], b. July 30, 1808	34
Almira, [d. James & Mary], b. Sept. 5, 1810	40
Amy Chapel, [d. Mathew & Harriet], b. Oct. 24, 1804	3
Anna, [d. Isaac], b. Sept. 11, 1788	25
Anna, [d. Guy & Grace], b. Dec. 7, 1800	28
Catherine, [d. Giles & Eunice], b. Sept. 25, 1816	34
Daniel*, m. Lois **BAKER**, d. Josiah, [ ] *(Probably "David")	25
David, b. Apr. 10, 1776; m. Lois **BAKER**, Nov. 26, 1797	16
David, [s. James & Mary], b. Sept. 30, 1821	40
David S., [s. David & Lois], b. July 27, 1804	16
Eliza, [d. David & Lois], b. Feb. 5, 1799	16
Elisabeth, [d. Isaac], b. Oct. 22, 1793; m. Samuel **COMSTOCK**, [ ]* *(In pencil in a later hand)	25
Elizabeth, m. Samuel **COMSTOCK**, Oct. 11, 1812	35
Emeline Smith, [d. James & Mary], b. May 5, 1825	40
Emily, [d. Guy & Grace], b. June 4, 1808; d. Jan. 25, 1818* *(In pencil in a later hand)	28
Giles, [s. Isaac], b. Oct. 21, 1783; m. Eunice **COMSTOCK**, [ ]* *(In pencil in a later hand)	25
Giles & Eunice, had s.[ ], b. Mar. 3, 1821; d. Apr. 27, 1821	34
Giles, Jr., [s. Giles & Eunice], b. Feb. 6, 1823	34
Guy, [s. Isaac], b. Jan. 9, 1778; m. Grace **COMSTOCK**, [ ]* *(In pencil in a later hand)	25
Guy, m. Grace **COMSTOCK**, Dec. 8, 1799	28
Harriet, [d. Mathew & Abigail], b. Feb. 8, 1800	3
Hariet Newell, [d. Jared & Nancy], b. May 24, 1817	34
Hubbard*, s. [Mathew & Harriet], b. Sept. 1, 1802 *("Nathaniel" written and crossed out)	3
Isaac, [s. Isaac], b. Apr. 5, 1786; m. Esther **COMSTOCK**, [ ]* *(In pencil in a later hand)	25
Isaac, [s. Guy & Grace], b. Oct. 12, 1806	28
James, b. July 13, 1781; m. Mary **BAKER**, July 14, 1805	40
James, of Waterford, m. Mary **BAKER**, of Montville, July 14, 1805, by Moses Warren, J.P.	3
James, m. Mary **BAKER**, d. Josiah, [ ]	25
James Henry, [s. James & Mary], b. Oct. 22, 1812	40
Jane Maria, [d. Giles & Eunice], b. Dec. 26, 1811	34
Jared, [s. Isaac], b. Apr. 1, 1790; m. Nancy **STEBBINS**, [ ]* *(In pencil in a later hand)	25
Jared, m. Nancy **STEBBINS**, June 7, 1810	34
John, [s. Mathew & Harriet], b. Oct. 15, 1816	3

MONTVILLE VITAL RECORDS   247

	Page
TURNER (cont.)	
Josiah B., [s. David & Lois], b. Apr. 10, 1801	16
Laura Ransom, [d. James & Mary], b. Feb. 19, 1815	40
Lucy Ann, [d. Giles & Eunice], b. Mar. 6, 1819	34
Lyman, [s. Mathew & Harriet], b. Sept. 1, 1809	3
Mary, [d. Isaac], b. Apr. 7, 1781	25
Mary Emily, [d. James & Mary], b. Jan. 10, 1807	40
Mary Louisa, [d. Guy & Grace], b. Apr. 26, 1815	28
Mathew, m. Abigail **CHAPEL**, July 19, 1795	3
Matthew, [s. James & Mary], b. Apr. 27, 1817	40
Mercy M.*, m. Gideon **PALMER**, July 11, 1813 *(Here follows in pencil "B. June 29, 1795")	35
Mercy Maria, [d. Isaac], b. June 29, 1795; m. Gideon **PALMER**, [ ]* *(In pencil in a later hand)	25
Nancy Maria, [d. Jared & Nancy], b. Oct. 20, 1814	34
Peregrine, [s. James & Mary], b. Aug. 10, 1819	40
Peter C., [s. Guy & Grace], b. June 15, 1804	28
Samuel Rathbone, [s. Giles & Eunice], b. Sept. 28, 1813	34
Sarah, [d Guy & Grace], b. Apr. 8, 1802; d. Dec. 20, 1817* *(In pencil in a later hand)	28
VERGUSON, Calvin, [s. Jonathan], b. Oct. 19, 1820* *(First written "1830" and crossed out)	42
Lyman, [s. Jonathan], b. Aug. 23, 1823	42
Nathan, [s. Jonathan], b. Nov. 16, 1830	42
VIBBER, Amos S., [s. William], b. Jan. 5, 1787	23
Betsey, [d. Nathaniel], b. Aug. 31, 1774	11
Dezire, [d. Nathaniel], b. Sept. 13, 1772	11
Fanny, [d. William], b. June 5, 1785	23
Lois, [d. William], b. July 2, 1779	23
Louisa, [d. Nathaniel], b. Sept. 16 ,1780	11
Mehitabel, [d. Nathaniel], b. June 15, 1785	11
Nathaniel, [s. Nathaniel], b. Jan. 13, 1783	11
Russel, [s. William], b. Nov. 26, 1788	23
WALDEN, William, Jr., b. Aug. 31, 1796	30
WHEELER, Ebenezer, [s. Ephraim & Anna], b. Feb. 28, 1788	27
Jerome, [s. Ephraim & Anna], b. [ ]* *(In pencil in a later hand)	27
Joshua, s. Ephraim & Anna, b. Oct. 29, 1779	27
Nancy, [d. Ephraim & Anna], b. [ ]* *(In pencil in a later hand)	27
Oliver, [s. Ephraim & Anna], b. [ ]* *(In pencil in a later hand)	27
Sally, [d. Ephraim & Anna], b. [ ]* *(In pencil in a later hand)	27
Topliff, [child of Ephraim & Anna], b. [ ]* *(In pencil in a later hand)	27
WHIPPLE, Isaac, m. Charlotte **BAKER**, d. Josiah [ ]	25
WHITE, Edward, m. Lois **BAKER**, Dec. 25, 1791	26
John, [s. Edward & Lois], b. Mar. 7, 1793	26
Joshua Paul, [s. Edward & Lois], b. Feb. 14, 1802	26
Lois, [d. Edward &Lois], b. Apr. 30, 1795	26
Lyman Joseph, [s. Edward & Lois], b. Sept. 5, 1797	26
Mary Ann, b. Mar. 3, 1810	49

	Page
WICKWIRE, Amy C., b. Nov. 25, 1809	49
Phebe, m. Joseph Lee **CHAPMAN**, Feb. 5, 1818	38
WILLIAMS, Clarasa, m. Frances **GREEN**, of Bozrah, Jan. 7, 1848*, by J. L. Chapman, J.P. *(Perhaps "1868")	45
WINCHESTER, Caleb Thomas, s. George H. & Lucy, b. Jan. 18, 1847	38
WOOD, Daniel Webster, [s. Willet R. & Julia Ann], b. Nov. 25, 1836	44
Julia A., [d. Willet R. & Julia Ann], b. July 22, 1833	44
Mary, had d. Irena **TORRY**, b. Feb. 17, 1781	52
Willet R., m. Julia Ann **READ**, July 4, 1830	44
WORTHINGTON, Daniel, m. Betsey **HASARD**, Mar. 28, 1790	49
Daniel, Jr., [s. Daniel & Betsey], b. Oct. 14, 1792	49
Robert, [s. Daniel & Betsey], b. July 17, 1791; d. Aug. 14, 1792	49
NO SURNAME, Nancy, m. Elkanah **NEWBERY**, s. Davis, [ ]	17

NAUGATUCK VITAL RECORDS
1844 - 1853

	Page
ADAMS, Betsey, m. Willard **HOPKINS**, b. of Naugatuck, May 12, 1851, by Rev. Charles S. Sherman	16
ANDREWS, ANDRUS, ANDRUSS, Caroline A., of Naugatuck, m. Benjamin **BOOTH**, of New Haven, Nov. 8, 1848, by Rev. A. K. Teele	10
Darwin C., of Norfolk m. Jane E. **COOK**, of Winsted, Dec. 26, 1853, by Rev. Charles S. Sherman	27
Elias C., m. Mary A. **BIGALO**, b. of Naugatuck, Nov. 29, 1847, by Rev. A. K. Teele	10
Joel N., of Naugatuck, m. Mary J. **DENNEY**, of New Milford, Oct. 21, 1846, by Rev. O. Hopson	8
Mary N., m. Horace **TREAT**, Jan. 19, 1848, by Rev. James Mackay	29
AUSTIN, Esther Jane, of Prospect, m. Edward H. **CLARK**, of Leicester, N.Y., Nov. 2, 1851, by Rev. Joseph Scott	23
BAKER, Sarah, of Naugatuck, m. George **DYSON**, of Waterbury, May 11, 1851, by Rev. Joseph Scott	18
BALDWIN, Jerusha M., of Naugatuck, m. Thomas K. **SMALL**, of Touro, Mass., Jan. 2, 1853, by Rev. C. S. Sherman	25
BARBER, Sarah, of Harwinton, m. Lewis **UMBERFIELD**, of Naugatuck, June 27, 1850, by Rev. Joseph Scott	14
BEARDSLEY, Nancy D., of Naugatuck, m. Daniel **PRATT**, of Southbury, Oct. 6, 1846, by A. K. Teele	8
BEECHER, Betsey, m. John **HOPKINS**, b. of Naugatuck, Oct. 20, 1844, by Rev. Reuben Torrey, of Prospect	1
BEERES, Philo S., of Naugatuck, m. Mariette **FENN**, of Middlebury, May 17, 1846, by Rev. O. Hopson	6
BENEDICT, Mary Ann, m. Smith **DELAVAN**, of Naugatuck, Oct. 21, 1849, by Rev. A. K. Teele	12
BENNETT, Asa L., of Oxford, m. Martha Ann **CARROLL**, of Naugatuck, Oct. 15, 1845, by Rev. O. Hopson	4
BIDWELL, George A., of Naugatuck, m. Harriet **PHILPS**, of Winchester, Nov. 26, 1846, by Rev. O. Hopson	8
BIGALO, Mary A., m. Elias C. **ANDREWS**, b. of Naugatuck, Nov. 29, 1847, by Rev. A. K. Teele	10
BISHOP, Polly M., m. Aaron **OSBORN**, of Naugatuck, Dec. 8, 1852, by Rev. C. S. Sherman	24
BOOTH, Benjamin, of New Haven, m. Caroline A. Andrews, of Naugatuck, Nov. 8, 1848, by Rev. A. K. Teele	10
Legrand M., of Hartford, m. Clarissa A. **HOTCHKISS**, of Naugatuck, Jan. 16, 1844, by Rev. O. Hopson	1
BOUGHTON, Thalia I., wid., m. W[illia]m C. **SCOTT**, b. of Naugatuck, Mar. 10, 1850, by Rev. Charles S. Sherman	13
BRADBURN, Abner, m. Sarah Ann **BRONSON**, b. of Waterbury, Dec. 18, 1851, by Stephen W. Kellogg, J.P.	21
BRONSON, Lester, m. Sarah **SCOVILL**, b. of Middlebury, June 18, 1848, by Rev. A. K. Teele	11
Sarah Ann, m. Abner **BRADBURN**, b. of Waterbury, Dec. 18, 1851, by Stephen W. Kellogg, J.P.	21

BARBOUR COLLECTION

	Page
BRONSON (cont.)	
William B., of Waterbury, m. Eliza A. **HOADLEY**, of Naugatuck, Oct. 25, 1846, by Rev. O. Hopson	8
BUCKINGHAM, John M., of New Milford, m. Ellen S. **HOADLEY**, of Naugatuck, Oct. 29, 1849, by Rev. C. S. Sherman	12
BUNDY, Joseph B., of Danbury, m. Sarah Ann **LORD**, of Brookfield, July 2, 1851, by Rev. Joseph Scott	19
CARROLL, Martha Ann, of Naugatuck, m. Asa L. **BENNETT**, of Oxford, Oct. 15, 1845, by Rev. O. Hopson	4
CHAMBERLAIN, Albert, m Sarah **KENNEY**, b. of Naugatuck, Mar. 7, 1847, by Rev. O. Hopson	9
CLARK, Edward H., of Leicester, N.Y. ,m. Esther Jane **AUSTIN**, of Prospect, Nov. 2, 1851, by Rev. Joseph Scott	23
Jennette, of Prospect, m. Harrison B. **TORREY**, of Naugatuck Feb. 23, 1848, by Rev. A. K. Teele	11
Maria P., Mrs. of Waterbury, m. Israel **UPSON**, Apr. 21, 1851, by Rev. C. S. Sherman	16
COOK, Dickerman, of Wallingford, m. Emily **SMITH**, of Naugatuck, Dec. 3, 1846, by Rev. O. Hopson	9
Jane E., of Winsted, m. Darwin C. **ANDRUS**, of Norfolk, Dec. 26, 1853, by Rev. Charles S. Sherman	27
Julius B., of Cheshire, m. Polly C. **HOPKINS**, of Naugatuck, Mar. 2, 1851, by Rev. C. S. Sherman	15
COUCH, Samuel A., of Danbury, m. Nancy **TOMLINSON**, of Newtown, Oct. 5, 1845, by Rev. O. Hopson	4
CRANE, Harvey, of Bethlehem, m. Cornelia **SPERRY**, of [ ], Nov. 25, 1851, by Rev. Charles S. Sherman	20
CULVER, Josiah, m. Mrs. Abigail **HOTCHKISS**, b. of Naugatuck, May 6, 1846, by Rev. O. Hopson	5
CUNSAN (?), Mary Ann, of Naugatuck, m. Reuben **HITCHCOCK**, of Prospect, Aug. 31, 1851, by Gideon O. Hotchkiss, J.P.	20
CURTIS, George, m. Harriet F. **JUDD**, b. of Naugatuck, Oct. 4, 1852, by Rev. Joseph Scott	24
DASCUM, Charles, of Woodbury, m. Clarinda **ROPE**, of Oxford, Dec. 22, 1851, by Gideon O. Hotchkiss, J.P.	21
DAVIS, Lydia P., of Naugatuck, m. John R. **TOMLINSON**, of Derby, Jan. 1, 1845, by Rev. O. Hopson	2
DELAVAN, DELEVAN, Martha, of New Haven, m. Henry **JOHNSON**, of Naugatuck, June 6, 1848, by Rev. A. K. Teele	10
Smith, m. Mary Ann **BENEDICT**, b. of Naugatuck, Oct. 21, 1849, by Rev. A. K. Teele	12
DEMEREST, Eliza Ann, of Woodbury, m. David Edson **PECK**, of Newtown, May 4, 1846, by Albert K. Teele	6
DENNY, DENNEY, Burr C., of Waterbury, m Matilda **MORGAN**, of Naugatuck, Sept. 8, 1850, by Rev. Joseph Scott	15
Mary J., of New Milford, m. Joel N **ANDRUSS**, of Naugatuck, Oct. 21, 1846, by Rev. O. Hopson	8
DOOLITTLE, Reuben, of Hamden, m. Laura **HORTON**, of Naugatuck, Oct. 24, 1848, by Rev. A. K. Teele	11
DOUGLASS, David K., of Naugatuck, m. Nancy M. **NEWCOMB**, of Plymouth, June 27, 1853, by Rev. Charles S. Sherman	26
Maria A., of Naugatuck, m. Wheaton S. **PLUMB**, of Wallingford, Oct. 10, 1853, by Rev. Charles S. Sherman	26

NAUGATUCK VITAL RECORDS 251

	Page
DYSON, George, of Waterbury, m. Sarah **BAKER**, of Naugatuck, May 11, 1851, by Rev. Joseph Scott	18
FENN, Mariette, of Middlebury, m. Philo S. **BEERES**, of Naugatuck, May 17, 1846, by Rev. O. Hopson	6
FORD, Eliza, m. John **SPRING**, b. of Naugatuck, Feb. 8, 1847, by Rev. O. Hopson	9
FRENCH, Ellen L., of Naugatuck, m. Earl A. **SMITH**, of Oxford, July 20, 1851, by Rev. Joseph Scott	22
GIBBARD, GIBBERD, Delight, m. Nathaniel **MERRILL**, b. of Naugatuck, Oct. 28, 1849, by Rev. Joseph Scott	14
William, of Naugatuck, m. Jane W. **HOTCHKISS**, of Prospect, Feb. 10, 1846, by Charles Nettleton, J.P.	5
GIPSON, Isabella, of New York, m. Eliza **THOMAS**, of Naugatuck, Mar. 23, 1851, by Rev. Joseph Scott	17
GLYNN, James W., of Meriden, m. Sarah E. **GOODYEAR**, of Hamden, Oct. 26, 1851, by Rev. Joseph Scott	23
GOODWIN, Mary, m. Jesse B. **WOOSTER**, b. of Naugatuck, Nov. 8, 1848, by Rev. A. K. Teele	10
GOODYEAR, Sarah E., of Hamden, m. James W. **GLYNN**, of Meriden, Oct. 26, 1851, by Rev. Joseph Scott	23
HALL, [see also **HULL**], Adeline, m. Burritt **HOTCHKISS**, Nov. 24, 1844, by Rev. J. Sloper	1
Harriet M., of Waterbury, m. Burnet H. **LEWIS**, of Naugatuck, Nov. 29, 1847, by Rev. A. K. Teele	10
Hiram L., of Watertown, m. Maria L. **LUCE**, of Naugatuck, Dec. 24, 1844, by Rev. O. Hopson	2
HARRINGTON, Mary, m. George W. **JOHNSON**, b. of Humphreysville, Nov. 14, 1844, by Rev. O. Hopson	2
Thomas, of Seymour, m. Susan M. **JOYCE**, of Naugatuck, July 17, 1851, by Rev. Joseph Scott	22
HAYS, Clarissa, m. Charles **ROGERS**, b. of Naugatuck, Mar. 10, 1851, by Rev. Joseph Scott	17
HICKOX, Jane M., of Bethany, m. W[illia]m H. **JOICE**, of Oxford, July 27, 1849, by Rev. A. K. Teele	11
HINE, Augusta, of Naugatuck, m. Samuel R. **NEWELL**, of Longmeadow, Mass., Sept. 26, 1849, by Rev. Joseph Scott	14
Emely E., m. Charles B. **HOTCHKISS**, b. of Naugatuck, Dec. 24, 1845, by Rev. O. Hopson	5
Robert B., m. Caroline **HOADLEY**, b. of Naugatuck, Apr. 26, 1852, by Rev. Joseph Scott	23
Sarah E., of Naugatuck, m. Willard W. **THORPE**, of Southington, July 27, 1851, by Rev. Joseph Scott	22
Sarah M., of Naugatuck, m. Henry **RATTLE**, of Akron, O., Apr. 16, 1846, by Rev. O. Hopson	5
HITCHCOCK, Nancy, of Prospect, m. Charles **MALLORY**, of Fair Haven, Oct. 22, 1848, by Rev. A. K. Teele	11
Reuben, of Prospect, m. Mary Ann **CUNSAN** (?), of Naugatuck, Aug. 31, 1851, by Gideon O. Hotchkiss, J.P.	20
HOADLEY, Caroline, m. Robert B. **HINE**, b. of Naugatuck, Apr. 26, 1852, by Rev. Joseph Scott	23
Eliza A., of Naugatuck, m. William B. **BRONSON**, of Waterbury, Oct. 25, 1846, by Rev. O. Hopson	8

BARBOUR COLLECTION

	Page
HOADLEY (cont.)	
Ellen S., of Naugatuck, m. John M. BUCKINGHAM, of New Milford, Oct. 29, 1849, by Rev. C. S. Sherman	12
HOLTON, Addie, m. James R. PITKIN, b. of Manchester, Conn., June 13, 1853, by Rev. C. S. Sherman	25
HOPKINS, Emily M., m. William H. PLATT, b. of Naugatuck, May 26, 1846, by Albert K. Teele	7
Enos, of Naugatuck m. Jane C. HOPKINS, of New Haven, Sept. 30, 1846, by A. K. Teele	8
Harriet A., m. Merit WOODING, b. of Naugatuck, Sept. 20, 1846, by A. K. Teele	7
Jane C., of New Haven, m. Enos HOPKINS, of Naugatuck, Sept. 30, 1846, by A. K. Teele	8
Jane E., m. Lawrence S. SPENCER, b. of Naugatuck, Nov. 24, 1847, by Rev. A. K. Teele	10
John, m. Betsey BEECHER, b. of Naugatuck, Oct. 20, 1844, by Rev. Reuben Torrey, of Prospect	1
Polly C., of Naugatuck, m. Julius B. COOK, of Cheshire, Mar. 2, 1851, by Rev. C. S. Sherman	15
Willard, m. Betsey ADAMS, b. of Naugatuck, May 12, 1851, by Rev. Charles S. Sherman	16
HORTON, Laura, of Naugatuck, m. Reuben DOOLITTLE, of Hamden, Oct. 24, 1848, by Rev. A. K. Teele	11
HOTCHKISS, Abigail, Mrs., m. Josiah CULVER, b. of Naugatuck, May 6, 1846, by Rev. O. Hopson	5
Burritt, m. Adeline HALL, Nov. 24, 1844, by Rev. J. Sloper	1
Charles B., m. Emely E. HINE, b. of Naugatuck, Dec. 24, 1845, by Rev. O. Hopson	5
Clarissa A., of Naugatuck, m. Legrand M. BOOTH, of Hartford, Jan. 16, 1844, by Rev. O. Hopson	1
Gilbert, of Prospect, m. Emeline WOOSTER, of Naugatuck, Oct. 13, 1845, by Rev. O. Hopson	4
Jane W., of Prospect, m. William GIBBARD, of Naugatuck, Feb. 10, 1846, by Charles Nettleton, J.P.	5
Milo, of Prospect, m. Eliza YOUNG, of Cheshire, Oct. 13, 1845, by Rev. O. Hopson	4
Noyes, of Bethany, m. Jane Caroline SACKETT, of Oxford, July 27, 1845, by Rev. O. Hopson	3
HULL, [see also HALL], Elizabeth, Mrs., m. Lawrence S. HULL, b. of Naugatuck, Jan. 31, 1847, by Rev. O. Hopson	9
Lawrence S., m. Mrs. Elizabeth HULL, b. of Naugatuck, Jan. 31, 1847, by Rev. O. Hopson	9
Nancy C., of Farmington, m. Elias F. MERRILL, of Naugatuck, Nov. 23, 1853, by Rev. C. S. Sherman	26
Susan, of Waterbury, m. Nathaniel MERRELL, of Naugatuck, July 6, 1851, by Rev. Charles S. Sherman	20
ISBELL, Aurelia E., m. Nathaniel I. NICHOLS, b. of Woodbury, June 23, 1844, by Rev. O. Hopson	1
JOHNSON, George W., m. Mary HARRINGTON, b. of Humphreysville, Nov. 14, 1844, by Rev. O. Hopson	2
Henry, of Naugatuck, m. Martha DELEVAN, of New Haven, June 6, 1848, by Rev. A. K. Teele	10

	Page
JOHNSON (cont.)	
Mary I., m. George T. **RICHARDSON**, b. of Middlebury, Sept. 15, 1851, by Rev Charles S. Sherman	19
JONES, Edward P., of Bridgeport, m. Caroline E. **LATHROP**, of Naugatuck, Sept. 25, 1849, by Rev. Joseph Scott	14
JOYCE, JOICE, Susan M., of Naugatuck, m. Thomas **HARRINGTON**, of Seymour, July 17, 1851, by Rev. Joseph Scott	22
W[illia]m H., of Oxford, m. Jane M. **HICKOX**, of Bethany, July 27, 1849, by Rev. A. K. Teele	11
JUDD, Charlotte A., of Naugatuck, m. Andrew J. **STILSON**, of Denmark, N.Y., July 19, 1846, in St. Michaels Ch., by Rev. E. E. Beardsley	7
Charlotte A., of Naugatuck, m. Joel **KEELER**, of Redding, June 16, 1851, by Rev. Charles S. Sherman	18
Harriet F., m. George **CURTIS**, b. of Naugatuck, Oct. 4, 1852, by Rev. Joseph Scott	24
Mary E., of Naugatuck, m. James **SHAW**, of Easton, Conn., May 8, 1853, by Rev. C. S Sherman	25
KEELER, Joel, of Redding, m. Charlotte A. **JUDD**, of Naugatuck, June 16, 1851, by Rev. Charles S. Sherman	18
KENNEY, Sarah, m. Albert **CHAMBERLAIN**, b. of Naugatuck, Mar. 7, 1847, by Rev. O. Hopson	9
KUNECK, Antone, of Naugatuck, m. Catharine **WIRGAND**, of Portchester, N.Y., Mar. 23, 1851, by Rev. C. S. Sherman	15
LAKE, Walter, of Bethelhem, m. Alma **NETTLETON**, of Naugatuck, Nov. 25, 1847, by George P. Prudden, of Middlebury	9
LANG, Mary A., m .Marshall **LINES**, b. of Naugatuck, Apr. 29, 1849, by Rev. A. K .Teele	11
LATHROP, Caroline E., of Naugatuck, m. Edward P. **JONES**, of Bridgeport, Sept. 25, 1849, by Rev. Joseph Scott	14
LEAVENWORTH, Joseph N., of Middlebury, m. Fanny **MANN**, of Naugatuck, June 3, 1851, by Rev. Joseph Scott	18
LEWIS, Amelia, of Naugatuck, m. Clark M. **PLATT**, of Waterbury, May 20, 1846, by Albert K. Teele	6
Burnet H., of Naugatuck m. Harriet M. **HALL**, of Waterbury, Nov. 29, 1847, by Rev. A. K. Teele	10
James, m. Mary Jane **OSBORN**, b. of Naugatuck, Apr. 25, 1852, by Rev. Joseph Scott	24
LINES, Marshall, m. Mary A. **LANG**, b. of Naugatuck, Apr 29, 1849, by Rev. A. K. Teele	11
Rebecca, m. Hial S. **STEVENS**, b. of Naugatuck, Feb. 18, 1850, by Rev. Charles S. Sherman	13
LORD, Sarah Ann, of Brookfield, m. Joseph B. **BUNDY**, of Danbury, July 2, 1851, by Rev. Joseph Scott	19
LUCE, Maria L., of Naugatuck, m. Hiram L. **HALL**, of Watertown, Dec. 24, 1844, by Rev. O. Hopson	2
McMILLUM, Alexander, m. Mary Jane **QUAIN**, b. of Naugatuck, July 3, 1851, by Rev. Joseph Scott	19
MALLORY, Charles, of Fair Haven, m. Nancy **HITCHCOCK**, of Prospect, Oct. 22, 1848, by Rev. A. K. Teele	11
Samuel M., of Woodbury, m. Mary E. **WARNER**, of Naugatuck, Feb. 9, 1845, by Rev. J. Atwater	2

	Page
MANN, Fanny, of Naugatuck, m. Joseph N. LEAVINWORTH, of Middlebury, June 3, 1851, by Rev. Joseph Scott	18
MANVILLE, Eli J., of Watertown, m. Mary POTTER, of Naugatuck, Mar. 15, 1846, by Rev. O. Hopson	5
MERRILL, MERRELL, Elias F., of Naugatuck, m. Nancy C. HULL, of Farmington, Nov. 23, 1853, by Rev. C. S. Sherman	26
Nathaniel, m. Delight GIBBERD, b. of Naugatuck, Oct. 28, 1849, by Rev. Joseph Scott	14
Nathaniel, of Naugatuck m. Susan HULL, of Waterbury, July 6, 1851, by Rev. Charles S. Sherman	20
MILES, Benjamin F., of Cheshire, m. Sarah M. STEVENS, of Naugatuck, Apr. 4, 1850, by Rev. C. S. Sherman	13
MORGAN, Matilda, of Naugatuck m. Burr C. DENNY, of Waterbury, Sept. 8, 1850, by Rev. Joseph Scott	15
NETTLETON, Alma, of Naugatuck, m. Walter LAKE, of Bethelhem, Nov. 25, 1847, by George P. Prudden, of Middlebury	9
NEWCOMB, Nancy M., of Plymouth, m. David K. DOUGLASS, of Naugatuck, June 27, 1853, by Rev. Charles S. Sherman	26
NEWELL, Samuel R., of Longmeadow, Mass., m. Augusta HINE, of Naugatuck, Sept. 26, 1849, by Rev. Joseph Scott	14
NICHOLS, NICHOL, David H. of Waterbury, m. Harriet D. WILLIAMS, of Naugatuck, Dec. 1, 1851, by Rev. Charles S. Sherman	21
Nathaniel I., m. Aurelia E. ISBELL, b. of Woodbury, June 23, 1844, by Rev. O. Hopson	1
OSBORN, OSBORNE, Aaron, of Naugatuck, m. Polly M. BISHOP, Dec. 1852, by Rev. C. S. Sherman	24
Cloe M., of Naugatuck, m. Erastus YOUNG, of Mansfield, Mar. 30, 1845, by Rev. O. Hopson	2
Jennett, of Naugatuck, m. George STAPLES, of Hartford, June 23, 1845, by Rev. O. Hopson	3
Mary Jane, m. James LEWIS, b. of Naugatuck, Apr. 25, 1852, by Rev. Joseph Scott	24
PAINTER, James, of Hamden, m. Mary A. SAXTON, of Middlebury, Oct. 6, 1851, by Rev. Joseph Scott	23
PATTERSON, Celestia, of Naugatuck, m. W[illia]m W. SMITH, of Bridgeport, Nov. 27, 1851, by Rev. C. S. Sherman	15
PECK, David Edson, of Newtown, m. Eliza Ann DEMEREST, of Woodbury, May 4, 1846, by Albert K. Teele	6
[PHILLIPS], PHILPS, Harriet, of Winchester, m. George A. BIDWELL, of Naugatuck, Nov. 26, 1846, by Rev. O. Hopson	8
PITKIN, James R., of Manchester, Conn., m. Addie HOLTON, of Manchester, Conn., June 13, 1853, by Rev. C. S. Sherman	25
PLATT, Clark M., of Waterbury, m. Amelia LEWIS, of Naugatuck, May 20, 1846, by Albert K. Teele	6
Samuel, of West Haven, m. Eliza Jane SMITH, of Naugatuck, Oct. 5, 1851, by Rev. Joseph Scott	22
William H., m. Emily M. HOPKINS, b. of Naugatuck, May 26, 1846, by Albert K. Teele	7
PLUMB, Wheaton S., of Wallingford, m. Maria A. DOUGLASS, of Naugatuck, Oct. 10, 1853, by Rev. Charles S. Sherman	26
POTTER, Angelina, m. Elias THOMAS, b. of Naugatuck, Aug. 3, 1845, by Rev. L. Baldwin	3

NAUGATUCK VITAL RECORDS 255

	Page
POTTER (cont.)	
Mary, of Naugatuck m. Eli J. MANVILLE, of Watertown, Mar. 15, 1846, by Rev. O. Hopson	5
PRATT, Daniel, of Southbury, m. Nancy D. BEARDSLEY, of Naugatuck, Oct. 6, 1846, by A. K. Teele	8
QUAIN, Mary Jane, m. Alexander McMILLUM, b. of Naugatuck, July 3, 1851, by Rev. Joseph Scott	19
RATTLE, Henry, of Akron, O., m. Sarah M. HINE, of Naugatuck, Apr. 16, 1846, by Rev. O. Hopson	5
RICHARDSON, George T., m. Mary I. JOHNSON, b. of Middlebury, Sept. 15, 1851, by Rev. Charles S. Sherman	19
ROGERS, Charles, m. Clarissa HAYS, b. of Naugatuck, Mar. 10, 1851, by Rev. Joseph Scott	17
ROPE, Clarinda, of Oxford, m. Charles DASCUM, of Woodbury, Dec. 22, 1851, by Gideon O. Hotchkiss, J.P.	21
RUSSELL, Charles M., of Naugatuck, m. Jennett H. WHITTLESEY, of Derby, July 29, 1849, by Rev. A. K. Teele	12
Munroe, of Birmingham, m. Julia A. WOODFORD, of Naugatuck, May 11, 1847, by Rev. A. K. Teele	10
Stern, of Naugatuck, m. Juliette WOODWORTH, of Middlebury, Mar. 16, 1851, by Rev. Joseph Scott	17
SACKETT, Jane Caroline, of Oxford, m. Noyes HOTCHKISS, of Bethany, July 27, 1845, by Rev. O. Hopson	3
SAXTON, Mary A., of Middlebury, m. James PAINTER, of Hamden, Oct. 6, 1851, by Rev. Joseph Scott	23
SCOTT, W[illia]m C., m. wid. Thalia I. BOUGHTON, b. of Naugatuck, Mar. 10, 1850, by Rev. Charles S. Sherman	13
SCOVILL, Sarah, m. Lester BRONSON, b. of Middlebury, June 18, 1848, by Rev. A. K. Teele	11
SHAW, James, of Easton, Conn., m. Mary E. JUDD, of Naugatuck, May 8, 1853, by Rev. C. S. Sherman	25
SHERWOOD, Nancy M., of Bridgewater, Conn., m. George WILETT (?), of Oxford, Dec. 13, 1844, by Rev. O. Hopson	2
SMALL, Thomas K., of Touro, Mass., m. Jerusha M. BALDWIN, of Naugatuck, Jan. 2, 1853, by Rev. C. S. Sherman	25
SMITH, Earl A., of Oxford, m. Ellen L. FRENCH, of Naugatuck, July 20, 1851, by Rev. Joseph Scott	22
Eliza Jane, of Naugatuck m. Samuel PLATT, of West Haven, Oct. 5, 1851, by Rev. Joseph Scott	22
Emily, of Naugatuck, m. Dickerman COOK, of Wallingford, Dec. 3, 1846, by Rev. O. Hopson	9
W[illia]m W., of Bridgeport, m. Celestia PATTERSON, of Naugatuck, Nov. 27, 1850, by Rev. C. S. Sherman	15
SPENCER, Francis, m. Harriet E. SPENCER, b. of Naugatuck, Apr. 16, 1848, by Rev. A. K. Teele	11
Harriet E., m. Francis SPENCER, b. of Naugatuck, Apr. 16, 1848, by Rev. A. K. Teele	11
Lawrence S., m. Jane E. HOPKINS, b. of Naugatuck, Nov. 24, 1847, by Rev. A. K. Teele	10
SPERRY, Cornelia, of [ ], m. Harvey CRANE, of Bethlehem, Nov. 25, 1851, by Rev. Charles S. Sherman	20
SPRING, John, m. Eliza FORD, b. of Naugatuck, Feb. 8, 1847, by Rev. O. Hopson	9

	Page
STAPLES, George, of Hartford, m. Jennett **OSBORNE**, of Naugatuck, June 23, 1845, by Rev. O. Hopson	3
STEVENS, Hial S., m. Rebecca **LINES**, b. of Naugatuck, Feb. 18, 1850, by Rev. Charles S. Sherman	13
Sarah M., of Naugatuck, m. Benjamin F. **MILES**, of Cheshire, Apr. 4, 1850, by Rev. C. S. Sherman	13
STILSON, Andrew J., of Denmark, N.Y., m. Charlotte A. **JUDD**, of Naugatuck, July 19, 1846, in St. Michaels Ch., by Rev. E. E. Beardsley	7
THOMAS, Elias, m. Angelina **POTTER**, b. of Naugatuck, Aug. 3, 1845, by Rev. L. Baldwin	3
Eliza, of Naugatuck, m. Isabella **GIPSON**, of New York, Mar. 23, 1851, by Rev. Joseph Scott	17
THORPE, Willard W., of Southington, m. Sarah E. **HINE**, of Naugatuck, July 27, 1851, by Rev. Joseph Scott	22
TOMLINSON, John R., of Derby, m. Lydia P. **DAVIS**, of Naugatuck, Jan. 1, 1845, by Rev. O. Hopson	2
Nancy, of Newtown, m. Samuel A. **COUCH**, of Danbury, Oct. 5, 1845, by Rev. O. Hopson	4
TORREY, Harrison B., of Naugatuck, m. Jennette **CLARK**, of Prospect, Feb. 23, 1848, by Rev. A. K. Teele	11
TREAT, Horace, m. Mary N. **ANDREWS**, Jan. 19, 1848, by Rev. James Mackay	29
UMBERFIELD, Lewis, of Naugatuck, m. Sarah **BARBER**, of Harwinton, June 27, 1850, by Rev. Joseph Scott	14
UPSON, Israel, m. Mrs. Maria P. **CLARK**, of Waterbury, Apr. 21, 1851, by Rev. C. S. Sherman	16
WARNER, Mary E., of Naugatuck, m. Samuel M. **MALLORY**, of Woodbury, Feb. 9, 1845, by Rev. J. Atwater	2
WHITTLESEY, Jennett H., of Derby, m. Charles M. **RUSSELL**, of Naugatuck, July 29, 1849, by Rev. A. K. Teele	12
WILLETT, George, of Oxford, m. Nancy M. **SHERWOOD**, of Bridgewater, Conn., Dec. 15, 1844, by Rev. O. Hopson	2
WILLIAMS, Harriet D., of Naugatuck, m. David H. **NICHOL**, of Waterbury, Dec. 1, 1851, by Rev. Charles S. Sherman	21
WIRGAND, Catharine, of Portchester, N.Y., m. Antone **KUNECK**, of Naugatuck, Mar. 23, 1851, by Rev. C. S. Sherman	15
WOODFORD, Julia A., of Naugatuck, m. Munroe **RUSSELL**, of Birmingham, May 11, 1847, by Rev. A. K. Teele	10
WOODING, Merit, m. Harriet A. **HOPKINS**, b. of Naugatuck, Sept. 20, 1846, by A. K. Teele	7
WOODWORTH, Juliette, of Middlebury, m. Stern **RUSSELL**, of Naugatuck, Mar. 16, 1851, by Rev. Joseph Scott	17
WOOSTER, Benjamin A., of New Haven, m. Esther **WOOSTER**, of Naugatuck, May 24, 1848, by Rev. A. K. Teele	11
Emeline, of Naugatuck, m. Gilbert **HOTCHKISS**, of Prospect, Oct. 13, 1845, by Rev. O. Hopson	4
Esther, of Naugatuck, m. Benjamin A. **WOOSTER**, of New Haven, May 24, 1848, by Rev. A. K. Teele	11
Jesse G., m. Mary **GOODWIN**, b. of Naugatuck, Nov. 8, 1848, by Rev. A. K. Teele	10
YOUNG, Eliza, of Cheshire, m. Milo **HOTCHKISS**, of Prospect, Oct. 13, 1845, by Rev. O. Hopson	4

	Page
YOUNG (cont.)	
Erastus, of Mansfield, m. Cloe M. **OSBORNE**, of Naugatuck, Mar. 30, 1845, by Rev. O. Hopson	2

www.ingramcontent.com/pod-product-compliance
Lightning Source LLC
Chambersburg PA
CBHW050844230426
43667CB00012B/2144